THE INSTITUTE FOR POLISH–JEWISH STUDIES

The Institute for Polish–Jewish Studies in Oxford and its sister organization, the American Association for Polish–Jewish Studies, which publish *Polin*, are learned societies which were established in 1984, following the First International Conference on Polish–Jewish Studies, held in Oxford. The Institute is associated with the Oxford Centre for Hebrew and Jewish Studies, and the American Association is linked with the Department of Near Eastern and Judaic Studies at Brandeis University.

Both the Institute and the American Association aim to promote understanding of the Polish Jewish past. They have no building or library of their own and no paid staff; they achieve their aims by encouraging scholarly research and facilitating its publication, and by creating forums for people with a scholarly interest in Polish Jewish topics, both in the past and in the present.

To this end, the Institute and the American Association help organize lectures and international conferences. Venues for these activities have included Brandeis University in Waltham, Mass., the Hebrew University in Jerusalem, the Institute for the Study of Human Sciences in Vienna, King's College, London, the Jagiellonian University in Kraków, the Oxford Centre for Hebrew and Jewish Studies, the University of Łódź, University College London, and the Polish Cultural Centre and the Polish Embassy in London. They have encouraged academic exchanges between Israel, Poland, the United States, and western Europe. In particular they seek to aid in training a new generation of scholars, in Poland as well as elsewhere, to study the culture and history of the Jews in Poland.

Each year since 1987, the Institute has published a volume of scholarly papers in this series, *Polin: Studies in Polish Jewry*, under the general editorship of Professor Antony Polonsky of Brandeis University. Since 1994 the series has been published on its behalf by the Littman Library of Jewish Civilization, and since 1998 the publication has also been linked with the American Association. In March 2000 the entire series was honoured with a National Jewish Book Award from the Jewish Book Council in the United States. More than twenty other works on Polish Jewish topics have also been published with the Institute's assistance.

For further information on the Institute for Polish–Jewish Studies or the American Association for Polish–Jewish Studies, contact <polin@littman.co.uk>.

THE LITTMAN LIBRARY OF
JEWISH CIVILIZATION

MANAGING EDITOR
Connie Webber

Dedicated to the memory of
LOUIS THOMAS SIDNEY LITTMAN
*who founded the Littman Library for the love of God
and as an act of charity in memory of his father*
JOSEPH AARON LITTMAN
יהא זכרם ברוך

'*Get wisdom, get understanding:
Forsake her not and she shall preserve thee*'
PROV. 4: 5

*The Littman Library of Jewish Civilization is a registered UK charity
Registered charity no.* 1000784

POLIN

STUDIES IN POLISH JEWRY

VOLUME SIXTEEN

*Focusing on Jewish Popular Culture in Poland
and its Afterlife*

Edited by

MICHAEL C. STEINLAUF

and

ANTONY POLONSKY

Published for
The Institute for Polish–Jewish Studies
and
The American Association for Polish–Jewish Studies

Oxford · Portland, Oregon
The Littman Library of Jewish Civilization
2003

The Littman Library of Jewish Civilization
Chief Executive Officer: Ludo Craddock

PO Box 645, Oxford OX2 OUJ, UK

—————

Published in the United States and Canada by
The Littman Library of Jewish Civilization
c/o ISBS, 920 N.E. 58th Avenue, Suite 300,
Portland, Oregon 97213–3786

A catalogue record for this book is available from the British Library

Library of Congress Cataloging-in-Publication Data applied for
ISSN 0268 1056
ISBN 1–874774–73–0
ISBN 1–874774–74–9 (pbk)

Publishing co-ordinator: Janet Moth
Production: John Saunders
Copy-editing: Laurien Berkeley
Proof-reading: Bonnie Blackburn
Index: Bonnie Blackburn
Design: Pete Russell, Faringdon, Oxon.
Typeset by Footnote Graphics Limited, Warminster, Wilts.
Printed in Great Britain on acid-free paper by
Biddles Ltd., Kings Lynn. www.biddles.co.uk

Articles appearing in this publication are abstracted and indexed in
Historical Abstracts and *America: History and Life*

Dedicated in love, admiration, and gratitude to

RAFAEL SCHARF

*one of the pioneers of the revival of interest in the
Polish Jewish past*

———

The publication of this volume of POLIN *was
supported by grants from*

WŁADYSŁAW T. BARTOSZEWSKI

TONY COREN

THE SEWERYN KOŃ AND
IRENA KOZŁOWSKA FOUNDATION

THE LUCIUS N. LITTAUER FOUNDATION

and the

MEMORIAL FOUNDATION FOR
JEWISH CULTURE

Editors and Advisers

Preface

THIS volume of *Polin* is centred around a core of chapters in Parts I and II, along with an introduction, devoted to Jewish popular culture. Two translations of works relevant to this section are to be found in Part II. As in previous volumes of *Polin*, in Part III, New Views, substantial space is given to new research into a variety of topics in Polish Jewish studies. These chapters include an analysis of the origins of antisemitism in Poland by Brian Porter; a discussion by Alex Rossino of what is known about the presence of German forces in the vicinity of Jedwabne in the summer of 1941; and an investigation by Andrzej Paczkowski of the vexed question of Jews in the communist security apparatus in Poland after 1944. Part IV, Reviews, includes an account by Andrzej Trzciński and Marcin Wodziński of a new book on the old Jewish cemetery in Kazimierz, an important discussion by Anna Landau-Czajka of what should be done about the paintings in Sandomierz Cathedral that represent an alleged ritual murder in the seventeenth century, an examination by Włodzimierz Rozenbaum of the 'anti-Zionist' campaign of 1968 and an extended review by Gunnar Paulsson of Jan Gross's book *Neighbors*.

Polin is sponsored by the Institute of Polish–Jewish Studies, Oxford, and by the American Association for Polish–Jewish Studies, which is linked with the Department of Near Eastern and Judaic Studies, Brandeis University. As with earlier issues, this volume could not have appeared without the untiring assistance of many individuals. In particular, we should like to express our gratitude to Dr Jonathan Webber, treasurer of the Institute for Polish–Jewish Studies; to Professor Jehuda Reinharz, president of Brandeis University; and to Mrs Irene Pipes, president of the American Association for Polish–Jewish Studies. These three institutions all made substantial contributions to the cost of producing the volume. The volume also benefited from grants from the Memorial Foundation for Jewish Culture, the Lucius N. Littauer Foundation, the Seweryn Koń and Irena Kozłowska Foundation, Władysław T. Bartoszewski, and Tony Coren. Volume 15 (published in 2002) also benefited from a grant from the Memorial Foundation for Jewish Culture which came too late for it to be acknowledged in that volume. As was the case with earlier volumes, this one could not have been published without the constant assistance and supervision of Connie Webber, managing editor of the Littman Library; Janet Moth, publishing co-ordinator; and the tireless copy-ending of Laurien Berkeley, Claire Rosenson, and Phyllis Mitzman. Additional thanks are due to a number of people who contributed their expertise to various aspects of the section on popular culture: Dr Paul Glasser of the YIVO Institute for Jewish Research, Professor Dan Ben-Amos of the University of Pennsylvania, Professor Joseph Davis of Gratz College, and the staff of the Tuttleman Library of Gratz College, including Eliezer Wise, Dr Hayim Sheynin, and Yisrael Meyerowitz.

Plans for future volumes of *Polin* are well advanced. Volume 17 will deal with Jews in smaller Polish towns, and future volumes are planned on Jewish women in eastern Europe, on Polish–Jewish relations in the United States, on 1968 in Poland, and on the history of the Jews in Kraków. We should welcome contributions for these issues as well as for our section New Views. We should also welcome any suggestions or criticisms. In particular, we should be very grateful for assistance in extending the geographical range of our journal to Ukraine, Belarus, and Lithuania, both in the period in which these countries were part of the Polish–Lithuanian Commonwealth and subsequently.

POLIN

Gentle Polin (Poland), ancient land of Torah and learning
From the day Ephraim first departed from Judah

From a selihah *by Rabbi Moshe Katz Geral
of the exiles of Poland, head of the Beth Din of the
Holy Congregation of Metz*

We did not know, but our fathers told us how the exiles of Israel came to the land of Polin (Poland).

When Israel saw how its sufferings were constantly renewed, oppressions increased, persecutions multiplied, and how the evil authorities piled decree on decree and followed expulsion with expulsion, so that there was no way to escape the enemies of Israel, they went out on the road and sought an answer from the paths of the wide world: which is the correct road to traverse to find rest for the soul? Then a piece of paper fell from heaven, and on it the words:

Go to Polaniya (Poland).

So they came to the land of Polin and they gave a mountain of gold to the king, and he received them with great honour. And God had mercy on them, so that they found favour from the king and the nobles. And the king gave them permission to reside in all the lands of his kingdom, to trade over its length and breadth, and to serve God according to the precepts of their religion. And the king protected them against every foe and enemy.

And Israel lived in Polin in tranquillity for a long time. They devoted themselves to trade and handicrafts. And God sent a blessing on them so that they were blessed in the land, and their name was exalted among the peoples. And they traded with the surrounding countries and they also struck coins with inscriptions in the holy language and the language of the country. These are the coins which have on them a lion rampant towards the right. And on the coins are the words 'Mieszko, King of Poland' or 'Mieszko, Król of Poland'. The Poles call their king 'Król'.

When they came from the land of the Franks, they found a wood in the land and on every tree, one tractate of the Talmud was incised. This is the forest of

Kawęczyn, which is near Lublin. And every man said to his neighbour, 'We have come to the land where our ancestors dwelt before the Torah and revelation were granted.'

And those who seek for names say: 'This is why it is called Polin. For thus spoke Israel when they came to the land, "Here rest for the night [*Po lin*]." And this means that we shall rest here until we are all gathered into the Land of Israel.'

Since this is the tradition, we accept it as such.

S. Y. AGNON, 1916

Contents

PART II
DOCUMENTS

BOOK REVIEWS

CORRESPONDENCE

OBITUARIES

Note on Place Names

POLITICAL connotations accrue to words, names, and spellings with an alacrity unfortunate for those who would like to maintain neutrality. It seems reasonable to honour the choices of a population on the name of its city or town, but what is one to do when the people have no consensus on their name, or when the town changes its name, and the name its spelling, again and again over time? The politician may always opt for the latest version, but the hapless historian must reckon with them all. This note, then, will be our brief reckoning.

The least problematic are those places that have a widely accepted English name, which we shall use by preference. Examples are Warsaw, Kiev, Moscow, St Petersburg, and Munich. As an exception, we maintain the Polish spelling of Kraków, which in English has more often appeared as Cracow.

Most other place names in east central Europe can raise serious problems. The linguistic and contextual diversity encountered cannot adequately be standardized by editorial formula, and in practice the least awkward solution is often to let subject matter and perspective determine the most suitable spellings in a given article. The difficulty is well illustrated by Galicia's most diversely named city, and one of its most important, which boasts five variants: the Polish Lwów, the German Lemberg, the Russian Lvov, the Ukrainian Lviv, and the Yiddish Lemberik.

A particular difficulty is posed by Wilno/Vilne/Vilnius/Vilna, to all of which there are clear objections: until 1944 the majority of the population was Polish; the city is today in Lithuania; 'Vilna', though least problematic, is an artificial construct. Our preference will be to use the common English form 'Vilna' until its first incorporation into Lithuania in October 1939, and 'Vilnius' thereafter.

In this volume of *Polin*, devoted to Jewish popular culture, context often dictates the use of Yiddish place names. In such cases the corresponding Polish (Ukrainian, Belarusian, Lithuanian, Russian) name is given in parentheses at first mention.

In all cases where context does not strongly suggest a preference, the following guidelines will apply by default for the period up to the Second World War:

1. Towns that were clearly part of a particular state and shared the majority nationality of that state will be given in a form which reflects that situation (e.g. Breslau, Danzig, Rzeszów, Przemyśl).

2. Towns that were in 'mixed' areas will take the form in which they are known today and which reflects their present situation (e.g. Poznań, Toruń, Kaunas).

Note on Transliteration

HEBREW

An attempt has been made to achieve consistency in the transliteration of Hebrew words. The following are the key distinguishing features of the system that has been adopted:

1. No distinction is made between the *aleph* and *ayin*; both are represented by an apostrophe, and only when they appear in an intervocalic position.

2. *Veit* is written *v*; *ḥet* is written *ḥ*; *yod* is written *y* when it functions as a consonant and *i* when it occurs as a vowel; *khaf* is written *kh*; *tsadi* is written *ts*; *kof* is written *k*.

3. The *dagesh ḥazak*, represented in some transliteration systems by doubling the letter, is not represented, except in words that have more or less acquired normative English spellings that include doubling, such as Hallel, kabbalah, Kaddish, rabbi, Sukkot, and Yom Kippur.

4. The *sheva na* is represented by an *e*.

5. Hebrew prefixes, prepositions, and conjunctions are not followed by hyphens when they are transliterated; thus *betoledot ha'am hayehudi*.

6. Capital letters are not used in the transliteration of Hebrew except for the first word in the titles of books and the names of people, places, institutions, and generally as in the conventions of the English language.

7. The names of individuals are transliterated following the above rules unless the individual concerned followed a different usage.

YIDDISH

Jewish popular culture in eastern Europe was overwhelmingly in Yiddish, the vernacular language of east European Jews. In this volume, reflecting this primacy, where there was a choice between Hebrew and Yiddish renderings, it was decided to use the Yiddish: *badkhn* and not *badhan*, *kheyder* and not *ḥeder*. Transliteration follows the standard YIVO system with the following exceptions. All proper names (including those of groups and institutions) are capitalized. A small number of Yiddish words that have been commonly transliterated in other ways here retain this transliteration: *rebbe* and not *rebe*, yarmulke and not yarmlke. In addition, in some places the transliteration follows dialectical or archaic forms. In the case of people's names, where an individual is known to have favoured a particular Latin form of his or her name, or if a particular version has gained currency, that form appears alongside the standard transliteration at the first mention of the name. In addition, occasional Hebrew titles or terms embedded in a Yiddish linguistic context have been transliterated using the YIVO system.

RUSSIAN AND UKRAINIAN

The system used is that of British Standard 2979:1958, without diacritics. Except in biblio-graphical and other strictly rendered matter, soft and hard signs are omitted and word-final -й, -ий, -ый, -iй in names are simplified to -*y*.

PART I

Jewish Popular Culture in Poland
and its Afterlife

Introduction

MICHAEL C. STEINLAUF

FROM about the middle of the nineteenth century Jewish life in the Polish lands began to undergo an extraordinary transformation that accelerated during the latter part of the century and the first decades of the twentieth. Our journal has examined many aspects of the Jewish engagement with modernity: the creation of new Jewish demographic centres in the largest Polish cities; the development of Jewish political parties and ideologies; changes in Jewish religious life; the multifaceted relations, in the realms of politics, culture, and society, between Jews and their co-territorial neighbours.

This issue of *Polin* is devoted to another aspect of this transformation, one that has hitherto received little attention in our journal, or, indeed, anywhere else. The Jewish engagement with modernity in the Polish lands brought masses of Jews out of their small-town communities and conceptions and into the tumult of urban life. A Jewish mass culture resulted that shaped Jewish life in Poland until its end. This culture was constructed above all around the possibilities of Yiddish, the vernacular language of Polish Jews. But the culture far transcended literature and included a diverse array of phenomena including mass-circulation newspapers and magazines, music, theatre, and material artefacts of various kinds. For several generations of Polish Jews, this culture defined the texture of everyday life.

These were Jews who lived in two worlds. On one hand, they could take for granted Jewish law and custom, folklore and legend, as these had developed for centuries in the Polish lands. Regardless of their degree of practice or even belief, they were intimately acquainted with this cultural storehouse; its contents were still instantly recognizable and—more or less ambiguously—still attractive. On the other hand, these were also Jews accustomed to trains, telegraphs, newspapers, and later radios, telephones, automobiles, ballot boxes, and public schools. By the inter-war period they were citizens of Poland; many felt themselves to be citizens of the world as well. They expected an equal share of the rights and comforts of modern societies.

Yet the popular culture these Polish Jews created to serve their daily needs is largely unknown. This is a consequence, first of all, of a well-known bias at the origin of modern Jewish scholarship. Studies of the culture of the Jews, the so-called people of the book, have focused in self-fulfilling manner on books and on the elites who produced them, be it the scholars of the pre-modern period or the secular writers of modernity. If the emphasis on the former reflected, after all, the preponderance of scholarship in the historical sources, the emphasis on 'great writers' and 'great works' in the modern period has been largely programmatic. The critical study of Yiddish literature, from its origins in the late nineteenth century, when Sholem Aleichem anointed Mendele Moykher Sforim the grandfather, *der zeyde*, of the entire literature, was a work of canonization, whose goal was to gain equal rights for the literature and its language, the scorned 'jargon', among Western cultures. In recent years this approach has merged easily with traditional methods of literary criticism, and the study of Yiddish literature has begun to find a niche in university departments of literature in the United States and Israel.

Meanwhile, during the past several decades the study of popular culture has increasingly attracted Western scholars. This has been part of a larger trend away from 'old-fashioned' political, military, and diplomatic history as documented in the relatively accessible sources of the rulers, and towards the history of daily life based on the more problematic records of the ruled. Even the popular culture created by east European Jewish immigrants in the United States has, ever since Irving Howe's magisterial *World of our Fathers*, become a subject of study. But studies of parallel phenomena in the *alter heym* (old home) have been nearly non-existent.

There are a number of reasons for this. First there is the problem of sources. The Nazis, as we know, targeted not only Jews but their culture; beyond the vast destruction of east European libraries and archives as a whole, Jewish records were particularly devastated. However much this destruction impeded all scholarship about Polish Jews, it made studies of popular culture the most difficult of all. For such scholarship depends on the most ephemeral of sources: flimsy pamphlets, leaflets, chapbooks, catalogues, postcards, and yellowing tabloid newspapers that were never intended, in the best of circumstances, to survive beyond their immediate use. East European scholars, moreover, have not shown the same interest in such artefacts as their Western counterparts; for the most part they still do not consider popular culture a serious subject of inquiry. Thus, for example, the growing Polish interest in the history of Yiddish theatre focuses largely on its more canonized forms. There has been, finally, a disinclination by Jewish scholars as well to approach the subject of popular culture. Prior to the Second World War a handful of studies of so-called folk culture appeared, but there was little interest in tracing the development of such phenomena under modern conditions. After the Holocaust the aura of martyrdom that has hung over the Polish Jewish world as a whole has discouraged investigations into its seemingly less exalted corners.

The result has been a distortion of what that world was about. However sublime the accomplishments of Yiddish literary artists from Mendele to Bashevis Singer, the Yiddish language, even in the modern period, retained its roots and its power in the spoken word. The appeal of modern Yiddish literature never rivalled that of Yiddish theatre, above all in its popular version, yet our knowledge of the former dwarfs our knowledge of the latter. Similarly, most of the limited studies of the

Yiddish press have focused on ideological issues, but it is serialized novels and political cartoons, not to mention classified ads, that doubtless drew most readers.

The first twelve chapters of this volume constitute a preliminary attempt to restore a certain balance in our approach to the lost world of Polish Jewry. The contributors examine phenomena from the ground up rather than the top down. They reflect a variety of disciplines: literary and cultural history, art history, anthropology, ethnomusicology. The subjects discussed are inevitably somewhat haphazard; their coexistence between the covers of one volume is often more the result of the momentary availability of scholarship produced by a handful of scholars than the fulfilment of an editorial plan. A crucial function of most of these chapters is the gathering of material, its retrieval from oblivion. Only after such work has progressed considerably will it begin to be possible to link phenomena in some larger theoretical and meta-historical narrative.

Studies by Ariela Krasney and Walter Zev Feldman conduct us into the scarcely known worlds of *badkhonim* (wedding jesters) and *klezmorim* (musicians), respectively, precisely at the moment when these performers were reinventing themselves and their craft under the conditions of modernity. Michael Aylward then examines one part of the technology that underlay such transformations: the early recording industry. Michael Steinlauf offers an overview of the history of Jewish theatre in Poland; François Guesnet analyses a bawdy parody of traditional Jewish elites probably intended for the popular stage; and Natan Gross traces Mordechai Gebirtig's passage from folk singer to cabaret performer in inter-war Poland. Seth Wolitz investigates the career of a piece of 'folklore' that turns out to have been a literary creation; Shalom Sabar traces the varying ways in which German Jews and Polish Jews created postcard images of themselves at the turn of the twentieth century. Four chapters about reading follow. Joshua Shanes examines the transformation of Orthodox Galician Jews into modern newspaper readers; Nathan Cohen tracks the contentious relations between popular literature, the tabloid press, and the Jewish intelligentsia in inter-war Poland; Ellen Kellman sketches a history of working-class Jewish libraries during the same period; Edward Portnoy recovers Jewish cartoon art and its creators in the Polish Yiddish press. These studies of the pre-war Jewish world are supplemented in Part II, Documents, by the first English translations from the work of two remarkable authors. A. Litvin, an early Jewish ethnographer, traipsed the remotest corners of eastern Europe to document the lifeways of the impoverished and the marginal caught up in irreversible change. The yeshiva *bokher* (student) Icek Boruch Farbarowicz chose a life of crime, then published his memoirs, a popular sensation in inter-war Poland, under the name Urke Nachalnik. Gwido Zlatkes provides an introduction to Nachalnik's writings and to the Polish Jewish underworld they uncover.

While it is much too soon for conclusions of any sort, the very act of locating these texts within a single volume produces resonances of various kinds. The geographical range covered by the research suggests that the ambiguous designation

'Polish lands' may nevertheless be the best approximation for the cultural territory of eastern Ashkenaz. A number of names, somewhat unexpectedly, keep reappearing. The numerous references to the Broder singers, for example, groups of performers who wandered the Polish lands during the second half of the nineteenth century, hints at the rewards of their further study. New perspectives also seem to emerge on the importance of hierarchy in Jewish life, be it among communal elites, hasidim, *klezmorim*, or thieves, as well as on efforts to reconstruct hierarchy under modern conditions using distinctions such as *kunst* (art) versus *shund* (trash). Most of all, these chapters suggest that in the realm of everyday life some of the distinctions that historians regularly make between traditional and secular, pre-modern and modern, need to be rethought. The Orthodox readers of the Galician Yiddish press or the urban Jews chortling at a cartoon in *Haynt* or a Gebirtig cabaret song or longing for a little 'Romanian' Jewish music seem to have been considerably less predictable ideologically than studies of Jewish political parties might have us believe. In the daily life of *yidn fun a gants yor* (average Jews) old and new seem to have coexisted and interacted in remarkably subtle configurations.

The final six chapters of Part I concern what can be termed the afterlife of the sorts of phenomena explored in the first twelve chapters. They track some of the traces of the popular culture of Polish Jews that managed to survive into and past the destruction of that culture in the Holocaust. If the Polish lands were already farflung, here the frontiers are global. Bret Werb and Barbara Milewski investigate the transformation of a popular Polish Jewish cabaret song in a Nazi concentration camp. Yaakov Mazor discovers the supposedly lost art of the *badkhn* among east European hasidim living in Israel. Alex Lubet traces the fusion of pre-war Jewish cabaret and contemporary blues, rock 'n' roll, and reggae music in the work of the Canadian Jewish singer–composer Wolf Krakowski. Jeffrey Shandler re-views the photographs of Roman Vishniac as post-war Jewish American cultural artefacts. Erica Lehrer traces the wooden figures of Jews produced in contemporary Poland from their creators to their consumers throughout the world and back again. Ruth Ellen Gruber focuses on the annual festival of Jewish culture in Kraków, the largest gathering of *klezmer* musicians and their fans in the world.

Are there continuities between the pre-war and the post-war world? What resonates across the great destruction? 'Ver vet blaybn, vos vet blaybn?' ('Who will last, what will last?'), the poet Avrom Sutzkever once asked. Such questions, which the construction of this volume is intended to provoke, are best left to our readers.

The *Badkhn*: From Wedding Stage to Writing Desk

ARIELA KRASNEY

INTRODUCTION

IN this chapter I discuss two key roles of the traditional Jewish entertainer known as the *badkhn*: as a performer on the wedding stage (*bimah*) at Jewish weddings and as the author of published versions of such performances. My goal is to examine, first, the *badkhn*'s techniques of expression and, secondly, the process through which, beginning in the mid-nineteenth century, the *badkhn*'s work began to move from oral performance to written literature.

The *badkhn* first emerged in Europe during the Middle Ages alongside comparable artists among other peoples. As Jewish society and Judaism evolved from the sixteenth century to the end of the nineteenth century, the *badkhn* adapted himself to the changing conditions. By the nineteenth century his identity had crystallized into that of a figure with two faces: one of riotous, chaotic, topsy-turvy jesting, rooted in ancient sacrificial traditions surrounding the god Dionysus and evincing a tendency towards social subversiveness; and the other of conservative, learned discourse rooted in the fixed system of halakhic *mitsvot* and serving as a mouthpiece for them.

The popular poetry of the *badkhonim* is noted for its simplicity, the language closely identified with the spoken idiom of ordinary people. Yet at the foundation of the *badkhn*'s poetry the holy, elevated language of the Bible is present in varying degrees. Alongside the prosaic features of this poetry are the repetitive sounds of rhyme, a widespread by-product of the strong rhythms that characterize oral art.

The art of the *badkhn* could not be expressed in isolation. It was meaningless without the participation in the artist's performance of those watching and hearing him. Because the encounter between the *badkhn* and his audience occurred at specific special events—family gatherings or holidays—the audience usually gathered for the event and not specifically to see the *badkhn*. None the less, the *badkhn* usually led the event and was at the centre of the celebration, though the audience was also active, often no less than the *badkhn*. Consequently, the *badkhn* had two possible

This chapter is based on my book *Habadḥan* (Ramat Gan, 1998).

approaches, not entirely distinct from each other, to participating in the event: he could allow himself to be swept up by the celebration and spontaneously follow the needs of his audience, their wishes and mood, or he could organize the event at the outset and play a more central role in determining its course.

Within his performance the *badkhn* was the final arbiter of the nature of the interaction between himself and the audience. Nevertheless, the audience too participated in the artistic situation; the *badkhn* and his audience were dependent on each other in a reciprocal process of creation that had its own rhythm, which they worked to maintain. Understanding the heart of the audience, its needs, and its mood was no less important than mastering artistic principles and techniques. The *badkhn* had to control communication between himself and the audience at all semiotic levels, including mimicry, gestures, and body language.

In addition to verbal language, the *badkhn* had to consider visual elements such as dress and mask, mimicry and movement. Theatrical elements—words, intonations, gestures, body language, and music—had to be harmonized into a cohesive language that could serve him just as it serves other performers.

In the second half of the nineteenth century the *badkhonim*, celebrated as directors of wedding ceremonies, entertainers of the bride and groom, and possessors of a diverse and multivalent oral repertoire that attracted varied audiences, began to publish their works. A literary genre tends to preserve its primary elements while incorporating innovations related to current needs. The genre undergoes many transformations, but it is never disconnected from its origins; it brings its past with it and therefore maintains unity and continuity in its literary development. The printed sources documenting the songs (*badkhones*) of the *badkhonim* are rooted in a literature that had been transmitted orally from generation to generation, and that finally metamorphosed and made its way into writing and print.[1]

Numerous booklets of *badkhones* appeared in Warsaw in the latter half of the nineteenth century; they quickly gained a large audience and were among the most popular books published at the time.[2] The fashion spread and soon engulfed the Jewish world.[3] Abraham Ber Gotlober, a contemporary Hebrew–Yiddish author, maskil, and occasional *badkhn*, tries to account for the phenomenon in his long poem 'Di farkerte velt' ('The Upside Down World'):

---

[1] On an analogous situation in early modern France, see M. Bakhtin, *Rabelais and his World* (Bloomington, Ind., 1984).

[2] J. Shatzky, *Geshikhte fun yidn in varshe*, vol. iii (New York, 1953), 266. Some of the booklets are: M. Shlayfshteyn [Badkhn oys Varshe], *Der bankrot oder di geshlogene tsayt* (Warsaw, 1884); M. Marakhovske, *Di yontevdike lider oder vokhedike lider mit yontevdike nigunim* (Warsaw, 1886); S. K. Levin, *Shirey khayim oder finf naye lebns lider* (Warsaw, 1891); A. Geller, *Sefer lemenatseyekh* (Transvaal, 1900); M. Taradeyke, *Di sheyne vitsn-lider fun di damen-hoyzn* (Piotrków, 1911); A. Fishzon, *Der zinger* (Vilna, 1913); L. Bergman [R. Mekhele Badkhn], *Der badkhn* (Warsaw, 1928). See also *Elyokem tsunzers verk*, ed. M. Schaechter, 2 vols. (New York, 1964).

[3] The *badkhn* Alter Fishzon addresses this phenomenon in his booklet *Der zinger*, 3.

> Many people write books;
> Some because they are poor . . .
> Some want to pass the time . . .
> Another writes a *muser*[4] book,
> Some like to write songs
> And riddles for Hanukah and Purim . . .[5]

Many *badkhonim* believed that the transition to writing had been forced on them by the society around them.[6] But among the *badkhonim*, whose work was oral, additional hidden creative potential had been seeking realization and now discovered an outlet in writing. They quickly understood the strength of the new medium and exploited it in the interests of their older medium, the performance of the comic artist standing on the stage, captivating his audience and directing them as his heart desired. At the same time they discovered in print the opportunity to develop their poetic talents as writers and not only as stand-up improvisers.

THE COMPLEXITY OF THE *BADKHN*'S IMAGE

The *badkhn* is mentioned in the Talmud,[7] and his image fixed itself in the Jewish world for centuries, although it changed form, wandered through many countries, and was called by other names.

The *badkhn* became an object of criticism by the Jewish religious establishment on one hand, and, in the nineteenth century, by the intellectual enlightened establishment on the other; however, he always awakened curiosity and attracted the masses. A fascinating ambivalence existed within this figure, which served as a canvas for popular artistic expression in a range of periods and places.

We can add the *badkhn* to the long line of comic artists emerging throughout Europe since the Middle Ages. In the Jewish world he was known as the *lets*, and,

[4] The term *muser* (Heb. *musar*) refers both to a ritualized form of moralizing, as in the phrase *muser-zogn* (saying *muser*), and to a genre of popular Jewish literature that developed from the middle of the 16th century to the beginning of the 18th century. *Muser*, a kind of early modern self-help literature, brought preaching and homiletics, steeped in a popular conceptual framework stemming from Lurianic kabbalah, to the average Jew. Hebrew *muser* books were translated into Yiddish, and some were written directly in Yiddish. The *badkhn*'s art was steeped in such texts. In the 19th century the Lithuanian rabbi Israel Salanter (Lipkin) founded a religious movement called Musar, which tapped into these traditions in an effort to renew Judaism.

[5] Abraham Ber Gotlober, 'Di farkerte velt', *Tsaytshrift* (Minsk), 5 (1931), 55. Here and in other citations from *badkhones* the original is in rhymed couplets.

[6] See N. Oyslender, 'Tsu b. slutskis "Badkhonim-shoyshpiler"', *Tsaytshrift*, 1 (1926), 261–2; Fishzon, *Der zinger*, introd., unpaginated.

[7] In BT, *Ta'an.* 22a *badkhones* is mentioned as a profession and there is reference to *anshei baduhei* (people who entertain). In *Hul.* 95b the art of *badkhones* is apparently well known and there is reference to the *shoteh* (fool).

like his Christian counterparts, the jester and the fool, he was a complex figure with multifaceted characteristics. The dualities and ambivalences of the comic event centre around this archetypal hero and his disguises. The comic artist is the fool or idiot:[8] he is the comic spirit, the crude figure wearing the ugly mask of jest or satire; he is also the possessor of primordial magical strength and can say his words without fear.[9] His audience too is in conflict: on one hand there is fear of his charismatic powers, but on the other there is laughter at his jests. Because the fool is adaptable, vital, able to absorb blows, and always marked, he can also be denied with impunity, rejected and beaten. Yet inevitably he rises again.

The jester appears as an anarchic figure, the possessor of unformed and unrealized energy.[10] He seems to act within a special framework of laws, an inversion of the daily social framework. He thereby possesses the potential to overturn the world order and introduce chaos by breaking all laws.[11] Given these tendencies, it makes sense that Jewish religious leaders reacted negatively to the *badkhn*, and emphasized his irresponsibility and frivolity.

Nevertheless, there was a qualitative difference between the *badkhn* and the Christian comic artist. This is because his function as a jester, what Mikhail Bakhtin has termed the carnivalesque, made up only one dimension of the *badkhn*'s art.[12] The other was expressed in the framework of commandments—*aseh velo ta'aseh* ('thou shalt and shalt not')—whose source was the strict system of Jewish law. These two dimensions of the *badkhn* were never independent of each other; the carnivalesque was always restrained by the halakhic dimension. The *badkhn* thereby moved between two functions—that of the *magid* (preacher) and speaker of *muser*, and that of the jesting clown. This ambivalent characterization and the ambiguous situation in which he found himself were inescapable. The two dimensions of the *badkhn*'s role were two dimensions of life, which exist side by side, with continuous tension between them. This tension was perfectly reflected, as we shall see, in the traditional wedding ceremony, over which the *badkhn* presided. For the *badkhn* differed from his Christian counterpart in his connection not simply to the halakhic system as a whole, but to a specific commandment, that of making the bride and groom rejoice.

---

[8] On the two comic figures appearing in the Middle Ages, see R. Navo, 'Hakomediyah', *Bamah* (Tel Aviv), 2 (Sept. 1959), 8. See also B. Slutski, 'Yidishe badkhonim-shoyshpiler', *Tsaytshrift*, 1 (1926), 257–61; Y. Shiper [Ignacy Schiper], *Geshikhte fun yidisher teater-kunst un drame fun di eltste tsaytn biz 1750*, 3 vols. (Warsaw, 1923–8); Y. Lipshits, 'Badkhonim un leytsim ba yidn: materyaln tsu a verterbukh', *Arkhiv far der geshikhte fun yidishn teater un drame* (Vilna), 1 (1930), 5–37; W. Willeford, *The Fool and his Sceptre* (London, 1969); Bakhtin, *Rabelais and his World*.

[9] On the image of the comic artist, see Shiper, *Geshikhte fun yidisher teater-kunst un drame*, i. 228–31.   [10] Ibid. 144–5.

[11] Willeford, *The Fool and his Sceptre*, 101; see also Bakhtin, *Rabelais*.

[12] Bakhtin, *Rabelais*. See also A. Ziv, *Personality and Sense of Humor* (New York, 1984); A. Zajdman, *Humor* (Tel Aviv, 1994).

THE *BADKHN*'S SUBVERSIVE LAUGHTER

The humour of the *badkhn* contained both seriousness and mischievousness, separate from each other and expressed through different artistic and performative means. The central ritual of the seating and veiling of the bride (a ritual known as *bazetsns*) prior to taking her under the *khupe* (wedding canopy) was accompanied by advice on ethical matters (*muser-zogn*) by the *badkhn* to the bride and groom, each separately. In this recitative the *badkhn* discussed weighty subjects such as life and death, sin and repentance, and the roles of the Jewish wife and the Jewish husband, as, for example, in the following:

> On the day of your wedding
> You must remember
> All of your sins,
> From the day you were created.[13]

His song elicited much emotion and weeping. In nearly every published version of this song the *badkhn* quiets the weeping women with the words 'Noshim zol zayn abisl shtil!' ('Women, let's be a little quiet!').[14] This command was easily parodied. Similarly, the *muser-zogn* itself could inspire hilarity, as in this concluding portion of a *bazetsns*:

> O little bride, weep, weep,
> In your mother's eyes you have such charm,
> And when your groom looks at you,
> He too will break into a terrible cry—and let us say amen.[15]

In order to understand the *badkhn* it was not enough simply to listen to his words. It was also important to appreciate his disguises and follow his gestures and movements. The communication was verbal, but the movements, along with the rise and fall of the voice, and its changing tones, were all a necessary part of his art. The gestures were a language that functioned parallel to speech and together with it, and were, in fact, the central means of communication. In the following quotations we see the *badkhn* on the stage:

Khaym Henkl puts on his yarmulke, gets up on the bench, and starts to say Torah, sharp words in rhyme . . .[16]

And Reb Borukh Badkhn got up on the table, folded his hands over his belly, and dropped his head, as when one mourns the dead, and began with the beautiful sad melody that can move a stone to tears.[17]

Leyzer Badkhn would perform a scene called 'Der erets yisroel yid' [the Jew from the land of Israel]. This performance would end in a special way. Leyzer had made a pair of stilts thanks

---

[13] Bergman, *Der badkhn*, 6.   [14] Ibid.

[15] Y. Makusmakher, 'Di vishkover kapelye', in D. Shtokfish, *Sefer vishkov* [Wyszków, Vishkeve] (Tel Aviv, 1964), 55–6.   [16] Ibid.

[17] Sholem Aleichem [Sholem Rabinovitsh], *Mayses far yidishe kinder*, vol. ii (New York, 1927), 46.

to which he looked extraordinarily tall. He would put on a long white robe [*kitl*] which made him look fatter, and in such attire he would end the performance of the 'Der erets yisroel yid' with an artful dance.[18]

> A celebration's in progress
> A time of rejoicing
> This one spins like a wind
> And that one pretends to give birth.
> This one is disguised as a Jerusalemite
> And that one as a priest.
> This one bangs on a basin—and that one
> Blows on a cane.[19]

Even those serious *badkhonim* who used neither costumes nor mimicry typically accompanied their performance with a symbolic act of disguise: turning their hats inside out and back to front.[20]

The *badkhn* made use of the full gamut of linguistic comic effects: images that are humorous in their own right; comic exaggerations; grammatical slips of the tongue, mistakes in vocabulary and the construction of sentences; transpositions of words; idiomatic mistakes; inappropriate metaphors. The *badkhn*'s repertoire ranged from stories that amused the simplest minds to sophisticated discourses whose comic intent could not be immediately grasped. Word games were particularly popular.

We can differentiate between the comic expressed in language and the comic created by language. With respect to the latter, Asher Avraham Druyanov puts forward two linguistic mechanisms as causes of laughter.[21] Linguistic commentary (*midrash lashon*) exploits the consonant or the syllable at the phonetic level, that is, upsets the surface elements of speech. This technique, obviously untranslatable because entirely bound by particular languages, was widespread among European jesters. More common among *badkhonim*, however, was commentary on thought or words (*midrash mahshavah* or *midrash milim*). For Druyanov this is a more advanced technique, as it uses combinations of meaning to create meaning on two levels, explicit and implicit; the jester moves his audience from the former to the latter.[22] Here the *badkhn* is greatly aided by a special tradition, that of parodying biblical

---

[18] Slutski, 'Yidishe badkhonim-shoyshpiler', 257–61.   [19] Ibid.

[20] Y. Indershteyn, 'Der letster badkhn', in B. Kaplinski (ed.), *Pinkes zhetl* [Zdzięcioł] (Tel Aviv, 1957), 276–7.   [21] A. A. Druyanov, *Sefer habedihah vehahidud*, vol. i (Jerusalem, 1939), 8.

[22] Dan Ben-Amos discusses this in his article 'Iyun mehudash bemusag humor yehudi', in D. Noy and Y. Ben Ami (eds.), *Mehkerei hamerkaz leheker hafolklor*, vol. i (Jerusalem, 1970), 26. He notes that the comparative research that has developed since the appearance of Druyanov's work *Sefer habedihah vehahidud* allows us to examine Jewish humour in a balanced way and concludes that in large part Jewish jokes nevertheless relate to the tradition of international jokes. See also Y. L. Kahan, *Shtudyes vegn yidisher folksshafung* (New York, 1952), 266–74; D. Noy, 'Hakayemet bedihat-am yehudit?', *Mahanayim*, 67 (1962), 48–56; H. Jason, 'The Jewish Joke: The Problem of Definition', *Southern Folklore Quarterly*, 31 (1967), 48–54.

verses. Yitskhok Yoel Linetski, for example, describes a *badkhn* who 'spread[s] out his hands and exclaim[s]':

Be still, gentlemen! I will amuse you with a sharp little commentary [*peshatl*][23] before the wedding gifts. In Scripture it's written 'Vayikaḥ korah ben-izhar'.[24] So in either case there's a problem. Was Korah a female? Then why does it say *ben-izhar* [son of Izhar]; it should say *bat-izhar* [daughter of Izhar] . . . But if he was a male, why did he take Izhar for a wife? . . . A youth and a male have to part ['a bokher mit a zeykher sheyt zikh dokh'] . . . The answer is: Korah was in fact a male, but Izhar was a female and the 'ben' means 'old', that is, 'old Izhar', and that's what Rashi means when he asks: 'Koraḥ shepike'aḥ hayah mah ra'ah lishtut zeh?' [Now Korah, who was prudent, why did he commit this folly?][25] You, clever Korah, how did you manage to be so stupid and marry an old maid?[26]

The underlying method of this commentary on words is to use combinations of meaning that are apparently connected by the thread of a particular logic. When the logic is drawn out, however, it emerges that there was really no thread at all and no basis for the connections. This is the technique of sophistry (*pilpul*), which appears to be rational, yet actually contains no real logic at all; one can attach to it all sorts of notions that seem to be meaningful but in reality have no meaning. The *badkhn*-sophist's apparent intention is not hair-splitting or sarcasm; he seems to think that his words arise only from deep levels of his text. In contrast, the ordinary jester rarely pretends to seriousness.

Abraham Ber Gotlober offers another such example of parody when he relates that he once heard a *badkhn* expound on the subject of hasidic *rebbes* who dance before the bride:

Why, when dancing with the bride, do the rabbis (the righteous [*tsadikim*] of the generation) not give her the corner of a handkerchief to hold and hold another corner themselves, as is the custom in dancing. Because these *tsadikim* are not ruled by the evil urge [*yetser hara*] nor will they see it before them, and with bare hands they take the hand of the bride and dance with her (and in childhood my eyes beheld many times how these *tsadikim* hugged the bride in full view of the congregation while dancing with her!). And the reason for this way of dancing was given in the words of the Talmud: 'Our rabbis taught: how does one dance before the bride'[27] . . . 'Before the bride': the meaning is in the letters that come before the letters

---

[23] *Peshat* is considered the first and most straightforward of the four traditional methods of interpreting scripture.

[24] This is the beginning of the weekly Torah reading known as *parashat* Korah (Num. 16: 1–18: 32), generally read in June. The entire verse is: 'And Korah, the son of Izhar, the son of Kohath, the son of Levi, with Dathan and Abiram, the sons of Eliab, and On, the son of Peleth, sons of Reuben, took men' (*The Pentateuch and Haftorahs*, ed. J. H. Hertz (London, 1981), 639). But in the Hebrew text 'took (*vayikaḥ*) is not followed by an object; the word 'men' was first supplied by ibn Ezra. The *badkhn* reads the text without this addition as: 'Korah took [i.e. wed] the son of Izhar.'

[25] *The Pentateuch and Rashi's Commentary*, ed. A. Ben-Isaiah and B. Sharfman, vol. iv (Brooklyn, NY, 1949), 167 (Num. 16: 7). Rashi is referring, of course, to Korah's folly in rebelling against Moses. In Hebrew the word *ben* can mean 'old' as in *ben sheloshim* (30 years old).

[26] Y. Y. Linetski, *Dos khsidishe yingl* (Vilna, 1897), 94.　　　[27] BT, *Ket.* 17a.

khaf-lamed-he, which are the letters *yod-khaf-dalet*, and in transposition *yod-dalet-khaf*. That is, they will take the bride[28] and not the handkerchief.[29]

The songs of the *badkhn* took shape in an atmosphere of strong familial and communal solidarity, which nurtured mutual trust between the *badkhn* and his audience. This intimacy encouraged the *badkhn* to address potentially explosive subjects, including settling scores with members of the audience, whether as individuals or as representatives of institutions. Although such attacks on individuals and institutions were often couched in strong language, they nevertheless served to reinforce the bonds between audience and performer. Dissatisfaction with existing conditions in the world was a source of creativity for the *badkhn* and his humour. Relationships among audience members, disputes between neighbours, the exploitation of the oppressed, the haughtiness of community leaders, slavish conformity to new fashions in social behaviour: all such issues could be addressed in this intimate atmosphere.

The nineteenth-century *badkhn* Moyshe Marakhovske, for example, could refer to the Jewish establishment as follows:

> Community leaders who pretend to be pious
> And all the town funds are in their pockets,
> Like wolves
> Who bite the lambs.
> They hear voices crying
> And do not look round.[30]

In a song he entitled 'Tehilim' ('Psalms'), Marakhovske echoes portions of Scripture most familiar to his audiences, but transforms them with a new addressee, new content, and new meaning. The song, as Marakhovske tells his readers, follows Psalm 119, 'Ashrei temimei derekh' ('Happy are they that are upright in the way'), but it quickly becomes clear that the supplication 'Ikh bet aykh!' ('I beg of you!') does not address an omnipotent God but denounces morally compromised human beings who are far from 'upright in the way'.

> I ask of you! I cry out [*shray gevalt*] for Jews
> Not to stray from the true path . . .
> I beg of you! Bankers! . . .
> I beg of you! Doctors! . . .
> I beg of you! Community leaders [*gaboyim*]! . . .
> See and consider the pains of today
> And leave a spark of love in your hearts.[31]

[28] The word *kala* (bride) is spelled *khaf-lamed-he*; *yod-dalet-khaf* can spell *yadkha* (your hand). The anecdote parodies hasidic *rebbes* (*tsadikim*).

[29] *Der dektukh oder tsvey khupes in eyn nakht* (Warsaw, 1876), 105.

[30] Marakhovske, *Di yontevdike lider*, 19.

[31] Ibid. 9–10.

The *badkhn* could even subject Jewish values as a whole to withering critique, as in this passage from the work of Yisroel Yitskhok Tsipershteyn:

> Lineage [*yikhes*] or money
> Throughout the whole world
> Play the only role.
> Whoever has them,
> One of these two,
> Goes from small to great.
> Honour and respect without end
> Cover his greatest failings.[32]

After a moment of initial discomfort, the *badkhn*'s audience, freed from the inhibitions that served as protection from such criticism, generally responded with laughter. The *badkhn*, moreover, was a product of the same social world as his audience. At the moment when the words of criticism passed his lips, he overcame his fear of the audience's response. When he heard their laughter, he knew not only that he had said what needed to be said, but that in doing so he had also gained esteem and strengthened his professional standing. Both audience and performer were thereby liberated from their shared fears of authority and shared social conditioning into a space of unrestrained laughter.[33]

THE *BADKHN* AT THE CENTRE OF THE JEWISH WEDDING

Making the bride and groom rejoice: this is a first-order *mitsvah* (commandment) and is frequently mentioned in traditional sources: 'It is a *mitsvah* to make the bride and groom rejoice, also to dance before the bride and to say that "she is beautiful and graceful" and we find that Rabbi Judah bar Illai used to dance before a bride.'[34] Talmudic discussion of how one dances before the bride includes not only the issue of elevating the *mitsvah* but also the dancing itself, in which rabbis are mentioned as participating.[35]

The wedding celebrations typically lasted for at least seven days. They began on the sabbath before the wedding, when in a ritual known as *oyfrufns* the groom was given public honour during the reading of the Torah in the synagogue. It continued on the sabbath after the wedding, when the bride was escorted to the synagogue, and culminated at the end of the seven days of festive meals after the wedding, when the seven ritual blessings (*sheve brokhes*) recited at the wedding were repeated. The *badkhn* was present on the evening after the *oyfrufns*, when all gathered for a banquet at the bride's house, and he was present with farewell rhymes for the bride

---

[32] Y. Y. Tsipershteyn, *Dray naye lider* (Warsaw, 1900), 12.

[33] See T. Reik, *Jewish Wit* (New York, 1962), 233–4.

[34] *Code of Jewish Law (Kitsur shulkhan arukh)*, ed. S. Ganzfried, trans. H. Goldin, vol. iv (New York, 1927), 13 ('Laws of Marriage' [Hilkhot ishut] 149: 9). [35] BT, *Ket.* 17a; see also *Ber.* 6b.

as she left her parents' home for that of her husband at the end of the celebrations
a week after the wedding. The wedding week comprised a number of ceremonies,
but the turning point, which essentially divided the week into two parts, was the
betrothal ceremony. The first half of the wedding was saturated with expectation
and anxiety. This tension peaked as the couple stood beneath the *khupe*. The breaking of the glass by the groom signalled a release of tension and an explosion of merri-
ment. The *badkhn* accompanied all these moments and channelled them by placing
himself at their centre. Before the *khupe* he stood before both the bride and the
groom and brought them to tears with words of *muser*. After the *khupe* this weeping
surged into a torrent of laughter and rejoicing, and the *badkhn* became a roisterous
jester. Throughout the wedding the duality of the *badkhn*'s experience was paralleled by the experience of the community: desire was acknowledged yet simultaneously limited by means of Jewish law, in this case, the ceremony of marriage.

On the wedding day itself the *badkhn* first greeted the bridegroom's parents
upon their arrival at the wedding hall. For example, in a play by Avrom Goldfadn
(Abraham Goldfaden), whose father was a *badkhn* and who himself had worked as a
badkhn in his youth, we find the following:

> Silence. A little more quiet! Make way, scholars and gentlemen,
> Here comes an in-law, a very wealthy woman.
> Her name is Brayne, the modest and the righteous,
> From a beautiful and fine family . . .
> And because of her honour and the honour of all the in-laws
> She will soon hand out cash [*mezumonim*].[36]

It was as the guests were arriving and just before the *khupe* that financial matters
were often settled and the *ksube* (wedding contract) was completed. Sometimes the
bride's father failed to pay all the dowry at this time, and financial disputes typically
erupted, leading to a variety of related arguments.[37]

At this time the *badkhn* began to speak words of *muser* to the bride. This section
of the wedding, the *bazetsns*, is also called *bazingen di kale* (singing to the bride) or
baveynen di kale (weeping over the bride). Although the women were admonished
about weeping, they were also encouraged to weep. If the bride or groom was an
orphan, the *badkhn* would note this with special verses. The *badkhn* spoke philo-
sophically, meditating on the meaning of life and the purpose of religious obligations and commandments. He presented the wedding day as the end of one cycle
and the beginning of a new one, and called upon the bride to repent, to cry to God
and ask that he bless the marriage. The *badkhn* also emphasized the importance of

---

[36] Avrom Goldfadn, *Di komishe khasene fun shmendrik mit di kale* (Warsaw, 1890), 30. Another
version of the last two lines may be found in A. Medvitski, 'Fun alts tsu bislekh', in Kaplinski (ed.),
Pinkes zhetl, 92.

[37] For a sarcastic view of the sorts of things that could happen during these moments, see Y. Zeevi,
'Shidukhim utenaim', in Y. Zeevi (Wilk) *et al.* (eds.), *Yizkor kehilot luniniec/kozhanhorodok* (Tel Aviv,
1952), 54–5.

the bride practising the three central *mitsvot* of a woman in her married life: taking
ḥalah when baking bread (a ritual symbolizing the setting aside of a portion of
dough for the *kohanim* (priests)) lighting sabbath candles, and observing *nidah*
(ritual purity in marital relations). Marriage was explicitly portrayed as analogous
to both birth and death:

> You are now
> Like a child that is born.[38]

> Also, bride, you must know
> That the day of *khupe*
> Is like the day of death.[39]

Weeping and rejoicing were linked and stressed as being dependent on each other:

> Therefore let your tears pour out
> So the Creator doesn't, God forbid,
> Spoil your wedding.[40]

And again:

> Today there is rejoicing for you,
> Today there is also complaint.[41]

Despite the seriousness of the moment, these were not words of chastisement, but
words of persuasion, more guidance than hard moralizing. Fear was mixed with
encouragement and hope:

> And pray further with
> Great weeping . . . with terror and fear . . .
> And delight and joy
> May you have both.[42]

The verses, moreover, were filled with terms of endearment and sincere wishes:

> This I wish you,
> Groom and bride both,
> That good luck should shine on you
> In heaven so bright.[43]

When the *badkhn* had completed his sermon to the bride, he turned to the groom,
holding in his hands the bride's gifts.[44] He then sang to the groom (*bazingen dem
khosn*), often beginning:

> A *badkhn* comes
> And brings the groom
> A present from the bride.[45]

---

[38] Bergman, *Der badkhn*, 4.　　[39] Ibid. 3.　　[40] Geller, *Sefer lemenatseyekh*, 42.
[41] Goldfadn, *Di komishe khasene*, 32.　　[42] Ibid. 44–5.　　[43] Ibid. 9.
[44] On the importance of these gifts, see Y. Elzet, 'Mit hundert yor tsurik', in Elzet, *Shtudyes in dem
amolikn inerlekhn yidishn lebn* (Montreal, 1927), 12–13.　　[45] Bergman, *Der badkhn*, 10.

In his sermon to the groom the *badkhn* also spoke of repentance on this great day, and compared it to Yom Kippur. He addressed the groom, as he did the bride, with terms of endearment, such as 'dear groom' and 'groom of my heart', and advised him to pray and not to hold back his tears, so that God would bless the match. The end was always optimistic and full of good wishes:

> And with good luck
> May this pair
> Approach the *khupe*
> With great fortune.[46]

These sermons were spoken in the spirit of traditional *muser* writings, which were popular Jewish moral and religious guides. Emphasis was placed on making oneself pure and holy, on repentance, and on turning to God in prayer, each of these seen as a way of overcoming the menace of the demonic world. In the *Kav hayashar* ('The Straight Line') it is said that if a man is careful to put up a fence, he is protected from demonic forces.[47] In his *muser-zogn* the *badkhn* directed the bride and groom towards this holy purpose of life. For Moses Hayim Luzzatto (Ramhal) in his celebrated *musar* work *Mesilat yesharim* ('The Path of Uprightness'), living in a holy way is of critical importance, but this holiness extends into every area of life: 'the matter of holiness is twofold: its beginning is work and its end is reward; its beginning is that which the man devotes to himself and its end is that which is dedicated to him . . . And, lo, the man who sanctifies himself in sanctification of his Creator, even his physical actions become matters of real holiness.'[48] But the *badkhonim* seemed to emphasize purity in a narrower sense, often reminding the couple, for example, of the importance of fasting on the day of *khupe* in order to encourage repentance.

Throughout each stage of the wedding ceremony the *badkhn* directed the action and its performers, as in the following example from Goldfadn. Here the *badkhn* first turns to the women dancing around the bride before the *bazetsns*:

> All of you have danced already,
> Now let's go and seat the bride!

The women gather around and plait her hair, and the *badkhn* continues:

> Now let's go and bring the groom,
> And have him cover the bride.
> May God today
> Wipe out all your sins.

---

[46] Goldfadn, *Di komishe khasene*, 39.

[47] Z. H. Kaydanover, *Kav hayashar* (first pub. Frankfurt am Main, 1705; Jerusalem, 1982), 42.

[48] Moses Hayim Luzzatto, *Mesilat yesharim* (first pub. Amsterdam, 1740; Jerusalem, 1965), par. 188, 190.

And he gives the groom the veil:

> Take this veil in hand, groom, like a king,
> And cover your bride's radiance.

He then clears a way for the bride and groom and brings them to the *khupe* with the words 'Make a path! In a propitious hour with the right foot under the *khupe*.'[49] And again:

> And if it's really this way,
> Let's not delay
> And put away the weeping motions,
> And you, musicians, play
> Really badly, I mean well [*Gor zeyer mis, meyn ikh zis*],
> And you, pious women,
> Don't be angry,
> Wipe the sniffle from your noses with care,
> Put aside your woe—
> And let us with good luck
> To the *khupe* go.[50]

Immediately after the *khupe* the role of the *badkhn* centred around the *vetshere* (evening meal). As Saul Tshernichowsky writes: 'And when the crowd finished their meal of fish and rested, Yosi the *badkhn* rose and stood on a high stool and gladdened the hearts of all the guests with words of jesting and wonders.'[51] This could be a time for speeches but also for magic tricks, pantomime, masked sketches, or anything the crowd enjoyed:

> As that *badkhn* sang:
> Some like to hear learned discourse,
> Some demand funny disguises,
> The *badkhn* can please them all.[52]

The *badkhn*'s repertoire included songs about the land of Israel, some of them strongly parodic, as in the following, entitled 'Lid fun dem terik' ('Song of the Turk'):

> When I saw that my prospects were few
> I became an Erets Israel Jew.
> In a red fez disguised
> And an ill-fitting coat
> Everywhere making money.[53]

---

[49] Goldfadn, *Di komishe khasene*, 33.   [50] Gotlober, *Der dektukh*, 117.

[51] Saul Tshernichowsky, 'Ḥatunatah shel elkah', in Tshernichowsky, *Shirim* (Jerusalem, 1952), 333–4.

[52] K. Liberman, 'Fun badkhonishn repertuar', in Liberman, *Ohel rokhl*, vol. ii (New York, 1980), 307–13.

[53] Ibid. 313. In this song one can hear echoes of events that occurred after the death of the Shabbatean rabbi Yehuda Hasid (1660?–1700) in Jerusalem. The Ashkenazim, who borrowed money and

More contemporary references included the Hibat Tsion movement, as in Elyokem Tsunzer (Eliakum Zunser)'s celebrated song 'Di sokhe' ('The Plough').[54] The infant Moses in his wicker basket was another theme characteristic of late nineteenth-century nationalist *badkhones*.[55]

The final role in which the *badkhn* could express himself artistically was as the announcer of wedding gifts in the *droshe-geshank* (gift sermon). He might begin with a parodic piece of casuistry and then continue to the heart of the business at hand:

> The *badkhn* nearly loses his voice crying:
> Hey! Behold, behold from the bride's side wedding gifts,
> Hey aunts and uncles, grandfathers and mothers,
> Good friends, broken beggars,
> Groom's side, groom's side, bride's side . . . [56]

Throughout the wedding the *badkhn* was also responsible for organizing and announcing dances. These dances were performed at various times during the wedding; there was no fixed custom. Chief among them were the *mitsve-tents* (*mitsve* dances), which included the women's *mazl-tov* (good luck) dance immediately after the veiling of the bride. The *mitsve* dances generally climaxed towards the end of the banquet, when the bride was placed in the centre of a circle of dancers. The *badkhn* would invite the participants one after another to dance with the bride, first the parents of the bride, the parents of the groom, and the groom himself, and then the other guests. This dance was sometimes known as the *kosher tants*, signifying the ritual purity of the wedding:

At the end of the banquet, when the special hour arrived, if the wedding was kosher the famous kosher dance was held. The bride stands in the middle of the hall with a kerchief in her hand. One by one the important men go before her; each takes hold of the kerchief and circles once with the bride.[57]

---

did not return it, were hated by the Sefardim, who forced them to wear Turkish clothes. See Moshe Yerushalmi, *Sefer yedei moshe* (Amsterdam, 1764), MS 63; Y. Barnai, 'Letoledot ha'ashkenazim be'erets yisrael bein hashanim 1721–77 ve hatemikhah hakalkalit bahem', *Shelem* (Jerusalem), 2 (1970), 193–230. On two *badkhonim* from Belarus who also included performances about the land of Israel in their repertoire, see Slutski, 'Yidishe badkhonim-shoyshpiler', 257–61.

[54] *Elyokem tsunzers verk*, i. 352–5; the poem was first published in 1888.

[55] Tsunzer's student Yankev Zizmer (1867–1922), for example, had in his possession the song 'Dort in a geflakhtene kerbl' ('There in a Woven Basket'), which Yosef Kohen-Tsedek heard at a wedding from the *badkhn* Asherke Fidler; see M. Gorali (ed.), *Di goldene pave* (Haifa, 1970), 74.

[56] Linetski, *Dos khsidishe yingl*, 100–1.

[57] A. A. Druyanov, 'Nosafot lema'amaro shel y. elzet "Miminhagei yisrael"', *Reshumot* (Odessa), 1 (1917), 361.

FROM PUBLIC TO PRIVATE CREATION

The *badkhn*'s art, as we have seen, was inseparable from his audience. Understanding the heart of the audience, its needs, its moods, its aims, and its nature, was no less important than mastering artistic principles and performing techniques. The audience itself, moreover, was a constitutive part of the *badkhn*'s performance. The passage for some *badkhonim*, during the second half of the nineteenth century, from the vivacious *badkhn*, standing on stage, able to move those around him, to the *badkhn* sitting at his desk, writing his songs and putting them into print, was therefore nothing short of revolutionary. It led to a new conceptual framework for these artists and a new genre: the *badkhones* booklet.[58]

One feature of this new genre was the *farrede*, the introduction that gave the artist the opportunity to present the new genre from his point of view. The *farrede* was not an invention of the *badkhonim*; they borrowed this literary form, which was conventional in exegetical (midrashic) literature, and transformed its function. The fact that all the *badkhonim* chose the word 'farrede' for the introduction to their books and not 'forvert' or 'faroysloyfung', more commonly accepted Yiddish words for 'introduction', points to their understanding their writing as part of a tradition in which the *droshe* (sermon) was referred to as a *rede* (discourse), and was conventionally preceded by a *farrede*, known in talmudic sources as *petiḥah*: 'Before Raba began the lesson he opened [*pataḥ*] with words that gladdened the heart and made the students happy. Afterwards when they were sitting seriously he began the lesson.'[59]

The serious and scholarly aspect of the *badkhn* thus resembled that of the preacher. In contrast to the preacher–scholar, who directed his expositions in the synagogue to an educated audience that was familiar with the holy tongue, the popular preacher, the *mokhiakh*, or *magid*, moved from place to place in order to preach before less educated people in Yiddish.[60] In order to engage this audience, the preacher did not limit himself to verbal elements but also employed theatrical means: 'It is known to all that the celebrated preachers who enchant the audience and bring it to terrible weeping and sometimes also to hearty laughter, did not accomplish this only by means of their profound words, but also through their songs, mimicry, and with the art of illustrating, performing things as living before one's eyes.'[61] The structure of the sermon, which wove together material from popular aggadic sources, tales, and legends with references to daily life and current events, developed over time, along with the *farrede*, as a means of focusing the emotions and curiosity of the audience at the beginning of the preacher's exposition.[62]

[58] On the differences between writing and performance, see H. Shoham, *Te'atron vedramah mehapsim kahal* (Tel Aviv, 1989), 10–20.

[59] BT, *Shab.* 30*a*; Y. T. Zunz, *Haderashot beyisrael vehishtalshelutan hahistorit* (Jerusalem, 1947), 172, 519. On the *farrede*, see J. Heinemann, *Derashot batsibur bitekufat hatalmud* (Jerusalem, 1882), 12–28.

[60] Zunz, *Haderashot beyisrael*, 203; 'Preaching', *Encyclopedia Judaica*, xiii. 1004.

[61] B. Parnas, *Far ale* (New York, 1929), introd., unpaginated; on preaching, see S. Y. H. Gliksberg, *Torat hadrashah* (Tel Aviv, 1948).   [62] 'Preaching', *Encyclopedia Judaica*, xiii. 996.

The *badkhonim* knew very well the importance of the *farrede* for the success of a sermon. They recognized the power hidden within it, and exploited that power to reach their audience in both traditional and innovative ways. Nevertheless, for most *badkhonim* the *farrede* marked a difficult transition. In 1892 the *badkhn* Peysekh-Eli published a booklet of songs that included material he had composed decades earlier. As an additional introduction he included a song in the form of a dialogue between the composer (*ferfaser*) and his songs (*lider*):

THE COMPOSER

Since you were born
Quite some years ago,
You've found favour.
Now it's high time
To meet the people.
So go out into the world.

THE SONGS

With our wares
We are afraid
To travel in the world.
We've lived for years
And don't know the way,
Raised in the village [*dorf*], in the village born.

THE COMPOSER

Do not fear,
Go out right now.
You will also find good friends
Like those in the village.
If they only have good thoughts,
They will not hate you anywhere.

THE SONGS

For who will give us shelter?
Who will be interested in us? [*Ver vet af undz zayn balonim?*]
A scholar or philosopher
Will certainly not let us in,
Only poor *badkhonim*.

THE COMPOSER

Go straight out now.
You'll see many greater fools than you
Among the greatest rich people.
Just look at them,
With golden letters on their spines,
In polished bookcases with glass doors.

THE SONGS

Why should we feel ashamed
If the world does not accept us?
For us it is certain that
For a hasid we lack hasidism [*khsides*],
For a maskil too much Yiddish.
Both will want us under the table.[63]

The first expressions of a new medium as well as the profoundly ambivalent feelings that accompany this development are contained in this remarkable song. Its
structure, that of an intimate dialogue between the poet and his creation, facilitates
the expression of the contradictions that the *badkhonim* experienced at a turning
point in their development. The movement from an oral to a written medium
removes a creation from the sole possession of its creator and places it in the public
realm. For the *badkhn* this transition is accompanied by the fear of baring his
creation before an audience of anonymous readers in place of the audience long
familiar to him: wedding participants with whom his connection was natural and
empathetic:

> With our wares
> We are afraid
> To travel in the world.

This fear is combined with the fear of the new dimension of the written work, and
hence the fundamental question about the new world, with which the artist could
no longer establish the traditional sort of dialogue: 'Who will be interested in us?'
Peysekh-Eli's song also follows the form of a father's blessing for the son who is
leaving home. The father must send him on his way with encouragement and support as he moves from the warm and safe ancestral home into the alien world outside.

Some *badkhonim* sought to use the *farrede* itself to inspire the continuation of a
traditional reciprocal relationship with their audiences. The *badkhn* Moyshe Marakhovske, for example, begins the introduction to his book as follows:

> Since I have heard
> Many readers say
> That there are no songs
> That are any good . . .
> I thought up
> Strange new songs.[64]

The *badkhn* Shmuel Khayim Levin clearly connects the continuation of his writing
to his readers' response:

---

[63] Oyslender, 'Tsu b. slutskis "Badkhonim-shoyshpiler" ', 261–2.

[64] Marakhovske, *Di yontevdike lider*, 3; see also B. Z. Rabinovitsh, *Der disput fun a shiler mit a kloyz-
nik* (Vilna, 1877), 3.

Read them through, my dear customers . . .
And I will want to write more . . .
Just don't remember me badly [*Nor mir tsu shlekhts nit dermonen*].[65]

At the same time, as a sign of the transformation of the *badkhn*'s art, the *farrede* itself sometimes became the subject of controversy. Thus, for example, the *badkhn* Alter Fishzon expresses his criticism of the new form by means of traditional rhetoric:

And I say that a *farrede* may be compared to a man who is hearty and hale
And walks in the street without being pale.
But when you look him over from top to bottom
You see that poverty never left him.
The book is like this too since the *farrede* can be very nice
But the book can make no sense at all.[66]

Some *farredes* also provide a window on the social and economic changes that led the *badkhonim* to write. In the introduction to his work Peysekh-Eli recounts his resistance to publishing his songs:

These songs (and many more) were written by me from 1850 to 1859 and I never wanted to have them printed. And though many of my friends and acquaintances called me timid [*nekhbo el hakeylim*], I didn't listen to them, for I know very well the fate of such authors in the new world.[67]

What finally convinced him to publish his songs was learning that they were being sold to other *badkhonim*. Theft of this type was not uncommon; there is ironic testimony to it in Alter Fishzon's *farrede*:

If you want to ask why I write, I will ask further why does that other one write, but I have a clear reason. I, Fishzon, first became a scribbler [*shrayberl*], and everyone knows it, because one has only to copy the other, and if you ask me who requires such things of me, I'll give you a simple answer . . .[68]

Fishzon also testifies to the strange new demands that have created a bustling book market:

I see, unfortunately, . . . how the bookshops are filled with people. On Friday the whole day it's as noisy there as a mill . . . Sell me books . . . sell me songs . . . give me a booklet to read for the sabbath. The bookseller yells . . . 'there are no more; if the writer writes there will be more'. As if for spite . . . there is not one author here, so meanwhile I became a writer.[69]

By the second half of the nineteenth century in eastern Europe a new audience of Jewish readers had emerged that no longer comprised scholars but included people who were less well acquainted with the holy word: women, men of limited education,

---

[65] Levin, *Shirey khayim*, introd.

[66] Fishzon, *Der zinger*, 3; see also Geller, *Sefer lemenatseyekh*, introd., unpaginated.

[67] Slutski, 'Yidishe badkhonim-shoyshpiler', 261.   [68] Fishzon, *Der zinger*, 3.   [69] Ibid.

and young people hungry for light and undemanding literature. To satisfy their needs a new popular literature developed, parallel to the literature aimed only at the scholarly, that combined education and entertainment.[70] The secularizing Jewish reformers, the maskilim, influenced by the European Enlightenment, wished to educate their people in the spirit of European humanism. But the works of the maskilim, which were primarily in Hebrew, focused on universal human values, and when they did write about Jewish issues, they presented them in the abstract and rarely addressed ordinary Jews. This literature captured the heart of some of the intelligentsia, but it was very remote from the Jewish masses. In contrast, the new popular literature was the product of a new intelligentsia rooted in or responsive to the lower classes. They included the *badkhonim*, but also the wandering performers known as *Broder zingers* (Broder singers), whose sketches and songs began to appear in inexpensive booklets at this time, and finally Avrom Goldfadn, a maskil and a *badkhn*, and the father of professional Yiddish theatre.[71]

The songs of the *badkhonim* were therefore one response to the poetry of the didactic and ideological Haskalah, which was reserved to the upper classes and never reached the masses. The *badkhonim* spoke to the people and for the people; their songs were beloved by the masses and offered them a path through a changing world parallel to the path the maskilim offered their readers.[72] Lower-class readers began to feel they too were part of the dynamic shaping of a new cultural reality.

Certainly, as hinted at in Peysekh-Eli's dialogue, creators of neither the old nor the new elite literature looked favourably upon the new literary genre. Despite the fact that most *badkhonim* were observant Jews and that *muser-zogn* required the preacher to be well versed in Jewish sources, rabbinic authorities treated *badkhones* as mockery and calumny, even if it was tastefully worded. They saw the *badkhn* as a sinner, nothing but a *komediantshik*, that is, a jester, an entertainer.[73] The maskilim similarly regarded the *badkhn* with contempt; the more extreme among them accused *badkhonim* of being former yeshiva students. Maskilic disdain is apparent in a song by Shimen Shmuel Frug:

> A singer [*meshoyrer*], a musician [*klezmer*], a *badkhn* is he,
> A rhyme and a joke, a little song, a tune [*nign*],
> A twist this way and a grimace that way,
> The audience should have some fun.

[70] As early as the 13th century the recognition that, since much of the public could not read books in Hebrew, Jews observed the *mitsvot* without full understanding, led to the creation of parallel works in the Yiddish language; see C. Shmeruk, 'Di altyidishe literatur', in *Pinkes far der forshung fun der yidisher literatur un prese* (New York), 3 (1975), 130–250.

[71] D. Sadan, 'Zamarei brod veyerushatam', in Sadan, *Avnei miftan* (Tel Aviv, 1962), 9–17. On the Broder Zingers and Avrom Goldfadn, see M. Steinlauf, 'Jewish Theatre in Poland', in this volume.

[72] A. S. Idelsohn, 'Badkhonim', *Bodn* (New York), 2 (1935), 62–6; Shatzky, *Geshikhte fun yidn in varshe*, iii. 266–71.

[73] Y. Lipshits, 'Yidishe farvayler af di layptsiger yaridn', *Arkhiv far der geshikhte fun yidishn teater un drame*, 1 (1930), 58.

Frug emphasizes the *badkhn*'s appeal to the masses:

> A Jew needs a musician with drums and dances,
> A *badkhn* with rhymes and jokes,

and contrasts it with the fate of the maskilic poet:

> He will be heard by the mountain
> And the valley . . .
> But by people—none.[74]

Nevertheless, and despite what the maskilim believed, once having entered the realm of the printed word, the *badkhn* had to concern himself with matters important to his upper-class counterparts as well. For the performing *badkhn*, the text was only a tool to help realize his performance on the wedding stage. Much of his energy was invested in non-verbal effects, and at times it seemed as if the text was swamped by the happenings on the stage. In contrast, when the *badkhn* moved to writing, his centre of gravity moved from performance to text, which became an end in itself. In writing about their transition from performer to author, some *badkhonim* therefore found themselves discussing matters such as literary style, language, and technique, but within the context of the *badkhn*'s craft. The *badkhn* Moyshe Shlayfshteyn, for example, characterizes the conventions of his songs as follows: first, a humorous style ('*ferfast mit sheyne vitsn* [made with nice jokes]'); secondly, plain language ('*un mit natirlekhe verter* [and with natural words]'); thirdly, a reason for every effect ('*gearbet yedes tsu der zakh* [everything done to the point]'); fourthly, everything presented in the best possible way ('*shtelt es dortn rikhtik for* [present it rightly]') and in the most complete manner ('*gearbet on shum feler* [crafted with nothing lacking]').[75] The *badkhn* Shmuel Khayim Levin refers to both the aesthetics and the content of his songs when he explains that he has '*gemakht im geshmak*' [made them rich in flavour] and '*gemakht . . . nokh undzer lebn* [taken them from real life]'.[76]

Yet even when freed from his direct obligations to the religious–spiritual world he had served for centuries, the *badkhn* could not easily divorce himself from its context. It was difficult for him to see his writing as something that existed for its own sake; an emphasis on religious purpose (making the groom and bride rejoice) and *muser-zogn* remained. This comes through well in the following lines, in which the *badkhn* Avrom Geller defines his craft:

> Not tales of painted *rebbes* and their hasidim,
> But true poetry and words of wisdom [*divrey lomdim*] to make each man rejoice
> At all celebrations and at all tables [*Ba ale simkhes un ba yedn tish*].[77]

---

[74] M. Pines, *Di geshikhte fun der yidisher literatur biz yor 1890* (Warsaw, 1911), 12–14.

[75] Shlayfshteyn, *Der bankrot*, 3.   [76] Levin, *Shirey khayim*, introd., unpaginated.

[77] Geller, *Sefer lemenatseyekh*, introd., unpaginated.

CONCLUSION

Badkhones was the performance of a *mitsvah* and in principle should not have involved the thought of reward. Nevertheless, *badkhonim*, of course, hoped to receive payment for their performances. Yet except for a small number who achieved renown and therefore commanded a comfortable salary for their performances, most could not rely exclusively on their craft to earn a living.[78] The typical *badkhn* was guaranteed nothing at a wedding, and received only what the hosts provided as a gift of good will and what guests might offer him and the musicians during the dancing.[79]

The publication of their work gave *badkhonim* the opportunity to become known outside their home towns without having to wander from place to place. They immediately comprehended the power of the new medium and exploited their introductions both to advance the sale of the booklets and to advertise their talents as wedding performers. The *badkhn* Moyshe Marakhovske, for example, ends his *farrede* as follows:

> I announce to readers
> Both poor and rich
> That I the 'author' come to all celebrations
> With my own songs.
> Whoever wants to hear me
> They should contact me
> In the author's name:
> *Min hamayim meshiseyhu*
> [From the water I drew him, i.e. Moyshe].[80]

Moyshe Shlayfshteyn writes as follows:

> And don't be stingy with your money
> But go and chase the booklets . . .
> I hope that you will
> Lick your fingers from them . . .
> I the writer [*ferfaser*] am certain
> That you will sing my songs
> With great pleasure.
> For this work is from me,
> Moyshe Shlayfshteyn the doll-maker.[81]

---

[78] Indeed, celebrated *badkhonim* sometimes avoided the very word *badkhn*, with its low social connotations; see S. Ernst, 'Tekstn un kveln tsu der geshikhte fun teater farvaylungen un maskaradn ba yidn', *Arkhiv far der geshikhte fun yidishn teater un drame*, 1 (1930), 5–37.

[79] On this, see Z. Fridhober, *Hamahol hayehudi* (Haifa, 1968); also E. Fosklinski, 'A khasene in shtetl', *Sefer porisov* [Parysów], ed. Y. Granatstein (Tel Aviv, 1971), 152–3.

[80] Marakhovske, *Di yontevdike lider*, 4. 'And she [Pharaoh's daughter] called his name Moses, and said: "Because I drew him out of the water"' (Exod. 2: 10). See also Taradeyke, *Di sheyne vitsn-lider*, 6.

[81] Shlayfshteyn, *Der bankrot*, 3, 5.

And Geller not only advertises his book but announces a sale price:

> Therefore young and old
> Should run right away
> *Sefer lemenatseyekh* ['The Conductor's Book'] to buy . . .
> And to find favour with all
> The price is now small
> So everyone will be enthralled.[82]

In the *farrede*, rooted both in talmudic tradition and in the transition to modern social relations, we rediscover the full complexity and ambiguity of the *badkhn*'s role. Here are verses that are peddled at the lowest price, but whose authors also concern themselves with the formal qualities of their verse and see themselves as fulfilling sacred commandments. In the same breath the *badkhonim* describe their art, hawk their wares, and fulfil the holiest of *mitsvot*. The confusion of the different worlds resonates wondrously and strangely.

In the short introduction at the beginning of the booklet *Der krumer marshelik mit a blind oyg* ('The Lame *Badkhn* with a Blind Eye') the anonymous author announces the new genre of printed *badkhones*: 'It is very lovely [*zeyer sheyn*] to read [*leyenen*] the songs that the *badkhn* has sung [*gezungen*]. And how he sang to the bride and groom [*khosn kale bazungen*] and they [the songs] have never before been printed.' And then, in the very next line, we encounter the following: '*Kukuriku* [Cock-a-doodle-doo]! The jester is here.'[83] Similarly, the *badkhn* Mordekhayele Taradeyke portrays himself in the introduction to his booklet as 'magnificent *badkhn* and author and also comic actor'.[84] Even as it made the problematic transition into modernity, *badkhones* managed to retain its traditional tensions. It remained both high and low, normative and blasphemous, sacred and profane.

Translated from Hebrew by Erica Nadelhaft and Benjamin Greenberg

---

[82] Geller, *Sefer lemenatseyekh*, 1, 5.

[83] *Der krumer marshelik mit a blind oyg* (Warsaw, 1873), introd., unpaginated.

[84] Taradeyke, *Di sheyne vitsn-lider*, introd., unpaginated.

Remembrance of Things Past: *Klezmer* Musicians of Galicia, 1870–1940

WALTER ZEV FELDMAN

INTRODUCTION

UNTIL the present time knowledge about the east European Jewish professional instrumentalist the *klezmer* and his music has related almost exclusively to eastern Ukraine. This is primarily because of accidents of research, commercial recording, and emigration. Material from the travels of S. An-ski and Joel Engel in Podolia and Volhynia in 1912–14, the commercial recordings of the Belf's Romanian Orchestra in 1911–14, the fieldwork of Moyshe Beregovski in the 1930s, much of the material published by Joachim Stutchewsky (1891–1982), the early American commercial recordings of Lieutenant Joseph Frankel (1885–1953), and the somewhat later recordings of the master clarinettists Shloimke Beckerman (1883–1974) and Dave Tarras (1897–1989), all contribute to our knowledge of the repertoire, style, and social history of *klezmorim* of eastern Ukraine, which was part of the Russian empire throughout the nineteenth century. *Klezmer* materials from the non-Ukrainian and non-tsarist territories of eastern Europe are far rarer. Although a few *klezmer* documents survive from eastern Galicia (ruled by Austria between 1772 and 1918), no attempt has hitherto been made to synthesize this material and assess its similarities to and differences from the better-known east Ukrainian *klezmer* patterns.

Yet some of the very earliest references to Jewish musicians—as distinct from the professionally undifferentiated medieval Jewish entertainers known as *letsonim*—concern the region between Kraków and Lemberg (Lwów, Lviv, Lemberik):[1] Małopolska and Galicia. The earliest known use of *klezmer* as a term for a musician (rather than *kley zemer* for the musical instrument) occurs in a Jewish community document from Kraków dating from 1595.[2] An agreement between the Jewish musicians' guild and the corresponding Christian guild dating from 1629 was published by Majer Bałaban in 1906.[3] From this document we learn, first of all, of the existence of a Jewish musicians' guild—an institution that apparently had not existed

---

[1] While the name Lemberik continued to be used by some Yiddish speakers, by the 20th century Lemberg seems to have become the more commonly used Jewish name for the city; it was used by my chief informant, Yermye Hescheles.

[2] Y. Rivkind, *Klezmerim: perek betoledot ha'omanut ha'amamit* (New York, 1960), 16.

[3] M. Bałaban, *Żydzi lwowscy na przełomie XVI i XVII wieku* (Lwów, 1906), 533–4.

in Germany or earlier in Poland. We also learn that most of the musicians worked part-time as craftsmen (such as hatters and gold-braid makers—both quite respectable professions), and that the Jewish guild musicians performed on violin, cimbalom,[4] lute, double bass, and drum. Except for the lute, which disappears from Jewish music entirely after the seventeenth century, the remaining instruments formed the basis of the *klezmer* ensemble through much of eastern Europe, and survived in this southern Polish region until after the First World War.

We have no information at all concerning the *klezmorim* of this region throughout the eighteenth century and up to the middle of the nineteenth century. From the second half of the century we have figures who are described by the Galician informants of Joachim Stutchewsky in his book *Haklezmerim*.[5] A number of memorial books dealing with Galicia mention the *klezmorim* active at the turn of the twentieth century. From this period also there are a few photographs that document the composition of the *klezmer-kapelyes* (bands) of such towns as Przemyśl and Rohatyn. Between 1908 and 1911 Columbia, Victor, and Odeon issued a limited number of commercial recordings of the traditional *klezmer* ensemble of the Lemberg region, featuring violin and cimbalom, or occasionally flute and cimbalom. In 1910 Favorite issued a recording of the theatre music of the noted *klezmer* Khone Wolfstahl of Tarnopol.[6] Between 1922 and 1927 Naftule Brandwein, the famous American clarinettist who originated from a family *kapelye* in Premishlan (Przemyślany) near Lemberg, issued a number of commercial recordings in New York. Of these, several represent the traditional repertoire of his home.[7]

[4] Cimbalom (Yid. *tsimbl*), a dulcimer: 'In many parts of the world, the dulcimer has a trapeziform box; its strings, commonly from two to six for each course, are unfretted, but some are divided into two segments by a partitioning bridge. The courses are usually set in intersecting horizontal planes. The player may hit the strings with hammers or pluck them with the fingers or a plectrum. Many scholars, however, reserve the term "dulcimer" for an instrument played with hammers, calling it a "psaltery" when the plucking technique is used' (D. Kettlewell, *New Grove Dictionary of Music and Musicians*, ed. S. Sadie (London, 1980), v. 695). 'The word Cymbal appeared during the seventeenth century and increased in frequency during the eighteenth century, especially in areas near Bohemia, such as Saxony, the Upper Palatinate, and Lower Austria, but also in Holland . . . Jewish musicians incorporated the Cymbal into ensembles with two violins and a bass by the middle of the seventeenth century. Since they also went in large numbers to Amsterdam, itinerant Jewish musicians may have had some responsibility for the spread of this instrumentation' (P. M. Gifford, *The Hammered Dulcimer: A History* (Lanham, Md., 2001), 69). 'Jewish association with the instrument in this region (Poland, Ukraine, Belarus, Lithuania, and Latvia) remained strong until the nineteenth and even twentieth century, especially in Poland, where it is still to some extent regarded as a "Jewish" instrument. This historical association accounts for similarities in both the design and tuning of traditional dulcimers found today in locations as disparate as Latvia and Greece . . . The singular Hungarian *cimbalom* and Yiddish *tsimbl* became the plural words *cymbały* in Polish, *tsymbaly* in Ukrainian, and *tsymbaly* in Belarusian' (ibid. 117).

[5] J. Stutchewsky, *Haklezmerim: toledoteihem, orah hayeihem veyetsiroteihem* (Jerusalem, 1959).

[6] Most Galician *klezmorim* Germanized the spelling of their surnames, a practice retained in this chapter. They used Polish transliteration for their given names, for which standard Yiddish transliteration has been substituted here.

[7] See *Naftule Brandwein King of the Klezmer Clarinet* (Rounder CD 1127, 1997).

In the 1980s Joel Rubin and Michael Alpert conducted a number of interviews with Naftule's nephew Leopold Kozłowski.[8] Between May 1998 and February 1999 I conducted a series of interviews with Yermye (Jeremiah) Hescheles, who had been the *kapel-mayster* (bandleader) of the *klezmer* ensemble of Gline (Gliniany), near Lemberg, during the 1930s. These interviews contain information about the status of *klezmer* music throughout the region of eastern Galicia—with most detailed information about Gline—from roughly the 1870s until 1936, when Hescheles left Poland for Italy and eventually the United States. Besides confirming certain data known from other sources, Hescheles' descriptions and explanations offer a unique synthesis of the various kinds of information about Galician *klezmorim* and *klezmer* music unavailable elsewhere. The picture I present here integrates other, more fragmentary, data with Hescheles' recollections.

In Stutchewsky's narrative two family *kapelyes* stood out in nineteenth-century Galicia: the Weintraubs of Brod (Brody) and the Wolfstahls of Tarnopol. In the first half of the nineteenth century the violinist Shmuel Weintraub left the town of Tshortkev (Czortków, Chortkiv) in south-eastern Galicia for Brod, located somewhat further north. Stutchewsky suggests that he might have been related to Shloyme Weintraub Kashtan (1791–1829), the leading east European *khazn* (cantor) who lived in Dubno, just north-east of Brod, but across the Russian border in Volhynia.[9] It is known that Shloyme's son Hirsch Weintraub, who succeeded his father in Dubno and then went on to become a well-known Reform *khazn*, also played the violin and left a manuscript containing *klezmer* fiddle tunes dating from 1822 to 1836.[10] It is tempting to connect Shmuel Weintraub to this family of fiddling *khazonim*, but no more positive evidence has been found. Shmuel and later on his son Yose-Vove became the nucleus of the Tshortkever *kapelye* of Brod, who competed with the two older *kapelyes* of the town, the so-called Black *kapelye* of the Topaz family and the Red *kapelye* of the Rosenblums.

The elder Weintraub performed mainly his own compositions and improvisations. One of these, 'Der hirshn-yagd' ('The Stag Hunt'), based on the lament of David for Jonathan, the stag or gazelle of Israel (*hatsevi yisrael*, 2 Sam. 1: 19), developed into an allegory of Israel hunted by the nations. According to Stutchewsky, 'Shmuel and his son immersed themselves in it and expressed the joy and sorrow of Israel, the terror of exile, the mercy of God, the love of the Torah, the yearning for the return, and the depths of prayer and supplications of the soul.'[11] Although Stutchewsky (probably quoting his local informant) states that 'its origin was a composition of one of the great composers of the nations (i.e. non-Jewish)', it seems more likely that the piece was based on a version of the programmatic stag hunt or foxhunt compositions known from European folklore, e.g. the Irish foxhunt pieces

---

[8] See also Yale Strom's documentary film *The Last Klezmer* (1995) about Kozłowski, who lives in Poland. [9] Stutchewsky, *Haklezmerim*, 124–5.

[10] H. Weintraub, Cantorial Manuscript (1822–1836), Hebrew Union College, E. Birnbaum Collection, no. 75. [11] Stutchewsky, *Haklezmerim*, 125.

for Uillean pipes. Apparently the Weintraubs would perform this piece in the synagogue at the close of the sabbath. Stutchewsky states: 'The light that fell from the
end of sabbath until nightfall was not a light of colour but a light of sounds—the
great violin of Shmuel Tshortkever and the little violin of Yose-Vove.'[12] In the later
nineteenth century Yose-Vove Weintraub was the pre-eminent *klezmer* of Brod;
marriages were arranged according to his performance schedule and his name
appeared in the marriage contracts.[13]

In the case of the Wolfstahl *kapelye* of Tarnopol it is known that its founder
Khone Wolfstahl (1853–1924) was the son of a cantor from Sismanicz in Stanisle
(Stanisławów) province in the extreme south-east of Galicia. Khone learned the
cello and played professionally in the local *kapelye*, thus marking the rather rare
shift from cantorial to *klezmer* lineage. He began to compose his own pieces, and,
together with his four brothers, he moved to Tarnopol and founded the Wolfstahl
Brothers' Band. The Wolfstahls travelled throughout the vicinity playing for Jews
and non-Jews and put on Hanukah concerts in the synagogues. Khone continued to
compose, and his tunes were either written down or transmitted orally not only in
Galicia but in Austria, Hungary, and Germany. In 1889 Y. B. Gimpel (the father of
the violin virtuoso Bronisław Gimpel) invited Avrom Goldfadn (Abraham Goldfaden) to present his operetta *Shulamis* in the Lemberg Theatre. Khone Wolfstahl,
who was then 36 years old, attended these performances and was so impressed that
he gave himself over to composing music for the Yiddish theatre. He composed the
music for Moyshe Shor's *Der tayvl als regent* ('The Devil Rules'), *Bas Yerusholayim*
('Daughter of Jerusalem') (which played successfully in Budapest), as well as *Dray
matones* ('Three Gifts'), based on the story by Y. L. Peretz.[14] Nevertheless, Wolfstahl's switch from *klezmer* to Yiddish theatre did not result in much material
success. He lived in poverty, and later became embittered as several of his songs
became hits on the Yiddish stage in America but produced no income for him in
Galicia.[15]

In Lemberg the most established *klezmer* family was the Schwiders. Apparently,
at the turn of the twentieth century five of the Schwider brothers (Stutchewsky
gives only the names Leyb, Zosya, and Nakhmen) established an all-cimbalom

[12] Stutchewsky (ibid.) adds significantly, 'The elder Tshortkever usually performed *his own compositions*' (my italics).

[13] The most striking fact that Stutchewsky relates about the other two local *kapelyes* is that the 'Red'
Rosenblums performed at the municipal Yiddish theatre that emerged out of the Broder singers. He
does not state that the *kapelye* actually accompanied the singers, but true to the *klezmer* tradition it
would seem that the *klezmorim* constituted a separate act, yet within a novel context created by the
singer–performers.

[14] Wolfstahl's overture for this play was recorded in 1910 in Lemberg; it can be heard on *Oytsres—
Treasures: Klezmer Music 1908–1996*, produced by J. Rubin (Wergo SM 1621–2, 1999).

[15] One of Wolfstahl's nephews became the first violinist of the Berlin Philharmonic, while another
played in the Vienna Opera, and a third was a professor of violin at the Lemberg Conservatory. The
latter two Wolfstahls converted to Catholicism. One of them was Yermye Hescheles' violin teacher.
See Stutchewsky, *Haklezmerim*, 142–3.

ensemble, seemingly the first of its kind. Like most *klezmorim* they also played other instruments. Stutchewsky also mentions a Schwartzmann family, but without any additional information. He relates that 'In Lemberg musical life began to become lively at the beginning of the twentieth century. New *klezmorim* and new Jewish ensembles were established and fulfilled their functions with success.' One of the most striking innovations in the Jewish musical life of Lemberg at the time was the *froyen kapelyes* (women's ensembles). According to Stutchewsky, the *klezmer* bassist Shapse Refoel established one of these ensembles. In 1912 Shloyme Kosch (1869–1940), a *klezmer* flute-player, founded another *froyen kapelye*. According to Hescheles, these women's ensembles were usually made up of the daughters of *klezmorim*. It was only from this period that Jewish women were allowed to perform music in public. They worked mostly in restaurants since Jewish celebrations were still the exclusive domain of their male relatives.[16]

According to Stutchewsky, Shloyme was the only son of Nisele Kosch, who was one of the most famous *klezmer* violinists in Galicia, especially favoured as the performer for the 'weddings and feasts of rabbis and *tsadikim*'.[17] Shloyme is doubtless the 'S. Kosch' who recorded two flute and cimbalom *doinas*, in the Romanian style much favoured by hasidim, in 1911.[18] What is surprising is that this same Shloyme Kosch, apparently from a religious and possibly hasidic home, at the mature age of 43 created a women's ensemble. He also learned the saxophone, and in 1922, at the age of 54, formed an innovative musical group. The variety in the career of this *klezmer* can only be seen as a sign of the rapid changes that overtook the musical world of the Jews of Lemberg and environs in the early twentieth century. What is most striking is that his ultra-traditional flute and cimbalom recording of 1911 and the founding of the *froyen kapelye* took place only a year apart.

The only other Galician *kapelye* to which Stutchewsky gives more than a brief mention are the Foyermans of Kolomey (Kołomyja). He includes the now famous portrait of Mordkhe Foyerman (1818–95), who he claims was the 'last Jewish cimbalom player in Warsaw'. There also exists a photograph of Mordkhe at a more advanced age, but playing what looks like the identical tiny cimbalom while dressed in the same Orthodox Jewish garb. But, as in Lemberg, the period after the First World War apparently brought vast changes to the *kapelye* of Kolomey. Both of the Foyermans of the next generation, Zigmunt the violinist and Emanuel the cellist, acquired classical training.[19]

Stutchewsky mentions in passing the Faust *kapelye* of Rohatyn, who are remembered today mainly because of their beautiful portrait photograph at the turn of the

---

[16] Ibid.   [17] Ibid. 142.

[18] See *Klezmer Music: Early Yiddish Instrumental Music, 1908–1927*, produced by M. Schwartz (Arhoolie Folklyric 7034, 1997), tracks 12–13. The *doina* (Yiddish: *doyne*) is a rubato melody, either sung or played instrumentally, originating in the pastoral folklore of Wallachia and Moldavia. During the 19th century it was adopted by Galician Jews, and particularly by hasidim, who attributed a spiritual value to such melodies.   [19] Emanuel (1902–42) died in New York.

Fig. 1. Faust *kapelye* of Rohatyn
Courtesy of YIVO Institute for Jewish Research

Fig. 2. Zimbler *kapelye* of Przemyśl
Courtesy of YIVO Institute for Jewish Research

century, when they were led by an Orthodox fiddler, with his brother-in-law on *sekund* (second violin), an Orthodox bassist and *badkhn*, with a modern-looking clarinettist, trumpeter, and flute-player (Fig. 1).[20] From the same era as the Faust family portrait is a photograph taken in 1905 of the Zimbler *kapelye* of Przemyśl. This six-man *kapelye* appears to have been a thoroughly hasidic group but is distinguished from the Fausts mainly by the totally traditional nature of the instrumentation. The band consists of four violins, a cimbalom, and a cello—an ensemble that could have existed in the early nineteenth century or even before (Fig. 2).[21]

THE EARLY RECORDINGS OF THE *KLEZMER* MUSIC OF GALICIA

Between 1908 and 1911 commercial record companies issued a few recordings featuring the traditional *klezmer* instruments. The labels are in German and it appears that the recordings were made in Lemberg. Several were also reissued in America on the Columbia and Okeh labels. In addition to the two flute and cimbalom *doinas* by Shloyme Kosch mentioned above, there are four sides by a certain H. Steiner with cimbalom accompaniment, and three by Leon Ahl, also with cimbalom. Two religious selections, a Kol Nidre and the hymn 'Mimkomkho Malkenu', were credited to Leon Ahl in Europe but were issued anonymously in America. A *doina* was also issued in both Europe and America under the name of Leon Ahl.[22]

---

[20] Most of this *kapelye* emigrated to America between the world wars. The photograph, housed in the YIVO Institute for Jewish Research in New York, was first used for the poster of the Dave Tarras concert I organized with the Balkan Arts Center in 1979, then for the *klezmer* reissue of the YIVO archive in 1981: *Klezmer Music 1910–1942 from the YIVO Archives*, produced by H. Sapoznik, notes by W. Z. Feldman, H. Sapoznik, and A. Statman (Folkways LP, 1981). Woody Allen, evidently having seen one of these reproductions, used it to represent the family of the hero of his film *Zelig* (1982).

[21] This photograph was reproduced on the cover of *Yikhes (Lineage/Stammbaum): Early Klezmer Recordings 1911–1939 from the Collection of Prof. Martin Schwartz*, notes by R. Ottens and J. Rubin (Trikont LC 4270, 1995).

[22] A useful catalogue of these early recordings appears in the private publication 'European Recordings of Jewish Instrumental Music 1911–1914 by Jeffrey Wollock with additional data by Cor van Sliedregt 1908–1930'. As the title indicates, this catalogue is an addendum to Jeffrey Wollock's study of the early Russian commercial recordings 'European Recordings of Jewish Instrumental Folk Music 1911–1914', *Association for Recorded Sound Collections Journal*, 28 (1997), 35–6. Unlike the situation of the recordings of Kosch, who can be identified with a known *klezmer* family and even with a particular individual, neither Steiner nor Ahl were names associated with *klezmorim* in Galicia. Furthermore, there is some confusion about to whom to attribute the recordings. Steiner recorded two sides of religious music, ostensibly associated with Hanukah, as 'Haneros Haluli' ('Hanerot halalu') and 'Mizmor Shir Hanuka' as well as two 'Potpourri jüddischer Melodien'. Joel Rubin (who reissued the latter on his CD *Oytsres*) writes that it was recorded in Lemberg in 1908 (*Oytsres*, track 2, p. 7), while Martin Schwartz (who reissued the first side of the Hanukah tunes on his Folklyric CD) claims that the Hanukah music was recorded in 1909 and the 'Potpourri' was recorded afterwards (*Klezmer Music*, track 10, p. 13). Kurt Bjorling (who reissued all of these recordings on a private cassette) writes: 'Some passages of this Doina [of Ahl's] so closely resemble passages on both parts of the recently discovered "Potpourri jüddischer Melodien" by H. Steiner that it is suspected that "Ahl" and "Steiner"

There is another small corpus of violin and cimbalom recordings from Poland: the four sides entitled *Rumänische Fantasien* recorded by the violinist Josef Solinski in 1911 and issued in Warsaw.[23] Like Ahl and Steiner, nothing at all is known about Solinski. Two of the four sides are *volekhlekh*, that is, Jewish melodies based ultimately on Romanian Gypsy (*lăutar*) *horă* and *joc* melodies.[24] Solinski's style is related but not identical to that of Steiner and Ahl. In keeping with the Romanian

are really the same person' (K. Bjorling (ed.), *Jewish Violinists*, rev. edn. (1997), vol. i). This does seem to be the case for the Ahl *doina* and the Steiner 'Potpourri', but not so for the Kol Nidre and 'Mimkomkho Malkenu', where both the fiddling style and the cimbalom playing differ in significant ways from that of 'Steiner' and 'Ahl' as heard on the *doina*. I confirmed this by playing all the recordings for Hescheles, who pointed out several differences on the two instruments. Thus it would seem that Steiner recorded the Hanukah pieces, the 'Potpourri' (in whatever sequence), and the *doina*, while Ahl recorded the other two religious items. Nevertheless, the fact that the style of all of these pieces is relatively close allowed the misattribution mentioned above. As Rubin concludes: 'That these violinists sounded quite similar points to a generic folk style of Jewish violin playing in the period leading up to the First World War. Their style was characterized by a non-classical tone, little or no use of vibrato and a highly refined sense of ornamentation' (*Oytsres*, 7). I agree with this except that I would substitute the word *klezmer* for 'folk'. There were many Jewish amateur, or folk, violinists, but the style of these recordings must reflect a professional rather than a purely folk usage. Likewise the cimbalom playing certainly reflects a unified Jewish *klezmer* style, rather more sophisticated in the case of Ahl's and Kosch's cimbalom playing, somewhat less so in the case of Steiner's. The cimbalom was rarely played at an amateur level by Jews—it was almost always a professional (i.e. *klezmer*) instrument. The rhythmic phrasing, ornamentation, tremolos, and range on these recordings have no close parallel in known styles of Ukrainian *tsymbaly* or Romanian *ţambal mic* playing.

[23] All four sides of the *Rumänische Fantasien*, pts. 1–4, as well as an alternative version of pt. 4, were issued by Kurt Bjorling on his *Jewish Violinists*, i. Solinski's pt. 4 can be heard on *Yikhes*, track 4; pt. 1 can be heard on Schwartz's *Klezmer Music*, track 19. An 'Orientalische Motiv II', credited to Solinski, was issued in Warsaw by Favorite in 1908, and reissued by Henry Sapoznik on his *Klezmer Pioneers* (Rounder CD 1089, 1993). However, as noted by Bjorling, 'the material and the performance are identical in nearly every detail with that of Oscar Zehngut'. The performance style of this track does not resemble that of Solinski, and it is accompanied by a piano, in contrast to Solinski's recordings, all of which use only cimbalom.

[24] In 1904 the Russian musicologist Ivan Lipaev observed how all of the foreign elements in the music of the *klezmorim* 'were gradually blended into a single harmonious whole and reworked within the crucible of the Jewish national feeling and soul . . . The only thing that was hardly touched was the song "Volokh", that is, "Wallachian", but even it in the end has become unrecognizable' ('Evreiskie orkestry', *Russkaia muzykal'naya gazeta*, 6 (1904), 170). These two *volekhlekh* of Solinski's are excellent examples of this process. Of special interest is the Fantasie no. 4, which seems to correspond to the improvised form called *gedanken*, and is found on no other recording. Another of his Fantasien (pt. 1) is a Jewish version of a Turkish *longa*—Romanian-style dances composed in Istanbul. The one performed by Solinski is based on the 'Nihavent Longa' by the woman violinist Kevser Hanım ('Nihavend Longa', in O. Akdoğu, *Türk müziğinde eser analizeri* (Izmir, 1993). Solinski's version, however, is almost identical to the version played in Iaşi (Jassy) by the *klezmer* violinist Avrom Bughici early in the 20th century. The Bughici manuscript may be lost, but its contents were recorded by the accordionist Izu Gott. A version of the tune resembling Bughici's is found in the repertoire of the Bessarabian clarinettist German Goldenshteyn (b. 1935), currently in New York. Kevser Hanım's tune is quite distinctive and became very well known in Turkey, where it is performed to this day. Considering that Solinski's recording dates from 1911 and already shows a distinct *klezmer* version, which became established among Moldavian *klezmorim* such as Bughici and Goldenshteyn, his source was probably one of those Moldavian or Galician *klezmorim* who had toured in Istanbul.

theme of these recordings, Solinski employs a series of ornaments more character-istic of Romanian Gypsy than of Jewish fiddling. He also shows elements of classi-cal Western bowing. The style of his cimbalom player, however, is completely in accord with that of the cimbalom players recorded in Lemberg. Indeed, despite the fact that the recordings were issued in Warsaw, Solinski and his accompanist were doubtless from Galicia.[25]

Taken together, these few duets for fiddle and cimbalom and flute and cimbalom give us priceless information about the state of *klezmer* music in Galicia just prior to the major cultural changes brought on by the First World War. It is also useful to compare them with the larger corpus of recordings issued in Warsaw and Kiev by Belf's Romanian Orchestra between 1911 and 1914. This 'orchestra' was a quasi-traditional *klezmer* ensemble with clarinet and violin who alternated as leader, accompanied by *sekund* fiddle, double bass, and piano. Other than the piano, this combination of instruments was not uncommon in small *shtetl kapelyes* in eastern Ukraine in the later nineteenth century. But the repertoire of the Belf ensemble and the Galician–Polish duets are utterly different. The Belf recordings are more 'democratic' in two ways: they almost never feature solo performance, but rather involve interaction of the two leaders, and they contain a number of folk dance and even folk song melodies, in addition to purely *klezmer* pieces of the *skotshne* type. Hasidic music is represented by a significant group of *khosidls*, which, in this geo-graphical area, meant a kind of religious instrumental dance tune.[26] Nothing in the large Belf catalogue[27] suggests purely religious or artistic music per se.

[25] During these years Syrena issued many recordings of Belf's Romanian Orchestra (Rumynskii orkestr Bel'fa), which was certainly not from Warsaw and seems to have originated in Russian Podolia. The fact that the label of Solinski's recording is in German also suggests that neither the musicians nor the recording originated in Warsaw. Stutchewsky avers that Mordkhe Foyerman was the last Jewish cimbalom player in Warsaw, and he died in 1895. A contemporary Warsaw recording from 1911 or 1912 features the 'Evreiskii svadebnyi orkestr' under the direction of Back, which was the kind of large brass and strings *klezmer* band we would expect to find in a large city within the Russian empire by the First World War (reissued in *Oytsres*, track 3). Thus, it is hard to accept that the combination of the classic violin–cimbalom duet, the Gypsified fiddle style, the traditional *klezmer* cimbalom style, and the Romano-Turkish *klezmer* repertoire could have originated in Warsaw at this time. It is much more likely that Solinski and his cimbalom player came from somewhere in eastern Galicia, probably towards the southern end, perhaps Tshortkev, Stanisławów, or Kolomey, since Hescheles did not regard Solinski's style as typical of the *klezmer* violinists that he had heard in the region of Lemberg (inter-view, 28 Sept. 1998).

[26] In some places the term *skotshne* meant a line dance such as the *freylekhs*, but in Ukraine it denoted a somewhat developed instrumental melody in dance form but used for listening. In Galicia the term *khosidl* (pronounced *khusidl*) was the standard term for Jewish line dance, equivalent to *freylekhs* in Ukraine or *hopke* in Lithuania. But elsewhere it referred to a slow *freylekhs* employed in religious or hasidic environments. Although only one of their recordings is entitled 'Khosidl', many of the extant recordings of Belf fit into the *khosidl* genre as it was known in eastern Ukraine. Examples are: 'Na rassvete', 'U rabina', 'Dem Rebns Gavdule', 'Noch Gavdule', 'Lipovetskaya', and 'Skvirskaya'; all may be heard on *V. Belf's Romanian Orchestra, 1911–1914*, a cassette issued by Kurt Bjorling.

[27] See Wollock, 'European Recordings'.

Despite the inclusion of two melodies that may be Yiddish folk songs among
Steiner's 'Potpourri', the repertoire of the Polish duets as a whole has a markedly
different character from the Belf recordings. Three elements predominate: para-
liturgical or even liturgical rubato melodies, artistic solos, usually of a *volekhl*, or
Romanian-derived, nature, and virtuoso dance pieces. The artistic and technical
standard of all of the performers on the Polish recordings is very high, far higher than
that of the Belf players. Despite the 'Rumynskii' in their name, Belf's Orchestra
performs almost no Romanian-derived items and their style shows no familiarity
with any kind of Romanian performance, whether Gypsy or Jewish. The Belf style
is evidently Jewish (this is also how it was perceived by Hescheles) but directed
towards a lower social class, probably the majority of Ukrainian *shtetl* Jews, which is
no doubt why these recordings proved to be such a commercial success. The slightly
earlier Polish recordings, while not 'Westernized' and undoubted appealing mainly
to the more Orthodox elements of the Galician Jewish population, are elitist in their
orientation, perhaps meant to appeal to a class of wealthy Orthodox merchants or
the better-off followers of the 'rabbis and *tsadikim*' who patronized Nisele Kosch of
Lemberg. It is probably no accident that fewer recordings of this type were issued
and that they were discontinued very soon, to be replaced by the Belf recordings,
which, according to Syrena's publicity, were 'shipped south' in large quantities.[28]

YERMYE HESCHELES AS A SOURCE FOR THE HISTORY OF GALICIAN *KLEZMORIM*

It is fitting that, with his many talents and keen mind, Yermye Hescheles also contributes to posterity something of his experiences in *klezmer* music. Hescheles is a
polymath. Primarily a poet, his two volumes *Lider* ('Songs') and *Sonetn fun tohu
vavohu* ('Sonnets from Chaos') come out of the avant-garde of Yiddish verse.[29]
From the 1940s until the paper's closure in 1971 Hescheles was a regular reporter
for *Der tog* in New York, which serialized his novel *Gitl di tsiganke* ('Gitl the
Gypsy'). After his retirement he acted as a resource for a number of scholars.[30]

Hescheles was born in Gline in 1910. His family was long-established in the
area. His grandfather was the accountant for the local Polish landowner, while his
father, Moyshe, ran a successful tobacco business. The family were all Orthodox
mitnagdic (non-hasidic) Jews. Moyshe Hescheles, while remaining Orthodox, was
independently minded. He studied both kabbalah and German literature and had a
keen appreciation for many kinds of music. He attended the Yiddish theatre in

---

[28]   See Wollock, 'European Recordings', 39.

[29]   Y. Hescheles, *Lider* (New York, 1957) and *Sonetn fun tohu vavohu* (New York, 1963). Hescheles
prefers the Hebrew pronunciation over the Yiddish 'toye-voye'.

[30]   Among them the noted Yiddishist Mordkhe Schaechter of Columbia University, Rabbi Abraham
Holtz of the Jewish Theological Seminary, New York, in his research on S. Y. Agnon, and the
Yiddishist Itsik Gottesman, now the assistant editor of the Yiddish *Forverts* in New York.

Lemberg. Before 1900 he travelled to America, where he became acquainted with the Yiddish theatre in New York. He returned to Gline permanently before the birth of his son Yermye. Yermye received an Orthodox elementary education in Gline, completing the Bnei Toyre school run by Mayer Schapiro from Shots (Suceava), who later became an important force among the Orthodox Jews of Poland. As a child Hescheles showed a strong inclination towards music, and when he was 10 years old his father furthered this by apprenticing him to the local *klezmer kapel-mayster*, Moshke Mikhl Dudlsack, a violinist and cimbalom player. Of course, as the son of a wealthy bourgeois household, there was never any thought of Yermye becoming a *klezmer*. Afterwards he took violin lessons with Hershele Kleinman, a younger son of Peysekh Brandwein, the *kapel-mayster* of Premishlan. After completing the Jewish *Gymnasium* of Lemberg, where he studied classical languages, Yermye enrolled in the Lemberg Conservatory, where he became the violin student of Morycz Wolfstahl.

The death of his father somewhat before 1930 prevented Yermye from completing his course of study. He returned home to Gline, and eked out a living by giving violin lessons. But at the same time his old teacher the *klezmer* Moshke Mikhl Dudlsack was planning to retire and take his whole family to Argentina to join his daughter. The only local *klezmer* capable of taking Moshke Mikhl's place was Yitskhok Katz, the nephew of Berish Katz, who had already emigrated to New York. But then Yitskhok's father died and his mother decided to take him with her to Palestine. This left Yermye as the most competent musician in Gline. Moshke Mikhl decided to train him for a year, and when he left for Argentina Yermye Hescheles, although not a hereditary *klezmer*, became the new *kapel-mayster* of Gline. He perfected his knowledge of *klezmer-loshn* (*klezmer* slang), in Galicia known as *labushaynski*, and he inherited the manuscript of the Gliner *kapelye*, which had probably been written by Psakhye Wolf, the old *kapel-mayster* who had emigrated to America before 1900. Thus Yermye Hescheles served as the new *kapel-mayster* of Gline from about 1932 until 1936, when he decided to enrol in medical school first in Prague and then in Pisa. When Italy passed antisemitic laws in 1938, Hescheles managed to obtain an invitation from an uncle living in Brooklyn to emigrate to America.

In America he immediately met his father's friend Berish Katz (1874–1966), formerly the trumpeter in the *kapelye* of nearby Radikhov (Radziechów, Radekhiv) and now a successful *klezmer* violinist in New York. But Hescheles declined his friend's offer to join his band, and instead looked for work as a journalist. Forming an instant dislike for the *klezmer* music of America, which was, he says, 'in the hands of the clarinettists', he gradually gave up his musical career entirely and focused on prose and verse writing. Shortly after arriving in America, Hescheles was filmed in a one-minute slot as the *kapel-mayster* in the 1939 film *Fishke der krumer* ('Fishke the Lame'), but this proved to be his swansong as a *klezmer*. He became a well-known figure in the New York Yiddish literary world, but only a few people were aware of his musical past. In the late 1980s Michael Alpert interviewed him for one afternoon, but he never pursued this research. During the late 1990s Itsik Gottesman urged me to interview Hescheles, and finally in May 1998 I began a series of interviews that continued until February 1999. By that time a close friendship had developed between us and we both preferred to use our time together for more purely social contact. Since September 1999 Hescheles' health has suffered a number of complications and interviews are no longer possible.

The material that Hescheles conveyed in approximately twenty-four hours of interviews covers a wide variety of topics concerning Yiddish culture and the various types of music in which Jews were involved in the region of Lemberg. The language of the interviews is predominantly English, which Hescheles speaks fluently. At times he speaks Yiddish, especially when quoting someone in Galicia or retelling an anecdote. He never uses *klal-yidish* (standard Yiddish) but only his Galician dialect. In addition he frequently quotes songs and remarks in Polish and Ukrainian, or mixtures of all these languages, sometimes with grammatical errors supposedly typical of Jews.

For present purposes I will confine myself to Hescheles' remarks on *klezmer* music proper. These can be divided into the following topics: the status system of the *kapelyes* of the Lemberg region, the inner working of the *klezmer-kapelye* and the ethos of the *kapel-mayster*, and the particular history of the Gliner *kapelye*. I will leave the issues of the *klezmer* repertoire and performance practice for treatment elsewhere.

THE STATUS SYSTEM OF THE GALICIAN *KAPELYES*

In Hescheles' discourse the concept of 'status' or 'standing' must be approached from two perspectives: legal and aesthetic. The latter often contains an ethical element as well. Issues of status are also connected with two key concepts for Hescheles: those of hierarchy and anarchy. He repeatedly points out how hierarchy in every social context was considered natural and good in Jewish society in Galicia. At the same time an important function of both the *klezmer* and the *badkhn* (wedding jester) was to challenge the social and religious hierarchy, but this challenging itself was an established part of the social system. The society Hescheles depicts was aware of unspoken boundaries within which this challenging could occur.

Hescheles views hierarchy as a two-edged sword; on one hand it ensured social continuity and with it the transmission of moral and aesthetic knowledge, but on the other hand it led to cruel abuses. His discourse is replete with examples of both functions. But the opposite of hierarchy is anarchy, and this he sees as an absolute evil. According to Hescheles, the anarchy in Jewish Galicia began in the last quarter of the nineteenth century with the massive emigration outward, then the Russian destruction of the Jews of Galicia during the First World War, followed by the disintegration of many Jewish institutions, including the *klezmer-kapelye*, during the inter-war era.

By the time Hescheles became a professional *klezmer*, the heyday of the major *kapelyes* of Galicia had passed. He continually refers to the music of the *klezmorim* as 'something that was on its way out'. He is able to speak about the *klezmorim* of Lemberg, Gline, Premishlan, Radikhov, and Belz (Bełz) from first-hand experience, but for the most part he is describing the world of Galician *klezmorim* as it had been in the generation before him. Thus my fieldwork with him was in part based on his reconstruction of the recent past of the musical world into which he entered when he became the *kapel-mayster* of Gline. Some of this reconstruction occurred when he emigrated to America and spoke to Berish Katz, who had been the trumpeter of the neighbouring Radikhover *kapelye*, and who had known Psakhye Wolf, the famous Gliner *kapel-mayster* of the late nineteenth century. But Hescheles avers that most of what he knows about the earlier situation of *klezmorim* comes from his first teacher, Moshke Mikhl Dudlsack. He had known Dudlsack first as a child of 10 and then as a young man while he was being groomed as the new *kapel-mayster* and hence needed to absorb more of the *klezmer* lore of Galicia, including its distinctive language. As he says now: 'Moshke Mikhl probably had a very vivid, a graphic way of telling a story. Because whatever he told me is engraved on my mind.'[31]

The *klezmer* map of Galicia is replete with boundaries. In Galicia every *kapelye* had its own *krayz* (territory) within which it could perform legally. It could perform outside the *krayz* when specifically hired by a rich man or a noted hasidic *rebbe*. Certain villages bordered on the *krayz* of more than one town, and for weddings in those villages something would have to be arranged with the *kapelyes* concerned. Gline controlled twenty-eight satellite villages to which the Gliner *kapelye* would naturally be invited to play at weddings. There were also a number of predominantly Jewish towns in the area which had no *kapelye*, such as Yaritshev (Jaryczów) and Golege (Gołogóry), and it was customary for the *kapelye* of Gline to play there as well. Several villages lay in the shared domain of Gline and Premishlan, which had a prestigious *kapelye* led by the Brandwein family, but also contained members of the Dudlsack *klezmer* family of Gline. The boundaries between the *kapelyes* were maintained by the norms of *khazuke* (title or tenure in Galician Yiddish) which specified the rights of individuals or groups to specific occupations. These rights were guaranteed by the *bezdn* (rabbinic court). *Khazuke* prevented any outsider from starting his own *klezmer-kapelye*, and it guaranteed the hereditary rights of the *klezmer* families within each *kapelye*. Hescheles quips that the term for the artisanal guilds, *yad kharutsim* (hand of the skilled), was turned into *yad rotskhim* (hand of the murderers) by those disgruntled with their economic limitations.[32] He stresses that in Galicia this system applied to other craftsmen as well,

---

[31] Interview, 28 Sept. 1998.   [32] Interview, 1 Sept. 1998.

such as shoemakers, candlestick makers, and butchers. He employs the word *tsekh*, meaning 'guild', for this system, and states that among several crafts the terms for apprentice (*lern-yingl*), journeyman (*khalatnik*), and master (*mayster*) were still in use.[33]

When Psakhye Wolf was in town, no barber could have practised that [fiddling]. He couldn't even have a fiddle on his wall. They were a power. This was a franchise. They called it *khazuke*. You couldn't start with them. They'd find ways to punish you. Because they had a guild, a *tsekh* . . . Not an official guild, but among the Jewish community. No one could touch a violin to go to a *khasene shpiln* (wedding gig) if he was not of the family. *Khazuke* was the most important thing.[34]

The ethnomusicologist Moyshe Beregovski's *klezmer* research, accomplished on the Soviet side of the border during the years when Hescheles was the *kapel-mayster* in Gline, reveals a social organization of music which had evidently developed out of a system not unlike that prevailing in contemporary Galicia, but which had changed in several crucial respects.

In a questionnaire published in Kiev in 1937 Beregovski alludes to this system with the following questions:

Were there occasions when the band took on weddings not in its own region?

Did the band that usually played in that area react?

Did the intruding band pay off the local band?

Did the band have to get permission from someone to play (the Jewish community, the state rabbi, police, etc.)?

These questions suggest that the *klezmorim* of eastern Ukraine indeed remembered a system similar to the one described by Hescheles in Galicia. The following questions suggest greater freedom in forming a *kapelye*:

How did you create your band? When did it begin?

Would it be possible for a second band to develop in a town that already had a band?[35]

Writing in 1904, Ivan Lipaev refers to the *klezmer* ensemble as 'kompaniya' and describes it as a collective enterprise without an absolute leader that could be formed with relative ease.[36] This was evidently the reason for the adoption of the term by Russian *klezmorim*. Beregovski explains the change by stating categorically that 'the Jewish community administration [*kahal*] had lost its power by that time [the second half of the nineteenth century], and *kapelyes* could be formed openly

---

[33] Interview, 24 Aug. 1998.   [34] Interviews, 24 Aug. and 1 Sept. 1998.

[35] M. Beregovski, *Yidishe instrumentale folksmuzik: program tsu forshn di muzikalishe tetikayt fun di yidishe klezmer* (Kiev, 1937), trans. in M. Slobin (ed.), *Old Jewish Folk Music: The Collections and Writings of Moshe Beregovski* (Philadelphia, 1982), 544–5.

[36] I. Lipaev, 'Evreiskie orkestry', 135.

everywhere'.[37] Hescheles' information stresses the strict control of traditional *klezmer* families over Jewish performance venues in *shtetls* and even in cities well into the twentieth century. And in Galicia the newer term *kompaniya*, with its open, commercial overtones, was not accepted. The *klezmorim* were called *kapelye*, *khevrise* (study group) in *klezmer-loshn*, or else the older term *di klezmer*.

The information that Stutchewsky furnishes about the establishment of the Weintraub *kapelye* of Tshortkev in Brod and the Wolfstahl *kapelye* in Tarnopol are enough to show that *kapelyes* had branched out and moved even in the Galicia of the mid-nineteenth century, but Brod and Tarnopol were small cities, and the latter was a regional capital. Thus the possibilities for musical work were comparatively greater, especially when one includes venues that were not specifically Jewish, such as restaurants or cafés, over which the Jewish system of *khazuke* had no control. On the other hand Hescheles' information about the tight control of the Schwider family in Lemberg, the largest city in eastern Galicia, suggests that even in the early twentieth century the movement of outsiders into the Jewish sphere of musical work was impossible in that city. Stutchewsky does not mention whether or not the movement of members of the Weintraub and Wolfstahl families was connected with marriage into one of the older *klezmer* families of Brod or Tarnopol.

Usually in Hescheles' narratives the rights of the *klezmer* families to an absolute monopoly over musical performance is represented as a good and moral custom that prevented the deterioration of musical standards. For example, after listening to a recording of Max Leibowitz, a Romanian Jewish violinist who became a well-known bandleader in the 1910s and 1920s in New York, Hescheles exclaimed: 'A man like this could only be a *kapel-mayster* in America. In Europe only in a town that had no good *kapelye*, like Belz. Anyone there could take up a fiddle—maybe a barber. But in Berzhan [Brzeżany], Premishlan, Tarnopol or Zlotshev [Złoczów]—never!'[38] But Hescheles does tell at length of at least one case where he acknowledges that the *khazuke* system led to great abuse. This occurred in Lemberg itself and concerned a dispute between the Schwider family of *klezmorim* and the fiddler Yankev (Koba) Fischer. Stutchewsky mentions the Schwiders as one of the principal *klezmer* families of Lemberg at the turn of the twentieth century, along with the Kosches. But in the 1930s Hescheles knew nothing of the once famous cimbalom ensemble of the Schwiders, which was apparently defunct by his time. He had heard the Schwider fiddlers perform, and he ranked them among the mediocre *kapelyes*, despite the size of their city. But Hescheles ranked Fischer as the only first-rate *klezmer* violinist in Lemberg. He grants that Fischer, who was born about 1912, had no classical training and could not even read music, but he apparently made up for it by his great talent. Hescheles considers Fischer a master of the indigenous *klezmer* virtuoso style; he compares him to Yoysef Drucker 'Stempenyu'

---

[37] M. Beregovski, 'Evreiskaya narodno-professional'naya (klezmerskaya) instrumental'naya muzyka — sostavnaya chast' evreiskogo fol'klora', in his *Evreiskaya narodnaya instrumental'naya muzyka*, ed. M. Goldin (Moscow, 1987), 18.   [38] Interview, 28 Sept. 1998.

(1822–79) and Avrom Kholodenko 'Pedotser' (1828–1902), the great *klezmer* fiddlers of Barditshev (Berdychiv).[39] Fischer appears as a rather modern figure because he chose to play the oldest and most authentic *klezmer* repertoire, which he picked up in his travels in the region, even though this repertoire was becoming less and less fashionable in his generation. He was not a hasid but had to perform for the Orthodox, the 'frime yidn', simply because no one else had much interest in this repertoire and style any more. But he was not a *kapel-mayster* or even an official *klezmer*, so the Schwider *kapelye* would only hire him on an 'adjunct' basis at a much lower pay scale. Otherwise Fischer could only play at small Orthodox weddings in *shtetls* such as Golege (where he hired Hescheles to form an ad hoc *kapelye*) or else in taverns or bordellos. He was very poor and lived in a basement apartment in Lemberg.

In Hescheles' narratives Koba Fischer appears as a true anomaly. By the inter-war era there were many professional Jewish musicians who were not *klezmorim* but had the techniques to perform in the newer venues, such as restaurants and silent-movie houses where the *klezmer khazuke* was not relevant. There were many middle-class amateur musicians who sometimes played a classical repertoire. There were also illiterate amateurs who merely scratched out a few folk songs. But Fischer was none of these—rather he was the kind of fiddler who would have been a major *klezmer* in more favourable circumstances. Indeed, in Russia nothing would have prevented him from starting his own *kompaniya*. But in Galicia he was condemned to a life of humiliating poverty, although it was he who preserved the repertoire and style that the city *kapelye* of Lemberg no longer maintained. Fischer, who had learned much of the Galician *klezmer* repertoire during his frequent travels around the province, must have imparted to Hescheles his own observations and musical judgements. He was Hescheles' contemporary and they had played together pro-fessionally.

It is largely based on the lore current among the local *klezmorim* of his generation that Hescheles presents his map of the *klezmer-kapelyes* of Galicia. First of all, we should note that he is concerned only with Galicia proper, what the Austrians renamed 'East Galicia'. Not once in his interviews does Hescheles speak of the *klezmorim* of Przemyśl, located only as far west of Lemberg as Tarnopol was east. Kraków, the central city of Małopolska, was evidently viewed as being in another country. He has no opinion at all of the *klezmer* music or traditions of these more westerly towns. Likewise, Bukovina, although also governed by Austria, was foreign territory.

Within Galicia proper in the generation of his teacher Moshke Mikhl and the previous Gliner *kapel-mayster*, Psakhye Wolf (roughly the 1870s to the First World War), he considers Tarnopol, Tshortkev, Radikhov, and Premishlan to have had the

[39] M. Beregovski, 'Klezmorim in the Nineteenth Century', in *Jewish Instrumental Folkmusic: The Collections and Writings of Moyshe Beregovski*, ed. M. Slobin, R. Rothstein, and M. Alpert (Syracuse, NY, 2001).

major *klezmer-kapelyes*. The next tier was Gline, Berzhan, Zlotshev. Then Keney-nitsh and Kamenka (Kamionka). Among the lowest were Belz, Busk, and other towns that he does not bother to mention. Strangely, he never mentions Brod. It is per-haps understandable that Kolomey and Stanisle (Stanisławow, Ivano-Frankivsk) were too far away to appear on his musical map. He agrees with Stutchewsky's Galician informants in stressing Tarnopol and Tshortkev. But they also mentioned Lemberg, Brod, Rohatyn, and Kolomey.

That Hescheles' judgements were common among the Jews of Galicia can be seen from the following anecdote told by Hescheles' uncle Avrom Yitskhok, who was the postmaster of Belz. Some time before the First World War the Belzer *rebbe* was celebrating the wedding of his daughter. Passing over the local *kapelye*, he hired the *klezmorim* of Radikhov, Tshortkev, and Kamenka. The absence of the Belzer *kapelye* was, of course, significant. Since it was highly unusual for these three *kapelyes* to perform at one wedding, there was no clear order of preference. To play first would be to acknowledge lower status. As Hescheles puts it: 'Would the Radi-khover play for the Tshortkover?' Finally, the Kamenka *kapel-mayster* began to play his violin, at which the Radikhover *kapel-mayster* turned to the Tshortkover *kapel-mayster* and remarked: 'Where can you find the courage of a nobody?' ('Oy, vi nemt men di harts fun a kaliker?').[40]

Hescheles is less explicit about the qualities that were desired in a *kapelye*, but a few points emerge clearly. All first-rate Galician *kapelyes* were strictly hierarchical and were always led by the first violinist. He was always a full-time musician, and often he was the only such one in the *kapelye*. So he determined the quality of the *kapelye*. Thus Hescheles speaks of the Premishlaner *kapelye* as essentially the vehicle for the violin of Eli Brandwein, just as the Radikhover and Tshortkever *kapelyes* were for their first violinists (whose names he does not remember). Secondly, the leading *kapelyes* 'had a tradition'. 'Tradition' seems to have been con-nected in part with the relative presence of social hierarchy in the town in which the *kapelye* was located. As an example, Hescheles frequently contrasts the situation in his own town, Gline, with that of nearby Premishlan: 'In our town there was more democracy. But in Premishlan they had castes like that. A tailor didn't talk to a shoemaker, a shoemaker didn't talk to a bathhouse attendant, a bathhouse attendant didn't talk to a carpenter. They had their separate guilds.'[41] Partly as a result, 'The Brandweins, the way Moshke Mikhl spoke about them, they looked down on the Gliner [*kapelye*] even in their heyday.'[42] He also adduces the presence of a more prestigious hasidic *rebbe* in Premishlan (to whom the Brandwein *klezmorim* were related) than the *rebbe* of Gline. He adds that although Premishlan's population was no larger than Gline's, it had the status of a district centre, a *powiat*. In the past it had had a higher status within the Va'ad Arba Aratsot (Council of Four Lands). In

---

[40] Interview, 24 Aug. 1998. *Kaliker* literally means 'cripple'; 'nobody' is Hescheles' own translation.
[41] Interview, 28 Sept. 1998.   [42] Ibid.

some way all of these secular and religious factors seem to have created the tradition of the Brandwein *kapelye* of Premishlan.

As another example he speaks of the tradition of Radikhov. A highly respected *rebbe* was resident there, and the first violinist of the previous generation had been a follower of his and a strictly observant hasid. The Radikhover *kapelye* was famed for its strict discipline and clear methods of instruction. The fact that Moshke Mikhl had studied cimbalom in Radikhov carried great prestige. On the other hand the fame of the Belzer Rebbe did not lead to comparable fame for its *kapelye*. Hescheles mentions only the marches learned or composed by the Belzer *rebbe* and otherwise does not cite him as a connoisseur or patron of music. In one place he also questions his qualifications as *rebbe*, even saying that a man of his mercantile family background could only have become a *rebbe* because of the prevailing cultural and social anarchy.[43] Hescheles considered himself a mitnaged and quite unsympathetic to hasidism. Nevertheless, he seems to suggest that the leading *kapelyes* of Galicia often drew some of their inspiration from an active and musical hasidic milieu.

THE INNER WORKINGS OF THE *KAPELYE*

Hescheles is acutely aware of the fact that the ideal *klezmer-kapelye* no longer existed after the First World War. He would have agreed with this statement by Joel Rubin: 'By the first decade of this century, when the recording industry had become a serious mass medium, the centuries-old tradition of the professional east European Jewish instrumentalists, known as *klezmorim*, was already a fragmentary one.'[44] Hescheles also knows that even prior to the First World War most *klezmorim* lived in considerable poverty, and their social status within the Jewish community was low. Nevertheless, he insists on a number of points which are rarely touched on in the available sources from the United States. As mentioned earlier, there were significant differences in both social and economic status among the various *kapelyes* of Galicia prior to the First World War. To perform with those *kapelyes* that had a tradition was a privilege and was by no means the least attractive work in the region. Secondly, *klezmorim* had a very high opinion of their profession, so that they preferred to maintain their own line of work rather than enter another. Indeed, the children of bourgeois families—the offspring of both businessmen and *khazonim*—sometimes entered the *klezmer* profession. Finally, the relative status of the *klezmer* instruments, with their particular aesthetic and moral connotations, maintained themselves until the First World War and even beyond.

The first point has been discussed somewhat in the previous sections, but we should note here the relationship among *klezmer*, barber, and other professions. Even in the seventeenth century, in the earliest document pertaining to *klezmorim*

---

[43] Interview, 28 Sept. 1998.   [44] Rubin, *Oytsres*, 2.

in Galicia (the Lemberg guild register of 1629), most musicians held down other occupations.[45] Evidently the hatters and gold-braid makers mentioned in the document made a considerable proportion of their living from music, as they are registered in that guild. And the two trades mentioned are both respectable. Both of these facts speak well of the economic status of those Jewish musicians in Lemberg at that time. Yet Hescheles, Stutchewsky, and many other sources for the late nineteenth to early twentieth centuries frequently connect the *klezmer* with the barber's profession, considered one of the lower ones among the Jews.

Hescheles states that in his time the barber was considered slightly below the *server*—the professional baker at weddings—and equal to the midwife. He is quite explicit about the connection between barber and *klezmer*. Even in his time it was still the case that, when the economy had sunk to the level at which local *klezmorim* could no longer make a living as musicians or in combination with other professions, they were allowed to become barbers as well. This was part of their *khazuke*. He speaks of the possibility of becoming a barber as a danger that hung over most *klezmorim*, commenting on the catastrophic situation of most *kapelyes* in Galicia after the First World War, when most of them were forced to become barbers, like the *kapelye* of Belz, which he visited in 1932. But he says that even members of the more famous and established *kapelyes* like those of Premishlan and Radikhov were becoming barbers in his day. He speaks approvingly of the late nineteenth century, when Psakhye Wolf would not allow any barber–musician to play Jewish weddings in the territory of Gline. Hescheles was almost reluctant to admit that in his own time a barber–musician, a flute-player, sometimes joined the regular Gliner *kapelye*. He even impugns this musician's Jewish pedigree by speculating that his surname, Kashevai, sounded somehow Gypsy. Above all it was essential that the *kapel-mayster* be employed exclusively as a *klezmer* and not allow himself to become a barber. To Hescheles the combination of barbering and fiddling resulted not only in less time to rehearse and practise music, but in a lowering of the moral stature of the *kapel-mayster*, which spelled the end of the prestige and tradition of a *kapelye*.

On the second point, it is important to see *klezmorim* as a group with a strong professional ethos, which in their own minds counteracted much of the negative view of them within the Jewish community. They spoke their own professional jargon (*labushaynski*) in which the ordinary Jew was termed a *yold*, or chump. Such a *yold* was clearly inferior in that 'his ear is stopped up' (*zayn oyer iz farshtopt*), 'he has tin in his ear' (*er hot a blekh in oyer*), he was bereft of that special ability to understand music fully. *Klezmer* fathers, especially the *kapel-mayster*, indoctrinated their sons with a sense of the special character and abilities of the *klezmer*. The daughters too shared something of this professional ethos—even though they could not perform in public until the twentieth century—in that they would be expected in most cases to marry a *klezmer*. An apprentice *klezmer* (a *klezmer-ying*) led a poor but com-

[45] Bałaban, *Żydzi lwowscy*, 533–4.

paratively free life, in which his sexual encounters with peasant and sometimes Jewish girls was considered one of the 'perks' of the profession.

The status of the more successful *klezmer*, moreover, did not depend on the Jewish community alone. He was also the musician for the local nobility, and in favourable circumstances he could turn this to his advantage through gifts of cash, a horse, land, a house, or tax exemptions. This contact with the nobility led some *klezmorim* to adopt a largely non-Jewish, popular, and light-classical repertoire. In both Russia and Poland this led some of the leading *klezmorim* to convert to Christianity. This had happened with one of the earliest Polish *klezmorim* known to us by name, Khayim Cimbalist, who died as the court musician for General Wallenstein during the Thirty Years War.[46] Thus there was an open-ended quality to the career of *klezmer* in comparison with most other Jewish crafts. But apart from these exceptional cases the situation of the *klezmorim* is aptly summed up by Hescheles' *landsman* Joseph Roth of Brod: 'Music is another hereditary profession. Some musicians earn great respect and a local reputation. The true musicians among them have no greater ambition than that.'[47]

Within the *kapelye* there was a sharp distinction between the first violinist, who was the *kapel-mayster*, and all the other musicians. The first violinist was usually the son or son-in-law of the previous *kapel-mayster*, and thus he inherited the moral authority of his predecessor. Although he was from eastern Ukraine, Stutchewsky defines this older traditional situation very clearly: 'The first violinist was the central personality within the ensemble. The others were only his accompanists. Occasionally this position was taken by an extraordinary clarinettist, but generally the violinist was the soloist, the solitary and unlimited ruler, the officially recognized leader of the ensemble.'[48] In Galicia the possibility of a clarinettist taking the position of *kapel-mayster* would seem to have been nil. But there may have been cases where the cimbalom player was the leader, as can be seen in the 1905 photograph from Przemyśl in which Yankev Zimbler, who was indeed a cimbalom player, is the father and leader of the *kapelye* composed of his sons or sons-in-law on violins (Fig. 2).[49] In fact, the status of the first violin seems to have risen as violin technique itself developed in the course of the nineteenth century. Too many names of famous cimbalom players have survived from the eighteenth to the early nineteenth century for us to conclude that the pre-eminent position of the first violin extended also to those earlier periods. Nevertheless, the situation described by both Stutchewsky and Hescheles was very much the case from the second half of the nineteenth century.

Practically speaking, this meant that the first violinist took 50 per cent or even more of the total fee for a wedding. Only by dint of this grossly uneven distribution could the violinist maintain himself as a full-time musician, learn or compose new

---

[46] A. Z. Idelsohn, *Jewish Music in its Historical Development* (1929; New York, 1967), 459.

[47] J. Roth, *The Wandering Jews*, trans. M. Hoffmann (New York, 2001), 45.

[48] Stutchewsky, *Haklezmerim*, 109.

[49] See n. 21.

repertoire, and teach it to the *kapelye*. While maintaining that he was a poor man, Hescheles never speaks of his teacher Moshke Mikhl as holding down any other job than musician. Likewise the previous *kapel-mayster*, Psakhye Wolf, was exclusively a violinist by profession. Hescheles insists on this prerogative of the *kapel-mayster* because of the limited economic freedom it granted him, but also because of the spiritual freedom. The *kapel-mayster* was not bound to any routine drudgery and so he could develop his mind and wit. He needed to be able to talk freely to anyone, whether a Polish nobleman, Jewish businessman, or hasidic *rebbe*. The reputation of the *kapelye* depended on him, and this extended to his personality and intelligence. Thus, not only the repertoire but the entire ethos and tradition of a *kapelye* was largely in the hands of its first violinist. The other musicians were not always as fully committed to the *kapelye* or to their development as musicians. Hescheles makes this clear in his image of Moshke Mikhl tuning the instruments of his cimbalom player and bassist, and in the reluctance of the latter to follow his instructions for accompaniment.

An unusual complement, if not a full member of the *kapelye*, was the professional dancer. This was not a required or even a customary professional slot. But Hescheles speaks very highly of Aron Leybele Dudlsack of Premishlan, who had flourished until the First World War as a member of the Brandwein *kapelye*. He also played the tambourine but does not seem to have been the regular drummer of that *kapelye* (if indeed they had one in that period). Hescheles, who knew Aron Leybele's son, who was also a drummer and dancer, states that Aron Leybele was a well-paid member of the Brandwein *kapelye* who performed as a soloist to the accompaniment of virtuoso *klezmer* dance tunes. Thus he was not a *tantslerer*, a teacher of European dances—a profession not unknown in Gline—but a virtuoso performer of *khusidls*. He was akin no doubt to the dancing *badkhonim* of Lithuania, who also specialized in virtuoso performances of traditional Jewish dances while wearing traditional Jewish garb.[50]

Despite the not infrequent lowering of *klezmorim* to the rank of barber–musicians, in Galicia *klezmorim* saw themselves as a completely distinct social and cultural group from the Gypsy musicians. This fact forms a sharp contrast with the situation of nearby Transcarpathia to the south, or Bukovina to the south-east, where *klezmorim* and Gypsies commonly performed together. Indeed in both Romanian and Russian Moldavia this kind of professional combination had been established practice at least since the late eighteenth century. Nothing of the sort seems to have developed in Galicia. There were several reasons for this. On one hand the Gypsy musicians were relatively recent newcomers from Moldavia, following the abolition of slavery there in the 1860s. They were not allowed to integrate themselves into the normal *klezmer* structure any more than non-*klezmer* Jewish musicians. Hescheles remembers them as mainly travelling musicians appearing at inns and sometimes

---

[50] Interview with Naftali Aharoni (Aronczyk) (b. 1918, Vilna), Jerusalem, May 2000.

at fairs. Their ensembles were composed of violins and double bass, rarely with cimbalom or flute.

The reports of the celebrated American *klezmer* clarinettist Naftule Brandwein playing with Gypsy musicians at taverns early in his career shows him as a freelancing individual, rather than a member of a family *kapelye*—thus a reverse of his actual status, which was typical of his temperament. Leopold von Sacher-Masoch's delightful scene of the Jewish cimbalom player playing for a peasant dance at a tavern does not mention Gypsies, who would have been relatively new to the territory. Nor does he suggest that his character Abrahamek the tailor was playing with a *klezmer* ensemble. This was a non-Jewish venue where a part-time musician like Abrahamek (who is described as a tailor, sign-painter, coachman, and cimbalom player) would expect to play with peasant musicians. When Sacher-Masoch describes Jewish weddings (in Kolomey), he mentions only Jewish musicians, even though he uses non-Jewish imagery to personify them.[51]

In contrast to his near-silence about Gypsy musicians, Hescheles has much to say about Ruthenian peasant musicians. It was understood that one source of livelihood for an apprentice *klezmer* was to play at Ruthenian weddings. Hescheles never suggests that mature *kapel-maysters* of the past performed in such venues, but in his own experience straitened economic circumstances induced him to play at such weddings even when he became the local *kapel-mayster*. Socially his participation was facilitated by the fact that both the local Ruthenian fiddler and the local cimbalom player had been students of Moshke Mikhl. He speaks very warmly about these musicians, named Vasily and Dimko, with whom he had both a professional and a social relationship. He stresses that such teacher–student relationships between *klezmorim* and Ruthenian musicians were common in Galicia, and that antisemitism, or indeed any ethnic or religious chauvinism, was alien to these musicians: 'If you played good music you were their friend and they took you to their bosom.'[52]

In Hescheles' discourse the pre-eminent instruments of Jewish music were the violin, followed by the cimbalom. These were the essential instruments; all others were embellishments. The status and prestige of Jewish violinists was well established in Galicia, as elsewhere in eastern Europe, among non-Jews as much as among Jews. But in addition, by the second half of the nineteenth century the *klezmer* violinists also benefited from the rise of virtuosity on the violin generally. It does not seem that *kapel-maysters* thought of themselves as folkloric fiddlers. In their social environment it was they who furnished some parts of the European art repertoire to the rural Polish nobility—and it was only the violin that could function so significantly both in Jewish and in European art music. Hescheles reports a noteworthy concert of Handel's *Water Music* performed by the Radikhover *kapelye* for the local Polish nobleman. In general, it would seem that it was mainly lighter

---

[51] L. von Sacher-Masoch, *A Light for Others and Other Jewish Tales from Galicia*, trans. M. T. O'Pecko (Riverside, Calif., 1994).   [52] Interview, 17 Aug. 1998.

parts of the European repertoire that found their way into a *kapelye*'s programme. But by the latter part of the nineteenth century, with most *kapel-maysters* musically literate, that cross-over repertoire grew steadily, regardless of the fact that the *kapelye* musicians frequently had to learn their parts by ear. The violins owned by *kapel-maysters* were sometimes unusual specimens, often with spurious signatures by Stradivarius and Amadi. Moshke Mikhl's violin was over 100 years old and featured a carved lion on its head. The high aesthetic level of the leading *klezmer* violinists is attested in a plethora of sources, from Sholem Aleichem's novel *Stempenyu* to anecdotes and interviews transmitted by Beregovski and Stutchewsky, and is, of course, enshrined in Chagall's painting of the fiddler on the roof.

Hescheles also insists on the centrality of the cimbalom as the 'soul of the accompaniment'.[53] He is not aware of any Galician *kapelye* lacking a cimbalom. The antiquity of the cimbalom among the *klezmorim* of Galicia is attested by the Lemberg guild document of 1629. This antiquity is further confirmed by the word for cimbalom in the *klezmer-loshn* of Galicia, *hakbreydl*, a reference to the German term *Hackbrett*, which was not otherwise used by Polish Jews.[54] In Galicia the Jewish cimbalom was usually a rather small instrument, as we see in the photograph of Mordkhe Foyerman mentioned earlier. It was light enough to be carried by a strap over the musician's neck while he walked in the wedding or other procession. Cimbalom players generally sat down while performing indoors, resting their instrument on a table or barrel, although folding cimbalom stands were also apparently known. In Hescheles' time the cimbalom player in Premishlan was Shiye Zimbler. The ensemble, under Hershele Kleinman (son of Peysekh Brandwein), consisted also of a clarinet, *sekund* fiddle, double bass, and drum.[55] Hescheles is not aware of a Jewish maker of cimbaloms in Gline or environs and he recalls that Moshke Mikhl's instrument was generations old.

Although subordinate to the first violin, the cimbalom had a large role in the dramatic wedding genre known as *kale-baveynen*, in which the violin and cimbalom alternated virtuoso rubato passages and cadenzas with the voice of the *badkhn*. Another genre that depended on the accompaniment of the cimbalom was the *gedanken* (meditations), a loosely defined species of improvisation, shifting from rubato to metrical passages. The violinist depended on the cimbalom player to follow his modulations and rhythmic changes on the spot, without the other instruments. Hescheles characterizes good cimbalom playing as 'witty', demanding both a chordal accompaniment as well as runs and cadenzas, alternating with snatches of melody. The cimbalom player did not play the melody along with the violinist, especially not in the same octave. As he says: 'That would have been considered competition.'

---

[53] Ibid.

[54] After about 1830 the *Hackbrett* was quite rare in Germany, so Polish *klezmer* use of the term *hakbreydl* must date at least from the 18th century, if not earlier. See Gifford, *The Hammered Dulcimer*, 71. [55] R. Ottens and J. Rubin, *Klezmer-Musik* (Munich, 2000), 97.

It is not known when the clarinet first appeared in the *klezmer-kapelyes* of Galicia, but it is clear that the relatively conservative traditions of these ensembles did not allow much scope for the development of the instrument. Whereas Stutchewsky admits that an exceptional clarinettist might perhaps become an ensemble leader—his own father was such an exception—nothing in the Galician evidence would suggest such a possibility. No source, including Stutchewsky, mentions a prominent clarinettist in Galicia, nor was one every recorded there (although the recordings are, admittedly, very few). Furthermore, Hescheles offers considerable evidence for why such an eventuality would not have been acceptable. He relates that the *klezmer* slang for clarinet was *marbeyn* (marrow bone). In his discourse the clarinet almost always appears as an unrefined instrument associated either with non-Jews or with the poor Jewish masses. Most *kapelyes* did not have a clarinettist, and if they did, his work was confined to dance music and processionals. He was not invited to play in the *kale-baveynen* or perform solo pieces at the table of the wealthy guests. Hescheles concedes that he once played with a clarinettist from the disbanded *kapelye* of Stryj, who was an artistic player with a largely classical repertoire. Hescheles also knows that under Psakhye Wolf the Gliner *kapelye* did indeed include a clarinettist, but he does not know his name or anything about him. Judging by the commercial recordings from Lemberg in the period before the First World War, it seems clear that the traditional Jewish audience was still attuned to the much older and more introspective tones of the violin and wooden flute, accompanied by the small cimbalom. We know from documentary sources that the *klezmer* culture of Moldavia of a far earlier period (over a century earlier) had already accepted the clarinet along with the violin and cimbalom. Yet Galicia and perhaps other regions of Jewish Poland stubbornly resisted this innovation, or else gave it grudging acceptance. It is perhaps paradoxical that one of the great stylists of the *klezmer* clarinet in America, Naftule Brandwein, was a Galician from the Lemberg region. But Naftule's absolutely original and idiosyncratic clarinet technique, resembling no other recorded *klezmer* clarinettist, suggests that he had to create a technique and style for himself without reference to any Jewish model.

THE *KAPELYE* OF GLINE

The memorial book of Gline has this to say about the local *klezmorim*: 'The *shtetl* also had its own *kapelye*, all natives of Gline. Not only were they the best and favourite *klezmorim* for boys and girls from Gline, but they also played weddings in all of the surrounding *shtetls* and villages. They had many pieces of their own composition.' In a list of typical occupations in Gline between 1825 and 1914 the author lists seven *klezmorim*, the same as the number of bakers.[56]

---

[56] H. Halpern (ed.), *Megiles gline* (New York, 1950).

Naturally Hescheles has the most precise data on the recent history of the Gliner *kapelye* and its sister *kapelye* in Radikhov. His narrative contains many instances of the social 'anarchy' that was engulfing life and music in Gline even prior to Hescheles' birth.

The earliest name of which Hescheles is aware is that of Psakhye Wolf, first violinist in the last decades of the nineteenth century. The Wolf family had been *klezmorim* for at least a generation or more prior to the birth of Psakhye. Some time prior to 1900 Psakhye emigrated to America. He settled in New York and changed his name to Paul Wolf. Remarkably, he achieved success as a popular violinist there and no longer made his living as a *klezmer*. He wrote a song in English entitled 'Golden Dreams', which apparently earned him some fame, but Hescheles is unable to explain where Psakhye acquired the reading skills and violin technique with which he accomplished this transformation. He had apparently written a manuscript of the *klezmer* repertoire, which probably contained some of his own compositions and which ended up in Hescheles' hands when he became the *kapel-mayster*. Wolf apparently was no longer alive when Hescheles emigrated to New York.

Berish Nussbaum had been the trumpeter in the Gliner *kapelye* and, like Psakhye Wolf, he emigrated to New York prior to 1900, where Hescheles met him after 1938. The other, much more prominent Berish in Hescheles' narrative is Berish Katz, formerly the trumpeter for the Radikhover *kapelye*. Katz's family had been involved in moneylending, and he was apparently the first to become a *klezmer*. Hescheles speaks highly of the Radikhover *kapelye* and particularly of the training they gave their apprentice *klezmorim*. It is not known whether Katz learned to play the violin in Radikhov or in Gline. He had close relations with Gline; he was a friend of Hescheles' father and had been an unsuccessful suitor of Hescheles' mother. Evidently his non-*klezmer*, bourgeois background put him on a more equal social footing with the Hescheles family. Katz too emigrated to New York sometime before 1900. Like Psakhye Wolf, he succeeded as a violinist there, but in his case within the *klezmer* world.

During the 1920s Katz collaborated with the violinist Abe Schwartz in founding the Boyberiker Kapelye, which is known mainly because of two recordings that it made in 1927.[57] Among its members was the new immigrant clarinettist Dave Tarras. According to a contemporary photograph, the drummer, named Gross, was the official leader of the group. Of course for the drummer to be the leader of a *klezmer-kapelye* was an impossible situation (in Europe a drummer was not usually even a paid member), so we assume Gross must have had important business connections for the group. Hescheles does mention that, when he arrived in New York in 1938, Katz was being marginalized within the ensemble because his taste was too artistic. In 1927 the Boyberikers were a small group by New York standards, with

[57] These items are reissued on *Klezmer Music 1910–1942*, track 15, and *Klezmer Music*, ed. Schwartz, track 9.

two violins, clarinet, trumpet, tuba, double bass, and drums. This was not a traditional Galician *kapelye*, as it lacked a fully independent violin, as well as a real *sekund* fiddle, and it had no cimbalom. Of course the personnel was mixed— Schwartz was Romanian and Tarras Ukrainian. The model for the ensemble was probably the Yiddish theatre more than any kind of *klezmer-kapelye*. However, the phrasing and rhythm of the group are among the most traditional and artistic of any of the groups recording in America at that time. Hescheles had nothing but praise for their 1927 recordings, and commented that Katz must have worked hard to get them into that shape.[58]

Unlike almost all other violinists of his generation who were marginalized or excluded from the *klezmer* scene in New York, Berish Katz maintained his position as a major bandleader for Jewish weddings. Hescheles remembers him from the 1940s, conducting his ensemble on such occasions, adorned with a red sash across his chest. He found that among the New York *klezmorim* his friendship with Katz produced immediate respect. The leading American-born *klezmer* clarinettist Max Epstein remembered Katz in a similar way, as a respected authority on European *klezmer* music, a fine performer, and also a good composer in the current New York *klezmer* style. Epstein's recording of 1995 opens with a bulgar composed by Berish Katz, a fine example of the American Jewish dance music of the 1940s.[59] This same ability to preserve something of the old music while adapting to the new no doubt was one of the secrets of his success in America, but it sometimes gave rise to conflicts with Hescheles. On more than one occasion Hescheles recalls arguments with Katz when he tried to 'correct' the rhythm of certain *klezmer* pieces they had learned in Galicia. Hescheles' final argument was usually 'but I learned this from Moshke Mikhl [Dudlsack]!'[60]

The Dudlsacks were one of the oldest *klezmer* families of the region, with strong representation also in Premishlan, where before the First World War, as mentioned, Aron Leybele Dudlsack was a famous drummer and professional *klezmer* dancer, and afterwards Shiye Dudlsack was the cimbalom player. As a child Moshke Mikhl received expert instruction from the cimbalom player of Radikhov. He also showed a strong interest in the violin, but was discouraged in this by the Radikhover *klezmorim*. Nevertheless, largely on his own, he picked up the violin.

---

[58] After 1927 Katz was not recorded again until the ethnomusicologist Ruth Rubin used him to perform examples of *kale-baveynen* melodies for her LP *The Old Country* (Folkways FS3801, 1963).

[59] 'Berish Katz's Bulgar', *The Epstein Brothers Orchestra: Kings of Freylekh Land—A Century of Yiddish-American Music* (Scott-Wergo Music, Mainz, 1995), track 1. The bulgar (Yiddish: *bulgarish*; Romanian: *bulgareasca*) is a line dance of Bessarabian origin that was adopted by Jews in America between about 1900 and 1970.

[60] Part of Katz's material success in America was ensured by his marriage to the daughter of a wealthy store-owner—in a sense he was returning to his original bourgeois *yikhes*. They lived in a comfortable home in New Jersey. Their son Milton changed his family name to Kay and became a successful pianist. Despite Katz's remarkable success as a *klezmer* in New York, however, he was deeply disappointed that Toscanini had rejected him for the New York Philharmonic.

He was being groomed to be the new cimbalom player of Gline when the emigration of Psakhye Wolf threw open the much better-paid position of first violin. Moshke Mikhl's family *khazuke* evidently gave him priority though he was not a properly trained violinist, even by *klezmer* standards. His confusion is evident from the fact that he too attempted to emigrate to America shortly thereafter. But a year spent in New York and Philadelphia convinced him that he did not have the technique or versatility to succeed there, so he returned to Gline, where he became the new *kapel-mayster*. In Hescheles' narrative it is clear that Dudlsack was unable to maintain the musical standards of the *kapelye* of Gline as they had existed under Psakhye Wolf, or on the level of Radikhov. Nevertheless, Hescheles admired his overall musicality, and his cimbalom playing, of which he was a master. Throughout his career as *kapel-mayster* he attempted to make up for his deficiencies as a violinist by studying the Hohmann series of books for violin students.

The cimbalom player of the group, Motke, was also a Dudlsack. Hescheles remembers him as a good singer but a mediocre cimbalom player. He had obtained his position in the group mainly through his family connections, and was unable even to tune the cimbalom without the help of Moshke Mikhl. His other profession was that of fowl merchant. The bassist was Yosl Bass, also of an old *klezmer* family, who had his position in the *kapelye* by right of *khazuke*. Hescheles describes him as the least musical in the *kapelye*. He also worked as a printer of cotton textiles in the Ukrainian villages. The drummer was Dovidl Poyker, who laid floor clay for a living. One of Moshke Mikhl's three sons, Shulem, played *sekund* fiddle and was also a fine dancer. The barber Peyshe Kashevai sometimes played flute with the *kapelye*.

In the previous generation Berish Nussbaum had been the regular trumpeter in Gline, but when he emigrated to America he was never replaced. Likewise at that time there had been a regular clarinettist, whose name Hescheles does not know. Afterwards there was no clarinet. So in the nineteenth century the Gliner *kapelye* had been a seven- to eight-piece ensemble, but by the First World War it had become a five- to six-piece group, actually more like the local *klezmer* ensembles from before the middle of the nineteenth century. But this seems to have been the result not of an aesthetic choice, but rather of a depleted economy and frequent emigration.

Around 1931, when Moshke Mikhl and his family emigrated to Argentina, Hescheles became the new *kapel-mayster* of Gline. He inherited Motke the cimbalom player, Yosl Bass on double bass, and Dovidl Poyker on the drum, and, as mentioned, sometimes Peyshe Kashevai joined them on flute. There seems not to have been a *sekund* violin. In playing for hasidim, the Gliner *kapelye* sometimes teamed up with Koba Fischer, the excellent violinist from Lemberg. This was the composition of the *kapelye* until Hescheles' emigration.

In Hescheles' time the Gliner *kapelye* usually played at weddings with Leybish Marshalik (Brand). Hescheles describes him as a good *badkhn*, with original lyric

poems that he recited for the weddings of the wealthy. But in the previous generation there had been a famous *badkhn* in Gline, Moyshe Shtam, known as Moyshele
Marshalik. Hescheles is able to recite many lines from Shtam's poems, which often
featured biting and subtle satire against the Jewish community. Although he never
knew Moyshe Shtam, Hescheles is familiar with his works because he once owned a
manuscript that included them.

During Hescheles' tenure as *kapel-mayster* the Gliner *kapelye* still performed at
weddings within its territory. But the traditional part of the repertoire became
increasingly restricted. They still played traditional dance melodies in the street on
the morning of the wedding. The *badkhn* directed the performance of *mazl-tov*
tunes for the bride and groom's parents; these varied according to their status. The
badekns (veiling of the bride) was performed in full, with melodies that varied somewhat according to the status of the bride's family. But modernity made itself felt
in two very significant ways. Dancing was no longer segregated by gender at most
weddings, so the traditional Jewish dances took second place to the mazurka,
krakowiak, or even tangos. Hescheles recalls the *khusidls* being requested mainly by
older men, who danced them as solos. And the music for the table at most weddings
featured light-classical items or even popular songs in Polish or Yiddish, including
the new songs by Jewish composers, using Jewish themes but in Polish. A broader
traditional *klezmer* repertoire, including virtuoso *gedankens*, was in demand mainly
among more Orthodox and hasidic communities, of which Golege was the principal
centre in the region of Gline. For this type of written repertoire Hescheles relied
mainly on the manuscripts of Psakhye Wolf or on the playing of Koba Fischer.

CONCLUSION

What is perhaps most striking about the composite picture of *klezmer* life in Galicia
is the retention of the guild-like and hierarchical structure of the *kapelyes* well into
the twentieth century. This alone distinguishes Galicia from eastern Ukraine
or other Russian territories. Along with this went the older combination of instruments and performance practice. Nevertheless, that this tradition was hardly flourishing even in the late nineteenth century can be seen from the fact that no source
mentions any significant composer of *klezmer* music, or any virtuoso performer,
whose reputation extended outside his native territory. Galicia has no figure to
compare with Stempenyu or Pedotser in mid- to late nineteenth-century Volhynia,
Marder Hagodol in Podolia, Khayim Fidler and Mile Lemisch in Bessarabia, not to
mention the legendary figures of earlier generations.[61] The last real *klezmer* com-

---

[61] On Marder Hagodol the only source is Stutchewsky, *Haklezmerim*, 116–17; on Khayim Fidler of
Orhei (Orgeyev), see M. Bik, *Klezmerim in orhei* (Haifa, 1964); on Mile Lemisch, see B. Kotlyarov,
Moldavskie leutary i ikh iskusstvo (1955; Moscow, 1989), 41–2, music examples 14–20. Three of the
compositions of Khayim Fidler are recorded on *Khevrisa: European Klezmer Music* (Smithsonian
Folkways Recordings SFW CD 40486, 2000), tracks 10, 13, 14.

poser of the region would seem to have been Shmuel Weintraub of Brod in the mid-nineteenth century. Khone Wolfstahl of Tarnopol, although a professional *klezmer*, was rather a composer of Yiddish theatre music.

The first blow to the integrity of *klezmer* music in Galicia seems to have been the massive Jewish emigration from 1881 to the early 1920s. In addition there was significant emigration from Galicia to Vienna and to Hungary. In Hescheles' narrative the theme of emigration, to the United States, Argentina, and Palestine, looms large in the history of the local *kapelyes* in this period and continuously until his own emigration in the 1930s. The disruptions and changes in personnel, including the unusual successions in the position of *kapel-mayster* in Gline, all had their origin in the heavy movement outward.

Thus, to Hescheles, not only his own period, but even that of his predecessor, Moshke Mikhl Dudlsack, was marked by decline in prestige among the *klezmorim*. Nevertheless, the oral tradition of the *kapel-maysters* was still transmitted to Hescheles and with it tales of the more glorious days of the *kapelyes* of Tarnopol, Radikhov, Premishlan, and Gline. At the same time Hescheles is able to evaluate certain changes in a more positive way. The fact that he, along with other *klezmorim* such as Hershele Kleinman in Premishlan, were getting access to conservatory training, either first- or second-hand, meant that they could tackle classical repertoire of greater complexity and on a higher technical level than the *klezmorim* of previous generations. As a former student of the Lemberg Conservatory, Hescheles certainly understands the value of such training. Thus, he often characterizes the inter-war period as one of great promise for the music of the *klezmer*, despite the overall disruptions. Stutchewsky likewise points to the early years of the twentieth century as a period of significant change in musical life, some of which, like the creation of the *froyen kapelyes*, represented a liberating force within Jewish society. We have only to consider the enigmatic figure of Shloyme Kosch, traditional *klezmer* flute-player and founder of one such women's ensemble, to realize the powerful musical potential of Jewish society in Galicia in the early decades of the twentieth century.

Early Recordings of Jewish Music in Poland

MICHAEL AYLWARD

FOR seven years I have been working on a discography of commercial recordings of Jewish music made in Europe on cylinders and shellac records. This project has now progressed sufficiently for a work-in-progress report to be issued. I will initially give a general account of the discography as it stands at present and then concentrate on those aspects that apply especially to Poland.

OVERVIEW OF THE DISCOGRAPHY

The aim of the project is to document as far as possible all commercial recordings of Jewish music made in Europe on cylinders or shellac records (broadly speaking, 78 rpm records). When complete, this discography will list them all, together with all standard discographical details such as record label, catalogue number, matrix number, disc size, artist name and title of recording (together with details of

I would like to thank the following: Janet Topp-Fargion and Jane Harvell, National Sound Archive, London; Ruth Edge and her staff, EMI Sound Archive, London; Ewa Krysiak and Pani Wróblewska, Biblioteka Narodowa, Warsaw; Alan Kelly (Sheffield), Arthur Badrock (Norwich), Bill Dean-Myatt (Sutton Coldfield), Paul Vernon (London), George Woolford (Wells-next-the-Sea, Norfolk), Joel Bresler (Lexington, Massachusetts), Helen Winkler (Calgary), Michael Gunrem (La Ferté-Milon), Dina Levias (Geneva), Valeria Ieseanu, Chişinău (Kishinev), Pekka Gronow (Helsinki), Dr Risto Pekka Pennanen (Göttingen), and John DeMetrick (Budapest) for much discographical information and advice; Joel Rubin and Rita Ottens (Berlin) for their generous support and advice and invaluable technical information on Jewish music and recordings.

The following are important sources for the work I have been doing: R. Gelatt, *The Fabulous Phonograph 1877–1977* (London, 1977); M. Kominek, *Zaczęło się od fonografu* (Kraków, 1986); J. Łętowski, *Magia czarnego krążka: ABC kolekcjonera płyt* (n.p., 1981); J. Wollock, 'European Recordings of Jewish Instrumental Folk Music, 1911–1914,' *Association for Recorded Sound Collections Journal*, 28 (1997), 36–55; S. Prizament, 'Yidish teater in Lemberg', in I. Manger, Y. Turkov, and M. Perenson (eds.), *Yidisher teater in eyrope tsvishn beyde velt-milkhomes: poyln* (New York, 1968); J. Gelston, 'Lwów i śpiewacy brodzcy', in A. Kuligowska-Korzeniewska and M. Leyko (eds.), *Teatr żydowski w Polsce* (Łódź, 1998); N. Sandrow, *Vagabond Stars: A World History of Yiddish Theater* (New York, 1986); I. Fater, *Yidishe muzik in poyln tsvishn beyde velt-milkhomes* (Tel Aviv, 1970); M. Fuks, *Muzyka ocalona* (Warsaw, 1989); J. Rubin and R. Ottens, *Klezmer-Musik* (Kassel, 1999); Z. Zilbertsvayg (Zylbercweig), *Leksikon fun yidishn teater*, 6 vols. (New York, 1931–69); H. Veigl, *Lachen im Keller: Von den Budapestern zum Wiener Werkel. Kabarett und Kleinkunst in Wien* (Vienna, 1986).

composers and arrangers where these are given), precise recording date and recording location, name of recording engineer, and details of any records on which the original recording was later reissued. Every effort will also be made to provide artist biographies and additional information of interest.

The range of musical genres covered by the discography is wide, but may be broadly defined as applying to traditional Jewish music. For example, it excludes works by Jewish composers working in the European classical tradition; art music, even if specifically Jewish in tone and content; and non-Jewish music performed by Jewish artists. It does, however, extend to non-musical recordings such as comic monologues and dramatic recitals. In addition, there are separate appendices dealing with categories such as 'Jewish' music performed by non-Jewish artists[1] and Jewish parodies performed by non-Jewish artists, the latter a fairly common genre among pre-revolutionary Russian recordings, but rare in Polish ones of the same era.

Tables 1 and 2 give a snapshot of the discography as it currently stands. Although enlightening, they by no means give a representative picture. This is merely a view taken at a particular point in time of a project that is constantly evolving and will, by the time this chapter is published, be hopelessly out of date. The data recorded in these tables is based only on those recordings that have so far been entered onto the database. In addition to the 1,753 recordings noted here, there remain a further 2,000 or so recordings from the Gramophone and Zonophone companies that need to be entered, and an additional 1,500 or so recordings from a range of other companies. Most of the additional 2,000 Gramophone and Zonophone recordings were made in Poland and Russia, but that number also includes about 500 titles, mostly comic routines, made by Jewish artists from the polyglot theatres of Budapest such as the Fővárosi Orfeum, where performances appear to have been conducted in a mixture of Yiddish, Hungarian, and German. Many of the 1,500 or so recordings on other labels derive from Vienna, particularly from the Yiddish theatre and Jewish music hall (notably by artists from the Budapester Orpheum-Gesellschaft, whose entertainers were mostly Jewish and where routines were performed in German but with a very heavy admixture of Yiddish).

It is important to stress that of the 1,753 records noted in these tables only 150-odd were recorded after 1914 and that on closer examination some of these may ultimately prove to be reissues of pre-First World War recordings. Furthermore, all the 3,500 recordings still to be added to the database derive from the period 1899 to 1914.

Bald statistics such as these are usually misleading and the data set out in these tables are no exception. For example, the thirty-six Budapest recordings of Yiddish theatre songs were recorded in 1909 and 1911 and were all made by the ubiquitous

---

[1] As, for example, a title such as 'Żydowski krakowiak z wystawy', recorded by the Polish folk group Orkiestra Wiejska for the Gramophone Company sometime before 1925.

Table 1. Breakdown of recordings by record company and musical type

Record company	Cantorial	Synagogue choir	Yiddish theatre song	Yiddish song	Yiddish theatre orchestra	Klezmer	Instrumental	Spoken word	Miscellaneous	Total
Anker	2	5	12	2						21
Beka	68		20	4						92
Cristal Electro	4			10					12	26
Edison	3			1			5			9
Favorite	48	5	141	3						197
Gramophone	339	18	173	171	15	48	12	23		799
Homocord	13		14	14						27
Imperial	24		14	22		4				64
Jumbo			34	3						37
Odeon			8							8
Olimpia				6						6
Parlophone	52		12	2						66
Polska Płyta				22					3	25
Scala	24		92	5	4					125
Syrena	10		2	14					14	40
USIBA									1	1
Zonophone	34		52	95	15		6	1	7	210
TOTAL	621	28	560	374	34	52	23	24	37	1,753

Table 2. Breakdown of recordings by location and musical type

Location	Cantorial	Synagogue choir	Yiddish theatre song	Yiddish song	Yiddish theatre orchestra	Klezmer	Instrumental	Spoken word	Miscellaneous	Total
Bucharest	4	3	18							25
Budapest	56		36	5						97
Czernowitz	26			23		8				57
Lemberg	5		354	1			4		1	365
London	82		13	84		4	2		1	185
Moscow				20			2	6		29
Nizhny Novgorod				4						4
Odessa						6		4		10
Paris				14						14
Poltava							2			2
St Petersburg	25	9		82			4	14	4	138
Tarnów	11			14						25
Vienna	196	2	25	6						229
Vilna	43	4	11	34	30	15	3			140
Warsaw	121	5	82	79	4	19	1		31	342
Unknown	52	5	21	8			5			91
TOTAL	621	28	560	374	34	52	23	24	37	1,753

Pepi Litmann, who was born in eastern Galicia and seems to have been constantly on the move throughout her career. Presumably these recordings were made while she was on tour in Hungary. The staggering lack of recordings made in Romania (with the exception of those made in Czernowitz, which was located in Austria-Hungary during the period in which most of these recordings were made) may perhaps be explained by the fact that so far I have had little luck in tracking down information on the Odeon recording company, which was very active in this area and whose catalogues, when finally located in sufficient quantity, may well completely change the picture. The complete lack of recordings from western Europe (apart from Great Britain) is explained simply by the fact that I have not yet investigated this area. In view of this, I will, therefore, refrain from drawing any but the broadest conclusions from this set of figures and even these should be regarded as tentative.

On the basis of present findings, however, we can say that prior to the First World War there was in Europe, and specifically in eastern Europe, a vigorous Jewish music recording industry. This was centred predominantly in Poland, but was also fairly active in Russia, mainly in St Petersburg (very few recordings seem to have been made in Moscow), as well as in Vienna. The main type of music recorded was Yiddish songs from either the Yiddish theatre or other sources. The second largest category was cantorial music, and bringing up the rear was a small number of instrumental recordings, not much more than 6 per cent of the whole, even if we combine the figures for Yiddish theatre orchestras, *klezmer*, and other instrumental recordings. Moreover, this percentage figure will reduce drastically once the 3,500 other recordings are added in, as these are overwhelmingly non-instrumental.

THE FIRST JEWISH RECORDINGS IN POLAND

On the 22 July 1902 the Russian branch of the British-controlled Gramophone Company, which for two years had already been recording in Poland, opened a shop at 30 Nowy Świat. This was initially under the management of Franciszek(?) Rafalski and subsequently under that of Konwitz (the shop moved premises on 26 February 1903 to 116 Marszałkowska). The very same year that the Warsaw branch of the Gramophone Company opened its doors, recordings of Jewish music began to be made by the company. These were the first of what proved to be a steady stream of recordings until 1915, when the German occupation of Warsaw resulted in the closure of the British company. The very first Jewish recordings made by this company in Poland appear to have been a set of ten cantorial pieces sung by the cantor Gershon Sirota and recorded in Warsaw in 1902.

In 1903 the Gramophone Company took over its American arch-rival, the International Zonophone Company, and from 1904 Zonophone became the Gramophone Company's budget label. To describe it in this way, and this is the usual way Zonophone is thought of, is to do it a major disservice. It may have been a budget label, but in the field of recordings of 'ethnic' music it made a substantial contribution. Between them the Gramophone Company and Zonophone issued from 1902 until 1915 about 3,000 Jewish recordings, about 90 per cent of which were recorded in eastern Europe, with Poland being the major recording centre.

They were, however, by no means the only companies active in this field. In December 1907 the German company Favorite-Record opened a branch in Warsaw at 2 Nalewki, moving in 1908 to 13 Graniczna. Even before setting up in Warsaw, the company had been actively recording artists from the Yiddish theatre in Lemberg (Lwów), and by December 1907 had already recorded at least eighty-nine titles by artists from this theatre. In subsequent years the company extended its Jewish recordings to Warsaw, where it recorded both cantorial and Yiddish theatre items.

By 1914 dozens of record companies were operating in Warsaw; many were branches of foreign-owned companies, but Polish companies were also making their mark. At this stage it is impossible to give a definitive accounting of which of these companies were issuing Jewish recordings. All that can be said is that the German-owned companies Beka, Jumbo, Odeon, and Scala were all active in this field to a greater or lesser extent. As regards Polish companies, the most significant was Syrena. Founded by Julius Feigenbaum, most probably in 1904, its shop at 153 Marszałkowska distributed a wide range of recordings of all types of music. Syrena has always had the reputation of having been a major source of Jewish music recordings, and it is believed that a substantial number were made. But documentary evidence concerning this company is notoriously difficult to come by and two weeks that I spent at the Biblioteka Narodowa in Warsaw in 1998 yielded information on only a handful of Jewish recordings. This lack of information has so far represented a major gap in our overall picture of recordings of Jewish music in Poland.

Miraculously, this gap is about to be filled. While the final draft of this chapter was being written, news arrived of the forthcoming publication of a complete Syrena discography written by the Polish discographer Tomasz Lerski. This three-part, 1,100-page magnum opus will appear under the title *Syrena Record: Pierwsza polska wytwórnia fonograficzna, 1904–1939* ('Syrena Record: The First Polish Phonograph Company, 1904–1939'). I am told by the author that it contains a very large number of Jewish recordings spanning the whole period. If so, then this work will contain detailed information (including artist biographies) on what was probably the only major source of Jewish recordings in Europe during the inter-war period.

THE RECORDED REPERTOIRE

As can be seen from the tables, the repertoire fell into two basic categories, cantorial and Yiddish theatre, plus a scattering of Yiddish songs and instrumental pieces.[2]

Cantorial

Recordings of cantorial music in Europe are dominated by two immensely prolific artists, Sawel Kwartin, based in Vienna, and Gershon Sirota, based in Warsaw and Vilna. Only twenty-nine of the 180 Polish cantorial items so far documented were not recorded by Sirota. These include recordings by the cantor Kipnis, who recorded six sides for the Gramophone Company in Warsaw 1902; Butzarski and Blacher, soloists of the Great Synagogue of Vilna, who recorded two sides for the Gramophone Company in Vilna in 1903, probably at the same session; the cantor Alter Melitzer,[3] who recorded eleven sides for the German Homocord company in Tarnów in 1908 and also several Yiddish songs both as soloist and in duet with his son Israel Melitzer; the cantor I. Icht, who recorded eight sides for Syrena Record before 1924, probably not in Poland; and the cantor Fainer, who recorded a series of non-cantorial items for the Gramophone Company in Vilna in 1903.

Yiddish Theatre and Other Songs

Under the heading 'Yiddish Theatre Songs' I include recordings by Broder singers. These were itinerant actors and singers who toured throughout Galicia and Romania and often much farther afield, performing in taverns and cafés. There is no firm dividing line between Broder singers and theatre artists. Broder singers often moved into the theatre for a while, only to revert later on to their former profession. Likewise, theatre artists would also spend periods as Broder singers.[4]

This needs to be borne in mind when we consider the overwhelming significance of Lemberg as a recording centre for Yiddish theatre songs. Of the 560 Yiddish theatre recordings so far identified, 354 were recorded in Lemberg and of these about 100 are by Broder singers such as J. Reissmann, S. Podzamcze, and especially the hugely prolific Pepi Litmann, who was, according to Zalmen Zilbertsvayg (Zilbercweig) a personal favourite of Mendele Moykher Sforim, at whose home in Odessa she was a frequent guest during the First World War.

The remaining theatre songs recorded in Lemberg are by artists which the record catalogues invariably, but rather vaguely, refer to as belonging to the Jüdisches Theater Lemberg. However, a glance at the roster of artists immediately reveals that this theatre, as one would expect, is Yankev-Ber Gimpl's company. This was the main Yiddish theatre in Lemberg, which was founded by Gimpl in 1889 and remained in the family's hands until 1939. All the most well-known and popular

---

[2] Names of performers and their works will follow the spelling in contemporary catalogues and record labels.   [3] Zilbertsvayg's theatre lexicon refers to him as a *badkhn*.

[4] On the Broder singers, see M. Steinlauf, 'Jewish Theatre in Poland', in this volume.

artists are represented on these records, including Julius Guttmann (for many years the theatre's artistic director), his wife, Salcia, J. Deutsch, Leon Kalisch, Helene Gespass, J. M. Thur, Jakob Fuchs, S. Schilling, Norbert Glimer, Adolf Melzer, Lina Karlik, and many others.

Even on the basis of these figures, these 250-odd recordings made during the period 1906 to 1909 must be regarded as a remarkable achievement, but the true situation is even more extraordinary. The 3,500 or so recordings that have not yet been put on the database and are available only in the form of catalogue pages contain an estimated additional 250 recordings by the artists of Gimpl's theatre, making a grand total of 500 recordings. Assuming an average playing time of 2½ minutes per recording, this would yield a total of almost twenty-one hours of continuous recorded music, an amazing prospect for students of the popular Yiddish theatre, assuming these records are ever unearthed in meaningful quantities. I can think of no parallel in the history of the early record industry where any artist or group of artists was the subject of such intense activity. The pioneering recording engineers of this era documented a complete sound panorama of one of the most important Yiddish theatres ever to operate in Europe and, what is more, captured it on disc during the period when it was at the very peak of its powers.

As regards the repertoire, scenes from the Yiddish operettas of Goldfadn and others predominate, but there is also a substantial number of comic songs and couplets. The instrumental accompaniment is usually piano, or piano and violin, but there are also a large number of recordings with full orchestral and choral accompaniment.

Most of the Yiddish theatre recordings from Warsaw simply note the artist as being from the Jüdisches Theater Warschau and so it is only by knowing the background of the individual artist concerned that we can identify which theatre this may have been. The main artists represented are S. Landau, Herrmann Weissmann, G. Feinstein, Lina Goldstein, P. Breitmann, S. Rotschein, J. Fiszelewicz, L. Braun, and Nadia (Estera) Nerosławska, the last four all from the Elizeum Theatre. As with Lemberg, the emphasis is on the Yiddish operetta, but with Goldfadn not nearly as apparent and far more recordings of works by composers from the American Yiddish stage, such as Yosef Rumshinsky ('Die Amerikanerin') and Boris Thomashefsky ('Die Neshume von main Volk').

There are a few Yiddish theatre recordings made in Vilna prior to the First World War, but there is no sign of any recordings made by Yiddish theatres in Kraków or Łódź.

Yiddish song is far more difficult to discuss, since it is represented by a large number of singers who recorded only a few titles that are difficult to analyse. Significantly, however, the standard repertoire of what nowadays is presented as Yiddish 'folk song' is completely absent. One will search in vain for a recording of 'Di mizinke oysgegebn', 'Di mame iz gegangen', or 'Der rebbe elimeylekh'. Even 'Rozhinkes mit mandlen' appears to have been recorded only once (by Leon

Abramovitch, London, 1904), which is surprising given the numerous recordings of Goldfadn's other songs. Finally, mention should be made of the mysterious group which recorded in Poland under the name Żydowski Kwartet, and in Russia as the Evreiskii Kvartet N. Pundika (N. Pundik's Jewish Quartet). Between 1902 and 1909 in St Petersburg, Moscow, and Warsaw this group made forty or more recordings of what seem to be mainly comic Yiddish songs. I have been unable to find any information whatsoever about them.

Yiddish Theatre Orchestra, Klezmer, *and Other Instrumental*

As mentioned previously, the most striking thing about this category is how little of it was recorded. Two possible explanations immediately spring to mind, only to be just as immediately countered by two forceful objections. The first explanation is that for technical reasons it was far more difficult to record groups of musicians than, say, a solo singer with just piano accompaniment. This is true, but it did not prevent record companies before the First World War from producing vast quantities of recordings of military bands, dance orchestras, salon ensembles, and every other combination of musical instruments—the Russian catalogues overflow with countless hundreds of such recordings. Besides, this technical problem did not prevent record companies from providing an orchestral accompaniment for many of their Yiddish theatre recordings. The second explanation is that there was no great market for purely instrumental recordings of Jewish music. This supposition, however, is soundly confuted if we take at face value a statement made in a Russian publication about the Syrena company's sales of recordings by Belf's Romanian Orchestra (Rumynskii orkestr Bel'fa), which performed a *klezmer* repertoire: 'And do you know how many of Belf's records the factory sells? Every day not less than two to three thousand items are shipped south, yet new orders pour in endlessly.'[5] Something is not right here. Either these figures are grossly exaggerated or there was some factor other than lack of demand which deterred companies from recording Jewish instrumental music to any significant degree.[6]

The earliest purely instrumental recordings that I have been able to identify is a series of four sides made in 1903 for the Gramophone Company by the Orkestr Vilenskago Bol'shogo Teatra (Orchestra of the Vilna Grand Theatre) conducted by Stupel. The first side is entitled 'Tsyganskaya serenada' ('Gypsy Serenade'), but the other three are entirely Jewish, being pot-pourris of themes from two Goldfadn operettas: *Shulamis* and *Di koldunye*. Stupel followed this set in March 1910 with a set of fifteen sides on the Gramophone label with the Dukhovoi Orkestr Vilenskago Gorodskogo Teatra (Brass Band of the Vilna Municipal Theatre). Again, with a

---

[5] *Grammofonnyi Mir*, no. 11, 25 June 1912; as cited in Wollock, 'European Recordings of Jewish Instrumental Folk Music'.

[6] I should point out that, apart from the Belf recordings, I have not incorporated any of the 193 recordings listed in Jeffrey Wollock's article noted above, so that what follows is entirely additional information on the subject of instrumental recordings.

few exceptions all the titles are Jewish, e.g. 'Der rebi hot geheissen lustig sein', 'A frehlichs "Sore schejndel"', a six-sided pot-pourri of Yiddish operettas, and so on. Yet more Stupel recordings were made in July 1913 in Vilna.

Who was Stupel and what was the status of the Bolshoi Teatr and the Vilenskii Gorodskoi Teatr as regards the Yiddish theatre? Documentation of the Yiddish theatre in Vilna prior to the advent of the Vilna Troupe is scant, but it seems that these theatres were shared by both Russian and Jewish companies. Perhaps in the course of time more light will be shed on this and many other matters concerning the less 'artistic' side of the Yiddish theatre in Poland.

The bulk of the Polish items that I have provisionally classified as *klezmer* is provided by two main groups, the first based in Vilna and headed by D. Olevsky. Three recording sessions have been identified so far: a single side in September 1910 for the Gramophone Company (actually under the name of A. S. Olevsky—perhaps a misprint, perhaps a completely different artist); a four-side set recorded on 8 and 9 July 1912 for the Zonophone Company; and a ten-side set recorded in July 1913 for the Gramophone Company. Roughly half the titles are Jewish, the others having an 'oriental' flavour or Polish motifs.

The other group, which recorded nineteen titles for the Gramophone Company in Warsaw on 5 and 7 March 1914, was Belf's Romanian Orchestra. This orchestra, almost certainly Romanian in name only, was in fact a Jewish ensemble, although its origins have long been the subject of speculation. Current opinion is that the group probably came from Podolia. Knowing that these recordings were made in Warsaw may cast some doubt on this theory, although recording location is a rough guide at best to the provenance of the recording artist.[7]

THE INTER–WAR YEARS

The period 1918 to 1939 saw a steep decline, we may even say collapse, of the recording of Jewish music in Europe. Although the catalogues of this era carry many Jewish lists, almost all on closer inspection turn out to be reissues of pre-war recordings.

In Poland the situation was no different. I have been able to find information on no more than 100 recordings made in Poland during this time, most on the Syrena, Homocord, and Polska Płyta labels, but these need to be treated with caution. For example, all the twenty-two Polska Płyta recordings are of Yiddish songs by anonymous artists, usually a sign that these are either reissues of extremely early recordings or are recordings pirated from other companies, in which case they may even be American in origin.

As regards Poland this picture will change greatly with the publication of Tomasz Lerski's Syrena discography, but it seems unlikely that even with the

---

[7] On the Belf orchestra, see also W. Feldman, 'Remembrance of Things Past', in this volume.

discovery of further sources the general European picture will change substantially. Why this collapse? We can speculate about a number of intersecting causes. First of all, loss of the Russian market after the revolution made the recording of Jewish music by big international firms such as the Gramophone Company a less attractive financial proposition. Meanwhile, domestic recording companies in the new, fervently nationalistic successor states of eastern Europe doubtless had little inclination to cater to the tastes of their national minorities. Moreover, from the mid-1920s onwards, Anglo-American music, in the form of either direct imports or recordings by local artists imitating the general style, began to shoulder aside all forms of indigenous music. An additional factor may have been that after the war the American Victor and Columbia companies vigorously began to market their American-recorded Jewish repertoire in eastern Europe. Such competition may well have discouraged local companies from making their own recordings for this specialized market.

CONCLUSION

Recordings of Jewish music were made on a massive scale in eastern Europe and especially in Poland prior to the First World War. So far, more than 3,000 such recordings have been identified, with the prospect of many more thousands being added in coming years as other major labels such as Odeon and Syrena are investigated.[8]

---

[8] By mid-2003 the number of items on the database had increased to approximately 5,500, but the additional material has done little to alter the overall picture presented in this chapter. Anyone who has any information whatsoever that may be relevant to this project is invited to contact the author of this chapter at 164 Loose Road, Maidstone, Kent ME15 7UD, England; fax +44 (0)870 0528675; email:<mikeaylward@last.demon.co.uk>.

Jewish Theatre in Poland

MICHAEL C. STEINLAUF

IN PRE-MODERN TIMES

TRADITIONAL Judaism, as frequently noted, is less concerned with doctrine than with practice. The practice is defined by Jewish law, *halakhah*. Originating in the Talmud, adapted by religious authorities from generation to generation for 1,500 years, *halakhah* (along with the associated system of *minhag*, or custom) made it possible for Jews to maintain an absolute distinction between Jewish and non-Jewish ways of doing nearly everything in life. *Halakhah*, in other words, is a kind of script for the observance of traditional Jewish life, and this life was richly performative. This was obviously true of the complex liturgy of the synagogue, but it also applied to the Jewish home, where sabbath meals and Passover *seders* were only the more obvious examples of densely detailed, carefully enacted ritual performances, and it also applied to the Jewish life cycle. All such ritual, whether part of the life cycle, the annual cycle, or daily life, was also linked to music, above all to the chanted melody, or *nign*. The taking of wedding vows, the benediction over food, the burial of the dead, the study of Torah, and countless other activities were all performed to characteristic *nigunim*: moreover, everyday Jewish conversation and gesture were punctuated with *nigunim* and cannot be imagined without them.

The centrality of performance in traditional Jewish life inspired the development of a class of specialized performers. They included the *khazn*, or cantor, who sang prayers on sabbath and holidays; *meshorerim*, singers who accompanied the *khazn* in larger synagogues; the *magid*, or travelling preacher, whose livelihood depended on the charisma of his sabbath sermons; *klezmorim*, the instrumental musicians who played at weddings and other celebrations; the *badkhn*, or *marshelik*, a professional jester and master of ceremonies at such celebrations. But the very specialization of such performers, their existence as a class apart, led to tension with normative Jewish society. Often itinerant, the Jewish performers were frequently not responsible to local religious and communal authorities. They were also not averse to practising their craft in secular contexts. *Khazonim* entertained in private

I would like to thank the Smukler/Lasch Family Trust for its generous support during the writing of this chapter. A Hebrew version appeared in I. Bartal and Y. Gutman (eds.), *Kiyum veshever*, vol. ii (Jerusalem, 2001), 327–50; a Polish version appeared in J. Tomaszewski and A. Żbikowski (eds.), *Żydzi w Polsce: Leksikon* (Warsaw, 2001), 498–512.

homes and taverns, and frequently wove non-Jewish material, such as folk songs and opera arias, into their singing; *klezmorim* performed with non-Jewish musicians and such mixed bands often played at both Jewish and Christian celebrations. Jewish performers were typically reproached as well for the sins of individualism: valuing their own craft at the expense of sacred ritual, using their craft to encourage unseemly levity or passion. In common with their counterparts in other cultures, they were also accused of living dissolute lives. 'Happy is the man who refrains' from attending celebrations where the *badkhn* is welcome, wrote one rabbi, and another, in the early eighteenth century, declared: '*Khazonim* will not be resurrected [in messianic times], for voice and melody is their only object [*kavanah*].'[1] Such denunciations, however, rarely resulted in communal prohibitions.

The case of theatre was different. Here rabbinical objections were enforced. The formula 'theatres and circuses' (*te'atrot vekirkasot*) in such proscriptions attests to their antiquity.[2] For the Greeks and Romans, theatre was connected to religious worship. Be it the cult of Bacchus or the emperor, such associations inclined the rabbis to regard theatre as idolatry (*avodah zarah*). Medieval European theatre was also largely religious in character and, moreover, often specifically anti-Jewish. Indeed, Passion plays staged in urban marketplaces at Easter time often inspired Christian attacks on the Jewish quarter. Theatre in itself was also doubtless threatening to the rabbis. In a society whose existence depended on maintaining a carefully tended border between 'us' and 'them', acting—allowing another identity, albeit temporarily, inside one—could only be perceived as socially and morally subversive.

But even theatre found a place in pre-modern Jewish societies. This was nearly exclusively as a result of its association with the Jewish holiday of Purim. Observed in February or March (the Jewish month of Adar), Purim is one of two holidays that celebrate post-biblical events and are therefore not stipulated in the Pentateuch; the other is Hanukah. Both holidays commemorate the Jews' victories over their enemies, and both became associated with decidedly this-worldly practices; gambling became traditional on Hanukah and plays were sometimes staged as well. But such tendencies were particularly pronounced during the holiday of Purim, and their aura extended throughout the month of Adar. Unlike Hanukah, which celebrates the reconquest of the Temple and its miraculous rededication, Purim commemorates events set entirely in the Diaspora and that are entirely the work of human hands. Indeed, the Scroll of Esther, the textual basis for the holiday, is unique in the Jewish canon in not containing a single reference to God. The scroll recounts how the Jews of Persia turn mortal threat into triumph, averting their

---

[1] D. Halevi, *Turei zahav*, cited in Y. Lifshits, 'Badkhonim un leytsim ba yidn: materyaln tsu a verterbukh', *Arkhiv far der geshikhte fun yidishn teater un drame* (Vilna), 1 (1930), 46; Z. H. Kaydanover, *Kav hayashar* (Frankfurt am Main, 1705), ch. 41, cited in J. Shatzky, 'An apologye fun khazones onfang 18tn yorhundert: yoel khazn un zayn *Reyekh nikhoyekh*', *Pinkes* (New York, 1927–8), 180.

[2] This formula occurs in BT, *AZ* 18*b*. For a collection of rabbinical rulings covering some 1,500 years, see S. Ernst, 'Tekstn un kveln tsu der geshikhte fun teater, farveylungen un maskaradn ba yidn', *Arkhiv far der geshikhte fun yidishn teater un drame*, 1 (1930), 6–17.

destruction at the hands of the king's counsellor Haman and having Haman executed instead. The Jews' saviour is the Jewish Queen Esther, who triumphs not through force of arms, as do the Hasmoneans commemorated on Hanukah, but through manipulation, deceit, and sexual relations with the non-Jewish king. These are the ambiguous virtues that permit Jewish survival in the Diaspora, in a profane world into which Jews have been exiled, according to the traditional formula, 'because of our many sins'.

The celebration of this story early became associated with practices typical of holidays of reversal, impulses that the Russian theorist Mikhail Bakhtin termed carnivalesque: the high dragged low, the serious mocked, the holy profaned, the forbidden permitted.[3] It should be stressed that such practices find parallels in the Christian societies amid which Jews lived: the medieval Feast of Fools and the German Renaissance farces called *Fastnachtspiel*, for example. The Jewish customs included the 'coronation' of a *purim-rov*, a yeshiva student chosen by his fellows and paraded down the main street with jeers and insults for all the town worthies. Such festivities typically included a Purim kiddush in which traditional Hebrew verses alternate with parodic and obscene Yiddish lines. Enjoined not to exult over the death of their enemies, on Purim Jews were encouraged to do so, and in as raucous a way as possible, including public drunkenness. The meaning of the latter custom is more fully disclosed when we recall the common Yiddish expression 'shiker vi a goy' ('drunk as a gentile'). Encouraging such behaviour, some rabbis interpreted it in a redemptive context: according to one tradition, in messianic times the only holiday that will continue to be observed is Purim.

Closely linked to the celebration of Purim in Ashkenazi communities at least as early as the mid-sixteenth century was the performance of a Purim play, or *purim-shpil*. The actors were yeshiva students or artisans; dressed as non-Jews and where necessary as women, the *purim-shpilers* marched through town, performing their play in the wealthier Jewish homes, occasionally on an improvised stage. In eastern Europe by the nineteenth century the *purim-shpil* had become the property of the lower classes; it was often staged annually by the same group of players, with parts and even costumes passed down from father to son. Some of these groups travelled and performed in neighbouring towns. The earlier *purim-shpils* were apparently skits parodying local events; from the mid-seventeenth century they began to be based on biblical stories. Most common, understandably, was the Purim story, but the selling of Joseph, as well as David and Goliath, were also popular. Sections of the plays (prologue, epilogue, actors' introductions) were formulaic. The plays were ribald and strongly parodic, mocking both local personages and the biblical heroes themselves.[4]

---

[3] M. Bakhtin, *Rabelais and his World* (Bloomington, Ind., 1984).

[4] On the early history of the *purim-shpil*, the indispensable work is C. Shmeruk, *Maḥazot mikra'im beyidish, 1697–1750* (Jerusalem, 1979), 13–152. For the 19th century, see the article in Z. Zilbertsvayg [Zilbercweig], *Leksikon fun yidishn teater*, vol. iii (New York, 1959), cols. 1653–1756.

NEW AUDIENCES

Traditional *purim-shpils* continued to be performed in Poland and throughout eastern Europe until the Second World War. But from the nineteenth century onwards the Jewish experience of theatre began to develop in a secular context as well. During the first half of the century, in a handful of east European cities and towns, a new Jewish commercial elite emerged, oriented towards west European trade and ideas. These circles provided a natural audience for the Jewish reformers known as maskilim. Small in number but increasingly influential, the maskilim were fiercely fought as heretics by the representatives of hasidism, which swept eastern Europe during this same period. The maskilim encouraged Jews to learn non-Jewish languages, study the sciences and humanities, and generally make themselves more 'productive'. They wrote in Hebrew and, apologetically, in the 'jargon' of Yiddish as well. They subjected the hasidim, the so-called representatives of darkness and superstition, to savage satires. These took the form of dialogues and occasionally plays, which, however, could not be staged because of the opposition of the hasidim.

By the mid-nineteenth century, touched by maskilic ideas, a Yiddish popular culture had begun to develop throughout eastern Europe. Literature intended for women and lower-class men was distributed by pedlars in chapbook form (*mayse-bikhlekh*); songs were written and performed by itinerant singers.[5] Above all, in Warsaw there is evidence of Yiddish theatre performances as well. As early as the 1830s Yiddish plays on biblical themes were staged before mixed Jewish and Christian audiences in a Warsaw dance hall. In 1868–70 Yiddish plays were performed in a permanent Jewish theatre.[6] Some of these performers were doubtless the so-called *Broder zingers* (Broder singers), who from the 1850s performed in restaurants, cafés, and beer gardens throughout eastern Europe. Their name suggests a link to the 'progressive' town of Brody, located on the Russian–Galician border, a crossroads where Jewish merchants travelling to and from the Leipzig fairs typically sought entertainment. The repertoire of the Broder singers consisted of songs and skits, often with a satirical thrust directed at wealthy Jews and hasidim. The songs were sometimes performed in appropriate costume; *farshtelt* (disguised) was the contemporary term.

During this period there is increasing evidence as well of Jews attending non-Jewish theatre. This was particularly apparent in Warsaw, where a Jewish plutocracy unprecedented in eastern Europe had developed. Financiers and industrialists who sought entry into Polish high society through education and occasionally intermarriage, they identified themselves with Polish cultural values and

---

[5] On the connection between Haskalah and popular culture in the 19th century, see M. Viner, *Tsu der geshikhte fun der yidisher literatur in 19tn yorhundert*, vol. i (New York, 1945), 319–21; D. Roskies, *The Jewish Search for a Useable Past* (Bloomington, Ind., 1999), 94–103.

[6] On the earliest Jewish theatre performances in Poland, see J. Shatzky, 'Di ershte geshikhte fun yidishn teater: tsu dr. y. shipers verk', *Filologishe shriftn* (Vilna), 2 (1928), 215–64; Redakcja [Z. Raszewski], 'Sześć głos do artykułu Jakuba Szackiego', *Pamiętnik Teatralny* (Warsaw), 41 (1992), 193–209.

became patrons of Polish literature, art, music, and theatre. Their presence in the front rows of the State Theatre (Teatr Wielki and Teatr Rozmaitości) was a function, above all, of the upper-class aura surrounding European theatre during this period; in western Europe, especially in Germany, the new Jewish bourgeoisie also crowded the theatres. But their presence in Warsaw theatres attested as well to the enormous national significance of Polish theatre. In Russian-occupied Poland after the 1863 uprising, theatre was the last remaining place where the Polish language was permitted public expression, and it therefore emerged as a bastion of national exaltation.

As the population of Polish cities, fed by arrivals from small towns and peasant villages, began to swell during the last decades of the nineteenth century, a new urban audience, like its counterparts in Paris, London, and New York, began to hunger for entertainment. The Jewish elite was joined in Polish theatres by a lower-class audience that also included Jews. Yiddish-speaking and traditionally dressed, they began to appear in the balcony seats (the so-called *paradyż*) of the Teatr Wielki. At the same time, in the summer 'carnival' of the new Warsaw 'garden theaters' (*teatrzyki ogródkowe*), in the words of Henryk Sienkiewicz, '[Amid] a mixture of voices, languages, social classes, manners, moods, a veritable Tower of Babel of people linked only by the hope of relaxation, freedom, and entertainment', one also heard 'the dialect of Franciszkaner Gasse [the Jewish quarter]'.[7] Language seemed little of an obstacle for these Jewish audiences, and in any case a large component of the popular plays consisted of singing and dancing.[8]

AVROM GOLDFADN

This was the context in which Avrom Goldfadn (Abraham Goldfaden, 1840–1908) launched a professional theatre from which all subsequent Yiddish theatre is descended. Born in Volhynia, Goldfadn's roots were in both traditional Jewish performance and the Haskalah. In his youth he performed his own songs in the *badkhn* tradition, but he was also educated at the crown rabbinical seminary in Zhitomir, an institution dedicated to training 'enlightened' rabbis. Indeed, at the seminary Goldfadn played the (female) title role in a student production of the maskilic play *Serkele*, written three decades earlier by Shloyme Ettinger (1801–56) but never staged. Goldfadn subsequently published several volumes of Hebrew and Yiddish verse, and edited short-lived Yiddish periodicals. In 1876 one such initiative brought him to Jassy (Iasi) in Romania. There he encountered the Broder singer Yisroel Grodner (1841–87), who had been performing Goldfadn's songs, and began to collaborate with him. Within a year Goldfadn was writing entire musical plays and

---

[7] H. Sienkiewicz, *Gazeta Polska* (1875), no. 115, cited in Sienkiewicz, *Chwila obecna*, vol. i (Warsaw, 1950), 171–2.

[8] See M. C. Steinlauf, 'Jews and Polish Theater in Nineteenth Century Warsaw, *Polish Review*, 32 (1987), 439–58.

staging them using actors he had assembled and trained himself. These early productions would often end with Goldfadn in a frock coat declaiming his poetry from the stage, accompanied by the singing of his cast. His enthusiastic lower-class audiences were augmented by fortune-seeking Russian Jewish military contractors and their entourages, who flocked to Romania with the start of the Russo-Turkish War in 1877. Goldfadn and his company performed in the larger Romanian cities and after the war moved to Odessa. There, in the legendarily godless centre of new urban life, his plays inspired a large and enthusiastic following. Using Odessa as a base, for several years he and his company toured Russian cities including St Petersburg.

Goldfadn's earliest plays were farces directed against the so-called forces of backwardness. Kuni Leml, in Goldfadn's *Di tsvey kuni lemls* ('The Two Kuni Lemls') is a viciously caricatured yeshiva student; he limps, he is blind in one eye, he stutters; he exclaims 'Shema yisroel' ('Hear, O Israel', the martyr's credo) when a girl tries to kiss him. By the play's end the attempt to arrange his marriage to the progressive young heroine is foiled, and the hasidim are expelled from her father's house by her enlightened true love and his university comrades. 'Lineage [*yikhes*] means nothing more than the educated man', resounds the final moral. Similarly, in *Di kishef-makherin* ('The Sorceress') the villainous Bobe Yakhne's black magic amounts to nothing more than exploiting the gullible. Increasingly Goldfadn turned to historical melodramas; the best-known are *Shulamis*, a love story set in the land of Israel and based on a talmudic legend, and *Bar kokhba*, whose hero is the leader of the last Jewish uprising against the Romans. Large-scale spectacle and the miraculous, *purim-shpil* writ large, frames all the action in these plays: angels wield fiery swords, spirits materialize amid 'Bengal lights', pilgrims crowd the temple steps in Jerusalem, and a wedding is celebrated in front of the altar; there are lions, battles, and massacres. Goldfadn devoted great attention to set design and stage effects; he was a master of contemporary stage technology.

No less important, perhaps more so, were the melodies that Goldfadn, who could not read musical notation, adapted for his plays. 'I was even ready to believe', the Warsaw writer Yankev Dinezon wrote, 'that it was not that [Goldfadn's] songs came into the world for the sake of the theatre, but that the entire Yiddish theatre was created for the sake of the songs.'[9] This music, like his plots and dialogue, was woven from a great variety of sources: from cantorial chants to Romanian military marches to Gypsy dances, mazurkas and Ukrainian folk songs to Handel, Verdi, and Halévy.[10] But the result of this dizzyingly eclectic craft was something whole: the creation, for several generations of popular audiences, of a solid theatrical tradi-

---

[9] Y. Dinezon, *Zikhroynes un bilder: shtetl, kinder-yorn, shrayber* (Warsaw, [1928]), 212. Dinezon (1856–1919) was a close associate of Y. L. Peretz.

[10] Y. Rumshinski, 'Der liber plagyator: vegn der opshtamung fun avrom goldfadns muzik', *Literarishe bleter* (Warsaw), no. 464 (24 Mar. 1933), repr. in A. Goldfadn, *Oysgeklibene shriftn* (Buenos Aires, 1963); A. Z. Idelsohn, *Jewish Music: Its Historical Development* (New York, 1992), 451–3.

tion. Fifty years after their debut Goldfadn's plays were still being acted and staged precisely in their original versions; a director would encounter opposition when he attempted to move a table from its 'traditional' location, which had attained the status of what one Yiddish critic termed 'Torah from Sinai'.[11] Goldfadn's characters, less individuals than types, along with his beloved melodies, moved beyond the stage, moreover, and rooted themselves in Jewish popular consciousness. 'Rozhinkes mit mandlen' ('Raisins and Almonds'), for example, a song from *Shulamis*, arguably became the single best-known Yiddish 'folk song'. Today, even where the melody fades (not to mention the memory of Goldfadn and his theatre), the song's title still functions as a sentimental trope for the whole of east European Jewish culture.

The newly created Yiddish theatre audience's appetite quickly spawned numerous competing companies. The most successful of these were those of 'Professor' Moyshe Hurwitz (1844–1910), Joseph Lateiner (1853–1935), and Shomer (Nokhem-Meyer Shaykevitsh) (1846–1905), who were capable of splicing together plots and melodies more efficiently than their nominal master Goldfadn. Meanwhile, presumably troubled by the mass nature of the new phenomenon, in 1883 tsarist authorities banned Yiddish theatre. During the following years, as Yiddish actors along with their audiences began to emigrate from eastern Europe, London, Paris, and above all New York became centres of the new theatre. On New York's Second Avenue it was the mass produced plays of Hurwitz and Lateiner that drew audiences, and Goldfadn found himself increasingly irrelevant. He spent the remaining years of his life moving between Europe and America, and died in dire poverty in New York in 1908.

POLISH–LANGUAGE JEWISH THEATRE

But Yiddish theatre, its growth impeded in eastern Europe, nevertheless managed to survive. In Romania and Galicia travelling companies continued to perform the Goldfadn repertoire. In the Russian empire such companies often bribed local officials and performed in 'German', that is, in a language that could pass for German in order to satisfy the authorities yet still be understood by Jewish audiences. In Russian Poland Goldfadn himself managed, despite the theatre ban, to plant the seeds of his theatre. In 1886 he arrived in Warsaw from Odessa and obtained permission to stage his plays, supposedly in German, in partnership with a Russian company. *Shulamis*, the most successful, played in a Warsaw garden theatre over 150 times before audiences that included non-Jews and numbered, particularly on Saturdays, several thousand. Goldfadn had already left Warsaw for New York when, in September 1887, *Shulamis* became the first Yiddish play to be

[11] Y. Mestel, 'Goldfadn als traditsye af der bine', in J. Shatzky (ed.), *Goldfadn-bukh* (New York, 1926), 12.

performed on the Polish stage. As *Sulamita*, the play attracted huge crowds of Jews and Poles, setting a garden theatre attendance record of 3,000 for a single performance. The play went on to a notable career on the Polish stage, as attested by a couplet popular among Polish actors: 'Jakby nie Sulamita | To by dawno z nami było kwita' ('If not for Sulamita, | we'd have been finished long ago').[12]

Following the success of *Sulamita*, *Di kishef-makherin* (as *Czarownica*) and *Bar kokhba* were also staged in Polish. Over subsequent years the hunger for theatre, unsatisfied by sporadic performances in Yiddish, led masses of Jews to the Polish stage. Responding to the needs of this audience, to the interest in Jews by Polish writers such as Klemens Junosza and Eliza Orzeszkowa, and to the prevailing fashion for *ludoznawstwo* (the study of folklore and ethnography), Polish popular theatres began to stage plays reflective of Jewish life. What one critic soon described as 'a small "current" in our literature' (*mały 'prąd' w literaturze naszej*)[13] was triggered by the huge success in 1897 of *Małka Szwarcenkopf*, a play by Gabriela Zapolska (1857–1921). The play, whose doomed heroine struggles against her 'ghetto' environment in the name of her freedom as a woman, became the most popular play in the history of the garden theatres and continued to be staged throughout Poland for decades to come. It inspired numerous others, including Zapolska's own sequel as well as several plays by the young Jewish writer Wilhelm Feldman (1868–1919), who would shortly abandon Jewish matters to become the pre-eminent critic of Polish neo-Romanticism. Yet even most of these plays, not to mention those by other, less fastidious playwrights (ferocious antisemites among them), were accused by Jews of exploiting long-established Polish stage stereotypes, above all that of the comical *żydek* (little Jew) speaking a mangled Polish known as *żydłaczenie*.

The 'small current' of Polish-language 'Jewish plays' climaxed in the work of Mark Arnshteyn (Arnsztejn *c.*1879–1943).[14] Raised in a middle-class Warsaw Jewish family, Arnshteyn was educated in both Jewish and Polish schools, and early in his life began writing about literature and the arts in both Polish (using the pseudonym Andrzej Marek) and Yiddish. He became a protégé of both Stanisław Przybyszewski and Y. L. Peretz, each a cult figure in their respective literary worlds. Early in his career Arnshteyn turned to theatre, producing 'Jewish plays' while denouncing the existing 'Jewish' fare in Polish theatres as dedicated to ridiculing Jews. Arnshteyn's efforts to create a new kind of Jewish theatre bore fruit in his popular play *Pieśniarze* ('Singers', later staged in Yiddish as *Der vilner balebesl*, 'The Little Vilna Householder') which premiered in Łódź in 1902 under his direction.

[12] Z. Zilbertsvayg, 'Goldfadn af der poylisher bine', in Zilbertsvayg, *Teatr mozayik* (New York, 1941), 231.

[13] G. Kempner, 'Ze scen letnich', *Przegląd Tygodniowy*, no. 29 (21 July 1900).

[14] See M. C. Steinlauf, 'Mark arnshteyn vehate'atron "hapolani–yehudi" bepolin shebein shtei milḥamot olam', in C. Shmeruk and S. Werses (eds.), *Bein shetei milkhamot olam: perakim miḥayei hatarbut shel yehudei polin velashonoteihem* (Jerusalem, 1997).

Here, as elsewhere, critics noted Arnshteyn's strength in the non-verbal aspects of stagecraft, in his ability to stage ritual and spectacle. The hero of his play (based on a semi-legendary nineteenth-century figure) is a Vilna *khazn* whose extraordinary voice leads him to a career on the Warsaw opera stage, the love of a Polish noble-woman, and finally the loss of his voice. This *khazn* is the earliest version of a rather significant symbolic figure: the Jewish artist torn between two worlds, whose final incarnation, several decades later in the United States, would be Al Jolson's Jazz Singer.

In Warsaw in April 1905 Arnshteyn staged his translation of Sholem Aleichem's (1859–1916) play *Tsezeyt un tseshpreyt* ('Scattered and Dispersed') as *Rodzina żydowska* ('A Jewish Family'). This was apparently the first venture in a plan to stage Jewish plays in Polish for primarily Jewish audiences. Arnshteyn's purpose was not to compete with and ultimately eradicate Yiddish theatre (which had been Wilhelm Feldman's goal), nor even to attract Polish audiences to the 'exotica' of 'Jewish' plays, but to enable Jewish audiences to experience new Yiddish plays that could not yet be staged in their original language. Polish here would function as an instrument adapted to the needs of Jewish culture. But the lapsing of the ban on Yiddish theatre over the following months eliminated for years to come the need for a Polish-language Jewish theatre.[15]

THE STRUGGLE FOR A CANON

Amid the first Russian revolution Yiddish companies flocked to Warsaw and began to perform at five different locations, including one theatre (Muranover (Ermitazh)) built especially for that purpose. This upsurge was part of a larger development: a modern mass Jewish culture with its capital in Warsaw sprang into being virtually overnight. Crucial to this change was the legalization in 1905 of the Yiddish press; by the following year there were five Yiddish dailies in Warsaw with a circulation of 100,000. Suddenly one could find not only international news in Yiddish, but the serialized works of favourite writers, Yiddish theatre schedules, and reviews. News-paper readers, traditional and secular, rich and poor, began to constitute a new kind of community. Encouraged by the new Yiddish journalists, they found it increas-ingly natural to think of themselves using the discourse of modern nationality: they were *dos yidishe folk* (the Jewish people or nation). The Jewish intelligentsia, many of whom had sought hitherto to have Jews assimilate into Polish culture, now increasingly 'returned to the people'. Spearheading this movement was the Yiddish writer, activist, and culture hero Y. L. Peretz (1852–1915), a close observer of Polish culture who was well acquainted, for example, with the work of the celebrated neo-Romantic playwright Stanisław Wyspiański.

---

[15] C. Shmeruk, '*Tsezeyt un tseshpreyt* lesholem aleichem vehahatsagot shel hamehazeh besafah hapolanit bevarsha beshanim 1905 ve-1910', in E. Mendelsohn and C. Shmeruk (eds.), *Kovets mehkarim al yehudei polin: sefer lezikhro shel paul glikson* (Jerusalem, 1987).

The new Jewish culture, proclaimed Peretz, must represent the Jewish people's highest aesthetic and moral aspirations. But in 1905, when he and his disciples visited the Yiddish theatre, they were aghast. The performers were poorly educated, even illiterate; performing styles, stage sets, and audience behaviour seemed grossly inappropriate; scripts and musical scores were plagiarized and spliced together from a variety of sources; the plays themselves, primarily from the American Yiddish stage, were mixtures of comedy, farce, and melodrama, vulgarly and irretrievably scrambled. Many of the theatres, it appears, had connections to the Jewish underworld; pimps and their women were a common sight in the front rows. Peretz declared war on this theatre; 'Ayngezunken zol es vern!' ('May the earth swallow it up!'), he proclaimed.[16] Peretz and his followers called such theatre *shund* (trash), and preached the creation of a 'new theatre' which would be 'literary', 'artistic', and 'refined'. Two of Peretz's followers, Noyekh Prilutski (Prylucki, 1882–1941) and A. Mukdoyni (Aleksander Kappel, 1878–1958), became the first professional Jewish theatre critics in Poland.[17]

At this very moment a talent of huge proportions emerged from the ranks of the old Yiddish theatre and briefly seemed capable of creating the kind of theatre of which Peretz dreamed. Ester-Rokhl (Halperin) Kaminska (1870–1926) was born to an impoverished family in a *shtetl* near Grodno; her father was a retired religious functionary. She received little formal education; as a young woman she moved to Warsaw, where she worked as a seamstress and was increasingly drawn to the theatre. In 1893 she married Avrom-Yitskhok Kaminski (1867–1918), a gaiter-maker and aspiring actor. Together they organized a series of companies with which, for over a decade, they staged the operettas and melodramas of Goldfadn and others under extremely constrained conditions throughout the cities and small towns of the Russian empire. In 1905 the Kaminskis returned to Warsaw, and amid the new freedom discovered a new kind of repertoire.

These were the plays of the dramatist Jacob Gordin (1853–1909), which had become the sensation of the New York Yiddish stage. Gordin, a Russian writer and Tolstoyan agrarian radical, emigrated to the United States in 1891, where, despite a poor knowledge of Yiddish, he began to write for the Yiddish theatre. Gordin's plays were the first attempt on the Yiddish stage to mirror contemporary social reality. In the eyes of Gordin and his audiences this reality was brutal and 'heartless', for it concerned above all the fate of the Jewish family under the pressures of nascent capitalism. *Got, mentsh un tayvl* ('God, Man, and Devil'), for example, chronicles the transformation of a poor and pious scribe who takes on the devil as a business partner. The scribe's good intentions lead only to evil: money corrupts him and his family; the *tales* factory he founds to bring prosperity to his town maims its workers; he ends as a suicide. Gordin's productions, which at his insistence were rehearsed

---

[16] Y. L. Peretz, 'Kleyne felyeton: dos fraye vort', *Fraytog*, no. 1 (1 Feb. 1907).

[17] See M. C. Steinlauf, 'Fear of Purim: Y. L. Peretz and the Canonization of Yiddish Theater', *Jewish Social Studies*, 1/3 (1995), 44–65.

rather than improvised according to contemporary practice, inspired critical as well as popular success. He was hailed in the American Yiddish press as a Jewish Ibsen, a purveyor of truth, social and psychological, on the Yiddish stage.

Gordin's melodramas were filled with powerful roles, especially for women. In Warsaw in 1905 Ester-Rokhl Kaminska discovered the first of many when she played the title role in *Khashe di yesoyme* ('Khashe the Orphan Girl'), about a great-hearted Jewish country girl brought to work in a modern middle-class family and finally destroyed by its hypocrisy. Several years later she played the title role in Gordin's *Mirele efros*, arguably the most popular play in the history of Yiddish theatre. Mirele, whom Gordin originally conceived as the 'Jewish Queen Lear', is a traditional Jewish woman of nobility and strength. The widow of a bankrupt merchant, she has managed to pay back his debts and expand the family business. But when her mercenary modern daughter-in-law insists that she relinquish the business to her, Mirele refuses to quibble, proudly consents, and suffering ensues. When Ester-Rokhl Kaminska, mother of three children, prematurely aged by a wanderer's life, a square and somewhat masculine stage presence, took on such a role, 'generations of *zogerins* [sayers], generations of mothers spoke out of her'.[18] In pre-modern times the *zogerin* led prayers in the women's section of the synagogue and preached to women out of an oral tradition. Performances such as these led to Kaminska's adoration by huge audiences, for whom she became the 'mother of the Yiddish theatre'.

With the upsurge of Yiddish theatre Mark Arnshteyn began producing 'better' Yiddish theatre in Warsaw. In 1907 he collaborated with Avrom-Yitskhok Kaminski to found the Literarishe Trupe (Literary Troupe), which included Ester-Rokhl Kaminska. With a repertoire of plays by Gordin as well as Dovid Pinski (1872–1959), Sholem Aleichem, and Arnshteyn, and even a translation of Ibsen's *A Doll's House*, the company toured the Russian empire. In 1908 and 1909 it performed in St Petersburg and was lionized in the Russian liberal press. Subsequently, Kaminska alone was engaged several times by the New York Yiddish stage. Even as her renown grew (and perhaps because of it) the Literarishe Trupe began to fall apart. Another such company organized by the writer Peretz Hirshbeyn (1880–1948) subsequently toured the Russian empire for several years without success. During the years prior to the First World War, Jewish mass audiences flocked to the older Yiddish repertoire, especially of the American variety. Stars of the American Yiddish stage, such as Boris Thomashefsky (1866–1939) and David Kessler (1860–1920), began to tour in Poland, a practice that continued in the inter-war period as well. But even Avrom-Yitskhok Kaminski, in the new theatre he built on Obożna Street in Warsaw in 1909 using his wife's American earnings, found that he could not afford to stage 'literary' theatre. In the meantime Y. L. Peretz, scorning the 'tainted' professional Yiddish stage, began to work with amateurs, better-educated young people intoxicated with the new Yiddish literature,

[18] A. Mukdoyni, 'Zikhroynes fun a yidishn teater-kritiker: yidisher teater in poyln fun 1909 biz 1915', *Arkhiv far der geshikhte fun yidishn teater un drame*, 1 (1930), 359.

to prepare the way for a different theatre. Throughout eastern Europe amateur Yiddish drama societies arose and thrived.

DYBBUKIADA

In 1916, a year after Peretz's death, one such group of young people in German-occupied Vilna received permission from the relatively tolerant authorities to perform professionally. In contrast to the norms of contemporary Yiddish theatre, where everything turned around the 'star' of the company, they organized themselves co-operatively. On the stage they favoured the ensemble approach that had been introduced into Russian theatre by Konstantin Stanislavsky in his pioneering productions of Chekhov at the turn of the century. The new company's productions of plays by Sholem Asch (1880–1957), Sholem Aleichem, Hirshbeyn, Pinski, Peretz, Arnshteyn, Gordin, and others were acclaimed by the intelligentsia. In 1917 most of the company, now known as the Vilner Trupe (Vilna Troupe), relocated to the Elizeum Theatre in Warsaw. There, on 9 December 1920, they opened a play that was to change the course of Yiddish theatre history: S. An-ski's *Tsvishn tsvey veltn: der dibek* ('Between Two Worlds: The Dybbuk').

An-ski (Shloyme Zanvl Rapoport, 1863–1920), a Russian Socialist Revolutionary whose reading of Peretz's tales had returned him to the Jewish *folk*, had written the play inspired by stories he had collected on an ethnographic expedition through the eastern Polish borderlands on the eve of the First World War. In the years before his death An-ski had tried unsuccessfully to have the play staged; at his open grave in the Warsaw Jewish cemetery Mordkhe Mazo (1880–1943), the manager of the Vilner Trupe, vowed to open *The Dybbuk* at the end of the traditional thirty-day period of mourning. Its premiere intended as a simple act of homage, *The Dybbuk* unexpectedly blazed an astounding career from the Warsaw stage to all the towns and cities of inter-war Poland, then into the repertoires of Yiddish companies throughout the world, and then beyond the Yiddish stage, translated into a dozen languages, the accredited emissary of Jewish theatre art to the world at large. Crucial to this development was the Hebrew production by the Habima company, which opened in Moscow in 1922, and later accompanied Habima on numerous world tours, including several visits to Poland.

In Warsaw *The Dybbuk* inspired an unprecedented kind of frenzy. The Yiddish press couldn't get its fill of what it referred to as the *Dybbuk* phenomenon, the Dybbukiada, the *Dybbuk* cult and psychosis. For over a year, rich and poor, secular and Orthodox, assimilationists and nationally minded Jews, as well as good numbers of Poles, streamed into the Elizeum Theatre, often on repeat visits, to 'sit quietly together and watch the stage with bated breath'.[19]

[19] Ben Levi [Avrom Levinson], 'Shmuesn: *dibek*, haftke un politik-makheray', *Haynt*, no. 16 (19 Jan. 1921).

The play was directed by Dovid Herman (1876–1937), a lapsed Polish hasid who had begun his career in pre-war Warsaw as Peretz's most devoted theatre disciple. As the lovers Herman cast Miriam Orleska (*c.*1900–42) and Alyosha (Eliohu) Shtayn (1890s–1940s), whose backgrounds were with Polish and Russian theatre, respectively, and who had had to learn Yiddish to perform with the company. Herman filled the stage with slow, solemn, ritualized speech and gesture, and with *nigunim* taken from hasidic traditions.

The play is a tale of two young people promised to each other before their birth by their fathers. Years later, innocent of their fated link, Leah and Khonen meet and fall in love, but Leah's father breaks his oath and betroths his daughter to another. As a result, Khonen dies, but his *dybbuk* (spirit) returns to possess the body of his beloved. After an awesome exorcism ritual the *dybbuk* is driven out of Leah's body, whereupon she too dies to rejoin her beloved. In the Warsaw production the voices of the living and the dead mingled in the *Song of Songs*[20] as the curtain slowly fell over Leah's body.

At the beginning of a new era in their history, marked on one hand by war, revolution, and devastating pogroms, and on the other by the promise of a modern, urbanized life in a parliamentary nation-state, Polish Jews responded most powerfully, it seems, not to attacks on superstition in the name of enlightenment nor to portrayals of social conflict, but to what contemporaries called a mystery play (Yiddish: *misterye*; Polish: *misterium*), a pageant rooted in folklore and the supernatural. For these Jewish audiences *The Dybbuk* was a mythic evocation of the most elemental Jewish sense of place—the cemeteries, synagogues, courtyards, marketplaces, and landscapes of eastern Europe where Jews had lived for centuries. It was an affirmation of cultural and national identity all the more powerful for being implicit.[21]

THE INTER-WAR PERIOD

With *The Dybbuk* the Vilner Trupe fulfilled Peretz's dream and demonstrated that Yiddish theatre was capable of producing world-class art. This example laid the foundation for the development during the inter-war period of a Yiddish dramatic theatre of very high calibre. With companies such as the VIKT (Varshever Yidisher Kunst-Teater, Warsaw Yiddish Art Theatre), founded by Zygmunt Turkow (Zigmunt Turkov, 1896–1970) and Ester-Rokhl's daughter Ida Kaminska (1899–1980) in 1924; the VNIT (Varshever Nayer Yidisher Teater, Warsaw New Yiddish Theatre), organized by Zygmunt's brother Jonas Turkow (Yonas Turkov, 1898–1988) in 1929; Yung-Teater (Young Theatre), founded by Michał Weichert

---

[20] 'For love is strong as death' (8: 6).
[21] See M. C. Steinlauf, 'Dybbuks on and off the Polish Jewish Stage', in S. Kapralski (ed.), *The Jews in Poland*, vol. ii (Kraków, 1999).

(Mikhal Vaykhert, 1890–1967) in 1932;[22] and the Vilner Trupe itself, particularly under the direction of Jakub Rotbaum (Yankev Rotboym, 1901–94) in the 1930s, it became possible for the Yiddish-speaking theatregoer to see dramatic productions of Yiddish classics, but also plays by Shakespeare, Hugo, O'Neill, and Dreiser, artistically on a par with any in Europe. 'Yiddish theatre must free itself from the black coat and leave the Jewish street where it's been stuck since Goldfadn's time, and rise to the broad highway of a "world" repertoire',[23] declared Zygmunt Turkow, who directed and starred, for example, in an acclaimed production of Molière's *The Misanthrope*. Turkow and other directors of the new companies, as well as many of the actors, had studied in Polish, Russian, or west European drama schools; they were thoroughly at home in modern European culture and were assiduous students of contemporary Polish theatre.

Nevertheless, despite its increasing maturity, there remained significant differences between Yiddish dramatic theatre and its Polish and west European counterparts. First of all, Yiddish theatre shared in the permanent economic crisis common to all Yiddish cultural institutions. Contemporary assessments of the state of Yiddish theatre continually despair at the lack of funding from either official Polish or Jewish communal sources. Even Jewish entrepreneurs, it seems, much preferred to invest in Polish theatres. In Warsaw, despite interminable efforts, Yiddish dramatic companies never managed to acquire their own theatre, and were forced to move from one locale to another at the whim of theatre owners, who found *shund* or Polish operettas more profitable. As a result, Yiddish dramatic theatre operated on a shoestring, its disorganized, discontinuous existence punctuated by intense soul-searching, recriminations, and the cry '*Toyevoye!*' ('Chaos!') Under such circumstances, the very notion of Yiddish art theatre remained problematic. In the words of Avrom Morevski (1886–1964), the celebrated actor who played the exorcist in the Vilner Trupe's *The Dybbuk*, 'Yiddish theatre often . . . flies into heaven, grasps at universality and—slips unavoidably back down—back to its own four cubits . . . "To eat in order to create" is to rise. Yiddish theatre on the whole *plays in order to eat* . . . And every attempt at a higher conception is—an *experiment*.'[24] Yet precisely because it had so little to lose, this theatre could occasionally devote itself to experiments which put it in the vanguard of contemporary theatre art; to cite only one example: Yung-Teater's 1933 production of Bernard Blume's *Boston*, a play about Sacco and Vanzetti, the anarchists whose murder trial in America had become an international cause célèbre. Forced to work in a very small space that prohibited even a stage, Michał Weichert produced something unprecedented: a

---

[22] After the Second World War Weichert became the subject of controversy when he was unjustly accused of using his wartime activity on behalf of a Jewish social service organization to collaborate with the Nazis; he emigrated to Israel in 1957. See D. Engel, 'Who is a Collaborator? The Trials of Michał Weichert', in Kapralski (ed.), *The Jews in Poland*, ii.

[23] Z. Turkow, *Di ibergerisene tkufe: fragmentn fun mayn lebn* (Buenos Aires, 1961), 17.

[24] A. Morevski, 'Nokhn crizis', *Literarishe bleter*, no. 1 (2 Jan. 1931).

sequence of forty-eight brief scenes illuminated by spotlights, separated by black-outs, staged on every side of the seated audience. Indeed, Yung-Teater itself was the kind of experiment to which Morevski alluded. Founded by Weichert first as a theatre studio for idealistic young performers, Yung-Teater specialized in avant-garde, politically radical productions that were hailed in the Polish theatre world and increasingly closed down by the police.

Secondly, in contrast to other European theatres, the core of whose audience was the middle and upper classes, the mainstay of Yiddish theatre, true to its origins, continued to be the Jewish working class. This audience, along with con-spicuous representatives of the Jewish underworld and the 'slumming' Jewish intelligentsia, swarmed to the *shund* theatres. In 1931, for example, at a time when Warsaw's only Yiddish dramatic company had disbanded, five theatres were staging *shund*.[25] Yiddish cultural activists, among them the so-called *folks-inteligentn*—self-educated intellectuals with roots in the lower classes—responded by attempting to educate their audiences. Particularly among the new generation of working-class and lower-middle-class youth, driven by an intense hunger for modern culture in any form, this process met with considerable success, and resulted in the creation of a permanent audience sensitive to the artistic intentions of the 'better' Yiddish theatre. American Yiddish actors, accustomed to seeing children accompanying their elders to the theatre and announcing at the box office in English, 'I'm sending my parents to your theatre', marvelled at the youth, enthusi-asm, and knowledgeability of the Yiddish theatre audience in Poland.[26] By the mid-1930s, supported by this audience, Yiddish dramatic theatre, particularly in comparison to the perceived crisis in Yiddish book publishing, libraries, and press, amid an economic depression and the competition of sound films, had scored notable successes. 'Finally, finally,' declared Nakhmen Mayzil in 1934, 'Yiddish theatre has now in all respects surpassed all other areas of Yiddish art and culture, both in the breadth of its creativity, and in the huge circle of its influence. Its scenic oral art [*kunst-shebalpe*] now surpasses Yiddish written art [*kunst-shebiksav*].'[27] Support for Yiddish dramatic theatre was, moreover, considerably stronger outside Warsaw, in the traditionally Yiddish-speaking towns and cities of central and east-ern Poland, as well as among the nationally minded Jewish intelligentsia in Kraków and Lwów. A frequent refrain in the memoirs of Yiddish actors is that of being 'saved by the provinces' whenever a troupe had to abandon Warsaw. Hundreds of amateur troupes throughout Poland also devoted themselves to 'better' Yiddish theatre.

[25] J. Turkow, 'Ver iz shuldik?', *Literarishe bleter*, nos. 14–15 (1 Apr. 1931); M. Melman, 'Teatr żydowski w Warszawie', *Warszawa II Rzeczypospolitej* (Warsaw, 1968), 394.

[26] N.M. [Nakhmen Mayzil], 'Yidish teater in amerike un in poyln (a shmues mit misha un lucy german)', *Literarishe bleter*, no. 35 (1 Sept. 1933). Mayzil (1887–1966) was an influential critic and the editor of *Literarishe bleter*.

[27] 'Nakhes funem yidishn teater', *Literarishe bleter*, no. 8 (23 Feb. 1934).

The constraints on the development of Yiddish dramatic theatre could not but affect its self-conception, and brought its creators to fulfil Peretz's dream in another way as well. Rather than involving themselves in purely 'theatrical' problems, they conceived of theatre as a force in the struggle for survival of Yiddish culture and of Polish Jewish society itself. For the new Yiddish directors, who could have made a career for themselves on the prestigious Polish stage, commitment to the 'poor' Yiddish theatre was the product of a conscious choice made for 'moral' and 'national' reasons. Yet however far from west European notions of art, such a conception reflected well its Polish milieu, in which theatre had long played a key role in national survival and renewal. In the enterprise of transforming Yiddish theatre, in the words of Michał Weichert, into 'a powerful weapon in the struggle for national, social and human liberation',[28] the tradition of Polish theatre, from Mickiewicz to Wyspiański to the innovative directors of the inter-war period, provided an influential model. Yet even as they profited from the Polish model, Yiddish theatre activists, in common with Yiddish writers, artists, and intellectuals, also worried about the lure of the sophisticated culture that surrounded them.

There was much to worry about. With over half of all Jewish children attending Polish public schools during the inter-war period, younger Jews, especially of the middle class but hardly exclusively so, tended to be fully bilingual, and some even began to prefer Polish over Yiddish. Jews streamed into Polish theatres; according to numerous contemporary assessments, they often made up the majority of the audience. The lively Polish popular theatre of the inter-war period as well as the powerful dramatic theatre created by figures such as Juliusz Osterwa, Leon Schiller, Stefan Jaracz, Aleksander Węgierko, Arnold Szyfman, and Aleksander Zelwerowicz owed much of its success, it seems, to the enthusiasm of its Jewish audiences. Increasing numbers of Polish actors were of Jewish descent as well. Linguistic assimilation, however, did little to counteract the growing disaffection of Poles and Jews caused primarily by the spread of virulent antisemitism. As a result, unlike in the pre-war period, 'Jewish plays' on the Polish stage proved controversial and were rarely staged. On the other hand, at a time when Polish attitudes to the Jewish culture flourishing in their midst generally ranged from indifference to hostility, the creators of Polish dramatic theatre, for the most part 'progressive' artists with left-wing sympathies, proved notable exceptions. Throughout the inter-war period they observed, supported, and occasionally collaborated in the work of their Yiddish counterparts. Thus, for example, on the eve of the Second World War, in a gesture of Polish–Jewish solidarity, Leon Schiller (1887–1954), along with the stage designer Władysław Daszewski (1902–71) and the choreographer Tacjanna Wysocka (1894–1970), worked with a Yiddish cast that included Avrom Morevski and Zipporah Faynzilber-Glikson (b. 1913) to stage the Yiddish version of Shakespeare's *Tempest* by the poet Arn Tseytlin (Aaron Zeitlin, 1889–1973).

[28] M. Weichert, *Zikhroynes: Varshe (1918–1939)* (Tel Aviv, 1961), 20.

Moreover, despite the affirmation, indeed the fortification, of borders, particularly in the realms of high culture, cultural borderlands continued to expand. One such borderland was cabaret. Warsaw cabaret specialized in two not entirely distinct sorts of entertainment: literary cabaret (*kabaret literacki*), emphasizing sketches, songs, monologues, parodies, often political in nature, and variety shows (*rewie*), including relatively more singing and dancing by scantily clad women. In comparison to the nineteenth-century 'gardens' with their popular audiences, cabaret between the wars was expensive and attracted a wealthier and more sophisticated audience; moreover, among its creators were numerous well-known poets, directors, and stage designers. For example, the poets Julian Tuwim (1894–1953) and Antoni Słonimski (1895–1976), both of Jewish descent, regularly wrote for cabaret. At establishments such as Qui Pro Quo and Morskie Oko a new genre of entertainment, the Jewish joke, monologue, or sketch known as *szmonces* became 'the universal method of reporting on everyday life' and 'the favourite means of communicating with the public'.[29] The *szmonces*, inevitably characterized by a more or less subtle *żydłaczenie*, at its best turned the pretentious Jewish assimilator or the harried Jewish tradesman into a universally accessible symbol of the dislocations of modern life; at its worst, it became vulgar antisemitic caricature. At the same time a sophisticated Yiddish *kleynkunst* theatre, modelled primarily on Polish cabaret, also attracted a considerable audience. The first was Azazel, founded in Warsaw in 1926, followed by Ararat, established by the writer Moyshe Broderzon (1890–1956) in Łódź in 1927. It was Broderzon who discovered Shimen Dzhigan (Dzigan, 1905–80) and Yisroel Shumakher (Israel Schumacher, 1908–61), who went on from Ararat to become the most celebrated Jewish comedy team in Poland.[30]

Another expanding borderland was the realm of Polish-language Jewish culture. Most highly developed was the Polish-language Jewish press, especially daily newspapers, but there were also numerous Polish-language Jewish schools and a growing literature in Polish written by and intended for Jews. Unlike at the turn of the century, when assimilationists dreamed of Polish literacy turning Jews into 'Poles of the Mosaic faith', Polish-language Jewish culture in the inter-war years largely reinforced Jewish national identity. This was the context in which Mark Arnshteyn brought to the stage, between 1925 and 1929, Polish versions of some of the most popular works of Yiddish theatre: An-ski's *The Dybbuk*, Sholem Asch's *Got fun nekome* ('God of Vengeance'), *The Golem* by H. Leivick (1888–1962), and Gordin's *Mirele efros*.[31] Most highly praised were his *Dybbuk* and *Golem* productions. The latter, the first Polish theatre production to make use of a circular stage, was a spectacle mounted in the Warsaw circus arena amid a constructivist set built

---

[29] R. M. Groński, *Jak w przedwojennym kabarecie: Kabaret warszawski, 1918–1939* (Warsaw, 1978), 43.

[30] See G. Rozier, *Moyshe Broderzon: Un écrivain yiddish d'avant-garde* (Saint-Denis, 1999), 159–94.

[31] Steinlauf, 'Mark arnshteyn vehate'atron "hapolani–yehudi"'. Arnshteyn also revived at this time Zapolska's *Małka Szwarcenkopf*.

by the Polish stage designers Andrzej Pronaszko (1888–1961) and Szymon Syrkus (1893–1964). The production also made use of the 150-member choir of Warsaw's Great Synagogue.

The Polish response to these endeavours ranged from charges of provocation and blasphemy in the antisemitic press to the liberal critic Tadeusz Boy-Żeleński's praise for a revelation of 'the soul of the nation with whom we are fated to coexist'.[32] But it was on the Jewish side that Arnshteyn discovered his most dangerous opponents. His work was attacked by the Turkows, Weichert, Mayzil, and others, particularly after a supporter suggested that the productions heralded a whole new kind of theatre, a Polish-language theatre for Jews. Struggling to prove how far Yiddish theatre had risen above *shund*, the representatives of Yiddish dramatic theatre could only regard Arnshteyn's Polish-language Jewish enterprises as a mortal threat to that theatre, as a project that would conquer Jewish theatre art for the Polish language while relegating Yiddish to the ghetto of *shund*. Insisting that his purpose was to familiarize Poles with Jewish culture, as well as to offer those Jews already distant from Yiddish a taste of modern Jewish creativity, Arnshteyn nevertheless terminated his initiative. While Yiddish plays continued to be staged sporadically in Polish, the notion of a Polish-language Jewish theatre fell, a casualty of the Jewish culture wars of inter-war Poland. Even as Polish nationalists ranted about Jewish pollution of Polish culture, Jewish cultural politics, in its own way, was about the same thing—fortification of the borders between what was Jewish and what was Polish, accompanied by raids on the expanding borderlands.

THE SECOND WORLD WAR

The Second World War and the Holocaust put an end to the millennial Jewish civilization of Poland in all its diversity. Jewish theatre was no exception; the overwhelming majority of its creators and audiences were murdered by the Nazis. But Jewish theatre continued, astonishingly, even amid the destruction, and it has also managed a kind of afterlife in post-war Poland.

In the Warsaw ghetto, for example, apparently as part of their plan to 'stabilize' the ghetto and exploit it economically, the Nazis permitted Jewish theatres to open.[33] By the end of 1941 five professional theatres were performing. Tickets were inexpensive; in the winter of 1942, when bread cost about 13 zlotys a kilogram, the price of a ticket was less than 2 zlotys. The theatres proved popular among a population starving not just for food, but also for a bit of distraction from the horror of

---

[32] *Głos Lubelski* on the Lublin production, cited in 'Di oyffirung fun h. leyviks *goylem* in lubliner poylishn shtot-teater', *Literarishe bleter*, no. 3 (20 Jan. 1928); *Kurier Poranny*, no. 296 (10 Oct. 1928), cited in Boy-Żeleński's *Pisma*, 28 vols. (Warsaw, 1956–75), xxiii. 520.

[33] R. Sakowska-Pups, 'O działalności teatralnej w getcie warszawskim', *Biuletyn Żydowskiego Instytutu Historycznego* (Warsaw), no. 69 (1969), 47–70.

the everyday. Conditions in the theatres were difficult. Carbide lamps were frequently the only illumination; heating was poor or non-existent. The audience sat in their coats while on the stage décolleté actresses shivered with cold. Technical installations were forgone; breaks between acts lasted very long.

Three of the theatres performed in Yiddish, primarily American Yiddish operettas but also some dramatic theatre. Jonas Turkow and his wife, Diana Blumenfeld (1906–61), a celebrated performer of Yiddish songs, were particularly active in the latter productions. With a number of fine actors from the Polish stage behind ghetto walls, two of the theatres performed in Polish. The larger of these was Mark Arnshteyn's Nowy Teatr Kameralny (New Chamber Theatre), which inaugurated its activity with an extremely popular production of Gordin's *Mirele efros* and scored another success with a revival of Arnshteyn's own *Pieśniarze* in March 1942, just four months before the 'liquidation' of the ghetto. Arnshteyn himself was captured during the Warsaw ghetto uprising and murdered shortly after.

AFTER THE HOLOCAUST

With the end of the war, Jewish survivors began to return to Poland, primarily from the Soviet Union. Political parties and cultural initiatives flourished, particularly in the western regions of Poland, annexed from Germany, where Jews had begun to settle. It briefly seemed as though Jewish life in Poland might regain the vitality if not the magnitude of pre-war days. But the violence and uncertainty of the post-war years combined with pervasive expressions of anti-Jewish hatred to convince most Jews to leave. By 1950 less than 100,000 Jews remained in Poland.

In 1944, with the Red Army still fighting German forces throughout Poland, Jonas Turkow and Diana Blumenfeld appeared in liberated Lublin, 'like Noah's dove returning with tidings', to stage, 'like an extraordinary religious act', a concert of Yiddish songs that marked 'the beginning of Jewish theatre art after the flood'.[34] By 1946 Yiddish theatres were performing in Wrocław and Łódź. Their activity was invigorated by the arrival of Ida Kaminska from the Soviet Union at the end of that year, and the return of Jakub Rotbaum from the United States in 1949.

By 1956 Ida Kaminska was back in Warsaw, but now as the director of the only state-funded Yiddish theatre in the world, named after her mother, Ester-Rokhl (Państwowy Teatr Żydowski im. Ester Rachel Kamińskiej). This achievement had a political price; her theatre would serve as an international showcase for what 'national minority cultures' could attain under communism. But in the small Polish Jewish community and among Holocaust survivors throughout the world she was revered, a figure who continued to create in the battered Yiddish language and represent its highest cultural aspirations. She also developed strong ties to the Polish

---

[34] D. Ginzberg [Shloyme Belis-Legis], 'A fertl yorhundert', in *25 yor yidisher melukhe-teater in folks-poyln* (Warsaw, 1975).

theatre world and, unlike in the pre-war years, her productions were reviewed and often acclaimed in the Polish press.

Her repertoire was a mixture of renewed Yiddish classics and adaptations from world literature, along with an occasional 'politically correct' piece.[35] It was a realistic theatre of powerful emotions, expressed through rhythmic word, evocative gesture, stylized movement. It was in addition a moral theatre, one that continually returned to the struggle between right and wrong. In these ways Kaminska's theatre remained true to the traditions of 'the mother' whose name it bore. But it was often also something else: a theatre, as the writer Adolf Rudnicki observed, of mystery plays in which millions of Polish Jews were remembered by 'a handful of those not burned, miraculously saved. Through the actors, to the rhythm of their sentences, songs, lamentations, those assembled honour[ed] the dead and their own youth.'[36]

In her own roles Kaminska portrayed a succession of wise and heroic women. She revived *Mirele efros* to great praise, but most acclaimed was her version of Brecht's Mother Courage, who wheels and deals and pulls her cart ever onward as the war she profits from claims all her children. Brecht intended his 'epic theatre' to create a didactic distance between audience and stage, but in this respect Kaminska subverted Brecht. Her Mother Courage was less a symbol than a solitary sorrowing woman.

I looked at Kaminska, the camp-follower Mutter Courage [declared the critic Andrzej Wróblewski, recalling a production in the 1960s], and I saw before me a Jewish King Lear, under whose feet the ground crumbles, who realizes, in the course of moving across this earth, that the world is one huge graveyard. Perhaps earlier, even fifteen years ago, Kaminska believed that the only stance worthy of a human being was to fight to the end. Now I had the impression that Ida Kaminska kept pulling the cart because what else remained to her?[37]

Even as her audiences in Poland shrank, particularly with the emigration of some 40,000 Jews in 1956–60, and remaining audiences increasingly availed themselves of translations through headphones attached to their seats, Kaminska began to tour the world. Her company was acclaimed in western Europe, Israel, Australia, and later in North and South America. In 1967, during the company's first appearance in New York, news emerged from Poland of so-called anti-Zionist agitation. Despite pleas for her to remain in the United States, Kaminska and her company returned to Poland. There they were swept up in an antisemitic campaign organized by the government, rooted in both byzantine party intrigue and decades of festering antisemitism. In 1968–70, 20,000 Jews emigrated from Poland, most

---

[35] On one such play, see S. Wolitz, 'Performing a Holocaust Play in Warsaw in 1963', in C. Schumacher (ed.), *Staging the Holocaust: The Shoah in Drama and Performance* (Cambridge, 1998).

[36] A. Rudnicki, *Niebieskie kartki* (Kraków, 1956), cited in S. Gąssowski (ed.), *Państwowy Teatr Żydowski im. Ester Rachel Kamińskiej* (Warsaw, 1995), 145.

[37] A. Wróblewski, 'Niobe', in *Ida Kamińska: 50 lat pracy artystycznej* (Warsaw, 1967), 46.

having been 'exposed' as 'Zionists' and fired from their jobs. Less than a year after their return to Poland much of the company, including Kaminska and her family, had emigrated.

But the State Yiddish Theatre has continued. In 1970 Szymon Szurmiej (b. 1923) became its director. Over the subsequent decades Polish actors have been trained to perform Yiddish theatre for audiences for whom pre-war Yiddish theatre is no longer even a memory. Among the theatre's most successful productions has been *A goldfadn-kholem* ('A Goldfadn Dream'), written and directed by Jakub Rotbaum. First staged in Wrocław in 1950 and revived frequently since, the play is a tribute to Goldfadn and his successors and the musical theatre they created.

While for decades political factors were chiefly responsible for the survival of the State Yiddish Theatre, its continuing existence also reflects Polish cultural needs, particularly since the fall of communism. In certain corners of Polish society the need has emerged for a new kind of history, not only of Poles but of all the peoples who once contributed to the cultural mosaic of the Polish lands. Jews are central in all such conceptions. In the words of the critic Stefan Treugutt: 'Can the gallery of figures in our folk plays [*szopki*] lack the Jew and the Jewish melody, the customs and humour of this nation? Without this element can we try to imagine the history of our common land? It is unimaginable.'[38] In 1992 the leading academic theatre journal *Pamiętnik Teatralny* devoted a special 500-page issue to the subject of Jewish theatre in Poland. On its front cover is a facsimile of the cover of Goldfadn's play *The Two Kuni Lemls*. This pioneering volume was followed by an international conference and the appearance of a number of similar volumes. The development of such scholarship and related initiatives, along with the survival of the State Yiddish Theatre, suggest that Polish traces of Jewish theatre will continue to lure audiences, however small, well into the foreseeable future.

[38] S. Treugutt, 'Spotkanie z Rotbaumem', *Teatr*, no. 7 (1984), cited in Gąssowski (ed.), *Państwowy Teatr Żydowski*, 275. The *szopka* was a kind of miniature puppet play carried into peasant homes and performed at Christmas.

A *Tuml* in the *Shtetl*: Khayim Betsalel Grinberg's *Di khevre-kedishe sude*

FRANÇOIS GUESNET

A PIECE OF *SHUND* THEATRE

THE comedy *Di khevre-kedishe sude, oder, Reb arye der bal-menagn* ('The Burial Society Banquet, or, Reb Arye the Musician'), which depicts the chaotic events surrounding the annual banquet of a burial society, was published in Warsaw in 1883.[1] This low-priced edition, with its dense typeface, cheap paper, and numerous typographical errors and irregularities, is a good example of the popular literature that Jews were soon to call *shund*. Here was a book that did not hide the fact that its readership was to be found among the less well-to-do, and that had no claims to higher spiritual (be it aesthetic or religious) values. Within the history of Yiddish literature, it represents a kind of pulp literature *avant la lettre*, as the term *shund* was not coined before the end of the nineteenth century.[2]

The play's author, Khayim Betsalel Grinberg, was from the town of Węgrów, a short distance from the provincial centre Siedlce, 50 miles due east of Warsaw.[3] He was born there in 1860, and already as a young man enjoyed a reputation as a

I am indebted to Michael Steinlauf for numerous bibliographical references and suggestions. I also wish to express my thanks to Jacob Barnai of Haifa University, whose wealth of knowledge of Jewish tradition was helpful to me in connection with many questions regarding intertextual matters. I am also grateful to Shaul Stampfer, Hebrew University of Jerusalem, for providing important bibliographical references; to Angelika Glau, Heidelberg, for assistance with special points in Yiddish semantics; and to Bill Templer of the Dubnow Institute, Leipzig, for his painstaking translation of this chapter.

[1] Publication was approved by the censor. The play was published by the printing house Meir Yehiel Halter, 2 Miła Street, Warsaw; the price was 15 copecks. The only copy of this edition I have been able to locate is in the National Library, Jerusalem. All subsequent citations follow this edition.

[2] On the etymology of the term, see C. Shmeruk, 'Letoledot sifrut ha-"shund" beyidish', *Tarbits*, 52 (1983), no. 2, 326. He localizes the first use of the term in an article by V. Vernik (1898), who commented that 'the period of the *shund* novel in Yiddish literature in America is finally over'.

[3] The following biographical notes are from Zalmen Reisin, *Leksikon fun der yidisher literatur, prese un filologye*, vol. i (Vilna, 1926), cols. 647–48, and *Leksikon fun der nayer yidisher literatur*, vol. ii (New York, 1958), cols. 404–5. These works mention as sources a 'private communication' from M. Holland, and N. Prilutski, *Mame-loshn* (Warsaw, 1924), 119. Grinberg is not mentioned in any other history of Yiddish literature or Yiddish theatre. Zalmen Zilbertsvayg, *Leksikon fun yidishn teater*, vol. i (New York, 1931), col. 532, is based exclusively on Reisin. A series of articles by A. Wieśniewski that analyses

prankster and jester (*khoyzek makher*). Even at that time he was starting to poke fun at the local authorities, the *shtetl* establishment, who presumably played a decisive role in Grinberg's probably not entirely voluntary decision to leave Węgrów for Warsaw.

In addition to *Di khevre-kedishe sude* Grinberg wrote another comedy, *Bintshe di tsedeykes, oder, Di ayngefalene bod* ('Bintshe the Pious Woman, or The Dilapidated Bathhouse'). Both were characterized by Zalmen Reisin (Reyzn) as 'showcase examples of popular satire, with a good-natured earthy humour, written in a juicy authentic folk idiom'. After publishing these two plays, Grinberg apparently went to Galicia, where we lose all further trace of him. Reisin emphasizes the popularity of his two plays, which is confirmed in an article written in 1890 by Ignacy Suesser on the Yiddish theatre and literary scene in Warsaw, where Grinberg is mentioned among the most popular repertoire authors of the Yiddish theatre.[4] Both his pieces were republished in 1911, further evidence of their continuing popularity.[5]

The dramatic format of *Di khevre-kedishe sude* is not that of a conventional stage play. The action is presented by a narrator external to the plot, and direct speech is for the most part embedded in the flow of the narrative. There are, however, more than two dozen interpolations to the reader, usually prefaced by 'My dear readers!'[6] It is highly probable that this text is the prose version of a theatrical comedy similar to the stage version, or a text that served as an actor's script or prompt book for improvised performances. Such a hypothesis is also suggested by the fact that Grinberg himself was an experienced actor. He performed in Warsaw with a troupe

the social and cultural situation of Polish Jewry also deals with the development of Jewish literature in Hebrew, Yiddish, Polish, and Russian and mentions Grinberg's play; see 'Kilka słów o Żydach', *Głos* (Warsaw), 31–2 (1889), 378–9, 387–9, 400–2.

[4] I. Suesser, 'Kilka słów o żargonie i teatrze żydowskim', *Izraelita*, no. 26 (1890), 255. This article marked a change of direction for this Warsaw weekly, which until then had completely rejected Yiddish. Now it began to regard Yiddish as a suitable means for enlightening the 'Jewish masses'. On Suesser, see M. Steinlauf, 'Fear of Purim: Y. L. Peretz and the Canonization of Yiddish Theater', *Jewish Social Studies*, 1/3 (1995), n. 45. On these developments, see also A. Cała, *Asymilacja Żydów w Królestwie Polskim (1864–1897): Postawy, Konflikty, Stereotypy* (Warsaw, 1989), 102–15. David E. Fishman's observation that the Russian ban on Yiddish theatre in 1883 was a 'devastating blow to the brief flourish of Yiddish theatre' clearly doesn't apply to Congress Poland and Warsaw; see his 'The Politics of Yiddish in Tsarist Russia', in J. Neusner, E. S. Frerichs, and N. M. Sarna (eds.), *From Ancient Israel to Modern Judaism*, vol. iv (Atlanta, Ga., 1989), 163–5. The regular diatribes by opponents of the Yiddish theatre in the Warsaw press in the 1880s evidence the continuing presence of the theatre in Yiddish; see *Izraelita*, no. 41 (1884), 328 (theatre performances in Warsaw in Yiddish); no. 8 (1886), 60 (the same); no. 32 (1886), 256 (the same); no. 34 (1887), 271 (performances in Łódź); no. 21 (1888), 186 (advertisements for Yiddish theatre); no. 30 (1888), 259 (performances in Warsaw).

[5] Pub. M. Knaster, 39 Franciszkańska Street, Warsaw, printed at Konkordia; there are only minor differences from the first edition.

[6] The first such remark, marked by a clear indentation on the page, states: 'Let us leave the two *balebatim* seated there and proceed on to the burial society. But first, my dear readers, I must explain the statutes governing the society' (*Di khevre-kedishe sude*, 6). Hereafter, page numbers will be given in parentheses in the text following the citation or reference to the play.

known as Di Broder, and then left with them for Galicia.[7] The name links them to
the so-called *Broder zingers* (Broder singers), groups of wandering performers who
emerged from Galicia in the late 1840s. Their performances were often staged in
taverns and characterized by intensive interchange with their audience, high spon-
taneity, and manifold improvisations. The themes of the songs and plays were
taken from everyday life, their barbs often aimed at the *sheyne yidn* (beautiful, i.e.
upper-class, Jews) and religious hypocrisy, especially among hasidim.[8] By the 1860s
they were performing in Warsaw, and they were also popular at the time Grinberg's
comedies were published.[9]

Numerous descriptions by contemporaries stress the direct and intensive participation in such plays of the audience, which was socially quite diverse.[10] For
example, Ignacy Suesser notes:

The first time I entered such a theatre I was struck by the loud conversations, the spectacle
on the stage, the cries and exclamations in Yiddish vernacular that flew like rockets through
the auditorium . . . Seated in the first row was the Jewish *haute volée*, the moneyed aristocracy,
here and there a non-Semite who had strayed into the audience, and the occasional detached
'educated' Jew, regarding his surroundings with an air of pity. . . . The gallery was packed to
the rafters, a colourful crowd composed of all the humanity one might encounter on the
pavements of the Jewish quarter. The orchestra strikes up the overture. Generally the bill
features serious stage plays or satirical melodrama. The music alternates, sometimes serene,
sometimes wild, loud, and booming, always full of originality and the requisite colour. It
puts the audience in the proper mood for the performance to come.[11]

It is hard to overlook the strong similarity between such scenes and the image of
the carnival as described by Mikhail Bakhtin: 'Carnival is not a spectacle seen by the
people; they live in it, and everyone participates because its very idea embraces all
the people.'[12] At the heart of carnival, as Bakhtin conceives it, is the culture of
laughter, a culture in which Grinberg, his audience, and his publishers were all
deeply immersed.[13] As will be shown, Grinberg achieved his objective by means of

---

[7] Reisin, *Leksikon fun der nayer yidisher literatur*, ii. 405.

[8] See Z. Turkov [Turkow], introd. to S. Prizament, *Broder Zinger* (Buenos Aires, 1960), 19–25.

[9] J. Szacki [Jacob Shatzky], 'Najstarsze dzieje teatru żydowskiego w Warszawie', *Pamiętnik
Teatralny* (1992), 181–2. In the 1883 edition of *Di khevre-kedishe sude* the text is followed by a page of
advertisements entitled 'If you want to be happy', which offered, among other things, printed versions
of the 'world-famous Broder songs': *Shirey zimro: draysig herlikhe broder lider mit melodyen vos zenen
bekant in der gantser velt*. On the Broder singers, see M. Steinlauf, 'Jewish Theatre in Poland', in this
volume.

[10] On the situation in the United States see I. Bialik, 'Audience Response in the Yiddish "Shund"
Theater', *Theatre Research International*, 13 (1988), 97–105, and Steinlauf, 'Fear of Purim', 53.

[11] Suesser, 'Kilka słów o żargonie i teatrze żydowskim', *Izraelita*, no. 25 (1890), 246, no. 26, 255.

[12] M. Bakhtin, *Rabelais and his World* (Bloomington, Ind., 1984), 7.

[13] On the page of advertisements noted above there are also titles such as *Der vaybersher yom kiper
oder der farshterter kol nidre in dray teyl . . . fun dem berimtn badkhn moyshe shlayfshteyn oys varshe* and
Naye zabaves af dem varshever plats by the same author. Worth mentioning is another work listed here
by Shlayfshteyn: *Der gehargeter kantortshik oder der umgerekhter toyt fun dem yungn albevistn feygelem vi*

an earthy humorous depiction of the hierarchies in the Jewish *shtetl*. However, this caricature never becomes a dispassionate lampoon by which the reader or audience member can feel superior to the figures burlesqued. Grinberg's description of religious practices is also strongly exaggerated. But in keeping with Bakhtin's view that the folk-cultural forms of the carnival and the culture of laughter are 'completely different, nonofficial, extra-ecclesiastical and extrapolitical . . . they built a second world and a second life outside officialdom', Grinberg targets not religious practice and belief as such, but rather human fallibility and its forgivable frailties.[14]

I will present a short summary of the play's plot, and then discuss some aspects of the textual structure, dramaturgy, and dramatis personae, as well as the social relations reflected in the play. A concluding section attempts to suggest the value and function of such a work of folk culture in the Polish Jewish context.[15]

THE PLOT AND ITS CONSTRUCTION

The annual banquet of the burial society in an unspecified *shtetl* generates enormous confusion. The unnamed head of the burial society, known here only as *gabe*,[16] has acquired the last barrel of brandy in town, a crucial part of the necessary provisions for the banquet evening. This angers Reb Shakhne, the woodcutter, and Reb Shloyme, the water-carrier, two *shtetl* residents who are returning home from a long day's work and are eager for a little drink (pp. 4–6). The two men, by dint of their occupations members of the lower class, decide to help themselves. The following morning they steal the barrel of brandy from the *gabe*'s house. In the meantime, after fasting for a day, the members of the burial society have gone to the ritual bath to purify themselves for the meal. After bathing they proceed to the synagogue for a hurried prayer (pp. 7–8). Upon returning home, the *gabe* learns of the robbery and soon discovers the culprits, who are lying in a stupor sprawled on a bed in the house of the water-carrier. This discovery leads to a scuffle between the *gabe* and the thieves, which ends with the arrival of the policeman who has been summoned. All three are taken into custody and brought before the local mayor,

tsvey koleges zayne shtshepinski un kleynyud hobn im baroybt dray toyzend rubel und ermordet arayn gepakt im in akasten un ekspedirt im af der viner ban nokh lodz bashribn un alid tsu zingen mit der melodye fun doktor almasado faryomert farklogt fun dem berimten badkhn moyshe shlayfshteyn oys varshe. The model for the melody mentioned was doubtless the operetta *Doktor Almasado, or, The Jews of Palermo* by Avrom Goldfadn, which was a great success throughout the Russian empire at this time; see 'Z Cesarstwa', *Izraelita*, no. 4 (1882), 32.

[14] Bakhtin, *Rabelais and his World*, 6.

[15] In keeping with Dan Miron's suggestion, that even in the case of authors who chose the *shtetl* as their setting one must first evaluate their works as *literature*, isolated references to the contemporary social situation in the *shtetl* with respect to housing, employment, nutrition, etc. will not be followed up here; see D. Miron, 'The Literary Image of the *Shtetl*', *Jewish Social Studies*, 1/3 (1995), 10.

[16] The head of any Jewish fraternity (*khevre*) was known as the *gabe* (Heb. *gabai*, president); see I. Levitats, *The Jewish Community in Russia, 1772–1844* (New York, 1943; repr. 1970), 105–22.

who has them gaoled (pp. 9–10). When the members of the burial society hear what has happened, they and the *gabe*'s wife rush to the court. But in vain: they cannot do a thing since it is already late evening. But in the meantime persons unknown make off with the banquet meal, which has been cooked by the *gabe*'s good wife and consists largely of gruel. Thus, after fasting a full day, the burial society's members have nothing to eat (pp. 10–11).

The wives of the two culprits, Dvoyre and Rivke, learn what has happened to their husbands. But their sorrow is muted; after all, they suffer daily beatings at the hands of their husbands and they can now enjoy a day of respite. However, they decide at least to bring the men in gaol something to eat. Provisions are hard to find since the *gabe* has acquired most of the food in the *shtetl* for the banquet—even parsley is scarce. While returning, the women are observed by burial society members. Misled by the pots they are carrying, they believe the two are responsible for the theft of the banquet meal (pp. 12–13). The women too are taken into custody and thrown in gaol.

The next morning the mayor interrogates the *gabe*. Only after some refreshment is he able to describe his view of the events (p. 14). While the water-carrier and woodcutter must return to gaol, the *gabe* is permitted to return home. There he finds all the members of the burial society awaiting him. They want to discuss how to arrange the banquet for a later date (pp. 14–15). This marks the close of the comedy's first section (pp. 4–15).

The second part (pp. 15–20) follows the efforts undertaken to locate the necessary funds for organizing the second banquet. It has been a bad year, and the fraternity, which has fixed rates for burial, is broke (p. 16). A respected member, Reb Getsl Pipik, has an ingenious idea: why not ask the older residents in town, anyway at death's door, to pay a portion of the expected expenses for their burial in advance? Keyltshe, the young wife of one such elderly Jew, Efroyim Toter (Tartar, i.e. barbarian), is looking forward to soon being rid of him. In his absence she pawns his best shirt to get the money for this advance payment (pp. 17–18). In another house the burial society members are attacked and beaten up: it appears that they had wanted to take a man still alive to his own burial, decked out in a shirt that resembled a shroud. In the meantime the two thieves receive their sentence. Shakhne the water-carrier and his wife, Rifke, are banned from entering the tavern for an entire year, while Shloyme the woodcutter and his wife, Dvoyre, are banished from the *shtetl*, since the woodcutter already has a criminal record (pp. 18–20).

In the third section (pp. 20–24) the owner of the pawned linen shirt, Efroyim Toter, returns to town after a busy week selling all sorts of goods in the peasant village. He notices that his shirt is missing and is furious. His wife tries to conceal the facts and pretends she has only lent his shirt to someone. Her irate husband orders her to get it back immediately (pp. 20–1). She is forced to redeem the pawned shirt from Reb Getsl by exchanging her hat for it. She comes back wailing and moaning, with a tale that her hat has been stolen. The next morning Reb Getsl's wife dons the pawned hat and wears it to synagogue. On her way home Efroyim sees her, recognizes his wife's hat, and rips it from the head of Reb Getsl's startled wife (pp. 22–3). Rumour of what has happened spreads like wildfire through the *shtetl*. Gimpl Shkope, a neighbour of Getsl's, denounces him to the rabbi, who rules that Keyltshe and Getsl are probably guilty of breaking the law. Reb Getsl is then expelled from the burial society (p. 24).

In the play's fourth and final section (pp. 25–30) the narrator briefly describes the strict hierarchy inside the burial society, mentioning that young members pay fines for thoughtless behaviour, which will now help finance the substitute banquet. The members of the society are called to assemble, including one Reb Yeshaye, who has a bellyache from eating too much *tsholnt* (a rich sabbath dish) and is suffering from diarrhoea. But when he hears the food is ready, he drags himself from his sickbed and comes to join the others at the table (pp. 25–6). Plagued by his diarrhoea, Yeshaye has to leave the room to answer nature's call, taking along his beloved pipe (for which he is nicknamed Yeshaye Tabatshnik). Reb Arye, who goes out to relieve himself at the same time, mistakes the pipe for a gleaming treasure. He hurls a heavy boot at the supposed treasure, following an old superstition which says that the treasure will thereby remain with the one who discovered it. The boot strikes Reb Yeshaye on the head, killing him instantly (pp. 27–8). The burial society quickly discovers the cause of this death and sentences Reb Arye to a fine of 5 roubles and the punishment of being called 'murderer'. But the dead Reb Yeshaye contributes his posthumous share to the second banquet, which, along with the income from another death in town, nets the burial society, to its unconcealed delight, a further 2 roubles. The valuable book containing the society's regulations, deathbed confessions, etc., *Ma'avar yabok*, is pawned, bringing two more roubles for the purchase of the new brandy. In accordance with the rules, the burial society fasts for another day. And then, after a few more prayers, it is able to sit down to enjoy the banquet meal, which now goes almost without a hitch (pp. 29–30).

The time of the action stretches over more than a week, since several weekdays are mentioned in the text (pp. 21–3, 29–30), from a Monday afternoon to Wednesday evening of the following week. The plot's structure is confusing, since several episodes develop in parallel and are presented in rapid succession. The finale, the banquet meal, surprises the audience by the unmotivated introduction of new characters unsupported by any new elements in the plot.[17] The explanations about the nature of the burial society (pp. 6, 11, 25 ff.) also complicate the presentation. In their absurdly objective tone, they serve to burlesque the burial society:

---

[17] One may wonder whether the character Avrom Yankev, the miller, who makes his appearance in a quite unmotivated manner in the final line of the play, is one of those 'unexpected guests' that Miron regards as a characteristic metaphor in *shtetl* literature. But Grinberg does not develop that figure in any of the directions suggested by Miron (emissary from heaven, saint, envoy from the land of Israel); see Miron, 'The Literary Image of the *Shtetl*', 28–9.

In the *shtetl* it has long been the custom to take 2 guilders for a dead infant. For a child up to the age of 5, the fee is 4 guilders. From 5 to 10, people pay 1 rouble, and for a young person 10 to 18 years old, 8 guilders. For the middle-aged the going rate is 10 guilders. From the elderly they take 2 roubles plus a swig of brandy. (p. 16)

This confusing plot is partially counterbalanced on two levels. First, there is the obvious primacy of comedy. Readers or members of the audience have constant reason to grin or laugh. As a rule, the source of humour here lies in the exaggeration of human foibles. Thus, the two *proste* (coarse) Jews are motivated by an excessive craving for brandy (pp. 4–6). Because of their egoism, the burial society members exclude all non-members from their ablution: after all, the wood used to heat the water belongs to the fraternity (p. 7). The members of this prestigious association are also intemperate, driven by their craving for brandy. Lusting for a drink, they rush through their prayers in unbecoming haste (p. 8). When 'the *gabe* . . . returned in a fright to the room and informed the fellows of his fraternity about the calamity that had occurred [the theft of the small barrel of brandy], a great commotion ensued. And it grew darker in the room than on Tisha Be'av. All scurried about, seized by grief' (p. 8).[18] But the other residents of the town are no better. While the burial society is standing by its leader, who is behind bars, 'others broke into his house and made off with all the food, the rolls included. They also took the cutlery. The house was left as pure as on Passover' (pp. 10 ff.). Individual members of the burial society are singled out for their gluttony, such as Yeshaye Tabatshnik, who has spoiled his digestion with too much *tsholnt* and none the less cannot resist the temptation of a banquet (pp. 25–6). The indomitable craving of the members for a second festive meal leads to the already mentioned attempts to find money for this substitute banquet. In one case those efforts end with the confusion surrounding Keyltshe's hat (pp. 17–18, 22–3), in another with a heavy thrashing for the society members:

There was such an uproar in the room that all the neighbours ran in. They started to berate Reb Getsl for having frightened people. Then they just grabbed hold of him and hurled him out of the house—with such force that he was left scrambling to find his teeth on the ground. Inside the room the same honour was accorded Reb Nokhem and Reb Toyvye. (p. 19)[19]

Grinberg depicts uncontrollable craving as something that has seized all social groups and strata, and leads to grotesque excesses. The grotesquerie peaks when the craving for food (in the person of Yeshaye Tabatshnik) and material gain (in the person of Arye) mesh, leading to Tabatshnik's accidental death. Grinberg amplifies this moment scatologically by having the two leave the meeting in order to relieve themselves: Yeshaye 'lights his pipe and goes to the toilet. Nor is it any wonder; if a person has diarrhoea, he has to go to the toilet constantly . . . that same moment,

---

[18] On Tisha Be'av Jews commemorate the destruction of the Temple in Jerusalem.

[19] After the fracas between the *gabe* and the brandy thieves this is the second violent confrontation in the satire.

Reb Arye also had to heed nature's call' (p. 27). In addition, Arye 'dirties his hands with excreta' (p. 28).

Another comic effect for the audience undoubtedly derives from the violent way in which the coarse husbands treat their wives, frequently beating or threatening them: 'You're going to have a black year! Go immediately and get that shirt, otherwise I'm going to kill you!', says Efroyim Toter to his wife, scaring her into rushing off to retrieve the pawned shirt (p. 21).[20] At that point in the plot the audience or reading public was probably less amused by the threat of force than by Efroyim's boorishness. The crude behaviour of the burial society is manifest not only in their hurried prayers but in their hand-rubbing delight over a burial that will bring them two more roubles for their substitute banquet: 'Soon the man died. The fraternity got to work, finishing the job quickly . . . They returned elated.' The violent end that meets Yeshaye Tabatshnik when brained by a thoughtlessly hurled boot utilizes the same register of humour (pp. 27–8).

A further source of humour is language, particularly the confusion of diverse discourses, which Bakhtin considers a distinctive feature of carnivalesque laughter.[21] In *Di khevre-kedishe sude*, Yiddish words are often replaced by Hebrew and Slavonic expressions. The high point of this language play is doubtless the complaint made by the *gabe* to the mayor, an alliterative ragout of Yiddish, Hebrew, and Polish:

> Poshet ten neveyle. Pitsh iz moye keyle.
> Yak on khtse pitsh. To ya ganev kshitsh. . . .
> I mnye vzol za nos. To yest tsali fardros. (p. 14)[22]

It is conceivable that these lines were sung as a song. The inclusion of non-Yiddish lexemes also served to mock manneristic ways of speaking: 'The *gabe* is certainly not a coarse boor. He knows what's written . . . It is a long-standing practice that custom overrules a court judgment . . . And there's a German saying: *delo po delam* [one thing at a time] . . . You just can't get round it, we're gonna have to organize a new banquet' (p. 15).[23] The wisdom of both Jewish tradition and the non-Jewish world—a 'German' saying in Russian—leads to the same result: the fraternity has to have its special dinner.

Finally, the only role played by erotic or even sexual elements in the play concerns one, rather conspicuous, moment. This is when Keyltshe, decked out in her hat, comes to visit Reb Getsl Pipik to redeem her husband's pawned shirt and is observed leaving his house with her head bare. This, combined with her comment,

[20] Additional threats of violence against spouses on pp. 6 and 12.

[21] Bakhtin, *Rabelais and his World*, 181–96.

[22] 'Off goes that bugger to drink out of my cup. When he tries to drink, I shout "thief"! . . . And he grabs me by the nose. That's my whole complaint.'

[23] The term 'German' here stands naturally for the acculturated Jew who has a European education, wears European clothing, and cultivates a knowledge of Russian.

overheard and reported by a neighbour, to the effect that she 'owes him a favour' (possibly of an improper sort), results in Reb Getsl's exclusion from the fraternity (pp. 21–3). In the dramatis personae, Getsl is listed as head of the community (*rosh hakahal*).[24] This is possibly an understated risqué allusion, in keeping with contemporary attitudes.[25]

The dominating comic element in the play's action and language thus helps to create a distinctive unity in the work. From start to finish readers or members of the audience are kept waiting in anticipation of the next joke, the next comical situation. In addition, unity is maintained by the constant flow of commentary, directed by the narrator towards the audience or readers. These interpolations have several functions: the narrator explains his way of narrating (pp. 6, 10, 20) or the background to the action (pp. 11, 22, 25, 27), and takes the audience from one scene to the next (pp. 6, 7, 8, 10, 12, 13, 23), often introducing a humorous meta-level to the narration: 'And now, dear readers, we have to return to our first two *balebatim* . . . You can't just leave them sitting there all alone, pining away' (p. 12). In these interpolations he looks into the past (p. 12) or the future (pp. 24, 25, 27) and comments on his audience's reactions: 'I assume my dear readers are satisfied with the first banquet, but I promise the second one will be more fun' (pp. 15–16, 19, 24). With his broad palette of interspersions into the flow of the action, the narrator functions both as a chorus and as an accompanying master of ceremonies. He serves the audience as the fixed point in a tale that lacks unity of time, place, or action.

REFLECTIONS OF THE *SHTETL*

Why did Grinberg choose the annual banquet of the sacred burial society as an occasion to denounce and lampoon the foibles of his contemporaries? What attracted him, like every satirist, was the discrepancy between the lofty claims of tradition and the social order on one hand, and the fallibility of those who appeal to these traditions and hierarchies on the other. By dint of their honoured place in society, the burial fraternities were especially suited as targets for satirical burlesque. Within traditional Ashkenazi Jewish society in central and eastern Europe, such societies (*khevres*) were a key component in the local hierarchies. In formal terms,

---

[24] A typical Jewish community (*kehile*) of Grinberg's time was administered by a state-recognized institution, the *dozór bóżniczy* (synagogue supervisory board), introduced in 1822 after the abolition of the autonomous *kahal* (community council). Despite this difference in legal terms and the anachronistic character of the term, the head of the community council in later times was still addressed as head of the *kahal* (*rosh hakahal*). See F. Guesnet, *Polnische Juden im 19. Jahrhundert. Lebensbedingungen, Rechtsnormen und Organisation im Wandel* (Cologne, 1998), 223–9.

[25] Shmeruk, 'Letoledot sifrut ha-"shund" beyidish', 327, points to the phenomenon of 'virtuous' trash literature. Steinlauf mentions the excesses by Jewish workers against houses of prostitution in 1905, the so-called 'Alfonsn pogroms'. These point to intolerance towards prostitution within the Jewish petit bourgeoisie and the working class in Warsaw.

they were voluntary associations, independent of the community council (*kahal*) and rabbinate, and invested with a large number of communal functions.[26] Central among these was the foundation of a cemetery, as a rule preceding the establishment of a formal community, along with the maintenance of this cemetery and the burial of deceased members of the community in keeping with religious regulations and precepts. In particular, this included preparing the corpse for burial and appointing a *vakher* (guard) to watch over it until the funeral. These tasks generated other areas of activity. Thus, the burial fraternities were frequently responsible for tending to the sick in the community if no other society existed for that purpose. A substantial portion of the income from the burials, to which Grinberg refers in caricature (p. 16), was set aside for aid to the needy. The burial societies often maintained schools for children from needy families and a communal shelter (*hekdesh*); they provided young brides with a dowry and served as institutional godparent for poor children. Not only was their annual banquet, as Grinberg describes, partially financed by the participants themselves (p. 6), it comprised but a small portion of the total expenses of the fraternity.

The influence exercised by such burial fraternities, based on the social scope and religious significance of their activities, was generally quite substantial in a community. The symbol of this social power was the burial fraternity's book of records (*pinkes*) mentioned by Grinberg (p. 17), in which sanctions against individual community members were recorded. Such sanctions might later be felt in various ways at an individual's burial, often many years after the original incident: large sums might be demanded from his family, the corpse might be buried in an unbefitting plot, or, worst of all, interred in a disgraceful public 'donkey burial' (*eyzls-levaye*).[27]

Membership in a burial fraternity was highly restricted. It was generally granted to a candidate only after a long waiting period and was based on co-optation. Thus, as a rule, the societies contained members from the most influential and respected families in the locality. Along with the burial society itself, such families formed an informal oligarchic centre within the community, subject to less public control than the *kahal*. At times this resulted in heated conflict between certain segments of the community and the burial society.[28] None the less, no community could exist without a *khevre-kedishe*. From the late eighteenth century in Prussia, it began to be driven into a corner by maskilim and the Christian authorities, utilizing administrative and police means. As a rule, under this pressure the fraternities were transformed into officially registered associations. In Congress Poland, in contrast, they

[26] A number of studies have appeared in recent years dealing in detail with burial fraternities. They also cite the older literature. See e.g. S.-A. Goldberg, *Crossing the Jabbok: Illness and Death in Ashkenazi Judaism in Sixteenth- through Nineteenth-Century Prague* (first pub. in French, 1989; Berkeley, 1996); Guesnet, *Polnische Juden im 19. Jahrhundert*, 303–25, 357–86; A. Reinke, *Judentum und Wohlfahrtspflege in Deutschland. Das jüdische Krankenhaus in Breslau 1726–1944* (Hanover, 1999), 17–131.   [27] Guesnet, *Polnische Juden im 19. Jahrhundert*, 315.

[28] Naturally there were also conflicts within the burial societies; these sometimes resulted in splits and the formation of rival societies; see ibid. 361–4.

continued to exist in their original form despite ongoing police harassment and persecution. The vast transformations in Jewish life in the late nineteenth century also affected the burial fraternities. One of the most significant transformations, the rise of large Jewish urban concentrations in east-central Europe (Warsaw, Łódź, Budapest), brought far-reaching disruptions in the influence of the fraternities. In these rapidly changing centres of Jewish life, consensus on the proper institutional framework for transmitting and implementing social norms quickly eroded.

With its burlesque of the burial fraternity, Grinberg's lampoon marks that historical juncture where the Jewish audience, though increasingly urban, was still aware of the formidable power and high moral stature of this institution. Grinberg situated his spoof in a believable *shtetl* setting. A reading or staging of the comedy in Warsaw could draw on this playful satirizing of familiar Jewish life and traditions, and on the deepening contrast between small-town community and rising metropolis. Grinberg caricatures the *shtetl* for its circumscribed horizon for experience. Take the narrow economic frame: the burial society banquet sufficed to exhaust the entire local supply of brandy and parsley, and to plunge the *shtetl* into the perils of a general price rise: 'The fraternity has bought up all the parsley in town . . . I'm afraid that because of the fraternity everything is going to go up in price here' (pp. 6, 11). The exchange relations between the peasant village and the Jewish *shtetl*, reflected in the goods Efroyim Toter sells (simple articles crafted by hand or from the factory) and those he brings back to the *shtetl* at the end of the week (only various foods), underscore the economic isolation of the *shtetl* (pp. 20–1). But the *shtetl* is the local burial fraternity's bailiwick: it sets the rates for burial there (p. 16), and seeks new sources of revenue in its confines (p. 17). The *shtetl*'s hierarchies are rooted in the burial fraternity's effective local monopoly and inescapable presence.

A specifically Jewish public sphere was also operative in the *shtetl*, perceiving, passing on, and evaluating events as they unfolded (pp. 23, 24). The blinkered nature of this experiential horizon is aptly expressed in the ironic sigh of the narrator as he comments on the predictability of what is to come: 'Six roubles have already been gathered for the banquet. There'll be enough money in the end, don't you worry. That's how it is in the *shtetl*' (p. 28). These conditions and their comic representation in *Di khevre-kedishe sude* were only comprehensible and hilarious for an audience familiar with this narrow horizon of experience—but not directly subject to its constraints. To laugh at the burial fraternity, you needed to come from the *shtetl*, like Grinberg himself, but view the world with an urban outlook and values. His ideal audience was made up of the new Jewish residents of a big city who knew the limitations of the *shtetl* and its distinctive forms of social control but were no longer affected by them. To this extent, the comedy deals with 'critical matters from a bygone world' (*kritishe zakhn fun di fartsaytishe velt*) (p. 1), as the subtitle announces. Yet this critique of the *shtetl*'s dysfunctionality is not one-sided ridicule of the *sheyne yidn* or the more numerous *proste yidn*. Nor does Grinberg mock religious observance. In contrast with the Broder singer troupes mentioned earlier, whose special target for biting satire was hasidic piety,[29] there are no comparable parodies or caricatures in Grinberg's plays. The fast days and prayers are kept by the fraternity, even when the craving for brandy threatens to overpower its members: 'Towards evening the entire fraternity came to the *gabe*. He recited *minkhe* [afternoon] prayers and read the weekly Torah portion, then they said *mayrev* [evening prayers]. Afterwards the *gabe* went to the pantry to get the brandy' (p. 8). This strict observance is also manifest after their trial in anticipation of the substitute banquet (p. 30).

The world doesn't turn topsy-turvy because the protagonists are religious fanatics or obsessed with tradition and rabbinical authority. The *tuml* (tumult) springs, rather, from the incompatibility between communal authority and responsibility. The insatiable craving for food and drink is the dominating motif of the action. Gluttony is a central topos in European folk culture. In its specific association with death in Grinberg's comedy it is at the very heart of that culture.[30] This linkage is initially forged on the level of motif through the burial fraternity as protagonist and its annual banquet as the key plot-shaping element. The nexus between food and death also appears in the important episode of Yeshaye Tabatshnik's accidental end, which is the event that makes the meal possible: the fine levied for his killing provides the rest of the money needed to arrange the banquet. The play's concluding scene, centring on a festive repast, is in keeping with a key criterion of folk artistry in Bakhtinian terms.[31] Yet the foibles of the protagonists are not something distinctive to the *shtetl* milieu, which is subjected here to external critique. Rather, the spoofing of the fallibility of all the fabula's participants allows the author to present the questionable character of the existing situation in the *shtetl*, yet without negating that situation: 'Carnivalesque parody . . . recreates its object in negation. As a whole, pure negation is totally alien in folk culture.'[32]

To the extent that all human beings are prey to the vices depicted, the author does not condescend in presenting his characters. As *khoyzek makher*, he himself is closely bound up with this folk culture even while able to reflect on its shortcomings: 'clowns and fools . . . represented a special at once both real and ideal form of life. They stood on the divide between life and art in a zone of transition of a special nature. They were neither simply eccentrics nor what is termed stupid in everyday language, nor were they comic actors.'[33] Here lies the fundamental qualitative difference between the comedy of the *khoyzek makher* Grinberg and later authors who made use of the *shtetl* as a canvas.

For Dan Miron, the *shtetl* is central to the Jewish literary landscape of eastern

---

[29] Prizament, *Broder Zinger*, 25.　　　　　　　　[30] Bakhtin, *Rabelais and his World*, 319.
[31] Ibid. 325: 'Due to its character of triumph and renewal, the festive meal often has the function of closure and completion in folk culture. A work of folk art never ends with death: if death appears toward the end of the book, then the obligatory funeral meal follows, a festive meal after burial . . . The reason for this lies in the ambivalence of all folk art: the end must bear within itself the seeds of a new beginning, as death bears within a new birth.'　　　　[32] Ibid. 60.　　　　[33] Ibid. 56.

Europe at the turn of the nineteenth century. The *shtetl* is constructed as the aesthetic extension of the original Jewish political homeland, Erets Yisroel, via an array of recurring metaphors, such as fire, departure from home, the unexpected guest. Through this myth it is connected with the continuum of Jewish sacred history, which ultimately contains a powerful component of anticipated redemption, whose specific outlook (emigration, Zionism, messianism) depended on a particular author's predilection.[34] For purely chronological reasons, Grinberg's work can be seen as a prototype of *shtetl* literature, a development Miron traces through the classic writers down to the 1930s. None the less, Grinberg deviates in every respect from this townscape of *shtetl* topoi.

The difference between Grinberg and his much better-known successors lies not in their respective aesthetic strategies but rather in their intentions. The parody in character names such as Efroyim Toter or Yeshaye Tabatshnik in Grinberg's play is obvious. But in contrast to, for example, Mendele Moykher Sforim, who (though Grinberg's contemporary) adhered to a maskilic value system and suggests a negative judgement of his characters merely by populating his world with towns with names like Kabtsansk (Pauperville) and Glupsk (Dopesville),[35] Grinberg restricts himself to point out individual faults as the target of his laughter. He thus distances himself less from the traditional Jewish community then did Mendele and his successors.

Another important element in the use of the *shtetl* as literary canvas is its representation as *yidishe melukhe*, or self-created Jewish state.[36] Yet that political dimension is also absent in Grinberg, who includes the non-Jewish world in his literary construction. Along with the already noted economic function of the peasant village, the non-Jewish world is represented by the police and administrative authorities, who end the first fracas, arrest the troublemakers (p. 10), and punish the theft of the brandy (p. 20). The narrator describes these events as appropriate even if the two wives are mistakenly also found guilty. He leaves no doubt that the theft of the brandy must be condemned and that recidivists must receive harsher sentences (p. 20). Nor is the collaboration between non-Jewish and Jewish institutions presented as comical or worthy of caricature:

The mayor soon handed down his verdict. Reb Shakhne and his wife are forbidden from entering the tavern for the duration of an entire year. Should they be found there or in another tavern, the magistrate is to notify the synagogue immediately that Reb Shakhne's wife is not permitted to enter its premises for two months, and that Reb Shakhne is banned for a similar period from reading from the Torah. Well, now we can understand why Reb Shakhne and his missis were afraid to drink any brandy for a whole year long. (pp. 19–20)

The threat of being excluded from synagogue prayers and the reading of the Torah is not something comical but the expression of a suitable punishment. Here too we can see the author's respect for religious observance. Other characteristic

---

[34] Miron, 'The Literary Image of the *Shtetl*', 35–6.   [35] Ibid. 18.   [36] Ibid. 3.

features of *shtetl* topoi as analysed by Miron are also absent in Grinberg: for example, tensions within the community are not developed according to the template of maskilim versus Orthodoxy or rabbinical Judaism versus hasidism. The ritual bath (*mikve*) and cemetery play little role here as symbols of a metaphysical bond between the *shtetl* and the continuum of Jewish history.[37] Grinberg's work is fully integrated into the complex and primarily Orthodox life-world of Polish Jewry. But it is totally worldly, non-metaphorical, indeed, anti-metaphorical.

CONCLUSION

Despite all its lampoonery, Grinberg's comedy is not a negative critique of the social order. Rather, it is a satire internal to and moving within traditional society. It offered the occasion for a good cathartic laugh, serving no purpose but that of a collective mental cleansing, therapeutic for coping with the peculiarities that crop up everywhere in life.[38] Though it interrogated the substance and legitimacy of existing authorities and hierarchies, it did not seek to overthrow them. Grinberg uses comedy within a controlled overstepping of the norms of good taste. The domains of religion and sexuality are largely excluded from this transgression. The 'powerful collective experience',[39] an essential characteristic of the popular Yiddish theatre, takes on a concrete social dimension here against the scaffolding of themes and stylistic means that Grinberg employs. As in a convex mirror, Grinberg's comedy reflects the immediate life-world of his public in a representation that both distorts and exaggerates. It mirrors what is above *and* below, holding up this image and all its facets as an object for therapeutic, liberating laughter. Herein lies the universal claim of Grinberg's artistry.

Translated from German by Bill Templer

[37] Miron, 'The Literary Image of the *Shtetl*', 32–5.

[38] One can certainly see a parallel here to the French *abbayes de maugouvert* and other fraternally organized associations in the French High Middle Ages and the early modern period as described by Natalie Zemon Davis ('The Reasons of Misrule', in her *Society and Culture in Early Modern France* (Stanford, Calif., 1987), 107–8); she characterizes the *abbayes* as a 'raucous voice of the conscience of the community'.   [39] Steinlauf, 'Fear of Purim', 53.

Mordechai Gebirtig: The Folk Song and the Cabaret Song

NATAN GROSS

WHEN does a song become a 'folk' song? Certainly not when it is written down, and not when it has only been sung for the first time. Only when it has been repeated once, twice, or three times—when it catches on and moves from the stage to the kitchen and its composer is forgotten. But even then it must survive the test of time. Scholars say it takes at least two generations.

A song's career can start on any stage, even an amateur one, and it need not be sung by a professional singer. But beginning on the professional stage, in an operetta or literary cabaret, gives a song a better chance. When first heard in cabaret or in the movies, it may become a hit, popular throughout a country or even throughout the world. Yet a hit song is not a folk song. Its popularity passes; it gives way to new fashions. Old people may still recall it with nostalgia, but it says nothing to new generations. It is different with a folk song, which enters the repository of national folklore and remains there. It becomes a part of folk culture, while its author remains anonymous or is known only to specialists.

Mordechai Gebirtig (1877–1942) engraved his name on the history of Jewish cabaret in Poland between the wars. Every singer had his songs in his or her repertoire.[1] These songs spread from the cabaret stages (*kleynkunstbine*) of Łódź and Warsaw to all of Poland and to the entire Jewish world. Even today they are alive on the stage and in Jewish homes; they are an indispensable part of the repertoire of Jewish singers. They are also arousing increasing interest among non-Jewish audiences in Poland, Germany, the Netherlands, Italy, and the United States. Since the destruction of European Jewry these songs have become a crucial means of learning about Jewish folklore and the life of the Jewish poor, matters inadequately recorded in Yiddish literature and other sources.

Mordechai Gebirtig (né Bertig) was born on 4 May 1877 in Kazimierz, Kraków's Jewish quarter.[2] After a few years of traditional instruction in a *kheyder* his father

Some parts of an earlier version of this chapter were published in A. Kuligowska-Korzeniewska and M. Leyko (eds.), *Teatr żydowski w Polsce* (Łódź, 1999).

[1] See Z. Turkow, *Di ibergerisene tkufe* (Buenos Aires, 1961), 106.

[2] Bertig (Bärtig) means bearded; Gebirtig suggests 'born again'. For other biographical information, see I. Fater, 'Uśmiech i łza Mordechaja Gebirtiga', in *Trubadur z Galicji: Pieśni Mordechaja*

apprenticed him to a carpenter. Gebirtig spent his youth among workers, and this environment shaped his political views, as he came under the influence of social democratic parties. There is a lack of information about this period in his life, but it is significant that he entered the political arena in December 1905 with a poem entitled 'General Strike' in the Kraków Jewish weekly *Socialdemokrat*.

By the age of 28 Gebirtig was an actor and possibly director in a Jewish amateur theatre organized by the association Bildung, which was dedicated to improving the taste of Jewish audiences. Gebirtig probably co-founded this theatre, which had a serious, literary repertoire whose standard is confirmed by reviews of its productions by the poet Avrom Reyzn (Abraham Reisen) in the Kraków daily *Dos yidishe vort*.[3] His brief acting career allowed Gebirtig to develop skill in constructing monologues and dialogues (duets), the forms that he would often employ in his later songwriting. For the moment, however, he was entirely engaged in the struggle for a better future. In his socially charged poems he attacked the wealthy Jewish classes and criticized injustice, yet he did not raise the slogan of class struggle.

During the First World War Gebirtig, who had a heart condition, served as a nurse in a military hospital in Kraków. This experience added a strong pacifist flavour to his political consciousness.[4] After the war, by now married and the father of three daughters, he worked in his brother's second-hand furniture store restoring old furniture. He was popular in Bundist circles and participated in the meetings of a Jewish writers' circle, where he read his poems, sometimes accompanying his reading or singing with a melody played on a simple pipe. These presentations, still not professional, prompted his Kraków friends to publish in 1920 a slim volume of his poems entitled *Folkstimlekh* ('Folk-Like').[5] At the same time his

Gebirtiga, programme of the E. R. Kaminska State Yiddish Theatre, Warsaw, 1991–2; J. Ficowski, 'Mordechaj Gebirtig', in M. Gebirtig, *Pieśni*, trans. J. Ficowski (Warsaw, 1992); N. Gross, 'Mordechaj Gebirtig—człowiek teatru', in J. Michalik and E. Prokop-Janiec (eds.), *Teatr żydowski w Krakowie: Studia i materiały* (Kraków, 1995); N. Gross, *Żydowski bard: Gawęda o życiu i twórczości Mordechaja Gebirtiga* (Kraków, 2000).

[3] H. Heierman's *Ghetto*, 24 Jan. 1905; Sholem Aleichem's *Tsezeyt un tseshpreyt*, 7 Mar. 1905; Y. Y. Lerner's *Di yidene*, 5 May 1905.

[4] His pacifist songs include 'Unter geyt di velt' ('The World Collapses') and 'Hershele', in his *Folkstimlekh: Lider* ('Folklike: Songs') (Kraków, 1920); 'Zog mir levone' ('Tell me, Moon', p. 60) and 'Krigsinvalid' ('War Veteran', p. 106), in *Mayne lider* ('My Songs') (Kraków, 1936); 'Dos letste vort' ('The Last Word', p. 125), 'A royter tseykhn' ('A Red Medal', p. 60), and 'A mabul shik!' ('Send a Flood!'), in *Mayn fayfele: unbekante lider* ('My Little Pipe: Unknown Songs') (Tel Aviv, 1996).

[5] *Folkstimlekh* contains twenty poems, without any music. Gebirtig saw only one other book published during his lifetime. This was *Mayne lider*, which appeared in 1936. Also published by a group of his Kraków friends, the book contains fifty-four songs with music; two of these, 'Kleyner yosem' ('The Little Orphan') and 'Viglid' ('Lullaby'), were reprinted from *Folkstimlekh*. Gebirtig did not read musical notation; the music in this volume was transcribed by his friend the composer Juliusz Hoffman. In 1945 the Wojewódzka Żydowska Komisja Historyczna w Krakowie (Provincial Jewish Historical Commission in Kraków) published a booklet entitled *S'brent* ('It Burns'), which includes the words to fourteen songs written during the war (with one exception; see n. 32), with music to three of the songs. Another volume of Gebirtig's songs appeared only recently. During the deportation of the

songs were performed at the workers' club Arbeter Heym (Workers' Home).[6] In the summer of 1921 these songs, notably 'Kinder-yorn' ('Childhood Years') and 'Hulyet, hulyet, kinderlekh' ('Play, Children, Play')[7] were introduced to the American Yiddish actress Molly Picon, who was performing in Kraków. Enchanted by the songs, she included them in her repertoire. Shortly after, the American theatrical agent Boaz Young bought the rights to the songs and included them in Moyshe Shor's operetta *Rumenishe khasene* ('Romanian Wedding'). The play had its premiere in Warsaw in 1923 and was later performed all over the world.[8] Gebirtig's nostalgic songs were instrumental in the play's success, and to no one's surprise they also conquered the cabaret stages. The royalties paid by Young were Gebirtig's first literary income, and pointed him on his way to his songwriting future as the 'Galician troubadour'.

The audience for Jewish cabaret was primarily from a working-class background. A Jewish tailor, carpenter, or factory worker of this period was culturally sophisticated; he or she read books, attended lectures, participated in amateur theatres or choirs, and went to the professional theatre, sometimes even at the expense of his or her daily bread. In such a social climate and with active organizations and political parties such as the Bund, the Folkists, and the Left Zionists for whom Yiddish was the language of choice, conditions were propitious for a Jewish artistic cabaret. By the beginning of the 1920s, stages presenting so-called miniature theatre (*kleynkunst*) emerged, supported by the celebrated Łódź literary group Yung Yidish. Well-known directors, writers, and actors also began to work with these small theatres. Cabaret Azazel was led by Dovid Herman, a prominent stage director of the Vilner Trupe (Vilna Troupe); one of his stars was Władysław Godik of the Habima troupe.[9] In Yitskhok Nożyk's cabaret, Sambation, Roza Gazel and Khane Grosbard reigned. An important place in the history of Jewish cabaret is occupied by Moyshe Broderzon, a poet, satirist, and author of skits that, together with the work of the American-based writer Moyshe Nadir, constituted the

Jews from Kraków in June 1942, just days before his death, Gebirtig handed his daughter Lola two folders containing eighty unpublished poems and songs. She passed them to Juliusz Hoffman's daughter Julia, who, with her sister Hanka, hid them during the war. After the war the folders were given to the Moreshet archive of Hashomer Hatsa'ir, Kibbutz Givat Havivah, Israel; part of the material went to the archive of the YIVO Institute for Jewish Research, New York. After more than fifty years these manuscripts were published as *Mayn fayfele: unbekante lider*, ed. N. Gross (Tel Aviv, 1996). For English translations of Gebirtig's songs, see G. Schneider (ed.), *Mordechai Gebirtig: His Poetic and Musical Legacy* (Westport, Conn., 2000); *Antologye fun yidishe folkslider*, vol. v: *Der mordkhe gebirtig band*, ed. S. Leichter (Jerusalem, 2000); *The Song that Never Died: The Poetry of Mordecai Gebirtig*, trans. S. Simchovich (Oakville, Ont., 2001).

[6] See N. Zucker, 'In der khaveyrisher svive fun mordechai gebirtig', in Zucker (ed.), *Gedenkbukh galitsye* (Buenos Aires, 1964). Zucker was the director of this literary theatre, which was linked to the Po'alei Tsion (Workers of Zion) movement.   [7] *Mayne lider*, 8, 10.

[8] See Y. Turkow-Grudberg, *Af mayn veg* (Buenos Aires, 1964), 74–84.

[9] After the Second World War Godik performed in a Polish army theatre in Łódź and with Teatr Polski in Warsaw.

fundamental repertoire of all Jewish cabarets. Broderzon established and directed the celebrated cabaret Ararat, which began in Łódź and later moved to Warsaw. Ararat was the birthplace of the best-known Jewish comedy team of Shimen Dzhigan (Dzigan) and Yisroel Shumakher (Israel Schumacher).[10]

The ensembles of these theatres were rarely stable. Cabarets closed and opened again, and actors moved from place to place (to meet finally in the 1930s in Di Yidishe Bande (The Jewish Gang), which featured Khayele Gruber, an actress–singer with a strong talent for comedy).[11] Though Gebirtig's songs were to be found in every cabaret programme, this did not necessarily improve his material situation. Despite the popularity of his songs, the finances of these theatres were generally lamentable, and copyright laws were usually ignored. And Gebirtig was the last person to fight for his literary rights.

When Gebirtig began to encounter large audiences, he realized that many of his listeners would not care for a militant proletarian repertoire. At the same time he avoided the genre known as *shmontses* (Polish: *szmoncesy*), with its titillating and tear-jerking texts—popular songs bereft of any ideology. Cabaret opened a path for him that was socially conscious but not narrowly political. The social criticism widespread in Jewish cabarets nurtured spontaneous creativity in a poet who came from the poor and never left them either physically or ideologically. 'Avreml der marvikher' (Avreml the thief), for example, 'the cleverest of thieves' who 'doesn't rob at fairs' but only from magnates, could have grown up to be a great man, but his childhood was hungry and cold and he was educated by the 'evil streets'.[12] The poor prostitute of 'Di gefalene' ('The Fallen One'), who stands at midnight under the streetlight, has a human heart. She too wants true love, but her consumptive cough scares her clients away:

> Far away a mother thinks:
> What has happened to my child?
> Blood would flood into her eyes
> If she could see her daughter now.

Similarly, there is the disabled veteran who received a medal from the emperor for his lost sight, but now must live by begging.[13]

Unemployment affects young people, especially young couples who cannot marry because of lack of money; and it also worries mothers who want to arrange

---

[10] See, among others, J. Malinowski, *Grupa 'Jung Idysz' i żydowskie środowisko 'nowej sztuki' w Polsce 1918–1923* (Warsaw, 1987); C. Shmeruk, 'Mojżesz Broderzon a teatr jidysz w Łodzi', in M. Leyko (ed.), *Łódzkie sceny żydowskie: Studia i materiały* (Łódź, 2000).

[11] Among prominent Jewish cabaret artists may be mentioned the singers Yosele Kolodny, Nadia Kareni and Józef Strugacz (a couple who specialized in Gebirtig's duets), and Lola Folman. The composers Henekh Kon and Dovid Beyglman (Beigelman) were the musical pillars of Jewish cabarets even though their musical interests were much broader. Yitskhok Turkow was the master of ceremonies at Azazel and wrote a memoir about his cabaret experiences (see n. 8).

[12] *Mayne lider*, 100.   [13] Ibid. 76.

wealthy matches for their daughters. But love is blind, and the girl's heart goes to the poor tailor's apprentice or to a young man with no future. The girl asks, 'Mameniu, an eytse!' ('Mother, some advice!'), but her heart does not want to follow this advice. Another girl lies to find out if her beloved's intentions are pure, whether he really loves her or just wants her dowry. Her heart is confused and poverty gnaws. 'Tirli, tirli', sings a bird, the only friend of the girl whose beloved has gone far away to look for work. He's doubtless in a strange town, far from his fiancée and family, and still unemployed. Gebirtig wrote many such texts.[14]

Gebirtig's work, shaped by social issues and Jewish folklore, voicing the everyday worries of a poor society but avoiding inflammatory rhetoric, had little in common with Polish cabaret lyrics, which, moreover, were probably unknown to him. The character of his work is particularly striking when we scan the titles of the most popular Polish cabaret hits of Hanka Ordonówna, Zofia Terne, and Zula Pogorzelska, such as 'Czy Pani mieszka sama?' ('Do you Live Alone, Miss?'), 'Ta mała piła dziś' ('This Baby had a Few Drinks Today'), 'Ja się boję sama spać' ('I'm Afraid to Sleep Alone'), with the songs written by Gebirtig and sung by Khane Grosbard, Malvina Rapel, or Diana Blumenfeld, whose repertoire was less inspired by cabaret than by folklore. His sources were generally Jewish, but occasionally non-Jewish as well. For example, 'Blumke mayn zhiduvke' ('Blumke, My Little Jewess') is a duet sung by a Polish shepherd and a Jewish girl who rejects his advances with the words 'You've got enough goyish girls in the village, why do you need a Jewess?' In the ballad 'Hey, tsigelekh!' ('Hey, Little Goats!') a nymph misses the boy she bewitched; now, as he lies at the bottom of the lake, she weeps on the shore. Truly romantic but also folklike is the tale of Dovidl from the slums, who's in love with Reyzele. 'Reyzele' is one of the most beautiful Jewish songs, humorous and at the same time innocent, tender, delicate, and sentimental.[15]

Sentimental songs were what made Gebirtig popular. Alongside 'Reyzele', which Gebirtig wrote as a wedding gift for his eldest daughter, Shifra, the song 'Dray tekhterlekh' ('Three Daughters') became a standard in every Jewish cabaret; Gebirtig dedicated the song to his wife, Blumke:

> Play, musicians! play away—
> The first daughter gone today.
> There still remain daughters two,
> What are we to do!
> Play, musicians, instruments in hand!
> Sound our joy throughout the land.
> Only God knows how we feel
> And those that have daughters.

---

[14] 'Oy narishe briye?' ('Oh, Stupid Girl', p. 38), 'Khanele un nokheml' (p. 42), 'Oreme shnayderlekh' ('Poor Little Tailors', p. 80), 'Farvos veynstu shayndele' ('Why do you Weep, Shayndele?', p. 102), in *Mayne lider*.   [15] *Mayne lider*, 50, 52, 66.

But when the third daughter is married:

> The last daughter is also gone
> What more is there to do?[16]

This vision was never fulfilled personally for Gebirtig, who was not to see his younger daughters under the *khupe*.

'Reyzele', 'Dray tekhterlekh', 'Kinder-yorn', 'Hulyet, hulyet, kinderlekh', and many other songs sprang from Gebirtig's personal experience. They were not initially intended for cabaret. The author performed them himself, and they were written with masculine grammatical forms. Once they reached the stage, they were most often sung by female singers dressed as men. I remember Khayele Gruber of Di Yidishe Bande in the marvellous role of Avreml the thief, clad in prison stripes. I also remember the song 'Ver der ershter vet lakhn?' ('Who will Laugh First?'), in which a wealthy young boy bets the son of a poor family that he will manage to make him smile. Shloymele is hungry. His father is out of work and Shloymele goes to school without breakfast. He cannot concentrate in the *kheyder* and the teacher whips him. Abramek wins the bet by offering Shloymele a roll with butter and a herring head. This brings a smile to his hungry friend's face. This duet was also sometimes performed by two actresses.

Here Gebirtig the socialist and defender of the oppressed can still be heard, though not as insistently as in his pre-cabaret works. At the beginning of the 1920s he evoked social reality in his lullabies.[17] Mothers rocking their children to sleep are poor and overworked: they would like to sleep too. The child is most often an orphan or raised without a father who has left for America looking for bread. Who knew if he still remembered his wife and children—perhaps he'd found another mate. But Gebirtig's late, beautiful lullaby 'Yankele', though it ends with the words 'It will take much more of your mother's toil and tears to make a decent person [*mentsh*] of you', is devoid of social undertones. It simply tells of a mother's dreams for her child's happy journey from the cradle to the *khupe*.[18]

Over the years Gebirtig's collaboration with cabarets grew closer; his works became more cabaret-like and specifically Jewish themes became more evident in them. For instance, in 'Kh'vil nisht aza khosn' ('I don't Want such a Groom') Gebirtig ridicules a young woman who dislikes Jewish boys with names such as Binyumin, Zalmen, Kalme-Zishe ('who speaks only Yiddish to boot—feh, shame!'). She rejects all the matchmaker's offers and finally finds herself a boy named Władek. But Jewishness intervenes after all. They cannot marry because the boy's mother's name is Sara, the same as that of her future daughter-in-law—which is contrary to Jewish custom. Among songs containing social satire is 'Nokh a glezl tey' ('Another Glass of Tea'), a conversation between a couple trying to decide on a

---

[16] *Mayne lider*, 88.

[17] 'Viglid' and 'Kleyner yosem' in the volume *Folkstimlekh*; 'Kivele' (p. 22) and 'Hungerik dayn Ketsele' ('Hungry is Your Kitten', p. 96), in *Mayne lider*.   [18] *Mayne lider*, 30.

name for their future son, which must be based, according to Jewish custom, on the name of a deceased family member. The dialogue turns into a quarrel as husband and wife invoke the pretensions of each side of the family. They end in compromise, however: perhaps there will be two boys. And perhaps even two girls—in which case, the entire discussion is irrelevant.[19]

Gebirtig was very musical and would often break into dance when performing new songs before groups of writers and friends. He liked to dance, but his heart ailment restrained him. In any case he was conservative in his tastes, and the fast modern dances were not for him. He laughed at affected Jewish girls who treated fashionable rhythms as the essence of their lives and tried to drag in their Jewish boyfriends, as in his famous song 'Kum, leybke, tantsn' ('Come, Leybke, Let's Dance'). In the 1920s the charleston was in and Gebirtig's 'classic' was born. An enthusiastic girl tries to teach her partner to dance: 'Either you learn the charleston, or we're through!' One can see from the first steps, she insists, who's fine, who's a bum, and who's a charlatan.[20] In the late 1930s Gebirtig returned to this topic from a different perspective. 'Undzer tokhter khaye' (our daughter Khaye) is getting married and we, her parents, don't know how to dance anything except the waltz. We absolutely have to learn modern dances so as not to embarrass ourselves at the wedding, says Khaye's mother. But the young couple is not spared either. Khaye is a bright girl, plays tennis and the mandolin ('she's so musical!'), she can type and speaks Polish, while her man is a sportsman. He swims like a fish, plays soccer, runs like a racehorse. And how much he can pack away! Eating is his best sport. The refrain, in tango rhythm, turns into a sketch:

> So let us then go and learn the tango!
> Dear Khayele just wants to tango!
> Every step a kind of longing,
> The music like a magic potion.
> So let's all together learn the tango,
> For us old folks there is only tango.
> The melody somehow wakes again
> The happiness and dreams
> That are long gone.[21]

Probably from the same period comes the cabaret song–monologue 'Gevalt! vel ikh shrayen' ('Bloody Murder! I will Scream'), a harsher social satire:

> Bloody murder! I will scream.
> Oh, people, I will lose my mind!
> I've got a husband who can only chew
> But earn a penny he can't do.

---

[19] Ibid. 46. [20] Ibid. 56. [21] *Mayn fayfele*, 174.

Everyone else is working, earning money; only her husband is indifferent to her worries and sufferings. The children are hungry, the shopkeeper refuses credit, and the landlady demands the rent:

> And my dear little husband, when I get angry and scream,
> Answers me calmly, like this:
> A time will yet come,
> When we, poor people all,
> We will turn the world on its head!
> Oh happy then will be
> All the poor, you see—
> We will be the bosses then.
>
> Bloody murder!
> Bloody murder, I will scream!
> Such stupidities you dream!
> But what, I ask, will we eat
> Until those times so sweet?
>
> The Jews, I complain,
> They comfort themselves in vain
> That messiah will come riding.
> Meanwhile there's only woe,
> They all suffer so,
> For now the times are only sad.

And then the husband sends his wife to the shop for a loaf of bread on credit 'one last time'.[22]

From the late 1930s there are also two songs about the bitter fate of a domestic servant. 'Ba gvirim a dinstmoyd tsu zayn' ('To be a Servant Girl for the Rich') is a complaint full of anger and bitterness against the 'madam' and her husband, who 'feels something' for the girl.[23] The second song is humorous and has a dance-like refrain, 'Ker, bezeml, ker' ('Sweep, Little Broom, Sweep'). It expresses a young woman's yearning for a home and children in place of sweeping up other people's rubbish. But only her employers' son can change her fate:

> They want to kick me out,
> But the son says to them
> That he loves me and will take me,
> Just exactly as I am.
>
> Sweep, little broom, sweep,
> I will serve no more!
> Madam as my mother-in-law,
> The master my father-in-law,
> So sweep, little broom, sweep![24]

---

[22] *Mayn fayfele*, 170.   [23] Ibid. 184.   [24] Ibid. 180.

In his memoirs from the early 1920s the Yiddish writer Nechemia Zucker (Cukier), who first gave Gebirtig an opening on the stage in the amateur theatre at the Arbeter Heym, recalls that he also wrote satirical songs based on current events such as wartime and post-war relief. Zucker also mentions militant songs that Gebirtig wrote for the Jewish militia organized to protect Kazimierz against hooligans. According to Zucker, these songs, soon outdated, were apparently of little importance to Gebirtig.[25] This is perhaps why they are not to be found in the recently discovered collection of Gebirtig's poems and songs.[26] Indeed, the only topical song preserved in these archives along with its music is 'Endekówna' ('Endek Lady'), written during the coup of May 1926, when Marshal Piłsudski seized power from a government headed by the Endek (National Democrat) Władysław Grabski. The 'Endek lady' of the song did well for herself when Grabski was in power, but now that Marshal Piłsudski has kicked her in the backside, she must go begging. And to whom? 'My Grabski used to say, Jak bida to do Żyda' ('To the Jew if you have to').[27] (Let us not forget the other half of this saying: 'A po bidzie całuj mnie w nos, Żydzie' ('And when the hard times are through, kiss me somewhere, Jew.') Older Krakovians remember this satire, which was performed on the cabaret stage but not included in Gebirtig's pre-war collection *Mayne lider*.[28]

Wine, women, and song is a traditional theme of operettas, often adopted in cabaret as well because it affords opportunities to stage singing and dancing. Gebirtig used this genre, but the students and army officers who sang such songs had different concerns from Gebirtig's. It is therefore hard to consider 'Hey, klezmorim!' among so-called drinking songs. It has an autobiographical character and its references to *klezmorim*, the traditional Jewish bands, and to the bottle allow us an insight into the poet's soul, his optimism even in deepest despair:

> Hey *klezmorim*, my good brothers,
> Here is something for some wine—
> Play for me a happy tune
> Chase away my gloom.
>
> Play for me a happy tune—
> You're playing somehow sadly today;
> The flute is weeping, fiddle too—
> All around me weeps.

'Hey, klezmorim!' exists in two versions. In the documents of the Kraków censor's office for December 1922 there is a longer version intended for the stage.[29] Fifteen years later, and substantially shortened, the song was published at the beginning of

[25] Zucker, 'In der khaverisher svive fun mordechai gebirtig'.
[26] See n. 5.   [27] *Mayn fayfele*, 146.
[28] It was recalled by Gebirtig's friend Józef Bosak in the Irgun Yotsei Krakov Beyisrael (Union of Krakovians in Israel).
[29] The censored copy is in the Moreshet archive of Hashomer Hatsa'ir; it consists of ten songs by Gebirtig, of which nine, sometimes thoroughly reworked, were later included in his volume *Mayne lider*.

the volume *Mayne lider* (p. 6). Gebirtig recalls the *klezmorim* several times in this volume, for instance in the cheery song 'Oy, briderl, lekhayim!' ('Oh, Brother, to life!'):

> Oh, brother, *lekhayim*!
> Drink a bit of wine,
> It banishes the gloom,
> All the care and pain.
>
> Now, brother, I drink too,
> And when my head is ringing,
> What do I care for all the world,
> I dance a hop, hop, hop.[30]

The nostalgic 'Dos lidl fun goldenem land' ('The Song of the Golden Land') opens with an appeal to a *klezmer*:

> Oh take, good *klezmer*, your fiddle in hand
> And play me the song of the golden land.
> Once long ago with heart and with feeling
> My mother would sing it. Oh play it, oh play!

Another song, 'Mayn yoyvl' ('My Jubilee'), is one of the few that can be precisely dated. It was written in 1927 for the artist's fiftieth birthday, to which he invited a *klezmer* musician.

Doubtless intended for cabaret, perhaps even commissioned by one, was the song 'Hey, tsigeynerl!' ('Hey, Gypsy!') modelled on fashionable tangos:

> Hey, Gypsy! Take your fiddle
> With Gypsy feeling!
> Of my little one, your sweet song
> On your fiddle play!
> Of my little one, your sweet song,
> Play, oh Gypsy, play!
>
> Play your song, play a little,
> Free me from my gloom!
> To your heart give a key,
> Is it still true to me?
> To your heart give a key
> Play again from the start.[31]

Gebirtig's work, both the folk songs and the cabaret songs, was ended by the Second World War. As bombs exploded, a different sort of song emerged.[32]

---

[30] *Mayne lider*, 74.   [31] *Mayn fayfele*, 167.

[32] The song 'Undzer shtetl brent' ('Our Town is Burning'), probably Gebirtig's best-known creation, was written in 1938 as a protest against anti-Jewish violence in Poland. The censor prohibited its performance in Kraków. It represents a new era in Gebirtig's work and foretells the coming catastrophe.

Gebirtig himself was shot in the Kraków ghetto in the course of the *Aktion* of June 1942. Cabaret died along with the past, but the songs have survived: in books, archives, and memories, and increasingly in performance once again.[33]

Translated from Polish by Gwido Zlatkes

[33] Gebirtig's work acquired new life on the stage with the performance, at the E. R. Kaminska State Yiddish Theatre in Warsaw, of *Der trubadur fun galitsye* ('The Troubadour from Galicia'), directed by Golda Tencer (premiered on 4 Apr. 1992), and at the Yidishpil Theatre in Tel Aviv of Yehoshua Sobol's *Gebirtig: a harts vos benkt nokh lider* ('Gebirtig: A Heart that Yearns for Songs'), directed by Shmuel Atzmon (premiered on 4 Jan. 2000). Gebirtig's songs are regularly performed in Polish, Hebrew, German, English, and Italian.

Simkhe Plakhte: From 'Folklore' to Literary Artefact

SETH L. WOLITZ

THE Polish Jewish folk motif and figure of Simkhe Plakhte deserves closer attention because of its wide popularity and extensive literary reworking among Polish Jews during the twentieth century. The putative folk tale of Simkhe Plakhte projects a character drawn from the *shtetl* underclass who not only subverts the established social order of the traditional Jewish world, but also earns respect from the non-Jewish ruling class of the old Polish Commonwealth. While the tale contains maskilic elements of anti-hasidic satire, it is also a conscious expression of Jewish fantasy and wish-fulfilment, reflecting a specific Polish Jewish milieu in the nineteenth century. These elements go far towards explaining the wide interest this material has sustained.

The basic narrative elements of the Simkhe Plakhte tale are the following: Simkhe Plakhte (*simkhe*, joyful time; *plakhte*, homespun or coarse cloth), a bachelor, is an amiable water-carrier who occupies the lowest rung on the traditional Polish Jewish social ladder. Urged to marry an orphan like himself by the *shtetl* elite, Simkhe finds domestic bliss and in consequence refuses to remain a water-carrier any longer. Looking for an easier way to earn a better living, he decides that, even though he is illiterate, his best option is to become a rabbi. Dressed in traditional rabbinical garments, Simkhe enters the woods to pray. There he encounters a passing Polish nobleman in search of his favourite horse, which has gone missing, and in response to the nobleman's enquiries Simkhe indicates that the horse can be found on the other side of the forest. The Polish aristocrat gallops off, finds his horse, and in gratitude returns to the *shtetl* to reward this Jewish miracle-worker. The *shtetl* knows of no such person, but the Polish lord insists; Simkhe Plakhte is finally brought forward, and the nobleman, declaring him to be a *vunder rebbe* (*tsadik*, hasidic wonder worker) honours him with riches.

This core tale is elaborated but not reshaped in several literary reworkings. Both the chapbook entitled *Simkhe plakhte* by Yankev Morgenshtern (1820–90) and the novel of the same name by Y. Y. Trunk (1887–1961) add a second major episode to this core, in which Simkhe Plakhte solves the mysterious theft of the Polish nobleman's treasure chest containing the parchment scroll setting out his family's pedigree, as well as a final episode in which the king of Poland himself comes to recognize Simkhe Plakhte's holy genius.

Not only has this material awakened literary interest, but its figure and motif have also attracted folklorists. In his *Studies in Jewish and World Folklore* (1968), the late Haim Schwarzbaum notes that Simkhe Plakhte is 'very current in Jewish folklore, especially in the Yiddish chapbooks entitled *Simkhe plakhte*, which that excellent Yiddish writer Y. Y. Trunk has heightened with his masterly touches'.[1] The theme of Simkhe Plakhte has unquestionably enjoyed considerable popularity in the twentieth century, as is evident from the many republications of Yankev Morgenshtern's chapbook, *Simkhe plakhte, oder, Der veltshvindler* ('Simkhe Plakhte, or, The Swindler of All'), the original of which appeared some time in the 1870s or early 1880s.[2] First published in Warsaw, *Simkhe plakhte* passed through multiple editions from at least five different publishing houses in various cities, including Vilna (1894) and Przemyśl, right up to the First World War.[3] It seems also to have given rise to a sequel entitled *Der gliklikher nar, oder, Der khaver fun reb simkhe plakhte* ('The Happy Fool, or, Reb Simkhe Plakhte's friend'), dated 1882.[4] In 1932 Yankev Preger (1887–1942) transformed this material into a play, *Simkhe plakhte*, which was first performed in 1935 by the Yung-teater in Warsaw, where it enjoyed great success and was subsequently performed in all the major cities of Poland. In 1936 Maurice Schwartz played the leading role in his Yidisher Kunst Teater version in New York under the title *Der vasertreyger* ('The Water-Carrier') and then toured the Americas with the play.[5] Its enduring popularity is proved by the

---

[1] H. Schwarzbaum, *Studies in Jewish and World Folklore* (Berlin, 1968), 54.

[2] This dating is made by Zalmen Reisin. See his *Leksikon fun der yidisher literatur*, vol. ii (Vilna, 1927), 329.

[3] Ibid. The first publishing house in Warsaw to publish the chapbook seems to have been L. Nisenkorn, *c.*1880. The text was reprinted by publishers in other cities at various later dates. The problem remains that there is no extant text which bears the date of the first edition. Nisenkorn republished the text as well, but without a date. It is this edition of Morgenshtern's work, which I found at the YIVO Institute for Jewish Research in New York, that I used.

[4] See Reisin, *Leksikon*, ii. 330. The popularity of the satire *Simkhe plakhte* most likely also led him to write the satire *Der gliklikher nar, oder, Oykh der khaver fun simkhe plakhte* (1882). As I have been unable to find any copy of this text, I am obliged to depend upon Reisin's assertion and dating.

[5] Preger's original published edition (Warsaw, 1932) is subtitled *Dramatishe poeme in 3 aktn*; for the Yung-teater, *Simkhe plakhte* is a 'komedye in 3 aktn', whereas the Schwartz version is a 'folks-komedye in 2 aktn'. Schwartz also replaced Henekh Kon's original and more sophisticated score with the more popularizing music of the American Yiddish composer Aleksander Olshanetsky. See Z. Zilbertsvayg [Zylbercweig], *Leksikon fun yidishn teater*, vol. iii (New York, 1959), cols. 1889–91. Zilbertsvayg's text provides two good photographs of the two productions. It also notes elements of possible *purim-shpil* (Purim play) influence, especially that of *Der khokhem mitn nar* ('The Wise Man and the Fool'). This latter text is reproduced in Y. L. Cahan, *Yidisher folklor* (Vilna, 1938), 222–9. The erudite endnotes by Yitskhok Shiper in Cahan's book point out that this *purim-shpil* was a '"Simkhe plakhte" motiv' and a 'rekrutn-shpil' element (p. 312), which reflect Broder singer anti-hasidic elements and especially the work of Velvl Zbarzher. Zilbertsvayg in his *Leksikon* suggests that there was a *purim-shpil* entitled *Der gliklikher nar, oder, Der khaver fun reb simkhe plakhte* in 1882. This is clearly an error; the work referred to is the narrative satire of the same date written by Morgenshtern.

fact that as late as 1979 the play could still be performed successfully by the Montreal Yiddish Theatre. In Buenos Aires in 1951 Y. Y. Trunk published his novel *Simkhe plakhte fun narkove, oder, Der yidisher don kikhot* ('Simkhe Plakhte from Narkove, or, The Jewish Don Quixote'). This expansive comic novel is an elaboration of Morgenshtern's text, and, in a tongue-in-cheek brotherly way, the narrator gives credit to Morgenshtern in the text. Trunk's narrative is the last Yiddish literary reworking of the material.

Since the beginning of the twentieth century the Simkhe Plakhte material has entered various generic structures of literary expression, all based on the supposedly rich folk tales surrounding this water-carrier. However, I have been able to locate only one late example of such a folk tale, 'Shimon Plakhtah', collected by Malkah Kohen, a professional folklorist, who published it as an oral record from a Czech Jew in Israel after the Second World War.[6] This charming version follows the syncretic core tale with some elaborations. Nevertheless, were this tale 'very current in Jewish folklore', as Schwarzbaum asserts, it should have appeared frequently in various collections of folk tales published during the last century. It does not. The folklorists, perceiving Simkhe Plakhte to be part of a widespread narrative type,[7] assert that Simkhe Plakhte is an exemplum that 'belongs to the inalienable goods of Jewish and international folklore together'.[8] Folklorists thus see in the figure the repetition of a 'current' narrative type, whereas literary scholars are concerned only with one particular tale and its leading character. The most important question raised by the claims of the folklorists, however, is the extraordinary rarity of the Simkhe Plakhte figure in extant published sources.

My investigation into the origins of the Simkhe Plakhte tale convinces me that, because of the huge popularity of both Morgenshtern's chapbook and Preger's play, we confront in the figure of Simkhe Plakhte the same transformation that was worked on the songs of the 'father' of Yiddish theatre, Avrom Goldfadn: folklorization. Doubtless the narrative material in Simkhe Plakhte has folkloric elements, but the actual construction of the figure of Simkhe Plakhte and the narrative surrounding him belong to exclusively written sources. I wish to suggest that it is Morgenshtern's text that serves as the basis of the oral folk tale, which, significantly enough, has been 'collected' in Israel but nowhere else. In other words, Morgenshtern's text was 'swallowed' as a folk creation, and Morgenshtern's name as its creator has been effaced.[9] If authorship is attributed at all, it is to the

[6] M. Kohen, *Mipi ha'am: sipurei am mipi edot yisrael*, vol. ii, ed. H. Schwarzbaum (Tel Aviv, 1975–6), 35–6, cited according to Arkhiv Hasipur Ha'amami Beyisrael, MS 13.114; source: Yaakov Nyuman from Chust, Czechoslovakia.

[7] A. Aarne and S. Thompson, *The Types of the Folktale (Index to Narrative Types)* (Helsinki, 1961). Type 1641: Doctor Know-All; type 1645b: treasure discovered by interpreting a dream.

[8] Kohen, *Mipi ha'am*, 35–6.

[9] This phenomenon can be witnessed in fact in relation to another of Morgenshtern's creations. A certain B. Shtern published six volumes of *Sheloshah ahim* (Jerusalem, 1964) in which he writes on the cover: 'Loyt di velt barimte vunderlikhe geshikhte, *Mayse meshlosha akhim*, eyns fun di sheynste un

playwright Yankev Preger, whose name is associated with the Simkhe Plakhte material in consequence of the immense success of his comedy, which played up the folkloric aspects of Polish Jewry to the delight of Jews in inter-war Poland. But even Preger's text was considered a reworking of 'folk material', drawn as it was from Morgenshtern's creation which, after only fifty years, had become 'folk matter', a phenomenon noted before as a part of Judaic oral tradition in which the author's name is removed in subsequently published chapbooks, and memory of the actual author is lost to the public. Disturbed by the rarity of Simkhe Plakhte oral folk retellings, I approached both Edna Hechal, head of the Yeda Am (Israel Folklore Archives) in Haifa, and Dov Noy, Israel's leading Jewish folklorist, and both confirmed for me in email correspondence that my hypothesis is very likely correct: Morgenshtern's chapbook is the probable source of all later recorded oral retellings and, of course, of the literary creations arising from it.[10] Thus we have in the Simkhe Plakhte narrative a good example of how, through the popularization of a regional Polish Jewish phenomenon, a successful written text becomes the common property of an ethnic culture. Khayim Leyb Fuks reinforces this point in his book *Lodz shel mayle* ('Łódź of the Heavens'), where he notes that, in the development of modern Yiddish literature, the author of *Simkhe plakhte* has not been given his due, for Morgenshtern's *Simkhe plakhte* is the progenitor of both Preger's work and that of Y. Y. Trunk.[11] Even in Morgenshtern's lifetime, according to Fuks, the publishers tried to obliterate his name: because they did not want him to enjoy the fruits of his work's popularity by demanding more money, they often omitted his name as the author of the published chapbooks.[12] Since Fuks attributes the Simkhe Plakhte material directly to the story by Yankl Lerer (Morgenshtern), it is clear that the tale's popularization went hand in hand with the deliberate effacement of its author.

The concerns of this chapter are, first, to search the storyline of the Simkhe Plakhte narrative for its deeper structural significance; secondly, to interpret how and why the main character is open to literary and ideological exploitation in the various literary treatments; thirdly, to examine the surface pattern of repeated episodes testing Simkhe Plakhte, and to link this pattern to the ideological intentions of the putative folk narrative.

---

interesantste bashraybungen. Bashribn un bearbet fun B. Shtern' ('Based on the well-known wonder tale *Mayse meshlosha akhim*, one of the best and most interesting narratives. Rewritten and reworked by B. Shtern'). The name of Morgenshtern, who wrote the original, is completely effaced. The original has been reduced to folk material. Plagiarism might be a more appropriate term, but the literary material is considered to be in the 'public domain' and 'popular', namely, folk material.

[10] In the year 2000 my random questioning of Polish Jewish survivors in Texas and New York about the Simkhe Plakhte material uncovered that, if the material is remembered at all, it is either related to Preger's play or to Trunk's novel, or to some popular folk story. None of my respondents could provide an even minimally coherent folk narrative. The term *folkstimlekh* (folk-like) was commonly used about the matter.

[11] K. L. Fuks, *Lodz shel mayle* (Tel Aviv, 1972), 15. Fuks devotes his entire first chapter to resurrecting the name and accomplishment of Yankev Morgenshtern.   [12] Ibid. 19.

The four texts of the Simkhe Plakhte story that we possess—Morgenshtern's chapbook, Preger's play (with minor variants from productions in Poland, the United States, and Canada),[13] the folk tale, and Y. Y. Trunk's novel—all reproduce the same personages, motifs, events, and patterns. Setting aside the generic distinctions through which the matter is developed, it is evident that the function of the chief character and the treatment of the various events and sequences are most affected by ideological perspectives. Schwarzbaum's interpretation of the Simkhe Plakhte 'folk tale' places it in the category of a folk-tale type known as Doctor Know-All.[14] Within the context of world folklore, this may be true. The various literary treatments of the Simkhe Plakhte material generally conform to this interpretation, in which the hero can be seen as a version of Molière's hero in *Le Médecin malgré lui*. This chapter, on the other hand, seeks to reveal in the hero and his adventures a rebuttal or subversion of the non-Jewish and rabbinic dominating realities of ordinary Jewish life in Poland during earlier centuries, and their implied continuation at the time of the material's various artistic re-creations. From internal evidence I aim to show that the successful comic hero material of Simkhe Plakhte the water-carrier comically subverts traditional Jewish and Polish power structures in order to express both the resentments and the suppressed desires of the Jewish lower classes. That is, the reworked narratives aim to reclaim the dignity of the Jewish folk from both the Jewish ruling class and the Polish overlord. This seeming impossibility is achieved through Simkhe Plakhte's luck, ruse, and subversion. There is at the same time a sharp implied critique of the hasidic world with its superstitious belief in the powers of the *vunder rebbe* and an explicit narrative critique of the Christian world and its discriminatory treatment of Jews.

All the texts are set in a self-contained *shtetl* ordered according to the traditional social hierarchy. The presumed locality, somewhere in the old Polish Commonwealth, becomes more important only in later texts. The setting, however, is never innocent. When Morgenshtern gave the name of the country in which he sets his narrative as Uts, he was seeking a generalized Jewish exilic setting using the biblical allusion to Erets Uts, the land of Job, which is intended to imply both anywhere and nowhere. In 1880 Poland per se did not exist except as a Russian dependency and a historic memory. Uts is therefore anywhere in the Jewish diaspora. Furthermore, the name of the *shtetl* in Morgenshtern's *Simkhe plakhte* is Narkov, or Fools' Town, a name that parallels the identical usage and function of Glupsk, Mendele Moykher Sforim's Russian Fools' Town. Through these allegorical names both writers were able to heap scorn upon the traditional *shtetl*, while the names more widely imply a manifestly maskilic perspective, with all Ashkenaz being subjected to scrutiny. Y. Y. Trunk turned Narkov into Narkove, giving the town a more specifically Yiddish flavour and explicitly insisting on its being located in Congress Poland: 'in

---

[13] These are available in the archives of the YIVO Institute for Jewish Research in New York.
[14] Aarne and Thompson, *The Types of the Folktale*, type 1641: Doctor Know-All.

same yidishn gedikhtenish fun fartsaytishn poyln iz gelegn gor a kleyn shtetele . . . narkove' ('in the most intensely Jewish setting of long-ago Poland lay a small town . . . Narkove').[15] But the connotations of the Polish Jewish setting are no less intense in Preger, who even employs the archaic Polish Yiddish dialect forms of the second-person singular *ets* and *enk* to heighten the characteristics of Polish Jewishness.[16] In Preger's treatment of Simkhe Plakhte, indeed, one can most fully appreciate the play's ideological drive to emphasize the uniqueness of Poland's Jews, a determination to celebrate their distinctiveness, setting them apart from, and making them quite unlike, the Jews of Lithuania, for example, and of course quite unlike the surrounding Polish Christian world.

The setting of the Simkhe Plakhte material always seeks to define an intact, traditionally ordered *shtetl* world sharply removed from the surrounding world of the Other. The *shtetl* is Jewish, organized and ordered by Jewish law and traditions, and seemingly safe. The world outside the *shtetl* is what the Jews consider *hefker*, wild and dangerous, a world of untamed nature and Polish gentry whose menacing *gzeyres* (evil decrees) are perpetually hovering. A dual perspective of space and perception runs throughout the narratives, separating not only two ethnicities, but also two wholly different world-views. The major events that define the successes of Simkhe Plakhte occur outside the milieu of the *shtetl*, distant from the everyday life of the town-dwelling Jew. What happens outside carries little weight inside the Jewish community unless it threatens the order of the *shtetl*. As each episode in the developing adventures of Simkhe Plakhte expands territorially from the forest to the court of the Polish nobleman to the palace of the king of Poland in Warsaw, the *shtetl* continues to remain tightly closed, uninterested in or scornful of the outside world.

Narkov, isolated by the surrounding forest, the traditional symbol of wild and uncontrolled nature, remains content in its aloneness. It accepts as given the fact that the Other surrounds it, but the *shtetl* refuses to interact with that Other except under the duress of economic necessity and political obedience to the overlord. The Polish nobleman's appreciation and enriching of Simkhe Plakhte has no meaning for the Jewish community as a whole. On the contrary, it underscores for the *shtetl* Jews the profound ignorance of the Polish nobility who can regard an illiterate water-carrier as a *vunder rebbe*. Simkhe Plakhte, a long-time resident of the town, wants the respect he feels he deserves, but the gifts of the Polish nobleman do not

---

[15] Y. Y. Trunk, *Simkhe plakhte fun narkove, oder, Der yidisher don kikhot* (Buenos Aires, 1951), 15.

[16] Preger, *Simkhe plakhte*, 20. One can feel the rich difference in the second-person singular familiar and the high tone of the formal *ets* in the following exchange:

MALKELE. Ober simkhe, vos hostu azoyns gezogt dem porets?

BEYLE. A tsadik veyst shoyn vos tsu zogn. Un ets zolt im nisht rufn simkhe, nor rebbe!

The dative of *ets* can be seen in this example:

YANKEL SHOYFER. Yakh [also dialectal for *ikh*] zog enk, yidn, az di mayse iz nisht glatik. (p. 21)

bring him the slightest recognition from the Jewish ruling class. In this way the narrative offers an implied critique of the traditional Jewish world: its spatial setting, by demarcating the physical boundaries separating *shtetl* Jews from Polish non-Jews, points out the constricted vision of the Jews.

The temporal frame is no less an indicator of signification. All the narratives situate their events in a *fartsaytishn Poyln* (long-ago Poland) that seems to be some time during the Poniatowski period when the Polish state still existed but the king dwelled insecurely in Warsaw. The texts with which I am dealing all use that past as a sort of Jewish 'Sarmatian' period when 'lost time' seemed more stable and ordered, and problems were small. But there is an interrelationship between the *fartsaytn* of the tale and the present of the text. Before the state's demise, Poland at the end of the eighteenth century indeed seemed 'pastoral' in retrospect, and is therefore used in deliberate contrast to the unstable and difficult present. This contrast could only have been a deliberate choice on the part of the writers. Morgenshtern's 1880 chapbook is written against the reality of a lost Poland and tsarist repression of both Poles and Jews; Preger's 1932 comedy indulges in a nostalgia for a lost Polish past at the very time when the Jews of inter-war independent Poland were experiencing economic and social upheaval as well as unprecedented antisemitism. Trunk's 1951 novel deploys its narrative voice with deft irony, deliberately confusing two periods, both of which imply *fartsaytishn Poyln*: Simkhe Plakhte's existence in the eighteenth century together with a last evocation of pre-Holocaust Jewish folk life. Both periods are *fartsaytn* for the author–narrator Trunk, a survivor who wrote his novel in New York and published it in Buenos Aires. The text consciously employs the comedic, with all the folklore it can possibly muster, to depict the past and to attenuate the pain of the omnipresent memory of a lost world. This sense of dual time—the past time of the story and the present time of the author and reader— forces upon the audience a consciousness that the story was always a wish incapable of fulfilment. This seemingly simple narrative's play with time poignantly articulates Proust's awareness that 'les seuls paradis sont les paradis perdus'.

In all the texts an earlier time frames the local setting, permitting both literary and aesthetic distance between text and reader as well as proffering both irony and appreciation of seemingly happier times. The texts all have comic endings that imply magical restoration, and the far-off time that all share obstructs the entry of the obtrusive present with its bitter insecurities in every way except through the irony of style. The surface of the texts in 'magical' time is escapist, but a closer reading hints broadly at the tensions running through the works.

The narrative can be divided into four basic sequences or motifs that repay attention: first, the marriage; secondly, the new career as *rebbe*; thirdly, the testing of the new holy man; and fourthly, the reward. All imply inversion: a reversal of a norm, a change in status, career, performance, and accomplishment, the transformation of failure into success, of movement from the bottom to the top. Each motif delineates an alteration, and each alteration is a linear improvement. In all four cases, when the tale opens, Simkhe Plakhte, the hero, is a lowly and exploited water-carrier, illiterate, ignorant of Judaism, an orphan, a bastard, mocked and insulted by being given empty plates to lick at weddings. He is also not very intelligent, standing closer to non-Jewish peasants than to *shtetl* Jews. His very name signifies his outcast condition.

The first sequence to develop the tale's action is Simkhe's unexpected marriage. He is too poor to marry but, for its own interests, the community underwrites the marriage, either seeking to perform a good deed to avert a threatened plague (as in the folk tale and the play) or to please the town rabbi's wife, who wishes to marry off an orphan girl under her protection (as in the prose texts). In all cases the ruling class of the *shtetl* community, which has hitherto exploited the water-carrier, effectively changes his civil status by sanctioning his marriage. This marriage removes him from the condition of pariah and makes him 'respectable'. He can now look forward to a better life. In his changed social condition the role of his new wife is crucial, for not only can she offer the comforts of domesticity and the knowledge of another kind of existence, but she also becomes her husband's 'co-conspirator' and worthy helpmate. In the literary texts, particularly, she is her husband's major supporter and chief motivator, for while she may be the realist who takes a full share in planning and scheming, she also knows when it is essential for her husband to find work because they need food.

The second motif is the hero's determination to embark on a new career. In the versions of Morgenshtern, Trunk, and the folk tale, Simkhe Plakhte's decision to don the *zhupitse* (robe) of a *rebbe* and to act as one is presented as comic, for it inverts the current structure, subverting the whole elitist social system of the community. By dressing up in a *zhupitse* and putting a *spodek* on his head, the traditional outfit of a Polish hasidic rabbi, Simkhe Plakhte assumes a disguise that not only underlines the essential Polish placement of the tale—a Lithuanian rabbi would wear a coat and hat with different cuts and shapes—but also mocks the classic rabbinic role itself, since that role is now presented merely as a matter of external costuming without any internal content. The costume itself is thus turned into a source of comic scorn through which Simkhe Plakhte's meteoric rise to eminence comes to express the resentment of the *shtetl*'s lower classes towards the class that governs them. Hence the playful quality of the tale sets up a carnivalesque mockery both of the conventional status of the *rebbe* and of the internal structure of *shtetl* life itself.

Preger's play employs the dream-sequence device made famous in Sholem Aleichem's Tevye stories, through which Simkhe's wife learns from her dead father that her husband's real calling is to be a *rebbe*. Taken in this context, the narrative appears as a maskilic attack that sets out to subvert hitherto unchallenged rabbinic authority. It mocks those religious activities that have sprouted into traditions, particularly the avid collecting of *pidyen*, the money given to the *rebbe* in return for his advice and blessings. This entire sequence is an extended ridicule of religious posturing. When Simkhe, clad in full rabbinical costume, appears for the first time before the townspeople, they vociferously deride him for having usurped a role that normally commands the highest respect. Only Simkhe himself believes in his bluff. He has learned the outward signs of how to act 'rabbinical'—the high comic moment—and attempts to pass as authentic by insisting that 'clothes make the man'. The double edge of his comic role is heightened by his ignorance of any real rabbinic substance, an ignorance that in turn implies that rabbinic 'substance' is in reality nothing at all. In the versions by Morgenshtern and Trunk the derisive *shtetl* forces Simkhe to flee to the woods, an area wholly outside Jewish jurisdiction. Once there, in a place beyond normative Jewish governance, Simkhe is transformed into a *vunder rebbe*.

The third motif, the testing of the new holy man, must of necessity take place in a forest, a place consistently symbolic, in folklore and its literature, of the untamed world of nature, wholly outside the control of humankind and operating according to its own laws, a world frighteningly perceived by the Jewish mind as *hefker*. In the wilds of nature all holy men must at some time or another in their lives isolate themselves and, in a state of self-encounter beyond the commonplace, alone with nature and with God, seek to discover their authenticity of self. So Simkhe Plakhte, bewildered, flees into the forest and prays like the Ba'al Shem Tov, facing a tree—itself a traditional symbol of communion with the transcendent and a key element in the hagiography of the Ba'al Shem. In this parodic context the native skills of the chief character, and his ability to deal with adversity, will be tested.

This forest motif can be divided into two parts: first, the encounter between the Polish nobleman and Simkhe; and secondly, the authentication of Reb Simkhe. When, in these woods, the Polish nobleman comes upon Simkhe Plakhte in the full costume of rabbinical office, two worlds and two wholly disparate classes meet. There are naturally misreadings on both sides. The nobleman's favourite horse has fled and is missing somewhere in the forest. The Polish aristocrat is desperate. The loss of his horse must be read as a personal loss of control and as a threat to his continued exercise of power. The situation of the horse that has escaped from its master into the forest parallels that of Simkhe, who has fled from the ordered *shtetl* into the wild woods, the emblem of freedom, of discarding human rule, of a primal state of being, and even of psychological chaos exemplified, for instance, in the opening lines of Dante's *Inferno*. Both Jew and non-Jew are in fact desperate. The self-esteem of both is at stake. Both need to get out of the forest, but only once each of them has achieved his objective. For the nobleman, to find his horse would restore his absolute power. For Simkhe, his self-construction as a revivified Ba'al Shem Tov would transform this forest experience into an essential rite of passage towards the establishment of his new career. He would acquire spiritual wealth, the inner correlative of his outer garments. The satiric thrust of this narrative matter, of course, derives from maskilic contempt for the absence of the real learning and genuine knowledge that should characterize a true rabbi. Simkhe's fear of the nobleman, and his announcement that the missing horse is on the other side of the forest being threatened by wolves, is a verbal expression of terror uttered in desperation to protect himself from and rid himself of the nobleman, a dangerous intruder. His panicky utterance can hardly be read as a prophecy, as it is taken to be by the nobleman. This naivety, however, is not what gives importance to this scene; rather, it is the emerging symbiotic relationship between the two: the Polish overlord needs his Jewish *vunder rebbe* and the Jew needs the nobleman's protection and support.

The parody of the Ba'al Shem Tov enacted by an ignorant water-carrier is intended to chastise if not to subvert hasidic authority. But the subversion undercuts both the Jewish and the non-Jewish authorities. In the forest men are abruptly reduced to their shared condition of human vulnerability and are made equals. The water-carrier, the lowest of the Jewish low in borrowed rabbinical robes, encounters the all-powerful ruling non-Jew, who bears life and death in his hands. The magical inversion of customary intercultural encounter and behaviour of Jew and Polish noble produces a carnivalesque compensation for the actual bitter reality outside the text.

Simkhe Plakhte's magical rise as a result of accidentally directing the nobleman to his missing horse produces a comic release. Simkhe will now become what he is not. The fact that the nobleman does indeed find his horse in exactly the way described by Simkhe Plakhte serves as the springboard for all the subsequent action, even though the way the truth emerges is treated in slightly different ways in the sources. In the folk-tale retelling, Simkhe has already sighted the animal and so has told the truth, which is then misinterpreted as a 'prophetic' insight. Morgenshtern and Preger reveal a Simkhe both hungry and frightened, who desperately wants to terminate this menacing encounter as quickly as possible and therefore tells a lie that turns out to be the truth. In Trunk's novel the new *shames* (sexton), Fayvl, interprets for Simkhe, and sends the nobleman off in the 'right' direction. In fact, throughout Trunk's narrative it is Fayvl who always speaks for Simkhe, not unlike the way in which Nathan of Gaza so often spoke for Shabbetai Tsevi. In all the narratives, however, the nobleman retrieves his horse, leading to a restoration that brings good fortune. The nobleman and Simkhe Plakhte are at all times ignorant of each other's nature, both as fellow human beings and with respect to their differing motivations. Hence their meeting in the forest is invested with symbolic appropriateness, for both are blind, lacking proper enlightenment.

The fourth motif treats the nobleman's rewarding of Simkhe Plakhte for the services he has rendered. The setting for this rewarding returns, significantly, to the *shtetl*, to the world of men, of hierarchy, of Jewish subordination and Polish overlordship. The Polish aristocrat 'ennobles' Simkhe Plakhte by investing him with the magical powers of a *vunder rebbe*. The rabbinic and ruling Jewish *shtetl* authorities do no such thing. The dividing line between Jewish and non-Jewish authority remains sharp and immovable. The Polish lord asserts his authority with de facto recognition of his chosen Jew which the Jewish *shtetl* elect must respect, but they are not obliged to grant that Jew de jure acceptance. Simkhe Plakhte's new wealth and honour leaves the community leadership astonished but not cowed. Nevertheless, in their subordinate position their hands are tied by the decisions of the ruler. Hence the carnivalesque inversion of Simkhe Plakhte's fortune, which slaps down the snobbery of the Jewish elite, and voices the suppressed anger of the folk (the ordinary reader), who can now vicariously exact a momentary and highly enjoyable revenge.

Ensconced in new living quarters in the town square and honoured by the nobleman, Simkhe Plakhte acquires hangers-on, and word spreads among the townspeople that he is a *lamed-vovnik* (a saintly figure, one of the thirty-six just men). Morgenshtern, Preger, Trunk, and the recorded folk tale all concur on this point. Simkhe is transformed into a holy figure. His presence on the town square symbolizes his new authority, and his dwelling becomes an alternative locus of power. Now another subtle critique emerges from the narrative event: the ruling elite is insensitive to the interests of the poor, so the *vunder rebbe* offers alternative advice that is neither more nor less useful. A fraud he may be, but he believes in himself; so the Jewish folk masses believe in him as well. The narrative's mockery of the elite gathers force through the emergence of a water-carrier, a non-person as it were, to a position of dignity and respect for which the masses themselves all yearn. The irony, of course, remains: an accident of luck, a costume, and a naive Polish lord all combine to confirm the reality of the new *rebbe* and, in doing so, expose the fraudulence of this venerated hasidic institution.

The storyline can be developed ad infinitum by variations on the third and fourth motifs. Indeed this is exactly the way both Morgenshtern and Trunk expand their respective narratives. With piquant folkloric flavour, Morgenshtern portrays the way Simkhe uses luck and subterfuge to solve the mystery of the stolen chest containing a parchment on which the nobleman's genealogy is written. Simkhe learns where the chest is hidden from Stefan, a gullible Polish peasant thief, and then 'proves' his wondrous powers once more by 'discovering' the chest the next day. Trunk reworks the same motifs of luck and fulfilment through subterfuge, again attributing the initiative to Fayvl, Simkhe's *shames*. By deliberately selecting as Simkhe's second 'test' the loss of the genealogy parchment, Morgenshtern evidently seeks to question the legitimacy of the nobleman's heritage. His version of the tale therefore challenges the authority of a hereditary aristocracy whose right to rule was founded originally on conquest and bloodshed.

In the versions of both Morgenshtern and Trunk, the fourth episode takes place in the capital, Warsaw. The king of Poland wishes to test the abilities of Simkhe the *vunder rebbe* so that he can be called upon to advise the kingdom. Terrified, Simkhe is about to reveal that he is not what he seems to be, but in doing so he uses metaphorical language that inadvertently unmasks the secret the king was going to ask him to reveal. The royal reward is massive, and the tale ends with Simkhe's restoration to happiness and triumph. The lowest-ranking Jew has reached the highest peak of respect, and his fraud has proved to be a complete success. Now both Poles and Jews honour him, despite the fact that the ruling Jewish elite consistently refuses to accept him. Simkhe's return to his *shtetl* can be read as both a personal triumph and a legitimization of the Jews in their own *shtetl* home.

The other characters in the narrative all serve as foils for Simkhe Plakhte. The *shtetl* rabbi, who radically alters Simkhe Plakhte's status by marrying him off to an orphan, personifies the Jewish community. While his new wife is supportive of Simkhe, his principal supporter is the Polish nobleman. These are the narrative's key figures, and they are in all cases clear-cut types with no psychological development and little significant presence except for their links to dramatic turning points, particularly in Preger's comedy. The elaborations of the literary texts include further figures that function chiefly as additional helpers. The figure of the Litvak appears first in Preger and is borrowed later by Trunk; he may well be an elaboration of the *shames* who teaches Simkhe some Talmud in Morgenshtern's version. The Litvak in Preger's play appears as an exploitative outsider and a figure of ridicule, emphasized by his comic accent, in which he pronounces every *shin* as 's': thus, for example, instead of *droshe* (sermon), the Litvak says *drose*.[17] This Litvak becomes Simkhe Plakhte's *shames*. Exploiting Simkhe's role as a *vunder rebbe* for his own dishonest ends, he and his partner in crime, the innkeeper Reb Yosele Parnas, steal the *pidyen* offerings for themselves. In Trunk's novel the figure of the Litvak is Reb Fayvke or Fayvl, the glib-tongued caricature of the learned Litvak, who joins Simkhe because he sees Simkhe's naivety as a path for himself into the wider world. In Trunk's novel Fayvl's role takes over the trickster aspects of Morgenshtern's Simkhe Plakhte; Fayvke the Litvak plays Sancho Panza to the sage fool Don Quixote Simkhe. If Preger's Litvak is comically negative, exposing contemporary tensions that were actually felt, particularly in Warsaw, with the influx into Poland of Lithuanian Jews at the end of the nineteenth century, Trunk's post-Holocaust novel assigns to the Litvak his stock role as rationalist and mediator, reflecting Trunk's wider purpose to capture the full panoply of rich east European Jewish life now destroyed for ever. In both Preger and Trunk the innkeeper or arendar appears as a tough businessman. Preger's innkeeper is a capitalist exploiter in cahoots with the crooked Litvak, but Trunk's innkeeper, following more closely the model established by Cervantes, offers a sheltering Jewish haven for Simkhe during his time of trials.

Apart from Simkhe, the *porets*, or nobleman, is invested with the widest variety of personality. In Morgenshtern the nobleman is presented as respectful of religious and mystical powers. In Preger he is a figure of comedy who plays the stock role of Christian antisemite but who, after finding his horse, becomes a *khosid* of Reb Simkhe. In Trunk the aristocrat is named Voytsekh Tshuplak-Tshaplinski and is depicted as a stereotypical patrician appreciative of Simkhe to the point of offering this *vunder rebbe* the formal attentions normally reserved only for other

---

[17] Preger, *Simkhe plakhte*, 3.

members of the Polish *szlachta*. All these personages are simply agents of various forces in society and human nature, and their functions in the narrative are merely to engineer the trials and reversals that must be overcome in order to bring about a happy conclusion.

The putative folk tale and all its literary treatments debunk the traditional hierarchy of both Polish and Jewish societies, exposing instead the raw truths of power and control. As the rabbi of the *shtetl* stands at the head of Jewish society and the water-carrier stands at its foot, so Stefan the peasant occupies the lowest rung on the Christian social ladder and the Polish aristocrat the highest. The established social structure is comically but severely shaken both by the marriage of Simkhe, initiated by the rabbi, and by the elevation of Simkhe to the status of *vunder rebbe*, initiated by the Polish nobleman. Both Jewish and non-Jewish leadership act with the sheer arrogance of power, unaware of the possible consequences of their actions. In the literary treatments Simkhe is able to break through the barriers of cultural difference through his personal subterfuge and intelligence, and through the widespread popular belief in the existence of magical powers that a 'holy figure' possesses. But the ironic use of the Polish nobleman as assistant uncovers the wholly surrealist and subversive aspect of the tale. The fact that they ignore Polish hegemony exposes not only the elitism of the Jewish communal leadership, but also their weakness in the face of real temporal power. This tale type, it is evident, elaborates the role of underdog who manages to succeed in two societies. It is worth attempting to understand the purpose of this role as personified in the figure of Simkhe Plakhte.

Morgenshtern's chapbook, the chief source of the tale's popularity, has as its subtitle *Der veltshvindler*, the world-swindler, or the swindler of all. All three episodes examined above reveal the swindler's luck, cunning, and success against improbable odds. The earliest critics of the work recognized its anti-hasidic bias, demonstrated in the water-carrier's excellent mimicry of the style of the *vunder rebbe* through telling gestures alone, without possessing any substantive Jewish knowledge. Although he is a bit of a coward when put to the test, Simkhe has abundant vitality and capacity for action, demonstrating his skills on his feet and achieving his victories. Morgenshtern wants simultaneously to entertain and to provide a cautionary tale. For him, Simkhe is a *veltshvindler* because he has dared to represent himself as a religious authority when he is in fact an ignoramus. On the sabbath, as a comic example, he gets so worked up in delivering his *droshe* that he eats the fish and meat that is supposed to remain for his followers to consume (*shirayim*).[18] Yet his 'swindle' is a success: he lives happily into old age surrounded by many children who do him honour by learning a trade and prospering.[19] Morgenshtern's tale thus concludes on a moralistic note. This maskilic conclusion rewards the reader by displacing the resentments against the oppressive social structure into the reader's

---

[18] Morgenshtern, *Simkhe plakhte*, 50. [19] Ibid. 53–4.

delight in empathizing with the nonentity Simkhe outmanoeuvring both the *zaydene yidn* (Jewish elite) and the Polish *szlachta*. But Morgenshtern makes a final appeal to hard work with a real trade, rather than to the hoodwinking of innocent people, as the best route to survival. No matter how successful Simkhe Plakhte's career may have turned out, it is in essence the career of a *luftmentsh*, the ne'er-do-well dreamer so brilliantly to be developed a short while later by Sholem Aleichem in the character of Menakhem Mendl. However, as a tale of wish-fulfilment show-ing the magically successful rise of the underdog it succeeds fully. As an exemplary tale as well, it debunks the traditional hasidic world by insisting that following a proper trade provides the best security for Jewish life in modern times. In fact this tale was written in the industrial city of Łódź, and first served as moral entertain-ment for that city's working class. Morgenshtern's Simkhe Plakhte is a burlesque of the hasidic *mayse nore*, or wonder tale, and a parody of hasidic hagiography.

Trunk's 1951 novel frames the above narrative by accepting all its events and pretending merely to elaborate the earlier text in order to flesh out the story. But Trunk also makes himself a sophisticated extradiegetic narrator who can be con-sciously intrusive, from time to time openly embedding Morgenshtern's text into his own version when he wants his text's folkic flavour to be particularly racy. At times he will even depart from the diegesis to allude to the reality of Morgenshtern's time, 1880, and even to 1938, when, in the impoverished Łódź neighbourhood of Bałuty, Trunk came upon an old beggar woman he was told was Morgenshtern's only daughter.[20] Trunk's tale therefore presents the comedic world of *fartsaytishn Poyln* as a far better place in which to have lived than the unbearable reality of the modern world outside the text, be it 1938 or 1951. Trunk is a self-conscious narrator—one might even suggest a kind of postmodernist—who teases his reader as he steadily transforms Morgenshtern's fifty-four-page chapbook into his own 370-page novel. This novel's play with time and chronology carries great weight, for while the text has explicitly stopped the clock in some 'Poland in days of yore', the reader cannot help but be conscious that the narratorial presence is the voice of a survivor speaking in the immediate aftermath of the Holocaust. The novel is a paean to the destroyed Polish Jewish world in general, and in particular to Morgen-shtern of Łódź, who is lauded for having captured so aptly the living spirit of the folk. Embracing his predecessor's version, Trunk also maintains continuity with the city of Łódź, to which he was himself strongly attached. While he plays with the earlier writer's aesthetic naivety, he nevertheless recognizes his predecessor's narratorial skills—which are actually better than Trunk's own—as well as his imaginative flair. The novel's structure, a deliberate imitation of the old Yiddish chapbook style, using very short chapters with very long chapter headings, also links this tradition back to the style of early Spanish novels, particularly to the adventures of Quixote, which serves as the secondary title of the work: *Simkhe*

---

[20] Trunk, *Simkhe plakhte*, 31.

plakhte fun narkove, oder, Der yidisher don kikhot. This secondary title completely reorients the text. Trunk promises an elaboration of Morgenshtern's sequences and motifs and, indeed, he keeps his promise, but his narrative perspective actually presents an entirely different viewpoint.

In Trunk's version Simkhe Plakhte is metamorphosed into a Jewish Don Quixote, a passive figure of the wise fool type—he is even compared to a golem—who needs the realistic eyes of Reb Fayvl, his Sancho Panza, as the practical man of action who alone is capable of overcoming obstacles. Trunk thus employs a *fin-de-siècle* interpretation of *Don Quixote* particularly prevalent in Slavonic cultures, where the Spanish work was much loved. Each chapter of his novel permits a flow of rich idiomatic folk Yiddish to pour out as every little scene of the various motifs portrays in loving detail the various individual figures brought into play, as if this presentation were to be one last wedding feast—as indeed it tragically was for Trunk. By using the stock comic figures of vanished east European Jewish life, he can indulge in a nostalgic review of what the old Jewish *eygns* (uniqueness) was really like, and he can permit his reader to share with him what has been lost for ever, warding off the pain by deploying the comic mode. Simkhe Plakhte is therefore airbrushed into a passive good-natured type who wants a better life and so decides to become a *rebbe*. Trunk manipulates the type to reflect a lost *shtetl* lifestyle, and thus evokes that Poland whose very provinciality Morgenshtern had so severely criticized.

If Trunk sought to prove that east European Jewry was a fusion of Simkhe's wise foolishness with Reb Fayvl's logical coolness, he failed. Rather, as in the Spanish novel, he shows them to be two different types of humankind, not just of Jewry. What does emerge from Trunk's reworking, however, is an aching effort to present Jews and Poles as jointly and fruitfully inhabiting the same land, and to show how two Jewish characters can enhance everyone's life in Poland. In this novel the pain and bitterness of the Holocaust is repressed by a fictional celebration of the way Simkhe and Fayvl overcome impossible odds. Becoming lost in this fictive Poland of yore permits the reader to embrace a simple, almost childish wish-fulfilment dream that brutal reality had wholly precluded. Yet none of this can entirely obscure the encroaching shadows. Trunk may well also have been influenced by the knowledge that what was left of his readership in 1951 would still have kept this story vividly in mind as a result of the successful play of the same name that so dominated Poland in the late 1930s. Preger's play thereby provides another link to the continuity and uniqueness of Polish Jewry.

The play, published in 1932, reached the stage of the Yung-teater in 1935, and it was then triumphantly performed in every important city in pre-war Poland as well as in the United States and elsewhere. This play empathized with the *doyiker* position of Bundism (commitment to the Diasporic *here* against the Zionist *there*) by celebrating a distinctive east European Jewish setting and a wonder tale with anti-religious bite. The play is in reality an operetta, an interface with early Goldfadn theatre, filled with an abundance of songs and dances and folk types. Today the libretto seems dated and awkward, but it enjoyed massive popularity in its own time. In the play Simkhe Plakhte is transformed into a passive figure—the source of Trunk's characterization, I suspect—who only wishes to eat and to sleep with the housemaid despite the fact that he is married. At the same time we are shown the would-be capitalists, the innkeeper and the Litvak, who desperately manoeuvre to protect Reb Simkhe, the goose that lays their golden eggs. By playing up the conflict between the folk masses and these capitalist exploiters, the play reeks of folk Marxism, which comes to a head when Simkhe casts off his *zhupitse* to rejoin the labouring masses and goes off in *plakhte* (homespun), leaving the maid to incite masses to sweep away the real *veltshvindlers*, the capitalist innkeeper and the Litvak. The play sneers at religion as an opiate, and reinforces class conflict as a fact of life. The surface comedy joins the deeper structure of the Simkhe Plakhte material boldly to express the bitter frustrations of the lower classes. In Preger's construction of a folk comedy that ends with the return of Simkhe to his origins and the victory of the Jewish folk masses over their capitalist oppressors, we see a desperate attempt to magnify awareness of a unique east European Jewish culture linked to a yearning for redemptive socialism which relieves genuine class resentment by submerging it in theatre fun.[21] Were one a Bundist in the 1930s, Simkhe Plakhte, a water-carrier who returns to his working-class origins, would have occupied an ideologically correct position. The play emphasizes the second motif, the new career, but reduces the first and third sequences to vestigial remains and makes the fourth, reward, impossible. Nevertheless, all the Simkhe Plakhte narratives share the lower-class frustrations exemplified in the basic storyline's deep structure.

The basic 'tale type' of Simkhe Plakhte is clearly not a folk tale at all, but a narrative conceived by the popular writer Yankev Morgenshtern of Łódź, whose story was so compelling on many levels that it entered the popular culture and the folk mind to become a putative folk tale that was subsequently elaborated by other Polish Jewish authors. The story succeeds as a wish-fulfilment fantasy, and serves to articulate the protest of the underdog, whose magical worldly success provides a much-needed comic catharsis for the masses. The tale, however, conceals a deep structure of frustration, resentment, and hostility. The adaptability of the narrative matter, its joyous surface optimism, and the worldly success of its hero must all have provided a remarkable release of tension in the difficult years of its most

---

[21] Nakhmen Mayzil (*Literarishe bleter* (1936), no. 1, 9) interprets the work as 'a burlesque, somewhere between a comedy and a parody'. M. Kitay ('Arum Simkhe Plakhte', *Literarishe bleter* (1936), no. 12, 192) argues that the play 'derfilt gevise sotsial-oysklerishes funktsyes velkhe zenen nokh haynt aktuel ba undz . . . shvindler un fanatiker' ('provides particular socially illuminating types which are still relevant in our own day . . . the swindler and the fanatic'). Abraham Cahan (*Forverts* (28 Dec. 1936), 5) expresses mixed feelings about the work but finally likes it. He sees it as a play built on 'an alter folks-mayse . . . gegn dem khsidishn obergloybn un gegn di neviyim vos nutsn im oys in zeyere gabe "biznes" ' ('an old folk tale . . . against hasidic superstition and against those [so-called] prophets who exploit it in their "business" of managing the *tsadikim*').

intense popularity, between 1880 and 1951. Simkhe Plakhte permitted Jews a full identification with one of their own. His tale reinforced the uniqueness of Polish Jewish identity and continuity. It also happened to be one of those rare Jewish narratives in which the Jewish underdog wins fully and unconditionally. In all its variants Simkhe Plakhte partakes wholly in what the Jewish folk masses of eastern Europe yearned for: *oysher vekoved* (wealth and honour).

Between Poland and Germany: Jewish Religious Practices in Illustrated Postcards of the Early Twentieth Century

SHALOM SABAR

THE BEGINNINGS OF THE ILLUSTRATED POSTCARD IN GERMANY AND POLAND

TOURISTS throughout the world buy millions of illustrated postcards every year, which they send to their relatives and friends, or save for themselves to remind them of the places they visited. In most cases the postcards are not saved for long. Some people pile them into shoeboxes, though with the passage of time they generally forget about them or why they bought them. This seems to have been case since illustrated postcards first came into use in the 1880s.[1] But this homely artefact knew days of splendour much grander than the age of the Internet, with its plethora of images. It was in the years 1898–1918 that the production and demand for illustrated postcards were at their peak. During these years the postcard business flourished as the fashion for postcard purchase and collection swept many sections of society. Publishers printed various series of cards that were individually numbered for the benefit of collectors; they were sold on special stands in the streets of large cities, and collectors' clubs specializing in various postcard themes sprang up in European and American cities.[2]

The production of Jewish postcards developed within this context, with the Jewish bourgeoisie seeking to imitate the trends within the wider society while strictly limiting the choice of subjects to those they felt were appropriate and

---

[1] On the early illustrated postcards, see J. R. Burdick, *Pioneer Postcards: The Story of the Mailing Cards to 1898* (New York, [1964]); F. Staff, *The Picture Postcard and its Origins* (London, 1966), esp. 53–63.

[2] On the phenomenon of the 'Postal Card Craze', a term coined by the journalist Julian Ralph in the Feb. 1902 issue of *Cosmopolitan*, see D. B. Ryan, *Picture Postcards in the United States, 1893–1918* (New York, 1982); W. Duval and V. Monahan, *Collecting Postcards in Colour, 1894–1914* (Poole, 1978). On 'the craze for collecting [postcards]' in this period, see Staff, *The Picture Postcard*, 64–81.

reflected their world. The fact that the Jews in this period wanted to participate in the postcard phenomenon carries an important social message, and, as is implied in the common Hebrew term for the postcard at the time, *mikhtav galui* (open letter), this desire was clear for all to see. The printing and acquisition of postcards signified acceptance of and support for the public image portrayed upon them. They are therefore a mirror of the ideology and values of turn-of-the-century Jewish society as that society wished to present them. At the same time the postcards contain valuable ethnographic information about the lives of Jews during those years: their appearance and dress, utensils and ceremonial objects, furnishings of homes and synagogues, and so on.

The production of Jewish postcards was concentrated in three centres: two in Europe (Germany and Poland) and one in the United States (primarily New York).[3] The American centre drew its inspiration to a great extent from Europe, although it also created a world of images specific to American Jews. My focus here, however, is on the two European centres, each of which produced a great number of original and unique postcards. Germany may be considered the birthplace of the Jewish illustrated postcard: the earliest examples known to us were produced there in the 1880s. Polish Jews followed the German lead, with publishers, primarily in Warsaw, engaging in the business during the first two decades of the twentieth century. However, this imitation of the German fashion was not always received with enthusiasm. In 1888 in the pages of the monthly *Izraelita*, for example, a periodical which promoted the integration of Jews into Polish culture, one writer spoke out against the use of ornate and ostentatious postcards for Rosh Hashanah because of their 'coquettishness' as compared to the 'modesty' of earlier generations. He strongly criticized both the amounts invested in buying and sending the postcards, as well as the images themselves.[4] Despite such views, the postcards were a great success, and the number of different cards produced in Poland far exceeded that in Germany.

ILLUSTRATING JEWISH RELIGIOUS PRACTICES IN GERMANY AND POLAND

Before we turn to the portrayal of Jewish religious practices in the postcards, it is useful to note some of the more general characteristics of such portrayals in the two countries. The primary source for such illustrations in German postcards was the celebrated series of pictures 'Bilder aus dem altjüdischen Familienleben' ('Scenes of Traditional Jewish Family Life') by Moritz Daniel Oppenheim (1800–82), the

[3] Cf. S. Sabar, *Past Perfect: The Jewish Experience in Early 20th Century Postcards* (New York, 1997), 7 ff.

[4] See J. Brańska, '*Na Dobry Rok bądźcie zapisani': Żydowskie karty noworoczne firmy Jehudia* (Warsaw, 1997), 12 ff.

Frankfurt Jewish artist who has come to be known as the first Jewish painter.[5] These images present a nostalgic view of the religious life of German Jews during the period of the artist's childhood and youth, and they were enormously popular among German Jews. They were first published in book form in 1866, and in the year of the artist's death a luxurious expanded edition appeared, accompanied by an introduction and notes by Rabbi Leopold Stein. Following the success of this edition, the entire series of prints was published as two series of postcards by the Frankfurt printers A. H. Hofmann and Paul Grödel.[6] They were printed in 1899–1900 in black and white, Grödel's series with captions in five languages on the back of each postcard, and Hofmann's with the titles in German, occasionally supplemented by other languages, generally English and Hebrew.

Oppenheim's series continued to be republished in Germany. In 1904 a company named Tomor issued the illustrated postcards in colour (with advertisements on the back for kosher margarine), and worked 'improvements' into Oppenheim's paintings. The series was marketed by means of advertisements that were distributed by the company among its Jewish customers.[7] The primary value of this series is what it tells us about the continuing popularity of Oppenheim's images. With respect to information about Jewish religious practices in Germany, a more significant series of postcards was printed by Grödel and based on pictures painted by other artists following Oppenheim. The most important of these was, interestingly, a Christian artist from Frankfurt named Hermann Junker (1838–99). Junker considered himself a student and disciple of Oppenheim, and in many cases Junker's pictures are imitations of his master's work. Junker expanded Oppenheim's series, however, and not only added new scenes to the ceremonies that Oppenheim had selected, but also painted entirely new subjects. His paintings, which did not receive the sort of acclaim inspired by his master's work, were seldom saved. Only two of his paintings are known at present; all the rest are known only from the postcards that were produced after his death.[8]

The majority of images in the German postcards were the creations of Moritz Oppenheim or his school. Indeed, hardly any images of Jewish ceremonies were

[5] Much has been written on Oppenheim's series 'Scenes of Traditional Jewish Family Life'. For recent studies, see the exhibition catalogues: R. Dröse, F. Eisermann, M. Kingreen, and A. Merk (eds.), *Der Zyklus 'Bilder aus dem altjüdischen Familienleben' und sein Maler Moritz Daniel Oppenheim* (Hanau, 1996); G. Heuberger and A. Merk (eds.), *Moritz Daniel Oppenheim. Die Entdeckung des jüdischen Selbstbewusstseins in der Kunst* (Cologne, 1999). For detailed descriptions of the paintings in English, see A. Werner, *Scenes of Traditional Jewish Family Life* (New York, 1976).

[6] Cf. M. Kingreen, 'Entstehung, Erfolg und Verbreitung des Zyklus', in Dröse *et al.* (eds.), *Der Zyklus*, esp. 107. And see there a reproduction of the standard envelope, which was made to contain the entire set of twenty Oppenheim postcards; the envelope is covered with advertisements for the cards in German, French, and English (but not in Hebrew); the price for the entire series was 2 marks.

[7] On the Tomor postcards, see ibid. 107; the postcards are reproduced in colour on pp. 108–9.

[8] On Junker and his postcards, see S. Sabar, 'In the Footsteps of Moritz Oppenheim: Hermann Junker's Postcard Series "Scenes of Traditional Jewish Family Life"', in Heuberger and Merk (eds.), *Moritz Daniel Oppenheim*, 259–71 (Ger. and Eng.).

painted specifically for postcards in Germany. Moreover, despite the popularity of the German postcards, far fewer were produced than in Poland before the First World War. While this apparently reflects the different demography of the two countries (the Jewish population of Germany was a fraction of that of Poland), it is noteworthy that the German Jews did relatively little to present publicly subjects taken from their private lives; Oppenheim's images gave an 'official' picture, encouraging respect and maintaining a certain distance. No doubt the general trend of the Jews of Germany to portray Jewish enlightenment, as well as their desire to integrate into German society by emphasizing what was common rather than different, contributed to this. With respect to illustrated postcards, this tendency was expressed, for example, in images dedicated to biblical subjects such as the binding of Isaac or Moses holding the tablets of the law, which were doubtless recognized and enjoyed in the general culture as well. The captions on such 'biblical' postcards are in German, which made the message immediately accessible to the wider society and also strengthened the universal import of the image.

The Jewish postcards from Poland are entirely different. Here biblical subjects are marginal, and in their place are detailed portrayals of the Jewish street, Jewish daily life, occupations, children, synagogues, houses of study, hospitals, cemeteries, public figures (writers, political leaders, actors), religious ceremonies, jokes, and even pogroms.[9] Intentionally or not the producers of the cards provided a broad and comprehensive picture of life in the *shtetl*—almost in the last generation in which it was possible to document this experience at first hand. And although during this period the Jewish demographic centre in eastern Europe shifted from the *shtetl* to the big city, only a small fraction of the cards show city life. Moreover, in contrast to their German counterparts, postcards showing images of the Jewish street are usually authentic photographs and not staged depictions of faces and places. The honourable and dignified faces portrayed on the German cards were often replaced in Poland by actual people and views, however nostalgic and sentimental. In general, therefore, the images from east European postcards provide an abundant source for research into various aspects of the Jewish culture of the period.

Another important issue is the intended audience. Producers of Jewish postcards in eastern Europe clearly intended them for internal Jewish use—primarily by Jews living in the big city, for whom these cards apparently fulfilled a nostalgic need, reminding them of the traditional world they had left behind. Evidence that the makers of the cards did not expect anyone who was not Jewish to acquire or view them may be deduced, for example, from the exclusively Yiddish captions on many of the postcards, and from the pervasiveness of images of Jewish suffering and anti-Jewish violence. German Jews, who sought the sympathy of German society during this period, did not dare to portray the relationship with their neighbours in such a

[9] A wide selection of these postcards, arranged by subject matter, has recently appeared: G. Silvain and H. Minczeles, *Yiddishland* (Paris, 1999). See also E. Duda and M. Sosenko, *Old Jewish Postcards* (Kraków, 1997).

critical manner. On east European postcards depicting pogroms, in contrast, there is often a direct appeal for help. And despite the fact that such appeals sometimes appear in various languages, it is clear that they were intended above all for well-to-do Jews, whether in Poland or abroad.[10]

Among the many publishers of postcards depicting Jewish life in eastern Europe, some were non-Jewish. But the great majority were Jewish publishing houses that also printed other materials for Jewish communal use, such as calendars, prayer books, and Passover haggadahs. Thus, for example, the publishing house Jehudia, which issued many Jewish publications, was owned by the Yiddish newspaper *Haynt*. Among other Jewish publishers active in producing postcards during the first two decades of the twentieth century were Verlag Central (Farlag 'Tsentral'), Synaj (or Sinai), Lebanon, Alt-naj-land, S. Resnik, and A. J. Ostrowski.[11]

The postcards depicting Jewish ceremonies doubtless constituted a sizeable portion of the Jewish postcards produced in eastern Europe. Unlike the photographic postcards that depict people and scenes on the street, the ceremonial postcards are generally staged. This is clear from the artificial postures and affected expressions of the figures. Indeed, the creators of these postcards—the most well known of whom was Khayim (Haggai) Goldberg (1890–1943), who worked for Jehudia as a graphic artist and designed many of its postcards of ceremonies—sometimes staged the scenes using amateur actors, who were dressed in appropriate clothing and placed in suitable settings.[12] Thus, for example, comparing two postcards produced

[10] A typical example is a postcard, printed in Paris, reproducing a photograph of the doctors and nurses of OZE (Society for the Protection of the Health of the Jews) in 'the pogromed district of Bobrouisk' (repr. in Silvain and Minczeles, *Yiddishland*, 488). The back of the card (not reproduced) bears a lengthy trilingual inscription in Yiddish, French, and English, which reads: 'After the pogroms . . . The bandits are gone. Doctors, their assistants, as well as nurses, have taken their place in the annihilated Jewish townlets [i.e. *shtetls*]. They are sacrificing their lives to rescue these unhappy beings. It is now up to you to find means to enable them to pursue their task.' For additional examples of pogrom postcards, see ibid. 477–91.

[11] On the printers of the postcards, see the brief remarks in Brańska, '*Na Dobry Rok . . .*', 17–18; Duda and Sosenko, *Old Jewish Postcards*, 9 ff., 154–62 (the authors provide the printer's name for every postcard reproduced). It is important to note that some of the more elaborate 'Polish postcards' were printed outside Poland, especially in Germany (for example, the coloured postcards of the Warsaw-based Verlag Central bear the caption 'Printed in Germany'). Obviously, this was done because of the advanced technology of postcard printing in Germany (the American Jewish printers of postcards, such as the Hebrew Publishing Company of New York, did the same; cf. Sabar, *Past Perfect*, 8–9).

[12] Goldberg was born in Łuków (Lublin province) to a hasidic family, and went on to study graphic arts in Germany. In 1912 he returned to Poland and settled in Warsaw, where he opened a studio named Grafikon and became involved in various fields of the visual arts as well as poetry. A few years later he started to design New Year postcards for Jehudia (and occasionally also for other printers, such as Resnik), which he signed in either Hebrew or Latin characters (see the many examples reproduced in Brańska, '*Na Dobry Rok . . .*', and Figs. 17 and 19 in this chapter). On Goldberg, see ibid. 22–3; *Leksikon fun der nayer yidisher literatur*, vol. ii (New York, 1958), 50; Sabar, *Past Perfect*, 8; id., 'Letoledot minhag mishlo'aḥ kartisei shanah tovah vehitpatḥuto ha'omanutit', *Jerusalem Studies in Jewish Folklore*, 19–20 (1998), 103 (Eng. summary, p. x); and E. Portnoy's chapter in this volume. Note, finally, that postcards with staged scenes were extremely popular in the general market at the time, especially New

Fig. 1. *Tsu kol-nidre* ('On the Way to Kol Nidre Prayers'), New Year card
(Warsaw: Jehudia, 1912–18). Biblioteka Narodowa, Warsaw.
Repr. from J. Brańska, '*Na Dobry Rok bądźcie zapisani*' (Warsaw, 1997), 60

by Jehudia, *Tsu kol-nidre* ('On the Way to the Kol Nidre Prayers') and *Erev yom-
kiper tsu minkhe* ('Going to *Minḥah* [Afternoon Prayers] on the Eve of Yom Kippur')
(Figs. 1 and 2), we see the same backdrop photographed from the same angle.[13]
Moreover, the grandfather and his grandchild appear almost identically in the two
postcards, while in place of the grandmother and granddaughter in the first postcard there appears in the second card a man carrying a *tales* under his arm. The

Year (Christmas) cards. Examples from Russia that closely resemble the Jewish postcards in technique
and general appearance are reproduced in Yu. Kombolin (ed.), *The Greeting Card in Russia (End of the
XIX Century–Beginning of the XX Century)* (St Petersburg, 1994) (Russ. and Eng.).

[13] Cf. Brańska, '*Na Dobry Rok . . .*', 60 and 62.

Fig. 2. *Erev yom-kiper tsu minkhe* ('Going to *Minḥah* [Afternoon Prayers] on the Eve of
Yom Kippur'), New Year card (Warsaw: Jehudia, 1912–18). Biblioteka Narodowa, Warsaw.
Repr. from J. Brańska, '*Na Dobry Rok bądźcie zapisani*' (Warsaw, 1997), 62

backdrop in these cards and most of the figures reappear in a postcard entitled *Di
bobe mit di eyniklekh* ('Grandma and the Grandchildren'), only this time without
the grandfather; on another occasion the same picture was printed with another
title, *In shul arayn* ('Going to Synagogue').[14] Even without the similarity between
the different postcards it is clear that these scenes must have been staged, especially
in the case of sabbath and holiday observances, which Jewish law proscribed from
being photographed. On the whole, the producers of Jewish postcards in Poland

[14] Ibid. 59 and 60. The same characters and background appear in many other postcards printed by
Jehudia (e.g. ibid. 56, 57, 70–2, etc.). See also L. Dobroszycki and B. Kirshenblatt-Gimblett, *Image
before my Eyes* (New York, 1977), p. 85, fig. 1.

preferred staged scenes, however 'authentic', over the German practice of reproducing more or less celebrated works of art. This preference was not coincidental, for, as we shall see, such 'authenticity' was imbued with strong social significance.

YOM KIPPUR CEREMONIES

At first glance there appear to have been fewer differences between Polish and German images of religious practices than between depictions of daily life; indeed, Jewish practices related to annual and life-cycle events have been standardized for centuries according to the *Shulḥan arukh* and other codifications of Jewish law. There were accepted differences between the practices of Sephardim and Ashkenazim, but both the Jews of Poland and the Jews of Germany followed *minhag ashkenaz* (Ashkenazi custom). However, as researchers into Jewish traditional life know well, alongside the official law there developed within particular communities many customs, often in a limited context of time and place.[15] And indeed there are Jewish postcards from both Poland and Germany depicting well-known ceremonies, such as *bris* (circumcision) or the Kiddush (benediction of wine) on sabbath eve, that also show variations in practice in each community. There are also a distinctly smaller number of postcards that depict practices particular to one community that were not generally known in the other.[16]

Yom Kippur customs depicted in the postcards present an interesting basis for comparison. Only a few postcards from Germany deal with the subject, and they are largely based, as has been said, on the works of Oppenheim and Junker. Oppenheim's celebrated painting of the subject, whose English caption, on the back of the postcard, is 'The Eve of the Day of Atonement', depicts a scene from an unusual angle: it places the viewer inside the beautiful Frankfurt synagogue, gazing outward through the large entrance onto the Jewish street (Judengasse, Fig. 3). The holiday atmosphere in the synagogue before the Kol Nidre prayer can be seen on the faces of those entering, greeting their neighbours. The men are dressed in white robes, known as *kitls*, symbolizing purity and cleanliness,[17] and between the two open doors a young couple can be seen—the husband, also dressed in the characteristic *kitl*, parting from his wife, who is about to ascend the back stairs to the women's section.

---

[15] For a general introduction to the *minhag* (custom) in Jewish tradition and its relationship to 'official halakhah' (law), see D. Sperber, *Minhagei yisra'el: mekorot vetoledot*, vol. i (Jerusalem, 1990), 9 ff. And see the subsequent six volumes in Sperber's series (Jerusalem, 1990–8) for studies of the origins and development of specific Jewish customs in various Jewish communities.

[16] For a wide selection of reproductions of postcards that depict Jewish religious practices from various communities, see P. Maser (ed.), *Jüdischer Alltag—Jüdische Feste* (Dortmund, 1982). See also G. Silvain, *Images et traditions juives: Un millier de cartes postales (1897–1917) pour servir à l'histoire de la Diaspora* (Paris, 1980), esp. 400 ff.

[17] The term *kitl* actually reflects the east European usage. In medieval Germany the preferred term was *Sargenes*. On the *kitl* and its symbolism in Jewish tradition, see I. D. Markon, 'Hakitel', *Mellila* (Manchester University), 1 (1944), 121–8.

Fig. 3. After Moritz Oppenheim, *Am Vorabend des Sühnetages*
('The Eve of the Day of Atonement') (Cleve: Tomor, 1904).
Joseph Hoffman Jewish Postcard Collection, Folklore Research Centre,
Hebrew University of Jerusalem

A German postcard that is even more representative of the subject is based on a painting by Junker (Fig. 4). The subject is based on a historical event: the prayer of Jewish soldiers on Yom Kippur near the city of Metz during the Franco–Prussian War in 1870. Hundreds of Jewish soldiers appear in an open field, while three figures read from a Torah scroll on an improvised *bimah* on top of the hill. The

Jom Kipur (Versöhnungstag) vor der Schlacht bei Metz 1870.

Postkarten-Verlag Paul Grödel, Frankfurt a. M. Gesetzl. geschützt

Fig. 4. Hermann Junker, *Jom Kipur (Versöhnungstag) vor der Schlacht bei Metz, 1870* ('Yom Kippur before the Battle near Metz, 1870') (Frankfurt am Main: Paul Grödel, 1899–1900). Joseph Hoffman Jewish Postcard Collection, Folklore Research Centre, Hebrew University of Jerusalem

Fig. 5. *'Kayres' in erev yom-kiper* ('Dishes on Yom Kippur Eve') 'In zkhus fun tsedoke, vos mir gebn | Tsu yeder tsayt, fun kleyn biz groys— | Farshrayb undz, got, in bukh fun lebn, | Un mek dos keynmol shoyn nisht oys . . .' ('For the merit of *tsedakah* which we give | On every occasion, from big to small— | Inscribe us, God, in the book of life, | And never wipe it out at all . . .') (Williamsburg, NY: Williamsburg Art Co. [*c.*1914–18]; first pub. Central: Warsaw). Joseph Hoffman Jewish Postcard Collection, Folklore Research Centre, Hebrew University of Jerusalem

image far exaggerates the historical reality. Apparently only a few soldiers took part in the ceremony, which was held in a small building and not in an open field, and they did not possess a Torah scroll.[18] Junker himself painted a more historically accurate version of the event,[19] but it was the painting described above that achieved great popularity; one version was printed on an ornamental cloth panel, many copies of which were distributed.[20] The text printed on the cloth in Hebrew and German, 'Have we not all one father? Hath not one God created us all?' (Mal. 2: 10), was intended to reinforce the moral: Jewish soldiers had contributed to the general war effort, and Germans had allowed the Jews to hold their ceremony without interference.[21]

In contrast to the portrayal of Yom Kippur in German postcards, which generally emphasize Jewish interaction with non-Jews, the postcards from eastern Europe are more direct and present a Jewish world that is more closed. First of all, there are a large number of postcards devoted to various practices connected to Yom Kippur, among them even pictures of women in traditional dress beating their breasts in repentance in the synagogue. Some of the postcards show less well-known customs; for example, the custom depicted on a postcard bearing the title *Kayres in erev yom-kiper* ('Dishes on Yom Kippur Eve'): two men in traditional dress sit behind a table covered with a red cloth upon which a number of dishes are placed, while several men and children approach the table to place coins in the dishes (Fig. 5). Each of the dishes is labelled with the purpose of the donations: *talmud toyre* ('community-funded school'), *lines hutsedek* ('hostel for the poor'), *hakhnoses kale* ('dowries for poor girls'), *khazn* ('cantor'), *erets yisroel* ('land of Israel'). The custom was that on the eve of Yom Kippur at the time of the *minḥah* prayers donations were raised in this way for the various organizations active in the town. In this generation there were also dishes for Keren Kayemet Leyisrael, the Zionist agency that purchased land in Palestine for Jewish settlement, as well as the Yishuv (Jewish community in Palestine) itself. A number of earthenware dishes of this type, often embellished with appropriate sayings, remain in various Judaica collections. A characteristic example is the *tsedakah* (charity) dish for the redemption of Jerusalem made of

[18] An eyewitness description of the event, written by one of the Jewish officers, has been preserved. For an English translation of his account, see R. Gay, *The Jews of Germany: A Historical Portrait* (New Haven, 1992), 163. [19] See Sabar, 'Hermann Junker', p. 266, fig. 8.

[20] The commemorative cloth panel was printed in several colours. See e.g. *Moritz Oppenheim: The First Jewish Painter* (Jerusalem, 1983), 55.

[21] I. Schorsch, 'Art as Social History: Oppenheim and the German Jewish View of Emancipation', in *Moritz Oppenheim: The First Jewish Painter*, 54–6; R. I. Cohen, *Jewish Icons: Art and Society in Modern Europe* (Berkeley and Los Angeles, 1998), 169–71; Sabar, 'Hermann Junker', 267–9. Another German postcard which illustrates Jewish military service in the German army is reproduced in Sivain and Minczeles, *Yiddishland*, 416. Dated 1914, this little-known image also shows numerous Jewish soldiers in the countryside participating in the service, which was conducted by 'Feldrabbiner Dr. Sonderling, Hamburg'; a postcard illustration of Dr Sonderling himself appears on the facing page.

Fig. 6. 'Lekhu venivneh
et ḥomat yerushalayim
velo nihyeh od ḥerpah'
('Come and let us build up
the walls of Jerusalem, that we
may be no more a reproach').
Glazed earthenware *tsedakah*
dish. Carpathian Russia,
late nineteenth century.
Wolfson Museum,
Hekhal Shelomo, Jerusalem

Fig. 7. *Malkot* on the eve of
Yom Kippur (Warsaw:
Jehudia, 1912–18)

glazed pinkish earthenware, inscribed with the verse 'Come and let us build up the walls of Jerusalem, that we may be no more a reproach' (Neh. 2: 17) (Fig. 6).[22]

Another interesting practice connected to Yom Kippur and depicted in at least two different postcards is the ritual of flagellation (*malkot*) (Fig. 7).[23] On a postcard printed by Jehudia a young man crouches on a tapestry spread on the floor, while a thick-bearded older man rains blows on his back with a small whip. The procedure of this beating is based on a passage in the Mishnah:

How do they scourge him? His two hands are tied to a post on either side of it. The superintendent of the synagogue lays hold of his garments . . . A stone is placed behind the offender on which the superintendent of the synagogue stands over him, [holding] in his hand a strap of calf-hide, made of one thong, one folded into two, and [the] two into four, and [another] two thongs running [as it were] up and down . . . He administers one-third [of the lashes] in front and two-thirds behind. He lashes him not in a standing or sitting posture but stooping . . . He who administers the lashes smites with his one hand and with his whole force . . . [24]

In biblical and mishnaic times this practice was unconnected to Yom Kippur, and was simply intended as punishment for an intentional transgression of a religious prohibition. The connection of the custom to Yom Kippur apparently developed in Ashkenaz only after the end of the gaonic period (mid-eleventh century); it is already mentioned in *Sidur rashi* from the eleventh to twelfth centuries.[25] According to this source, flagellation was a central feature in the preparations for Yom Kippur; it was intended to humble the heart and awaken repentance.[26] From the eighteenth and nineteenth centuries a number of visual testimonies to the custom have survived, both in the books of Christian Hebraists and in Jewish art (Fig. 8).[27]

[22] The plate was formerly in the collection of Heshl Golnitzki of Haifa; see his book *Bemaḥzor hayamim: mo'ed vaḥol ba'omanut uvafolklor hayehudi* (Haifa, 1963), p. 46, fig. 48. The Golnitzki collection was acquired by and is now housed in the Wolfson Museum, Hekhal Shelomo, Jerusalem (see Y. L. Bialer and E. Fink, *Jewish Life in Art and Tradition*, 2nd enlarged edn. (Jerusalem, 1980), 186). Another *tsedakah* plate in the Golnitzki collection (repr. in Golnitzki, *Bemaḥzor*, p. 46, fig. 49, and Bialer and Fink, *Jewish Life in Art and Tradition*, 186) bears a moralistic verse: 'Vanity of vanities, vanity of vanities, all is vanity' (Eccles. 1: 2). A more ornate metal plate, painted in green and bearing coloured inscriptions (for Rabbi Meir 'Ba'al Hanes' along with a verse concerning Jerusalem (Ps. 137: 6)) is preserved in the private collection of Yitshak Einhorn, Tel Aviv. It must be noted that the maskilim emphasized the addition of the plates for Erets Yisroel as characterizing the activity of the early Zionist group Hovevei Zion. See e.g. the reference to Leon Pinsker in this matter by Ahad Ha'am, *Al parashat derakhim* (Tel Aviv, 1947), 43.

[23] The other postcard, issued by Verlag Central, is reproduced in S. Sabar, 'Letoledot minhag mishlo'aḥ kartisei shanah tovah', pl. 9.   [24] *Mak.* 22b.

[25] See *Sidur rashi*, ed. S. Buber and Y. Freimann (Berlin, 1911), p. 97, no. 211.

[26] The custom also took root in other Jewish communities, including among the Sephardim and the Jews of Islamic lands. In fact, Joseph Karo mentions it in the *Shulḥan arukh* (*Oraḥ ḥayim*, 607: 6) as a general custom, incumbent on all men in the congregation.

[27] Some examples: F. A. Christiani, *Der Juden Glaube und Aberglaube* (Leipzig, 1705), pl. VII; J. Bodenschatz, *Kirchliche Verfassung der heutigen Juden sonderlich derer in Deutschland* (Erlang, 1748), pl. VIII. Considerably reduced reproductions of these two illustrations are in A. Rubens, *A Jewish Iconography*, rev. edn. (London, 1981), p. 50, no. 503, p. 58, no. 597). A Jewish example is a coloured

Fig. 8. *Kaparot* (above) and *malkot* (below) on the eve of Yom Kippur. Engraving in F. A. Christiani, *Der Juden Glaube* (Leipzig, 1705). Library of the Jewish Theological Seminary of America, New York

The whipping was held on the eve of Yom Kippur after the *minḥah* prayer at the synagogue. Usually each of those praying took part[28] with a whip made, as described in the Talmud, from a strip of calfskin that was folded twice and entwined with two strips of donkey skin, following the verse 'The ox knoweth his owner and the ass his master's crib' (Isa. 1: 3). According to tradition, the one to be beaten was to pros-

paper *mizraḥ* plaque from late 18th-century southern Germany, which features folk motifs related to the Jewish holidays (preserved at the Israel Museum, Jerusalem; see I. Shachar, *Jewish Tradition in Art: The Feuchtwanger Collection of Judaica* (Jerusalem, 1981), p. 50, no. 107, and the colour plate following p. 15). The *mizraḥ* is a plaque hung on the eastern wall of traditional Ashkenazi homes to indicate the direction of prayer and of Jerusalem.

[28] There were, however, varying customs to determine who would do the whipping and who would be whipped; for eastern Europe, see below.

trate himself, his face to the north and his rear to the south.[29] At the hour of the whipping he recited the *vidui* (confession), while the whipper recited the verse

> But He, being full of compassion, forgiveth iniquity, and destroyeth not;
> Yea, many a time doth He turn His anger away,
> And doth not stir up all His wrath.
>
> (Ps. 78: 38)

The verse contains thirteen words and is read three times, for a total of thirty-nine words, which correspond to the thirty-nine blows which it was the custom to strike, according to the verse 'Forty stripes he may give him, he shall not exceed' (Deut. 25: 3), which the Talmud interprets as 'forty minus one' (*Mak. 22b*). A good description of this practice in eastern Europe in the second half of the nineteenth century can be found in the childhood memoirs of the Zionist leader Shmaryahu Levin (1867–1935), who was brought up in Sislevitsh (Świsłocz, Svislach) in Belarus.

After the *minḥah* prayer on the same day [Yom Kippur eve] . . . with my own eyes I saw how aged Jews prostrate themselves on the floor of the synagogue while Eliezer the psalm-sayer, or, as he was called because of his craft, Eliezer the bath attendant, stands over them with the whip and whips them without mercy. Of course I knew that this whipping was the ceremony of *malkot*, but in my heart memories of the *kheyder* spontaneously awakened. And the blows were delivered in perfect order: one below, on the part of the body designed for punishments, that was fair prey for the *rebbe* and his whip in the *kheyder*, and the second above, on the back. And then he would do it again and count: one, one and one, one and two—sometimes fifteen times. And my amazement grew sevenfold when I saw the whipped one rise and throw some copper coins into the plate that Eliezer the bath attendant offered. Truly it was a wonder and will be wondered: men are whipped and pay for the whipping![30]

---

[29] According to two Polish authorities, David ben Shmuel Halevi (1586–1667) and his grandson Yeshayahu ben Abraham (d. 1723), the preference of the south–north over the west–east axis stems from the idea that one should not turn his buttocks in the direction in which the divine presence (Shekhinah) resides. See their respective commentaries, *Magen david* and *Ba'er hetev*, to the aforementioned section in the *Shulḥan arukh*. And why should one turn one's face specifically to the north? Their reply: 'Since the essence of man's impurity stems from money, as it is written: "Out of the north comes gold" (Job 37: 22), therefore he humiliates himself in that direction to proclaim the source of his impurity.'

[30] See S. Levin, *Mizikhronot ḥayai* (Tel Aviv, 1944), pt. 1: Yalduti, 75–6; there is an abridged English translation: *Childhood in Exile*, trans. M. Samuel (New York, 1929), 91. Another interesting testimony is that of Yehezkel Kotik (1847–1921) of Kamieniec Litewski (Kamyanets) in Belarus. According to Kotik, the synagogue floor was covered with hay, to make it more comfortable for those being whipped. In addition, not everyone was 'rewarded' with whipping, but only the 'more important *balebatim*'—and even among them there was a certain hierarchy: the more affluent were whipped first while the others had to wait their turn patiently. Moreover, the extremely poor were not whipped at all, because they could not afford 'to pay the *shames* good money for his work'; see *Mayne zikhroynes* (Berlin, 1922), pt. 1, 203–4 (Heb. edn. *Mah shera'iti . . . : zikhronotav shel yeḥezkel kotik*, ed. and trans. D. Assaf (Tel Aviv, 1998), 254).

   Thus the Jews of Poland had no problem depicting on their postcards a custom that was accepted and natural in the context of religious and daily life. The Jews of Germany, on the other hand, found it unacceptable to depict the custom of *malkot* on their postcards, despite the fact that in earlier generations visual representations of the custom had been produced in Germany. It is likely, in light of what has already been noted about German Jewish postcards, that this subject was simply not 'representative' or 'cultured' enough to appear on postcards accessible to all, and, moreover, the custom was largely disappearing for the same reason.

   Another custom connected to Yom Kippur which I will discuss only briefly here because much has already been written about it, is that of *kaparot* or *shlogn kapores*.[31] As we know, this custom was already controversial in the rabbinic literature of the Middle Ages. From an anthropological perspective, the ritual of *kaparot* functions as a magical ceremony whose purpose is to 'capture' sin and expel it into the body of a chicken.[32] And, indeed, the belief that it is possible to transfer illnesses, blemishes, sins, and various maladies from one living body to another (or even to inanimate objects, such as rocks or branches) has been common among many peoples.[33] Authorities such as Solomon ben Aderet (Rashba, *c.*1235–1310) and Moses ben Nahman (Nahmanides, 1194–1270) declared that this custom contained a type of superstition, while Joseph Caro (1488–1575), author of the *Shulḥan arukh*, called the custom stupid and wanted to suppress it. However, despite these opinions, Moses Isserles (Rema, 1525/30–1572) of Kraków strongly defended the practice because it was *minhag vatikin* (a pious custom), and detailed its meaning and the various ways of carrying it out.[34]

   The postcards depicting this custom in Germany and Poland present an interesting contrast. Oppenheim did not portray *kaparot* at all in his work, and neither, it seems, did his student Junker. However, in the series of Junker's postcards there is one entitled *Kapores-Schlagen vor Jom Kipur* ('Performing the *Kaparot* Ritual

---

[31] *Kaparot*: literally 'expiations'. On the custom of *shlogn kapores* (beating expiations) and its origins, see J. Z. Lauterbach, 'The Ritual for the *Kapparot* Ceremony', in S. W. Baron and A. Marx (eds.), *Jewish Studies in Memory of George Alexander Kohut, 1874–1933* (New York, 1935), repr. in Lauterbach, *Studies in Jewish Law, Custom and Folklore* ([New York], 1970), 133–42; id., 'Tashlikh: A Study in Jewish Ceremonies', *Hebrew Union College Annual*, 11 (1936), 207–340, repr. in Lauterbach, *Rabbinic Essays* (Cincinnati, 1951), esp. 354 ff. See also Y. Reifman, 'Toledot minhag hakaparot', *Hadarom*, 28 (1968), 242–8, and notes, 246–8, by M. Herscovics.

[32] Cf. J. Trachtenberg, *Jewish Magic and Superstition* (New York, 1930), 162–5.

[33] The classic study on this issue is still J. Frazer, *The Golden Bough: A Study in Magic and Religion* (London, 1933), pt. IV: 'The Scapegoat', and see esp. ch. 1, 'The Transference of Evil', 1–71. The *kaparot* ceremony, which according to Frazer is the modern Jewish version of the biblical rituals of the scapegoat (Azazel; cf. Lev. 16: 5–24), is discussed on p. 210. Note that this association occasionally appears also in Jewish sources, e.g. *Mahzor vitry*, ed. S. Hurwitz (Berlin, 1889–93), 373.

[34] Caro's opinion that it is 'a stupid custom' appeared in the early editions of the *Shulḥan arukh* (1st edn. Venice, 1565); later editions only contain the warning to avoid this custom (*Oraḥ ḥayim*, 605: 1). Isserles, on the other hand, elaborates on the custom, explaining that a cock should be used for a male and a hen for a female; in both cases a white fowl should be preferred (based on Isa. 1: 18); the intestines are to be put on the roofs or thrown outside for the birds, etc. (*Hagahot harema* on *Oraḥ ḥayim* 605: 1).

Kapores-Schlagen vor Jom Kipur

Fig. 9. *Kapores-Schlagen vor Jom Kipur* ('Performing the *Kaparot* Ritual before Yom Kippur') (Frankfurt am Main: Paul Grödel(?), 1899–1900). Joseph Hoffman Jewish Postcard Collection, Folklore Research Centre, Hebrew University of Jerusalem

before Yom Kippur') (Fig. 9).[35] No artist is credited for the picture, and it portrays its subject in a modest manner lacking drama: three figures stand in a simply furnished room; the father of the family holds the chicken over the head of the wife, who holds an open book in her left hand; next to them stands their small daughter. The calm and dignified expression of the faces and the peaceful atmosphere in the room hardly suggest the dramatic character of the ceremony displayed.

The subject of *kaparot* in Polish postcards holds a far more central and honoured place than in the German cards. One postcard by Khayim Goldberg portrays the purchase of chickens on the eve of Yom Kippur (*Ba kapores koyfn*); another depicts a father raising a chicken over his son's head; a third, a mother with a chicken over

[35] The association of this postcard with the Junker series (it is probably no. 29) is uncertain since the name of the series' publisher, Paul Grödel, is missing (though the design of the postcard follows closely that of the others). Note, however, that the figures and the interior of the house certainly reflect the world of German Jews.

Fig. 10. *Kaparot* (Budapest, 1910–20?). 'Yesimkha elohim ke'efrayim vekhimenasheh, kesarah, rivkah, raḥel vele'ah' ('May God make you as Ephraim and as Manasseh [Gen. 48: 20], and as Sarah, Rebecca, Rachel, and Leah'). 'Leshanah tovah tikatevu' ('May you be inscribed for a good year'). 'Boldog ujévet' (Hungarian: 'Happy New Year'). Joseph Hoffman Jewish Postcard Collection, Folklore Research Centre, Hebrew University of Jerusalem

Fig. 11. Yom Kippur cock (publisher unknown, *c.*1905–10). Possibly an American reprint of a Polish or Hungarian card. Joseph Hoffman Jewish Postcard Collection, Folklore Research Centre, Hebrew University of Jerusalem

her daughter's head.[36] Other postcards portray greater numbers of participants in the ceremony or single figures in traditional dress holding the chicken, with the caption 'This is my substitute'. A number of postcards dealing with this subject were also printed in Romania and Hungary (Fig. 10), and the subject may be found also on postcards printed for east European immigrants in New York.[37] The subject is found as well in humorous contexts, additional testimony to the central place of the ritual in the lives of Polish Jews. On one postcard the sole image is a large rooster, taking up the right half of the postcard (Fig. 11).[38] This image is embossed; the rooster's body is gold and on its head burns a red comb. On the left side of the card are the verses that traditionally accompany the ritual according to the Ashkenazi custom (Ps. 107: 10, 14, 17–21; Job 33: 23–4). But they include the words that are recited not for a man but for a woman, around whose head a hen and not a rooster would be swung! Another humorous postcard, put out by Verlag Central, shows a small boy with black earlocks and an impudent look riding a huge rooster in the *shtetl* streets (Fig. 12). In the caption the boy is referred to as *der kleyner mazik* (the little mischief-maker); he holds in his hands the reins of the rooster and a sign that says, 'This is my substitute, this is my expiation'. On another postcard we see a hasid in traditional dress reading from a prayer book, which he holds in one hand, while in the other he grasps a rooster, whose head (by means of an early use of photo-montage) is that of Tsar Nicholas II; the caption reads 'This is my substitute, this is my counterpart, this is my expiation' (Fig. 13).[39]

[36] For these postcards, published by Jehudia, see Brańska, '*Na Dobry Rok . . .*', 53–4. Some of the Yiddish verses on these cards read, for a boy: 'Der hon er geyt tsum toyt atsund | Un mir—tsum lebn un gezunt . . .' ('The rooster now goes to his death, and we to life and health . . .'); for a girl, 'Di hun, di hun zi geyt lemise | Un mir—tsu lange yorn, zise!' ('The hen, the hen, it goes to die, and we to years long and sweet!')

[37] Additional Polish examples are reproduced in Duda and Sosenko, *Old Jewish Postcards*, p. 91, no. 9.9; Sabar, *Past Perfect*, p. 21, no. 15 (from Kraków, 1903); Dobroszycki and Kirshenblatt-Gimblett, *Image before my Eyes*, p. 85, fig. 3; Silvain and Minczeles, *Yiddishland*, 382–3, 387. An American example, from a painting by the artist Stanislaus Bender, is in Maser, *Jüdischer Alltag—Jüdische Feste*, 86. Other extant examples have not been published.

[38] It should be noted, however, that the association of this postcard with eastern Europe is uncertain. As the information on the back is given in English (but without the publisher's name), the card was printed either in the United States or in Europe for the American market. A similar card, with the blessing for the New Year in Hungarian, is reproduced in Sabar, *Past Perfect*, p. 87, no. 86.

[39] This curious postcard does not contain a date or the name of the publisher (perhaps intentionally). The only non-Hebrew text on it—and significantly it does not appear on all the extant cards—is in English, but it does not seem to have been printed in the United States. (Many cards intended for the American Jewish market were commonly printed in Europe, mainly in Germany, but also in Poland.) As for the date, it is likely that the card was printed before the fall of the tsar in 1917; this dating is supported also by the design and typography. But how was it possible to mail a postcard with so subversive an image in tsarist times? The answer apparently lies in the fact that all the extant cards with this image that I was able to examine have an unusual feature in common: damaged edges, showing some loss of the upper layer of the postcard. It appears, therefore, that the cards were distributed with another piece of paper pasted onto the postcard, concealing the image from hostile eyes. A version of this card with the figures drawn—rather than photographed—by an unknown artist is extant (but unpublished) in some collections as well.

Fig. 12. *Der kleyner mazik* ('The Little Mischief-Maker'). 'Der kleyner mazik shlogt kapores | Un rayt tsuglaykh oykh afn hon . . . | O, shenk im, got, a freylekh lebn | Un shrayb im lange yorn on!' ('The little mischief-maker *shlogt kapores*, | And rides the rooster at the same time . . . | Oh grant him, God, a happy life | And write down long years for him!'). (Warsaw: Central, 1910). Author's collection

The large number of Polish postcards on the subject of *kaparot* testifies to the pervasiveness of this practice and its centrality in the lives of the Jews of the *shtetl*; this is also reflected in the writings of contemporary east European rabbis, who strongly defended the custom. For urban Jews, who, as mentioned earlier, were apparently the main consumers of these postcards, such representations fulfilled their needs for 'picturesque' scenes of *shtetl* life. In contrast, the urban Jews of Germany in this period chose to play down the custom, and the postcards indeed reflect this tendency. As with *malkot*, this attitude becomes even more obvious in light of the fact that almost all the visual depictions of the custom of *kaparot* prior to this period were made in Germany.[40]

---

[40] See the images referred to in n. 27 above.

זה חליפתי. זה תמורתי. זה כפרתי.

Fig. 13. 'Zeh ḥalifati, zeh temurati, zeh kaparati' ('This is my substitute, this is my counterpart, this is my expiation') (Poland(?), publisher unknown, *c*.1917). Joseph Hoffman Jewish Postcard Collection, Folklore Research Centre, Hebrew University of Jerusalem

UNIQUE PRACTICES IN POSTCARDS

Alongside the shared practices that are presented, with varying emphases, in German and Polish postcards, there are a few depictions of practices apparently unique to the communities that documented them. This generally relates to customs that originated, developed, and were preserved in a particular region or community but were not practised or known in other areas. In certain cases this also means images that have no precedent in the art of earlier generations—whether in the illustrations accompanying the books by Christian Hebraists (or in other Christian sources), or in Jewish sources. Moreover, there are occasions when the image on the postcard is the sole visual portrayal of the ceremony known to us.

In the case of Germany, it appears at first glance that there is nothing unique in the postcards since they are copies of pictures. However, here too the postcard doubtless played an important function in spreading knowledge of a ceremony and

Fig. 14. Moritz Oppenheim,
Das Schuletragen . . .
The First Time to Synagogue
(Frankfurt am Main:
A. J. Hoffman, 1899–1900).
Author's collection

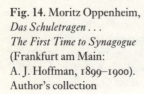

Das Schuletragen. Le porter de la Mappeh au temple.
The first time to synagoge. מפה
Nach dem Original-Gemälde von Prof. M. Oppenheim.

Ges. gesch. deposé, registred D.G.I.F. Nº 2

the manner of its performance. Some of Oppenheim's paintings are the only representations we possess of certain practices; the mass publication of these images in postcard form doubtless served to preserve and memorialize vanishing pieces of folklore among German Jews. Thus, for example, Oppenheim's picture *Das Schuletragen* ('Carrying [the Little Boy] to Synagogue') is the sole visual depiction (with the exception of Junker's subsequent copy) of a German Jewish ritual connected to a boy's first visit to the synagogue (Fig. 14).[41] In this ceremony an

---

[41] On Oppenheim's painting, see Dröse *et al.* (eds.), *Der Zyklus*, 58–9. On the custom as it appears in the painting, cf. J. Gutmann, '"Die Mappe Schuletragen": An Unusual Judeo-German Custom', *Visible Religion*, 2 (1983), 167–73, repr. in A. Weber, E. Friedlander, and F. Armbruster (eds.), *Mappot . . . blessed he who comes: The Band of Jewish Tradition* (Osnabrück, 1997), 65–9; with additional articles, in English and German, on the German Torah binders (*Wimpels*). For Junker's postcard version of Oppenheim's image, which is entitled *Schule-Tragen*, see Sabar, 'Hermann Junker', 262–3 and fig. 2.

embroidered or painted Torah binder, known as a *wimpel* or *mapah*, usually made by the mother from the swaddling cloth used during the circumcision ceremony, was presented to the synagogue. In the picture, as in the postcard produced from it, we see the father standing on the *bimah*, the child in his arms, guiding the child's hands to the Torah finials (*rimonim*) and the scroll tied up by the *wimpel*. The mother looks on from the women's gallery (it was also customary for her to throw the *wimpel* she had prepared onto her husband and son as they stood on the *bimah*). This custom was not known at all among Polish Jews, since it originated among the Jews of Germany relatively late, about the beginning of the sixteenth century, when cultural distinctions between the two communities had solidified.[42]

Although the postcards based on Oppenheim's well-known paintings do not tell us anything new about Jewish practices, Junker's postcards do. Precisely because Junker's work received less attention among his contemporaries, the postcards made from his works, nearly all of which have been lost, are of particular interest. The Christian Junker clearly imitated his Jewish master in many respects, but his paintings of Jewish ceremonies are much less nostalgic and formal than Oppenheim's. Some contain details that appear to be trivial but offer important information about contemporary Jewish practices. One postcard, for example, portrays the members of a family decorating a sukkah with colourful paper chains. While this custom is quite prevalent today, this is its earliest visual depiction.[43]

A number of postcards in Junker's series depict even older customs for the first time. For example, one postcard portrays the ceremony of Hollekreisch (also written Holegrasch or Holekraasch), or, as it is described on the back of the postcard, 'Namensverleihung des Mädchens (Holekraasch)' (Fig. 15).[44] In this ceremony, widespread among the Jews of Germany since the Middle Ages, a baby was given its non-Hebrew name (for a boy, in other words, additional to the Hebrew name given at the circumcision ceremony). In early sources the ceremony is associated only with boys. It was held in the child's home, usually on the fourth sabbath following his birth. The mother would invite children home and prepare candy, fruit, and nuts for them. The children would gather round the baby's cradle, which was decorated with a siddur, *tales*, and pages of the Gemara. They would raise the cradle three times to the cry of 'Hollekreisch, Hollekreisch, what name shall we give the baby?', whereupon the mother would announce the name. This ceremony was also adopted in a number of versions for girls, and is first mentioned by the noted fifteenth-century rabbi of Mainz (and other German towns) Moses ben Isaac Mintz.[45] In later generations the ceremony was increasingly identified with girls,

---

[42] Cf. J. Gutmann, *The Jewish Life Cycle* (Leiden, 1987), 8.

[43] The postcard is entitled *Das Schmücken der Laubhütte* ('The Decoration of the Sukkah'); see Sabar, 'Hermann Junker', 264 and fig. 6.   [44] Ibid. 264–5 and fig. 7.

[45] *Responsa Mintz*, 1st edn. (Kraków, 1617), responsum no. 64; on Rabbi Mintz, see the entry by S. Tal in *Encyclopedia Judaica* (Jerusalem, 1972), vol. xii, cols. 65–6. The most detailed account of the Hollekreisch ceremony is B. Hamburger, *Shoreshei minhag ashkenaz*, vol. i (Benei Berak, 1995), 415–55, and see there pp. 433–41, on the Hollekreisch customs relating to girls.

who, in contrast to boys, were generally given only a non-Hebrew name. An illustration of the ceremony for boys can be found in a manuscript of a prayer book from Nuremberg dated 1589,[46] but Junker's postcard is the first depiction of the ceremony for a girl. Around the baby's cradle stand only girls, while the parents look on from the side adoringly (Fig. 15).

On the last postcard in Junker's series a cat appears in the left corner as a cherished house pet. Without a doubt this detail bears witness to the changes in Jewish life that the artist was trying to document.[47] But another postcard in the series bears witness to change even more clearly. The title of this postcard is *Geburtstags-Feier*; in other words its subject is a birthday (Fig. 16). The postcard depicts a typical German Jewish family, including the grandfather and grandmother, sitting outside their house in a sukkah decorated with floral wreaths;[48] the table is covered with a cloth upon which light refreshments are set, and hanging above the table is the typical star-shaped sabbath lamp (*Judenstern*) of German Jews. A maid approaches from the right, a cat at her side, carrying additional refreshments. To appreciate fully the significance of this image, which is included in the series 'Scenes of Traditional Jewish Family Life', it is important to realize the non-traditional nature of this ceremony. In ancient times men's birthdays were not granted special importance in the Jewish world. In fact, the opposite was the case; according to the book of Ecclesiastes, 'A good name is better than precious oil; and the day of death than the day of one's birth' (7: 1), and the only biblical figure whose birthday is honoured with a feast is Pharaoh (Gen. 40: 20). In talmudic sources birthday celebrations are mentioned in a pagan context.[49] Indeed, birthday celebrations were common in the Roman world, and were connected with astrology and other practices (candles, cake, etc.), some of which have survived until today.[50] Over the course of centuries, however, such traditions infiltrated European Jewish practice, and the birthdays of various figures, from Isaac and Moses to celebrated rabbis of modern times, began to be determined and

[46] Germanisches Nationalmuseum, Nuremberg, MS Hs. 7058, fos. 43ᵛ–44ʳ; cf. Gutmann, *Life Cycle*, 8, 26, and pl. xva–b; the two pages are reproduced in colour in G. Cohen Grossman, *Jewish Art* ([New York], 1995), 136.

[47] Ultra-Orthodox Jews to this day do not keep pets. On the negative approach to cats and dogs in early Jewish sources, see J. Schwartz, 'Dogs and Cats in Jewish Society in the Second Temple, Mishnah and Talmud Periods', in *Proceedings of the Twelfth World Congress of Jewish Studies*, div. B (Jerusalem, 2001), and 'Cats in Ancient Jewish Society', *Journal of Jewish Studies*, 52 (2001), 211–34. On the gradual adaptation of general (or secular) modes of daily life among German Jews, see A. Shohat, *Im hilufei hatekufot: reshit hahaskalah beyahadut germaniyah* (Jerusalem, 1960).

[48] The sukkah is somewhat surprising. In fact, the scene is nearly identical with another postcard in the series, *Unterhaltung in der Laubhütte* ('Conversation [or Entertainment] in the Sukkah') (no. 36), which is evidently the work of the same artist. The main difference between the two images is the floral wreaths that decorate the sukkah in the birthday painting. The birthday probably occurred during Sukkot and was therefore celebrated in the sukkah.

[49] *AZ* 10a; see also the discussion in *JT, AZ* 1b.

[50] See W. Schmidt, 'Geburtstag im Altertum', *Religionsgeschichtliche Versuche* (Giessen), 7 (1908), 1. On the birthday in various cultures, see the brief entry 'Birthdays', in *Funk and Wagnall's Standard Dictionary of Folklore, Mythology and Legend* (New York, 1972), 144.

Fig. 15. *Namensverleihung des Mädchens (Holekraasch)* ('Name-Giving for a Girl')
(Frankfurt am Main: Paul Grödel, 1899–1900). Joseph Hoffman Jewish Postcard
Collection, Folklore Research Centre, Hebrew University of Jerusalem

Fig. 16. *Geburtstags-Feier* ('Birthday Party') (Frankfurt am Main: Paul Grödel, 1899–1900).
Joseph Hoffman Jewish Postcard Collection, Folklore Research Centre,
Hebrew University of Jerusalem

noted.[51] In Germany a son's date of birth was marked upon the *Wimpel* mentioned above. Nevertheless, celebrating the birthday of an ordinary family member (not necessarily an eminent individual) is a clear sign of the changes undergone by Jewish society at the end of the nineteenth century.[52]

Although there are many more postcards from Poland depicting Jewish ceremonies than from Germany, there are few portraying practices unique to Poland. There are many, however, that depict characteristic details of known customs. Thus, for example, in a postcard portraying the ritual of Havdalah, which closes the sabbath, we see the head of the family extinguishing the braided candle with wine that has overflowed the Kiddush cup onto the plate, while two figures touch their eyes with the wine remaining in the cup (Fig. 17). The former custom derives from the Talmud: 'A person in whose house wine is not poured like water has not attained the state of blessedness' (*Eruv.* 65*a*). The Kiddush cup that overflows at the end of the sabbath is therefore a sign of blessing and plenty at the beginning of a week of work and daily worries. The wine touched to the eyes is an attribute of wisdom, according to the verse 'The commandment of the Lord is pure, enlightening the eyes' (Ps. 19: 9); this verse can be found on many Havdalah plates made of silver or porcelain, especially from Germany.[53]

Finally, I will briefly touch on the world of children as depicted in the postcards. Children appear, indeed, on many of the postcards from eastern Europe, primarily in a religious context. Frequently they are accompanied by the rest of the family, as in scenes of sabbath meals or Havdalah. However, they often play a more central role in scenes associated with their world in east European Jewish tradition, such as in the extremely popular portrayals of the making of flags for Simhat Torah or the blessing of sons on sabbath eve. Another typical example is a New Year postcard entitled in Hebrew and Yiddish *Habeḥinah (Farheren)* ('The Examination'), which is clearly adapted from the famous painting *Der Besuch des Rabbi* ('The Rabbi's Visit', *c.*1886), by the Hungarian Jewish artist Isidor Kaufmann (1853–1921), who specialized in scenes of the *shtetl* (Fig. 18).[54] The image on the postcard, which

[51] See E. Weinberger, 'Yom huledet le'or hamekorot', in S. Y. Zevin and Z. Warhaftig (eds.), *Mazkeret: kovets torani lezekher . . . harav yitshak halevi hertsog* (Jerusalem, 1962); T. Preschel, 'Yom hahuledet etsel gedolei hatorah', *Hado'ar*, 48 (1968–9), 196–7; id., 'Yom huledet shel meḥabrim gedolei torah', *Hado'ar*, 51 (1972), 430; id., 'Yom huledet shel benei torah', *Hado'ar*, 52 (1973), 439; I. Ta-Shma, 'Al yom hahuledet beyisra'el', *Zion*, 67 (2002), 19–24. All this applies only to European Jewish communities; in the Islamic world Jews neither noted nor remembered their birthdays.

[52] And perhaps it is not accidental that the ceremony marking a boy's thirteenth birthday, namely the bar mitzvah, was created in Germany—though centuries earlier. In this case as well scholars see the influence of the surrounding society on the Jews. Cf. Gutmann, *Jewish Life Cycle*, 9–10; and S. Sabar, 'Tekes bar hamitsvah bamasoret uvaomanut shel edot yisra'el', *Rimonim*, 5 (1997), 61–77.

[53] Some examples: Golnitzki, *Bemaḥzor hayamim*, pl. 19, fig. 26; I. Shachar, *The Jewish Year* (Leiden, 1975), pl. VIIc.

[54] On Kaufmann and his work, see the comprehensive exhibition catalogue: G. T. Natter (ed). *Rabbiner, Bocher, Talmudschüler. Bilder des Wiener Malers Isidor Kaufmann, 1853–1921* (Vienna, 1995). *The Rabbi's Visit*, one of Kaufmann's most popular paintings, was frequently exhibited and reproduced in the 19th century (it was first shown in the respected Wiener Künstlerhaus as early as 1886). See ibid. 23, 180–1.

Fig. 17. Khayim Goldberg, *Havdalah* ('Prayer at the end of the sabbath') 'Hamavdil bein kodesh leḥol, | Ḥatoteinu hu yimḥol | Zareinu vekhaspenu yarbeh kaḥol | vekhakokhavim bal-ailah' ('[He] who differentiates the holy from the profane, | May he also pardon our transgressions. | May he multiply our seed as the sands | And as the stars at night' (part of the Havdalah prayers) (Warsaw: S. Resnik, *c.*1912–14). Joseph Hoffman Jewish Postcard Collection, Folklore Research Centre, Hebrew University of Jerusalem

Fig. 18. After Isidor Kaufmann, *Habeḥinah (Farheren)* ('The Examination'). 'Leshanah tovah tikatevu' ('May you be inscribed for a good year'). (New York(?): publisher unknown, n.d.; repr. Germany *c.*1910–20). Author's collection

deviates in significant details from the painting, shows the little boy in traditional dress standing shyly before the rabbi and his father, who are quizzing him on what he has learned, while his mother and brothers—missing in the painting—tensely watch the scene from outside the door.[55]

A more unusual custom appears in another postcard designed by Khayim Gold-berg, entitled *'Krishme' ba a kimpetorn* ('The Reading of the Shema for a Woman in Childbed'). (Fig. 19). Lying on a bed in an inner room on the left is the woman who gave birth (to a boy, according to the signs hanging above her), guarded by two women, one sitting in front of the room and the other standing in the doorway beside her. On the right a group of children is led by a young *melamed* (school-teacher) in the prayer. This custom is connected to the deep fears that accompanied childbirth in the past. The mortality of infants during birth or the first days of their lives necessitated various means of protection. In all Jewish communities, from Germany to Morocco and from Italy to Iran, amulets were traditionally employed against the demon Lilith, who was believed to kidnap infants.[56] In eastern Europe the amulets were handwritten, printed, or designed as ornate and colourful paper-cuts, which were hung in the birthing room at least until the eighth day in the case of a boy (the circumcision ceremony on this day was considered protection from then on).[57] Three amulets of this type, known in Yiddish as *kimpet-brivl* or *shir-hamaylesl* (Song of Ascents; following the opening words of the 'protective' Psalm 121, which is written on them), are seen hanging on the curtain in front of the room and over the birthing bed. The writing on them, 'mazl-tov, zokher' ('good luck [for the birth of a] male [child]'), is characteristic of the many printed amulets that remain in various collections (Fig. 20). The praying children document a custom unique to Poland: on the *vakhnakht*, or the night before circumcision—considered the most dangerous, for it is Lilith's last opportunity to attack the male baby before the protective circumcision ceremony—*kheyder* boys were brought by their *melamed* to the mother in childbed to recite the Shema and other prayers, and in this way defend the baby and express the hope that it will grow to be like them.[58] This is the

[55] Cf. ibid. 363; Sabar, *Past Perfect*, p. 48, no. 65. The name of the folk artist who transformed Kaufmann's painting into the postcard illustration in about 1910 is not known.

[56] On Jewish childbirth amulets from various communities and their artistic ornamentation, see S. Sabar, 'Childbirth and Magic: Jewish Folklore and Material Culture', in D. Biale (ed.), *Cultures of the Jews: A New History* (New York, 2002).

[57] For reproductions of east European childbirth papercut amulets, see G. Frankel, *The Art of the Jewish Paper-Cut* (Tel Aviv, 1996), 80–7; Y. and J. Shadur, *Jewish Papercuts: A History and Guide* (Berkeley, 1994), figs. 77, 92, and col. pl. 8, 26, 27.

[58] This custom is reported, for example, by Rabbi Shabbetai Lipschutz (1845–1929; b. Rohatyn, Galicia) in his book on the laws of circumcision, *Sefer sharvit hazahav heḥadash* (1st pub. Munkács, 1898; Brooklyn, NY, 1995), 24 ('Kuntres leil shimurim', par. 13). Lipschutz claims that the prayers of the little boys have the power to remove the evil shells (*kelipot*) from the room of the woman in child-bed, because of the purity of the boys (called *tson kadoshim*). Cf. Y. D. Weisberg, *Sefer otsar haberit: dinei uminhagei milah*, vol. ii (Jerusalem, 1991), 211–12.

Fig. 19. Khayim Goldberg, *'Krishme' ba a kimpetorn* ('The Reading of the Shema Prayer [*keriat-shema*] for a Woman in Childbed') (Warsaw: S. Resnik, *c.*1912–14). Author's collection

Fig. 20. Childbirth amulet, eastern Europe, late 19th–early 20th cent. Author's collection

only known visual depiction of this custom, which, significantly enough, survived only on postcards.[59]

CONCLUSION

The postcards that were produced and used during the golden age of illustrated postcards open a fascinating window onto the past. The Jews of Germany, and following them the Jews of Poland, exploited this medium well for their needs. The postcards that were produced in each of these communities present a broad spectrum of subjects that reflect not only the realities of the time but also the desires and ideals of the people. A limited selection of practices and the ways of presenting them on postcards demonstrate some of the differences between the two communities: differences in norms and customs, and also in social outlook and the image of themselves that they wished to present to the world. In both cases the context is nostalgia, but while the German postcards present a relatively distant past edited to create the impression of an enlightened and educated Jewry, the postcards from Poland deal more directly and boldly with religious and daily life. The reality they depict, however, was not, by and large, that of the big-city Jews for whom these cards were largely produced. During this period Polish Jewry witnessed the culmination of a remarkable process of urbanization, and the consumers of these postcards were apparently searching for nostalgic views of the *shtetl* they had left behind. But for us the postcards fulfil another function, one already apprehended by the Jewish intelligentsia of the time, who sensed that a world was quickly disappearing. For us there is as much value in the carefully posed postcard pictures as in the many memoirs written by maskilim about the world of their childhood.[60] In the postcards discussed here, and in hundreds of others, there is, without doubt, source material of great and rare value for more exhaustive investigation of the Jewish experience during these critical years.

Translated from Hebrew by Erica Nadelhaft

---

[59] Goldberg's depiction of this ceremony was issued, like many of his other postcards, in several versions (monochrome sepia, coloured, and coloured with gold highlights, as in my example). An earlier version, a postcard from Kraków, 1902, which is labelled in German 'Krischme leinen bei Wöchnerin', apparently served Goldberg when he staged his scene. For this rare card, see B. Purin, *Die Welt der jüdischen Postkarten* (Vienna, 2001), p. 38, no. 33.

[60] Cf. David Assaf's assessment in his introduction to the memoirs of Yehezkel (Yekhezkl) Kotik (*Mah shera'iti*, 68): 'In the year 1912, facing the rapid process of modernization, large-scale immigration, urbanization, industrialization, and secularization, it was clear to many Jews that the old *shtetl* was on the verge of disappearing. This is the background for the burst of nostalgia and desire for preservation which encompassed many circles, including those who saw themselves as the radical-secular avant-garde—nationalist, Zionist, Yiddishist or socialist.'

Papers for the *Folk*:
Jewish Nationalism and the Birth
of the Yiddish Press in Galicia

JOSHUA SHANES

JEWISH nationalism in Galicia, like its Viennese counterpart, was initially a movement largely of the secular intelligentsia, especially students. Raised in a Polish cultural (and educational) milieu, Jewish students tended at first to identify strongly with Polish nationalist aspirations, but the increasing rejection they experienced from Polish nationalists, among whom antisemitism was sharply rising, made them choice targets for Zionist propaganda. Galician Zionists attacked their 'assimilationist' rivals ferociously, and tried to inspire Galician Jews to support the rebirth of a Jewish national culture instead. At first they relied on the German-language Viennese organ *Selbst-Emanzipation*, but by 1892 they had begun to publish their own Polish-language literature, including a party organ, *Przyszłość* ('The Future').[1]

By the mid-1890s the Jewish nationalist movement, with dozens of associations and roughly 4,000 members throughout the province,[2] had achieved a strong foothold among the secular intelligentsia in Galicia. It could hardly claim to represent the hundreds of thousands of traditional Jews in the province, however. Zionists occasionally debated reaching out to these Jews, but the focus of Zionist efforts continued to be the Jewish intelligentsia. Lecture topics were oriented towards those with little to no background in Jewish history, for example, and Zionist publications continued to reflect a secular readership. Most Jews, after all, could read neither Polish nor German, and anyway would have been alienated by the Zionist publications' largely secular orientation.[3]

The author gratefully acknowledges the generous support of the George L. Mosse Endowment at the University of Wisconsin which made this work possible.

[1] *Selbst-Emanzipation*, founded by Nathan Birnbaum in 1885, appeared regularly until mid-1886, when it was discontinued, and then again appeared regularly from 1890 to 1893.

[2] M. Ehrenpreis, 'Vor Herzl und Mit Herzl', in T. Nussenblatt (ed.), *Theodor Herzl Jahrbuch* (Vienna, 1937), 185.

[3] Nor could most read literary Hebrew. Thus, although a number of Hebrew-language journals appeared in the 1880s, many Zionist-oriented, their readership remained Jews already committed to the Haskalah, and not the more traditionally minded masses.

Partially as a result of this political vacuum, a new kind of literature emerged in Galicia in the early 1890s: a populist nationalist press published in the Yiddish language.[4] These papers, published and edited by Zionists (and often supported by Zionist associations), represented an early, major effort of outreach beyond the secular intelligentsia, and constituted a revolutionary advance for the Jewish nationalist movement. Anticipating the eventual dominance of the Yiddish-language press in Galicia, although pre-dating it by over a decade, they helped to lay the foundation for popular acceptance of Yiddish as a modern language worthy of its own press.[5] More importantly, they made a critical contribution to the trans-formation of Jewish self-consciousness from an essentially religious to a national orientation, through the appropriation of religious norms which their readers shared. Papers such as *Dos folk*, *Der folksfraynd*, the *Yidishe folkstsaytung*, and the *Yidishes folksblat*, while they often survived just one or two years, collectively pro-vided a forum, in the vernacular language, for nationalists to convince the masses not only that the Jews constituted a nation, but that they needed to become politi-cally active to win the same rights other nations enjoyed.

Despite the fact that the vast majority of Galician Jewry read only Yiddish, the decision to publish in the Jewish tongue did not come naturally to Jewish national-ists. As Dan Miron has shown, until the 1880s at the earliest, Jewish intellectuals (including the founders of Yiddish literature itself) generally viewed Yiddish as ugly and inappropriate for literary purposes. Hebrew, on the other hand, was revered as aesthetically perfect, even divine.[6] Only after 1881, when despondency over the possibility of emancipation and immigration led to the rise of Jewish national ideologies, could Jewish intellectuals begin to approach Yiddish not as a regrettable means with which to influence the masses, but as a cultural heritage in itself.[7]

---

[4] For a brief discussion of some of these papers, see J. Toury, *Die jüdische Presse im österreichischen Kaiserreich* (Tübingen, 1983), 131–8. The following papers published before 1897 will be discussed here (the German name, usually appearing on the masthead, is given in parentheses): *Yidishe folkstsay-tung* (*Jüdische Volkszeitung*), ed. David Silberbusch and Leibel Taubes (Kołomyja, 1890–1); *Izraelitishes folksblat* (*Israelitisches Volksblatt*), ed. Efraim Laufer (Kołomyja, 1890–1); *Der folksfraynd* (*Der Volksfreund*), ed. Alter Teicher and Leibel Taubes (Kołomyja, 1891–2); *Yidishes familienblat* (*Jüdisches Familienblatt*), ed. Shevach Knöbel (Tyśmienica, 1893–4); *Yidishes folksblat* (*Jüdisches Volksblatt*), ed. Shevach Knöbel (Tyśmienica, 1894); *Ha-am/Dos folk*, ed. Leibel Taubes (Kołomyja, 1895–7). The last of these papers appeared originally as separate Hebrew and Yiddish publications, beginning in 1892. In 1895 the Yiddish paper alone began to be published under the combined name.

[5] The percentage of Jewish papers in Galicia published in Yiddish continued to rise over the next two decades, so that by the First World War the vast majority of Jewish papers were Yiddish; see Toury, *Die jüdische Presse*, 138.   [6] D. Miron, *A Traveler Disguised* (New York, 1973), 47 ff.

[7] The most important agent in this transformation was Sholem Aleichem, who essentially created a literary history for the Yiddish language through the articles in his short-lived literary journal *Di yidishe folks-bibliotek* (1888–9); see Miron, *A Traveler Disguised*, 27–33. Two other Yiddish journals appeared in the 1880s in Russia: the *Yidishes folksblat* (1881–90), ed. A. Zederbaum, and *Der hoyz-fraynd* (1888–9, 1894–6), ed. M. Spektor.

Jewish intellectuals in Galicia exhibited no greater affinity for Yiddish than their Russian counterparts.[8] Thus, the Jewish press in Galicia through the 1880s included German, Hebrew, and eventually Polish papers, but Yiddish-language papers were conspicuously absent.[9] The emergence of these Yiddish papers in the 1890s, then, reflected an independent and still radical view that recognized the need for Yiddish-language propaganda to reach out to the Orthodox masses. They were not, however, merely isolated attempts at such outreach, but rather represented a co-ordinated effort by a small number of educated, dedicated nationalists. Some of the papers were associated with mainstream Zionist associations. The first two to appear, the *Yidishe folkstsaytung* and the *Izraelitishes folksblat*, said so explicitly in their programme statements. Both were available for sale at the offices of the three major Zionist groups then in existence,[10] and both printed news of those groups' activities.[11] Moreover, papers often joined together in united subscription campaigns. Subscribers to either of the above papers, for example, automatically received its partner 'so they should have a paper [to read] every sabbath', as the *Folksblat* banner explained.[12] The *Yidishes familienblat* and the *Yidishes folksblat* were both edited by Shevach Knöbel,[13] who did not offer the two papers for the price of one, but did cross-advertise subscriptions between them. Leibel Taubes (1863–1933), whose agitation for Yiddish propaganda led to the birth of this press in the first place, launched as many as three papers and even recycled material between them.

[8] For a detailed history of the Jewish press in Galicia since 1848, see Toury, *Die jüdische Presse*, 25–35, 58–69, 122–38.

[9] Some German-language papers appeared in Hebrew characters, including the Zionist *Drohobyczer Zeitung* (1883–1914). Hebrew journals included the maskilic anti-Zionist *Ivri anokhi/ Ha'ivri* in Brody (1886–90), as well as the Zionist *Haharshu/Hashemesh* in Stanisławów (1888–9). (Journals often alternated names to avoid the Austrian tax on weekly papers.) The latter was edited by Hirsh Gottlieb, later an agent for the *Yidishe folkstsaytung*; see G. Bader, 'Hatenuah hale'umit bekerev aheinu benei yisrael begalitsiyah', *Aḥi'asef* (1894–5), 173. Bader writes that none of the Hebrew journals achieved significant circulation in Galicia.

[10] Namely, Tsion (Lemberg), Shoḥerei Tushiah (Stryj), and Ha'ivri (Drohobycz).

[11] Tsion later renounced its association with the *Yidishe folkstsaytung* when the paper suddenly endorsed the 'assimilationist' candidate Emil Byk over Joseph Bloch in the 1891 parliamentary elections. The paper's editor, Leibel Taubes, had left town for a week and his substitute apparently accepted a bribe to print the endorsement. Although Taubes immediately issued a correction and continued to endorse Bloch in future issues, Tsion did not back down, and the paper folded soon after; see n. 12. On the election campaign, see further below.

[12] This relationship eventually went sour when the *Folksblat* discovered that Hirsh Gottlieb, the agent for the *Yidishe folkstsaytung*, had absconded with their subscription money; see *Izraelitishes folksblat* (23 Aug. 1891). On the heels of the Byk endorsement fiasco, the *Yidishe folkstsaytung* simply folded and Taubes (with Alter Teicher) launched his second paper, *Der folksfraynd*, which became the *Folksblat*'s new partner; see *Der folksfraynd* (1 Sept. 1891).

[13] I have been unable to discover any information about Shevach Knöbel; the name may well have been a pseudonym.

Nevertheless, these papers were not a part of the Zionist movement per se—they were not the organs of any Zionist association[14]—and the most obvious sign of their ideological independence was their attitude towards the Yiddish language. Generally speaking, the Zionist movement, even in Galicia, clearly considered Hebrew to be *the* Jewish national language. Zionist associations, from the beginning, invested a great deal in Hebrew language courses, and generally regarded 'jargon' to be a gutter dialect of High German. An article in *Selbst-Emanzipation* in 1885, for example, reporting on the formation of a new Jewish trade union, commented, 'The language of the group is, of course, jargon, since the young men are unfortunately not yet at the level of the intelligentsia and able to make use of a modern language.'[15] In 1891 the paper recommended to those wanting to protest the census (which did not allow one to identify oneself as speaking a Jewish language) that one should at least write in Hebrew rather than Yiddish.[16]

The position of the Yiddish press on the language question was far more ambiguous. On the one hand, the papers officially championed Hebrew as the language of the Jewish people. Within the Yiddish press itself all references to 'our holy language' self-evidently referred to Hebrew. *Der folksfraynd*, for example, in a piece entitled 'On our National Language', argued this point at length, insisting that Hebrew was neither dead nor impossible to revitalize as a modern spoken language.[17] More fundamentally, the article exclaimed, Hebrew embodied the Jewish spirit, which it alone had protected from assimilation in exile.

[Many nations] have lost the rights to their fatherland, but they preserve their language with body and soul. They found linguistic associations to cultivate their language and its science, and they hold lectures in order to maintain their language . . . but why among us Jews is our language [so neglected]; our holy language, the first codified language with which the world was created, why have we neglected it so? Why do our young people study all foreign languages day and night, and not look at our language once?[18]

At the same time, however, these papers were deliberately and unapologetically Yiddish organs, 'genuine' Jewish papers written 'for the people' in the 'language of the people'. It is in these terms that they justified their existence. *Der folksfraynd*, the same paper quoted above commending Hebrew as the Jews' 'national language', had emphatically rejected it as an appropriate medium for a Jewish newspaper just as it rejected Polish and German.

[14] The *Yidishe folkstsaytung* did at first receive financial support from Tsion in Lemberg, but it was edited independently. The party organ of Galician Zionists, as noted above, was *Przyszłość*, although in 1893 they did make a short-lived attempt to publish a party organ in Yiddish called *Der karmel/Der veker*. The Yiddish papers were published not in the main cities but in the provincial south-east (see n. 4).   [15] *Selbst-Emanzipation*, no. 2 (1885).

[16] *Selbst-Emanzipation*, no. 1 (1891). On the census, see below.

[17] The position that Hebrew could become a spoken language was no less radical than the view that Yiddish could be employed as a literary language. It was just thirteen years earlier, after all, that Eliezer Ben-Yehuda had written the first article arguing that Hebrew could become a spoken language 'if we only wish'. See C. Rabin, 'The National Idea and the Revival of Hebrew', in J. Reinharz and A. Shapira (eds.), *Essential Papers on Zionism* (New York, 1996), 750.   [18] *Der folksfraynd* (15 Nov. 1891).

Just as we certainly do not aim to speak and write to our people in Polish or German, so we do not attempt to speak and write only Hebrew. Our people, by which we mean the ordinary public, the majority of the people . . . don't understand Polish, don't understand German, and don't understand Hebrew. With these people we need to speak ordinary Yiddish, as we are used to speaking from childhood on, and as we speak in our neighbourhoods and in business, plainly and straightforwardly [*on khokhmes*].[19]

It was not merely pragmatism, however, that dictated this decision. Most of the papers, including *Der folksfraynd* and the others more closely affiliated with the Zionists, regularly described Yiddish as the Jews' 'national language'. This position arose from the papers' populist orientation, but it also reflected an important campaign, which they initiated, for Jews to declare Yiddish their *Umgangssprache*, or language of daily use, to the Austrian authorities. The Austrian constitution guaranteed certain national minority rights, but only for its officially recognized nationalities.[20] Austrian law, however, defined nationality by linguistic criteria and did not accept Yiddish as a legitimate language.[21] Galician Jews, overwhelmingly Yiddish-speaking, were usually incorrectly registered as Polish.[22] As a result, they did not qualify for national rights, and were not even counted as a nationality in the Austrian census. Jewish nationalists thus had a tremendous stake in asserting Yiddish to be the Jewish national language, for in a system in which the existence of a nationality was determined by a unique 'language of daily use', Hebrew could not possibly achieve any legitimacy.

The real importance of Hebrew, then, seems to have been as a nationalist icon on which to ground a national identity among the Jewish masses. Indeed, Yiddish itself was also a symbol, albeit one laden with practical ramifications, above all, inclusion in the census, and the papers freely fluctuated between the two depending upon the context. Joshua Fishman's observation that vernacular literature 'provided the masses with the emotionalized link between language and nationalism that exists for elites at the level of ideological program' rings true for Galician Jewry.[23] However, in this case, whereas the innovation of Yiddish as a print medium was vital, Yiddish as a symbol of Jewish nationhood did not supplant Hebrew but joined it. By publishing in Yiddish the papers could simultaneously venerate Hebrew

[19] *Der folksfraynd* (1 Jan. 1891).

[20] These included the 'inalienable right' of every people (*Volkstamm*) to 'preserve and cultivate its nationality and language', and the equal rights of all languages in schools, government administration, and public life.

[21] For a detailed discussion of the issue of *Umgangssprachen* in Austrian censuses, see E. Brix, *Die Umgangssprachen in Altösterreich zwischen Agitation und Assimilation* (Vienna, 1982).

[22] In 1869 Jews were still generally recorded as German, but with the Polonization of the state bureaucracy in the 1870s Galicia's 'German' population steadily declined in favour of the Polish: 60.4% of Galician Jews were 'Polish' by 1880, 74.6% in 1890, 76.5% in 1900, and by 1910 over 92% were registered Poles (see M. Rosenfeld, *Die polnische Judenfrage* (Vienna, 1918), 147). Poles strongly opposed the recognition of Yiddish because they used the Jews to claim numerical superiority over the Ukrainians in Galicia; without the Jews, Poles and Ukrainians were roughly equal in number.

[23] J. Fishman, *Language and Nationalism: Two Integrative Essays* (Rowley, Mass., 1972), 52.

as the Jews' national language while passively proving that Yiddish was also the (or a) Jewish national language. The very existence of the press, whatever its actual content, testified to the reality of the Yiddish language, and thus by extension (at least in the Habsburg empire) of a Jewish nation.

This same ambiguity in regard to mainstream Zionism is echoed by the papers' treatment of Erets Yisroel (the land of Israel). To a certain extent, the papers' attitude towards Palestine did reflect the official programme of Galician Zionists as formulated in their 1893 party platform.[24] The Jüdisch-nationale Partei Galiziens (Jewish National Party of Galicia) adopted at that time its so-called 'dual programme' which viewed the rebuilding of a Jewish homeland in Palestine as a long-term goal, but directed its current activities towards the nurturing of 'Jewish national consciousness' and the securing of Jewish national rights in Galicia.

The Yiddish press of the early 1890s, particularly those papers more directly affiliated with the Zionist associations, repeatedly described Palestine as the Jewish fatherland, and called for its resettlement, especially through the support of the colonization association Admath Israel in Stryj.[25] Such support, however, never entailed negating the Diaspora. On the contrary, the papers' Zionist agenda seems closer to the Western model of Palestine as a refuge for Russian (and Romanian) Jewry alongside local patriotism for themselves as emancipated Jews.[26] Thus the same papers that proclaimed Palestine the Jewish fatherland could simultaneously refer to Galicia as the Jewish motherland in defence of their domestic political agenda. Indeed, the papers' Diaspora orientation allowed them to formulate arguments of Polish patriotism framed in Jewish national terms. To those Jews who feared Polish reprisals for the assertion of Jewish national rights, for example, the *Yidishe folkstsaytung* argued that Jewish nationalism offered the best framework within which Galician Jews could work for the betterment of their shared homeland (i.e. Galicia) for all of its inhabitants (note again the reference to Yiddish as the language of the Jews):

For surely we can live with our Polish brothers in a truly brotherly [fashion] even if we acknowledge that we know we are of the people of Israel? For surely we can foster our Polish language as the language of the land and of our cherished Polish literature, even if we say that

[24] In Apr. 1893 Galician Zionists, led by their flagship association Tsion in Lemberg, formed the Jüdisch-nationale Partei Galiziens (Jewish National Party of Galicia). Those associations that maintained the colonization of Palestine as their primary task joined the Vienna-based Zion, Verband der öster-reichischen Vereine für die Kolonisation Palästinas und Syriens (Zion Union of Austrian Associations for the Colonization of Palestine and Syria). See A. Gaisbauer, *Davidstern und Doppeladler* (Vienna, 1988), 66, 77–8, and N. M. Gelber, *Toledot hatenuah hatsionit begalitsiyah* (Jerusalem, 1958), 166 ff.

[25] The association was founded in 1891. Its leader, Abraham Salz, became an important figure in the Austrian Zionist movement.

[26] S. Almog, *Zionism and History: The Rise of a New Jewish Consciousness* (Jerusalem, 1987), 184. The papers characteristically expressed extreme reverence for the Austrian emperor, Franz Joseph, whom they credited with Jewish emancipation and whom they exonerated of any fault in the Austrian political system. This was probably somewhat tactical, catering to Habsburg Jewry's adoration of Franz Joseph, but it was likely quite sincere as well.

our own language is Yiddish? Yes, even those Jews who say truthfully that they are a special nation can still be good Polish patriots; they can love the land of Galicia as their motherland and the Polish nation as [their] sister nation. We have one interest in common with our Polish brothers: their good is our good and we can work together for the betterment of the land, 'for the good of our beloved motherland'. We can and should respect and love the language of the land, the language of our sister nation. Of course, the Poles should also reciprocate as brothers, as brothers from one mother, and [treat] our nation as a sister nation.[27]

As with its reverence for Hebrew, the purpose of invoking the land of Israel was symbolic, a tool designed to generate a national identity among Galician Jewry. Erets Yisroel was a natural focus for early Jewish nationalists. Like Hebrew, it appealed to religious sensibilities (religious Jews after all prayed daily for the gathering in of the exiles to the land of Israel), while simultaneously answering secular critics who argued that the Jews' territorial dispersion meant that they no longer constituted a nation. The papers often contrasted Palestine with America or Argentina (popular alternatives to migrating Jews), which they argued were foreign, while in Erets Yisroel Jews enjoyed both physical and spiritual familiarity.

Our only place of refuge is the land of Israel. This land is not foreign to us, thank God ... In this land every Jew feels at home, every corner, every stone is known to him, instils in him holy feelings, every mountain and every river speaks to him in brotherly language, reveals to him beautiful, elevated secrets and gives him greetings from his fathers, from his prophets, his kings and his heroes.[28]

Ha-am/Dos folk, Leibel Taubes's third and most successful Yiddish paper, highlights the loose relationship most of these papers shared with the Zionist movement. Taubes was not only a dedicated Zionist but also one of the movement's best orators.[29] In 1896 the paper wrote a glowing review of Theodor Herzl's *Der Judenstaat*, and even published a Yiddish translation of the work the following year. *Ha-am* even offered itself to be the new organ of the World Zionist Organization, which Herzl was then founding.[30] Nevertheless, Ha-am's detailed programme statement included no hint of political Zionism and did not discuss Palestine. It addressed instead 'political, national, religious, and economic' questions of Jewish life in Galicia. It sought the realization of Jewish civil rights as guaranteed by the constitution, as well as national minority rights for the Jews, which were theoretically

---

[27] *Yidishe folkstsaytung* (1 Dec. 1890).

[28] *Yidishe folkstsaytung* (1 Jan. 1891). The myth of Jewish intimacy with the land of Israel played a critical role in the Zionist movement throughout Europe, an example of what Anthony Smith has identified as the need by nationalists to draw upon a 'golden age' in order to establish its eternal and organic connection to the community's 'historic space' (see A. Smith, 'The "Golden Age" and National Renewal', in his *Myths and Nationhood* (New York, 1997)).

[29] On Taubes, see his short memoir, *Zikhroynes fun leybl toybes* (Vienna, 1920).

[30] J. Toury, 'Herzl's Newspaper: The Creation of *Die Welt*', *Zionism*, 2 (Autumn 1980), 163. Of course, Herzl could never have accepted the offer; his organ, with which he wanted to target the 'upper echelons' of Jewry in the West as well as Western governments, had to be fully Western, bourgeois, and above all in the German language.

protected by the constitution, but only if Jews could win recognition as a nationality. The principal objective of the paper, it concluded, was to 'awaken' the Jews' national pride and convince them that they must claim their national rights.[31]

Ha-am, as well as all of the other papers, repeatedly called for unity among Jews. Such calls not only made the Jewish nationalist movement the key to unity, a traditional Jewish value, but inherently placed these editors and their papers almost above political division; the Yiddish press became the focus of Jewish national identity. In other words, the ideology of Jewish unity presented by these papers was most often based in support of the papers themselves; subscribing to these 'genuine' Jewish organs became the hallmark of a true, national Jew. *Ha-am* said as much in concluding its programme statement:

we hope and expect that all those who have good intentions towards our people, that all who are moved by the present terrible condition of the Jews and strive to improve it, all true friends of our people will stand by us with their payment and also with their action, that all will support us and our undertaking.

The *Izraelitishes folksblat* (and its sister paper the *Yidishe folkstsaytung*) even linked its subscribers to the project of resettling the land of Israel by donating one-tenth of its income to the colonies.

To support strongly, dear readers, the holy undertaking of settling the land of Israel, our [paper] has made the decision to donate one-tenth of the proceeds of our paper in order to support our unfortunate Russian brothers and to help the colonization of Palestine. We request the Jewish reading community, even those who have newspapers in other languages, to subscribe to our paper, which strongly represents Jewish interests.[32]

In this light, delinquent subscribers, an endemic problem for all of these papers, did not merely threaten the viability of the newspaper, but constituted a direct attack on the persecuted Russian Jews whom the papers supported.

Now dear readers and subscribers to our paper! You deserve credit for the great thing you do in subscribing, and particularly that you pay promptly. Know that with that alone you support the Russian refugees who are so unfortunate that no pen can describe the circumstances of their troubles. And he who reads the paper and does not pay . . . he should know that he thus robs hundreds of thousands of unfortunate families who are wandering with such difficulty in darkness before the entire world.[33]

In order to establish their authenticity, the papers carefully positioned themselves as 'organs of the people' written in 'simple' Yiddish to represent the 'Orthodox' interests.[34] Thus whereas *Selbst-Emanzipation*, courting largely assimi-

---

[31] *Ha-am/Dos folk* (24 Sept. 1895).   [32] *Izraelitishes folksblat* (8 July 1891).

[33] *Yidishe folkstsaytung* (1 July 1891). Ironically this was the *Folkstsaytung*'s last issue.

[34] This is self-evident, above all, in the papers' names themselves, so many of which included the word *folk*. Here it is important to distinguish between Knöbel's papers, which were specifically 'Orthodox' in orientation, and Taubes's, which sought to take the 'golden mean' between religious reform and 'those religious Jews who close themselves to the modern world' (*Ha-am/Dos folk* (24 Sept.

lated, secular Jews, remained obsessively focused on the radically pro-Polish 'assimilationist' association Agudas Achim (Union of Brothers), gloating over its final demise in 1893, the Yiddish press rarely mentioned it. It focused more often on the decline of religious observance, especially among Jewish girls, who were frequently sent to state schools, which it equated with national betrayal. Generally, the papers portrayed themselves as the solution to this malaise.

Shevach Knöbel, the editor of two papers, is perhaps the best example of this convergence of religious orthodoxy and national consciousness. In the summer of 1894 Knöbel travelled throughout eastern Galicia to encourage subscriptions to his papers. An article signed by his 'friend' 'Shmilkye Hasid' describes the visit to his home town.[35] Welcoming Knöbel to his *shtetl* dressed in sabbath clothes, Shmilkye arranges a meeting with the wealthy Jew Reb Shakhne. Knöbel tries to explain that he is the 'redaktor' (editor) of a newspaper, but Reb Shakhne hears him say 'dokter' and wants to know what Knöbel wants. 'No, Reb Shakhne,' he explains, 'I am a *redaktor*, that is, one who publishes a newspaper. I publish a Jewish newspaper, the *Yidishes familienblat*, which represents Orthodox interests, and as you are a genuine Jew, you must support such a paper and order it.' But Reb Shakhne doesn't understand what 'Orthodox' means either, and so Knöbel explains, 'That is those Jews who hold fast in their faith and don't demand any innovations.' Knöbel tells him to ask his daughter about such issues, and the rich man responds, 'What should I ask my daughter? She is continually reading *Menores hame'or* [a traditional devotional text], [and] there it does not talk about this.' Finally Knöbel loses his temper:

An honest Jew like yourself is always engaging in Torah and acts of kindness, but needs sometimes to have this world in mind also, for by having nothing [of this world] in mind and neglecting your children, especially your daughters, they will soon not be as religious as you. Since you don't look into this at all, she is not reading the *Menores hame'or*, she is reading a German book [i.e. Haskalah literature], and such books make no good impression on young people . . . [until] the daughter wants only a 'doctor' for a husband and laughs off all of Judaism and Jewish customs.

One must be more attentive to one's children, he continues. Not all such books are harmful, but one has to be alert, and the *Yidishes folksblat* with its Orthodox orientation helps parents reach their children, for example, with its biographies of great Jews, 'For young people know the lives of Schiller, Goethe, Shakespeare, and Chekhov, as well as of the apostates Heine and Börne, but [not] of great Jews.' In the end he convinces the man, who immediately subscribes to the paper and goes to look at what his daughter is reading.[36]

1895)). Thus Taubes, for example, more openly supported Jewish educational reform, a topic which Knöbel left alone.

[35] On Shmilkye or Shmueli Hasid, see below.

[36] *Yidishes folksblat* (29 June 1894). The story was probably fabricated. It provided Knöbel with a subtle means of explaining to his readers what a *redaktor* did, what it meant to be Orthodox, and what services an Orthodox newspaper could provide. Elsewhere he defined assimilationism as well.

Similarly, an article in the *Yidishes familienblat* written in a heavy Galician dialect (doubtless to suggest authenticity) blames parents for sending their children to schools where Jewish learning is neglected. Again the newspaper is presented as the solution. 'The best cure for the time being is the newspaper, which can teach them who they are, make them somewhat familiar with Jewish history.'[37] Knöbel did not invent the idea that a newspaper constituted a religious literature vital to every 'genuine' Jewish home. The very first Galician Yiddish papers, the *Izraelitishes folksblat* and the *Yidishe folkstsaytung*, combined so that subscribers 'should have a paper [to read] every sabbath'. In this way, the editors subtly entered the newspapers into the religious canon appropriate for sabbath study.[38]

The idea of influencing the Orthodox masses through the press was not an original one, even in Galicia. The ultra-Orthodox party Maḥzikei Hadas (Defenders of the Faith) had attempted this over a decade earlier, on the eve of the 1879 elections.[39] But the party published its paper (other than its first issues) in Hebrew. Even by the 1890s the idea of a Yiddish-language paper was still considered radical. The Galician Yiddish papers had to justify their use of Yiddish, ironically not to any government censor, but to the Jewish public itself. The papers fought to transform traditional Jews into newspaper readers, and therefore had to explain to the public the purpose of a Yiddish paper.

In a lead article in November 1895, for example, an editorial in *Ha-am* complains that the Jew is too interested in foreign politics and human interest stories from abroad, and argues that he needs to focus more on Jewish politics, 'that is, the politics that he does not have'. This was the purpose of a Yiddish newspaper. 'The Jew does not yet know and does not want to know what he has to look for in a Yiddish newspaper. Therefore the Yiddish newspapers have fewer readers and their effect is small; therefore they have less support and their existence is miserable.' The author describes how he went to a certain businessman, a 'modern, educated Jew', and asked him to subscribe. 'I already get the [Viennese] *Neue Freie Presse*', the man responded. The author is indignant: 'As if we want to compete with the *Presse*. As if we consider that our poor, small paper for 70 kreuzer a quarter should, God forbid, threaten the *Neue Freie Presse*, which costs 8 guldeny a quarter.' The papers have different purposes, he explains. A Yiddish newspaper is a mirror to the Jewish nation, an alarm call to a people so oppressed that it doesn't even recognize its oppression, so beaten that it has become indifferent to the humiliation it suffers.[40]

---

[37] *Yidishes familienblat* (8 Dec. 1893).

[38] Significantly, the Gerer *rebbe* (R. Avraham M. Alter), despite endorsing the formation of an Orthodox daily (*Der yid*), specifically asked his hasidim not to read the paper on the sabbath. See G. Bacon, *The Politics of Tradition: Agudat Yisrael in Poland 1916–1939* (Jerusalem, 1996), 62.

[39] On Maḥzikei Hadas, see R. Manekin, 'Tsemiḥatah vegibushah shel ha'ortodoksiyah hayehudit begalitsiyah: ḥevrat maḥzikei hadat 1867–1883', Hebrew University Ph.D. thesis, 2000.

[40] *Ha-am/Dos folk* (1 Nov. 1895).

Knöbel intuitively sensed the importance of a Yiddish paper as an instrument to strengthen Jewish national feeling. A leader in his *Yidishes familienblat*, essentially a subscription appeal, reasserted the need for the 'jargon paper' along these lines. Against those who say that foreign-language papers are enough, he writes:

But in truth whoever can read a newspaper in other languages must first understand that every people must have a newspaper that every single person can understand, for not everyone can understand Hebrew, German, or Polish—but jargon everybody understands, the most highly educated as well as the ignorant.

Indeed, Knöbel went even further, suggesting that his paper had the potential to be a new public forum to unite the Jewish people. To what purpose were newspapers founded? Not to bring the news—that was incidental. Rather it was either to advance a party goal or else simply to unify a people.

Our Galician Jews still need a newspaper to join the people together, to discuss in the paper what they lack, how exactly one can help. A newspaper is such, for example, that if one is having a meeting, one can give advice, one can discuss in every city or association what the meeting needs [to accomplish]. Likewise a newspaper is a meeting place for many [people] from hundreds of cities. With the newspaper one can unite small strengths, and, most importantly, advise individuals together . . . [For] each person who reads the newspaper, all the news that is happening in the world [and] the life stories we present will awaken in that reader an honourable feeling [that] he is proud to come from such a people, such great men, such sages and geniuses . . .[41]

Other papers defined themselves in precisely the same terms. *Der folksfraynd*, for example, in its mission statement, emphasized above all its role as a public forum:

It has already been felt for a long time in many—very many—quarters that we Jews in Galicia need to have our own Jewish newspaper, which is not specifically about the news normally conveyed in the newspapers. No, not only about this—this is totally a side issue; the main thing is, we Jews need to have an organ for our people, a newspaper for our own interests, in order to hear one another's opinions and advise one other about our situation— our position, our economic situation, our communities, and the like.[42]

The papers often referred to other nationalities, especially the Ukrainians, in Galicia known as Ruthenians, who had already begun to challenge Polish domination through effective political organization. Jewish nationalists noted that the Ruthenians had begun to secure national rights only because they had organized themselves and demanded such rights; the Jews needed to do the same. Usually, however, such comparisons were based not on admiration, but on embarrassment. That is, instead of arguing that Jews ought to learn from the other nationalities, the papers emphasized that even these others, who ranked so much lower than the Jews, had won minority rights; how much more should the Jews have them?

---

[41] *Yidishes familienblat* (19 Jan. 1894).   [42] *Der folksfraynd* (1 Jan. 1891).

Ruthenians (as well as Romanians in Bukovina) were respected national minorities, stated an editorial in *Ha-am*,

yet even the Jews' worst enemy will recognize that in terms of intelligence we tower above both of these nations. We are in general much more intelligent than [both] the Ruthenians and the Romanians. Then why is it that we are so low politically! Simple—political rights are not demanded, so we don't have them; since we don't demand them, they don't give them.[43]

Other 'non-historical' nations (i.e. nations with no history of political independence) fell victim to similar arguments. The following appeal, for example, came from the *Izraelitishes folksblat* several years earlier.

The Serbians and Bulgarians who are simple, crude pigs who stand thousands of rungs below us, they are moved to struggle for a nationality and for a fatherland, to achieve their freedom, yet we Jews who have the most glorious history of all peoples, with our holy fatherland, which is respected and held to be holy by all nations . . . we are totally sleeping—we are completely not moved, we should also achieve some kind of freedom . . .[44]

As Shmuel Almog has pointed out, such comparisons were especially pronounced in the Habsburg empire, where Jews could point to other non-historical nations who had won recognition as nations and conclude that the Jews' claim was at least as sound.[45] Thus the tenacious Zionist claim of direct continuity between the 'glorious' past of ancient Israel and contemporary Jewry, a connection which the papers' appropriation of Hebrew and Erets Yisroel as symbols essentially sought to strengthen, would ultimately form an important basis of the Jews' claim to nationhood.

Rather than merely arguing that the Jews constituted a nation, however, the papers simply assumed it as a given and mocked the Jewish secular intelligentsia for denying the obvious. Because the nature of this national identity was in any case based in traditional values (Jewish unity, Hebrew, the land of Israel), it was relatively natural to claim that all 'genuine' Jews believed in Jewish nationhood; it merely entailed transforming the language of an existing identity. By associating denial of Jewish 'nationhood' with the secular Jewish elite, and confirmation of it with the ordinary, streetwise Jew, the newspapers greatly eased this transformation:

There are small things which a simple farmer who has a healthy human understanding will understand well, while people who have some education, yes, even great sages, can't get into their head the simplest part of such a concept . . . Suddenly great sages have begun to break their philosophical heads and have discovered a new type of question about Jews, a question at which every simple Jew totally laughs, poking at him while he laughs. Have you heard such a question: Are the Jews a people or just a religious community, that is, only a society

---

[43] *Ha-am/Dos folk* (24 Sept. 1896).
[44] *Izraelitishes folksblat* (8 July 1891).   [45] Almog, *Zionism and History*, 32.

which has its own statutes? Obviously the people who argue such nonsense are simply crazy; they ought to be sent to the mental asylum. Again! Everyone who looks at just the first pages of world history knows that we are the oldest people among all the peoples who exist today, that at that time when we had our land and our government, our king and our laws, all the other peoples did not yet exist.[46]

Thus wealth and secular education are linked to assimilation and national betrayal. In one article the *Izraelitishes folksblat* actually defines 'intelligentsia' as 'the assimilationists'.[47]

The papers' self-identification as 'organs of the people' played a critical role in their attempt to transform Jewish nationalism into a popular ideology. For this reason, all of these papers, but especially Knöbel's 'Orthodox' press, emphasized their role as a popular forum for all of the people. To this end they did not print just polemical editorials, but also included nature articles, essays on Jewish history, serialized fiction, and even word puzzles to which readers could send in solutions and win prizes.[48] In this way the publishers created a complete newspaper culture, a new public sphere in which traditional (if not ultra-Orthodox) Jews could safely participate.[49] Above and beyond the papers' platforms the very act of transforming religious Jews into newspaper readers was in itself a political act. It implied not only a cultural transformation, but also a transformation in the Jews' perception of themselves as members of a larger community. The papers, after all, included news about Jewish communities throughout the world. This too fostered a broader sense of a transregional Jewish national identity.

Moreover, beyond these family features, the main editorials (for the articles were little more than editorials) were carefully constructed to make the average Jew feel at home. There is no better example of this than the *Yidishes familienblat*'s frequent contributor 'Shmueli Hasid'.[50] In his debut he writes:

For a long time I have had the desire to be a contributor to some newspaper, for it is a real pleasure to be published in a paper, so that the whole world knows that I am also in the world. But I am—and it shouldn't happen to you—an unlucky person. I have had the misfortune to be born to a father who is called by the German name 'Hasid' and so I should

---

[46] *Yidishe folkstsaytung* (1 Dec. 1890).   [47] *Izraelitishes folksblat* (23 July 1891).

[48] Again, Knöbel's papers pioneered this format much more than the others. The first three papers, founded largely to fight for Joseph Bloch's 1891 re-election (see below), included very few such features, while Knöbel's *Familienblat* practically catered to them. Nature articles included lessons about exotic animals such as elephants and crocodiles; history pieces discussed the biography of Moses Maimonides (Rambam), the history of Jewish migration to Poland, and the story of Napoleon's Sanhedrin; and *Ha-am* even serialized a story of Sholem Aleichem's. The word puzzles were a *Familienblat* exclusive; winners received a prize of ten *seforim* (books on religious subjects). The paper insisted that all solutions be submitted in 'pure Hebrew'; see *Yidishes familienblat* (22 Dec. 1893).

[49] Unlike Maḥzikei Hadas, none of these papers included regular Torah lessons.

[50] This is Shmilkye Hasid, mentioned above, Shmilkye and Shmueli both being diminutives of the name Shmuel. Shmilkye–Shmueli was a frequent contributor to both of Knöbel's papers. The editor himself may have been hiding behind this persona.

really also be called Shmueli Hasid—now, how do you like that, dear editor? I tried to write an article for a German paper, [but] they answered me plainly and simply: we take no articles from a Hasid. I turned red with shame, like a beet. I had, *nebekh* [sadly], to burn the article in shame. I then tried to write articles for Hebrew newspapers, but everyone mistreated me, giving me the same answer. I saw that a Hasid remains a Hasid, and that I must sit with my articles and blow wind at home—such troubles, such worries . . . But how I thrilled, all my limbs simply became limp, when I saw that the *Yidishes familienblat* had such a tolerant editor who takes articles from a Hanak,[51] *nu*, he will surely accept an article from a Hasid.[52]

Much of the folksy flavour is lost in translation, but it should be clear that this was a populist style designed to convince its readers that a Yiddish paper could be a forum for the common people, and thus worthy of support.[53] Indeed, it could be a forum not only for the common people, but for hasidim, who constituted the vast majority of Galician Jewry. The article itself is a bitter lament over the problem of declining religious observance, but even here it managed to infuse this typically contemporary anxiety with populist significance. The government was considering legislating, as in Russia, that all community rabbis be required to attend state-sponsored seminaries. Shmueli attacks these so-called 'doctor rabbis', that is, the university-educated (*gebildete*) rabbis, not for their lack of a proper Jewish education, but because of their distance from the people. The article questions their ability to speak Yiddish and make 'simple Jews' feel at home:

It has always been a puzzle to me why the three, a medical doctor, a lawyer, and a rabbi, are all given the title 'doctor'. Only when I look at the contemporary 'educated' rabbi are all three questions answered for me: the first knows the disease, the other makes the disease, and the third is the disease! Only in the meantime, until the new [Reform] rabbis are ready, I am still a bit of a *mentsh*. I [can still] come to the town rabbi with my friends, we drink a bit of wine and say 'lekhayim', we hear words from the Torah, we celebrate with him and he with us, he doesn't look at whether I am dirty, or [have] a torn kaftan. I am a hasid; I may go as I please. When I come to the rabbi to ask a question, he answers me as I understand in a simple Yiddish. Ah, how bitter and dark it will be for me that I will have to come to the doctor rabbi, knock on the door, my hat under my arm; maybe I will even have to give him a kiss on the hand. *Nu*, and how exactly will I express myself in Polish: 'Es hot gegeybn a kap khaylev ofn kigl, a shprits milekh of der yokh?' ('A candle [made of un-kosher tallow] dripped into the pudding, a drop of milk into the chicken soup?') [daily questions of *kashrut* typically brought to the town rabbi]. Honestly, I don't know where to begin. Will he possibly understand Yiddish? I am highly doubtful![54]

51 Hanak refers to Zvi Chanak, a regular contributor to the paper.

52 *Yidishes familienblat* (4 May 1894).

53 It was typical of this press that each new paper claimed finally to fill the need of the Jewish people for a Yiddish paper, ignoring its predecessors, some of which were still in print, which had already done so.

54 Ibid. Similarly, *Der folksfraynd*'s objection to these 'rabbis of the future' included their 'German' pronunciation of Hebrew (the *komets* vowel, pronounced 'u' in Galicia, being turned into a *pasekh*, pronounced as a long 'a'), which was 'not like us' in Galicia; see *Der folksfraynd* (1 May 1891).

Many of these papers, by declaring in their manifestos that they were filling the need of Orthodox Jewry for a 'kosher' paper in a 'simple' Yiddish, could later assert near-religious authority in calling their readers to political action. In other words, the early nationalist papers were Orthodox not just to promote sales, important though this was, but also because the idea of genuine Jews standing up against assimilationists coalesced Orthodox and nationalist interests.[55] If a paper kept a distance from secular, anti-religious rhetoric (and associations), it could successfully promote the strengthening of Jewish national identity and Jewish national institutions.

A good example of such a 'kosher' campaign by the papers was their call for Jews to declare Yiddish their *Umgangssprache* in the 1890 census. As Emil Brix has noted, the census forced Austrian citizens to choose not merely a nationality, but a linguistic nationality.[56] Traditional Jews, who might have felt uncomfortable identifying themselves as members of the Jewish nation, doubtless felt more at ease identifying their language of daily use as Yiddish. In a society in which linguistic singularity defined nationhood, this could not help but have a transformative effect on Jewish identity, despite the fact that the campaign was unlikely to succeed in winning recognition for Yiddish (i.e. Polish census-takers would simply mark 'Polish' instead).[57]

The census campaign also provided an opportunity to remind Jews of the practical benefits of achieving recognition as a nationality, namely, that although Jews enjoyed equal civil rights, they still suffered from inequality because Yiddish was not recognized as an independent language. As a result, the government was not required to publicize proclamations in Yiddish, as it was required to do in other languages, and even Yiddish contracts were not legally binding. But Jews cannot

[55] Michael Silber has pointed out the peculiar congruence of ultra-Orthodoxy and modern Jewish nationalism in Hungary based on the ideologies' shared rejection of acculturation. This congruence came together in the person of Akiva Hirsch Schlesinger, who had already developed a fully fledged Zionist ideology in the 1860s and 1870s. See Silber, 'Pa'amei lev ha'ivri be'erets hagar', *Cathedra*, 77 (1995), 84–105. Rafael Mahler, in his classic history of the conflict between hasidism and the Haskalah, quotes hasidic leaders from the Napoleonic period who opposed Austria's attempt at Germanization on similar grounds. One rabbi (Menahem Mendel of Rymanów) cited a *midrash* quite popular with nationalists in the modern period, that Jews were redeemed from Egypt only for the merit of not having changed their names, their language, or their dress. Another rabbi decried the prohibition of Hebrew-language legal documents and the supplanting of Yiddish by German: 'Keep your children as much as possible from foreign tongues and God will bring his nation to speedy deliverance in our day as he did for our forefathers in Egypt' (Rafael Mahler, *Hasidism and the Jewish Enlightenment* (Philadelphia, 1985), 14). Of course, neither of these early figures constructed a modern Zionist ideology along the lines of Schlesinger. [56] Brix, *Die Umgangssprachen*, 114.

[57] Joshua Fishman's broad study of 'positive ethnolinguistic consciousness' identifies such calculations among a wide range of nationalist groups. Such campaigns may entail a difficult struggle, he writes, 'but the struggle itself presents possibilities for both direct and indirect rewards. Not only may the avowed beneficial end goals of the struggle ultimately be attained, but the very process of pursuing such a struggle for dignity is community creating, consciousness raising and language stimulating' (see J. Fishman, *In Praise of the Beloved Language* (New York, 1997), 76).

blame the government, cautioned *Der folksfraynd*. 'We are ourselves guilty' for not answering census-takers truthfully.

Nu, so all of us Jews who speak Yiddish and write Yiddish should ourselves not be foolish [but] clearly tell the census-taker what is the truth—that we are Jewish Jews, that is, we belong to the Jewish nation and we speak Yiddish; then the government will know that the Jewish nation lives and our language is not dead. Our Yiddish documents will become valid and the ledgers of Jewish businessmen will have some worth.[58]

The *Yidishe folkstsaytung*, annoyed at Jewish indifference towards the census, sharply attacked Jews too lazy to do their national duty for their people:

[The census-taker] asks 'What is a Jew?' 'A Jew is a Jew!' [the Jew answers]. He writes 'Mosaic religion'. Then comes the other question . . . 'What language do you speak, Mr. So-and-So?' 'To what nation do you belong my dear Jew?' But these other questions the Jew doesn't hear at all, or he is indifferent to them. 'Write whatever you want. I have no time, I need to get ready for the sabbath. My wife is already getting angry with me for dawdling so long.' The Jew was not at all moved to say, 'nationality, Israel', 'language, Yiddish'. Understand that one must do this, for otherwise how is one supposed to know that a Jew is a Jew from the people of Israel and speaks the Yiddish language. But the official who decides on a law that Jews are not a nation and their language is not a language already knows exactly how to fill in the census card: he writes 'nationality, Polish', 'language, Polish', or, very rarely, 'language, German'.[59]

A bolder campaign by the papers was their call, after a series of antisemitic incidents in Greece, to boycott Greece as a supplier of the *esrogs* (citrons) required by Jews for the Sukkot holiday each autumn. The boycott was designed both to punish Greek farmers for the attacks and to support Jewish colonists in Palestine, who had just started to produce *esrogs* themselves. Above all, however, it was an opportunity for the papers to draw traditional Jews into a political campaign, to appropriate a religious activity and fill it with political meaning. *Der folksfraynd*, among others, assumed religious authority in calling for the boycott, claiming that it was an extra *mitsve* (meritorious deed) to use only *esrogs* from the land of Israel. Taking their support from the chief rabbi of Vienna, Dr Güdemann (hardly someone whose authority traditional Jews in Galicia would normally have respected), the paper assumed the authority to demand that Galician rabbis forbid the use of Greek *esrogs* not only on political grounds, or even national grounds (i.e. to support Jews in Palestine), but on religious grounds, that Greek *esrogs* should be declared *posl*, ritually unfit for use.[60] A month later the *Yidishe folkstsaytung* announced that Hungarian rabbis had forbidden the purchase of *esrogs* from Corfu, and called on merchants to buy only from the Jewish colonies. It even included a five-stanza

---

[58] *Der folksfraynd* (1 Jan. 1891).   [59] *Yidishe folkstsaytung* (1 Dec. 1890).
[60] *Der folksfraynd* (1 June 1891). Taubes repeated this 'ruling' several years later, writing that God intended the commandment only for an *esrog* from Israel (see *Ha-am/Dos folk* (30 July 1896)).

poem in support of the campaign.[61] The same day an anonymous article in the *Folksfraynd* chastised Galician rabbis for remaining silent, claiming that all Jews had agreed that *esrogs* should be purchased only from Palestine.[62] Only in September, when the editors may have feared they had gone too far, or seen that they were being ignored, did they modify their view. *Der folksfraynd* conceded that Greek Jews would also suffer from a boycott, and in any case the supply from the Jewish colonies could not meet European demand, and a boycott could drive up the price of *esrogs* beyond the means of many Jews.[63]

Even Knöbel's papers, which specifically defined themselves as Orthodox, appropriated religious values for nationalist purposes. A story from his *Yidishes familienblat*, for example, tells of two sons of a wealthy Jew who went to a *Gymnasium* (secular secondary school). The younger son remained religious, while the older one Polonized his name and left Judaism altogether (except on visits home so as not to jeopardize his inheritance). The article praises the younger brother's piety, but also his patriotism to the Jewish people, while the older brother is reminded that Christians do not really love him, but hate him even more than his brother, whom they at least respect for not trying to imitate them and deny who he is. The younger son says:

As a Jew I must hold on to all commandments and prohibitions; with this I show that we are a people. The *tefilin* [phylacteries] show that 4,000 years ago we were already teaching all peoples the faith in the One, and that, before all other peoples, we were a civilized people. We learned from the past for the future that we were created for greatness, and just as putting on *tefilin* shows that God is One, so are we a single people![64]

The younger brother does not rebuke his sibling for denying God's Torah; rather he focuses on his brother's denial of the glory of the Jewish national language, and mocks his attempt to assimilate into Polish circles—this from the *Yidishes familien-blat*, a declared defender of Jewish Orthodoxy.

Other papers were even more inclined to view Jewish religious observance in nationalist terms. A leader in the *Izraelitishes folksblat*, for example, explains that while Christian holidays merely celebrate religious memories, Jewish holidays celebrate the Jewish nation, 'springing out of its achievement of political, material, and spiritual freedom'. Thus, Passover, according to the paper, was principally about political freedom, Sukkot was about thanking God 'for the bounty of our Fatherland', and so on.[65] These were certainly not radical interpretations, but they were narrowly focused to elicit nationalist meaning.

Still, the fact that they did not stray far from normative religious values empha-sizes the sincerity of the publishers of these papers. These were not assimilated Jews cynically manipulating religious themes in order to entice Orthodox Jews into

---

[61] *Yidishe folkstsaytung* (1 July 1891).

[62] *Der folksfraynd* (1 July 1891).   [63] *Der folksfraynd* (15 Sept. 1891).

[64] *Yidishes familienblat* (21 Sept. 1893).   [65] *Izraelitishes folksblat* (8 Oct. 1891).

their movement. Rather, they were Jews raised in a traditional milieu, who had come to Zionism as a means of entering the modern world without abandoning their deeply entrenched Jewish identities. They genuinely viewed Zionism as the natural and most authentic interpretation of Judaism. Their strong support of Jewish colonies in Palestine, for example, grew naturally from religious liturgy, filled with longing for the return to Zion.[66] 'Jewish nationalism', Ehud Luz has noted, 'drew its legitimacy from the Jewish religion.'[67] Nationalist ideas and religious motifs formed a seamless whole, upon which the writers drew freely; it was therefore not at all disingenuous for Jewish nationalists to frame their nationalist identity within religious themes.

Perhaps the most obvious example of this mixture of religious authority and nationalist rhetoric was the 1891 campaign of Joseph Bloch (1850–1923) for re-election to the Austrian parliament.[68] A battle of major political significance, it probably stimulated the emergence of the Yiddish press in the first place; in Kołomyja alone at least three new Yiddish papers began publication during the campaign.[69] No other Jewish nationalist entered parliament before 1897, or came close to matching Bloch's widespread popularity. His outspoken Jewish pride made him the darling of the early nationalist movement, and his election campaigns generated tremendous activity among Galician Jewish nationalists. Support for his re-election was increasingly seen as a religious duty, a badge which proved one's Jewishness. The 1891 election in particular highlighted how the Yiddish press linked religious authenticity and Jewish unity on the one hand, and support for their papers and their candidate on the other.

In 1891 Bloch once again faced Emil Byk (1845–1906), whom he and his supporters had already portrayed in previous campaigns as a lackey of the dominant

[66] Of course, the added component of human action to hasten such a return was an important innovation. Nevertheless, they still saw such action as fulfilling the divine plan, and opposition to it as hindering that plan. Tsion's first Yiddish publication, for example, subtitled 'Lamentations for *Tisha Be'av*', wrote that the prayers of religious Jews who mourned over the destruction of Jerusalem without supporting its rebirth were like 'chatter without heart and feeling' (see *Der kantshik* (Lemberg, 1890), 17).

[67] E. Luz, *Parallels Meet: Religion and Nationalism in the Early Zionism Movement (1882–1904)* (Philadelphia, 1988), p. x.

[68] Bloch had soared to popularity as a result of his successful refutation of the antisemitic pseudo-talmudist August Röhling, and in 1883 won a special election in the Kołmyja–Buczacz–Śniatyn parliamentary district. Bloch became an outspoken champion of Jewish rights and opponent of antisemitism in the Reichsrat, fighting especially against the problem of *Mädchenraub*, the kidnapping of young Jewish women by the Church in Galicia. Ultimately Bloch did not join the Zionist movement, although Jewish nationalists continued to rally behind him despite this. After briefly flirting with Jewish nationalism, he ultimately preached an identity of Jewish pride as Austrians *sans phrase*, the only true Austrian citizens in an era of hypernationalism. See J. S. Bloch, *Der nationale Zwist und die Juden in Österreich* (Vienna, 1886), 41. For Bloch's own account of his election bids, see his memoirs: id., *My Reminiscences* (New York, 1923), 78–9, 209–26, 259–71.

[69] Namely, the *Yidishe folkstsaytung*, the *Izraelitishes folksblat*, and *Der folksfraynd*. Toury also locates the roots of these papers in Bloch's re-election campaign, coverage of which constitutes the bulk of his analysis (see Toury, *Die jüdische Presse*, 133).

Polish parliamentary faction known as the Polenklub (Polish Club).[70] The papers allotted tremendous space to the campaign; two full supplements to the third issue of *Der folksfraynd*, for example, were filled with endorsements of Bloch. Letters such as the following from Rabbi Solomon Buber[71] added a religious imperative to supporting him:

It is a holy obligation according to the law that all rabbis and sages of Galicia stand by the wise Herr Dr Bloch, and preach in public in every city that every person who fears God in his heart should choose only the rabbi Dr Bloch, and every person who opposes him is sinning against God and man. Because God has sent him for our sustenance, he is an angel sent to his nation, and he is putting his life in danger to wage God's war against those who rise up against us.[72]

Similarly, at a political rally held in the large synagogue in Kołomyja, the president of the community council, H. Shlomo Hirsch, and the deputy mayor, Joseph Funkenstein, spoke on the vital necessity of re-electing Bloch for the good of all Israel:

The entire group of Jews agreed with one voice that anyone who stepped outside the community and gave their vote to someone else—he should suffer all the curses in the rebuke [of Moses] in the holy Torah. And he who voted for the Jewish fighter, the rabbi Dr Joseph Samuel Bloch, he should receive all the blessings in the Torah—to this the entire auditorium said 'Amen' and then they blew the shofar—the holy effect which this had on all of those gathered is indescribable.[73]

---

[70] Byk was a staunch opponent of Jewish nationalism, and had also opposed Bloch in 1883 and 1885. Initially pro-German and anti-Polish, in 1885 he reversed his position and became a leading supporter of Jewish integration into the Polish nation.

[71] This was Martin Buber's grandfather, the celebrated scholar of *midrash*. In using Buber, the paper probably hoped to ground its religious imperative to support Bloch in a traditional rabbinical authority. Besides, Buber was also a respected banker in Lemberg, one-time president of the Lemberg Chamber of Commerce, and a board member of the Lemberg *Kultusgemeinde* (*kahal*) since 1870.

[72] *Der folksfraynd* (1 Feb. 1891). Buber's letter, as well as several others, was written in Hebrew. Note that the spiritual mentor of the ultra-Orthodox Maḥzikei Hadas association, the Belzer Rebbe (R. Joshua Rokeah), endorsed the Polish Christian candidate against Bloch. In 1885 the *rebbe* had merely directed his hasidim not to take part in the election. Gershom Bader claimed that the rebbe declared, 'If the choice is to support such a Jew as Bloch, it would be better to have a *goy*!' See A. L. Shusheim, 'Yidishe politik un yidishe parteyen in galitsye', in *Pinkes galitsye*, ed. Nechemia Zucker (Buenos Aires, 1945), 44.

[73] *Yidishe folkstsaytung* (1 Mar. 1891). This was not the first time such religious invectives were levelled at political opponents. Maḥzikei Hadas pioneered the practice in 1883, when it cursed and literally excommunicated anyone who voted for the liberal, pro-Polish Jewish candidate Filip Zucker, who was running for re-election to the Galician parliament. Agudas Achim, of which Zucker was a prominent member, launched a massive counter-campaign against the Orthodox party, which ended in the government confiscating 15,000 copies of the issue of their paper containing the excommunication. The paper's editor was sentenced to one month in prison. See Manekin, 'Tsemiḥatah vegibushah', 227–53.

According to one paper, even Byk himself supported Bloch's candidacy. Why, then, was Byk opposing him? Putting words into Byk's mouth that he clearly never uttered, the *Izraelitishes folksblat* suggested a reason:

The party of Dr Emil Byk, however, says thus: Yes, it is admittedly true, we know this [that Bloch needs to be re-elected] and we want Dr Bloch to enter parliament again as before, for we also know how necessary [it is that] one must have him as a representative; *we feel just as Jewish as all Jews*. Only, there are electoral districts besides our own: let another electoral district show that they know what Dr Bloch is—not just Kołomyja, which has already shown it twice.[74]

In other words, only those who support Bloch are true Jews. Similarly, when Byk decided to drop out of the election, *Der folksfraynd*, which had been defaming him for weeks, suddenly began to applaud his noble action, which somehow returned him to the Jewish fold. Writing that Byk had acted so honourably, so Jewish, 'as a true son of our holy fathers Abraham, Isaac, and Jacob', the paper called on all of his supporters to back Bloch. Dr Byk's withdrawal from the race, it concluded, was done for the sake of unity, in order that Jews would not fight one other. Thus the way to national unity, including inter-class unity, was to support the nationalist candidate:

We may be proud of our representative, who saved the honour of God and all Israel, the honour of our holy Torah and our sages, the honour of our rich Jews and our poor working men, the skilled handworkers; we may be proud of our representative who is known by all of Jewry, from one corner of the world to the other.[75]

Election day violence, already infamous throughout the empire, could not over-come Bloch's popularity. Despite an outbreak of pogroms in Kołomyja and Śniatyn, and an extraordinary degree of electoral corruption, the district's Jewish majority ultimately united behind Bloch, who won with 2,128 votes, defeating the 'Christian' candidate by 350 votes.[76] Jewish nationalists, and the Yiddish press, could celebrate at least one victory.

CONCLUSION

Ultimately, it is difficult to measure the impact of the Yiddish nationalist press on Galician Jewry. Clearly, none of these papers could claim serious financial success. Aside from the obvious fact that they only lasted for a short time, all made it pain-fully clear that they were struggling to survive. They all complained bitterly in nearly every issue of their dire financial straits, about the problem of insufficient subscriptions and of subscribers who had not paid their dues; *Ha-am* even printed a blacklist of delinquent subscribers.

---

[74] *Izraelitishes folksblat* (8 Feb. 1891; my italics).
[75] *Der folksfraynd* (15 Feb. 1891). Byk ran instead in Brody, a seat he won that year and held until his death in 1906.   [76] *Der folksfraynd* (15 Mar. 1891).

Absolute circulation of the papers is difficult to gauge because the government, unable to distinguish between Hebrew and Yiddish papers, compiled circulation statistics for the 'Hebrew or Hebrew letter' press as a whole. As a result, Hebrew, Yiddish, and German papers printed in Hebrew characters all appeared as a single statistic. Fortunately, however, the statistics did classify papers according to frequency of publication, and because all of the Yiddish papers appeared as bi-weeklies, it is possible to estimate the extent of their circulation. Over the course of the years 1890–7 the 'Hebrew letter' press averaged between 10,000 and 14,000 bi-weekly papers each per year, roughly the same as the Ukrainian bi-weekly press during those years, although dwarfed by the Polish bi-weekly press, which printed between 50,000 and 100,000 papers each per year.[77]

Other evidence also suggests that the Yiddish papers enjoyed some influence. Zionist and other libraries, where a single subscription would be picked up by large numbers of readers, figured among the list of subscribers. In addition, papers circulated informally among friends. An agent for the *Yidishes folksblat* complained that he had had difficulty selling subscriptions in a certain *shtetl* because the entire town shared a single subscription.[78] Moreover, although short-lived, many of the papers achieved widespread distribution. The *Yidishes familienblat*, for example, listed agents in Romania (Bacău and Iaşi), Stryj, Borysław, Przemyśl, and Kraków. One can assume it was also sold in Lemberg (Lwów), the provincial capital, and Kołomyja, among other reasons because firms from both cities advertised in the paper, as did some from Vienna. To this extent, the papers' claim to have forged a single Jewish community across Galicia seems to support Benedict Anderson's ideas about the construction of modern national identities.[79]

In sum, the Yiddish nationalist press of the early 1890s represented a revolutionary advance for the Jewish nationalist movement. Written in a populist style, often in a heavy Galician dialect, these papers proclaimed themselves to be 'organs of the people', defenders of Orthodoxy and the common Jew. They appropriated Orthodox themes in order to convince traditional Jews to view themselves as a modern nation, and to organize politically to secure national minority rights. In this way, they attempted to transform Jewish identity from a religious to a national one. Their readers, whose history has been largely overlooked by scholars, became an increasingly powerful Jewish voice over the coming decades.

[77] See J. Myśliński, 'Nakłady prasy społeczno-politycznej w Galicji w latach 1881–1913', *Rocznik Historii Czasopiśmiennictwa Polskiego*, 4/1 (1965), 115–33, and 4/4, 80–98.

[78] *Yidishes folksblat* (13 July 1894).

[79] Anderson emphasizes the role of 'print-languages' in laying the foundation for national consciousness. The print media, he writes, allowed otherwise isolated individuals (or communities) to become aware 'of the hundreds of thousands, even millions, of people in their particular language-field, and at the same time that *only those* hundreds of thousands, or millions, so belonged. These fellow-readers, to whom they were connected through print, formed . . . the embryo of the nationally imagined community' (B. Anderson, *Imagined Communities: Reflections on the Origins and Spread of Nationalism*, rev. edn. (New York, 1991), 44, emphasis in original).

Shund and the Tabloids: Jewish Popular Reading in Inter-War Poland

NATHAN COHEN

THE POLISH TABLOID PRESS

IN the first third of the twentieth century, as the Polish press was developing rapidly, sensationalist newspapers began to proliferate. While this type of press had been widespread in the United States and western Europe since the middle of the nineteenth century, it first emerged in Poland only in 1910, with *Ilustrowany Kurier Codzienny* ('Illustrated Daily Courier') in Kraków. In Warsaw the first tabloid newspapers, *Kurier Informacyjny i Telegraficzny* ('Information and Telegraphic Courier') and *Ekspres Poranny* ('Morning Express'), appeared in 1922. In 1926 *Kurier Informacyjny i Telegraficzny* changed its name, now printed in red, to *Kurier Czerwony* ('Red Courier'). In time the colour red became emblematic of sensationalist newspapers in Poland, and they were nicknamed *czerwoniaki* (Reds), similar to the 'yellow' press in the West.[1]

There was originally little difference between mainstream and sensationalist newspapers other than the latter's small format (four pages with four columns on each page), compression of information into the fewest lines possible, concentration on the criminal world, and the publication of readers' surveys. Popular subjects, such as film, theatre, fashion, and sport, and titillating reading, such as serialized novels, were featured. Little by little photographs, advertisements, and letters from readers were also included. After a number of years the division between the newspapers became much clearer, with the Reds using banner headlines for the more shocking news items. Such articles were printed on the inside pages and contained detailed descriptions of the events.

The rapid growth of sensationalist newspapers increased the competition between them, and each innovation made by one was immediately copied by the others. In their slant towards the lowest common denominator of readers the newspapers defined themselves as apolitical. There were no political editorials, and their

This chapter is based on a chapter of my *Sefer, sofer ve'iton: merkaz hatarbut hayehudit bevarshah 1918–1942* (Jerusalem, 2002); a shorter version was published in *Kesher*, 11 (1992), 81–94.

[1] A detailed description and classification of these Polish newspapers appears in W. Władyka, *Krew na pierwszej stronie* (Warsaw, 1982); see also A. Paczkowski, *Prasa codzienna Warszawy w latach 1918–1939* (Warsaw, 1983), 194; and cf. H. Herd, *The March of Journalism* (London, 1952), 222–74.

comments on political and social matters contained no real opinions, consisting mainly of slogans, such as one promoted by the Reds in the 1930s: 'Obrona Polski i Polskości' ('For the defence of Poland and Polishness').[2] The average price of a Red paper was 5 groszy, and the cheapest, which was blatantly antisemitic, cost only 2 grosze, as reflected in its name, *Dwa Grosze*. Wiesław Władyka, who researches the Polish sensationalist press, suggests that, except for its Catholicism and extreme Polish nationalism, this press was not significantly different from sensationalist papers in the West, despite its late appearance.[3] A good example is the newspaper *Mały Dziennik* ('Little Daily') founded in 1935 and published by the Franciscan brotherhood. Its editors were avowed antisemites, who did not hide from readers their goal of defending Polishness by attacking the Jews, the masons, and the communists.[4] A daily sold mostly in Warsaw, *Mały Dziennik* had a circulation of 190,000 in April 1938.[5] The Church was thereby able to use the sensationalist press to reach the masses in its struggle for their spiritual and ideological life.

Six years before the appearance of *Mały Dziennik*, on 30 September 1929, newspaper vendors on the streets of Warsaw hawked a new paper, *Ostatnie Wiadomości* ('Latest News'), that was filled with startling headlines and weak, emotive articles. It contained information on the strikes and struggles of workers (in the spirit of those days of economic crisis), readers' surveys, and a column consisting of intimate letters to the editor. Within a short time its distribution reached 65,000, transforming it into one of the three most widely read newspapers in Warsaw.[6] Its publisher was Shmuel-Yankev Yatskan (1874–1936), founder and editor of the leading Yiddish daily *Haynt* ('Today').[7] To the credit of his new Polish paper, it faithfully preserved political neutrality and refrained from publishing antisemitic material. The nature of the newspaper, along with its well-known publisher, drew antagonism from the journalists of the Bundist *Di naye folkstsaytung* ('New People's Newspaper'), who described Yatskan as caught up in *shund*,[8] sensationalism, and

---

[2] Paczkowski, *Prasa codzienna*, 194–200.

[3] C. Bainbridge (ed.), *One Hundred Years of Journalism* (London, 1984), 287–8; cf. Władyka, *Krew na pierwszej stronie*, 75–86.   [4] Władyka, *Krew na pierwszej stronie*, 89–93.

[5] A. Paczkowski, 'Nakłady dzienników warszawskich w latach 1931–1938', *Rocznik Historii Czasopiśmiennictwa Polskiego*, 15 (1976), 95.

[6] Paczkowski, 'Nakłady dzienników warszawskich', 87–95; id., *Prasa codzienna*, 208–11.

[7] As early as May 1906 Yatskan had attempted a sensationalist Yiddish newspaper, *Yidishes tageblat*, which the Jewish bibliographer Avrom Kirzhnits described as 'dos ershte gele bulvar-bletl in yidish' (*Di yidishe prese in der gevezener rusisher imperye (1823–1916)* (Moscow, 1930), 100). The *Tageblat* antedated its Polish counterpart by four years; it appeared until Jan. 1911. Yatskan may have used the American Yiddish press as a model, but more probably the Russian press; see J. Brooks, *When Russia Learned to Read: Literacy and Popular Literature, 1861–1917* (Princeton, 1985), 118–41.

[8] The source of the term *shund*, which played a crucial role in Yiddish cultural history, is the abattoir. The term originally designated the stench of a skinned animal carcass. In 19th-century Germany *shund* was used in a literary context for a work of low artistic value that was considered morally harmful to its readers and therefore, it was often argued, ought to be banned. From the end of the 19th century the term was also used in this context in the Yiddish literary environment. See C. Shmeruk, 'Letoledot sifrut ha-"shund" beyidish', *Tarbits*, 52 (1983), 325–54.

pornography.[9] The Bundists were especially annoyed with his daughter, who worked on the editorial board of the new paper and had once reprimanded a member of the Yidishe Literatn un Zhurnalistn Fareyn (Union of Jewish Writers and Journalists) who had spoken to her in Yiddish: 'In a Polish paper we speak Polish!' 'This is how the daughter of the Zionist founder of *Haynt* permits herself to speak', retorted the *Naye folkstsaytung*.[10]

THE YIDDISH TABLOID PRESS

During the years between the two world wars the Jewish press in Poland experienced unprecedented development. Between 1919 and 1922 there were more papers for Jews per capita than for any other national minority in Poland. In 1922 Jewish publications comprised 14 per cent of all the publications in Poland and 23 per cent of those in Warsaw. By the 1930s this rose to 50 per cent in Warsaw.[11] In mid-1935 in Warsaw there were no fewer than eleven Yiddish dailies, as well as two Jewish dailies in Polish and a weekly in Hebrew.[12] The total distribution of all these newspapers was more than 180,000 copies per day.[13] These statistics did not much impress Jews in Vilna, where in 1926 the Warsaw press had been compared to a prostitute sitting in her brothel and counting her profits. The press was characterless, was the complaint. 'It is neither yellow nor sensational. It is simply uninteresting. This is the sweet swamp that poisons the air for miles around.'[14] This and worse was claimed by Nahum Sokolow at the conclusion of a visit to Warsaw in 1933: 'Our system of journalism is threatened here. You will find virtually no news item that is accurate and unbiased . . . Everything is scented, dressed up, and exaggerated. It's difficult to distinguish the dozens of noon, afternoon, and evening newspapers, each more sensationalist than the other.'[15] What led Sokolow to write

[9] 'Yatskan, "adek", un di "poylishe berte" ', *Di naye folkstsaytung* (10 Oct. 1929).

[10] Ibid. The Bundists were also angry that no one from Orthodox circles protested the paper's appearance on Yom Kippur. On Christmas Eve Yatskan was attacked again over the large amount of space dedicated to the Christian holiday, and the writer scornfully added that it was lucky that the holiday did not occur on Yom Kippur (*Di naye folkstsaytung* (24 Dec. 1929)).

[11] A. Paczkowski, 'The Jewish Press in the Political Life of the Second Republic', *Polin*, 8 (1994), 184.

[12] For details of the newspapers, see C. Shmeruk, review of M. Fuks, *Prasa żydowska w Warszawie*, *Kiryat sefer*, 55 (1980), 591.

[13] Paczkowski, 'Nakłady dzienników warszawskich', 91, 93. The figures are for July 1937.

[14] 'Der groyser zump', *Kunst un lebn*, no. 4 (1926). Jewish literary relations between Vilna and Warsaw have not yet been researched and are deserving of it.

[15] The original criticisms, written in German, were directed to Berl Loker and are in the Arkhiyon Tsiyoni Merkazi (Central Zionist Archive), Jerusalem, S25/1918. The ones dealing with the press are on pp. 4–14. Their translation into Hebrew is in *Sefer sokolov* (Jerusalem, 1943), 195–272. The citation here is on p. 215. On the same subject, see also J. Kuts, 'Nahum sokolov ve-"hafunktsiyah harishmit" shel ha'itonut ha'ivrit', *Kesher*, 2 (1987), 23–38.

in such strident tones? Had sensationalism really captured the entire Jewish press in Warsaw at the beginning of the 1930s?

Two clearly sensationalist Yiddish afternoon papers had indeed appeared in Warsaw for many years, with a content that infuriated many. They were brought out by the publishers of *Der moment* ('The Moment', 1910–39) and *Haynt* (1908–39), the two best-established Yiddish dailies in Poland. From the final days of the First World War the editorial board of *Der moment* occasionally published a special edition with the latest news. In December 1924 they began to publish a regular afternoon paper, *Der varshever radyo* ('Warsaw Radio'), edited by the journalist Shmuel Yanovski (1890–1935). In its early years it did not differ substantially from other papers, although the information in it was more condensed and it was only four pages long. In May 1925 the format was slightly shortened and the number of columns on each page reduced from six to four, although after several years the newspaper returned to its original format. The first two pages contained international news and news about the Jews in Poland. The two inside pages were dedicated to short international items and humorous pieces by Avrom Rozenfeld (Bontshe; 1884–1940s). The fourth page consisted of a column called 'Varshever khronik' ('Warsaw Chronicle'). On Fridays the newspaper added another two to four pages with short stories from well-known authors such as Avrom Reyzn and Yoel Mastboym, or translations of non-Jewish authors such as Anatole France and Osip Dimov, along with a humourous column and a sports section. The price of the newspaper ranged from 10 to 15 groszy. In the first years the newspaper was not particularly sensationalist, although the editor did not hesitate to come up with attention-grabbing headlines along the lines of 'Zelbstmord fun a yidishn soykher' ('Suicide of a Jewish Merchant'; 12 August 1925) or 'Shreklekhe katastrofe in dorem-amerike . . . Di erd efnt zikh un shlingt ayn fil mentshn' ('Terrible Tragedy in South America . . . The Earth Opens and Swallows Many People"; 26 December 1926). In the summer of 1926 the newspaper raffled off prizes of two week-long holidays at a hotel, 200 cinema tickets, two radios, and twenty-five pairs of shoes. There were no prizes of books, the norm for similar competitions in other newspapers. After the death of Yanovski in 1935 Sholem Gotlib, the *Moment* representative in Lwów, was appointed editor of *Radyo*. There he published a serialized novel, *Di geheymnisn fun viner hoyf* ('Secrets of the Viennese Court').[16]

Perusal of issues of the newspaper from the 1930s shows that it developed a discernible sensationalist style of writing much like that found in its Polish counterparts. Thus, for example, it declared that communist revolution was about to break

---

[16] It is almost certain that this title was based upon 'Di geheymnise fun rusishn kayzerlikhn hoyf', a series of pamphlets translated by A. Tanenboym that first appeared in New York in 1892 and comprised the beginning of the 'plague of the pamphlets' there. On this phenomenon and its implications, see Shmeruk, 'Letoledot sifrut ha-"shund" beyidish', 334–7. It is important to point out that *Hayntike nayes* also exploited the genre; one of the first novels it published was entitled 'Geheymnisn fun lebn fun rusishn tsar nikolay dem tsveytn' (1930). For more on the serialized novels, see below.

out in Britain (16 May 1933); it published an article entitled 'Groyser khurbn in erets yisroel' ('Great Catastrophe in the Land of Israel'; 3 January 1935) following a minor earthquake in the country that did little damage; and covered the alleged marriage of Hermann Goering to a Jewish woman (3 January 1935). With the growing fear of war with Germany, the newspaper proclaimed: 'Hitler geferlekh krank—der driter khaloshes atak in farloyf fun der letster tsayt. Di umheylbare haldz krankayt. Doktoyrim haltn az er ken oyshaltn di krenk nokh 18 khadoshim' ('Hitler mortally ill. Third recent fainting spell. Incurable throat disease. Doctors estimate that he will last another 18 months'; 12 May 1939). On the second page of the same edition a London medium was quoted as claiming that 1941 would bring the final defeat of Hitler and Mussolini.

At the beginning of 1939 *Radyo* announced a number of new and exclusive features, including a column on graphology, to which each reader could send his handwriting for analysis, and a section on the supernatural intended for lovers of magic. At the same time the newspaper announced an event the likes of which had never been seen before: a competition for the title of *di oremste kale* (the poorest bride). The winner would be awarded a dowry of 1,000 zlotys. In order to participate, families had to submit detailed requests that were published anonymously; the readers would then choose the poorest bride. The competition continued for four months. The prize was ultimately won by Perl Fayner of Sosnowiec (15 June 1939). Yet at the same time the popular author Avrom Zak (1891–1980) was writing for *Radyo* (under the initials A.P. or the pseudonym Alfa), and three times a week there appeared an editorial by Shaul-Yitskhok Stupnitski (1876 -1942), a senior journalist at *Der moment* and head of the Yidishe Literatn un Zhurnalistn Fareyn.

Since *Radyo* only appeared six days a week, the editors felt a need to provide sensational news on Saturday as well, and did so with a Saturday evening newspaper entitled *Gut vokh* ('Good Week', 1930–1),[17] which was very similar to *Radyo*. In *Gut vokh* one might read about a man married to 283 women (18 April 1931), night clubs in London (6 June 1931), the underworld in Poland and elsewhere, and theatre and film. The newspaper also published jokes and three sensational novels in instalments. One of the novelists, writing anonymously of course, was Dovid Mitsmakher (1904–41), a communist author who had dedicated himself to eradicating just this type of literature.[18]

The second and younger of the two best-established sensationalist papers was originally called *Letste nayes* ('Latest News') and belonged to the co-operatively run *Undzer ekspres* (on which, see below). When the co-operative encountered financial

[17] I was able to see only a few issues of this newspaper at the library of the YIVO Institute for Jewish Research in New York. The YIVO catalogue notes that it appeared between 29 Nov. 1930 and 14 Nov. 1931. But in Y. Szeintukh, *Preliminary Inventory of Yiddish Dailies and Periodicals Published in Poland between the Two World Wars* (Jerusalem, 1986), 50, the dates given are 10 Jan. 1931–16 Apr. 1932. I believe the YIVO dates are correct.

[18] M. Fuks, *Prasa żydowska w Warszawie* (Warsaw, 1979), 195 ff.

hardship, the publishers of *Haynt* bought the newspaper and changed its name to *Hayntike nayes* ('Today's News'). On the opening page of the first edition (17 December 1929) there appeared no less than eight sensationalist headlines. The inside pages contained similar material: two serialized novels and a column entitled 'Intime shmuesn' ('Intimate Conversations'), in which readers poured out their hearts to the editor. A column of this sort was one of the defining features of the Polish tabloid press in Warsaw.[19] Columns on theatre and film, sport, popular medicine, the weekly Torah portion (*parshe*), as well as a humour supplement and a supplement for women, were added over time. One of the most popular services catered to the unmarried reader and was called the 'Shidukhim vinkl' ('Matchmaking Corner'). An announcement inserted in the 30 August 1930 edition claimed that the paper's variety and trustworthiness made it the widest-circulating Jewish newspaper in Europe—an inflated claim, of course, but one that reflected the publishers' satisfaction with demand for the newspaper, at least in Poland.[20] At this time readers were also lured with the promise of a large lottery that would distribute record players, cameras, raincoats, perfumes, candlesticks, shoes, and even books. The scope of *Hayntike nayes* was similar to that of *Varshever radyo* and its price was 10 groszy, the average price for Yiddish newspapers of this sort. From 1932 the first instalment of each new novel was published in a separate eight-page pamphlet. Many copies of these pamphlets were distributed free of charge in Warsaw and other towns, or inserted in the Friday edition. Later, as we shall see, advertisements replaced novels in such newspapers.

Simkhe-Bunim Pietrushka (1893–1950), who had been a correspondent for *Haynt* in Palestine until 1927, edited *Hayntike nayes*. He and Avrom Gliksman (1883–1943) usually wrote the editorials. One writer for the newspaper was the reformed criminal Urke Nachalnik, who found great success writing in Polish, and whose one novel was serialized in *Hayntike nayes* in 1933.[21] Another was Shloyme Rozenberg (1896–1975), Sholem Asch's secretary, who serialized his own novels in *Hayntike nayes* while he sent his employer's, from the latter's residence in Nice, to *Haynt*.[22] Yankev-Kopl Dua (1898–1942) was the most prolific of the *Nayes* writers (although politically he was close to the Bund); from 1931 he published dozens of novels, based primarily on Jewish history. Dua was paralysed and spent most of his time at home, writing.[23]

In addition to *Hayntike nayes*, *Haynt* brought out a number of other popular publications. One of them was the weekly *Velt shpigl* ('World Mirror', 1927–32,

[19] Paczkowski, *Prasa codzienna*, 196. A similar column appeared in the *Forverts* in New York.

[20] The large income that *Nayes* brought to the coffers of *Haynt*, and from 1932 to the co-operative Alt-Nay, helped to maintain *Haynt* itself, which often experienced financial difficulties.

[21] On Urke Nachalnik, see A. Karpinowicz, 'Sipuro hamufla shel urke naḥalnik', *Kesher*, 18 (1995), 93–101. See also the excerpts from his autobiography in this volume.

[22] K. Finkelshteyn, *Haynt—a tsaytung bay yidn, 1908–1939* (Tel Aviv, 1978), 298–9.

[23] On his rich literary production, see *Leksikon fun der nayer yidisher literatur*, vol. ii (New York, 1958), cols. 459–62.

1938–9). In its first years it consisted largely of photographs, occasionally of scantily clad women. The novels it published had titles such as *Vi azoy bin ikh antlofn fun harem* ('How I Fled the Harem'; begun in no. 2 (1927)), and *Der heyliker tayvl: rasputin un di froyen* ('The Holy Devil: Rasputin and the Women', begun in no. 46 (1931)). Short stories with similar titles could be found alongside stories by such literary authors as Zalman Shneur, Zusman Segalovitsh, and Osip Dimov. The usual sections on fashion and cosmetics could also be found, as well as a popular science section containing information on, for example, the dangers of smoking, the sleeping habits of fish, and the age of the world. While such sections retained a popular format, the material found in them was somewhat more serious and included political commentary. Another publication, weaker in content and quality, was the weekly *Intimer fraynd* ('Intimate Friend'), which appeared from August to October 1931, at a time of particularly intense competition among tabloids (see below). Like *Der moment*, *Haynt* also attempted to publish a newspaper on Saturday evening, *Ekstra nayes* ('Extra News'), but it lasted only two editions (17 and 24 October 1931).

On 25 August 1926 a major new daily of a somewhat less sensationalist nature began to appear in Warsaw under the title *Varshever ekspres* ('Warsaw Express'). In its first edition the editorial board declared that the newspaper's goal was to provide for the worker and 'the ordinary man a new tone, a new sound, and a new [written] word'. On the front page of this issue appeared a picture of a family of seven who had been evicted from their home for not paying rent; soon, however, such pictures became less political. The main headline of the second edition announced that the hasidic owner of a restaurant at 17 Nalewki Street had been feeding his customers non-kosher food for years. From the start each edition included a coupon for coal, which readers were told to keep for the winter.

Following a dispute between the publisher, M. Goldberg, and the staff, a strike broke out on 20 December 1926. Members of the editorial staff, journalists, and printers put out a number of editions on their own that were printed at the publishing house of the *Naye folkstsaytung*, until on 9 January 1927 the paper changed its name to *Undzer ekspres* ('Our Express') and began to be published regularly under co-operative management. This arrangement, which lasted until the war, set a precedent among Yiddish newspapers in Poland.[24] Although it had a generally Zionist slant, the Undzer Ekspres co-operative declared itself independent, without ties to any particular political party. The newspaper was edited by Lazar Kahan (1885–1946) and Elkhonen Tseytlin (1902–42), who, unlike their counterparts in other sensationalist newspapers, provided editorials and weekly political analyses. The paper's successful entry into the market, coupled with the prestige of the name

[24] For details (not always accurate) about the beginnings of the newspaper, see M. Flakser, '*Undzer ekspres*', *Fun noentn over*, 3 (1957), 366–72. On 24 Jan. 1928 Goldberg tried to publish *Varshever ekspres* again, but succeeded for only a few days. *Der moment* became a co-operative after a long strike in the summer of 1930; *Haynt* became a co-operative two years later. The first Jewish newspaper that began to function as a co-operative was the 'bourgeois' Polish-language *Nasz Przegląd* in 1923.

Tseytlin (Elkhonen was the son of the philosopher Hillel Tseytlin (1872–1942) and the younger brother of the Yiddish and Hebrew poet Arn Tseytlin (Aaron Zeitlin, 1889–1973), who also wrote for the paper), were enough to enrage the competing newspapers (except for *Der moment*, the newspaper for which Hillel Tseytlin wrote) and led them to attack it at every opportunity.[25]

In the late 1920s there were already five Yiddish dailies in Warsaw. In order to compete with them it was necessary for the new paper to attract attention and provide reading material not found in the other newspapers. Its layout certainly attracted the eye: its title, and often the main headline, were printed in red, like its Polish counterparts; its size was slightly smaller than the average and the number of pages greater than in other Yiddish newspapers; its price was higher than that of *Radyo* and *Hayntike nayes*, but lower than that of the morning papers (except for *Di naye folkstsaytung*): 15 groszy (and for a short period only 10). The red headlines announced international news, and news of Poland and of the Jewish community; the emphasis was on international disputes, military confrontations, crime, natural disasters, and other tragedies. Thus it was possible to find headlines such as 'Di shreklekhe nest fun oysgelasnkayt' ('The Terrible Nest of Licentiousness'), about brothels that employed 14-year-old Jewish girls (29 January 1928), or 'Dershosn dem shtarkstn mentsh in varshe—dem yidishn alfons avrom "poyer" fun panske gas' ('Strongest Man in Warsaw Shot—Jewish Pimp Avrom "the Peasant" of Pańska Street'; 1 June 1928). After the 1929 pogroms in Palestine the newspaper's headline of 27 August 1929 proclaimed 'Taykhn yidish blut in gants erets yisroel' ('Rivers of Jewish Blood throughout the Land of Israel'), and on the following day: 'Ratevet undz! Alarmirt men fun yerusholayim' ('Save Us! They Implore from Jerusalem'). On 19 May 1935 passers-by glancing at a Warsaw kiosk would have surely been surprised by the headline 'Atntat af hitlern' ('Attempt on Hitler's Life'), but closer inspection would have revealed the small print above the headline: 'Opgeleyknt di falshe klangen vegn' ('False Rumours have been Rebutted About'). In contrast to the mainstream newspapers, whose sources were the Polish press, Polish information services, and the Jewish Information Agency, popular newspapers did not usually give sources of their information. If they did, they would use the formula 'exclusively from our writers' or 'an exclusive for our newspaper'—dubious proof that hardly contributed to the credibility of the newspapers or their writers.

Two serialized novels, described in their subheadings as 'sensational', 'thrilling', or 'intimate', were regularly found inside the pages of *Undzer ekspres*. Alongside them were literary works, feuilletons, and various columns by authors such as the Tseytlin brothers, Isaac Bashevis Singer, Yoel Mastboym, Avrom Zak, Efroyim Kaganovski, Zelig Melamed, and Yakir Varshavski. One of the most widely read sections appeared daily and received a full page on Fridays. This was 'Unter fir

[25] See *Di naye folkstsaytung* (3 Dec. 1926, 30 May 1929); B. Yeushzon [Moyshe-Bunim Yustman], 'Etlekhe verter fun a lezer', *Haynt* (10 July 1927); Lorento [Moyshe-Bunim Yustman], 'Zhurnalistn = shantazhistn', *Haynt* (1 and 7 Jan. 1931).

oygn' ('Under Four Eyes', i.e. private matters), a selection of personal letters from readers to the editor.[26] Another feature *Undzer ekspres* shared with the Polish sensationalist press was readers' surveys.[27] In January 1932 one such survey was undertaken asking the question 'Do Jews still need to wear long *kapotes* [black coats]?', and in August 1933 the question who killed the Zionist leader Chaim Arlozorof was asked.[28] In December 1934 large announcements proclaimed a new survey on the subject of whether the Jewish state would be established in Palestine or Birobidzhan. On Fridays, like all other papers, the newspaper included a full page of jokes and caricatures and, from 1933, a discussion of the weekly Torah portion. On Sundays there was a sport section, a section on family health, and an insert for women. In March 1930 the paper announced a competition to choose a beauty queen, and before almost every holiday it raffled off prizes. These prizes only occasionally included books. For Passover 1932 the newspaper organized a trip by sea to Palestine, and in August 1933, a trip to the Zionist Congress in Prague for the low price of only 140 zlotys. The large advertising section, primarily composed of classified ads for housing or employment, printed daily on the back page of the newspaper, contributed significantly to its distribution and its revenue. A section of this size was new to the Yiddish press.

The success of *Undzer ekspres* on the Jewish street and its successful competition with the established newspapers led its editors to try and publish an evening newspaper, *Varshever kuryer*, launched on 5 May 1929. The paper appeared daily at four in the afternoon, was four pages long, and cost 10 groszy. It was dedicated to news about natural disasters, crime, scandals, and tragedies. A 'sensational' survey was published in the very first edition: 'Tsi volt men gedarft opshafn dem kheyrem derabeynu gershom?' ('Should the [eleventh-century] ban of Rabbenu Gershom [concerning bigamy] be annulled?'). Despite the fact that the newspaper lasted less than three months, it began the serialization of two novels: *Der man iz nisht in der heym* ('The Husband is not at Home') and *Der shreklekher sod fun an opgehaktn froyenkop: a roman fun libe, laydnshaft, mord un raykhtum* ('The Terrible Secret of a Severed Woman's Head: A Novel of Love, Passion, Murder, and Riches').

Despite the failure of *Varshever kuryer*, the management of *Undzer ekspres* did not abandon the idea of publishing another paper. Indeed, they immediately began to plan the publication of an afternoon paper, and asked Shmuel Yatskan, the publisher of *Haynt*, to print it. He agreed, on condition that *Haynt* be a partner. The new paper was called *Letste nayes*, and the first edition appeared on 9 August 1929. It was edited by Menakhem Flakser (1898–1978) and Leyb Draykurs (1894–1941), its price was 10 groszy, and it was four pages long. The main head-

---

[26] A column of this sort with the same name ('W cztery oczy') appeared in Yatskan's *Ostatnie Wiadomości*. According to Flakser ('*Undzer ekspres*', 283), this column was copied from the *Forverts*.

[27] On this subject, see Paczkowski, *Prasa codzienna*, 194.

[28] Arlozorof (1899–1933) was a left-wing Zionist who was assassinated in Palestine, apparently by right-wing Zionists. His murder caused a political storm throughout the Jewish world.

lines primarily concerned politics. An editorial, sometimes signed by Lazar Kahan or Avrom Gliksman, at other times unsigned, was included almost daily. The rest of the newspaper's content was of a sensationalist nature and focused particularly on Jewish street life, e.g. 'Zun fun a lodzher khsidish manifaktur-soykher vil zikh shmadn tsulib a gasn-froy' ('Son of a Łódź Hasidic Manufacturer Wants to Convert because of a Prostitute'; 12 August 1929), 'Yom kiper tsvishn di khevre-layt fun der untervelt' ('Yom Kippur with the Boys of the Underworld'; 15 October 1929). The newspaper published many photographs. While its back page usually featured women (variously clothed or not), commissioned portraits of rabbis and other Jewish leaders often appeared on the first pages. The newspaper offered a serialized novel as well as a number of short series such as the memoirs of the famous Warsaw gravedigger Pinkert, followed by miraculous tales of the Gerer Rebbe.[29]

At first, distribution of *Letste nayes* reached 15,000 and even 20,000 copies a day; within a few months, however, its distribution declined, and *Undzer ekspres* withdrew from the partnership. Yatskan allowed the newspaper to continue under his ownership and renamed it, as we have seen, *Hayntike nayes*. Meanwhile, after nine months of recovery, *Undzer ekspres* published large announcements about the 'birth' of another new afternoon paper, *Ekstra blat* ('Extra Paper').[30] It was six pages long but was sold at the same price as the other sensationalist newspapers. The aim of the editors was to supply an 'interesting and exciting' newspaper while avoiding obscenity.[31] In order to demonstrate their seriousness, they published at the start the names of the novels and series that would appear, such as 'Di libe avantures fun barimte froyen' ('The Romantic Escapades of Famous Women'), 'Barimte tiranen' ('Famous Tyrants'), and 'Soydes fun a varshever dokter' ('Secrets of a Warsaw Doctor'). In its first issue the newspaper published the survey 'Tsi meg men onnemen mitlen kegn shvangershaft?' ('Is it Permissible to Use Contraception?'). On 10 October 1930 *Undzer ekspres* issued a short statement that for 'technical reasons' *Ekstra blat* would cease publication.

But *Undzer ekspres* recovered from this failure as well, and on 12 April 1931 offered the market *Yidisher kuryer* ('Jewish Courier'). Like its predecessors, this paper sought sensational headlines and ran a serialized novel, *Fraye libe: a roman fun shtarke emotsyes* ('Free Love: A Novel of Powerful Emotions'). The most outstanding new feature of the newspaper was its price: only 5 groszy. The paper published a Saturday night edition entitled *Ekstra kuryer* ('Extra Courier') (generally appearing at the same time as *Der moment*'s *Gut vokh*) and offered a daily matchmaking section. This newspaper lasted longer than its predecessors; its final edition was published on 28 February 1932.[32]

---

[29] The series appeared in successive issues on 18 Aug.–15 Dec. 1929.

[30] I have not been able to examine this newspaper; the information about it is from advertisements in *Undzer ekspres*.   [31] *Undzer ekspres* (2 Sept. 1930).

[32] During these years there was yet another sensationalist daily published in Warsaw but not connected to the major newspapers. It was called *Roman tsaytung* ('Novel Newspaper'), later renamed *Naye morgn-tsaytung* ('New Morning Journal'), and appeared from 24 July to 29 Sept. 1931.

The success of *Yidisher kuryer* spurred the board of *Undzer ekspres* to try to publish a third paper, a renewed *Letste nayes*,[33] for which *Undzer ekspres* readers were issued a coupon that allowed them to receive the new paper at no charge. On 30 October 1931 *Undzer ekspres* announced that newspaper distributors in Warsaw had been threatened by the editorial board of *Haynt* and *Der moment* for distributing the new paper. Two days later it threatened to seek legal recourse regarding the matter. *Haynt* and *Der moment* disregarded these threats and *Haynt* announced that from 4 November 1931 a special edition of the newspaper would appear every evening at five o'clock and include a section for merchants. It is not clear if this edition began as a direct response to *Letste nayes*, but its appearance certainly affected the distribution of the latter, more expensive, paper. The last edition of *Letste nayes* was published on 11 December 1931.[34]

The Bundist *Di naye folkstsaytung* was justifiably presented by its editors and publishers as an honourable and serious paper. Yet despite the widespread negative coverage the newspaper gave to the publishing war in the sensationalist press, it appears that the editors of the *Folkstsaytung* were greatly tempted to publish a popular afternoon paper of their own. This was *2 ba tog* ('2 p.m.'), which first appeared on 24 April 1932, a short time after the disappearance of *Yidisher kuryer*. The new paper was four pages long, cost 10 groszy, and, in contrast to the *Naye folkstsaytung*, was published only six days a week. Even though the newspaper aimed at the lowest common denominator in terms of journalistic standards, it still retained signs of its sponsorship. The headlines often concerned political issues and made reference to such subjects as strikes and workers' demonstrations. Three novels were published simultaneously: *Di letste nakht* ('The Last Night', about the martyred Hungarian Jewish workers' leader Hersh Yablonka); *Dos lebn un toyt fun aleksander ulyanov* ('The Life and Death of Alexander Ulyanov', Lenin's brother, a revolutionary executed in tsarist times); and *Der tron in flamen* ('The Throne in Flames', on the revolutionary movement in tsarist Russia). The newspaper also included short series of stories and reportages; here one might find anecdotes from the closed ward in the Jewish hospital in Warsaw, or secrets from behind the scenes of the city's rabbinate. Nearly every issue included an editorial, and once a week a feuilleton by Borukh Shefner (1896–1977) appeared. Unique to the newspaper was *Undzer entsiklopedye* ('Our Encyclopaedia'), a section on science, history, and culture. The newspaper also published readers' letters attacking the competing newspapers *Varshever radyo* and *Hayntike nayes*. Despite its innovations and attempts to draw readers, the fact that *2 ba tog* was affiliated with a party representing a particular section of the population prevented it from truly competing with the two other papers. It ceased publication after the 113th issue (2 September 1932).

[33] I have not been able to see this newspaper; the details about it are from *Undzer ekspres*.

[34] In addition to the above-mentioned dailies, *Undzer ekspres* also published a humorous weekly, *Der sheygets* (May 1929–June 1930); on this and similar publications, see below.

After 1932 few sensationalist papers were published. The two oldest and most well-established papers, *Varshever radyo* and *Hayntike nayes*, still survived, and demand for them remained constant. This stemmed, to a great extent, from increasing antisemitism and growing economic pressure on the Jews of Poland, and, to a lesser extent, from events in Germany. In a letter the writer Yisroel Shtern (1894–1942) described the changes in tone and atmosphere of newspapers, including the two leading afternoon papers:

The entire front page is taken up with telegrams, with current events, which means with sufferings and afflictions [*yesurim un puranyes*]. And by the time a reader has finished a whole column of Jewish sorrows [*yidishe tsores*]—the entire first column and sometimes its continuation in the middle of the paper too—it's enough to make him lose his appetite for all the idiocies of the adorable 'novels'.[35]

In Shtern's opinion this was also the reason for the publication of these novels in separate pamphlets (see more on this below). It seems that only one more short-lived attempt was made to publish an afternoon paper in Yiddish. This was *Dos 5 groshn kleyne blat* ('The 5 Groszy Little Paper'), which appeared from 6 to 28 November 1934. It was published seven days a week with blaring headlines; the real news, which it drew from the morning papers, was given half a column on the last page.

THE POLISH–LANGUAGE JEWISH TABLOID PRESS

Alongside Shtern's persuasive explanations for the limitations of the sensationalist Yiddish press, it must be remembered that there were undoubtedly Jewish readers (whose numbers cannot be estimated) who increasingly preferred the Polish sensationalist press to its Jewish counterpart. On the Polish street the sensationalist competition with established newspapers was much fiercer; this was reflected in the failure of most of the new competitors. Yatskan's *Ostatnie Wiadomości*, discussed above, was not considered a Jewish newspaper, although it was understandably read by many Jews. But there were also Jewish afternoon papers published in Polish. The first attempt to publish such a paper was initiated by the Polish-language Jewish daily *Nasz Przegląd* ('Our Review'). The new paper was *Nasz Głos Wieczorny* ('Our Evening Voice'), which was printed seven days a week from 16 April 1929. It was originally eight pages long and then decreased to four. While it contained material of a political nature, its headlines often concerned crime and the courts ('Krwawa zagadka w mieszkaniu sędziego śledczego' ('The Bloody Puzzle in the House of the Examining Magistrate'; 19 April 1929); 'Wstrząsający dramat w hotelu Słowańskim: Kochanek zabija kochankę i popełnia samobójstwo ('Shocking Drama in Hotel Słowański: A Man Kills his Lover and Commits Suicide'; 26 September 1929)). There was a serialized novel which primarily took place in courtrooms, a feuilleton

[35] Y. Shtern, 'Dos bisele shund zol gornit untergeyn', *Literarishe bleter*, no. 44 (1937), 700.

series entitled 'Behind the Walls of the Warsaw Prison', and memoirs of the Dreyfus affair. In addition the newspaper focused on anti-Jewish sentiments in Poland and Palestine. The stormy contents of *Nasz Głos Wieczorny* attracted enough readers to justify its existence until 30 June 1932, about the time when the Yiddish tabloid wars were winding down.

On 18 March 1931 a new Jewish paper, *Piąta Rano* ('5 a.m.'), was published in Polish. This was a Zionist newspaper that appeared seven days a week and lasted until the outbreak of war. It can be presumed that its success stemmed from the talents of the editor and publisher, Stanisław Świsłocki, who was also the first editor of *Ostatnie Wiadomości*. The few issues I was able to examine showed evidence of a newspaper with higher standards than the average sensationalist paper. The eight-page newspaper contained, in addition to the usual loud headlines, two novels and a variety of other sections, including ones for women and children. The only Jewish paper of its kind, *Piąta Rano* enjoyed wide distribution and longevity.

Between 21 December 1937 and March 1938 the co-operative Di Prese of *Der moment* also attempted to publish a Polish-language newspaper called *Nowy Głos* ('Our Voice'). Its goal was to decrease the co-operative's debt and stop the flight of readers to the Polish press.[36] According to the announcements of its publication it was to be 'an exciting newspaper, practical and absorbing' that would bring more detailed news from the Jewish world. Like *Piąta Rano*, *Nowy Głos* was a morning paper published seven days a week. It promised to publish instalments of two novels, short stories, and feuilletons each day. It was also to publish advertisements for all branches of trade and industry and to provide, like its older competitor, sections for women and children.[37]

There was no Hebrew tabloid press in Poland; indeed, after 1931 there was no Hebrew daily newspaper at all. The Hebrew reader always knew at least one other language and, if he or she was hungry for sensationalist news, could find it in another language.

SHUND IN THE TABLOIDS—AND THE STRUGGLE AGAINST IT

As this survey of the sensationalist newspapers demonstrates, serialized popular novels were an integral part of this press. There is even room to surmise that readers bought the newspapers primarily to learn what happened next in a given

[36] Tsvi Prilutski, memoirs written in the Warsaw ghetto, Yad Vashem Archives, Jerusalem, AR II/175, 279–82.

[37] I was unable to see this newspaper; the information about it is taken from an advertisement in *Der moment* (10 Dec. 1937). At one point in 1929 it seems that *Haynt* also attempted to publish a Polish-language Jewish paper of its own, *Nowy Czas* ('New Time'), presumably as a competitor to *Nasz Głos Wieczorny*, but I was unable to find any information about it.

novel.[38] Much importance was attached to the titles of the novels and to the adjectives in their subtitles ('suspenseful', 'sensational', 'thrilling', 'erotic', etc.), all of which were meant to capture the attention of the potential reader. The association of popular novels with the Yiddish daily press is as old as that press; even Sholem Aleichem, as evidenced by Y. D. Berkovits, was forced to come to terms with it.[39] *Haynt* and *Der moment*, considered the most prestigious newspapers, attracted readers by drafting in well-known authors such as Sholem Asch, Zalman Shneur, and Zusman Segalovitsh on one hand, and printing loud headlines on the other. In *Undzer ekspres* the sensationalist novel was an inseparable part of the newspaper. These included *Fun libe tsu shande* ('From Love to Shame', 1928), *Libe, laydnshaft un farbrekhn* ('Love, Desire, and Crime', 1930), and *Libe tsu farkoyfn* ('Love for Sale', 1932). In *Radyo* the novels had names such as *Heys blut* ('Hot Blood', 1933) and *Dos geshrey ba nakht* ('The Scream in the Night', 1938); and in *Hayntike nayes*, *Di zindike froy* ('The Sinful Woman', 1931) and *Di geheymnisn fun shikago* ('The Secrets of Chicago', 1935). Even the Bundist *Naye folkstsaytung*, which, as we have seen, could not refrain from publishing a sensationalist afternoon paper, also drew readers by means of novels such as *Dray teg libe* ('Three Days of Love', 1931) and *Dos hintishe gesl* ('The Nasty Lane', 1933).

In his remarks in 1932 on the subject of the serialized novel the influential editor Nakhmen Mayzil stated that, where literary authors had once written for the daily press, 'what rules now in the Yiddish press is generally a cheap sort of novel that is written not by artists but by novel-makers [*romanen-makher*]'.[40] According to Mayzil's study of thirty out of fifty Yiddish daily papers in the world, within one year no less than 300 serialized novels were published. Not all of them belonged in the same category, of course, but the clear majority were 'mass-produced pieced-together "novels" made according to a definite "recipe" by anonymous novel-makers or by writers who are ashamed to put their real names on this suspect merchandise'.[41] Mayzil explains that newspaper editors assigned the job of writing novels by lot or according to a rotating list, and, on occasion, a novel was written by a number of different people in sequence. This also happened when 'creations' of this type were taken from existing novels in foreign languages and adapted to fit the contemporary time and place.[42] A year earlier Mayzil had warned of the damaging

---

[38] Support for this opinion can be found in Y. L. Kahan, 'A tsaytung gezen durkh a prospekt', *Di naye folkstsaytung* (23 Apr. 1935). For an interesting survey of the overwhelming growth of serialized novels in the Western press, see M. Lyons, 'New Reading in the Nineteenth Century: Women, Children, Workers', in G. Cavallo and R. Chartier (eds.), *A History of Reading in the West* (Cambridge, 1999), esp. 313–21.

[39] Y. D. Berkovits, *Harishonim kevenei adam* (Tel Aviv, 1938–47), 806, 812; see also Shmeruk, 'Letoledot sifrut ha-"shund" beyidish'.

[40] N. Mayzil, 'Undzer tsaytung-roman', *Literarishe bleter*, no. 38 (1932), 599. The term *romanen-makher* is very similar to the term Władyka employs years later: *pisarz technik* (*Krew na pierwszej stronie*, 222).   [41] Mayzil, 'Undzer tsaytung-roman', 601.

[42] A. Pshepiurke writes about this sort of 'formula' in 'Vi azoy makht men an ekht sensatsyoneln roman?', *Dos naye vort* (12 Oct. 1937); there he also suggests suffusing the novel with eroticism. For

effects of sensationalist journalism, which fattened the reader with provocative material until he or she no longer had any appetite for other reading and became apathetic to the struggle for education, quality literature, and serious theatre. At the same time he warned of the continuous flow of Jewish readers to the Polish press, which was much less expensive than its Yiddish counterpart. He called for an all-out war on the phenomenon of *shund* literature,[43] but the response to his call was extremely limited. In 1933 he returned again to the subject, claiming that the situation had become much worse, primarily because talented writers were also being forced to take part in cheap writing for the daily press.[44]

Mayzil's claims were confirmed some decades later by two different literary authors. Avrom Arye-Leyb Yakubovitsh (A. A. Akavia) confessed that he contributed sensational writings to *Haynt* as early as 1909, under the watchful eye of Yatskan.[45] Isaac Bashevis Singer mentions more than once in his autobiographical writings that newspaper editors would return stories he had written with the suggestion that in their place he write, or rewrite for them, sensationalist novels. On one occasion the editor of *Radyo* offered him 200 zlotys a week to write a *shund* novel,[46] an unimaginable sum for one who was still a relatively unknown writer, and an offer he could not refuse: 'I took home a German novel over a thousand pages long. Besides the fact that it was pure *shund* . . . it was old-fashioned in style and unrelated to anything contemporary . . . Jews will read this trash . . . I myself because of my circumstances led them to it, but it tormented me.'[47]

Other important and prolific authors in Poland were also forced for economic reasons to 'make' inferior literature. Yehoshua Perle wrote novels for *Der moment* between 1926 and 1933, which he signed with three typographical stars, and Yisroel Rabon wrote for *Haynt* and the *Lodzher togblat* ('Łódź Daily'). In contrast to Perle, Rabon did not always hide his identity and even rose to the defence of *shund* literature and its writers (see below). The poet Itzik Manger fiercely attacked these two writers. He called them 'literary blackmailers' (*literarishe shantazhistn*) who adorned themselves with high artistic aspirations while corrupting the taste of the reader. According to Manger, there would come a time when the two would be called to

more on the latter issue, see below. The anonymous translation and adaptation of novels from foreign languages for publication in the daily press or as separate pamphlets was accepted practice in the Polish literary world as well (see A. Martuszewska, 'Literatura obiegów popularnych', in A. Brodzka *et al.* (eds.), *Słownik literatury polskiej XX wieku* (Wrocław, 1992), 582).

[43] N. Mayzil, 'Vu haltn mir mit undzer togprese in Poyln?', *Literarishe bleter*, no. 22 (1931), 415–16.

[44] N. Mayzil, 'Mikoyekh dem shund-roman', *Literarishe bleter*, no. 45 (1933), 709–10. This phenomenon was well recognized among Polish authors as well; see Martuszewska, 'Literatura obiegów popularnych'.

[45] C. Shmeruk, 'Te'udah nedirah letoledoteihah shel hasifrut halokanonit beyidish', *Hasifrut*, 32 (1983), 13–33.

[46] Y. Varshavski [Isaac Bashevis Singer], 'Fun der alter un nayer heym', *Forverts* (25 Oct. 1963); Y. Bashevis [Singer], 'Tsvishn gloybn un tsveyfl', *Forverts* (30 July 1976, 10 Feb. 1978).

[47] Y. Varshavski [Isaac Bashevis Singer], 'Der shrayber klub', *Forverts* (30 June 1956).

judgement and condemned with the mark of Yiddish literary disgrace, the name Shomer, recalling the author Nokhem-Meyer Shaykevitsh (1846–1905), whose pseudonym had become a synonym for *shund*.[48] In 1927 Yisroel Shtern wrote an imaginary conversation with Shomer in which Shtern admitted that, in the years since Shomer's death, his type of writing had won a great victory.[49] Shtern continued to fight against sensationalist novels and warned readers of the 'literary criminal' who had the power to corrupt the good qualities of those who were caught in his net and to damage all ethical and cultural values in society.[50]

Arn Tseytlin was also vilified on the suspicion that he took part in writing *shund* novels for *Undzer ekspres*. Tseytlin was the chairman of the Yiddish PEN Club in Poland and the editor of the periodical *Globus*, which sought to publish Yiddish literature of the same quality as that of other respected world literatures. He also fought against the politicization of the literary environment—a position that drew further criticism of him from other writers and from Bundist and communist activists, who missed no opportunity to recall his 'sins' and accuse him of passivity in the face of the hard economic situation of many Warsaw writers.[51]

In 1928 the leftist monthly *Oyfgang* ('Rising') called upon all young proletarian writers who had hitherto been paralysed by the '*shund* bacteria' to mobilize and fight against the destroyers of literature and rebuild positive relationships with their readers.[52] A number of years later the editorial board of the *Literarishe tribune* ('Literary Tribune') proclaimed that, thanks to Perle, Tseytlin, Bashevis Singer, and Asch, 'Today in Poland there is almost no bourgeois newspaper that is not "adorned" with a juicy pornographic novel . . . All is measured here by the number of times a hasidic girl is raped in each instalment.'[53] In the *Naye folkstsaytung* and the Orthodox *Dos yidishe togblat* the serialized novels were also labelled 'pornographic'.[54] When Perle's book *Yidn fun a gants yor* ('Everyday Jews') appeared, K. S. Kazdan sought its pornographic origins in the novels that Perle had written for *Der moment*.[55] In truth,

[48] I. Manger, *Getseylte verter* (Kraków), no. 4 (1930), 1–2. On Shomer and his place in Yiddish literature, see S. Grace-Pollak, 'Leor *shomers mishpet* leshalom aleichem', *Ḥuliot*, 5 (1999), 109–59.

[49] Y. Shtern, 'Dialog vegn zayn mayestet—shund', *Vokhnshrift far literatur, kunst un kultur*, no. 2 (1931), 2–4; no. 3 (1931), 2–4.

[50] See e.g. Y. Rapaport, 'Troyeriker mut', *Vokhnshrift far literatur, kunst un kultur*, no. 34 (1931). There Perle is accused of pornographic writing and Tseytlin of working for a newspaper of 'prostitution and extortion' in which he attempted to write a *shund* novel. See also Y. Pat, 'Umglik ba tog un znus ba nakht', *Vokhnshrift*, no. 37 (1932); Y.R. [Rapaport], 'Zey iz dos nokh nisht bakant . . .', *Vokhnshrift*, no. 21 (1934); id., 'A kurtse festshtelung? A groyser lign!', *Vokhnshrift*, no. 23 (1934), 4. See more on this subject in Y. Szeintuch, 'Sifrut, politikah vehumor: hapulmus bein yitsḥak bashevis ve'aron tseytlin orkhei hayarḥon *globus* levein hashavuon *vokhnshrift* vehayarḥon *literarishe tribune*', *Kesher*, 26 (1999), 67–78.

[51] Y. Shtern, 'Undzer lezern, oder: shomer hot gevunen', *Literarishe bleter*, no. 14 (1927), 265–8.

[52] M. Mintser, 'Ver, oyb nisht mir?', *Oyfgang*, no. 4 (1928), 1–2.

[53] A. Krakovski, 'Patsifikatsye durkh shund', *Literarishe tribune* (Łódź), 23 (1931), 4–5.

[54] B. Shefner, 'Der moderner shund-roman', *Di naye folkstsaytung* (17 Apr. 1931); see also *Yidishe togblat* (8 May 1934), and below.

[55] K. S. Kazdan, 'A bukh fun a gants yor', *Di naye folkstsaytung* (18 Oct. 1935).

the novels in the newspapers were usually far from pornographic, limiting themselves to sporadic hints of eroticism, and were, indeed, more modest and much less
violent than their counterparts in other languages.[56]

In 1925 Moyshe Gros made an early, serious attempt to understand the public's
demand for popular literature. According to Gros, the wider public was not able to
understand the coded nature of modern Yiddish literature, which hovered on the
border between 'literature and abstract mysticism' (*abstrakte kabole*) and was therefore understood primarily only by an elite subset of the reading public.[57] He felt
that the biggest problem of Yiddish literature was that average writers were trying
to imitate the exceptional ones and thereby creating a weak literature lacking content; Gros uses the term *shtum-loshn* (mute language). Therefore, the sole option
left for the popular readership was the *shund* literature that spoke to them in their
own language and presented them with the minutiae of everyday life. One of the
few to defend popular writing openly as having inherent value was Shmuel-Yankev
Imber. According to Imber, stories of suspense were popular throughout the world,
and allowed writers such as Edgar Allen Poe to achieve high esteem. Only the
Jewish environment, claimed Imber, despised this genre and rejected it as *shund*,
thus preventing the healthy and normal development of Yiddish literature.[58]

In the rooms of the Yidishe Literatn un Zhurnalistn Fareyn one could meet, side
by side with the 'makers' of sensationalist novels of various types, serious authors
who wrote low-quality literature for economic reasons, as well as those for whom
writing of this type was totally out of the question. In the 1930s there were heated
arguments within the union about the right of popular literature to exist in Yiddish
and the place of that literature's creators. At the general meeting of members of the
Yiddish PEN Club in 1933 the poet Kadya Molodowsky suggested taking significant steps against members who wrote novels under pseudonyms. This idea met
with strong resistance, as others defended those writers who were forced to 'sin'
because of economic hardship. According to Molodowsky, she suddenly found
herself on the defensive, and the suspicion crept into her mind that 'soon members
who did not write *shund* would be expelled from the PEN Club'.[59] Not only did

---

[56] Shmeruk, 'Letoledot sifrut ha-"shund" beyidish', 327. On violence in German *shund* literature
see R. Schenda, *Die Lesestoffe der kleinen Leute. Studien zur populären Literatur im 19. und 20.
Jahrhundert* (Munich, 1976), 105–20. The Polish novels published in newspapers or accompanying
pamphlets could also not be called 'pornographic'; see A. Martuszewska, 'Topika literatury obiegów
popularnych', in Brodzka *et al.* (eds.), *Słownik literatury polskiej XX wieku*, 1104–10.

[57] M. Gros, 'Kunst, shund un shtum-loshn', *Literarishe bleter*, no. 39 (1925), 4. Gros's writings
began in no. 38 and continued in nos. 42, 43, 46, 48, and 58.

[58] S. Y. Imber, 'Di moyre far shund', *Haynt* (16 Jan. 1931). See also S. Babad, 'Di kriminale literatur', *Dos vort* (30 Oct. 1936), and Schenda, *Die Lesestoffe der kleinen Leute*, 105–20.

[59] K. Molodowsky, 'Di khvalye fun vidershtand', *Literarishe bleter*, no. 46 (1933), 730. The conference was held on 11 Jan. 1933. On the same subject, see also Molodowsky's letter to Yoysef Opatoshu of
24 Nov. 1933 (YIVO Archives, New York, Opatoshu Collection) and her article 'Tsvey naye shund-
firmes', *Der fraynd* (16 Nov. 1934).

the Bundist Kazdan defend Molodowsky, seeing *shund* as a by-product of a corrupt bourgeois society, but both the pro-communist Nakhmen Mayzil and his Zionist rivals Moyshe-Bunim Yustman and Nekhemye Finkelshteyn also supported her.[60]

The struggle against sensationalist novels and their authors was really part of an ongoing struggle against the sensationalist Yiddish press that had begun in 1924. In that year a number of illustrated popular periodicals appeared in Warsaw and Łódź that reminded Yehoshua Perle of 'a narrow filthy courtyard somewhere on Nalewki Street where heaps of little shopfronts are piled with cheap goods and dizzy shopkeepers'.[61] Two inexpensive weeklies stood out: *Der sheygets* ('The Smart-Alec', literally 'The Gentile Boy') and *Der mazik* ('The Mischief-Maker'). From these names it is clear that the editors did not intend to provide serious reading material; indeed much of the writing was truly vulgar. These weeklies primarily contained jokes—almost always at the expense of women—caustic caricatures, and short stories with lurid titles: 'Der yeshive bokher durkhn shlisl lokh' ('The Yeshiva Boy [Peeks] through the Keyhole'), 'Der galekh un di sheyne yunge almone' ('The Priest and the Beautiful Young Widow'), 'Mitn gelibtn un man in shloftsimer' ('With the Husband and his Beloved in the Bedroom'), etc.[62] Such writing had never before been seen on the Jewish street and the literary faithful made war on these newspapers.

Predictably, the vanguard of the fighters was *Undzer folkstsaytung*, which called for the exclusion of newspapers of this type from the 'literary camp' and a boycott of those who wrote for them.[63] *Der sheygets* was quick to respond, claiming that such publications existed all over the world, that there was no reason to be ashamed of them, and that it would be better for the 'purest of the pure' to deal with 'their daughters' *live shkotsim* [non-Jewish boyfriends] than take on the paper *sheygets*'.[64] The Bundist newspaper replied that the nations of the world were not the concern of Jews: did the existence of brothels all over the world mean that Jews should have them too? *Der moment* and *Literarishe bleter* soon joined the fray and attacked the leadership of the Literatn Fareyn for not taking significant steps against the weeklies' editors.[65] At the same time the Literatn Fareyn published an announcement which claimed that none of their members were connected to the weeklies; one person who was in fact connected to them, apparently their editor, Pinkhes Kats (1891–1942), had been forced to resign from the union.[66]

---

[60] K. S. Kazdan, 'Der vidershtand fun der shund-khvalye', *Vokhnshrift far literatur, kunst un kultur*, no. 45 (1933), 3; N. Mayzil, 'Shaft take dos lebn bloyz shtof far shund-verk?', *Haynt* (25 May 1934); B. Yustman, 'Shund un ver iz derin shuldik?', *Haynt* (15 June 1934); N. Finkelshteyn, 'Mikoyekh dem shund-roman', *Literarishe bleter*, no. 48 (1934), 849.

[61] Y. Perle, 'In undzer vayngortn', *Literarishe bleter*, no. 6 (1924), 2.

[62] *Der sheygets*, nos. 7–9 (1924).   [63] 'Kegn pornografye', *Undzer folkstsaytung* (24 Aug. 1924).

[64] *Der sheygets*, no. 10 (1924); emphasis in original.

[65] *Literarishe bleter*, no. 17 (1924), 6; see aso Emanuel [Y. Heftman], 'In kamf mit shmuts', *Der moment* (29 Aug. 1924).   [66] Notice in *Undzer folkstsaytung* (24 Aug. 1924).

Der mazik appeared only twice, while *Der sheygets* published ten issues.[67] But their editor, who in the years 1915–23 had edited the humour column of *Haynt* and in the 1930s would serve on the editorial board of *Radyo*, did not give up. On 31 October 1924 Pinkhes Kats began a new weekly, the *Varshever velt kuryer* ('Warsaw World Courier'), whose contents were no different from its predecessors. Only three issues of this publication appeared. From them one can learn that Mussolini was really a Polish Jew, that a Jew sold his wife for two oxen and a bag of potatoes, and that a 22-year-old woman became a man.[68] In January 1926 the leadership of the Literatn Fareyn decided to readmit Kats as a regular member. In response, Israel Joshua Singer announced his resignation from the organization.[69] Kats continued to edit humorous magazines such as *Velt ekspres* ('World Express', January–February 1926); *Der blofer* ('The Bluffer', published by *Haynt*, July 1926–August 1930), the only publication of this type with any sort of longevity; and *Der mekhabl* ('The Destroyer', June 1935–July 1936).[70]

In order to compete with the sensationalist press, in August 1930 the editorial board of the *Naye folkstsaytung* launched a campaign to increase distribution of the newspaper with the slogan 'Friends! Remember that you are opening wide the door to the *shund* papers if you do not subscribe to and distribute your *Naye folkstsaytung*'.[71] The newspaper, which had attempted to keep its price at 15 groszy, lower than its competitors, now reduced it to 10 groszy for a limited time to keep readers from purchasing the 'inferior' publications. In 1932 the Bund's literary and cultural weekly, *Vokhnshrift far literatur, kunst un kultur* ('Literature, Art, and Culture Weekly'), ran a survey on ways to identify *shund* using excerpts from serialized novels in the daily press.[72] Readers' responses were published over several months.

Another newspaper that devoted much attention to the war against the *shund* press was the Orthodox *Dos yidishe togblat*, which announced a project on the eve of the high holidays in 1930 dedicated to purifying the souls of young people and eliminating the affliction of the *shund* press from among the God-fearing public. The newspaper declared that during the intermediate days of Sukkot girls from the Orthodox Beys-Yankev (Beis Ya'akov) schools would visit Jewish women in order to persuade them to keep the yellow press out of their homes. It was girls who had been recruited for this work because, according to the *Togblat*, they were the primary victims of the tabloids, which threatened the modest daughters of Israel with disgrace.[73] The Orthodox leadership had also decided to join the struggle, wrote

---

[67] *Der mazik* (10 Oct., 14 Nov. 1924); *Der sheygets* (June–Aug. 1924).

[68] *Varshever velt kuryer*, nos. 2, 3 (1924).

[69] Singer's announcement was published in *Literarishe bleter*, no. 90 (1926), 70. Details of the Literatn Fareyn meeting can be found in *Folkstsaytung*, single edn. (17 Jan. 1926).

[70] This was the third attempt at a weekly with the name *Der mekhabl*; earlier versions appeared for three months in 1919 and two months in 1928.   [71] Notice in *Di naye folkstsaytung* (8 Aug. 1930).

[72] *Vokhnshrift far literatur, kunst un kultur*, no. 37 (1932). An earlier survey (in no. 27, 1932) was concerned with defining the terms 'graphomaniac' and 'graphomania'.

[73] A. Zonenfreyd, 'Di yidishe tokhter in kamf mit der shund-prese', *Dos yidishe togblat* (17 Oct. 1930).

Avrom-Mordkhe Rogovi, the editor of the *Togblat*, and from now on the fight against *shund* would gain in strength.[74] About the same time the following year the *Togblat* held a similar campaign in conjunction with the Agudes Yisroel youth publication *Ortodoksishe yugnt bleter* ('Orthodox Youth Pages').[75] In support of the *Togblat*, the Strikover Rebbe (Stryków) called for a gathering of rabbis to co-ordinate a campaign against *shund*.[76] A number of days later Rogovi again declared that the affliction of the yellow press was already in every home. Today, he complained, older hasidim, young men, and schoolchildren went into the streets and shamelessly buried their heads in the pages of the *shund* newspapers.[77] Again that year Sukkot was devoted to building awareness of the *shund* menace. From 12 December 1931 the *Togblat* published letters from rabbis and hasidic leaders calling for a fight against the sensationalist press. Afterwards, at the request of several rabbis, these letters were translated from Hebrew into Yiddish for women.

It is not clear how the Orthodox community responded to these appeals, since there is no mention of any response in the *Togblat*. This is particularly odd, since there were regular reports concerning the large public response to the campaign against breaking the sabbath in Warsaw. Moreover, at the precise moment of the campaign against yellow journalism the *Togblat* announced the publication in the near future of a serialized novel that would be a 'shpanend un hekht sensatsyonale dertseylung' ('thrilling and highly sensational story').[78] Seven years later it also slipped in a novel entitled *Farn shturem* ('Before the Storm'), which angered both *Der moment* and the rabbis of Agudes Yisroel. Its printing was stopped a few days after it began.[79]

In 1937 both *Haynt* and *Der moment* began to publish serialized novels in separate pamphlets for 5 groszy each. The newspapers usually inserted the first instalment in the Friday edition at no charge, and when the reader was 'hooked' he could continue to read the story without buying the newspaper. The novels were named after their heroines, *Sabine* (*Haynt*) and *Regine* (*Der moment*); these names became synonymous with *shund* literature of the 'lowest' type. As is to be expected, the *Naye folkstsaytung* hurried to warn its readers of the poison being spread in the streets by *Haynt*.[80] In a satirical article Itzik Manger compared the two *shund* 'heroines' to two prostitutes emerging from the cellars of two respected newspapers that were proud of publishing Asch and Shneur. Manger accused the bourgeois press of fostering *shund* and corrupting the taste of the reader.[81] Borukh Shefner

[74] Editorial, *Dos yidishe togblat* (5 Oct. 1930).

[75] *Dos yidishe togblat* (13 Aug. 1931).   [76] *Dos yidishe togblat* (18 Aug. 1931).

[77] *Dos yidishe togblat* (21 Aug. 1931).   [78] *Dos yidishe togblat* (26 Aug. 1931).

[79] Y. Yefet, 'Arop di maske', *Der moment* (24 Jan. 1938). *Dos yidishe togblat* responded on the same day; the notice in *Der moment* was on 4 Apr. 1938; see also Beys Shin [Borukh Shefner], 'Di zmires zingern fun "mizrokhi" un lize fun gerer "togblat"', *Di naye folkstsaytung* (17 Jan. 1938).

[80] 'Der *haynt* farshpreyt gift af der yidisher gas', *Di naye folkstsaytung* (3 Sept. 1937).

[81] I. Manger, 'Sabine un regine', *Di naye folkstsaytung* (22 Oct. 1937).

suggested that perusal of these pamphlets would incline the foreign reader to think that the majority of Polish Jews were immoral and that even the women were blood-thirsty and wanton. Only the poor orphaned girls, the only positive figures in these novels according to Shefner, remained to redeem the corrupted image of Polish Jews.[82] Jonas Turkow (Yonas Turkov) claimed that only in the Jewish environment did popular literature reach such frightening proportions that it threatened the existence of serious literature itself; he called for the establishment of a special authority to fight against *shund* publications.[83] Alter Katsyzne (Kacyzne) and the playwright Ayzik Ruskolenker framed the phenomenon in medical terms: the *shund* epidemic, they suggested, should be fought with antibodies of similar pamphlets offered to the public at the same price but in smaller doses and in a controlled manner.[84]

An entirely different response was that of Yisroel Rabon. From his perspective it was preferable to have a public that read inferior literature to one that didn't read at all or only read political propaganda pretending to be literature. According to Rabon, the Jewish reader would never have reached the level of good literature if he or she had not read Shomer fifty years earlier. Indeed, every literary system included *shund* literature, because otherwise it could not be called literature. Rabon rejected the claim that the newspaper novels were pornographic and accused the Bund activists of exaggerating the problem in an attempt to make political capital.[85]

At the beginning of 1938 the Yidishe Literatn un Zhurnalistn Fareyn in Vilna issued an appeal to its counterpart in Warsaw, to the Jewish printers' union, and to newspaper distributors and editorial boards in both cities. The union proposed a joint effort to remove the sensationalist novels from the press, stop the printing of the pamphlets, and call a national conference to mobilize for a war against *shund*.[86] The only response, it seems, was from *Dos yidishe togblat*.[87]

[82] B. Shefner, 'Dos ponim fun poylishn yidntum', *Di naye folkstsaytung* (21 Nov. 1937).

[83] J. Turkow, 'A mageyfe vos ruft zikh: shund', *Literarishe bleter*, no. 2 (1938), 27. See also A. Pshepiurke, 'Der sfinks—di gas', *Dos naye vort* (3 Sept. 1937), and Shtern, 'Dos bisele shund', 700. On the war against German *shund* literature and its national, educational, and economic implications, see Schenda, *Die Lesestoffe der kleinen Leute*, 78–97.

[84] A. Katsizne and A. Ruskolenker, 'Sabine mit regine, oder, Di klole fun nisht organizirikayt', *Mein redndiker film*, no. 11 (1937), 7–12; A. Ruskolenker, 'Mayn inflatsye fun gasn-literatur', *Os*, no. 6 (1937), 33–6.

[85] A. Ringel [Yisroel Rabon], 'Der gayst fun zhelekhov', *Os*, no. 6 (1937), 40. Rabon also exploited the discussion to even scores with Manger, who, Rabon claimed, put Jewish biblical heroes to cheap use in his Bible and *Megilah* poems, lowering them to the level of 'erotic tales in the yellow newspapers' (see 'Di mase un di dikhtung', ibid. 40–6).   [86] Notice in *Undzer tog* (12 Jan. 1938).

[87] D. Flinker, 'Vegn der aktsye kegn shund in der yidisher prese', and S. Shtokhamer, 'Di plog fun shund', *Dos yidishe togblat* (13 Jan. 1938).

CONCLUSION

According to the press historian Andrzej Paczkowski, the Polish sensationalist press always had a clear advantage over the traditional Polish press in Warsaw. In 1938 the average distribution of the eleven mainstream newspapers in the capital was approximately 25,000 copies per newspaper. But at the same time the average distribution of the seven afternoon papers reached about 70,000.[88] In the Jewish context the sensationalist press was never so predominant: first, because the more respected newspapers themselves published serialized popular novels; secondly, because the sensationalist Polish press could be read by the Jewish reader; and thirdly, because the weakening political, social, and economic status of the Jews in Poland had, as suggested above, depressed the appetite of the reader for sensationalist writing. Nevertheless, in 1938 *Sabine* and *Regine* achieved distribution in greater numbers than any Jewish newspaper.[89]

Despite the relatively low proportion of sensationalist literature in Yiddish publishing as a whole (especially as compared to its availability on the Polish street), there is no doubt that it grew in volume during the inter-war years and that it achieved wide popularity. At the same time it must be emphasized that this literature, including its pamphlet form, was connected to and dependent upon the daily press. Books or pamphlets of this type were no longer sold in bookshops in the numbers in which they had been thirty and forty years earlier.[90] Imber and Rabon are correct in their estimation of the phenomenon in its entirety.[91] Indeed, the latter cites the words of Y. L. Peretz from 1905, referring to the new Yiddish popular culture: 'Ikh bin dafke tsufridn mit di bitere kraytekhtser, vos heybn on shprotsn in undzer gan-eydndl . . . Dos iz der bester bavayz az mir antiviklen zikh, az undzer

[88] Paczkowski, *Prasa codzienna*, 262–7, and 'Nakłady dzienników warszawskich'.

[89] In Shmeruk's article 'Letoledot sifrut ha-"shund" beyidish', 333, it is estimated that *Sabine* was distributed in about 100,000 copies. Even if this number is somewhat exaggerated, it is undoubtedly much greater than the average daily circulation of a mainstream Yiddish newspaper, which was 15,000–25,000.

[90] Lists of books issued by established publishing houses do not include *shund* literature; I have not found comparable lists for small and marginal publishers. From the yearbooks *Urzędowy wykaz druków w Rzeczypospolitej Polskiej* (Warsaw) and *Bibliografishe yorbikher fun YIVO*, vol. i (Warsaw, 1928), one can draw out a relatively small number of titles that can definitely be termed *shund*. In comparison, in 1889 the works of Shomer constituted 35% of all books published (see *Yidishe folksbibliotek* (1889), 135–9). By 1912 their proportion had declined to less than 4% (see M. Shalit, 'Statistik fun yidishn bikhermark', in *Der pinkes: yorbukh far der geshikhte fun der yidisher literatur un shprakh, far folklor, kritik un bibliografye* (Vilna, 1913). Shmeruk, 'Letoledot sifrut ha-"shund" beyidish', mentions the 'plague of the pamphlets' in America as a precedent; however, it is more reasonable to assume that the immediate model for this imitation was closer, in Poland itself. There pamphlets of this type began to appear as supplements to the newspapers in the first years of the 20th century; these complete creations could run to over 2,000 pages (see Martuszewska, 'Literatura obiegów popularnych', 580–1). Another possible model is Russian (see Brooks, *When Russia Learned to Read*, 141–62). Unfortunately, I have been unable to examine even one of the early Yiddish pamphlets.

[91] See nn. 58 and 85.

literatur antviklt zikh' ('So I am pleased with the bitter weeds that have begun to sprout in our little Garden of Eden . . . This is the best proof that we are developing, that our literature is developing').[92]

Translated from Hebrew by Erica Nadelhaft and Benjamin Greenberg

[92] Y. L. Peretz, 'Der tog', in his *Ale verk*, vol. ix (New York, 1947), 94.

Dos yidishe bukh alarmirt!
Towards the History of Yiddish
Reading in Inter-War Poland

ELLEN KELLMAN

If we wish to measure the cultural level and cultural needs of a country or population, we must take into consideration the extent of its book production and the
number of libraries and readers it possesses. Material conditions, socio–political
relations, the general state of child-rearing and education, and the role of the press,
theatre, cultural organizations, and the trade unions also have much light to shed
on the subject.

NAKHMEN MAYZIL, *Geven a mol a lebn*

INTRODUCTION

IN the lead article of its January 1939 bulletin the Bundist organization Kult-bukh
bemoaned the wretched financial state of the Yiddish book market in Poland and
appealed to several organizations—the Yidishe Literatn un Zhurnalistn Fareyn
(Jewish Writers' and Journalists' Union), the Yiddish PEN Club, the Tsentraler
Yidisher Shul-Organizatsye (Central Yiddish School Organization, TsIShO), the
YIVO Institute, and the Bibliotekn-tsenter (Library Centre) of the Bundist
Kultur-lige—to proclaim a Yiddish book month. Its aim was to revive the book
market and to make the reading public aware of the role it could play in ensuring
that Yiddish books would continue to be published in Poland.[1]

The weakness and vulnerability of the Yiddish book market on the eve of the
Nazi destruction of east European Jewish life points to a variety of adverse forces
that were in play at that fearful moment in history: economic depression, anti-
Jewish government policies, the omnipresence of entertainment fiction in the
Yiddish daily press, and the rapid linguistic assimilation of Polish Jewish youth.

I would like to thank the following colleagues for their suggestions and help in locating research materials
for this study: Zachary Baker, Małgorzata Barcikowska, Alina Cała, Leo Greenbaum, Urszula Grygier,
Samuel Kassow, Herbert Lazarus, Kenneth Moss, Antony Polonsky, Jeffrey Salant, Jeffrey Shandler,
Michael Steinlauf, Rafał Żebrowski, and Olga Zienkiewicz.

[1] M. Tsanin, 'Dos yidishe bukh alarmirt!' ('The Yiddish Book Sounds the Alarm!'), *Bikher-nayes*
(Jan. 1939), 1–2.

Jewish public libraries played a pivotal role in working-class Jewish culture in the period between the wars. Since many young people typically left school in their early teens to enter the workforce, libraries and the cultural activities that took place in and around them enabled young people to continue to develop intellectually.

The symbiosis between the Yiddish book industry and Yiddish libraries in inter-war Poland meant that the relative health or infirmity of libraries strongly affected the book industry. Thus, when the Yiddish book sounded the alarm in 1939, it was an indication of the troubled state of the libraries as well.

Although the twenty-year interlude between the two world wars was an extremely difficult period for Polish Jewry, one that, with hindsight, we may see as characterized by significant losses, it was also distinguished by the tremendous creative energy of its cultural activists. Their determination to build a viable modern Yiddish culture in the face of formidable obstacles has inspired this study.

THE RISE OF SECULAR YIDDISH LITERATURE AND CULTURE

Public libraries did not become part of east European Jewish life until the early years of the twentieth century, and took hold firmly only after the First World War. They arose as a means of disseminating secular Jewish culture among Jewish workers and young people.

As the Haskalah became a pervasive force in east Europe in the mid- to late-nineteenth century, a new, secular Jewish literature developed in Hebrew, Yiddish, and the predominant non-Jewish languages of the region: Polish, Russian, and German. Literacy rates, always unusually high among east European Jews in comparison with their non-Jewish neighbours, grew steadily during this period, especially among women, and formulaic fiction in Yiddish became exceedingly popular. The leading exponent of this fiction was Nokhem-Meyer Shaykevitsh (1846–1905), known by the pen name Shomer. The readership of his sentimental romances mainly comprised artisans, servants, and factory workers of both genders.[2] These works were originally published in chapbook editions. After the turn of the twentieth century, as the Yiddish press established itself in eastern Europe, formulaic fiction of the type popularized by Shomer came to be published in serial form in daily newspapers.[3]

During the final two decades of the nineteenth century Yiddish became, for the first time, a linguistic medium for a number of other genres as well. Original works of poetry, satire, drama, serious fiction, political theory, geography, and natural history were written in Yiddish. By the end of the first decade of the twentieth

---

[2] Zalmen Reyzn [Reisin] wrote of Shomer's impact: 'For the mass readership, Shomer was the most popular author of his time, and to a great extent, he created that readership. His conception of literature was, to put it mildly, quite naive, but he correctly sensed the new cultural needs of the Jewish masses in that transitional period' (*Leksikon fun der yidisher literatur, prese un filologye*, vol. iv (Vilna, 1929), 768).

[3] On this and related issues, see the chapter by Nathan Cohen in this volume.

century all of these genres had found their way into the Yiddish periodical press. As a result, book publishers found themselves in sharp competition with newspapers and magazines for the patronage of readers. Like their counterparts in North America, Yiddish writers in eastern Europe often turned to journalism as a means of making a living while continuing to produce serious literature on the side.

READING NETWORKS AND LENDING LIBRARIES UNDER TSARIST RULE

The Haskalah shaped modern Jewish culture in many ways, one of the most important of which was to foster an urge towards secular education. We know from memoirs describing east European Jewish life at the beginning of the twentieth century that a youth culture revolving around autodidacticism flourished. Young men and women whose social position afforded them access to some degree of secular education often acted as catalysts, establishing networks of readers and teaching each other Polish, Russian, and German in order to read works of literature, political theory, and natural and social science in these languages.

In a memoir of his youth in the predominantly hasidic *shtetl* Strikov (Stryków), near Łódź, in the mid-1890s, Avrom Pinkhes Unger (b. 1880) described his participation in a clandestine network of teenage boys and girls who exchanged secular books in Yiddish and Hebrew with one another.

During this time my friend Avrom-Alter Yona and I became even more active in distributing *haskole-bikhlekh* [secular books] I convinced Berish, Reb Rafoel's son and a grandson of the Strikover *rebbe*, that he should borrow one of these books from me and read it. He was very happy with it. Berish could read and write *loshn-koydesh* [Hebrew-Aramaic] very well. I gave him a book of Mapu's writings. I no longer remember the title of the book. A few weeks later I persuaded Reb Rafoel's elder son, Avrom, to accept books from me. Thus did the Haskalah penetrate even the *rebbe*'s court.[4]

Unger and his friends read unsystematically, acquiring books whenever they could from itinerant *moykher-sforimnikes* (booksellers). Both the booksellers and their young customers were at pains to keep their business transactions secret.

Booksellers who had *sforim*, *tfiln*, *taleysim*, *mezuzes*, and other wares to sell frequently came to Strikov. Secretly they also sold *mayse-bikhlekh* [secular Yiddish stories in chapbook format], making sure that no hasid would see. I learned of this from my friend Shloyme Spitsek, who had bought several *zhargonishe* [Yiddish] *mayse-bikhlekh* from the bookseller. He told me that I should keep the information strictly secret, because if people found out about it they would run the *moykher-sforimnik* out of town.[5]

---

[4] A. P. Unger, *Mayn heymshtetl strikov* (New York, 1957), 66. Abraham Mapu (1808–67) was the creator of the modern Hebrew novel.   [5] Ibid. 44.

Other books were lent to the young readers by members of a small group of adult maskilim in town, the Khevre Mefitsey-haskole (Society of Disseminators of the Enlightenment). There was no Jewish public lending library in Strikov during this period, so Unger and his friends often met secretly at the home of one of the adult maskilim to read secular books and Hebrew newspapers.

Every day, after I had finished my lesson in *gemore* [Talmud] and worked on committing the text to memory, I took time to visit my friend Shmuel Bretshnayder and read a newspaper or a secular book. Avrom Bretshnayder's house was already known in town as a place where boys and girls gathered to read *treyfene bikhlekh* [heretical books].[6]

Unger's memoir portrays girls and young women as active in the underground network of readers of secular literature that flourished in Strikov. In addition to reading in Yiddish and Hebrew, the young autodidacts of Strikov were eager to learn Polish, Russian, and German, so as to gain access to non-Jewish literature. In this realm the girls in the circle, whose parents had them tutored in non-Jewish languages to prepare them to run family businesses, served as teachers to the boys.

Unger was the orphaned son of a prominent talmudist in Strikov. A bright student, he was tutored in *gemore* by a succession of learned hasidim. In the course of visiting the home of one of his tutors to receive his lessons, he was taught to read and write Russian and Polish secretly by the man's daughter, a young woman in her late teens. Unger was then 15 years old.[7]

Rokhl Holtman, who was born in 1882 and grew up in Plungyan (Plunge), a *shtetl* in north-western Lithuania, wrote about the evening courses and library that she, along with other girls in their late teens, organized in her town at the turn of the twentieth century. From the age of 9 to 11 Holtman had attended a two-year elementary school for Jewish girls in her town. There she developed a thirst for knowledge, and later educated herself beyond the elementary level of her formal education by reading all the Russian literature she could lay her hands on.

Our *shtetl* was in an impoverished, secluded corner of the country. Apart from the girls' school that I had attended, there were no other educational institutions. It is true that there were several *khadorim* and a yeshiva, but these did not count because they were not open to girls. . . . Those who could afford it would hire private teachers for their children. These pupils had hour-long lessons in Russian three times a week. Those, however, who couldn't afford to pay, and there were many of them, had no opportunity to study. Therefore, several of us girls took it upon ourselves to open an evening school. It was illegal, because the police would not provide a permit for such an undertaking. The pupils in our school were young Jewish workers, male and female alike. We taught them to read and write Yiddish, to do arithmetic, and to write enough Russian and German to enable them to address a letter.

We girls went around town, collected several hundred books, and opened a library, which was also illegal. We set up our collection at my grandmother's house because we were afraid that if we kept the books in the centre of town they might be confiscated. My grandmother

---

[6] Unger, *Mayn heymshtetl strikov*, 58.   [7] Ibid. 64–5.

lived on the outskirts, where our library didn't attract too much attention. Our desire to bring a bit of light into the *shtetl*, which, at the time, was our whole world, motivated us to organize the courses, the small library, and a reading circle.[8]

Some lending libraries that were established illegally under tsarist rule endured over many years, through war and changes in government. One of these was the Dovid Frishman Jewish Library in the industrial town of Zgierz, near Łódź. Founded in 1907 by a group of young intellectuals and autodidacts, the library's primary purpose was to 'awaken an interest in education and knowledge in the common people'.[9] Its founders intended it to be an independent institution whose purpose was Jewish cultural education. Legalized in 1917, during the German occupation of Zgierz, the library was able to broaden its activities and advertise them freely. After acquiring its own premises it organized a variety of public events, such as literary readings, anniversaries of the deaths of Jewish writers and artists, and commemorative programmes, to celebrate important historical events. Members taught courses there in Hebrew, elementary mathematics, non-Jewish languages, and general sciences. The library became a second home for the Jewish youth of Zgierz, many of whom frequented it against the wishes of their hasidic parents. It remained the central cultural institution in the Jewish community of Zgierz until the outbreak of the Second World War.[10]

THE RAPID DEVELOPMENT OF YIDDISH CULTURE IN INDEPENDENT POLAND

The establishment of the Second Polish Commonwealth in 1918 brought Jews from the former Austro-Hungarian, German, and Russian empires together as part of a new political entity, creating dialectal and cultural diversity in the Jewish communities of the larger cities and fostering intensified contact between writers, educators, artists, and political and cultural leaders in the various regions of the new Poland. These new configurations sparked an enthusiasm for rebuilding institutions and organizational ties that had been lost during the war.

The *kultur-tuer* (cultural activist) Nakhmen Mayzil (1887–1966) commented as follows on the process whereby a million Galician Jews, a million Polish Jews, and a million Jews from the eastern *kresy* (borderlands) came to regard themselves as members of one community, with common political, social, and cultural concerns:

It was not so easy for these separate 'tribes' to live together. Often they did not willingly fall into the Jewish melting-pot or let themselves be drawn into the circle of Jewish concerns and

---

[8] R. Holtman, *Mayn lebns-veg* (New York, 1948), 29–30.

[9] V. Fisher, 'Yidishe bibliotek untern nomen dovid frishman', in D. Shtokfish (ed.), *Seyfer zgerzh: tsum ondenk fun a yidisher kehile in poyln* (Tel Aviv, 1975), 283 (quoting Fabian Grinberg, in *Lodzher folksblat* (4 July 1915)). David Frishman (1859–1922), one of the first major writers in modern Hebrew literature, was born in Zgierz.   [10] Ibid. 282–3.

influences. But perhaps without even realizing it or choosing to do so, each section of the Jewish masses that became part of Wielkopolska began to contribute its characteristic traits (both positive and negative) to the general Polish Jewish organism.

'Polish Jewry', as we are accustomed to calling the Jews who lived in independent Poland, without a doubt benefited greatly from the influx of 'foreign' Jews.

This was felt especially strongly in the metropolis of Poland, in the largest Polish Jewish community, Warsaw, to which were drawn intellectuals and prominent leaders in the most varied fields of endeavour. Wherever one turned, in the Yiddish press, in the arts, in theatre, in leading political circles, everywhere one found Jews from Galicia, Lithuania, Volhynia, and White Russia.[11]

YIDDISH LIBRARIES IN THE EARLY YEARS OF POLAND'S INDEPENDENCE

The flowering of a network of Yiddish libraries in inter-war Poland owed much to the cultural ferment engendered by the new social and political conditions there. Scores of Yiddish libraries were founded under German occupation during the First World War and during the first years of Polish independence.[12] Of these, the majority were connected with political movements, but some were private, profit-making enterprises. In an article written in 1934 on the history of Jewish libraries in Warsaw the librarian Bashe Temkin noted the founding dates for the leading public Yiddish libraries in the capital and the most important private libraries with Yiddish collections.[13]

Of the *efntlekhe* [public] *gezelshaftlekhe* [institutional] libraries that are still in existence, Hazomir Bibliotek, founded in 1914, was the first. Later, during the period of German occupation and the first years of Poland's independence, the following libraries came into existence: the Grosser Library (1915), Merkaz (1917), the Borokhov Library (1919), Dos Lebn, and several others.

We also have exact information about the existence of a number of other private lending libraries that had collections of Yiddish or Hebrew books during this period. Some of them,

---

[11] N. Mayzil, *Geven a mol a lebn* (Buenos Aires, 1951), 17.

[12] The German occupation enabled much socially progressive activity to take place. In 1922 the literary journal *Bikher-velt* ('Book World') published statistics for sixty-six provincial *arbeter-bibliotekn* (workers' libraries) in Congress Poland. Of these, 91% were founded after the collapse of the tsarist regime. See D. Meyer, 'Bibliotek-vezn', *Bikher-velt*, no. 3 (May–June 1922), 331.

[13] A variety of terms were used by contemporary commentators to refer to libraries. Most frequently encountered in the literature are: *gezelshaftlekhe bibliotek* (a library organized and run by a cultural institution), *oyslay-bibliotek* (a lending library), *hant-bibliotek* (a library whose books are non-circulating), *efntlekhe bibliotek* (a library that is open to the public, i.e. not restricted to the members of the organization that runs it), *birgerlekhe bibliotek* (a library run by a bourgeois organization, i.e. a Zionist organization), *arbeter bibliotek* (a library run by a workers' party or organization, whose clientele consists mainly of workers), *shtotishe bibliotek* (a municipal library), and *folks bibliotek* (a people's library).

Another term that poses a problem to the translator is the adjective *yidish*, which can refer to the language spoken by Jews in eastern Europe or to characteristics of the Jewish people in general. In each case, I have relied on the context in translating the adjective.

such as Vayner's and Kultura, were later closed down; others, such as Bresler's (now called Lektura), Konfer's (now called Humanité), and Kontarovitsh's (now called Verbum), are still in existence today.[14]

The holdings of the Warsaw libraries were quite small during the early 1920s. In 1922, for instance, the Hazomir Bibliotek reported holdings of 2,300 books, of which 51 per cent were in Yiddish. The Bronisław Grosser Bibliotek had 3,300 volumes, 91 per cent of which were in Yiddish, and the Ber Borokhov Bibliotek had 3,700, 56 per cent of which were in Yiddish.[15]

Similarly, a survey of sixty-six *arbeter-bibliotekn* (workers' libraries) in provincial towns conducted in 1921 reported that forty of these had fewer than 1,000 volumes, six had between 1,000 and 2,000, and eight had between 2,000 and 8,000. The largest collections were in Białystok (7,640) and Łódź (4,581).[16] Yiddish books predominated in the collections of most of these libraries, but many offered books in Polish as well. (The survey included scant information about holdings in Hebrew, Russian, and other languages.) Half of the libraries surveyed had reading rooms.

THE GROWTH OF YIDDISH PUBLISHING AND ITS IMPACT ON YIDDISH LIBRARIES

The early years of the 1920s saw rapid growth in the Yiddish book industry in Poland and a rapid rise in the number of Yiddish libraries in the country. Figures published in the journal *Bikher-velt* for the years 1921–3 show that approximately 300 Yiddish books appeared in Poland in each year, about 70 per cent of the world total.[17] In addition to books written originally in Yiddish in a variety of genres, many translations into the language were brought out. In 1922, for example, over 25 per cent of the 400 Yiddish books published in lands formerly held by the Russian tsar (i.e. Poland, Lithuania, and Latvia) were translated works.[18] The demand for works of world literature in Yiddish translation rose as secular education became more widespread among Jewish youth.[19]

---

[14] B. Temkin, 'Di yidishe bibliotekn in varshe in likht fun tsifern', *Dos virtshaftlekhe lebn*, nos. 6–7 (Sept.–Oct. 1934), 21.

[15] D. Meyer, 'Yidishe bibliotekn in poyln', *Bikher-velt*, nos. 4–5 (July–Oct. 1922), 470.

[16] D. Meyer, 'Bibliotek-vezn', 334.

[17] N. Mayzil, 'Dos yidishe bukh in yor 1923', *Bikher-velt*, no. 6 (Nov.–Dec. 1923), 51.

[18] N. Mayzil, 'Dos yidishe bukh in 1912 un in 1922', *Bikher-velt*, no. 5 (Sept.–Oct. 1923), 403.

[19] Evidence of the popularity of translated works is found in the publication lists of predominantly Yiddish publishing houses. For instance, on the back page of *Bikher-velt* no. 1–2 (1923) the publishing house Yidish advertised, among other offerings, the following works for sale: Leo Tolstoy's *Di geshikhte fun mayn kindheyt* ('Childhood'), Mark Twain's *Geveylte dertseylungen* ('Selected Stories'), Guy de Maupassant's *Shtarker fun toyt* ('Fort comme la mort'), Jack London's *Di shtim fun blut* ('The Call of the Wild'), and Victor Hugo's *Dos 93ste yor* ('Quatre-Vingt-Treize').

Yiddish libraries began to increase their holdings and attract more patrons, whenever possible providing space for reading rooms where readers could avail themselves of newspapers, magazines, and non-circulating books. A survey of 138 libraries was made in 1922 by TsIShO, which included data concerning the holdings of each library in Yiddish, Polish, Russian, and Hebrew and the number of its registered patrons. While the holdings of a few of the larger libraries had grown rapidly since 1921, only eight of them had more than 4,000 volumes.[20] The original purpose of the survey was to identify public libraries that would receive shipments of Yiddish books published in the United States gratis from the American Jewish organization People's Relief.[21] Many of the smaller libraries in Poland were thus able greatly to increase their holdings.[22]

THE ROLE OF THE KULTUR-LIGE IN YIDDISH PUBLISHING

Transplanted from Kiev, the Kultur-lige (League for Culture) burst upon the Warsaw scene in March 1921 and quickly made a place for itself in the forefront of Yiddish publishing in Poland. Its history exemplifies the impact of the sudden influx of so-called 'foreign' Jews on the development of Polish Jewish culture, as described above by Nakhmen Mayzil.

Founded in May 1918 in Kiev, the Kultur-lige functioned for nearly three tumultuous years during a time of revolutionary ferment and civil war in Ukraine. In the months leading up to the October revolution of 1917, revolutionary activity in the Ukraine brought a body known as Tsentralna Rada (Central Council) to power. The Tsentralna Rada granted certain powers of autonomy to minority groups living in Ukraine, including the Jews. In January 1918 a Ministry of Jewish Affairs was established, with the socialist leader Moyshe Zilberfarb as minister. By July of that year a counter-revolutionary coup dissolved the Rada and the Ministry of Jewish Affairs with it.[23]

[20] D. Meyer, 'Yidishe bibliotekn in poyln', 467–75.

[21] People's Relief was an organization established by Jewish-led labour unions in the United States to bring material aid to east European Jews who were dislocated and victimized during the First World War and its aftermath.

[22] Ties between American Jewish and Polish Jewish organizations were often close. An example is found in a small advertisement placed in the third issue of *Bikher-velt* (May–June 1922). The management committee of the library of the Textile Workers' Union asks their fellow textile workers in America to send Yiddish books to add to their collection: 'To All Textile Workers in America! During the past seven years, we have, through hard toil and strenuous effort, created a library (named after Avreml Shtriker) for our members. We built this library with our *groshns*, and the collection has now reached 2,500 books. However, our collection is lacking in scientific and belletristic works that have been published in America. We have weathered all our crises without asking for help from you, our friends, fellow textile workers, and *landslayt* (fellow townsmen). Now we turn to you: help us build and secure our cultural circle! Send us books! With proletarian greetings, the Management Committee of the Professional Union of Textile Industry Workers in Warsaw.'

[23] H. Abramson, *A Prayer for the Government* (Cambridge, Mass., 1999), 33–66.

Established at the same time as the Ministry of Jewish Affairs, the Kultur-lige sought to carry on its educational and cultural work in the politically volatile climate of revolutionary Ukraine.[24] Not affiliated with any political party, the organization professed the general goal of fostering an international movement for Yiddish culture. Although it was vulnerable to the vicissitudes of a succession of political regimes, the Kultur-lige still managed to operate on many cultural fronts throughout Ukraine. It has been described as 'a kind of education ministry, with 105 departments and around 300 institutions active in all realms of Yiddish cultural activity'.[25] Among the institutions it founded were schools of music, art, and drama, a publishing house, and a central library. The Kultur-lige also published literary and pedagogical journals.[26]

In late 1920, having gained control of Ukraine, the Soviet government issued a decree removing from office the non-communist members of the Kultur-lige's central committee, and in 1921 the entire organization was closed down. Some leaders left for Warsaw at that time, intending to continue the cultural and political work they had begun in Kiev in the Polish capital. Their group included Moyshe Zilberfarb, the former Minister of Jewish Affairs, A. Litvak, Yankev Leshtshinski (Khmurner), Zelig Melamed, Khayim-Shloyme Kazdan, and Nakhmen Mayzil. Litvak, Kazdan, and Leshtshinski were prominent Bundists, Zilberfarb had been a member of the central committee of the Fareynikte Yidishe Sotsialistishe Partey (United Jewish Socialist Party), while Melamed and Mayzil were not affiliated with any political party.

Once settled in Warsaw, the newly re-formed executive of the Kultur-lige launched an ambitious programme to create a secular Yiddish culture rooted in tradition but shaped by modern thought. The first publication of the Kultur-lige in Poland was an anthology that appeared in April 1921, only a month after the arrival of the leadership from Kiev. The first page carried an article entitled 'Vos iz di kultur-lige?' ('What is the Kultur-lige?') The first portion of the article reads as follows:

The Kultur-lige is a communiqué from the broad Jewish masses, who are emerging from that dark place behind the oven into the bright sun of the modern cultural world. Masses of new people will begin to create and benefit from modern culture in its full panoply, with all its branches and subtleties.

There has been a lot of talk about the new Yiddish culture for more than twenty years, but up to now we have seen only an outline, only glimpses, of what this culture might be. Up to now the field of our culture has been strewn with old fragments of the tablets of the Ten Commandments. Up to now we have had vast wastelands untouched by the plough. To create a far-reaching modern culture with all its colours and shadings—this is the great task of the Kultur-lige.

[24] K. S. Kazdan, 'Di kultur-lige in ershtn period', in *Di geshikhte fun bund*, vol. iv (New York, 1972), 333.

[25] 'Zelig melamed', in *Leksikon fun der nayer yidisher literatur*, vol. vi (New York, 1965), 17.

[26] Mayzil, *Geven a mol a lebn*, 11–12.

In the past hundred years quite a few so-called non-historical nations have joined the family of modern peoples, and each time it has been a great and important event. More important still is the cultural revival of the Jewish people. Our roots go back to the grey dawn of humanity. Along with the dust of many generations, we have accumulated the nectar of generations. We neither wish to, nor can, tear ourselves out by the roots. We wish to shake off the ancient dust and take into ourselves the ancient and powerful nectars. Creating a new branch of the great family of world cultures out of the Jewish nation does not mean translating world culture into Yiddish. Neither does it mean simply allowing universal human culture to filter through the temperament of a particular nation. It means much more: transplanting the new culture into an old soil, creating a union of our history, which lives in us, with the culture of the new age.

The centrepiece of the Kultur-lige's programme was the publication of modern Yiddish literature. Supplementing donations from several wealthy comrades from Ukraine,[27] the leadership borrowed considerable sums of money and applied for help from People's Relief to re-establish their publishing house, Farlag Kultur-lige, on Polish soil. During its first year of operation the publishing house released seventy titles, including literary anthologies, poetry, novels, short stories, textbooks, chrestomathies, and children's literature. Among these were two collections of poetry by Peretz Markish, *Stam* ('Without a Reason') and *Di kupe* ('The Heap'), I. J. Singer's experimental drama *Erd-vey* ('Earth Pangs'), H. Leivick's drama *Der goylem* ('The Golem'), and Yoysef Opatoshu's novel *In poylishe velder* ('In Polish Woods'). The last-mentioned became a bestseller in the Yiddish book market in Poland, going through fifteen editions in the course of several years. With these successes, Farlag Kultur-lige assumed a leading role on the Yiddish cultural scene in Poland.[28]

From 1922 the Kultur-lige revived its bi-monthly journal of literary criticism and bibliography *Bikher-velt* ('Book World'), five issues of which had appeared in Kiev in 1919–20 under the co-editorship of Nakhmen Mayzil and A. Litvak. Among the topics that were regularly covered in the pages of *Bikher-velt* were the problems of the Yiddish book market and the organizational difficulties facing Yiddish libraries in Poland and elsewhere in eastern Europe.

Financial problems soon arose, hindering the work of Farlag Kultur-lige.[29] *Bikher-velt* came out four times in 1923.[30] In debt and facing bankruptcy, the editors published a double issue of the journal in winter 1924 (dated January–April), after which they were forced to suspend publication. At the same time shifting political allegiances among the six émigré leaders of the Kultur-lige caused serious tensions to develop among them,[31] with the result that by 1924 the two remaining non-Bundist members of the executive, Nakhmen Mayzil and Zelig Melamed, left the organization.

---

[27] K. S. Kazdan, *Mayn dor* (New York, 1977), 119–20.

[28] Mayzil, *Geven a mol a lebn*, 45–52.   [29] Kazdan, 'Di kultur-lige in ershtn period', 337.

[30] The first two issues published in 1923 were double issues (Jan.–Apr. and May–Aug.).

[31] Moyshe Zilberfarb had allied himself with the Bundist members of the executive by this time.

The Kultur-lige thus came under full control of the Bund. Its press became one of the two most important publishing houses for modern Yiddish literature in inter-war Poland, and the Kultur-lige played a key role in organizing a network of *arbeter-bibliotekn* during the 1920s and 1930s.

After a hiatus of four years the Kultur-lige again revived *Bikher-velt*, this time with Moyshe Zilberfarb, K. S. Kazdan, and Yankev Leshtshinski as co-editors. The magazine came out as a monthly from April 1928 to August 1929 before ceasing publication permanently because of a lack of funds.

LITERARISHE BLETER AND THE PROBLEMS OF THE YIDDISH BOOK MARKET AND LIBRARIES

In April 1924 a new journal of literature and the arts entitled *Literarishe bleter* ('Literary Leaves') appeared. Nakhmen Mayzil was a co-founder and co-editor along with the writers I. J. Singer, Peretz Markish, and Melekh Ravitsh.

Although *Literarishe bleter* was published in Yiddish and emphasized the problems and achievements of contemporary Yiddish literature, its editors were at pains to make readers aware of important trends in modern literature in non-Jewish languages as well.[32] They also published articles on music, theatre, and the visual arts.

Continuing the practice that was begun in *Bikher-velt*, *Literarishe bleter* frequently carried reports on the vicissitudes of the Yiddish book market and the problems of Yiddish libraries. Mayzil and others wrote regularly about reading trends among Polish Jews. They addressed difficult questions, such as why young readers preferred to read works translated into Yiddish from world literature over original Yiddish works, the harmful effects of fiction serialized in the newspapers on the Yiddish book market and on the literary tastes of Yiddish readers, and the alarming rate at which young Polish Jewish readers were switching to Polish altogether.[33]

Literarishe bleter was *umparteyish* (not affiliated with any political party or movement). After the first year of the magazine's existence the editors persuaded Boris Kletskin, the wealthy proprietor of the Kletskin Farlag in Vilna, to become its publisher. Widely read and highly respected, the magazine appeared weekly from the time of its introductory issue in April 1924 until the German invasion of Poland in September 1939.

Around the time that Kletskin assumed responsibility for publishing *Literarishe bleter*, the Kletskin Farlag opened an office in Warsaw with Mayzil as manager and

---

[32] For instance, *Literarishe bleter* (19 Feb. 1926) carries a front-page article by Stefan Zweig on the genius of Romain Rolland, whose novels were extremely popular with Yiddish readers at the time.

[33] See e.g. Y. Shtern, 'Undzer lezern oder shomer hot gevunen', *Literarishe bleter* (8 Apr. 1927), 265–8; N. Mayzil, 'Di yidishe literatur in 1927', *Literarishe bleter* (6 Jan. 1928), 1; anon., 'Vifl hobn mir yidishe lezer un ver zenen zey?', *Literarishe bleter* (24 Aug. 1928), 1.

editor. The *umparteyish* Kletskin Farlag and its competitor and rival the Bund-allied Farlag Kultur-lige became the two most important publishers of modern Yiddish poetry and prose in inter-war Poland.[34]

YEARS OF CRISIS

The rapid growth that Yiddish publishing had enjoyed during the early 1920s soon dissipated. By the middle of the decade the Yiddish book industry was said to be in crisis. Writing in *Literarishe bleter* in 1925, Nakhmen Mayzil asserted that the problem did not lie with the size of the reading audience. There were plenty of ardent Yiddish readers in Poland, but few of them could afford to buy books.

Yiddish publishing is suffocating not because of a dearth of readers, but rather because of a dearth of buyers. . . . Some hold the opinion that the present crisis in the Yiddish book market is justified. They argue that its anaemic performance is the result of too-hasty, unnatural growth. It doesn't take much to realize how false these opinions are. We have a large number of devoted, loyal, honest readers everywhere. The number of available books does not satisfy the demands of readers. The most important and necessary works in various fields of human knowledge and creativity are not available in Yiddish. There are huge gaps that need to be filled immediately. We shouldn't be speaking about an excess of books, but rather the opposite. And it follows from this that the urgent need is to expand and strengthen Yiddish publishing at once, with both original and translated works.[35]

There were many organizational problems in the Yiddish book industry that exacerbated the crisis. In an article entitled 'Farleger un bukh' ('Publisher and Book'), which appeared in *Bikher-velt* in 1923, *kultur-tuer* Mikhal Vaykhert (Michał Weichert) analysed some of them.[36] He compared the conventional practices of mainstream book publishers with those of Yiddish publishers, finding the latter woefully behind the times. The essential problem, according to Vaykhert, was that publishers of Yiddish books still relied on methods of production and distribution that had worked well enough in the mid- to late nineteenth century but were now outmoded. The few works of Yiddish literature that were published in that early period were distributed to inhabitants of the small towns along with *ruml-sforim* (prayer books, Bibles, Talmuds, and the like) by *pakn-tregers* (itinerant booksellers).[37] Being religiously observant, the majority of *shtetl* dwellers needed to buy religious books. The presence of secular Yiddish books among a *pakn-treger*'s wares meant that they could be seen and purchased by the same clientele. For instance, the works of Ayzik Meyer Dik, the maskilic author of didactic stories,

[34] M. Vaykhert, *Zikhroynes*, vol. ii (Tel Aviv, 1961), 197.

[35] N. Mayzil, 'Der krizis fun yidishn bukh—an ofener briv tsu farleger, bukhhendler, bibliotekn un fraynd fun yidishn vort', *Literarishe bleter* (28 May 1925), 1.

[36] M. Vaykhert, 'Farleger un bukh', *Bikher-velt*, no. 6 (Nov.–Dec. 1923), 457–64.

[37] The term *ruml* is an acronym for *sifrei rabanim umelamdim*, which means 'texts of rabbis and teachers'.

reached a mass audience in this way. Dik produced hundreds of chapbooks during the third quarter of the nineteenth century, many of which sold thousands of copies.[38] Apparently, nineteenth-century publishers of Yiddish works made little effort to promote or advertise their merchandise. Potential purchasers learned of its availability by word of mouth or while perusing a *pakn-treger*'s book display.

Contemporary conditions in the field of book publishing, warned Vaykhert, demanded an entirely different approach. Successful mainstream publishers specialized in certain areas, selected manuscripts that they believed would appeal to particular audiences, and made potential buyers aware of their availability through advertising. Publishers of Yiddish books, however, were neither sufficiently enterprising nor particularly scrupulous. After buying an author's manuscript for as little as possible, such a publisher would reprint the book as many times as the market would bear, without paying the author additional fees. Yiddish books were poorly edited and printed, and distribution was still being handled by the purveyors of *ruml-sforim*, who cared little for modern Yiddish literature and whose business practices were often less than solid.

Vaykhert called for the reorganization of the Yiddish book publishing business. He pointed out that 'the Jew, who has achieved miracles of organization in every area of production and trade, has shown himself to be so terribly small-minded and shopkeeper-ish in the publishing business'.[39] He attributed this small-mindedness to the Jewish merchant's lack of faith that Yiddish literature and culture would continue to develop and thrive. Urging the Yiddish press to open a forum for discussion of the problem, he wrote: 'It is time [for the press] to begin to take an interest in the Yiddish publishing business, which until now has not even merited a serious article. In large measure the existence and future of Yiddish culture depends on the direction the developing Yiddish publishing business will take.'[40]

EFFORTS TO MODERNIZE THE DISTRIBUTION OF YIDDISH BOOKS

In 1926 the publishers' co-operative Bikher (Books) was founded in Warsaw on the initiative of the Kletskin Farlag and Farlag Tsentral (itself a publishers' cooperative). Its primary goal was to consolidate the Yiddish publishing business and introduce modern methods of distribution.[41] The Bikher co-operative soon became the most important distributor of Yiddish books in Poland. Its quarterly illustrated catalogue contained book listings from a score of publishing houses in Warsaw,

---

[38] Literary historian Dan Miron has estimated that Dik's chapbooks may have sold as many as half a million copies from the 1850s to the 1870s (Miron, personal communication).

[39] Vaykhert, 'Farleger un bukh', 464. [40] Ibid.

[41] Farlag Tsentral was founded in 1911. In partnership were: Binyomen Shimin's *farlag*, Ben-Avigdor's Farlag Tushiyah, S. Shrebrek's *farlag* in Vilna, Y. Lidski's Farlag Progres and Farlag Yidish, and M. Kaplan's Hashakhar.

Berlin, Paris, Vienna, and New York. In 1931 the co-operative claimed to represent 90 per cent of the world Yiddish book market.[42] Even before it was taken over by the Bund, the Kultur-lige had been operating a publishers' co-operative for book distribution. The two co-operatives now competed with one another sharply, and the Kultur-lige accused its rival of using commercial tricks to try to destroy it.[43]

Publishers' co-operatives were not, however, able to solve the distribution problem. Outside the major cities there were very few bookshops that would handle Yiddish books, which meant that the majority of potential buyers could not examine the merchandise before purchasing it. The co-operatives had thus to rely on mail order sales for the bulk of their business.[44]

POVERTY, LINGUISTIC ASSIMILATION, AND *SHUND*

Problems of distribution notwithstanding, the main obstacle to the growth of the Yiddish book industry during the inter-war period was the extreme poverty of Polish Jewry. The primary reading audience for Yiddish books was made up of working-class youth, many of whom had attended school for only a few years and who were most comfortable reading in their mother tongue. Their interest in self-education was very keen, and they read extensively in Yiddish, mainly in the areas of modern Yiddish literature, world literature in Yiddish translation, political theory, and the social and natural sciences. They could not, however, afford to purchase books. Thus, the main consumers of Yiddish publications were not in a position to contribute financially to the development of the book market.

At the same time members of the Polish Jewish middle class, who had more years of schooling and much better reading skills in Polish than did their working-class counterparts, increasingly preferred to read in Polish rather than in their mother tongue. The rapid rate of language assimilation in this segment of Polish Jewish society resulted in a significant loss of audience for the Yiddish publishing industry.

Competition from Yiddish newspapers created another major stumbling block for the book market. The practice of serializing popular fiction in the Polish Yiddish press began in 1908 in the newspaper *Haynt* ('Today'). Formulaic entertainment novels eventually became an obligatory feature of every Yiddish daily. During the inter-war period the book market suffered acutely as newspapers

---

[42] *Ilustrirter bikher-katalog kooperativ 'bikher', varshe*, no. 9 (Warsaw, 1929), 1. I have seen only three of the quarterly catalogues produced by the co-operative. These are dated 1927 (no. 4), 1928 (no. 7), and 1929 (no. 9), and are found in the microfilm collection of the YIVO Institute.

Halina Shimin-Shnayderman discusses the founding of the Bikher co-operative in 'Zikhroynes vegn binyomen shimin un andere varshever farlegers', *Dos amolike yidishe varshe* (Montreal, 1966), 805.

[43] *Bikher-velt* (1929), no. 2, cited in K. S. Kazdan, 'Di bundishe prese', *Di geshikhte fun bund*, vol. iv (New York, 1972), 384–5.   [44] Vaykhert, *Zikhroynes*, ii. 199–200.

competed sharply with one another by providing readers with plenty of *shund* (trash) fiction on a daily basis. This cheap and easily accessible source of pleasurable reading badly eroded the audience for Yiddish books, so much so that most writers of belles-lettres in Yiddish were not able to make even a meagre living from their artistic work. Many resorted to writing *shund* fiction for the newspapers to support their families. Throughout the inter-war period a bitter polemic raged among Yiddish writers in Poland concerning the moral obligation of a writer to edify his or her audience rather than pander to its vulgar, socially regressive tastes. Writers accused one another of producing *shund*; several talented and successful novelists were virtually hounded out of the community of Polish Yiddish writers by enraged, envious colleagues.[45]

YIDDISH LIBRARIES AND THE BOOK MARKET: A SYMBIOSIS

Efforts to strengthen Yiddish libraries and ensure their financial viability began in the mid-1920s, as cultural activists like Nakhmen Mayzil and the publishers themselves came to understand that the main purchasers of Yiddish books were in fact libraries. It was clear that, without a stable network of libraries, the book market would not be able to sustain itself for very long.[46]

The term *efntlekhe bibliotek* denotes a library that was open to the public, in the sense that one did not need to be a member of the organization that sponsored the library in order to hold a borrower's card. An *efntlekhe bibliotek* might be run by a labour union or by a political organization, such the Bund or Po'alei Tsion Left, in which case it was usually called an *arbeter bibliotek* (workers' library), or by a cultural organization without direct political ties, such as Hazomir, frequently called a *gezelshaftlekhe* (institutional) *bibliotek*.

These were not public libraries as we know them in the United States and Great Britain today; they received no government funds and were administered entirely by groups within the Jewish community. They often suffered from poor organization and inadequate finances. Borrowers' fees were paid monthly. The revenues raised from these fees were used to rent the library premises, keep books in repair and buy new ones, purchase furniture, establish and maintain a card catalogue, and, in some cases, to pay salaries. These fees were low, but not insignificant for most borrowers.[47] Privately owned lending libraries, such as Lektura and Humanité in Warsaw, charged higher borrowers' fees, which made them largely inaccessible to working-class readers.

[45] See Nathan Cohen's chapter in this volume. Attacks on the writers Israel Joshua Singer and Yehoshua Perle were among the most vicious.

[46] N. Mayzil, 'Der krizis fun yidishn bukh', *Literarishe bleter* (28 May 1925), 1.

[47] For instance, in 1928 the monthly membership fee for the Hazomir Bibliotek in Warsaw was 1 zloty. During the 1930s the monthly fee for the Grosser Bibliotek in Warsaw was 50 groszy, or half a zloty, but the fee was waived for unemployed and underemployed readers.

The problems of organizing and financing the smaller *efntlekhe bibliotekn* were exacerbated by the lack of co-ordination and co-operation among libraries operating in the same locality. In fact, in the small towns, and even in the larger ones, libraries competed with one another for readers. If, for example, a local chapter of the Bund opened up a library, the local Zionist or communist organization, hoping to attract new members, was likely to follow suit. Debating clubs, lectures, discussions, theatrical societies, and even sports teams were organized in conjunction with libraries.[48] The library frequently served as a meeting place for these groups. As a result of the competition among them, libraries associated with rival political organizations did not share resources, and often duplicated each other's holdings.

A description of this sort of rivalry is found in the memorial book of the town of Vishegrod (Wyszogród), near Płock. A group of young Zionists organized a lending library there during the early 1920s. The library, named Merkaz Hatsioynim (Zionists' Centre), started with a collection of fifty books, which grew to over 1,000 volumes in Hebrew and Yiddish. Political meetings and cultural events took place there as well.

During the same period a communist-leaning youth movement came into existence in Vishegrod and competed with the Zionist group for the allegiance of the youth. According to Menakhem Zilbershteyn, a contributor to the memorial book, this rivalry precipitated political conflicts among the youth of the town, which came to be centred on the question of which group would control the library.

Merkaz Hatsioynim became the object of these conflicts. Each side sought to dominate in [the running of] the library. . . . After a number of years of disputes and discussions, the young Zionists won out. Forced to withdraw from Merkaz Hatsioynim, the left-leaning group founded its own library, to which they gave the name Arbeter Bibliotek. This library became, in truth, the centre for communist activity in the Vishegrod area.[49]

---

[48] Writing in the *Szydłowiec Memorial Book*, Yankl Silberman describes the discussion groups and drama clubs associated with the Bund library in Szydłowiec, near Radom: 'One of the first things the Bund did was to open a library. The library committee arranged discussions with readers, as well as *kestl* evenings. . . . a week before the event they hung up a *kestl* [box] into which people could drop written questions. At the *kestl* evening the questions were answered by the library committee. Part of the cultural activities was a dramatic section that put on plays (by Leonid Andreev, Gordin, and Lateiner). . . . The dramatic groups of the Bund and other parties were important financially and culturally. Both the players and the audiences derived a great deal of artistic pleasure from the performances' ('The Bundist Movement in Szydłowiec', in B. Kagan (ed.), *Szydłowiec Memorial Book* (New York, 1989), 82.

To attract young readers, the directors of the Jewish public library in the town of Ostrin organized a sports club in the spring of 1938. In order to qualify for participation in the various athletic activities offered by the club, one had to belong to the library and attend the lectures on Yiddish literature and Jewish history that were held there. See 'Autobiographies of Jewish Youth in Poland', Record Group 4, no. 3519, YIVO Archives, New York.

[49] M. Zilbershteyn, 'Tsienizm in vishegrod', in *Vishegrod: a bukh a matseyve far di kedoyshim fun vishegrod* (Tel Aviv, 1971), 253–6.

THE PROBLEM OF LIBRARY LEADERSHIP

With respect to the factors impeding the advancement of libraries in the provincial towns, one of the prime problems that had to be addressed was the dearth of trained librarians capable of managing the *arbeter-* and *gezelshaftlekhe bibliotekn*. The Kultur-lige activists recognized that poor organization hindered the development and sustainability of Yiddish libraries. Most libraries were run by untrained volunteers, since almost none had funds to pay the salaries of professional librarians. In an effort to give some direction in this area, the Kultur-lige published information about existing Yiddish libraries in Poland through its literary magazine, *Bikher-velt*.

In the March–April 1922 edition of *Bikher-velt* the editors announced that henceforth they would regularly print news and statistics about Yiddish libraries under the heading 'Bibliotek-vezn' ('Library Affairs'). In a series of three articles (*Bikher-velt*, nos. 2, 3, and 4–5 (1922)) they published statistics gathered in 1921 pertaining to the holdings and readership of Jewish public libraries throughout Poland. *Bikher-velt* no. 2 contained a questionnaire for librarians. It asked for information about the founding of each library, its sources of funds, its readership, its holdings, how its card catalogue was organized, and what titles were most frequently requested and most widely read. Ten libraries responded to the questionnaire, but the results were not published.[50] The 'Bibliotek-vezn' column disappeared after issue no. 4–5 (1922). In 1923 the editors turned their attention to the problems of the Yiddish publishing industry in Poland and abroad.

The weekly *Literarishe bleter* continued the effort to reach lay librarians after *Bikher-velt* folded in 1924, publishing guidelines for various aspects of library organization under the heading 'Bibliotekn-firer' ('Library Manager'). In the issue dated 5 March 1926, for instance, a brief article entitled 'Putting Books on the Shelves' gives directions for organizing a collection when a card catalogue is lacking.[51] 'Bibliotekn-firer' for 7 May 1926 describes how a card catalogue system should be set up, warning that 'without these catalogues, the library is "a cemetery for books", which no one reads because no one knows about them'.

In addition to providing practical advice to lay librarians, *Literarishe bleter* prevailed upon them to gather vital statistics about their readers, the languages in which they preferred to read, and the types of books that were in greatest and least demand. The results of a 1926 survey of three Warsaw libraries and three provincial ones yielded an alarming statistic: schoolchildren were reading as many books in Polish as in Yiddish. The well-established Sholem-Aleichem Bibliotek in Białystok reported that between 1924 and 1925 the percentage of Yiddish books borrowed fell from 58.5 to 48.5 per cent, while that of Polish books rose from 27 to 34.7 per cent.[52]

[50] *Bikher-velt*, nos. 4–5 (1922), 475.   [51] *Literarishe bleter*, no. 96 (5 Mar. 1926), 162.

[52] See articles entitled 'Undzere bibliotekn in di statistik fun di leyener', *Literarishe bleter*, nos. 117 and 123 (30 July and 10 Sept. 1926).

Statistics such as these were important not only for library planning, but for the Yiddish publishing industry as well. In an article written in 1929 Nakhmen Mayzil argued that Yiddish book publishers should combat the encroachments of *shprakh-asimilatsye* (language assimilation) by bringing out more and more works of world literature in Yiddish translation. In this way, he hoped, Yiddish-speaking youth who were learning Polish in school would opt to do their extra-curricular reading in Yiddish, thus ensuring a continuing role for Yiddish publishing and Yiddish libraries on the Jewish street in Poland.[53]

THE EFFORTS OF THE PO'ALEI TSION LEFT TO STRENGTHEN YIDDISH LIBRARIES

While Nakhmen Mayzil and his colleagues on the staff of the *umparteyish Literarishe bleter* played an important role in publicizing the organizational needs and problems of Yiddish libraries, the most sustained and developed efforts to train lay librarians and improve the functioning of Yiddish libraries came from two political parties, the Po'alei Tsion Left and the Bund.[54]

Eliezer Vays (1903–30) and Bashe Temkin-Berman (1907–53), both activists in the Po'alei Tsion Left, made important contributions to the development of Yiddish *arbeter-bibliotekn* in inter-war Poland. The son of working-class parents, Vays did industrial work as a teenager but managed to attend *Gymnasium* at the same time. He later completed a degree in jurisprudence and worked as a lawyer in Kraków. As a member of Po'alei Tsion, he became involved with library work, serving as chair of the Peretz-Bibliotek in Kraków and secretary of Po'alei Tsion's library centre. His librarianship skills were self-taught. In 1926 he went to Warsaw to teach a training course for lay librarians. In 1929 he co-authored *Hantbukh far bibliotekn* ('Handbook for Libraries') with Y. Roykhfleysh, which was published by the adult education section of Po'alei Tsion Left, Ovnt-kursn far Arbeter (Evening Courses for Workers).[55] The handbook offers instruction in the many technical

[53] N. Mayzil, 'Velkhe verk vern ammeystn itst geleyent—di originel-yidishe tsi iberzetste?', *Arbeter tsaytung*, no. 24 (13 June 1929), 4–5.

[54] Founded in 1897, the Algemeyner Yidisher Arbeter Bund (General Jewish Workers' Alliance) came to be associated with devotion to Yiddish, autonomism, and secular Jewish nationalism. It was sharply opposed to Zionism, envisaging a socialist Jewish future in eastern Europe. The Po'alei Tsion (Workers of Zion) party, on the other hand, pursued the goals of establishing a socialist Jewish homeland in the land of Israel and fighting for Jewish national rights in the countries of the Diaspora. Founded in 1907, the party split into two factions at its world conference in 1920 over the question of whether or not to affiliate with the Third Communist International (the left-wing faction favoured the affiliation). Po'alei Tsion Left also promoted the use of the Yiddish language in the land of Israel. While the Bund and Po'alei Tsion differed over many political issues, their approach to cultural and educational work was similar.

[55] Gezelshaft Ovnt-kursn far Arbeter (Society for Evening Courses for Workers) was the central cultural organization of Po'alei Tsion Left.

topics pertaining to the administration of a library, such as book purchase, binding and conservation, book display, taking inventories and maintaining a catalogue, regulations for borrowers, and library statistics. It also addresses the crucial issue of the need for intensive pedagogical training for the corps of lay librarians who ran the *arbeter-bibliotekn* in provincial towns throughout Poland on a volunteer basis.

The second chapter of *Hantbukh far bibliotekn*, entitled 'Di oyfgabn fun bibliotekar' ('The Tasks of the Librarian'), charges lay librarians with the responsibility for educating working-class Jewish youth.

In writing this chapter we are taking into account the fact that in 100 per cent of our workers' libraries the librarians have had no special preparation for their heavy responsibilities. It is no secret that, until now, there have been no opportunities to prepare for these positions. Should we have to go on putting up with these conditions in the future? . . . The key to setting the workers' libraries to rights lies primarily in the hands of the librarian. He is the . . . driving force behind the library. He is the officer in the army battling for knowledge. . . . Jewish workers certainly need many such good and experienced officers.

In western Europe and now in the Soviet Union the role and importance of workers' libraries has long been understood. . . . With the help of special institutions of librarianship, courses, periodicals, handbooks for librarians, and instructors, the required number of people has been trained to assume responsibility for directing the [workers'] library. The concept of the librarian as merely a technical functionary who acquires and distributes books has disappeared. He has become the teacher, educator, and guide for the readers.

In our social order we cannot, for obvious reasons, expect any help in this sphere. The ruling classes have a bloody interest in maintaining the workers' lack of consciousness. They know that knowledge is power and that the consciousness of the working class deals capitalism a death blow. Therefore, the workers have had to organize their cultural institutions by themselves.

Jewish workers' organizations have not lagged far behind, but they haven't persevered with the work to its conclusion. We have created libraries, but haven't made the effort to create librarians, leaders of the libraries. . . . In our circles the work of the librarian is still limited to technical functions.

The Jewish working-class reader who has never been to school knows neither what to read nor how to read, but he finds on the staff of the library an automaton who only distributes books. These technical functions can be carried out by anyone, without special preparation or qualifications.

Just as in school, so too in the library: a librarian must be a teacher. He must be in constant contact with the readers. He must be aware of each one's intelligence, knowledge, and level of development. Through his instructions and explanations he must guide the reader through an accessible, planned programme for deriving knowledge from books . . .[56]

In setting such high standards for *arbeter-bibliotekarn* (librarians of workers' libraries), Vays could point to his own academic achievements and those of many others in his party as examples. However haphazard the education of working-class

---

[56] Y. Roykhfleysh and L. Vays, *Hantbukh far bibliotekn* (Warsaw, 1929), 9–10.

Jewish autodidacts might have been, they could claim impressive accomplishments. Why, then, not set out to train a cadre of socialist teacher–librarians through
evening courses and instructional guides?

Bashe Temkin-Berman was born into a scholarly but impoverished hasidic family in Warsaw. Determined to acquire a university education, she worked her way
through the Wolna Wszechnica (Free University) of Poland, where she studied
social science and library science. Feeling a strong bond with the Jewish working
class and dreaming of a socialist land of Israel, she became active in Po'alei Tsion
Left during her student years, serving as secretary of the students' union Yugnt
(Youth). She met the activist Adolf Berman there and later married him.[57]

After acquiring a diploma in library science, she became an administrator in
the Warsaw public library system. For a number of years she worked in the Jewish
division of the Polish Biblioteka Narodowa (National Library) as an administrator
responsible for questions pertaining to Yiddish books. In 1934 she published an
article which reviewed the history of Jewish libraries in Warsaw during the nineteenth and twentieth centuries, entitled 'Di yidishe bibliotekn in varshe in likht fun
tsifern' ('Jewish Libraries in Warsaw in the Light of Statistics').[58] It was the first
study to focus on the achievements of the *gezelshaftlekhe* and *arbeter-bibliotekn* and,
more importantly, the first to attempt to formulate contemporary demographic
profiles of their users and elucidate the problems they were facing.

In his memoirs Adolf Berman wrote that his wife 'had a passionate love for the
Yiddish language, its literature, folklore and folk music, and the Yiddish book'.[59]
Her Yiddishist orientation can be seen in the observations Temkin-Berman makes
about the state of Yiddish libraries and Yiddish reading in Warsaw in the mid-
1930s. A variety of factors, she notes, chief among them the influence of public
education on assimilation, were having an unfavourable effect on Yiddish libraries.
She points out that working-class readers were the major consumers of Yiddish
library books, while middle-class readers tended to prefer reading in Polish. She
laments the fact that while young people of working-class origin read intensively
and systematically, adult readers, and especially women, used libraries much less.

---

[57] Berman was in the leadership of Po'alei Tsion Left and editor of its Yiddish-language weekly
Arbeter tsaytung. As a leader of the Jewish underground during the Nazi occupation of Poland, he was a
member of the presidium of the Żydowski Komitet Narodowy (Jewish National Committee) and its
representative to the Polish underground. He left the Warsaw ghetto after the mass deportation of Jews
to Treblinka in the summer of 1942, working with left-wing resistance groups on the 'Aryan side' of the
city. He fought in the Warsaw uprising of 1944, and after the war became president of the Centralny
Komitet Żydów Polskich (Central Committee of Polish Jews). In 1950 he emigrated to Israel with his
family and was elected to the Knesset as a member of Mapam in 1951.

[58] B. Temkin, 'Di yidishe bibliotekn in varshe in likht fun tsifern', *Dos virtshaftlekhe lebn*, nos. 6–7
(Sept.–Oct. 1934), 20–7. The article was also published as an offprint.

[59] A. A. Berman, *Vos der goyrl hot mir bashert* (Israel, 1980), 43–7. Other biographical material about
Temkin-Berman used here appears in R. Auerbakh, *Varshever tsavoes* (Tel Aviv, 1974), 261–71, and Jonas
Turkow, 'Kemfern fun varshever geto geshtorbn in yisroel', *Der tog-morgn zhurnal* (4 June 1953), 8.

In contrast, Temkin notes, the number of Polonized, middle-class women making use of private lending libraries surpassed that of men. She remarks that, while the state of workers' libraries in Warsaw had improved somewhat in recent years, owing to efforts to reorganize them, the often uncomfortable, cramped, and unhygienic premises of many workers' libraries discouraged potential users from coming in. More hopefully, she notes that the total number of Yiddish readers in the capital was many times greater than the number of library subscribers because each book that was borrowed might be read by several members of a subscriber's family. She concludes by calling for more comprehensive research into the achievements of Yiddish libraries and the challenges they faced.[60]

Bashe Temkin-Berman is chiefly remembered for her heroic work as an organizer during the Nazi occupation of Warsaw, both in the ghetto, where she cared for orphaned children, and on the 'Aryan side', where she aided Jews in hiding and participated in the work of Emanuel Ringelblum's Oyneg Shabes, the secret project that documented the lives of Polish Jews under the occupation. In November 1940, as the ghetto was being established, Temkin-Berman organized an illegal children's library at Leszno 67, on the premises of a branch of the Warsaw Public Library that had been forced to evacuate. Aware that permission to establish a bona fide library would not be forthcoming, she applied for a concession to establish a play centre for children under the aegis of Centos, the Jewish children's aid society of which her husband, Adolf Berman, was director. The space was furnished with toys and decorated with children's art. Through the efforts of the publisher Leyb Shor, who was in the process of organizing a secret lending library for adults at the time, she obtained a great many children's books in Yiddish and Polish from the collections of several *gezelshaftlekhe bibliotekn* that had been closed since the beginning of the German occupation.

The library served both Yiddish-speaking children who still lived with their families and orphaned children, supplying small collections of books to approximately fifty orphanages, children's food centres, centres for homeless and refugee children, children's clinics, and quarantine centres. It became an active Yiddishist cultural centre in the ghetto, where children and adults gave public readings of Yiddish literature.[61] Many of the 700 individual subscribers who used the library were unaccustomed to reading in Yiddish. In order to combat the language assimilation that was widespread among schoolchildren, Temkin-Berman encouraged them to read in their mother tongue by lending each child two books at a time, one in Yiddish and a second in Polish.[62] The children's library was closed on 5 August 1942, during the second phase of the great deportation, when all the residents of Leszno Street between Żelazna and Karmelicka Streets were forced to vacate their

---

[60] Temkin, 'Di yidishe bibliotekn in varshe in likht fun tsifern', 27.

[61] B. Temkin-Berman, 'Tsu der geshikhte fun yidishn bukh in poyln: yidishe bibliotekn in varshe', in *Pinkes varshe* (Buenos Aires, 1955), 382.

[62] Auerbakh, *Varshever tsavoes*, 262, 267–8.

premises so that the German armaments-manufacturing firm Toebbens could take them over.[63]

Temkin-Berman survived the ghetto and her perilous work in the Jewish underground. After liberation she was appointed director of the main Jewish library in Poland. With the help of several colleagues, she travelled through formerly occupied Poland salvaging thousands of books from Jewish libraries that had been closed or partially destroyed by the Nazis. This collection eventually came to form the core of the library of the Żydowski Instytut Historyczny (Jewish Historical Institute) in Warsaw.[64]

The three title pages reproduced in Figures 1 to 3 are from books saved by Temkin-Berman in the post-war years, and illustrate some important aspects of the history of Yiddish books and libraries in inter-war Poland. Figure 1, from a Yiddish translation of Charles Dickens's *David Copperfield*, was part of the collection of the large private lending library Humanité in Warsaw, which offered books in eight languages. Interestingly, the book was published in Kiev in 1928 by Farlag Kultur-lige. After the non-Bolshevik leaders of the Kultur-lige left Kiev in 1921, the organization continued to operate the publishing house that had been established by the earlier group. Figure 2 shows the title page of a critical study of the works of Sholem Asch by Nakhmen Mayzil. It was published in Warsaw in 1926 by the Kletskin Farlag, which Mayzil then managed. The book was originally part of the collection of the Sholem Aleichem Yidishe Bibliotek in Radomsk. In the upper left-hand corner of the title page is stamped the slogan 'shoynt di bikher' ('take care of the books'), part of the campaign by librarians to get the reading public to treat library books with respect. The stamp of the library of the Żydowski Instytut Historyczny, to which the book now belongs, appears in the upper right-hand corner. Figure 3 shows the title page of *Fonye ganev* ('Fonye the Thief'; idiom for the Russian government) by Avrom Zak, which was published in Warsaw in 1929. The book originally belonged to the Jewish Library and Reading Room in Konin. The stamp in the centre right shows that during the Nazi occupation the book was appropriated by the Institut der Nationalsozialistische Deutsche Arbeiterpartei zur Erforschung der Judenfrage Abteilung Ostjudentum Litzmannstadt (National Socialist German Workers' Party Institute for Research on the Jewish Question, Section for Eastern Jewry, Litzmann-stadt (Łódź)). It now belongs to the library of the Żydowski Instytut Historyczny, as indicated by the stamp in the upper right-hand corner of the title page.

HERMAN KRUK AND THE BUND'S VISION FOR YIDDISH WORKERS' LIBRARIES

Herman Kruk (1897–1944) is best known as the director of the library in the Vilna ghetto, which was located on the premises of the former library of Mefitsey-haskole

[63] Auerbakh, *Varshever tsavoes*, 264.
[64] Temkin-Berman, 'Tsu der geshikhte fun yidishn bukh in poyln', 386.

Fig. 1. Yiddish translation of *David Copperfield*, with the stamp of the private lending library Humanité, Warsaw
Courtesy of the Jewish Historical Institute, Warsaw

Fig. 2. *Sholem Asch* by Nakhmen Mayzil, with the stamp of the Sholem Aleichem Yidishe Bibliotek, Radomsk
Courtesy of the Jewish Historical Institute, Warsaw

Fig. 3. *Fonye ganev* by Avrom Zak, with the stamp of the Jewish Library and Reading Room, Konin, and the insignia of the Institut der Nationalsozialistische Deutsche Arbeiterpartei zur Erforschung der Judenfrage Abteilung Ostjudentum Litzmannstadt, Łódź
Courtesy of the Jewish Historical Institute, Warsaw

(Disseminators of Enlightenment). His *Togbukh fun der vilner geto* ('Diary of the Vilna Ghetto') is an important Holocaust document.[65] Born into a middle-class family in Płock, Kruk attended *kheyder* but was unable to study beyond the elementary level owing to his family's impoverishment, his father's early death, and the outbreak of the First World War. Płock was under German occupation during the war, and the young Kruk supported his mother and two siblings by working for the occupying forces, first in road construction and later in a vegetable-canning factory. During these years he read the classics of Yiddish literature avidly, borrowing books from the local Hazomir Bibliotek and participating in various cultural and political activities that took place there. Thus began his lifelong commitment to both autodidacticism and Yiddishism.

After several years' involvement with communist-leaning organizations, Kruk joined the Bund in 1920 and remained an active Bundist until the end of his life. He found his vocation as a cultural worker during the 1920s, establishing the central cultural department of the Bund's youth organization Tsukunft (Future) in 1925. The department's goals were to encourage young workers to undertake programmes of self-education and to offer them direction in their studies. One of his projects as secretary of the cultural department was the creation of *vander-bibliotekn* (mobile libraries), collections of books that were sent to various Bund-related organizations around the country in order to make educational materials more readily available to their members. On a more ambitious scale, he organized *referentn-shuln* (schools for cultural workers), two-week intensive courses of instruction in social science, history, and the labour movement for members of Tsukunft who lacked formal schooling. The *referentn-shuln* took place in Warsaw in 1926–7 and 1930, drawing participants from a variety of provincial towns in Poland. Kruk also mounted regional *referentn-shuln* in such cities as Białystok, Lublin, and Łódź.

Kruk taught himself library science skills and was appointed head of the Kultur-lige's library centre. In 1930 he was named director of the Kultur-lige's central library in Warsaw, the Grosser Bibliotek. Named after the Bundist leader Bronisław Grosser (1883–1912), the Grosser Bibliotek was founded in 1915. It operated on a small scale during the first fifteen years of its existence. In 1930 the Bund launched a campaign to combine several smaller libraries and greatly expand the holdings, physical space, and activities of the Grosser Bibliotek. In the mid-1930s, under Kruk's leadership, the library boasted a collection of 30,000 volumes, a reference room, a reading room for periodicals in fourteen languages, a research room for scholars, a children's library, a lecture hall, and 4,000 regular readers. The logo of the Grosser Bibliotek was a proletarian figure with an open

Fig. 4. Logo of the Grosser Bibliotek, Warsaw

---

[65] Trans. as *The Last Days of the Jerusalem of Lithuania* (New Haven, 2002).

book in his raised hand (Fig. 4). The library's motto read 'Visn iz makht' ('knowledge is power').

Kruk's biographers in *Doyres bundistn* ('Generations of Bundists') wrote of his efforts to acquire professional expertise through self-education as follows:

Through laborious effort and persistent self-education over many years, Herman Kruk reached the level of an educated and specialized cultural activist and librarian. His numerous articles and his Yiddish and Polish brochures about cultural work and library affairs became very popular in hundreds of towns and cities. His work also became known in the community of Polish library professionals.[66]

A variety of extant documents and periodicals attest to the fact that, in the nearly ten years during which he directed the Grosser Bibliotek and the library centre of the Kultur-lige, Kruk worked tirelessly to strengthen and develop the *arbeter-bibliotek* as an institution and to create aids for self-education that would advance the collective project of autodidacticism among Jewish workers in Poland. He maintained contact by letter with the librarians of hundreds of small libraries throughout the country, offering them guidance on the technical, organizational, and educational problems they faced in their work. He published a special supplement to the Bund's literary paper, *Vokhnshrift far literatur, kunst un kultur*, entitled *Bibliotek, lezer un bibliotekar* ('Book, Reader, and Librarian'), whose intended audience was these same librarians.[67] Articles that appeared there supplied news and statistics of libraries affiliated with the Kultur-lige and emphasized the need for the non-professional librarians of *arbeter-bibliotekn* both to improve their technical skills and to begin to regard themselves as educators.

In the first edition of *Bibliotek, lezer un bibliotekar* Kruk exhorts his readers to understand that a librarian 'is obligated to help himself . . . to broaden and deepen his library knowledge through self-education. The printed word, and the periodical press especially . . . can be instrumental in this. General library management, library technology, social-educational questions that pertain to the Yiddish library, reading, and methods of reading must all be dealt with.'[68]

The supplement frequently carried advice for librarians on the careful management of scarce resources. For instance, in an article that appeared under the heading 'Di bibliotek in ir tog-teglekhkeyt' ('The Library in its Daily Operation') on 27 January 1933, Kruk addresses three topics he considers crucial for small *arbeter-bibliotekn* in provincial towns: book selection, purchase, and maintenance. He advises librarians not to buy books on the cheap from travelling salesmen, but rather to order directly from publishing houses, using lists of recommended books

---

[66] J. S. Hertz (ed.), *Doyres bundistn*, vol. ii (New York, 1956), 337. Other biographical material about Kruk used here appears in the biographical introduction to Kruk's *Togbukh fun vilner geto* (New York, 1961), pp. xiii–xlv, written by his younger brother, Pinkhes Shvarts.

[67] The supplement appeared approximately every four to six weeks between 25 Dec. 1931 and 15 Dec. 1933.

[68] H. Kruk, 'Mir muzn zikh lernen!', *Vokhnshrift far literatur, kunst un kultur* (25 Dec. 1931), 6.

and book reviews to make their selections. He charges that provincial libraries are full of *shund-literatur*, and that librarians and library boards are guilty of catering to readers' demands for entertainment fiction when they should be making better literature available and persuading library subscribers to read it. Kruk also has advice for librarians on the vexing subject of vandalism:

We have written more than once about the terribly lawless attitude of Yiddish readers towards books. The physical condition of a book in a Yiddish library cannot be compared with that of a book anywhere else. The book gets torn, smeared with grease, and defaced with graffiti by people who either curse the author or argue against a political opponent. Readers are often not only vandals but tremendously disrespectful of the library itself. [When book vandals and those who refuse to pay their library dues are eventually barred from using one library, they simply sign up as readers in another. After a time they return to the first library and enrol as new readers. Since few records are kept, they can get away with it.]

We must put a stop to this. Every library must introduce a 'blacklist' by means of which it will always be possible to tell if a new reader is really new. Such a list can be easily established. When a reader's name is removed from the list [of library members in good standing], his membership card should not be destroyed but filed alphabetically with those of other book vandals. When such a [blacklisted] person comes in again to enrol in the library, a quick perusal of the cards of book vandals is sufficient to catch him red-handed.[69]

Kruk and his colleagues in the Kultur-lige brought out several publications (in addition to the supplement in *Vokhnshrift far literatur*) whose purpose was to aid the non-professional librarian in selecting books for purchase and to advise library subscribers on their choice of reading material. In the spring and summer of 1930, as the Grosser Bibliotek was being reorganized under the aegis of the Kultur-lige, the organization's library centre published three issues of *Bukh un lezer: khoydesh-zhurnal far bikher-retsenzyes* ('Book and Reader: A Monthly Journal of Book Reviews').[70] *Bukh un lezer* printed reviews of newly published books in Yiddish, in Yiddish translation, and in Polish. On the first page of the first issue the editors formulated the journal's goals as follows: 'The need for such a journal has been felt for a long while. It is, however, extraordinarily important for our libraries. The journal *Bukh un lezer* can and should become a guide for librarians and library boards in filling out their collections and recommending books to readers.'[71]

Herman Kruk also developed lists of recommended books for the use of librarians and students. Two such lists, one on the subject of trade unions and the other on antisemitism, were published together as a sixteen-page pamphlet in 1937.[72] In

---

[69] H. Kruk, 'Di bibliotek in ir tog-teglekhkeyt', *Vokhnshrift far literatur, kunst un kultur* (27 Jan. 1933), 6.

[70] The editorial board of *Bukh un lezer* consisted of Sofie Dubnow-Erlich, D. B. Malkin, and Khayim-Shloyme Kazdan (Kruk was not a member).   [71] *Bukh un lezer*, no. 1 (May 1930), 1.

[72] H. Kruk, *Rekomendir-reshimes fun lektur af di temes: (1) profesyonele fareynen; (2) antisemitizm* (Warsaw, 1937).

his brief introduction to the pamphlet Kruk wrote: 'Today it is not enough to learn to read. We need to be shown how and what to read. Illiterates are not only those who don't know the alphabet, but also those who cannot make proper use of books.'[73]

Kruk's heartfelt desire to provide appropriate educational guidance to young Jewish workers found its most concrete expression in his *Heft far notitsn iber geleyente bikher* ('Notebook for Comments on Books one has Read').[74] This thirty-two-page pamphlet is subtitled *Tsuhilf dem leyener un zelbstbilder* ('An Aid for the Reader and Autodidact'), and aims to teach its user how to read in a systematic, disciplined way. The pamphlet contains the following general instructions: (1) make a reading plan for yourself, rather than reading whatever books come to hand; (2) choose books that really interest you; (3) work with a reading group, so that you will be able to discuss your reading with others; (4) don't read only belles-lettres, but also memoirs, history, geography, natural science, and popular books on current events; (5) read slowly and thoughtfully, and take notes on the difficult and important sections of each book; (6) reread a book after a certain amount of time has passed; (7) read aloud as often as possible; (8) keep a dictionary at hand and look up unfamiliar words. A section on the 'hygienics' of reading follows, with instructions on proper physical positions for reading, times of day when reading should be avoided, protecting one's eyesight while reading, and avoiding reading at times when one cannot give one's full attention to it.

The largest section of *Heft far notitsn iber geleyente bikher* is entitled 'Musterplan far notitsn iber geleyente bikher' ('Sample Plan for Notes on Books one has Read'). Five sets of pages on which to take notes are provided. Each is divided into ten sections, where the reader is instructed to record: (1) the title, contents of the book jacket, and number of pages in the book; (2) a summary of the book's contents; (3) a list of the main characters, brief character sketches, and a discussion of which character the reader would choose as a role model; (4) a list of characters and events that are similar to those the reader has encountered in daily life; (5) the book's main idea; (6) the ideas in the book that impressed the reader most; (7) whether the book was interesting or boring; (8) a list of similar works that the reader has read; (9) the length of time it took to read the book, and whether or not the entire book was read; (10) anything in the book that was difficult to understand.

Upon completing a set of extensive notes on a book, the autodidact would be able to make comparisons with other works and review the content at a later date, thus advancing his or her knowledge even without the guidance of a teacher or librarian.

Kruk and his associates laboured throughout the 1930s to strengthen the Yiddish libraries within their purview and aid workers in their efforts towards self-education. They achieved certain successes, among them the Grosser Bibliotek in

[73] Ibid. 2.
[74] H. Kruk, *Heft far notitsn iber geleyente bikher*, from a work by Y. V. Vladislavlev, adapted for the Yiddish reader by Herman Kruk (Warsaw, 1932).

Warsaw, the membership of which grew enormously during that decade.[75] Yet by January 1939, when they declared the need for a Yiddish book month, they were forced to admit that the Yiddish book was in danger of disappearing altogether in Poland.

INTER-PARTY COMPETITION AND DUPLICATIONS OF EFFORT

Three important spheres of activity in support of Yiddish libraries in inter-war Poland have been discussed here: that of the *umparteyish* journal *Literarishe bleter*, the socialist Bund, and the labour Zionist Po'alei Tsion. Intelligent, dedicated people worked hard at their task but faced an uphill battle against linguistic assimilation, poverty, and the popular fiction that flooded the daily Yiddish press. The scarcity of monetary resources forced cultural activists to curtail many of their plans to aid Yiddish libraries. The Bund and Kultur-lige, for instance, initiated several publications that they were unable to sustain.[76] In addition, competition among libraries associated with rival political organizations frequently resulted in duplications of holdings and of efforts. An article that appeared in the bulletin of the Kultur-lige's library centre in February 1939 gives evidence of this. The anonymous author complains that:

A very bad custom has developed in our little cultural world: wherever a new group is formed, the first thing [its members do] is found a small library. There are small towns where one can count several little libraries. . . . There are about 650 cities and towns in Poland, and among them about 400 have Jewish populations. None the less, there exist in Poland 700–800 small Yiddish libraries. Libraries are growing like mushrooms after the rain, and they are all tiny: the majority have no more than 200–300 books.

Is it any surprise that these libraries are poor? The town is small. It's impossible to buy books. One can't live, but no one wants to die—and of course one can't get along without a library!

Combine resources into a large centralized library—who would agree to such a thing? So lots of spindly little libraries appear and all groan that they can barely draw breath.

The library has no funds. How, under these circumstances, is it possible to buy books? But if these *arbeter-* and *folks-bibliotekn* were to merge, then not only would the buying power of such libraries undoubtedly be increased and strengthened, but so would the scope of the work of [such a] unified library.

Unified, centralized library activity, centralized in towns and cities, would be the salvation of this very neglected area of our cultural work.[77]

---

[75] In 1936 the Grosser Bibliotek in Warsaw had 4,000 borrowers (3,000 adults and 1,000 children).

[76] For example: the revived *Bikher-velt* (Apr. 1928–Aug. 1929); *Bukh un lezer* (May–July 1930); and *Vokhnshrift far literatur, kunst un kultur* (Jan. 1931–July 1935), which carried Herman Kruk's supplement. [77] *Bibliotekn-tsenter ba der gezelshaft kultur-lige*, no. 2 (Feb. 1939), 1.

It must be said that this notion of unifying forces across organizational lines came late and out of desperation. One need only compare the documents presented in the previous sections to see the close similarities between the library work of the Bund and the Po'alei Tsion Left. Had they seen fit to collaborate, they might have achieved more success. The competition between the Bikher co-operative and the publishers' co-operative of the Kultur-lige may also have hindered the growth of the book market.

CONCLUSION

In light of the many obstacles faced by the cultural activists who concerned themselves with the welfare of Yiddish libraries and publishing houses, their achievements were quite remarkable. With great devotion they built not only libraries in inter-war Poland, but a vibrant educational culture, much of whose history is still to be written.

Exploiting Tradition: Religious Iconography in Cartoons of the Polish Yiddish Press

EDWARD PORTNOY

SINCE the thirteenth century Jews have borne the force of an antisemitic caricature that has grown in ferocity from its medieval inception to the modern period.[1] By the early twentieth century, when vast numbers of east European Jews began the process of secularization and modernization, the progeny of such anti-Jewish caricatures were standard fare in the satirical press in both Europe and America. It was also at this time that, alongside the mainstream press, a Jewish satirical press began to flourish in the Yiddish language in both eastern Europe and America. In addition to jokes, humorous stories, poems, and many parodies, Yiddish satirical journals would come to include numerous cartoons and caricatures. Never having been seen previously in Jewish life, such visual parody was an unprecedented innovation among Yiddish-speaking Jews in Poland, partly because of its sheer novelty and partly because art without a religious connection was discouraged among Jews.[2] Moreover, the vast majority of Jewish texts, particularly those used on a daily basis, did not contain illustrations of any kind. The cartoonists of the Yiddish press were therefore engaged not only in a radical subversion of Jewish tradition but also in a reassessment of what Jewish caricature should be, as opposed to the antisemitic caricature of the non-Jewish satirical press. In addition, Jewish cartoonists frequently applied traditional Jewish themes to critical commentary on current cultural and political events. By appropriating a popular format that had not appeared before in Jewish life and filling it with Jewish content, the cartoonists of the Yiddish press in Poland were able to furnish a wide audience with a form of visual commentary that referenced the texts and traditions of their own minority culture. It is this use of traditional material in cartoon form, ranging from biblical quotation to religious articles, obligations, and folklore, that will be explored here.

[1] For examples and historical insight into such caricatures, see, among others, E. Fuchs, *Die Juden in der Karikatur* (Munich, 1922); E. Lucie-Smith, *The Art of Caricature* (Ithaca, 1981); J. Trachtenberg, *The Devil and the Jews* (Philadelphia, 1983).

[2] S. Wolitz, 'Experiencing Visibility and Phantom Existence', in S. Goodman (ed.), *Russian Jewish Artists in a Century of Change: 1890–1990* (New York, 1995), 14.

As works of graphic parody and artistic social commentary, these cartoons lay at a crossroads between art and literature, and politics and culture. What is unique about them is their distinctly Jewish orientation and their reflection of modern Jewish history and politics as their central feature during a wave of secularization and construction of national identity. Additionally, they are an important example of internal Jewish dialogue in a particularly factious, chaotic political and cultural environment. As documents representative of a wide array of attitudes towards an equally wide variety of subjects, the cartoons of the Yiddish press reflect virtually all aspects of Jewish political and cultural life from their inception just after the turn of the century to their ultimate disappearance in the wake of the Holocaust. This is of import not only because a significant portion of the artists and their audience was destroyed, but because the cartoons evoke long-forgotten attitudes on myriad political and social issues in the life of Polish Jewry that have been left out of both popular and academic histories.[3] For these reasons, they are a unique form of cultural and historical documentation of an urban Jewish history, which itself has barely been explored.

If, as is frequently argued by its scholars, critical study of the field of cartoons and caricature has been neglected until recent times, such study within the realm of Yiddish culture has been scarcely touched.[4] Not quite art, nor literature, cartoons contain elements of both, though their primary feature is an often insolent form of social commentary. They belong to what Adam Gopnik calls an 'underbelly culture, a tradition of social criticism or raw, outlaw drawing'.[5] Cartoons and caricatures often take cheap shots and aim for cheap laughs. In spite of being a widespread phenomenon, they may have been neglected because of an association with low culture. But the most serious complication is that the 40- to 90-year-old cartoons of the Yiddish press have entirely lost their topicality and, as a result, their efficacy. Moreover, the destruction of their audience and its culture has played a key role in their neglect. These problems, combined with the fact that many of the minor details of Polish Jewry's political and cultural past have been forgotten, have caused this entire genre of Jewish creativity to fade deep into the background of Jewish history.

A great many of the cartoons that appeared in the Yiddish press of Poland were extremely rich in their synthesis of traditional and folk material with modern

[3] As Marian Fuks notes, the satirical press can be a rich, if peculiar, place to study the history of the Jews of Poland (see Fuks, 'Żydowska prasa humorystyczno-satyryczna', *Biuletyn Żydowskiego Instytutu Historycznego* (Warsaw) (1980), nos. 2–3 (114–15), 31–54).

[4] Although academic work in the field of cartoons and comics has increased over the past decade, nearly every text begins with a lament about the lack of attention the field receives. The subject of Yiddish-language cartoons has been considered in depth in the following works: J. Fishman, 'Cartoons about Language: Hebrew, Yiddish and the Visual Representation of Sociolinguistic Attitudes', in L. Gleinert (ed.), *Hebrew in Ashkenaz* (New York, 1993); S. Stein, 'The Creation of Yiddish and Judeo-Spanish Newspaper Cultures in the Russian and Ottoman Empires', Stanford University Ph.D. thesis, 2000, esp. ch. 5, in which she analyses the sudden appearance and disappearance of cartoons in the pages of *Dos lebn/Der fraynd* in the wake of the 1905 Russian revolution.

[5] K. Varnadoe and A. Gopnik, *High and Low: Modern Art and Popular Culture* (New York, 1990), 11.

secular and political life. Although this fusion of Jewish folk culture and modern expression is often attributed to celebrated Jewish artists such as Boris Aronson, Marc Chagall, and El Lissitsky, this same synthesis initially appeared early on in cartoons of the Warsaw Yiddish press.[6] What Seth Wolitz writes about these artists applies quite well to the cartoonists of the Yiddish press:

By creating their own artwork, Jewish artists in Russia brought to an end the monopolization by the Other of the visual definition of the Jew. Jewish artists asserted their own gaze, removing Jews from their marginalized condition by reading them into the center of their cultural representation . . . Thus, Jewish artists constructed Jewish cultural identity from their own gaze, beholden neither to the Other nor to Tradition as defined by the shtetl leadership. Jewish artists acquired by their performance their own voices and authority.[7]

Like these respected, 'high' artists, the cartoonists of the Yiddish press also 'constructed Jewish cultural identity from their own gaze'. But instead of 'normalizing . . . the Jewish body and its cultural presence', they contorted and stretched it in directions previously unknown. Engaging in appropriations and reinventions of tradition and applying them to new experiences, they mined the rich quarry of Jewish tradition as fodder for their satire. The cartoonists of the Yiddish press, most of whom had been raised in a traditional Jewish environment, exploited customs and folklore in order to create biting political and social commentary. Items ranging from folk tradition to talmudic quotation to daily and holiday liturgy to cult objects were employed in order to invent a unique and new form of Jewish commentary. By applying Jewish symbols—together with the values that are associated with them—to their work, they created cartoons that reflected a deeply Jewish sensibility.

The Yiddish satirical press was a significant phenomenon within the Yiddish press as a whole: from 1862 to 1916 satirical publications comprised fully 25 per cent of the Yiddish press of the Russian empire.[8] However, it should be noted that that figure does not include other popular humorous publications such as joke booklets and *badkhonishe bikhlekh* (booklets by *badkhonim*, 'wedding jesters'), both of which were extremely popular and published in large numbers during the nineteenth century.[9] Most Yiddish satirical journals nevertheless appeared after the Russian revolution of 1905. This reflects the severe restrictions placed on the publication of Yiddish periodicals by the tsarist regime: if daily and weekly newspapers were not permitted through the 1890s, it makes all the more sense that

---

[6] R. Apter-Gabriel, *Tradition and Revolution: The Jewish Renaissance in Russian Avant-Garde Art, 1912–1928* (Jerusalem, 1987), 11.

[7] Wolitz, 'Experiencing Visibility and Phantom Existence', 14.

[8] This statistic is based on a close survey of A. Kirzhnits, *Di yidishe prese in der gevezener rusisher imperye, 1823–1916* (Moscow, 1930).

[9] J. Shatzky, *Geshikhte fun yidn in varshe*, vol. iii (New York, 1953), 268 n. 11. David Roskies's bibliography of I. M. Dik's publications includes at least ten joke books published by Dik. See 'An Annotated Bibliography of I. M. Dik', in M. Herzog (ed.), *The Field of Yiddish*, vol. iv (Philadelphia, 1980). On *badkhones*, see also Ariela Krasney's and Yaakov Mazor's chapters in this volume.

satirical journals, with their penchant for stripping emperors bare, would be banned outright.[10] Ironically perhaps, the Yiddish press in America was more developed than the Yiddish press of tsarist Russia at the turn of the century.

In spite of the restrictions on the Yiddish press in general, and on the humorous press, satire and parody were already common fare in Yiddish literature. Parody was, in particular, central to maskilic propaganda. Moreover, satire had been central to the beginnings of modern Yiddish literature. Its most significant contributors, Sholem-Yankev Abramovitsh (Mendele Moykher Sforim) and Sholem Aleichem, based much of their work on bitingly satirical portrayals of east European *shtetl* Jewry. Satirical journals published in Yiddish continued this tradition of internal criticism, and their contents ran the gamut from crude jokes to clever satire to vicious invective. They contained stories, poems, and parodies of nearly every type of religious text. Many of these one-time journals (known in Polish as *jednodniówki*) were published to coincide with major Jewish holidays and based much of their humour on issues relating to the holiday during which they appeared.

The tradition of printing a journal on holidays was partly an outgrowth of Yitskhok Leybush Peretz's *Yontev-bletlekh* ('Holiday Leaves'), a series of subversive literary journals disguised as religious material which were published on Jewish holidays to circumvent the tsarist ban on periodical literature in Yiddish.[11] Titles that denoted Jewish holiday imagery typically reflected a liturgical, cultural, or culinary element of the relevant holiday. Titles of issues of the *Yontev-bletlekh*, such as *Grins* ('Greens'), *Der shoyfer* ('The Shofar'), *Heshaynes* ('Willow Twigs'), *Lekoved peysekh* ('In Honour of Passover'), and *Homen-tash* ('Purim Cookie'), would later also be used as titles of satirical journals.[12] Indeed, the majority of these journal titles denote some relationship to traditional Jewish life. This suggests the importance of tradition and religion in nascent modern Jewish popular culture. It also stands in direct contrast to the titles of Polish and Russian satirical journals in the period following the failed revolution, the majority of which were connected in some way with violence or horror. This marks a sharp distinction in the cultural orientation of co-territorial satirists and artists. The contrast is evident not only in the titles of the journals, but also in their cartoons: Polish and, even more so, Russian journals of the period after 1905 contain numerous cartoons of horrific violence.[13] Such images were a rarity in the Yiddish press.

[10] On the tsarist restriction of the Yiddish press, see D. Fishman, 'The Politics of Yiddish in Tsarist Russia', in J. Neusner, E. S. Frerichs, and N. M. Sarna (eds.), *From Ancient Israel to Modern Judaism: Intellect in Quest of Understanding. Essays in Honor of Marvin Fox*, vol. iv (Atlanta, Ga., 1989).

[11] M. Bernshteyn, 'Yontev-bletlekh un humoristishe oysgabes ba yidn', *Yidisher kemfer* (New York) (29 June 1962), 22.

[12] There are also a number of stories by Sholem Aleichem that share titles with satirical journals. They include *Arbo koyses*, *Akdomes*, *Der seyder*, and *Blintses*.

[13] For examples of Russian titles and images, see M. Betz, 'The Caricatures and Cartoons of the 1905 Revolution', City University of New York Ph.D. thesis, 1984; S. Isakov, *1905 god v satire i karikature* (Leningrad, 1928); D. King and C. Porter, *Images of Revolution* (New York, 1983).

Unless earlier examples are found, the first cartoons in the Yiddish press of Russian Poland seem to have appeared in Heshl Epelberg's Warsaw-based *Peysekh-blat*, a magazine of Passover-related poems, short stories, and historical sketches published in 1904, which closed with a small humorous section entitled 'Kneydlekh' ('Matzah Balls'). One of the cartoons was a caricature of Jews' heads on the bodies of two crows, another a non-caricatured image of a traditional Jew reading a newspaper that was combined with humorous text.

These images, however, do not appear to have been created specifically for Epelberg's *Peysekh-blat* but were appropriated from outside sources.[14] Their origins can be traced to a satirical journal entitled *Der yidisher pok* ('The Jewish Puck'), published in New York by Shomer (Nokhem-Mayer Shaykevitsh) from November 1894 to June 1896.[15] These early cartoons are not typical of those that would eventually appear in the Yiddish press in Poland, nor is their quality exceptional. They are simply the first and therefore warrant attention. That they were not drawn for the journal, but were lifted from another, was a common occurrence in the industry.

The failed revolution of 1905 provided the atmosphere in which the satirical press flourished throughout the empire. It was during this period that preliminary press censorship ended, albeit temporarily. Almost immediately an unruly, snowballing satirical press began to savage the rulers of Russia and their minions. From late 1905 to early 1907 over 400 of these journals appeared in nearly all the languages of the empire. Approximately forty satirical journals appeared in Yiddish during this period, most during 1906 and 1907.[16] But whereas Russian and Polish satirical journals were rife with original cartoon art, the Yiddish satirical press, for the most part, was not. However, desirous of keeping up with current publishing trends, editors of such journals who could not afford to hire Jewish artists began to appropriate caricatures from Russian and Polish journals and translate their captions into Yiddish.

It was in 1906 that more efforts were made by a few Yiddish publications to provide original cartoon art by Jewish artists rather than reprint and translate non-Jewish cartoons. As such, the three main satirical periodicals that were published during 1906—*Der fraynd* ('The Friend')'s humorous supplement, *Der bezem* ('The Broom'); *Der sheygets* ('The Smart Alec') in St Petersburg; and the Warsaw-based *Di bin* ('The Bee')—all contained original cartoon art drawn specifically for the magazines.[17]

---

[14] Heshl Epelberg was the publicist who devised the idea of publishing *Yontev-bletlekh* to circumvent the tsarist ban on Yiddish periodicals, and whose idea Y. L. Peretz borrowed to print his own.

[15] *Der yidisher pok* (its editors rendered it as the *Hebrew Puck*) was a vaguely socialistic, humorous monthly, and eventually weekly, which contained cartoon images mainly stolen from the popular American and German-language satirical press and re-captioned in Yiddish.

[16] See Kirzhnits, *Di yidishe prese*; King and Porter, *Images of Revolution*; Isakov, *1905 god v satire*.

[17] Although *Der fraynd* (including its incarnation as *Dos lebn*) with its *Bezem*, as well as *Der sheygets*, were published in St Petersburg, most of their staff, as well as their audience, was based in Warsaw and elsewhere in Congress Poland. Additionally, *Der bezem* moved its operations to Warsaw in 1908, to be followed a year later by its parent, *Der fraynd*.

The Yiddish satirical journals, including periodicals and one-time publications, were typically printed on 23 × 30 centimetre pages and ranged from four to sixteen pages, the latter being more common. Their print runs ranged from 1,000 to 17,000, although the average was 5,000. Of the nearly 300 Yiddish satirical journals published in Russian-ruled and independent Poland between 1889 and 1939, more than two-thirds were published in conjunction with Jewish holidays. Of these, only eight were printed specifically for Rosh Hashanah, as opposed to twenty-five for Sukkot, eight for Hanukah, thirty-six for Purim, thirty-nine for Shavuot, and seventy-seven for Passover.[18] It should be noted that more one-time journals appeared in the period that preceded the First World War than during the inter-war period, mainly owing to the appearance thereafter of more successful humorous weeklies,[19] as well as the inclusion of regular Friday humour pages in the daily press. Many journals that called themselves 'illustrated' would often have only a cartoon on the cover. Journals that were published as supplements to major dailies, or were connected to papers in some other way, typically had more original cartoon art than one-time publications, a fact that can be attributed to better financial support.

The appearance of cartoons and caricature was evidently such an innovation in the Jewish publishing world that Warsaw's popular *Roman tsaytung* ('Novel–Newspaper') published an unsigned article in May 1908 explaining what caricature was and the purpose behind it. It commented that 'caricature has played a great role in the life of all civilized peoples, but with us Jews, as with many other things, it has, until recently, been practically unknown'.[20] This article was the first acknowledgement of graphic satire in Yiddish. Cartoons had quickly become a natural occurrence in the Yiddish press without much notice on the part of its usually vociferous critics.[21]

THE CARTOONISTS

Despite the large number of Jewish artists and the brief vogue for cartoons in the Russian and Polish press, few Jewish artists wished to dirty their brushes with the unholy ink of caricature, particularly in obnoxious satirical journals, where their

[18] Statistical information regarding the publication of satirical journals was culled from Kirzhnits, *Di yidishe prese*; Y. Szeintuch, *Preliminary Inventory of Yiddish Dailies and Periodicals Published in Poland between the Two World Wars* (Jerusalem, 1986); and the card catalogues of the YIVO Institute for Jewish Research, New York, and the New York Public Library. There were undoubtedly more journals published that are not catalogued in these sources.

[19] Weekly humorous journals such as *Der takhshit*, *Der mashkhes*, and *Der blofer* continued to publish special holiday issues similar to those of the one-time journals.

[20] 'Karikaturn', *Roman-tsaytung*, no. 17 (1 May 1908), 538–9.

[21] A. Mukdoyni (Aleksander Kappel) wrote apparently the only article on Yiddish satirical journals during the pre-war period. His 'Undzere vits-bleter' appeared in *Der vokhnblat* (suppl. to *Der fraynd*), no. 22 (7 Feb. 1913), 2–4. It is extremely critical of the state of both textual and caricatural material.

work might get them into trouble with the authorities and, possibly, with their colleagues. The first political cartoons that appeared in the Yiddish daily press of eastern Europe did so in *Dos lebn* ('The Life', the temporary name of *Der fraynd* from December 1905 to July 1906). These simple black-and-white cartoons, mainly relating to the revolution, appeared on an almost daily basis from February to June 1906. All were drawn by Arnold Lakhovsky, who also contributed cartoons to *Der bezem* and *Der sheygets*, as well as a number of Russian satirical journals. Interestingly, very few of the cartoons he drew for *Dos lebn* touch on Jewish issues. In fact, they are a decidedly un-Jewish element within the most important Yiddish daily of the time.[22] Specifically Jewish subject matter was reserved for the paper's newly separated satirical supplement, *Der bezem*.[23] In stark black and red ink Lakhovsky drew cartoons of political protest that considered the general and Jewish political predicament. Evidently the only Jewish cartoonist in St Petersburg, he also drew for *Der bezem*'s local competitor, *Der sheygets*. Lakhovsky's cartoons disappeared from *Der bezem* in mid-1908, when he left St Petersburg to teach drawing at the Bezalel School of Art in Jerusalem.[24]

In March 1906 Shmuel Yatskan, then publisher of *Yidishes tageblat* ('Jewish Daily Paper'), Warsaw's first 1 copeck daily and the first glimmer of sensationalistic journalism in Yiddish, began to publish *Di bin*, a monthly satirical journal with original cartoon work. Not to be outdone by his St Petersburg competitors, Yatskan hired the well-known Warsaw artist Yankev Vaynles (Weinles) to draw cartoons for *Di bin*. In fact, prior to the appearance of the first issue, advertisements appeared in *Der fraynd* and *Yidishes tageblat* announcing the forthcoming publication in Warsaw of a new humorous journal 'illustrated by the famous artist Y. Vaynles'.[25] This phrase was in bold print, suggesting that cartoons would be an important element of the new journal. Vaynles, a popular artist known for his sympathetic portrayals of traditional Jewry, drew simple, yet cutting, cartoons for *Di bin* that addressed Jewish cultural and political issues.[26]

Although *Di bin* got off to a strong start with Vaynles's cartoons, they disappear from the journal after the fourth issue in favour of cartoons appropriated from outside, probably Polish, possibly Russian sources. A few unsigned, amateurish cartoons also appear. It is likely that either Vaynles tired of drawing cartoons or Yatskan tired of paying him. Whatever the case, it was evidently easier for Yatskan

---

[22] This, perhaps, reflects the brief unity of nationalities behind a banner of Russianness following the events of 1905. For a closer look at this notion, see Stein, 'The Creation of Yiddish', 142, on what she calls the 'rossiiskaya' orientation of *Dos lebn*'s cartoons. It may also be that Lakhovsky intended to 'double-dip' and publish these cartoons in both Yiddish and Russian publications.

[23] *Der bezem* had appeared yearly, since 1903, within the body of *Der fraynd*. In March 1906 a separate journal was created out of it. See Stein, 'The Creation of Yiddish', ch. 5, for an analysis of the sudden appearance and disappearance of cartoons in *Dos lebn*.

[24] J. Bowlt, 'Jewish Artists and the Russian Silver Age', in Goodman, *Russian Jewish Artists in a Century of Change*, 45. [25] See *Dos lebn*, no. 49 (1 Mar. 1906), 4.

[26] See Y. Sandel, *Plastisher kunst ba poylishe yidn* (Warsaw, 1964), 83–7.

to lift cartoons from the Polish- or Russian-language press than to create original work for his journal. *Di bin* folded about a year after it began, and cartooning in the Yiddish press seemed to suffer a temporary decline throughout 1907. It may be that cartoons were seen as diminishing the importance of the written word. With so many writers eager to get into print, a cartoon took up much-needed space. Additionally, in the period after the failed revolution censorship was reinstated and it may have been problematic to print political cartoons, which can often be understood without the benefit of text.

After Lakhovsky and Vaynles left the scene, younger, Warsaw-based artists soon began to contribute to the satirical journals. The cartoons that followed Lakhovsky's departure contain more Jewish content and are also far more inclined towards physical distortion and caricature than his more realistic work. One wonders whether this was the difference between 'Jewish Warsaw and goyish St Petersburg', a charge levelled at Shaul Ginzburg regarding the absurdity of publishing a Yiddish newspaper in the Russian capital, where comparatively few Jews resided at the time.[27]

In mid-1908 cartoons and caricatures signed by Warsaw-based artists Leyb Brodaty, Khayim Goldberg, and 'Homunkulus' began to appear in *Der bezem* and in other, less well-known one-time journals and periodicals. Brodaty (1889–1954), who left Warsaw for Russia in 1915, would eventually achieve fame as a Soviet caricaturist: he published the first political cartoon to appear in *Pravda* in 1917 and founded the first Soviet satirical journal, *Krasnyi d'yavol* ('Red Devil') the following year. He later published caricatures in *Krokodil* ('Crocodile'), illustrated numerous books, and taught at the Moscow Polygraphical Institute. Biographical sketches about Brodaty are terribly vague about the period preceding the First World War and only note that he lived in Warsaw and was arrested there in 1914 for participating in an 'illegal gathering'. After that he lived illegally in Petrograd.[28] Yet from 1908 to 1915 Warsaw's Yiddish satirical press was replete with his caricatures. In 1908 he had evidently stepped in to fill the shoes of Lakhovsky at *Der bezem*. His cartooning style differed greatly from that of Lakhovsky and bore a greater sense of caricature and a humour based on wild incongruousness. Indeed, he was the only cartoonist praised by the critic A. Mukdoyni in his otherwise caustic review of the Yiddish satirical press.[29] Along with Lakhovsky, Brodaty was responsible for creating some of the earliest caricatures of Yiddish writers, thereby helping to advance the concept of Jewish celebrity into the Pale of Settlement.

[27] S. Ginzburg, *Amolike peterburg* (New York, 1944), 192. When it became known that Ginzburg had obtained permission to publish a Yiddish newspaper in St Petersburg, he wrote that the Warsaw writers complained, 'Why in Petersburg and not in Warsaw? The place for a Yiddish newspaper is not in goyish Petersburg, but really in Jewish Warsaw!'

[28] Biographical sources on Brodaty include S. Vavilov (ed.), *Bol'shaya sovetskaya entsiklopediya*, vol. vi (2nd edn., Moscow, 1951), 123; J. Milner, *A Dictionary of Russian and Soviet Artists, 1420–1970* (London, 1993), 90; *Mastera sovetskoi karikatury* (Moscow, 1990), 1–4; *Rossiskaya evreiskaya entsiklopediya*, vol. i, ed. H. Branower (Northvale, NJ, 1998), 213.

[29] Mukdoyni, 'Unzere vits-bleter', 4.

But, in spite of these contributions to cartooning in the Yiddish press, Brodaty has been remembered only as a Soviet caricaturist.

Khayim Goldberg, who worked under the pseudonym 'Khogay', also got his start in cartooning following Arnold Lakhovsky's departure from *Der bezem* in 1908. Goldberg, who was born in 1890 to a well-off hasidic family in Lukov (Łuków), attended yeshiva until he left to study graphic art in Germany. Upon returning to Poland, he became one of the most important figures in Jewish graphic art, his work appearing in nearly every Hebrew and Yiddish periodical publication that contained illustration. He founded the Grafikon, a zincography studio where nearly every cartoon that appeared in the Yiddish press during the inter-war years was prepared for publication. In addition to cartoons and graphics, in 1922 Goldberg published an article calling for the graphic reform of the Jewish alphabet, which apparently had some influence in the Yiddish printing industry.[30] He was also a founder of the Yidishe Artistn Fareyn (Jewish Artists' Union) in Poland. At the outbreak of war in 1939 he left Warsaw for Białystok, where he disappeared without trace in 1941.[31]

Another important figure, particularly in inter-war Yiddish cartooning, was Shaye Faygenboym, who was born in 1900 in Warsaw and perished in Treblinka in 1942.[32] His cartoon work is probably the most widespread of any artist that contributed to the Yiddish press. Unfortunately, very little is known about him. He was the artistic director of the periodical *Ilustrirte vokh* ('Illustrated Week') throughout the mid-1920s and participated in art exhibitions in Warsaw throughout the 1920s and 1930s. The scant biographical information available notes that Faygenboym 'occasionally did caricatures'.[33] This is an understatement: the Yiddish press is loaded with his cartoons from about 1918 to the end of the 1930s. In addition to contributing to many one-time journals, his cartoons appeared on Fridays in *Der moment* and he was a member of its editorial staff. However, he also drew a set of completely different cartoons for *Haynt*, which appeared as part of their Friday humour section. Faygenboym's work was so ubiquitous that an article in *Haynt* in 1931 complained that there was 'only one artist doing all the caricature' in the Warsaw press.[34] To a great extent, this complaint was legitimate.

[30] See K. Goldberg, 'Vegn reformirn dem yidishn alef-beys', *Bikher velt*, 4–5 (July–Oct. 1922), 379–84.

[31] Y. Sandel, *Umgekumene yidishe kinstler in poyln* (Warsaw, 1957), 83–4, and 'Khayim goldberg', in R. Feldshuh, *Yidisher gezelshaftlekher leksikon* (Warsaw, 1939), col. 660.

[32] According to Khayim Finkelshteyn, he perished in the Warsaw ghetto (see *Haynt: a tsaytung ba yidn* (New York, 1967), 227).

[33] J. Maurin-Białostocka *et al.* (eds.), *Słownik artystów polskich*, vol. ii (Wrocław, 1975), 187; this article cites an entry for Faygenboym in Feldshuh's *Gezelshaftlekher leksikon*, which only goes up to the letter *vov*. Perhaps J. Sandel, the writer of the entry, had access to an MS copy of the apparently unpublished volume.

[34] S. Shpigl, 'Di yidishe politishe karikatur', *Haynt*, no. 147 (26 June 1931), 7, continued in no. 153 (3 July 1931), 7.

Yoysef Tunkel (Der Tunkeler, 1881–1949), the most important Yiddish satirist of the inter-war period, was a unique exception to the circle of Warsaw cartoonists, having founded two important and successful satirical journals in New York.[35] Tunkel attended art school in Vilna in 1905–6 but left the Pale for New York at the end of 1906, where he joined up with the bohemian literary group Di Yunge (The Young Ones). Together with some of these writers he founded *Der kibitser*, a monthly forum for cartoons and satire. *Der kibitser* was a great success in New York and quickly became well known in Poland for its cartoons, many of which were initially drawn by Tunkel.[36] In its later incarnation as *Der groyser kundes* ('The Great Prankster') it became the most successful Yiddish satirical journal in any country, renowned for its plethora of original cartoon art.[37] But by the end of 1909 Tunkel had returned to Poland, lured back by Shmuel Rozenfeld to work at *Der bezem* in Warsaw.[38] As it turned out, *Der bezem* was published infrequently during 1910 and by the end of that year Tunkel accepted a position at the new daily, *Der moment*, writing a humorous column called *Der krumer shpigl* ('The Crooked Mirror'), which appeared weekly until August 1939. The column was initially accompanied by cartoons drawn by Tunkel, though by the inter-war period he generally left this to Shaye Faygenboym. In addition, Tunkel produced a number of one-time humorous journals from 1911 to the early 1920s. Although his skill as a satirist outweighed his drawing talents, Tunkel none the less applied his sharp wit to cartoon work.

A number of other artists, some of whom later became famous, also contributed cartoons to the Yiddish press in Poland. They include Artur Szyk (1894–1951), Yoysef Budko (1888–1940), and Menakhem Birnboym (1893–1944). In spite of the fame that some of them later achieved, their contributions to the Yiddish satirical press were sporadic and thus do not warrant close attention in this overview.[39] Additionally, as Fuks notes in his article on the Yiddish satirical press, many of the cartoons went unsigned and it is almost impossible to determine who drew them.[40]

[35] For more information on Tunkel, see Y. Szeintuch, *Sefer hahumoreskot vehaparodiyot hasifrutiyot beyidish* (Jerusalem, 1990).

[36] Tunkel left *Der kibitser* after eight issues and founded a new journal with the poet Yankev Marinov called *Hakibitser hagodl*, the title of which was changed in the following issue to *Der groyser kibitser*, and again to *Der groyser kundes*.

[37] Avrom Reyzn noted that no Yiddish satirical journal had as many cartoons as did *Der groyser kundes*. See 'Khayim gutman—der lebediker', in A. Mukdoyni (ed.), *Der lebediker yoyvl bukh* (New York, 1938), 25.   [38] Szeintuch, *Sefer hahumoreskot*, 26.

[39] All of these artists contributed during 1912–13. Some of the finest cartoons and caricatures of Jewish literary and political figures were drawn by the Berlin-based artist Menakhem Birnboym and appeared in *Der ashmeday*, of which he was the art editor. Allegedly, nine issues were published, but only five are extant. For more information on *Der ashmeday*, see Y. Szeintuch, 'Bere'i ha'ashmedai', *Ḥuliyot* (Haifa, 2000), 397–429.

[40] Fuks, 'Żydowska prasa humorystyczno-satyryczna', 42.

CARTOONS

The importance of cartoons that relate to or exploit Jewish religious or folk themes lies in the fact that these images Judaized cartooning. They allowed the Jewish reading public to enjoy cartoons *in der heym*, that is, in the privacy of their cultural home. The religious iconographies they used were uniquely imbued with a Jewish sensibility, and had not been seen previously in cartooning. As such, they allowed cartoonists to create their works within a Jewish symbolic framework. With the rise of national consciousness, Jewish readers naturally anticipated Jewish images and concepts in their press. During a period usually noted for secularization, symbols common to the Jewish experience were necessarily exploited in order to provide a humorous Jewish commentary on all manner of events. One of the significant cultural aspects of east European Jewish 'secular' humorous journals was that much of the humour relied heavily on traditional and religious themes. Evidently, the satirists not only found it necessary to build jokes and parodies on traditional texts, but clearly wanted to, as evidenced by their frequency. Moreover, the secularism of the humorous journals relied on a tradition that was not at all reviled, but, in fact, went hand in hand with the parent that spawned it. This secularism was of a type unlike the revolutionary secularism of political parties that rejected religion out of hand, but one that relished it and used it to great advantage. Even parodies of religious texts in Yiddish satirical journals did not ridicule the original texts, but used the widespread familiarity of their forms to satirize other subjects. It is likely, therefore, that such journals appealed to a wide readership, not only secular, but also religious.

It is unknown whether there was any religious opposition to these journals, nearly all of which parodied all manner of religious material, both textually and visually. While the Orthodox press itself never contained cartoons, parodies and humorous material were published by and for traditional audiences. In spite of the apparent frivolity of the satirical press, there was evidently wide social approval of such publications.

Some of the cartoons in the Yiddish press are simple and can be easily understood by any reader with a modicum of Jewish knowledge. Others are obscure and require research to comprehend their meaning and purpose. The discussion that follows includes examples of both. Because all the cartoons employ traditional Jewish symbols as part of their texts, I will organize my discussion around Jewish holidays, limiting myself to cartoons concerning the holidays of Rosh Hashanah, Yom Kippur, Hanukah, Passover, and Shavuot.

ROSH HASHANAH AND YOM KIPPUR

The high holidays were a time for serious reflection, not for humour. If a satirical journal appeared during this time of year, it usually did so in conjunction with

Sukkot. More than double the number of journals appeared on Sukkot than during the high holidays. Nevertheless, a small number did appear in connection with Rosh Hashanah and Yom Kippur. Moreover, these journals, like all the other holiday *jednodniówki*, exploited religious texts and icons for political and cultural commentary.

One of the most familiar images connected to Rosh Hashanah is that of the sounding of the shofar, the ram's horn, which has come to symbolize the ushering in of the New Year. The drama of this moment has been reproduced by both Jewish and non-Jewish artists. One unsigned cartoon (Fig. 1) makes use of folklore relating to the shofar and attempts by the devil to confound its sounding.[41] The image, from a publication called *Der shoyfer* dated September 1923, is entitled *Der sotn hot zikh farleygt* ('Satan Sat himself Down'), and portrays a character labelled 'Folkspartey' sitting in a shofar inscribed with the words *natsyonal-blok* ('nationalities bloc'). The shofar is being blown by the leader of Poland's General Zionists, Yitskhok Grinboym (Grünbaum). The caption reads, 'Blow harder, Reb Itshe, and you'll drive this Satan away from the Jewish street'. Satan, in this case, appears to be portrayed by a tiny caricature of Noyekh Prilutski (Prylucki), leader of the Folks-partey, and Grinboym's political adversary.[42] Although he is labelled 'Folkspartey', and not Prilutski, the caricature resembles him enough to warrant a clear connection. Grinboym, on the other hand, is seen blowing the metaphorical shofar of the National Minorities Bloc, the parliamentary coalition which included Ukrainian, German, and Belarusian parties, among others. It is of note that he is dubbed Reb Itshe, a folksy appellation reminiscent of a *shtetl bal-tkiyo* (shofarblower). This diminutive contrasts the Zionist leader Grinboym, imagined here as one of the common folk, with Prilutski, head of the party that allegedly promoted the way of the folk. The basis behind this role reversal is that the Folks-partey, in the November 1922 election, refused to join the National Minorities Bloc due to ideological disagreements with the other Jewish parties and also chose to remain outside the Koło (Jewish Circle) in parliament.[43] Although other Jewish parties also refused to join the Minorities Bloc, Prilutski bore the brunt of public reaction from its supporters.[44] As the cartoon indicates, the success of the Minorities Bloc

---

[41] Although unsigned, this cartoon was most likely drawn by Shaye Faygenboym.

[42] As an example of their personal animosity towards one another in connection to their ideological and political battles, Grinboym and Prilutski got into so fierce an argument in the cafeteria of the Yidisher Literatn un Zhurnalistn Fareyn (Union of Jewish Writers and Journalists) at 13 Tłomackie Street in Warsaw that it concluded in their throwing ashtrays at each other. Though 'they didn't aim for the head', the fight was memorable enough to warrant a mention in a biographical sketch of Prilutski by Melekh Ravitsh, then secretary of the Fareyn. See Ravitsh, *Mayn leksikon*, vol. i (Montreal, 1945), 176.

[43] For more on Prilutski and the Folks-partey, see K. Weiser, 'The Politics of Yiddish: Noyekh Prilutski and the Folkspartey', Columbia University Ph.D. thesis, 2001.

[44] A. Haftke, 'Dos politishe lebn fun yidn in poyln', in Haftke (ed.), *Yidisher gezelshaftlekher leksikon* (Warsaw, 1939), cols. 168–72.

Fig. 1. *Der sotn hot zikh farleygt* ('Satan Sat himself Down'), unsigned; probably drawn by
Shaye Faygenboym. *Der shoyfer* (September 1923)

depends on blowing Prilutski and his Folks-partey out of the shofar and out of the
Jewish political scene.

The cartoon is based on the page in the Talmud (*Rosh Hashanah* 16*b*), which
explains that the shofar is to be sounded while standing, in order to create sounds
loud enough to confound Satan. Undoubtedly aware of this, Satan, in turn,
attempts to thwart the blowing of the shofar in some manner. That Satan would sit
in the shofar to block its sounding was planted deeply in the folklore that surrounds
the sounding of the shofar. Such themes were further expanded upon in the
medieval *Sefer ḥasidim* and by later kabbalists, and became part of hasidic folklore
relating to the shofar. The cartoon also plays upon what Finesinger notes as the
dual usage of the shofar: one to announce the arrival of a new order (a new political
base in the National Minorities Bloc) and the other to scare off Satan (Prilutski and
the Folks-partey).[45] Additionally, the cartoon parodies traditional, ornate shofars,

[45] S. Finesinger, 'The Shofar', *Hebrew Union College Annual* (Cincinnati), 7–11 (1931–2), 194.

which were often inscribed with special blessings, by ironically inscribing it with the words *natsyonal-blok*, a thoroughly unreligious concept in which Jews were seen to be uniting with non-Jews for the unholy purpose of political gain.[46]

The cartoon is accompanied by a story entitled 'Kateyreg hasotn' ('Accuser of Satan'), and is subtitled *khsidish* ('Hasidic'). Written by the editor of the journal, Avrom Rozenfeld, under his pen name, Bontshe, it is a story told in the style of a hasidic *mayse* (tale) about how Satan attempted to obstruct the shofar on Rosh Hashanah, but was foiled as a clever congregant surreptitiously brought in a new one. The traditional story is offered in full, without the injection of humorous commentary. However, a note following the story comments: 'What's it worth? Later on didn't they find the half a challah and three squashed prunes in the neck of the first shofar? . . . Yeah, yeah. That's how far it had got . . .'.

Rozenfeld evidently felt the need to bolster the image with its 'authentic' hasidic folkloric variant. But he also offered a rational (and humorous) afterword to the story that defeats the concept of the hasidic miracle. After all, this was an allegedly secular satirical journal. To print a hasidic *mayse* without a secular punchline would have been sacrilege to the gods of humour.

The cartoon is an example of how traditional Jewish folklore, even that which reached back to ancient times, was able to serve a newly modern, often secular Jewry. Whether a majority of the readers of this 1923 cartoon was actually aware of the folk origins on which the humour is based is unknown. One imagines that knowledge of such folklore was duly pervasive, even among secular Jews. If readers were not familiar with the folklore, the 'hasidic' story below the image served to inform them of it.

Another popular image common to the high holidays was that of *shlogn kapores* (Hebrew: *kaparot*). This ritual, performed by men and women on the eve of Yom Kippur, in which a rooster (for the man) or a hen (for the woman) was waved above the head of the supplicant and then killed in order to expiate his or her sins, had received only ambivalent support from rabbinic authorities. It was, however, deeply ingrained in folk culture and commonly practised. The ritual is at least 1,000 years old and mentioned in ninth-century geonic sources.[47] In spite of numerous injunctions against it by an array of rabbinic luminaries, such as Moshe ben Nahman (Ramban) and Joseph Caro, who opposed the practice as superstitious, others, most notably the kabbalist Isaac Luria and the Kraków rabbi Moses Isserles (Remu), promoted it as an integral part of the Yom Kippur ritual. By the late nineteenth century *shlogn kapores* was a familiar sight on the eve of Yom Kippur throughout

---

[46] Trachtenberg, *Jewish Magic and Superstition*, 113. Trachtenberg also includes a report from 18th-century Frankfurt that, when a shofar does not function, it is the result of Satan sitting in the horn. For a similar report, see Y. H. Zehavi, 'Rosh-hashone folklor', *Der moment*, no. 216 (14 Sept. 1928), 11.

[47] J. Z. Lauterbach, 'The Ritual for the Kapparot-Ceremony', in S. Baron (ed.), *Jewish Studies in Memory of George Kohut* (New York, 1935), 414.

east European Jewish communities. It was portrayed by artists such as Hermann Junker, whose painting was reproduced as a postcard, an indication that the ritual was extremely well known.[48]

In 1913 the satirist Yoysef Tunkel exploited the image of *shlogn kapores* as a basis for commenting on the furious verbal brawl that was taking place in Warsaw's daily press between *Haynt*'s editor, Shmuel Yatskan, and the columnist Hillel Tseytlin (Zeitlin) of *Der moment*. Appearing on the cover of his one-time Rosh Hashanah journal *Kapores*, the drawing (Fig. 2), possibly one of the crudest ever to appear in the Yiddish press, seems appropriate to the atmosphere created by the mud-slinging writers. Drawn by Tunkel, it shows Yatskan performing *kapores* with a rooster on which Tseytlin's head has been drawn. The rooster, or Tseytlin, wreaks his revenge on Yatskan by defecating on him. The caption reads, 'Did you ever see such a rooster? I tried to *shlog kapores* with him and he goes and pulls this trick on me . . .'.

The story behind this cartoon image has its origins three years earlier, in November 1910, when Tseytlin, a popular columnist then at Yatskan's newspaper, *Haynt*, decided to move his column to the newly established daily *Der moment*, a decision that created a great deal of animosity between the two men. In addition, the two papers were in direct and often fierce competition with each another. This resulted in frequent accusations and sniping in polemical articles in both papers.

By late summer of 1913 Tseytlin, a secular intellectual who had 'returned' to traditional Judaism, became the centre of this increasingly heated press rivalry when he was attacked by the normally reserved daily *Der fraynd*. The first Yiddish daily in the Russian empire (it began publication in 1903), *Der fraynd* had been losing circulation to the newer, more sensationalist papers. The editor, Shmuel Rozenfeld, writing under his pseudonym 'R', lambasted Tseytlin for the latter's frequent polemical and critical attacks on other Yiddish writers. Tseytlin was also attacked for hypocrisy and accused of writing on the sabbath and eating pork on Yom Kippur. Coming from the editor of the secular *Der fraynd*, the accusations were difficult to believe. In fact, the overblown rhetoric of *Der fraynd* was probably a last-ditch effort to raise circulation. If that was the case, it didn't work, since the paper went out of business shortly thereafter. *Haynt* quickly picked up the mantle from *Der fraynd*; articles attacking Tseytlin began to appear ever more frequently. Pouring fuel on the fire, this time with an eyewitness, a report appeared in *Haynt* in which a correspondent from Pinsk reported that Tseytlin had been seen in a railway station restaurant eating pork.[49] Somehow this 'eyewitness' report seemed more

---

[48] See S. Sabar, 'Between Poland and Germany', in this volume.

[49] There is confusion regarding the dates and places of this affair in the memoir literature. According to Finkelshteyn (*Haynt: a tsaytung ba yidn*, 160), the event occurred in late 1910. In his article '*Der moment*', in *Fun noentn over* (New York, 1956), 248, Mendl Mozes writes that the correspondent was from Białystok. The original 'report', signed by Yokhenen Fridland, appeared in *Haynt*, no. 201 (11 Sept. 1913), 4.

Fig. 2. *Kapores* (1913), cover, drawn by Der Tunkeler (Yoysef Tunkel)

believable than Rozenfeld's initial foray. As such, it was a serious accusation about an observant writer who was seen as a hero by many traditional Jews. It created much turmoil among Tseytlin's readers, particularly in the provinces. Further articles accused him of hypocrisy in maintaining a façade of religiosity while promoting adherence to religious obligations.[50] Articles attacking Yatskan and Rozenfeld began to appear in *Der moment*, in addition to hundreds of letters and thousands

---

[50] See e.g. R [Shmuel Rozenfeld], 'Arop di maske!', *Der fraynd*, no. 188 (28 Aug. 1913), 2.

of signatures in support of Tseytlin. The controversy became so vociferous and rancorous that even the Polish press began to write about it. It was at that point that many felt the affair was becoming an embarrassment to the Jewish community, and arbitration between the two parties was attempted, mediated by the Zionist leaders Yitskhok Grinboym and Heshl Farbshteyn. To no avail: the two papers continued to snipe at each other. Only when the Beilis blood libel trial began in October 1913 did the rhetoric begin to recede.[51]

Tseytlin's alleged hypocrisy, his constant polemicizing against the secular, as well as his appearance, with a head of long, bushy hair and a wild, unkempt beard, contributed to his being a controversial figure and made him a frequent target for caricature. This, therefore, was not the first time that he had been lampooned. Although Tunkel was employed at *Der moment*, in his cartoon he does not appear to take sides in the matter. He does, however, call it as he sees it: an exceptionally vulgar affair. He uses the Tseytlin affair as a launch pad for commentary on how common invective was in Jewish press culture. The feud between the two writers was such a popular theme that 10,000 copies of *Kapores* were published, a significantly higher number than the usual 1,000 to 2,000 print run of the average one-time publication of preceding years.[52]

HANUKAH

There is no question that the foremost symbol of Hanukah is the menorah. One cartoon, drawn by Leyb Brodaty, is entitled *Undzere khaneke likhtlekh* ('Our Little Hanukah Lights') (Fig. 3), and appeared on the cover of the one-time journal *Khaneke-gelt* ('Hanukah Money') in December 1910. It features the most celebrated writers and critics of modern Yiddish literature as the 'lights' of the menorah. These writers include Y. L. Peretz, Sholem Asch, Hirsh Dovid Nomberg, A. Mukdoyni, Mordkhe Spektor, David Frishman,[53] Hillel Tseytlin, and, apparently, though the text is illegible, S. An-ski. On the surface, it would seem, the cartoon's intention was to lionize these artists as the beacons of a modern Jewish culture. But this is not the case. Instead, the image juxtaposes the notion that these writers were the 'brightest lights' of modern Yiddish literature and the folk insult 'You should be like a lamp, burning all night and snuffed out in the morning'. The traditionally garbed Jew to the right of the menorah cocks his thumb at the writers as if to comment ironically, 'So these are the best and brightest we've got?' The cocked thumb also recalls the emphatic gesture that accompanies a talmudic argument.

[51] Mozes, '*Der moment*', 249.

[52] Kirzhnits, *Di yidishe prese*, 110. The average print run for similar journals of the same year was 5,000.

[53] The token Hebrew writer, though Frishman also published in the Yiddish press and, of course, writers such as Peretz and Tseytlin published in Hebrew.

This argument, essentially that modern Yiddish culture literally cannot hold a candle to traditional Jewish culture, is made explicit in the poem below the image.

> What kind of new Hanukah lamp is this?
> What kind of candles are these? What kind of fire?
> How weak and foreign their shine?
> For them I should make a blessing, you say,
> To recall the heroism and wonder of the past,
> And they should be holy to me! . . .
>
> These measly candles—they should replace
> That once holy fire, the light of ancient times,
> That lit our way,
> That comforted me and gave me strength
> And kindled hope and yearning in my heart
> For better, happier days.
>
> No, little flames, your shine is for naught,
> Your winding, jumping, and dancing, for nothing—
> I know you and I know your strength!
> It won't be you in this dark, burdensome exile,
> You won't light our way,
> You will not light up my night! . . .

The lights of the Hanukah menorah provided a useful metaphor for derisive commentary on some of the foremost creators of modern Jewish literature, who by the time this journal appeared, in 1910, had attained celebrity status in the Yiddish-speaking community. The belletristic and essayistic works they published, primarily in the Yiddish press, shaped the new Jewish national culture that emerged after the 1905 revolution, and posited them as the de facto leaders of that culture, particularly in light of the increase in Jewish secularism. An important element of the Jewish secularism reflected in this cartoon is the creation and recognition of modern Jewish celebrity. There is little question that a person must be of some significance if he or she is caricatured; hence, the caricature, even if it denigrates, serves as a sort of backhanded compliment. With the concept of celebrity in mind, it is notable that there is no *shames* (principal candle) on this menorah. All egos, they are all *shamosim*—a pointed reference to their ultimate failure as leaders of the new Jewish culture.

What is fascinating about this particular cartoon and the accompanying poem is its heavy, even overbearing, emphasis on the superiority of traditional religious culture. The attack on modern Yiddish literature as being unable to serve the Jews as cultural sustenance is an interesting and ironic point, since the use by the anonymous author (probably Tunkel) of a modern visual semiotic that includes caricatured images, not only of well-known Jewish writers but also one representing traditional Jewry, betrays both its medium and its message. The cartoonist wrangles with the possibilities for modern expression in Yiddish and concludes that it is futile, although he himself utilizes a thoroughly modern vehicle, a mass-medium

Fig. 3. *Undzere khaneke likhtlekh* ('Our Little Hanukah Lights'), drawn by Leyb Brodaty. *Khaneke-gelt* (December 1910)

illustrated satirical journal. This represents, on a small scale, the negotiations Jews made and attempted to make while struggling to reconcile tradition and modernity. The contradiction within the cartoon reveals the importance of the role of traditional Judaism, even in the new secular Jewish world. It is as if it is saying that, without the basis, without the grounding in an all-encompassing traditional Jewish culture, secularism is a meaningless endeavour. As such, the cartoon reflects the conflict between traditional content and modern expression within Jewish culture: it is the modern sensibility of publicistic caricature in a mass medium grafted onto Jewish tradition, clearly a troubling issue for the producers of such conflicted works.

PASSOVER

As noted, more one-time satirical journals appeared during Passover than at any other time of year. Of all Jewish religious texts, none has been parodied more than the Passover Haggadah, beginning as early as the thirteenth century.[54] Its

[54] I. Davidson, *Parody in Jewish Literature* (New York, 1907), 16–17.

popularity, familiarity, and fixed structure allowed for easy substitution of words or sections, and it became a mainstay of Jewish parodic literature.

Unlike other Jewish ritual texts, the Haggadah typically contains illustrations. These illustrations, which appear both in medieval illuminated manuscripts and in the popular booklets of the modern era, provided a basis for cartoonists to parody. The most common visual parody that appeared in the one-time Passover journals was that of the four sons (*arbo bonim*). In the Haggadah these sons—the wise, the wicked, the simple, and the one so ignorant as to be unable even to ask a question—represent four approaches to asking about the story of the Exodus. In cartoons the sons provided an excellent structure for satirists to mock a selection of politicians, actors, writers, and other public figures.

In *Der afikoymen*,[55] a Passover journal published by *Haynt* in 1925, the four sons are transmogrified into cartoon caricatures of Warsaw's Jewish daily newspapers (Fig. 4). Ostensibly about the founding of the Hebrew University in Jerusalem, this unsigned rendering brings in a number of issues unrelated to that event. At the time the founding of the Hebrew University was a major Jewish press event and had received a great deal of attention in the Warsaw Yiddish- and Polish-language Jewish press. Under the question 'What do our four sons say about the university in Jerusalem?' the sons appear with newspapers as bodies. The wise son, on the right, portrayed by *Haynt*, is a rotund, self-satisfied Jew in a bowler hat. This reflects *Haynt*'s position as the most successful daily, less worried about competition or influence. Referring to the other papers, he says, '*Nu*, who's still the wise one—me or them?' The caption, playing on the importance of the founding of the Hebrew University, confirms *Haynt*'s support for Zionism, especially during the founding of a Jewish university in Jerusalem. Next to him stands the wicked son, the Bundist *Folkstsaytung*, depicted as a skinny and hatless character with a thin moustache and a scowl, offering his comments in Soviet-style orthography, incorrect though it may be, to indicate the Bund's anti-Hebrew stance.[56] He says, 'University, shmuniversity. *Zi ligt undz in der linker peye* ('We care about it as much as our left sidelock [a traditional idiom and image here entirely misplaced]'). Come to our meeting this Saturday.' The words play on the Bund's anti-Zionism, as well as its willingness to hold meetings on the sabbath in order to spite religious tradition. The simple son is the second most popular Yiddish daily, *Der moment*, portrayed as a thin, yet sturdy, bearded Jew in boots and the cap typically worn by Gerer hasidim. The latter, who wielded great political influence as a solid Orthodox block of voters, tended to read *Der moment* rather than *Haynt*, mainly because they were opposed to *Haynt*'s strident Zionism. Also suggested in the image of the thin, threadbare, traditional Jew is *Der moment*'s links to the nationalist but anti-socialist

[55] Refers to the piece of matzah whose eating concludes the Passover *seder*. Traditionally it is hidden by the adults, then searched for by the children, who 'sell' it back to the adults.

[56] Yiddish orthography in the Soviet Union was 'proletarianized' to rid it of its Hebrew component and spell all words phonetically; this practice was institutionalized in the 1930s.

Fig. 4. *Vos zogn undzere arbo bonim tsum yerusholayimer universitet?* ('What do our Four Sons Say about the University in Jerusalem?'), unsigned. *Der afikoymen* (April 1925)

Folks-partey, which appealed to the Jewish lower-middle class. He says, '*Mekhteyse* [be my guest]. There should be a Hebrew University too', suggesting that *Der moment* is hardly against such 'national' accomplishments, though its main focus is the Diaspora. Both *Der moment* and *Folkstsaytung* look askance at *Haynt*, an indication of their jealousy of the leading paper's success. The son who is unable to ask a question is the Polish-language daily *Nasz Przegląd*, who appears as a clean-shaven, thin man, with an odd look on his face and wearing plaid trousers. Depicted as an assimilated bourgeois imbecile dressed in caricatured Polish fashion, he says, in transliterated Polish, 'All right! Let's do university! There will be photos of it in our illustrated supplement.' *Nasz Przegląd*'s popular weekly supplement published a multitude of photographs with little text. Here the cartoonist pokes fun at the importance of the supplement at the expense of real news, at the paper's ignorance of events in the Jewish world, and at its eagerness to publicize whatever it happens to stumble across.[57]

[57] See M. Steinlauf, 'The Polish Jewish Daily Press', in A. Polonsky (ed.), *From Shtetl to Socialism: Studies from Polin* (London, 1993), 346.

As is evident, it was with great ease that Yiddish parodists connected the four sons of the Haggadah to the metaphor of the four sons of the Warsaw Jewish press, and inserted the news of the day into one small segment of the Haggadah structure in order to create multi-level social commentary on issues ranging from the original story—the founding of the Hebrew University—to local newspaper competition, Jewish socialist culture, and assimilation. The incongruity of seeing the traditional four sons portrayed as Warsaw's top daily newspapers furthers the humour by attributing varying levels of intra-ethnic attire to the papers as well as their readers. This superficially simple rendering of the four sons suggests the complexity, diversity, and fractiousness of inter-war Polish Jewish life.

SHAVUOT

Shavuot was second only to Passover in the number of satirical publications it inspired; Purim was third. All three major holidays take place in the latter half of the Jewish ritual year, during spring or its approach. Purim is specifically associated with parody and merry-making; the Passover *seder* is a particularly popular observance; and Shavuot, associated with the giving of the Torah, occurs in a joyous atmosphere. The symbolism of all three seems to lend itself more easily to parody, both visual and textual, than that of the other holidays.

The two main symbols of Shavuot are green plants, a gesture to its connection with spring, and images of the Torah. Both were exploited in the holiday *jedno-dniówki*. Above all, however, the image of the tablets of the Ten Commandments provided grist for the parodists' mill during this time of year. This image was common, of course, not only to Jews, but to the whole of European culture, east and west.[58] It figured prominently in the Christian artistic tradition and can be found in every graphic rendering of biblical events, most notably the engravings of Doré. In Jewish iconography the tablets are extremely prevalent, frequently found on the title-pages of books and often crowning synagogue arks. The ubiquity of the tablets was due not only to their importance in Jewish tradition, but to the fact that they did not involve a human figure. They were therefore an easy and useful format for cartoon parody, both Jewish and non-Jewish.[59] What differed in the Jewish use of the image was the fact that it appeared only at a specific time of year—in journals that were published around the time of Shavuot.

In the satirical journals the tablets often appeared with someone holding them, mimicking the traditional image of Moses on Mount Sinai. The parodies included,

---

[58] For examples of the frequent use of the Ten Commandments tablets as political metaphor in post-revolutionary French art and caricature, see J. Ribner, *Broken Tablets: The Cult of the Law in French Art from David to Delacroix* (Berkeley, 1993).

[59] They even appeared locally in the antisemitic and reactionary daily *Novoe vremya* in 1906 as a comment on British imperial arrogance in a cartoon entitled 'The New Moses'; repr. in R. Douglass, *Great Nations Still Enchained* (London, 1993), 169.

Fig. 5. *Di nayste eseres-adabres (fun an endek)* ('The Latest Ten Commandments (of an Endek)')
by Shaye Faygenboym. *Der nayer mekhabl* (13 June 1919)

among others, the ten commandments of modern women and the ten commandments of summer vacations. A cartoon drawn by Shaye Faygenboym and published
in the *Der nayer mekhabl* ('The New Destroyer') on 13 June 1919 is an example of
the exploitation of the tablets for political parody (Fig. 5). It is of particular interest
because of its focus on Polish–Jewish relations. Entitled *Di nayste eseres-adabres (fun
an endek)* ('The Latest Ten Commandments (of an Endek)'), it shows a Pole with the
ubiquitous moustache favoured by the Polish gentry, wearing the four-cornered
konfederatka hat. The hat implies that he is a Polish nationalist, or, in this case, a
supporter of the Endecja (National Democratic Party), the primary nationalist
and antisemitic political party, who, as Brian Porter has written, 'were brutal antisemites with a hateful, violent rhetoric'.[60] The cartoon was published on the heels
of reaction to the Paris peace conference in early 1919, at which the Allies demanded

---

[60] B. Porter, 'Social Darwinism without Empiricism, Romanticism without Ethics: Polish National
Democracy and the Concept of the "The Nation", 1863–1905', University of Wisconsin Ph.D. thesis,
1994, 900–1.

that minority rights be protected in Poland as well as other successor states, as well as after eight months of rising antisemitism including pogroms and other violence against Jews in Poland.[61] The tablets held by the Endek read as follows:

> You may not travel on any train.
>
> You may not have a beard.
>
> You may not go on any pedestrian crossing.
>
> You may not speak jargon [Yiddish].
>
> You may not demand any rights.
>
> You will allow pogroms to be made on you.
>
> Do not protest abroad.
>
> Do not request any commissions.
>
> You may not vote for Prilutski.

Most of these 'commandments' do not require an explanation. They can be viewed as versions of Endek ideology writ absurdly into law.[62] 'You will allow pogroms to be made on you' reflects the popular belief that the Endecja was behind the pogroms of 1918–19. The Yiddish press reported on articles in the Polish nationalist press that were allegedly responsible for aggravating Polish–Jewish relations and fomenting pogroms. The commandments regarding not travelling on trains, using pedestrian crossings, and wearing beards are connected to anti-Jewish violence particularly committed by Polish troops commanded by General Józef Haller.[63] Traditionally dressed Jews were particular targets of attack; they were thrown out of moving trains and their beards were cut off. After pogroms in late 1918 Jews requested the United States Department of State to set up a commission of investigation. The Endecja consistently denied that any pogroms had taken place and heatedly opposed foreign commissions of inquiry in Poland. The references to 'not request[ing] any commissions' and 'not protest[ing] abroad' refer to these matters.

With the exception of a small group of assimilationists, the secular Jewish political parties all fought for minority and cultural rights, hence the commandment 'You may not demand any rights'. When this cartoon was published, the minority rights portion of the Versailles Treaty was causing much consternation in parliament. In spite of considerable opposition, the Poles had little choice but to sign the

[61] See I. Lewin, *A History of Polish Jewry during the Revival of Poland* (New York, 1990), 57–60, 171–5.

[62] While the Jews did indeed fear the Endecja as a political and cultural force, it did not stop the nine Jewish deputies in parliament from acting as a swing bloc and electing the Endek Trąmpczyński as speaker of the house in 1919. They argued that he was the least antisemitic of the fielded candidates (see Lewin, *A History of Polish Jewry*, 102–3).

[63] J. Tomaszewski, 'Polish Society through Jewish Eyes', in R. Scharf (ed.), *The Jews in Poland*, vol. i (Kraków, 1992), 409; see also Lewin, *A History of Polish Jewry*, 156–7.

treaty, which was ratified, with the minority rights segment intact, at the end of June 1919.[64] 'You may not vote for Prilutski' refers to Noyekh Prilutski, the leader of the Folks-partey and one of the most popular Jewish politicians in Poland at this time. Prilutski incurred the wrath of the Endecja for his staunch advocacy of Jewish minority rights in numerous speeches in parliament.

CONCLUSION

In a way, it seems strange to spend so much time researching and interpreting events that Jewish newspaper readers of the day understood immediately. Yet this is our only entry into ephemeral materials that have been overlooked as inconsequential both by their contemporaries and by subsequent historians. While they were taken for granted, the cartoons were hardly unnoticed in their time. Indeed, they were an essential part of the cultural landscape of Jewish Poland. Cartoons that appeared on magazine covers were undoubtedly displayed at news-stands throughout Jewish neighbourhoods. Individual issues of the satirical journals were passed from hand to hand. There is no dispute about their popularity; as early as 1909 in Łódź a play by Yitskhok Katsenelson entitled *Karikaturn* featured a *Gymnasium* student whose library consisted exclusively of satirical journals.[65]

Moreover, as Marian Fuks has rightly noted, the Yiddish satirical press has great value as a historical source, reflecting the wide variety of social, moral, and political issues that affected the daily lives of Polish Jews.[66] Central to these journals and their cartoons, as we have seen, was a powerful bond to traditional Jewish culture. The ubiquity of references to traditional texts and customs points to the complexity of Jewish experience during this period: one may have lived a thoroughly 'modern' life, but one's roots still extended powerfully into the traditional past. Beyond our simplistic polarities of 'secular' versus 'traditional', these forgotten Jewish cartoons hint at a far more complex—and interesting—world than the materials hitherto at our disposal have allowed us to imagine.

[64] Lewin, *A History of Polish Jewry*, 207–9; R. Watt, *Bitter Glory: Poland and its Fate: 1918–1939* (New York, 1979), 359.

[65] Published in Warsaw in 1909, Katsenelson's play was performed by the Lodzer Fareynikter Trupe (Łódź United Troupe) in 1910.

[66] Fuks, 'Żydowska prasa humorystyczno-satyryczna', 31.

From 'Madagaskar' to Sachsenhausen: Singing about 'Race' in a Nazi Camp

BRET WERB and BARBARA MILEWSKI

AMONG the many remarkable cultural artefacts to come to light after the Second World War is a large and varied repertoire of songs created by Polish prisoners in Nazi concentration camps. Most common of these compositions are parodies of songs popular before the war.[1] The prevalence of this genre in the camps (as elsewhere) may be accounted for by the fact that parody is one of the easiest of processes for generating a new work, requiring only that the author add newly minted lyrics to a pre-existent melody. But while the formula of invention for parody song is fairly straightforward, its psychological effect on a knowing listener can be rather more complex. Indeed, one can hardly imagine the resonance of such music heard in the setting of a concentration camp. Drawing on well-known melodies and familiar styles such as the tango, waltz, or foxtrot, prisoners who listened to, created, and performed these songs could reclaim, if only for a moment, some part of their lost popular culture. Yet paradoxically, and as many survivors attest, these same songs, with their unsparing depictions of camp life, helped prisoners push aside thoughts of life before captivity and so preserve their mental balance during those difficult years.[2]

A shorter version of this chapter was presented at the 1997 meeting of the International Musicological Society in London. The authors are grateful to Leon Tadeusz Błaszczyk, Tomasz Lerski, Jacek Nowakowski, and Robert Rothstein for generously offering their knowledge of popular musical culture in inter-war Poland, and to Robert Kuwałek for his help in trying to secure Polish sources relevant to this study.

[1] In musicological parlance this sense of 'parody' is termed *contrafactum*, defined as 'replacement of the text with or (more often) without the implication of caricature' (W. Apel, *Harvard Dictionary of Music*, 2nd edn. (Cambridge, Mass., 1969), 203).

[2] Cf. A. Kulisiewicz, 'Polish Camp Songs, 1939–1945', trans. R. Hirsch, *Modern Language Studies*, 26/1 (Winter 1986), 3–9: 'Creating the songs permitted the composers to defy the terrible fate confronting them and it gave them the will to struggle to survive and the patience to wait for the day that vengeance would be theirs. . . . Occasionally listeners would pay serious attention to the songs, and what would always be most important at such a time was the content of the song. . . . Powerful and regenerative, the camp songs provided the prisoners with a means of psychological resistance, and kept them from falling into complete despair and resignation, and from committing suicide by flinging themselves on the electrically charged wire.' Kulisiewicz also cites fellow survivor Adolf Gawalewicz's study *Refleksje z poczekalni do gazu: Ze wspomnień Muzułmana* (Kraków, 1968) in which Gawalewicz

In this chapter we look at one parody song, 'Heil, Sachsenhausen', and also examine the song parodied, 'Madagaskar', itself a satirical consideration of the Jewish predicament in inter-war Poland. We speculate that 'Heil, Sachsenhausen' served not only as a narrative of camp experience, but also as a darkly comic condemnation of Nazi 'racial purity' laws. Finally, we suggest that this parody song may have functioned as a zone of inquiry for the author's personal reflections on German–Polish and Polish–Jewish relations before and during the Second World War.

*

'Heil, Sachsenhausen' was written by a Polish political prisoner, Aleksander Kulisiewicz, in the concentration camp Sachsenhausen in 1943. A journalist by profession, Kulisiewicz, born in Kraków in 1918, had been denounced for anti-fascist writings and was arrested soon after the German takeover of Poland. Sent to Sachsenhausen, near Berlin, he wrote by his own tally fifty-four songs over the course of nearly six years at the camp. He was liberated in May 1945 and devoted most of the rest of his life to gathering and documenting the songs and music created in concentration camps.[3] After his death in 1982 the Kulisiewicz Collection was acquired by the archives of the United States Holocaust Memorial Museum in Washington.[4]

Kulisiewicz's own songs were written in response to personal and communal experiences within Sachsenhausen, or were motivated by news from the outside world that had filtered into the camp. A local tragedy was the immediate inspiration for 'Heil, Sachsenhausen'. In his commentary to this song Kulisiewicz informs us that the event in question took place in July 1943 in the Sachsenhausen subcamp of Oranienburg, where Franz Zahn, director of the camp motor pool, had been caught forwarding letters from a Polish prisoner, Jan Kobiela. Zahn, a civilian, was arrested and sent to the camp *Strafkompanie*, the prison within the prison. Further investigations by the Gestapo incriminated Zahn's 15-year-old daughter, Eliza, as the party who had actually posted the letters and who (the story goes) was in love with

states: 'An important purpose of the camp songs, little understood, and therefore condemned by outsiders, was to convert the macabre into the frivolous. The frivolous and even obscene treatment of the macabre realities that undermined the psyche of the prisoner helped to strengthen the prisoner's will, to preserve his psychological stability, and to maintain his will to survive.'

[3] A. Kulisiewicz, 'Jak umierał mój głos' ('How My Voice Died'), US Holocaust Memorial Museum, Washington, RG-55.001.02.

[4] The Kulisiewicz Collection is, by any measure, a work of encyclopaedic proportions. Fifty-five feet of archival material consisting of annotated song texts, music notation, poetry, original artwork, photographic material, and scripts for puppet plays, it also includes cassette and reel-to-reel tape recordings of interviews with fellow survivors concerning music in the camps, as well as songs performed by survivors who either composed these musical creations or sang them during imprisonment. Some 500 songs that represent the musical activity of thirty-six different camps make up the bulk of the collection. Despite the fact that it touches on a variety of issues relevant not only to music scholarship but also to contemporary European history, the Kulisiewicz Collection still remains little known among scholars.

Kobiela. Suspected of having had 'more intimate contacts' (*bliższe intymne kontakty*) with Poles, Eliza was interrogated and tortured, and died soon afterwards under mysterious circumstances. Kulisiewicz speculates that she may have committed suicide in the camp. Franz Zahn survived until 1945, when he was shot by German soldiers during the evacuation of Sachsenhausen camp.[5]

Kulisiewicz called 'Heil, Sachsenhausen' an 'odd' (*dziwaczna*) song, noting that it protested, among other things, *Rassenschande* (race defilement), an ambiguous concept which in Germany, for practical purposes, referred to sexual relations between Germans and Jews, illegal after 1935.[6] Marriage between German and Slavonic nationals, however, had also been prohibited in the Third Reich on the principle that such liaisons would lead to the diminution of 'pure' Aryan stock.[7] Further decrees enacted during the war outlawed sexual relations between Germans and (primarily Slavonic) prisoners of war, the offenders being subject to quite stringent penalties.[8] Whether Eliza Zahn was, in fact, tried for 'race defilement' remains unclear. To the Gestapo and camp command, the act of abetting a prisoner to communicate illegally with outsiders may, in fact, have been considered the more serious crime. But to Kulisiewicz the charge was *Rassenschande*, and the incident provoked him to create 'Heil, Sachsenhausen', a model send-up of many assumptions dear to the Nazi German world-view:

Heil, Sachsenhausen

Jestem sobie na wpół dziki,	I'm a half-wild savage, you know,
Scheissen-Poluś, cham.	A shit-caked, Polish clod.
Und warum denn do Afryki?	Why then sail off to Africa?
Tu kolonię mam!	I have a colony right here!
Kupili cię, chłopie,	They bought you like a slave, boy,
Kupili z gnatami—	Bought you—lock, stock, and barrel.
Krew ci z mordy kapie,	Blood drips from your mug, and
Alles scheiss-egal!	Everything is equal crap!

[5] A. Kulisiewicz, 'Polskie pieśni obozowe 1939–1945', US Holocaust Memorial Museum, Washington, Music Collection, unpub. typescript, pp. 1688–95. Regarding the subject of 'Heil, Sachsenhausen', Kulisiewicz also includes the following information: 'The song was created in the *Schuhfabrik* at the end of July, 1943. . . . [It] was introduced, among other places, in block 33, where it received great applause for its exotic rhythm from the "audience". The song was sung with guitar accompaniment.' Cf. also Peter Wortsman's notes to Kulisiewicz's recording of 'Heil, Sachsenhausen', on *Songs from the Depths of Hell* (Folkways FSS 37700).

[6] Kulisiewicz, 'Polskie pieśni obozowe', 1691. For a helpful discussion of *Rassenschande*, see 'Racial Infamy', in C. Zentner and F. Bedürftig (eds.), *Encyclopedia of the Third Reich* (New York, 1991), 748. On the Nuremberg laws and their implementation, see J. Noakes and G. Pridham (eds.), *Nazism 1919–1939*, vol. i (New York, 1984), 535 ff.

[7] For information on Nazi policy regarding intermarriage, see minister of the interior Wilhelm Frick's, instructions to marriage registry officials, in *In Pursuit of Justice: Examining the Evidence of the Holocaust* (Washington, [1997]), 40–1.

[8] J. Noakes, *Nazism 1919–1945*, vol. iv (Exeter, 1998), 384–5.

Aj, Sachsenhausen!	Oh, Sachsenhausen!
Kolonia gwarna, parna—	Loud and sweltering, melting—
Germania *richtig* dzika . . .	A Germany that's *truly* wild!
Heil, Sachsenhausen!	*Heil*, Sachsenhausen!
Giry tycie jak bambusik,	Our legs are thin as bamboo shoots,
Trupie łebki, to kaktusy.	The 'death's heads' look like cactuses.
Heil! Es lebe Kulturkampf!	*Heil !* And long live *Kulturkampf!*
Mädchen sobie zafunduję,	I'll treat myself to a nice German girl,
Polaczysko ja . . .	Crummy Pole that I am . . .
Gibt's denn so was? . . . wy bestyje!	Imagine the nerve of the brute!
Śliczne oczka ma.	She has such lovely eyes.
A z tej *Mädchen*-matki	She, the sweet young mummy,
I z durnego tatki	Me, the stupid daddy,
Będą *Kindchen* w kratki:	We'll make a few striped babies—
Schwarz und weiss und rot . . .	Black and white and red . . .
Aj, Sachsenhausen!	Oh, Sachsenhausen!
Błogosławiony raju—	Heavenly paradise you are,
Wszak wielbi ciebie ludzkość . . .	Why, humanity adores you . . .
Heil, Sachsenhausen!	*Heil*, Sachsenhausen!
A jak będę jutro zdychać,	And if, tomorrow, I should croak,
Lewą nóżką ci zafikam:	With my left leg I'll drum for you:
Heil! Es lebe Kulturkampf!	*Heil!* And long live *Kulturkampf!* [9]

'Heil, Sachsenhausen', then, was a veiled retelling of a particular camp narrative. It was also a denunciation of German nationalist and racialist theories, the consequences of which Kulisiewicz found disturbing enough to risk commemorating in song. (According to the author, prisoners caught performing such 'dangerous' material were subject to torture or even execution.) By exploiting the layered medium of parody, 'Heil, Sachsenhausen' also functioned as a place of psychological retreat where the author could evaluate his situation as a prisoner, as a Pole, as a human being. In order to appreciate more fully this aspect of 'Heil, Sachsenhausen', we must turn to the song on which it is based, 'Madagaskar', a *szmonces* (Jewish-themed) entertainment written by Mieczysław Miksne for the cabaret artist Bolesław Norski-Nożyca.[10]

[9] Text and music are provided in Kulisiewicz, 'Polskie pieśni obozowe', 1688–9, Notation Notebook VII (31–2), unpaginated. All Polish translations are our own unless otherwise indicated.

[10] On *szmonces*, see M. Steinlauf, 'Polish-Jewish Theater: The Case of Mark Arnshteyn. A Study of the Interplay among Yiddish, Polish and Polish-Language Jewish Culture in the Modern Period', Brandeis University Ph.D. thesis, 1987, 258–61. Steinlauf defines *szmonces* as a 'Jewish joke, monologue or sketch inevitably characterized by a more or less subtle *żydłaczenie* [Yiddish-inflected Polish] of speech and gesture', and cites cabaret historian Ryszard Groński's depiction of the genre as having become, for the urban Jewish public in the 1930s, 'the universal method of reporting about everyday life'. The *szmonces* genre awaits its scholars. While lamenting the near universal absence of information on this topic and acknowledging our own failed attempts to turn up relevant archival material, we echo Steinlauf's assessment that research into *szmonces* will 'doubtless prove quite rewarding' ('Mr Geldhab and Sambo in *Peyes*: Images of the Jew on the Polish Stage, 1863–1905', *Polin*, 4 (1989), 128 n. 97).

Fig. 1. 'Heil, Sachsenhausen!' Source: A. Kulisiewicz, 'Polskie pieśni obozowe: 1939–1945', Notation Notebook VII (32), US Holocaust Memorial Museum, Music Collection, unpub. typescript, unpaginated. Score notated by A. Kulisiewicz with corrections in the author's hand

'Madagaskar' was conceived in 1937 or 1938 as a satiric response to a plan to resettle the Jews of Poland on the French island colony off the east coast of Africa.[11] This scheme did not originate in Poland; it had first been advanced by British and Dutch antisemites, who saw in it a remedy for every misfortune antisemites traditionally ascribe to the presence of Jews. But Poland's Sanacja regime was

[11] Norski-Nożyca's recording (with orchestral accompaniment) on the Syrena record label dates from 1938. No copy, however, is known to have survived. The authors are very grateful to Tomasz Lerski of Warsaw for providing biographical and discographical information included in his forthcoming monograph, *Syrena Record: Pierwsza polska wytwórnia fonograficzna 1904–1939*.

Fig. 2. 'In the Green Room of Café Esplanade Sienkiewiczall. Today and every day. Splendid political satire entitled "We're off to Madagascar . . . or, A Gay Voyage to the Promised Land"). Written by Roman Dobrzyński. Puppets by S. Tabak. [Cast.] Departure from the port at the Esplanade every day at 7.30 and 9.15. Ship ticket including food, 2.25 zlotys.' Advertisement in *Nasz Przegląd* (5 Mar. 1938), 1

the first national government to take the proposal seriously (anticipating Hitler's own Madagascar plan by about two years), and in 1937 it dispatched a delegation on a fact-finding mission to the island. On its return this committee—two of whose members were Jews—reported to Warsaw its finding that the resettlement scheme was essentially unworkable.[12]

Meanwhile, the satirist Miksne lampooned this grotesque proposal—and the mindset behind it—in his topical song. Indeed, he was not alone in doing so. As early as May 1937 the Polish Jewish daily *Nasz Przegląd* began publishing humorous commentaries (as well as straight reportage) concerning the resettlement scheme. By March 1938 the paper was running advertisements promoting 'a splendid political satire' (*kapitalna szopka polityczna*) at the Kawiarnia 'Esplanada' (Esplanade Café) entitled *Jedziemy na Madagaskar . . .* ('We're off to Madagascar . . .').[13]

While this chapter is no place to review the history of Polish–Jewish relations, some small background information may be in order. The question 'Who is a Pole?' concerned many in newly independent Poland, a country possessed of substantial territories formerly controlled by imperial Germany, Austria, and Russia, now bor-

---

[12] L. Yahil, 'Madagascar Plan', *Encyclopedia Judaica*, vol. xi (Jerusalem, 1972), cols. 678–9.
[13] For other Madagascar-related items published in *Nasz Przegląd*, see e.g. (28 May 1937), 5; (1 Mar. 1938), 8; (2 Mar. 1938), 9; (5 Mar. 1938), 6; (10 Mar. 1938), 13; (29 Mar. 1938), 8.

dered west and east by these same nations incarnated as powerful, belligerent dictatorships. Furthermore, and underlying any reasonable anxieties about nationality, was the age-old Polish obsession with Jews. Comprising about 10 per cent of the country's total population by the late 1930s, Jews remained, to a great extent, a distinct community within Poland. Quite aside from their elective 'otherness' as a religious group, they were kept apart from greater Polish society by a series of exclusionary laws, and as the 1930s progressed found their numbers increasingly restricted from universities, government posts, radio, and the press.[14] When the government in Warsaw lent credence to its Madagascar plan, it affirmed the role that state-sanctioned antisemitism would play in the struggle to uphold Polish culture against its traditional antagonists. A number of Jews, too, and with some foresight, seem to have debated the merits of the resettlement scheme. But for Miksne and Norski-Nożyca, the proper response—at least for culturally assimilated, Polish-speaking, urban Jews like themselves—was to treat the whole idea as a preposterous joke:

Madagaskar

Ja się czuję na wpół dziki,	I feel like a half-wild savage,
Ludożerca sam,	A proper cannibal,
Bo ja jadę do Afryki,	'Cause I'm headed for Africa,
Tam kolonię mam.	I have a colony there!
Kupię sobie słonia	I'll get myself an elephant
I dzikiego konia	And a wild pony—
Albo jest kolonia,	If I've gotta live there,
Albo nie ma jej!	I'm gonna do it right!

Refrain

Oj, Madagaskar!	Oh, Madagascar!
Kraina czarna, parna,	Dark and sweltering, melting—
Afryka na wpół dzika!	An Africa that's half-wild!
Oj, Madagaskar!	Oh, Madagascar!
Orzechy kokosowe i drzewa bambusowe,	Coconuts and bamboo trees,
Tam są dzikie szczepy,	The tribes there all are savage,
To mi może będzie lepiej,	I may just find it's better,
Bo tam gdzie kultura,	'Cause where there's culture,
Tam jest kłótnia, awantura!	There is fussing, and there's fighting.
Oj, Madagaskar!	Oh, Madagascar!
Kraj ukochany,	Beloved country,
Niech żyje czarny ląd!	Long live the dark continent!

---

[14] On exclusionary laws, see S. Rudnicki, 'From "Numerus Clausus" to "Numerus Nullus"', *Polin*, 2 (1987), 246–68.

Do Murzynki się rozpalę,	I'll make a pass at a lovely Negress—
Ja mam sposób swój,	You know, I have my ways.
Będę czarnę miał na białym,	With her it will be black on white,
Bo to typ jest mój.	'Cause that's just what I like.
Z takiej czarnej matki	Such a black-skinned mummy
I białego tatki,	And a white-skinned daddy,
Wyjdą dzieci w kratkę,	Will turn out chequered babies,
I będzie *all right*!	And it will be all right!

Refrain

Mykwę sobie wybuduję,	I'll build myself a *mikveh* right there—
Łaźnia musi być!	A bathhouse is a must!
Czegoż ja się tak krępuję?	Why should I stand on ceremony?
Sam się będę myć!	I'll wash there myself!
Restaurację także	I'll open my own restaurant,
Otworzę, a jakże,	Of course! Why shouldn't I?
Przyjdziesz do mnie, szwagrze,	You'll come to me, dear brother-in-law,
Na kojsę i na rum!	For kosher schnapps and rum![15]

Unfortunately, we were able to discover little about Norski-Nożyca and Miksne, sources for information on Jewish entertainers who chose to address Jewish themes in the Polish language being decidedly scarce.[16] Miksne, reportedly born in Łódź in the early 1890s, wrote a series of popular topical songs, among them 'Jestem chory' ('I am Sick'), 'Moniek Przepiórko', 'Komorne' ('Rent'), 'Abysynja' ('Abyssinia'), and 'Madagaskar'.[17] He was also a stage personality, performing in *Kleinkunst* (cabaret) theatres in Łódź and Warsaw. It is presumed that Miksne died during the occupation, although we have no solid evidence to this effect.[18] The popular singer–songwriter and monologist Norski-Nożyca, born near Lublin about

[15] Polish text and music printed in S. Wielanek, *Szlagiery starej Warszawy: Śpiewnik andrusowski* (Warsaw, 1994), 161–3. Wielanek recorded 'Madagaskar' for his LP *Szmonces i liryka* (Polskie Nagrania, 1990) and also included it more recently on his CD, *Party na Nalewkach* (ZicZac Music [distributed by BMI Poland], 2001). For reviews of his book and the CD, see later in this volume.

[16] For data on Miksne and Norski-Nożyca we have primarily relied on individuals with access (or second-hand access) to copies of contemporary theatrical publications, such as the cabaret broadsheet *Trubadur Warszawy*. We have not yet personally examined these publications.

[17] In the case of 'Madagaskar', the song's clever rhymes and catchy melody assured it a measure of popularity long after the Madagascar controversy had stopped making news. A Yiddish paraphrase appeared soon after the Polish original; as recorded in Argentina around 1950 by Max Perlman, its lyrics include a reference to Birobidzhan, the east Asian territory marked by Stalin for settlement by Soviet Jews. By the 1960s 'Madagaskar', absent its satirical sting, had become a favourite nonsense verse among young Jews in Poland; many recall singing it, with a pronounced Yiddish accent, at summer camp. We are grateful to Teresa Pollin of the US Holocaust Memorial Museum, Washington, Eleanor Mlotek of YIVO, and Herman Taube of the Yiddish *Forverts* for the information in this note.

[18] Miksne's discography is more detailed than his biography. The Syrena catalogue (Lerski, *Syrena Record*) lists twelve compositions over a twenty-two-year span.

1910, was also active in Polish Jewish cabaret.[19] The Polish historian Marian Fuks places him in the Warsaw ghetto in 1941, where, alongside notables like Dawid Zajderman, Wiera Gran, Diana Blumenfeld, and Władysław Szpilman, he offered entertainment to the ghetto inhabitants.[20] Although he was rumoured to have escaped the ghetto during a round-up and made his way to Lublin, his final fate is unknown.[21]

If Miksne's and Norski-Nożyca's biographies remain maddeningly obscure, the message of their artistic collaboration 'Madagaskar' need not be. Indeed, it is spelled out in the lines '*Bo tam gdzie kultura* | *Tam jest kłótnia, awantura!*' ("Cause where there's culture, There is fussing, and there's fighting!'), a catchphrase at the heart of Miksne's satire. The author makes this unavoidably clear by placing this text at a structurally critical point in the music, at the 'turnaround' leading to the partial repeat in the refrain. Noting that his government could consider deporting Poland's Jews for the good of the nation, Miksne questions his society's pretensions to culture, musing that it might not be such a bad idea to reject such culture in favour of a better, more 'savage' world.

At Sachsenhausen, Kulisiewicz interpreted and misinterpreted Miksne's lines. He had heard the song for the first time only in the camp, having learned it from a fellow prisoner in the *Schuhfabrik* (shoe factory). Perceiving the plight of Poles at the hands of Germans as similar to the plight of Jews at the hands of Poles, Kulisiewicz was quick to connect the song's critique of nationalism and the 'Jewish question' with the Germanic concept of *Kulturkampf* (cultural struggle). The term had originated in Bismarck's Prussia, where it was first applied to the government's efforts to suppress the Catholic Church. This policy soon after, however, also came to embrace the struggle against the Polish minority in Prussian Poland. Beginning in the 1870s and ending only with the First World War, Poles became subject to an ever-increasing series of restrictive legal measures, including bans on the use of the Polish language in public discourse and in schools, forced relocations to areas outside Prussia, and the confiscation of private property.[22]

---

[19] The Warsaw bandleader Stanisław Wielanek includes several songs by Miksne, Norski-Nożyca, and their contemporaries in his songbook *Szlagiery starej Warszawy*.

[20] See M. Fuks, *Muzyka ocalona* (Warsaw, 1989), 159. See also: J. Tarkow, *Azoy iz es geven . . . khurbn varshe* (Buenos Aires, 1948), 205; B. Engelking and J. Leociak (eds.), *Ghetto Warszawskie: Przewodnik po nieistniejącym mieście* (Warsaw, 2001), 556, 564.

[21] Letters Norski-Nożyca sent from a sub-camp of Majdanek situated within the city of Lublin confirm only that he was still alive in Dec. 1942. See R. Sakowska (ed.), *Archiwum Ringelbluma: Konspiracyjne archiwum getta Warszawy*, vol. i: *Listy o zagładzie* (Warsaw, 1997), 293, 312, 314.

[22] For a detailed study of the *Kulturkampf* in Prussian Poland, see L. Trzeciakowski, *The Kulturkampf in Prussian Poland*, trans. K. Kretkowska (New York, 1990). Other informative discussions of *Kulturkampf* ideology and Prussian–Polish relations can be found in R. Blanke, *Prussian Poland in the German Empire (1871–1900)* (New York, 1981); W. W. Hagen, *Germans, Poles and Jews: The Nationality Conflict in the Prussian East, 1772–1914* (Chicago, 1980); and H. K. Rosenthal, *German and Pole: National Conflict and Modern Myth* (Gainesville, Fla., 1976).

Aleksander Kulisiewicz regarded Nazi German treatment of the Poles as a perhaps more radical, but still recognizable, form of the *Kulturkampf* ideology. And he identified this continuum of oppression by defiantly proclaiming 'Es lebe Kulturkampf!' ('Long live *Kulturkampf!*'), daring the Nazis to break his Polish spirit. But more to the point, with his parody of 'Madagaskar' Kulisiewicz conflated the German–Polish and Polish–Jewish situations, each sanctioned by long tradition, now exposed in all their fraudulence by the war. Such reflections on culture, nationalism, humanity, had actually begun for Kulisiewicz a year earlier, in 1942. Prior to his captivity Kulisiewicz had been (in the words of his former wife) a 'typical Polish antisemite'. By his own admission, his transforming experience had been an encounter at the camp with a Jew, the Polish-born choir director Rosebery d'Arguto, whose 'Jüdischer Todessang' (a parody of an old Yiddish counting song) made a profound impression on Kulisiewicz when he heard it performed at a clandestine rehearsal of d'Arguto's Jewish men's choir. D'Arguto, who had befriended Kulisiewicz through a bond of music, asked him to remember his camp song, and to sing it to the world for the rest of his life. Through it Kulisiewicz would tell of Jewish suffering in the death camps.[23]

With his own creation 'Heil, Sachsenhausen', Kulisiewicz not only confronted the German persecution of Poles, but, we suspect, also came to understand— through an acquired empathy for other victims—something of the Jewish experience of persecution at the hands of the Poles. That empathy was repeatedly demonstrated in his post-war mission to document music-making by prisoners in the Nazi camps, in his writings, recordings, and performances. Together with d'Arguto's poignant 'Jüdischer Todessang', the humble *szmonces* 'Madagaskar' had conceivably provided a common chord.

---

[23] D'Arguto, born Martin Rosenberg, was also a well-known composer of children's and workers' songs in pre-war Germany. He and the members of his Jewish prisoners' choir were later transported to Auschwitz-Birkenau, where most perished in the gas chambers. For Kulisiewicz's retelling of this incident, see 'Polskie pieśni obozowe', 1825–45.

The *Badkhn* in Contemporary Hasidic Society: Social, Historical, and Musical Observations

YAAKOV MAZOR

THREE individuals inspired the research for this chapter: Benjamin Kluger, former librarian at the Jewish National and University Library in Jerusalem; the late Dr Bathja Bayer, chief librarian of the music department at the same library and lecturer in the musicology department of the Hebrew University, Jerusalem, who initially guided me in the fundamental aspects of Jewish music; and the late Professor Chone Shmeruk of the Yiddish department at the Hebrew University. Kluger was my intercessor in the court of the Kretshiner Rebbe in Rehovot, R. Menahem Eliezer Ze'ev (b. 1948), and with his assistance I received permission to record the wedding of the *rebbe*'s brother Zayde Shmuel Smelke (now the Bitshkover Rebbe, in Jaffa), which was held in Rehovot in 1971. At this wedding the late *badkhn* Yosef Grinvald presided over the *mitsve-tants* ceremony, which concludes the public events of the wedding night. He invited important guests to dance with the bride by reciting written verses that he had composed. I was surprised to witness this, for it had commonly been assumed by contemporary scholars in Israel and abroad that the practice of *badkhones* was a relic of the past. Bayer and Shmeruk were no less surprised than I, and encouraged me to continue recording *badkhonim* at hasidic weddings because of their value for the study of Yiddish culture. Shmeruk even recommended that I devote most of my time to 'this holy task'. At that time I was researching hasidic dance melodies for weddings and other celebrations, and the activity of the *badkhn* appeared to be of lesser importance. But, after speaking with Shmeruk, I made sure I recorded the *badkhonim* I came across and documented their activities.[1] In the 1980s, with the linguist Moshe Taube, I conducted research on the 'inviter', who fulfils a comparable function to the *badkhn* at hasidic

Research for this chapter was supported by the Memorial Foundation for Jewish Culture, the Jewish Music Research Centre, Jerusalem, and the Centre National de Recherche Sociale in Paris. The original version appeared in *Dukhan: me'asef lemusikah yehudit* (Jerusalem), 15 (2000), 41–80.

[1] All the recordings are catalogued at the National Sound Archives (NSA) in the Jewish National and University Library, Jerusalem.

weddings in Jerusalem.[2] What follows are preliminary findings in my research on the *badkhn* in contemporary hasidic society.

THE *BADKHN* IN JEWISH HISTORY

According to the most commonly held view, a *badkhn* (Hebrew: *badḥan*) is someone who composes texts in rhyming verse (Yiddish: *gramen*) and sings them before an invited audience on special ritual occasions.[3] In the past, according to Ashkenazi (Franco–German) sources, *badkhonim* were referred to by other names, such as *narn* (clowns, fools), or *leytsonim* or *leytsim* (jesters, jokers). But it is not clear which of these terms was used to refer to the people who composed the verses and which to those who performed as jesters.

In eastern Europe the term *marshelik* was also widespread. Some recent folklore studies consider *marshelik* to be synonymous with the versifying *badkhn*. Yitskhak Rivkind and Ariela Krasney believe that *badkhn* and *marshelik* were two different vocations, although the terms have tended to be used interchangeably.[4] This is also the opinion of many of those I interviewed. In contrast, both in hasidic writings and oral traditions the term *badkhn* most often indicates a versifier and jester alike.[5] In the terminology of the contemporary hasidic world a *badkhn* is primarily someone who composes and recites rhymed verses, either spontaneously or by preparing them in advance and reciting them from a written text.[6]

---

[2] Y. Mazor and M. Taube, 'A Hasidic Ritual Dance: The *Mitsve Tants* in Jerusalem Weddings', *Yuval*, 6 (1994), 164–224; Y. Mazor and A. Hajdu, 'The Hasidic Dance *Nigun*: A Study Collection and its Classificatory Analysis', *Yuval*, 3 (1974), 136–235. On hasidic dance melodies, see A. Hajdu and Y. Mazor, *Otsar haḥasidut: 101 nigunei rikud hasidiyim*, 3rd edn. (Jerusalem, 2000).

[3] M. Idit, 'Badḥan', in *Encyclopedia Judaica*, vol. iv (Jerusalem, 1971), 73–5.

[4] Y. Rivkind, *Klezmerim: perek betoledot ha'omanut ha'amamit* (New York, 1960), 13, 15–16. The problem of jesters is also not completely clarified in Ariela Krasney's book *Habadḥan* (Ramat Gan, 1999). According to her (pp. 9–10 and 26), *badkhonim* and *leytsonim* of different types coalesced during the 19th century in the form of the jester–*badkhn* who served in east European communities. In earlier centuries the scholar–*badkhn* and the *marshelik*, a kind of master of ceremonies, were in competition until the former took the place of the latter (pp. 38 and 76–7, but contradicting the source on p. 168). But the *marshelik* was also a versifier, according to Idit, 'Badḥan'; A. A. Druyanov, 'Habadḥan shelanu', *Ha'aretz* (27 Feb. 1937), 3, 16; Y. Tunkel, *In gutn mut* (Warsaw, 1936), 215; A. Yaari, 'Sifrei badḥanim' and 'Miluim lesifrei badḥanim', *Kiryat sefer*, 20 (1960), 126; 21 (1961), 266–7; and the author of *Shulḥan shelomoh* (see N. Cottler, 'Leitsanim o simḥat ḥatan vekalah', *Hamodia* (11 Mar. 1988), 9).

[5] A. Cohen-Reiss, *Mizikhronot ish yerushalayim* (Jerusalem, 1967), 53; N. Cottler, 'Habadḥanut beyisra'el', *Hamodia* (2 Mar. 1988), 8; id., 'Leitsanim o simḥat ḥatan vekalah', 9, 16.

[6] A hasidic source (Y. A. Vays, *Hakdamat hasefer hakadosh imrei yosef* (New York, 1974), 20) refers to the *badkhn* as a *tants mayster* (master of dance) because he directs the *mitsve-tants*. The Bobover Rebbe, R. Shelomo Halberstam, ordered the *badkhonim* in his court to recite the verses from a written text, lest they misspeak and offend the guests (interviews with the *badkhn* Shaul Hooterer, Antwerp, 28 Jan. 1997, and 5 Feb. 1997 (with Jean Baumgarten)).

There are differing views about when it became established custom to have a *badkhn* at a Jewish wedding. Hasidim claim that the custom stems from ancient times, and find textual support in the Talmud and rabbinic literature of the Middle Ages.[7] Some quote the Zohar, which refers to King David as *badhin d'malka* or *badhana d'malka* (*badkhn* of the king) because he knew how to delight the supernal king and queen—respectively, the male and female *sefirot* (emanations), Tiferet (beauty) and Malkhut (Kingdom) in the Godhead—with his music.[8] This is considered the proof-text justifying the importance of the *badkhn*'s role in entertaining the bridal couple because their coupling on earth is understood to reflect and bring about a parallel process in the upper world, namely the supernal unification of the Godhead.[9] The earliest source explicitly to permit buffoonery to entertain the bride and groom is found in the sixteenth-century book *Sefer maharil*.[10] The earliest documentation of *badkhones* (the *badkhn*'s art) also dates from that century.[11]

Scholars have therefore concluded that the art of jesting verse developed in western Europe and then spread to eastern Europe. While this art declined in the old lands of Ashkenaz in the eighteenth century and subsequently disappeared by the mid-nineteenth century, it blossomed in eastern Europe in the nineteenth and early twentieth centuries in communities of hasidim and of mitnagedim (rabbinic opponents of hasidism) alike.[12] Jewish folklorists, who have generally relied upon written sources, have rushed to lament the decline of *badkhonim* before the Second

[7] Apparently referring to the talmudic saying 'The merit of attending a wedding lies in the words [of congratulation addressed to the bride and bridegroom]' (BT, *Ber.* 6*b*). This saying, together with the accompanying warning that 'whosoever partakes of the wedding meal of a bridegroom and does not gladden him transgresses against the five voices mentioned in the verse: "The voice of joy and the voice of gladness, the voice of the bridegroom and the voice of the bride, the voice of them that say, 'Give thanks to the Lord of Hosts' [Jer. 33: 11]" ' (*Ber.* 6*b*, trans. I. Epstein, *Babylonian Talmud*, vol. i (London, 1961), 27, 29), teaches the importance of the commandment to delight the bride and groom even by means of jokes.

[8] Y. M. F. Rotenberg, *Zameru lishemo* (Jerusalem, 1996), 252, par. 346; 281, par. 388. On the place of humour and *badkhones* in the Zohar as a means of exaltation and worship, see Y. Liebes, 'Zohar ve'eros', *Alpayim*, 9 (1955), 82–3.

[9] Y. Tishby, *Mishnat hazohar*, vol. ii (Jerusalem, 1961), 607 ff. Furthermore, the hasidim base the custom of having the *badkhn* eavesdrop on the bride and groom in the *yihud* room (where they are secluded immediately after emerging from the *khupe*) on King David, who similarly discovered words of union which the supernal groom taught the supernal bride; see Rotenberg, *Zameru lishemo*, 252, par. 346.

[10] According to the author of *Sefer maharil* (Jerusalem, 1989), jesting alone is forbidden, 'but for the joy of grooms it is a *mitsvah* to clown before them and entertain them'; see 'Hilkhot aseret yemei teshuvah', 310, par. 17.

[11] See 'Bride's Songs', in *Sefer mitsvot nashim* (Venice, 1588), and *Sefer minhagim* (Venice, 1593). See also Y. Rivkind, 'Mipinkaso shel hazan ubadhan', in *Minhah liyehudah* (Jerusalem, 1950), 235–7.

[12] See Rivkind, 'Mipinkaso', 236, 238; Cottler, 'Habadhanut'. During his supposed decline in the West, the *badkhn* was so popular that those who had the means would invite several *badkhonim* to their celebrations, while those who looked unfavourably upon *badkhones* made efforts to ban it. Thus, for example, in 1767 the number of *badkhonim* (known as *shaltin* in western Yiddish) was restricted to two in the town of Smikhof (Smíchov) near Prague ('Takanot shenitaknu bekehilat kodesh smikhof bishnat tav kuf kaf zayin [1767]', *Kerem shelomoh*, 19/3 (27 Feb. 1996), 53).

World War and their disappearance after the Holocaust.[13] Such scholars were apparently unaware both of the *badkhonim* who practised in the land of Israel before the war, and of the renewed flowering of their art in hasidic communities in the United States, Israel, and Europe after the war.[14]

The fact is that the *badkhn* never lost his important role in the hasidic wedding. While *badkhones* sometimes came to be regarded negatively by Jews outside the hasidic world,[15] similar attitudes have never prevailed in hasidic society. On the contrary, hasidic leaders from the early days of the movement until the present have granted ideological legitimacy to *badkhones* at weddings.[16] This attitude may have been derived from the hasidic conception that joy, melody, and dance are fundamental in worshipping God,[17] as well as from the hasidic notion that the relations between bride and groom reflect those between God and Shekhinah.[18] In addition,

[13] See Druyanov, 'Habadhan shelanu', 17; Rivkind, 'Mipinkaso' 235–6, and *Klezmerim*, 13, 15–16; Y. T. Lewinsky, 'Badhan', *Entsiklopediyah shel havai umasoret bayahadut*, vol. i (Tel Aviv, 1970), 53; Idit, 'Badhan'; E. Lahad, 'Habadhanim', *Tatslil*, 20 (1980), 51–7. This mistaken view of the *badkhn* in the 20th century is similar to laments about hasidic society written by two historians of the hasidic movement after the Holocaust and in the 1960s (see D. Asaf, 'Hebetim historiyim vehevratiyim beheker hahasidut', in Asaf (ed.), *Tsadik ve'edah* (Jerusalem, 2001), 9, 31, and n. 42).

[14] See Cohen-Reiss, *Mizikhronot*, 53. In the NSA there are recordings of more than thirty *badkhonim*, the majority of them residents of Israel. Those of *badkhonim* outside Israel include the late Yom Tov Erlich, Shalom Kessler (a Bobov hasid), and Shelomo Yaakov Gelbman (a Satmar hasid) of the United States; Yaakov Miller, who emigrated from Israel to Monsey, New York; Shaul Hooterer (a Bobov hasid) and Mordechai Shtoyber (a Satmar hasid) of Antwerp, who perform regularly at the court of the *tsadik* of Przeworsk in Antwerp and at the courts of *tsadikim* in the United States; and Yisrael Shtern (a Belz hasid) of London.

[15] Krasney, *Habadhan*, 33–4; R. Glantz, 'Der kamf kegn badkhonim un klezmorim in daytshland onheyb 19tn yorhundert', *Yivo bleter*, 28 (1946), 394–7. Rabbi Hayim Bachrach (1630–1702) defined a *mitsvah* banquet with a *badkhn* as *moshav letsim* (frivolous company), and the first maskilim derided the *badkhn* (see Druyanov, 'Habadhan shelanu'). In our own day *badkhonim* have been denounced as well; see A. M. Izrael, 'Aldevar peratsot behatunot', *Hamaor*, 24/5 (Apr.–June 1972), 15–16. For similar opposition to 'words of jest' in Israeli communities originating in the Muslim world, see Rotenberg, *Zameru lishemo*, pars. 398–9.

[16] See Nahman of Bratslav, *Likutei etsot* (Jerusalem, 1976), 42; id., *Sihot haran* (Jerusalem, 1992), 85, par. 80. The founder of Habad hasidism, R. Shneur Zalman of Liady, permitted 'milei divdihuta shel inyanei hevel' ('joking about vain matters') because it is inspired by the supernal worlds. And more recently some people have invited a *badkhn* 'even if he is not God-fearing' (Rotenberg, *Zameru lishemo*, pars. 399, 401; Cottler, 'Leitsanim').

[17] See Y. Tishby and Y. Dan, 'Torat hahasidut vesifrutah', in *Entsiklopediyah ivrit*, xvii. 10–11; A. Rubinstein, 'Hasidism', in *Encyclopedia Judaica*, vii. 1390–1432; Y. Mazor and A. Hajdu, 'Nigunei simhah verikud shel hahasidim' (first record in the series Anthology of Jewish Musical Traditions) (Jerusalem, 1977); Y. Mazor, 'Koho shel hanigun bahagut hahasidit vetafkido bahavai hadati vehahevrati', *Yuval* (Jerusalem), 7, Studies in Honour of Israel Adler (2002), 23–53 (Heb. pagination). On dance as worship in hasidic theory and its use by *tsadikim*, see Yaakov Yosef of Polonoye (Polonne), *Tsofnat pa'ane'ah* (Korzec, 1782), 32*b*; A. Wertheim, *Halakhot vehalikhot bahasidut* (Tel Aviv, 1960), 104; Landoy, 'Hamahol veharikud', 54–62; Y. T. Lewinsky, 'Rikud, ma'asiyah, zemer betorat hahasidut', *Mahanayim*, 46 (1960), 98–103; id., 'Al meholot mitsvah lesugeihen', ibid. 48–9.

[18] See Z. M. Rabinovitsh, *Hamagid mikozhnits* (Tel Aviv, 1947), 127–9; Meir of Keristshov, *Me'ir einei hakhamim* (Sedeh Lavan [Białopole], 1823), 282–3; *Kuntres birkot hatanim* (Vitebsk, 1828–9), 65, par. 14; MS 3444, HNUL, Jerusalem.

both older and more recent hasidic tales relate that the founder of the hasidic movement, Israel Ba'al Shem Tov (Besht; 1700–60), as well as *tsadikim*[19] of subsequent generations such as R. Naftali Tsevi Horowitz of Ropshits (Ropczyce), Jacob Isaac Horowitz (the Seer of Lublin), R. Moshe Leib of Sassow, and R. Yosef Meir Weiss of Spinka (Săpânţa), are said to have served as *badkhonim* at weddings.[20] Other *tsadikim* supported well-known *badkhonim* that are said to have been noted for their piety. These included Hershl of Ostropol, *badkhn* of R. Borukh of Mezhibozh (Międzybórz); Yitskhak Ayzik of Homle (Gomel), disciple of R. Dov Ber (Duber) and the Tsemah Tsedek, both of Lubavitch (Lyubavichi); and Yona Aharon of Ostrodets (Ostrozhets, near Rovno), companion of the *rebbe* of Neskhiz.[21] Another celebrated *badkhn*, Yosl Broder, was associated with R. Uri of Strelisk. After the death of his *rebbe* this *badkhn* transferred his allegiance to the court of Israel of Ruzhin.[22] Whatever the reason, *badkhones* certainly came to flourish as the hasidic community re-established itself after the Holocaust.

THE *BADKHN* IN HIS SOCIOCULTURAL CONTEXT

The *badkhn* performs primarily at weddings. His chief role is to orchestrate the *mitsve-tants*[23] at the close of the celebrations on the day of the wedding by summoning several male guests, mostly relatives of the couple's families, to dance with the bride (or rather 'in front of the bride', as the traditional formula has it, since only the bride's father and her new husband have direct physical contact with her, in accordance with the rules of modesty that govern contact between the sexes in the hasidic world). The *badkhn* may also compose and sing verses on a moral theme to

According to these and other sources, certain wedding customs and events are perceived to reflect or to bring about processes in the upper world. As a consequence of this notion, the hasidim developed special prayers to be said by the bride and groom, related to specific parts of the wedding ceremony: a prayer recited by both bride and groom before the *khupe*, a prayer recited by the groom when the bride circles him, and a prayer recited by both before they enter the *yihud* room (Efrayim Deutsch, interview, 16 July 1987).

[19] The terms (used interchangeably here) *tsadik* (i.e. righteous) and *rebbe* (my teacher) designate hasidic leaders, descendants of dynasties founded from the late 18th to the 19th century. A more recent term is *admor*, an abbreviation of 'our master, teacher, and rabbi'.

[20] See *Shivhei habesht* (Tel Aviv, 1947), 132*b*; *Ohel elimelekh* (Landsberg, 1948), 66, par. 157; B. Landoy, 'Hamahol veharikud bitnuat hahasidut', *Mahanayim*, 48 (July–Aug. 1960), 59; D. Pintshevski, 'Apta utkumat hahasidut', *Sefer apta* (Tel Aviv, 1966), 52–4; Vays, *Imrei yosef*, 12 and 20, par. 7; Rotenberg, *Zameru lishemo*, 293, par. 402; 314–16, par. 434; 'Habadhan hasagfan', in M. Brot (ed.), *Sihat hashavua* (Kefer Habad, 17 Mar. 1995), 428.

[21] See *Entsiklopediyah ivrit*, i. 957; A. Z. Cantor, 'Divrei yonah badhan', *Reshumot*, 3 (1947), 128; 'Imrat hashavua: badhanut leshem mitsvah', in Brot (ed.), *Sihat hashavua*, 428.

[22] Interviews with Akiva Brilant, a hasid of Byan (Boyany), Jerusalem, 1993, 1998; cf. Krasney, *Habadhan*, 94.

[23] A *mitsve* (Heb. *mitsvah*) is a biblical commandment. Here the word describes the culminating ritual dance in the hasidic wedding ceremony; see Mazor and Taube, 'A Hasidic Ritual Dance'.

the groom while he is with his male friends and family at the *kaboles-ponim* (reception) that precedes his going to veil the bride in the ritual known as *badekns*.[24] Sometimes he may also perform to entertain the guests at the wedding banquet. In such cases, some *badkhonim* make specific reference in a *droshe-geshank* (literally, 'gift sermon') to the wedding gifts, following the practice common at weddings in eastern Europe in previous generations.[25]

According to written sources, *badkhonim* were also invited to perform at the *khosn-mol* (groom's banquet) on the day before the wedding, to the bride and groom's parties on Friday night and at the close of the sabbath preceding the wedding (*forshpil*),[26] and to the celebratory *sheve brokhes* (seven benedictions) banquets in the week following the wedding. In Israel the *forshpil* and the *khosn-mol* take place only at weddings of a *rebbe*'s family members; the *forshpil* is limited to the close of the sabbath before the wedding, and the *khosn-mol* to the day of the wedding. The *forshpil* is held only for the groom; the bride merely invites other young women to join her at the third of the sabbath meals (*shaleshudes*, an important hasidic tradition). In rare cases *badkhonim* are also invited to other family events.[27] They also play a particularly important role during the holiday of Purim: in the *purim-shpil* (Purim play) and in the Purim banquets (*tishn*) organized around the *tsadik*. According to one source, among the hasidim of Sants (Nowy Sącz) a second *tish* was held on the afternoon of Purim. On this solemn occasion the *badkhn* usually performed, conveying a moral message.[28] Scholarly literature and memoirs note additional events in which *badkhonim* took part in the past.[29] Some of these occur in present-day hasidic society in a different form or under a different name; some have been shortened. For example, the practice of the *badkhn* admonishing the bride during a special ceremony during which the bride is seated (*bazetsns*) has been reduced to reciting moralizing verses while the bride sits on a special 'throne' to

[24] At some weddings the *badkhn* also prepares special verses on the bride's behalf, sung from a text by a female family member. In only one wedding did the *badkhn* himself sing the verses, after the veiling ceremony and before the bride was led to the canopy. We still do not know in which dynasty, if any, this sermon to the bride has been an accepted custom. On the veiling ceremony, see further in n. 30 below.

[25] See *Kol mevaser*, no. 9, suppl. to *Hamelits* (5 Mar. 1866), cols. 136–7; A. B. Gotlober, *Zikhronot umasa'ot*, ed. R. Goldberg (Jerusalem, 1976), 95–6, 104. According to Krasney, *Habadhan*, 8, 85, 203, the *badkhn* was able to show off the extent of his talent during such gift announcements. Moshe Bik (*Hatunah yehudit, asufat manginot vezikhronot* (Haifa, 1964), 23) also transcribed the music of such an announcement.

[26] See J. Stutchewsky, *Haklezmerim: toledoteihem, orah hayeihem veyetsiroteihem* (Jerusalem, 1959), 156; Cottler, 'Habadhanut'; Druyanov, 'Habadhan', 16. According to Lewinsky, 'Hatunah', in *Entsiklopediyah shel havai umasoret bayahadut*, i. 214–28, *forshpil* was a synonym for either *khosn-mol* (groom's banquet) or *nadn mol* (bride's banquet).

[27] Druyanov ('Habadhan shelanu', 16) notes the *marshelik*'s performance during the procession of the bride to the *mikve*.

[28] Interviews with the *badkhn* Shaul Hooterer, Antwerp, 28 Jan. 1997, 5 Feb. 1997 (with Jean Baumgarten).

[29] See Y. Zizmor, 'Amolike khasenes', in Z. Reyzn (ed.), *Pinkes far der geshikhte fun vilne* (Vilna, 1922), 873–6; Stutchewsky, *Haklezmerim*, 156, 159–63, 166–7; Rivkind, 'Mipinkaso', 240 n. 13; Idit, 'Badhan', 73–5; Yaari, 'Sifrei badhanim', 109; Cottler, 'Habadhanut'; Krasney, *Habadhan*, 81, 85–6.

receive women guests at the reception immediately prior to her ritual veiling before the wedding ceremony.[30]

Another issue concerns the relationship between *badkhonim* and musicians. Stutchewsky, relying on literature from the late nineteenth century, describes *klezmer* bands that included a *badkhn* who told parables, *badkhonim* who led *klezmer* bands, and *badkhonim* who played instruments. In such cases the *badkhn* assumed several additional roles, such as marching at the head of the wedding procession with the musicians, cymbals in his hands, as they led the bride and groom to the *khupe* (wedding canopy), or signalling to the musicians to begin the *khupe-marsh* (the march to the *khupe*).[31] In hasidic weddings documented in Israel no remnants of such practices are to be found. There have been cases in which the *badkhn* and the musicians were requested by family members to collaborate during the *mitsve-tants*, but it was apparent that they were not accustomed to doing this. It is not yet clear whether such changes are due to conscious innovation or rather to the erosion of tradition over time.

While the status of the *badkhn* in hasidic society is generally solid and respectable, it is clear that, even so, quite a range of attitudes exists. These attitudes may be affected by such factors as the *badkhn*'s personality, his musical ability, his talent in constructing verses, his mastery of textual sources, his sense of humour, his ability to make skilful use of acronyms and *gematriyes* (numerical combinations),[32] and

[30] According to Lewinsky, ('Ḥatunah', 221), among east European Jews the *badkhn* recited his verses after the *budekns*, not before. For Krasney (*Habadḥan*, 19, 74–7, 79–81, 134, 149, 165, 168, 194, and 202), the terms *bazetsn*, *baveynen*, and *bazingen* are synonyms for *muser zogn*, i.e. the performance of moralizing verses which the *badkhn* sings to the bride and groom before they go to the *khupe*. In the few writings I have perused (Zizmor, 'Amolike khasenes', 874; Y. Tunkel, 'Dos naye kale-bazetsenish', in his *In gutn mut* (Warsaw, 1936), 215; Rivkind, 'Mipinkaso', 241; Bik, *Ḥatunah yehudit*, 8–9, 11; Stutchewsky, *Haklezmerim*, 157, 159–62; P. Taytl, 'A shvartse khasene in apt', in *Sefer apta* (Tel Aviv, 1966), 106–7), it appears that *kale-bazetsn* usually related to the entire ceremony and not specifically to the *badkhn*'s activity (according to Gotlober, *Zikhronot umasa'ot*, 100–3, the central part of the ceremony was cutting off the bride's hair); *kale-baveynen*, on the other hand, related to the *badkhn*'s verses and sometimes to the ceremony, and the term *bazingen* to the *badkhn*'s verses intended for the groom. (Y. Elzet, 'Miminhagei yisra'el', *Reshumot*, 1 (1918), 357, no. 46, uses *bazingen* also for the bride). Krasney does not feel it is anything beyond a matter of semantics. Rivkind ('Klezmerim', 18) has observed that 'wedding customs in every region, sometimes in particular cities, towns, and *shtetls*, took on a local form and a specific colouring'. It is possible that the different terms are related to these differences in ceremony and custom, and thus there is a need for renewed investigation into the terms and their relationships. In any event, prudent use of them would prevent many of Krasney's contradictions, especially regarding the '*bazetsns* song' (see Krasney, *Habadḥan*, 19 and 229 n. 29).

[31] Elzet, 'Miminhagei, 360; Stutchewsky, *Haklezmerim*, 61–2 and n. 106, 77, 121, 164, 166–7; cf. Cottler, 'Habadḥanut'; Krasney, *Habadḥan*, 39, 102, 107–8, 146, and *passim*.

[32] Since the letters of the Hebrew alphabet have numerical values, it is possible to transform words and phrases by discovering others with their equivalent numerical value. A well-known example is the equivalence between *arur Haman* ('cursed be Haman') and *barukh Mordekhai* ('blessed be Mordechai') in Purim observances. This practice is known as *gematriye* (Hebrew: *gematriyah*). The *badkhn* makes use of it in constructing blessings, attributes, comical inversions, or even quotations from classical sources out of the names of the wedding participants.

the expectations and preferences of particular audiences. The following examples illustrate the range of attitudes. It is well known that at weddings of the Husakov (Gusakov), Koson (Kaszony, Mezokaszony, or Kosyno), and Spinke dynasties family members often serve as *badkhonim*. In conversation with me, the eldest son of the Husakover Rebbe emphasized the importance of the *badkhn*'s role by mentioning the names of various *tsadikim* who had served as *badkhonim* at weddings. But at the wedding of a *badkhn*'s daughter I encountered a different attitude as well. This woman's first marriage had not been consummated for tragic reasons, and at the second wedding, instead of conducting herself modestly during the *mitsve-tants* as is customary (the bride barely moves), she danced ecstatically and joyously with her father. One of the men present, clearly shocked by the behaviour, commented on it to his neighbour, to which the latter replied: 'And what do you expect from a *badkhn*'s daughter?'

Of more than thirty *badkhonim* documented in hasidic weddings in Israel,[33] at least sixteen could be described as professionals, since they support themselves as *badhkonim* or serve as *badkhonim* on a regular basis. The others, amateur *badkhonim*, usually perform at the weddings of family members or close friends.[34] This classification, however, ignores considerations of quality or style. Some *badkhonim* claim that the main role of the *badkhn* is to entertain and make jokes, while others see their role as means of disseminating religious and ethical messages. The former constantly strive to amuse their audience with stories, anecdotes, and jokes, mostly without singing them. *Badkhonim* of the second type avoid such things, and only occasionally weave little threads of irony into verses aimed at the person invited to dance with the bride or at family members.

Another type of classification distinguishes between *badkhonim* who are related to a specific hasidic community or dynasty and those who move between different communities. According to our evidence, even this classification does not yield clearly distinctive groups. For although a *badkhn* may be connected with one dynasty, another dynasty may influence his musical repertoire. Likewise, the *badkhn*'s life experiences, his relationship to the hasidic community, his education, and his economic status may influence his craft, and the verses and melodies he performs. As illustrations, we will consider three *badkhonim*: two professionals and one amateur.

[33] See n. 14.

[34] In a number of communities it is customary to collect *shabes gelt* (sabbath money) from those who have the honour of dancing with the bride during the *mitsve-tants*, even if the *badkhn* is not a professional. In general, the role of collecting the money is the *badkhn*'s (at one wedding the *tsadik* performed this role). Prior to or following the dance the *badkhn* announces this with a sentence that includes the word *shabes*, e.g. 'Der mekhutn vet gebn shabes', 'Der zeyde vet gebn shabes gelt' ('The father-in-law, or the grandfather, will give sabbath money'), or he merely chants the word *shabes*. Some donate this money to charity (cf. 'Imrat hashavuah'). On the talmudic basis for this solicitation, see H. Lieberman, 'Al "shabat" ha'alufah sod', in his *Ohel raḥel*, vol. iii (New York, 1984), 426–31. On the musical fragment sung with the word *shabes* (as a remembrance of this custom) during the Jerusalem *mitsve-tants*, see Mazor and Taube, 'A Hasidic Ritual Dance', 174.

Yosef Grinvald (1924–73), known as Yosl Ramler, was born in Hungary. He considered himself a hasid of Kretshinef (Crăciuneşti), a 'sub-dynasty' of Nadvorne (Nadvornaya), even though he had not grown up in a Kretshinef home. As an adolescent and until his emigration to Israel in 1949, he wandered throughout Europe and heard many different *badkhonim*. In Israel he lived in the small town of Ramla (hence his nickname), but he used to spend sabbaths and holidays at the court of the Kretshinefer *tsadik*, R. Moshe David Roznboym (1924–69), in Rehovot. He performed regularly at weddings of the Kretshinef and Nadvorne dynasties, but did not earn enough from this to support his family.[35] He always accepted invitations to perform at weddings of other dynasties, and supported himself by anything that came his way. It is no wonder, then, that no connection can be found between his melodies and the musical culture of a specific community. His verses did not demonstrate great knowledge of the scriptural sources, and they often lacked the depth of those of the great *badkhonim*, whether professional or amateur. However, he took his role seriously, restrained his humour, and was known to have disapproved of *badkhonim* who told too many jokes and anecdotes. He felt they should more properly be referred to as *badranim* (entertainers in the more secular sense) rather than *badkhonim*.

Borukh Mordechai Geiger (1920–96) was a distinguished Vizhnitser (Vyzhnytsya) hasid. He was born in Kashoy (Czechoslovakia), emigrated to the land of Israel in 1949, performed in the courts of R. Hayim Meir Hager (1888–1972) and his son R. Moshe Hager (b. 1916), and was considered the *badkhn* of the Vizhnits community in the Orthodox town of Benei Berak. He did not need to support himself through *badkhones*, and donated the money he received during his performances (*shabes gelt*) to charity. Although he therefore did not have any economic reason for doing so, he accepted invitations from hasidim of other dynasties to conduct the *mitsve-tants* at their weddings, apparently because he loved doing it. Geiger composed his verses extemporaneously. Like Grinvald, he used a variety of melodies (*nigunim*), although in fact one particular *nign* was his favourite, and he used the others only for variety. The source of this melody is unknown, and it has not been found in the repertoires of other *badkhonim*. Stylistically it resembles the Ashkenazi melodies for the *kines* (lamentations) for the fast of Tisha Be'av, and it is in some ways similar to the unmeasured tunes (lacking fixed metre and distinctive rhythm) of the sabbath songs of Vizhnits. As is well known, setting an improvised text to an existing measured tune invariably violates the tune's rhythmic structure. *Badkhonim*, who are guided by their musicianship, acknowledge this phenomenon and try to minimize rhythmic discordance. However, Geiger never let this bother him. Often his verses are extremely long, though sometimes they are very short. For this reason, Geiger's frequent use of an unmeasured recitative

[35] R. Meir Roznboym (1852–1908), founder of the Kretshinef dynasty, was the son of R. Mordechai (d. 1895), the son of R. Yisakhar, founder of the Nadvorna dynasty; see Y. Alfasi, *Haḥasidut* (Tel Aviv, 1974), 45–6.

melody illustrates the distinct freedom he permitted himself in relating text to music. This suggests that for Geiger the tune was merely a technical means to allow the words to be heard, not an equivalent mode of expression. Another characteristic of Geiger's *badkhones* was his tendency to rhyme his verses in homiletic fashion, like a preacher. Members of the Vizhnits community also relate that on special occasions he would repeat the *tsadik*'s sermon in verse. His uniqueness therefore appears to have derived at least in part from his being a Vizhnitser hasid.

Yeshaya Meshulam Faysh Rotenberg (b. 1962), son of the Kosony *rebbe* in the United States and a relative of the Spinker Rebbe in Jerusalem, does not consider himself a professional *badkhn*. But since he has proven talents in this direction, he is often asked to act in this capacity for the *mitsve-tants* at family weddings. As a scion of a family of *tsadikim*, he has vast knowledge of the scriptural sources and is totally at home with hasidic literature. He is very musical, and generally leads the prayers for his community. He has a collection of recordings of various *badkhonim* and possesses a critical awareness of the differing standards of their musicianship, their talents at versification, the contents of their verses, and the degree of correspondence between words and music. According to Rotenberg, a good *badkhn* tries not to be funny but rather to compose verses that convey hasidic ethics and incorporate quotations from rabbinic and hasidic sources. The main function of the *badkhn*, in his view, is to convey a message, so he prefers to use melodies that are spiritually uplifting and express the messages of his verses.

THE *BADKHN*'S MELODIES: THE PROBLEM OF SOURCE, FUNCTION, AND GENRE

Analysis of the *badkhn*'s melodies must consider such ethnic, cultural, and social aspects as non-Jewish or regional influences, connection to a specific hasidic dynasty, and musical genre while also investigating their functional roles. On this level, one must distinguish between specific *badkhn nigunim* intended primarily for this purpose and melodies that are borrowed from other contexts and genres.

The issue of ethnographic sources is complicated. Only in rare cases is there direct evidence in this matter; stylistic analysis can be helpful in identifying the source, but largely through hypothesis. So far, a few *nigunim* have been identified as originating in the folk melodies of Romania,[36] but for the most part there is no clue to their ethnographic source. That being said, the majority of tunes have already been identified as pan-hasidic melodies (*velt nigunim*, as the hasidim say), i.e. melodies used by various hasidic dynasties, while not a single melody has been identified as exclusive to one dynasty.

[36] One possible explanation for the Romanian influence is that after the First World War many Hungarian hasidim found themselves within the borders of an expanded Romanian state. See A. Rubinstein, 'Ḥasidut', in *Entsiklopediyah ivrit*, xvii. 767–8.

The recordings I analysed yielded only a small number of specifically *badkhn* tunes. The remainder included tunes of popular Yiddish songs, melodies of hasidic contemplation and meditation (*dveykes nigunim*) aimed at achieving mystical union with God, hasidic melodies for rejoicing and ecstatic dancing, and tunes whose original functions have not yet been determined.

My findings so far indicate the eclectic nature of the *badkhn*'s repertoire; in most cases it does not reflect the musical repertoire of his own community. Comparative analysis of the repertoires used by different *badkhonim* will probably reveal additional dimensions of the musical personality of the *badkhn*, and his personal tastes and inclinations, and perhaps enrich our knowledge about his direct or indirect association with other *badkhonim*.

THE *BADKHN* DURING THE RECEPTION

During the *kaboles-ponim*, the reception that precedes the formal veiling of the bride (*badekns*) before the actual wedding ceremony (*kidushin*) performed under the *khupe*, *badkhonim* usually address moralizing verses to the groom, since, according to the hasidic view, the role of the *badkhn* at this stage is to prepare the groom mentally for the sanctity of the wedding ceremony.[37] A preliminary survey of recordings of such receptions in the National Sound Archives in the Jewish National and University Library in Jerusalem suggests that here the differences among *badkhonim*, both textual and musical, are not significant. Every *badkhn* stresses the holiness of the impending ceremony and the need to approach it with a pure heart and thoughts cleansed of sin. In order to arouse the groom to repentance, the *badkhn* equates the wedding day with Yom Kippur and the day of one's death. He directs the groom's attention to the *kitl* (white linen robe) he is wearing, and reminds him that on this day all his deeds are judged before God, but that, with repentance, all of his sins are forgiven. The *badkhn* also reminds him that the souls of his deceased ancestors will come to the wedding and participate in his joy.[38] Accordingly, many

---

[37] In hasidic writings the wedding and reception are seen as symbols of processes in the Godhead. For example, the marriage blessing (*birkat hakidushin*) of the groom is a symbol of a spiritual marriage between God and the people of Israel (see Rotenberg, *Zameru lishemo*, 194, par. 250). The groom must therefore be prepared for this. Moreover, traditional wedding customs in general gained greater force under hasidism because of the mystical interpretation given to them; which is to say, their performance with proper intention (*kavanah*) could influence the supernal processes (ibid., pars. 239–49, 251–5, 258). This hasidic conception is grounded in *midrashim*. See O. Meir, 'Noseh haḥatunah bemishlei hamelakhim be'agadat ḥazal', *Folklore Research Center Studies* (Jerusalem), 4 (1974), *Studies in Marriage Customs*, 9–51.

[38] On the remission of sins, the participation of souls of the departed at weddings, and the wearing of the *kitl* as a reminder of the day of one's death, see Rotenberg, *Zameru lishemo*, 203–8, pars. 262–73; 211, par. 277; 235, par. 305. On the *badkhn*'s reference to remission of sins and on the *kitl* in pre-hasidic society, see Rivkind, 'Mipinkaso', 250–1. We can conclude that most of the subjects to which hasidic *badkhonim* referred while addressing the groom were the legacies of prior *badkhonim* as described by Krasney. But rhymes addressed to the bride (Krasney, *Habadḥan*, 19–20, 74, 79) were by and large

hasidic communities customarily adopt here a set formula of inspiring verse, which is sung from a text usually by one of the groom's unmarried male friends with a good voice.

The number of melodies used to accompany such texts is small, and most of them are in dirge-like recitative style. Some resemble the melodies used for the *kines* on Tisha Be'av (possibly as a continuation of the old custom of bringing the bride to tears, *kale-baveynen*), and others are similar to tunes accompanying the *bazetsns*, which are not specific to hasidic society.[39]

THE *BADKHN* DURING THE *MITSVE-TANTS*

In my article on the *mitsve-tants* at hasidic weddings in Jerusalem I pay particular attention to the historical and social background of the ceremony.[40] I show that:

1. The ceremony of the *mitsve-tants*, which concludes the public events of the wedding night, is exceeded in importance only by the ceremony of the *khupe*.

2. It is not clear whether the term *mitsve-tants*, sometimes known as *kosher tants*, and others that appear in the literature concerning the dancing at wedding celebrations in the Ashkenazi communities in eastern Europe before the appearance of Beshtian hasidism in the second half of the eighteenth century, refers to variants of a single type of dance, or whether various wedding dances were all considered *mitsve-tents*.

3. Using rhymed verse declaimed extemporaneously or prepared in advance, the *badkhn* invites male relatives and men of high status (for example, the *rebbe* or the head of a yeshiva) to dance with the bride. The fathers-in-law determine in advance who is to be invited to dance in this way and the hierarchical order in which they will be summoned.

4. According to hasidic thought, dance, like music, is a potentially powerful means for serving God, and the *mitsve-tants* is considered to possess theurgical or magical potency that can influence the upper worlds.[41] Nevertheless, some oppose holding this ceremony for reasons of modesty, as it involves men dancing with a woman.

different in style and substance from those of the hasidic *badkhonim*. On the earlier *baveynen* custom in its hasidic transformation in the *badkhn*'s verses to the groom, see Rotenberg, *Zameru lishemo*, pars. 277, 434.

[39] M. Beregovsky [Moyshe Beregovski], 'Evreiskaya narodnaya instrumental′naya muzyka', in M. Goldin (ed.), *Sovetskii kompozitor* (Moscow, 1987), 13 and 55; Bik, *Ḥatunah yehudit*, 11.

[40] Mazor and Taube, 'A Hasidic Ritual Dance', 164–6.

[41] Meir of Karistshev, *Me'ir einei ḥakhamim*, 287–8; *Kuntres birkot hatanim*, 65, par. 14, incipit of '*sos tasis* (*vetagel ha'akarah*)'. On the magical and theurgical conception of music in hasidism, see M. Idel, 'Haperush hamagi vehate'urgi shel hamusikah betekstim yehudiyim mitekufat harenensans ve'ad laḥasidut', *Yuval*, 4 (1982), 33–63 (Heb. pagination); Mazor, 'Koḥo shel hanigun'.

5.   The selection of words and melodies for the Jerusalem *mitsve-tants* reflects the social outlook and cultural characteristics of hasidic society.

This last point is also true with respect to the *badkhn*'s performance during the wedding reception and the *mitsve-tants*. Yet, as opposed to the unity of music and text that generally characterizes the *badkhn*'s versification before the veiling ceremony, the words and music used during the *mitsve-tants* (which commonly lasts for several hours) often manifest a wide range of styles. Since the *badkhn* thus displays the fullest range of his talents, stylistic differences among *badkhonim* become very apparent. There are those, such as Grinvald and Geiger, who weave many *gematriyes* (wordplay based on the numerical value of letters) and acronyms into their texts, while others, such as Rotenberg, use them sparingly. Some interject jokes and anecdotes even in the midst of their verses (Geiger and Yisrael Shtern, for example), while others restrict themselves to inserting humorous verses only in appropriate places.[42] A comparative analysis of the sung texts will allow us to see the stylistic differences between *badkhonim* in greater detail, and relate them to the *badkhn*'s self-image and education, and the influence of other *badkhonim*. It will also reveal the idioms that are unique to each individual *badkhn*, and perhaps illustrate the atmosphere that generated such idioms, as well as the attitude of particular hasidic dynasties towards the *badkhn*'s performance.

In the following section I will examine several aspects of the textual and musical formulas of the *badkhn*'s verses, focusing on the *mitsve-tants* documented in 1971.[43] A full textual analysis would examine the language of the text, the dialect, the contents of the text, its structure and versification, relation to sources, acronyms, and *gematriyes*. Here, however, I will limit myself to those areas that are directly connected to musical analysis.

OBSERVATIONS FROM TEXTUAL ANALYSIS

At the *mitsve-tants* it is customary to summon the male guests to dance with the bride in a specific order. The first of the dancers is the grandfather on the groom's side; and after him, the grandfather on the bride's side; then, the father of the groom and the father of the bride; and after them, the uncles and other relatives in descending order, according to their relationship to the couple. The groom is the

---

[42] On Yisrael Shtern, see n. 14. Time and content limits are imposed on the *badkhn*. Time limits are imposed on him 'because of the strain on the audience', so that the ceremony does not extend into the small hours of the morning. Likewise, some *tsadikim* are opposed to jokes and other expressions of humour that are not sung. Others, such as the *tsadik* of Makhnovka, who dislike the praises which the *badkhonim* heap upon them (which the *tsadik*, for example, sarcastically terms *hespedim* (eulogies)), instruct the *badkhonim* to reduce them, and focus instead on the meaning of the ceremony and on citations from traditional sources.

[43] NSA YC 314–15. For the transcript of the full text, see the original Hebrew version of this chapter, app. A, pp. 67–79.

last to be summoned. If the *rebbe* is present at the wedding, he is summoned first, even before the grandfather on the groom's side. There are no fixed rules regarding invitations to heads of yeshivas or other respected figures who are not relatives; it seems that their place in the order of invitation is determined by their standing in the community.

At this particular wedding, at which the host was the Kretshiner Rebbe, in Rehovot, Yosef Grinvald was faced with a difficult dilemma as *badkhn*: all the relatives on the groom's side were *tsadikim* from the Nadvorne dynasty. According to custom, they should have been invited according to family hierarchy, which in this particular case would have paralleled their status in hasidic society. The trouble was that in this hierarchy two of the groom's brothers at the end of the list were young leaders of the Kretshinef sub-dynasty. Grinvald, himself a follower of the Kretshiner Rebbe in Rehovot, was not happy about giving such a lowly place to his own admirable *rebbe* and his brother, and he resolved this dilemma by using text and music in a way that would highlight their status without altering the traditional hierarchy. He did this by formulating the versified invitations to the older, venerable *tsadikim* in respectful yet standard language, with the exception of the address to the great-grandfather of the groom, the first to be invited, calling him *ekhod yokhid umeyukhod* ('unique and exceptional'). In contrast, he invited his own *rebbe* with the much more glorifying words *kevoyd kedushas adoneynu moreynu verabeynu shlit″e* ('Our holy master, teacher, and rabbi, may he have a long and good life, amen').[44]

In addition, by means of textual arrangement, the *badkhn* constructed a second, ascending hierarchy alongside the descending family hierarchy. In summoning the *rebbe* of Kiryat Gat, R. Yisrael Nisan (b. 1948), the younger of the two brothers, he used nine verses; he then honoured the elder brother, the leader of the Kretshinef hasidim, with eighteen verses, while for the groom he used twenty-four verses.[45] In contrast, he prepared only three verses for the great-grandfather of the groom, who was supposed to dance first.[46] As the latter was not present, he allotted four verses to the grandfather of the groom, who actually danced first, and two for each additional *tsadik*.[47] It is interesting to note that the father of the bride, the rabbi of Jaffa, who was not a hasidic *rebbe*, was invited by the *badkhn* through verses in a language resembling that of the invited *tsadikim*. However the *badkhn* allotted him five verses, more than each veteran *tsadik* and less than what he had prepared for the

[44] NSA YC 314/18.

[45] This hierarchical structure was cut short by the dance of an uncle who had unexpectedly arrived from the United States, whose invitation to dance was unplanned but requested by the older *rebbes* after the dance of the young *rebbe* from Kiryat Gat. However, the *badkhn* improvised for him only two verses, as he did for the older *rebbes*.   [46] NSA YC 314/4.

[47] Three of the verses are a combination of the verses which the *badkhn* prepared for the great-grandfather and the other grandfather who were not present. The fourth verse was new and had been composed a short time before the *mitsve-tants*. Similar hierarchy appears during the *mitsve-tants* in Jerusalem. There it is expressed through the number of melodies and their total length in the dance of each honoree guest (see Mazor and Taube, 'A Hasidic Ritual Dance', 198, 202–3).

two Kretshinef brothers. In this way, through the language of the invitation and the length of the text, the *badkhn* demonstrated his own attitude towards the younger *tsadikim*.

The *badkhn*'s attitude to the various participants was also expressed through the verses themselves. The older *rebbes* received merely routine blessings, while in the invitations to the father of the bride and the brother of the groom the *badkhn* proclaimed that the groom's father, recently deceased, had descended from heaven to dance with them and bless them. In his blessing of the *rebbe* of Kiryat Gat the *badkhn* included the wish that his community grow and prosper. In his invitation to the *tsadik* of Kretshinef, the *badkhn* mentioned the *tsadik*'s humility, saying that he did not consider himself worthy to dance on his own merit, but only as substitute for his deceased father. On the other hand, the *badkhn* affirmed that, as the successor to his father, the young *tsadik* was indeed worthy to dance on his own merit. Accordingly, the *badkhn* invited every deceased *tsadik* of the dynasty, including the founder of the dynasty, R. Meir of Premishlan (Peremyshlyany) (d. 1773), and even the Besht, to descend from heaven to join the *rebbe*'s holy dance with the bride. In addition, in verses that followed, the *badkhn* instructed the bride to remain motionless during the *tsadik*'s dance, and explained at length how it is possible to dance without moving. In his invitation to the groom the *badkhn* praised him and the education he received 'as the son of holy ones', and dared to add that he was sure that his dance would leave an impression in the higher spheres—something which was not said in honour of any of the older, venerable *tsadikim*.[48]

ASPECTS OF MUSICAL ANALYSIS

In this ceremony Yosef Grinvald invited each of the nine dancers with a different melody. The first, third, and fifth melodies are well-known *nigunim* for *badkhones*. The second melody is the tune of a Yiddish song entitled 'Eser sfires' ('Ten *sefirot*').[49] However, the fact that it was interwoven with a *purim-shpil* composed by Bobover hasidim suggests its connection to a *badkhn* repertoire, owing to the traditional involvement of the *badkhn* in composing and performing *purim-shpils*. The fourth melody is related to the Bobover *purim-rov* (Purim rabbi).[50] The sixth and

[48] The *badkhn* prepared more verses for *tsadikim* who did not stay for the *mitsve-tants*. They were included in this hierarchy as well, for the *badkhn* allocated two verses, in conventional language, for each of them. According to this hierarchy, the *badkhn* allocated only one verse to the unmarried younger brothers of the groom, who were told to dance together as one person with the bride.

[49] See *Zemirot yisrael: leket nigunei yere'im vehasidim beyidish* (on the title page: 'Leket shirim yekarim une'imim malhivim levavot le'avodat habore yitbarakh shemo') (Benei Berak, 1963), lyrics pp. 7–8 (Heb. pagination), melody p. 3 (Latin pagination).

[50] In hasidic and other communities it is customary to appoint someone with a sense of humour to the role of 'Purim rabbi' at Purim banquets. This person is given complete freedom to jest and make the crowd laugh in any way he can: reciting the 'Purim Kiddush' (a parody of the benediction over wine), composing rhymes, and performing skits. He is allowed to select any subject and display it in a distorted mirror.

seventh melodies are hasidic dance tunes. The former, sung to the words 'Tsaveh yeshuot yakov' ('Command the salvation of Jacob', Ps. 44: 5), does not have a specific ritual function. The latter, 'Ketsad merakdin' ('How does one dance [before the bride]?', BT, *Ket.* 17*a*), is a well-known wedding melody. The eighth is the tune of the Yiddish song 'Eyzehu mekoymen shel zevokhin?' ('What is the place of sacrifices?'), which concerns the Temple service and its substitute, prayer.[51] The ninth is the tune of a shepherd's song which hasidic tradition connects to the revelation of the first Kalever Rebbe, Yitskhok Ayzik Toyb (1744–1821). The Yiddish version opens with the words 'Vald, vald, vi groys bistu' ('Forest, forest, how vast you are'), which is apparently a translation from the non-Jewish source. An alternative opening verse is also known: 'Golus, golus, vi groys bistu' ('Exile, exile, how vast you are'), an esoteric interpretation of the pastoral text, attributed to the Kalever Rebbe. The song became famous in the hasidic world, and its tune was joined to different texts in various hasidic communities.[52] The first five tunes, therefore, are specifically *badkhn* melodies, or at least connected with *badkhonim* and folk humour. Three are hasidic melodies (nos. 6, 7, and 9), and one is the tune of a Yiddish folk song (no. 8). The Romanian source of two of the melodies (nos. 5 and 9) is beyond doubt. And the third melody, which was very popular among the *badkhonim* of Hungarian hasidim, is a modern Russian popular genre known as *chastushka*.

In other words, most of the repertoire Grinvald sang at this wedding was connected to the musical world of the *badkhn* and not to a specific hasidic dynasty's repertoire. On the other hand, the selection of tunes supported the ascending hierarchical ladder the *badkhn* had created by his verses. The opener was a traditional *badkhn* melody. After that came *nigunim*, which, for the most part, are also connected with traditional *badkhones*; some of them are '*nigunim* of rejoicing', which are connected to joyous occasions such as *purim-shpils* and weddings. Two special melodies were reserved by the *badkhn* for the end of the ceremony, for the invitation to the *tsadik* of Kretshinef, head of the community and brother of the groom, and the culminating invitation to the groom to dance with his bride.

This selection of melodies was far from arbitrary: the tune of 'Eyzehu mekoymen', which has served for many years as a *badkhn* tune, is quite close in terms of style and mood to the hasidic genre known as *dveykes nigunim* (tunes of cleaving [i.e. to God]), which are meant to help the hasid enter a meditative state of union with God.[53] In addition, the song itself deals with the offering of sacrifices in the Temple

---

[51] See *Zemirot yisrael*, lyrics, pp. 11–12 (Heb. pagination); tune, p. 4 (Latin pagination); every stanza of the song concludes with the words 'What is the place of sacrifices?' (Mishnah *Zev.* 5).

[52] On the song and its origin, see Idelsohn, 'Haneginah haḥasidit', in *Sefer hashanah shel yehudei amerikah* (New York, 1931), 78–9. For the second version and the music, see *Zemirot yisrael*, p. 3 (Heb. pagination) and p. 1 (Latin pagination); A. Hajdu and Y. Mazor, 'The Musical Tradition of Hasidism', in *Encyclopedia Judaica*, vii. 1428, ex. 2. On the appropriation of non-Jewish melodies in hasidism, and on this particular tune, see Mazor, 'Koḥo shel hanigun', 46–8 (Heb. pagination).

[53] On this topic, see Mazor, 'Koḥo shel hanigun', 23, 40–2 (Heb. pagination).

and their substitute, prayer, while the fourth stanza speaks of Jerusalem as immersed in the Shekhinah (Divine Presence, seen as a female emanation). According to the hasidic view, the prayer of the *tsadik* with its kabbalistic intentions is in itself divine service. This is also true of his dance with the bride, symbolizing a dance with the Shekhinah through which the *tsadik* also achieves supernal unions. It follows that from the perspective of the original text of the song, as well as its genre (*dveykes*), this song is directly linked to the divine service of the hasidic *tsadikim*. This is what the *badkhn* intimated when he proclaimed that the dance of his *rebbe*, the *tsadik* of Rehovot, alone was worthy to be considered 'actual divine service' (*avoyde mamesh*) that influenced the higher worlds.

A similar reason lay behind the selection of the tune of 'Vald, vald' for the verses used in summoning the groom. According to hasidic tradition, the shepherd's song and its melody were revealed by a *tsadik*, who sensed their latent holiness. The subject of the song is said to be the exile of the Shekhinah. And in counterpoint, the dance of the groom with the bride is a preparation for their coupling, which symbolizes, according to the hasidic idea grounded in kabbalah, the supernal coupling of God and the Shekhinah—a coupling which causes divine abundance to fill all the upper spheres, and hastens the repair of the world (*tikun*) and the end of exile.[54] In other words, the melodies which the *badkhn* chose for the verses inviting the *tsadik* of Kretshinef from Rehovot and the groom to dance were, in contrast to all the other tunes he used, linked to the theurgical function of the *mitsve-tants*.

THE RELATIONSHIP BETWEEN WORDS AND MUSIC

With respect to the relationship between words and music, an interesting question arises: which comes first? Does the *badkhn* mould the melody around a text which he has composed, or does he match words with tunes appropriate to them? According to recorded interviews with Grinvald in 1971, it seems that both methods were acceptable. Moreover, in many cases Grinvald could not decide which came first, claiming that the text and the tune were 'born' in his head at the same time.

An analysis of the relationship between words and music can occur on the following five planes: melodic sections, phrases, accents, rhythm, and melodic motifs. Such an analysis of the performance I have been examining[55] suggests that, whether the tune preceded the text or vice versa, Grinvald was so conscious of a tune's structure, in terms of sections, phrases, and phrase divisions, that he could not but consider such structures when composing verses, and always sought a complete correspondence between text and tune structures. And yet it appears that Grinvald did not invent new textual structures, but rather adopted known ones. And when he could not find a familiar textual repertoire to fit a specific tune, he did not hesi-

---

[54] See above, and Tishby, *Mishnat hazohar*, 607 ff.
[55] See the Hebrew version of this chapter, pp. 59–62.

tate to fit the tune to several structures, or to solve the problems deriving from his quest for complete correspondence between text and tune by means of audience participation in singing musical sections or phrases without text, or even through changes to the tune itself.

CONCLUSION

Hasidic society, as a matter of course, does not approve of radical innovations in relation to religious custom, and this is certainly true of the activities of *badkhonim* at weddings. Nevertheless, the hasidic leadership has been able to channel such activities into preferred directions, in accordance with its own conceptions and usages. Earlier practices that clashed with hasidic customs and beliefs have been discarded. On the other hand, mystical interpretation has invested some traditional values with new meanings. The *badkhn*'s position has thus been strengthened, thanks to the legitimization of his activity from a religious point of view. The same is true of the *badkhn*'s verses and the accompanying music. It would appear, however, that the shift of emphasis from form to content, to the inner meaning of the *badkhn*'s activities, has resulted in the formation, on one hand, of rigorous new constraints and, on the other, of new possibilities for the creation of local or even individual, personal styles, depending on the relative involvement of the *tsadikim* in such activities. The overt neutrality of the spiritual leadership to the musical aspect of the *badkhn*'s work, even on the part of leaders known for their involvement in shaping their community's repertoire,[56] and the emerging phenomenon of itinerant *badkhonim*, wandering from one hasidic court to another, has reinforced the eclectic nature of the *badkhn*'s music, but has also enabled him, if he so desires, to use his music as an expression of social hierarchy. An analysis of the relationship between music and text on additional levels, as well as a musical and textual analysis on every social and cultural level, will yield further conclusions that will contribute to our comprehension of the *badkhn*'s function.[57]

Translated from Hebrew by Glenn Dynner

[56] See Mazor, 'Merkaziyuto shel ha'admor behithadshut hahayim hamusikaliyim bahatsar vishnits bevenei berak (1950–1972)', *Dukhan*, 12 (1978), 130–58.

[57] Cf. Mazor and Taube, 'A Hasidic Ritual Dance', esp. 214–15, 118–19, 202–3.

Transmigrations: Wolf Krakowski's Yiddish Worldbeat in its Socio-Musical Context

ALEX LUBET

INTRODUCTION: THE LAST YIDDISH BLUESMAN AND THE MUSICIAN OF LUBLIN

I LOVE Wolf Krakowski. His legendary CD *Transmigrations*[1]—the first example of Yiddish worldbeat—is my favourite. I admit this freely, although I am by day a tenured full professor of Western classical music who swims in the sea of assimilation, Jewish self-loathing, and politely restrained antisemitism that is mid-western academe and for whom this confession might be received as ranging from eccentric to foolish to professionally risky. But, as the 1929 Michalesco recording says, 'A yid bin ikh geboyrn' ('I was born a Jew').[2] Jewishness defines me whether I like it or not (and I do) and *Transmigrations* speaks to and for our generation of North American Jews like nothing else, whether we know it or not (and we should).

Wolf is one of my dearest friends. A copy of *Transmigrations* and the stream of Krakowski–Lubet email that flowed constantly between Northampton, Massachusetts, and Lublin kept me sane while I was living in Poland in 1999. Lublin, a Jewish ghost town, was home to the great Romantic composer–violinist Henryk Wieniawski, a personal hero, a nineteenth-century Jewish Jimi Hendrix who, like Wolf, was a man of eclectic tastes and strong popular cultural sensibilities.

It was also, of course, inspiration to I. B. Singer. Isaac Bashevis Singer Street is a single, empty block facing the 'New Jewish Cemetery', by far the worst-kept Jewish cemetery or memorial I saw anywhere in Poland, in the shabbiest part of town. If my woefully inadequate Polish served me right, the word *żydowski* protrudes accusingly from any sentence it inhabits; one of my futile attempts to enter the cemetery was met with ridicule by a couple of toughs in a manner that strongly recommended my swift retreat. Majdanek is a suburb of Lublin. Its western border is a

---

[1] Wolf Krakowski, *Transmigrations* (Kame'a Media, 1996); rereleased on the Tzadik label in August 2001. A second CD, entitled *Goyrl* ('Destiny') was released by Tzadik in July 2002.

[2] 'A yid bin ich geboiren', *Dave Tarras: Yiddish-American Klezmer Music, 1925–1956* (Yazoo, Miss., 1991).

forest of tiny dachas whose owners must somehow have arrived at some kind of peace with the 125,000 Jews murdered there. I will never understand.

This is the context in which I lived and taught Jewish contributions to American musical culture in 1999 at Marie Curie-Skłodowska University. Prior to that time I had negative interest in east European travel, regarding the region almost exclusively as Holocaust Central, hardly a unique feeling among Jews. I was recruited, on the basis of my teaching prowess, rather than any particular subject, to apply for an exchange professorship in Lublin. My Polish colleagues invited me on the condition I teach Jewish music, an interest I had hitherto pursued as an artist and scholar, but never in the classroom.

Although not exactly by design, it is probably best I do not teach Jewish music at the University of Minnesota. I hold all things Jewish sacred and find it emotionally wrenching to share them with those, usually composition students, who do not and are merely seeking novelty, or who relate to Judaism through their Christianity. By contrast, my Polish students and colleagues, all devout Catholics or at least intimately familiar with others' devotion, respected my sacred space in a way that made sharing what I hold dear surprisingly less problematic and much more pleasurable than it had ever been at home.

My residency was extremely successful. I made numerous wonderful friendships with Polish colleagues and students who were anything but antisemitic. But being a solitary, thoroughly exposed, even celebrity Jew, charged with representing his people and faith to a non-Jewish public in a city at once so Jewish and Jewless, was among the most emotionally draining experiences of my life. I owe much of my spiritual sustenance in that challenging time to Wolf Krakowski.

JEWS IN (CYBER)SPACE

At the time of writing Wolf and I have not met and have spoken by phone only occasionally. Yet we regard ourselves as dear friends—a testament to the Internet in general and email in particular. If virtual, the Internet is also a most natural instrument of Jewish community. It is the nexus of contemporary secular Ashkenazi music, if not all Old World Ashkenazi culture which—tightly bounded by Israel, Orthodoxy, assimilation, and antisemitism—occupies, more than ever before, no physical space of its own.

Jewish life has been virtual for a very long time, in ways both awful and elegant. There is Diaspora—*golus*, Israel without place. But there is also Torah, Written and Oral: Israel as conversation with God. For me, the most life-affirming representation of Jewish virtuality is the Passover Haggadah, whose declaration that 'in every generation, every man must think of himself as having gone forth from Egypt' defies both space and time.

Wolf found me on the Internet. The most important web site for *klezmer* and other secular Jewish musics is Ari Davidow's KlezmerShack.[3] Davidow also maintains the listserve World Music from a Jewish Slant.[4] In the absence of significant electronic or print media or an ongoing presence in important performance venues (despite the widely touted worldwide Jewish dominance of all major media, governments, and financial institutions), these two adjoining cybershtetls with their one-man *kehile* (council), neither a musician nor a Yiddish speaker but a maven of *webkayt*, assume great importance in our little world of Yiddish music.

In 1995 I introduced myself on the web site as, among other things, an author who had reviewed Yiddish music recordings for the journal *Ethnomusicology*. Having read my posting, Wolf sent me *Transmigrations*, requesting a review.

YIDDISH WORLDBEAT: REGGAE OF AGES

At the time I ignored Wolf's request. *Transmigrations* struck me as wrong for *Ethnomusicology*; it was neither archival nor an attempt to revive with fidelity a historical style. When reviewing *klezmer* revival recordings for this journal, I always tried to balance my enthusiasm for innovative post-modern bands with the journal's scholarly mission. I sensed that Wolf's self-proclaimed Yiddish worldbeat lay beyond the pale of *Ethnomusicology*.

Yet even prior to hearing the album I was excited by the prospect of a New Yiddish fusion music, a 'Jewsion', that boldly went where even John Zorn and the Klezmatics had never gone. The album makes one contemplate the ontology of Jewish music as little else can. If only for that reason—there are many others—it must be taken seriously. That it was a first, remains unique, and combines many apparently disparate elements, invites the label 'experimental', although it is anything but abstruse or self-consciously avant-garde.

Definitions of Jewish music are elusive and contested. Debates may focus on which parts of the Jewish soundscape, such as chanted prayer, are 'music',[5] but are more typically framed by what musics are Jewish. I doubt broad consensus will ever be reached, particularly regarding secular music, which lacks the imprimaturs of sacred text or religious praxis that wield authority over the Jewish identity even of heretics and non-believers (whose Jewish peoplehood is still largely defined by their association with and even response to a creed to which they do not adhere). Still, lines are rarely clear or fixed between sacred and profane in Jewish life. After all, the Ashkenazi instrumental dance genres that are central to what is now called *klezmer*, the mainstream of contemporary Yiddish secular music, had their genesis in the wedding ritual which celebrates one of Judaism's most sacred commandments.

Transmigrations comprises principally secular songs, although these are at times referenced, as is nearly unavoidable in chronicles of Jewish life. Two songs,

---

[3] <www.klezmershack.com>.   [4] <jewish-music@shamash.org>.

[5] A. Shiloah, *Jewish Musical Traditions* (Detroit, 1992), 75–80.

'Shabes, shabes' and 'Zol shoyn kumen di geule' ('Let the Redemption Come'), are traditionally devotional, if non-liturgical. The songs that address the Holocaust and other Jewish suffering pose basic spiritual questions that Jews must ask, though not in formal prayer.

In determining any music's Jewishness, lessons from the sacred repertoire of Judaism may be applied. On utilitarian grounds, all settings of sacred Hebrew texts for use in Jewish worship are Jewish music. This principle extends to all Yiddish song, since Jewish languages are tools of Jewish community. This includes all twelve songs on *Transmigrations*.

Two of my mentors in Jewish music, the cantors Morton Kula and Max Wohlberg, while flexible in such matters as harmony and rhythm, insisted that sacred Jewish melody retain appropriate traditional *nusekh*, or mode.[6] While *nusekh* is a principle of sacred music, grounding in modes of Ashkenazi prayer, however intuitive, resulting in appropriation of melodic motifs of the synagogue, also lies at the heart of Yiddish vernacular music.[7]

Transmigrations—an album of Yiddish folk songs and works by Yiddish theatre and literary artists, its melodies forthrightly Jewish—is a product of this environment. Yet the album defies expectations of Yiddish song in broader aspects of style. Simply put, it's a rock album. More accurately, it combines influences of guitar-driven popular musics of the post-Second World War English-speaking world: 1960s counter-culture rock and folk-rock, hard-edged country, and reggae, with a nearly ubiquitous female chorus rooted in gospel and rhythm and blues. Blues is a subtle, yet pervasive, inspiration. This marriage of eclectic sources is harmonious and grooving, wedded under a *khupe* of Yiddish melody. The cantors who mentored me would be pleased.

But if my teachers would have sanctioned Krakowski's rebirthing of these great Jewish songs, I initially did not. My first response to Yiddish worldbeat was excitement at the concept but hesitation about the product. I was not at once convinced of a successful merging of musical worlds. Jews in *golus* have always absorbed their neighbours' musical practices. It is unlikely that much other than shofar-blowing—if that—is uninfluenced by Diaspora. The music Jews make may be unparalleled in its breadth of influences. In terms of historical precedent, then, *Transmigrations* seemed perfectly natural, neither new nor alarming. Intuitively, though, I was struck that Krakowski's 'Jewsion' differed greatly from others I had embraced with pleasure and affection.

---

[6] A mode may be regarded as a set of characteristics, usually melodic, that identify a genre or style. The defining elements of the blues offer a familiar example of modality.

[7] See J. Frigyesi, 'The Historical Value of the Record *Maramaros*', notes to the CD *The Lost Jewish Music of Transylvania* (Hannibal, Mo., 1993).

EAST SIDE STORY: THE AMERICANIZATION OF JEWISH MUSIC

Other *golus*-tinged eclecticisms of North American Yiddish music emerged from more organic, communally nurtured, decades-long interactions between Jews and other urbanites. Henry Sapoznik's 1992 CD anthology *Dave Tarras: Yiddish American Klezmer Music, 1925–1956*[8] chronicles over three decades of eclectic musics once simply called 'Jewish', modelled on operetta, musical comedy, Tin Pan Alley, and swing, yet grounded in *nusekh* and traditional Ashkenazi idioms. These infusions of light classical music and Jazz Age glitter are less assimilation than expression of the aspiration to enhance Jewish social status through absorption of stylistic intricacies of western Europe and the American 'Golden Land'.

The Klezmatics, the most eclectically post-modern *klezmer* revival band, rejuvenated that tradition with rock, jazz, and worldbeat influences of their native New York. Reviewing their 1992 *rhythm + jews*, I observed that

For all their diverse influences, the Klezmatics' sound is a seamless, essentially emic fusion. The sources from which they draw are native to the musical world of American Jewish intellectuals of the 'boomer generation'. Jewish interest in both Middle Eastern and American vernacular culture is both strong and long-standing enough for their imprint upon contemporary klezmer music to seem entirely natural.[9]

With emendations to accommodate generational difference, the same applied to the great clarinettist Dave Tarras. For the Klezmatics, though, the aspiration is no longer upward mobility, but cultural autonomy as American Jews, diasporites who do not require Zion for self-definition. Tarras was the musical heart of Jewish America; the Klezmatics are the revival's bright children. Both exemplify larger socio-musical movements; they are perhaps different moments in a single process.

I first heard *Transmigrations* as juxtaposing disparate, unrelated, Yiddish and American musical elements. The mix seemed a stretch: rural American, Jamaican, Latin; things one would instantly classify as un-Jewish. Yet every incursion of Diaspora music and culture (provisionally) accepted into Jewish life must once have seemed peculiar and met resistance. Jewish reggae or outlaw country are arguably far more natural—and less toxic—than German Lutheranism's influence on the music of Reform Judaism. Given the many genres born of Diaspora contacts and the great and varied successes of 'mainstream' Jewish musicians, what is finally unnatural about Krakowski's interpretations of Yiddish song is not his chosen path of rough-hewn Anglo-African American vernacular, but that he has had to go it alone.

Or has he? The 'conversion experience' through which I came to advocate Wolf's music occurred not through listening to *Transmigrations*, but through our

---

[8] (Yazoo, 1991). The music is accompanied by Sapoznik's essay 'Dave Tarras: Father of Yiddish-American Klezmer Music'. [9] *Ethnomusicology*, 39 (1995), no. 2, 340–3.

first extended exchange of email, which began on Davidow's listserve and quickly went private. Wolf and I were engaged in the sort of ultra-heated debate that non-Jews are often shocked to see occurring among people who regard themselves as friends. Topics ebbed and flowed, as we finally arrived at our mutual admiration and passion for the work of Lenny Bruce. Bruce was the epitome of the outlaw social critic, a recurrent figure in much of the world's history and lore, from Gandhi and King to *Till Eulenspiegel's Merry Pranks*[10] and *The Signifying Monkey*.[11] Recognizing Bruce as the Jewish exemplar of the tradition—and acknowledging the outlaw nature of *golus* in general—and hearing Wolf as he hears himself—as Bruce's musical *doppelgänger* (a few decades removed)—as Yiddish outlaw compatriot of Bob Marley, Willie Nelson, and Jerry Garcia—all this made beautiful sense. Allowing once more for generational difference, Lenny Bruce himself said it best in his classic 'Jewish and Goyish': 'Dig: I'm Jewish. Count Basie's Jewish. Ray Charles is Jewish.'[12]

Wolf Krakowski's *Transmigrations* is outrageously Jewish.

Earlier, better times for Yiddish culture spawned art song, opera, musical comedy, popular song, jazz, dance genres, folk song, and liturgical traditions. Much was undertaken; everything seemed possible. That Wolf may be the one true Yiddish rocker owes not to eccentricity, but to that ultimate aberration in Jewish life and Yiddish culture, the Holocaust. That Wolf has no peers owes much to the devastation of *yidishkayt*, all but replaced by the diverse, flourishing culture of Israel, Zionism, and modern Hebrew.

But globalization means that physical proximity is no longer the criterion for influence or even community. Were Yiddish thriving now, its song would surely include rich responses to rock, hip hop, everything, everywhere.[13] Its artists would feel less if any need for the *klezmer* revival which currently dominates secular Jewish American music. *Transmigrations*, uninfluenced by past or present *klezmorim*, would have been made with few if any changes had the *klezmer* revival never occurred.

BEYOND *KLEZMER*: *DOS LEBN IN AMERIKE* (LIVIN' IN THE USA)

The son of Polish Holocaust survivors, born in Saalfelden Farmach Displaced Persons' Camp in US-occupied Austria, raised in Eskilstuna, Sweden, and Toronto,

---

[10] A tone poem by the composer Richard Strauss portraying the great trickster of German folklore.

[11] A reference to the West African legend that is the title of Henry Louis Gates Jr.'s magnum opus on the literatures of African peoples (New York, 1989).

[12] W. Novak and M. Waldoks (eds.), *The Big Book of Jewish Humor* (New York, 1981), 60.

[13] See K. Malm, 'Music on the Move: Traditions and the Mass Media', *Ethnomusicology*, 37 (1993), no. 3, 339–52; M. Slobin, 'Micromusics of the West: A Comparative Approach', *Ethnomusicology*, 36 (1992), 1–87.

Wolf resides in Northampton, Massachusetts, with his wife, the Yiddish vocalist Fraidy Katz. A truly native Yiddish speaker, his singing sends a thrill of authenticity straight to the hearts of co-linguists, for whom artistic truth is manifest in the use of a timelessly eloquent vernacular. While enamoured of Yiddish song from childhood, Krakowski never internalized the traditional dance rhythms of *freylekh*, *bulgar*, or *sher*. A late twentieth-century Anglo–North American, Wolf's heart beats to 'blues-based rhythm music', anything (good) played with steel-string guitars in the English-speaking world.[14]

Thus, passion for Yiddish song, which, as Henry Sapoznik observes, Wolf understands culturally and linguistically as few of his peers,[15] is coupled with discomfort with the 'smiley-face' *klezmer* revivalism he fears is more performed than felt.[16] Armed with great Yiddish songs from beyond the *klezmer* revival repertoire, *Transmigrations* rages against the legacy of the Holocaust on behalf of the culture Hitler couldn't quite destroy. With the Lonesome Brothers, a kicking, altogether empathetic band, Wolf rocks an Ashkenaz struggling for survival on a few web sites and the leavings of JCC budgets hell-bent for Zion.

Characteristically modest about his post-modernization of Yiddish song, Wolf refuses to call himself anything more than an 'arranger'. I regard his transformation of the musical environment in which these melodies reside as nothing less than recomposition. He transforms his material to the same magnitude that Aaron Copland recast the Shaker hymn 'Simple Gifts' in his ballet *Appalachian Spring*. Their respective methods, however, result in very different sociocultural statements. Copland took the plain-spoken melody and placed it into a medium associated with social prestige and economic power. This required not only developmental methods of Western art music, but filling in 'awkward' melodic gaps in the original hymn, now often 'corrected' Copland-style even by professional 'folk singers'.[17] Hearing a Shaker rendition, one senses how Copland and others, embarrassed by the 'missing teeth' of this poor relation, 'improved' it with classical music's equivalent of cosmetic dentistry,[18] recalling Julia Roberts's made-over working-class heroines in the films *Pretty Woman* and *Erin Brockovich*.

Wolf wears his proletarian past and present proudly. Previous recordings of the songs on *Transmigrations* are full of schmaltz. I do not mean the emotionality that links cantorial singing to Horowitz to Hendrix (as attractive to the pink-haired as to the blue-),[19] but the melding of simply harmonized vernacular music (in this case,

---

[14] Two exceptions among Wolf's favourites, Jose Feliciano and Willie Nelson, play nylon-string guitars.

[15] H. Sapoznik, *Klezmer! From Old World to Our World* (New York, 1999), 253.

[16] See e.g. the 1995 PBS documentary *In the Fiddler's House*.

[17] e.g. the Armstrong Family's version on *The Wheel of the Year: Thirty Years with the Armstrong Family* (Flying Fish, 1992). [18] In musical terms Copland fills in skipped passing notes.

[19] On the relationship of rock to the Romantic tradition in classical music, see S. Frith, *Music for Pleasure* (New York, 1988).

Jewish melody) to such large gestures of Western art music as lush orchestration, classically trained voices, and four-part choral texture.[20]

When art music notions of elegance are grafted onto folk or popular miniature forms minus classical music's thematic development, the result is 'easy listening', the dominant aesthetic of white American popular music of the McCarthy 1950s, continued in the industry's self-censoring propagation of such non-talents as the 'anti-Elvis' Pat Boone. 'Jewish' too was prone to the 'vanilla' sound. Yaffa Yarkoni, popular Yiddish singer of the 1950s and 1960s, used Johnny Mathis's arranger, Glenn Osser, for her string orchestrations. (Jewish writers, arrangers, and promoters such as Osser were ubiquitous in early rock.)

Among the most familiar schmaltz is classic Motown: string-based orchestration, immaculate vocal harmony, and studied choreography. Early Motown's visual signature included formal evening wear and big hair (on women). Motown even schooled its artists in elegant on- and off-stage deportment in its 'finishing school'.[21] Not at first overtly political, Motown's images of African American affluent beauty, widely televised, embodied hope and possibility.[22]

LIKE A ROLLING *SHTEYN*

In contrast, Bob Dylan, musical herald of white (largely Jewish) support of the civil rights movement, employed wrinkled shirts, faded jeans, blue notes, an orchestra of one, and attempted working-class deportment (often countered by cryptic high-art lyrics). Like jazz-influenced George Gershwin, Dylan was a crucial mediator of African American and European–American idioms.[23]

Despite the importance of Dylan's songs, his performance may have been even more influential. Charles Keil's theory of 'participatory discrepancies' (PDs) argues that 'Music to be personally involving, must be "out of time" and "out of tune"',[24] ' "out of time and out of tune" only in relation to music department standardization and the civilized worldview, of course'.[25] Music needs slight (or, like Dylan, not-

---

[20] For a discussion of 'Jewish harmony', see A. Idelsohn, *Jewish Music in its Historical Development* (New York, 1967). In *Folk Song Style and Culture* (New Brunswick, NJ, 1968), Alan Lomax cites vocal timbre as a most unchangeable marker of a music's cultural origin. Thus, despite Jewish melody and harmony, an 'operatic' vocal quality might identify a performance as Western art music.

[21] See e.g. the 1995 WGBH (Boston) documentary *Rock 'n' Roll*.

[22] Oprah Winfrey has spoken of the importance to her youthful self-esteem of seeing the Supremes on television.

[23] Some of the white folk singers most identified with the civil rights movement and with Dylan's songs, like Joan Baez and Peter, Paul, and Mary, were little influenced by black music. Perhaps this lack of cultural common ground was an early indicator of the fragility of the coalition. Rock, much of it British, deeply assimilated African American influence.

[24] C. Keil, 'Participatory Discrepancies and the Power of Music', *Cultural Anthropology*, 2 (1985), no. 3, 275–83.

[25] C. Keil, 'The Theory of Participatory Discrepancies: An Update', *Ethnomusicology*, 39 (1995), no. 1, 4.

so-slight) variances in tuning (blue notes), rhythm (swing), and nuance (wobbling, cracking voices, and amplifier distortion), to vibrate with life. Dylan imported PDs from the blues into Anglo-American folk tradition.[26] Given the contrast between the music of 1960s white and African American progressives—white Blues People,[27] African Americans refusing the blues—small wonder the alliance was so fragile.

The music of the 1960s was as formative of Krakowski as the lyric poetry of the world the Holocaust destroyed: Dylan, the Grateful Dead, outlaw country, reggae, gospel-driven Stax-Volt/Atlantic R & B, and the blues singers then new to white audiences. Neither Motown nor schmaltzy Yiddish music—both born of rising expectations and attempts to claim a piece of the mainstream, though not quite to join it—is in the mix. Wolf's eclectic influences are pure urban working class, a flat rejection of post-Second World War Jewish suburban flight.

Jews were born to rock: from Lieber and Stoller, Phil Spector, and Allan Freed to Carole King, Dylan, Simon, Kiss, and Phish. Wolf Krakowski embeds Yiddish melody in the PDs of the New World's struggling class. He rocks, reggaes, R & Bs, and rhumbas—sometimes in several grooves at once. That the Lonesome Brothers are Wolf's Band of Goyim[28] is irrelevant except in so far as their obvious dedication to *Transmigrations* is all the more righteous. Confronted with Yiddish song, a band more fluent in the Old Country grooves Wolf eschews might have got it—or wanted to get it—wrong.

The women's chorus on *Transmigrations* is another matter. Their American accents and textbook diction distinctly contrast with Wolf's native fluency and Łódź accent.[29] Alan Lomax's theory of cantometrics observes that a culture's organization of singing voices reflects its social order.[30] But Yiddish worldbeat is the music of Wolf's utopia only, his imagined community where Yiddish (and that language's only worldbeat vocalist) rocks and rules. In soul music a single-sex, usually female, chorus signifies sexual prowess. Aretha Franklin's 'Respect' is the paradigm. This sexual dynamic operates in *Transmigrations*, as Wolf, centre-stage, the power and the glory, is backed by a chorus that has learned his tongue to amplify what he says. Here is a welcome, timely reversal of Woody Allen–Jerry Seinfeld–*Mad About You*–*Bridget Loves Bernie shikse*-lust constructions of Jewish masculinity. As they caress his seering Yiddish vocals, the women also lend irony and empathy in the great Yiddish literary tradition, creating a wash of macho posturing that

[26] The African Americanization of many Jewish musicians does not imply that Jewish music lacks PDs. One of the clarinet virtuoso Naftule Brandwein's best-known pieces is 'Der heyser bulgar' ('The Hot *Bulgar*'): *heys* is what PDs are about. Despite *klezmer's* low-status origins, Jews embrace their musical roots through ethnicity rather than class.

[27] A reference to the classic book on jazz *Blues People: Negro Music in White America* (New York, 1983) by Amiri Baraka (Leroy Jones).

[28] A reference to Jimi Hendrix's (all black) Band of Gypsies.

[29] I thank Michael Steinlauf for this observation.

[30] Lomax, *Folk Song Style and Culture*.

can never be taken as entirely literal in a historical context of Diaspora ambivalence and powerlessness.

ONE JEW'S BLUES

While *Transmigrations* has been widely praised within and beyond the Jewish community,[31] its first widely seen review was less than kind and fomented much rancour in our little cybershtetl. On his web page Ari Davidow took Wolf to task for commemorating the Holocaust with defeatist laments, while avoiding songs of overt resistance.[32]

Davidow didn't get it. Simply stating the nature of the crime, these laments— 'Varshe' ('Warsaw'), 'Friling' ('Springtime'), 'Yeder ruft mikh zhamele' ('Everyone Calls me Zhamele'), and 'Blayb gezunt mir, kroke' ('Fare thee Well, Kraków')— were acts of defiance and courage. Words suited to soapboxes fare less well as song. Compare Barry McGuire's 'Eve of Destruction' or Sgt Barry Sadler's 'Ballad of the Green Berets' to Dylan's 'Blowin' in the Wind' or Billie Holiday's 'Strange Fruit'. Recalling Exodus, the spiritual 'Go Down, Moses' assails black slavery with no direct reference to it in over twenty verses.

In Benzion Witler's 'Varshe' melodic and rhythmic contours depict struggle almost viscerally, a fatigue that refuses to capitulate to exhaustion or worse. Phrases are short, declamatory, almost breathless. The melody rarely moves in anything but the smallest intervals, mostly consecutive scale steps in a very narrow range, usually falling. Returns to the main (tonic) note are frequent; the singer never gets very far. Short phrases are often repeated, sometimes slightly varied; despite adversity, the struggle for life goes on. No white-flag-waving, Witler's lyrics scream injustice, recall the complex beauty of old Varshe, Venice of *yidishkayt*. And then the chorus dares to prophesy not just a Jewish quarter or a large Jewish population, but that a Jewish city will rise once again.

Witler's powerful lament is Krakowski's tour de force. After a brief instrumental introduction the opening lines haltingly proclaim lost love as surely as any blues:

| In hartsn do ba mir brent a fayerl | In my heart burns a flame |
| Af dem vos iz avek— | For that which is gone—[33] |

The laboured tempo slows further to a series of stop-times; the band halts as vocals lament. Perhaps *Transmigrations*' most moving gesture is a litany of Warsaw places:

---

[31] I. Johansson, review, *Djembe* (Copenhagen) (Oct.–Dec. 1998), 43–4, and id., 'Musik som mame-loshn', *Judisk Kronika* (Stockholm) (1998), 22–3; R. Kafrissen, 'The Last Yiddish Bluesman', MS, 1998; S. Rogovoy, 'Beyond the Pale: Wolf Krakowski's Shtetl-Rock', in his *The Essential Klezmer* (Chapel Hill, NC, 2000), and id., 'A Blues for Yiddish', *Der pakn-treger* (Winter 1998), 8–9.

[32] The review currently on Davidow's web site, dated 21 Sept. 1997, is a revision, following protests from Wolf and others about the original review's vitriol.

[33] Trans. Wolf Krakowski and Fraidy Katz.

| Krokhmalne un di nalevke, | Krochmalna and Nalewki, |
| Un di smotshe un di lazhinke. | And Smocza and Łazienki. |

Wolf intones these lines in rhythm: dirgelike, short, narrow-ranged, descending repeated riffs echoed by the chorus, rhythmically out of sync with themselves and the band, spoken, then sung. Chaos, were it not so evocative of a city of ghosts: an extreme, unique PD, expressing this textual moment, rare in rock, though typical of the avant-garde choral writing of vintage Penderecki. Later, stop-time continues; the chorus coalesces into a rhythmic unit, forthrightly supporting the lead vocal for the duration.

Two more lines litanize, the subject now the variety of Jewish types who inhabit Warsaw streets:

| Khsidimlekh, negidimlekh, | Hasidim, rich men, |
| Tsienistelekh, bundistelekh. | Zionists, Bundists. |

Witler makes use of the Yiddish diminutive -*lekh* in naming these subjects. Its use can be either endearing or contemptuous—like so much of Yiddish, it can go either way—and is certainly intended to evoke folk character in the midst of great lyric sophistication. The total effect is one of head-nodding, world-weary irony.

Next, harmony changes briefly on *gekemft* (struggled), a verb implying motion, ending the litany:

Gekemft dortn gor on an ek.   Struggled there without an end.

Here, Krakowski forges a powerful conceptual link to two Willie Dixon blues, 'Hoochie Coochie Man', best known in the performances of Muddy Waters:

> I got a black cat bone
> I got a mojo too
> I got the Johnny conkeroo
> I'm gonna mess with you[34]

and 'The Seventh Son', whose performance by Mose Allison is legendary:

> I can tell your future, it will come to pass,
> I can do things to ya, make your heart beat fast,
> Look in the sky, predict the rain,
> I can tell when a woman's got another man.[35]

As in 'Varshe', stop-time, a single repeated chord on the most basic beats, supports a litany, a standard formula at the beginning of numerous blues choruses. Here, as often, the list signifies masculine power. For Waters, this is represented by the possession of powerful charms, for Allison a soothsayer's magic powers. But in Krakowski's 'Varshe' signification, the proclamation of attitude and strength occurs in the lines following the litany. In the analogous place Waters declares him-

[34] *The Best of Muddy Waters* (Chess, 1958).   [35] *The Seventh Son* (Prestige, 1973).

self the Hoochie Coochie Man, Mose Allison, the Seventh Son. Witler's signification is gender-neutral, unrelated to sexual prowess:

Ikh vil probirn fargesn haynt	Today I will try to forget
Vos hot tsu dir geton der faynt	What the enemy did to you

Stop-time resumes, although, as the text changes to full sentences, voice and violin
obbligato, conveying activity, abandon riffs for rhapsody. Real harmonic motion
finally ensues with the first real contrast in mood, a call to action:

Un zogn itst tsu dir	And saying now to you
Mit bitokhn	With faith
on a shir	without an end

which continues in the refrain:

Varshe mayn, du vest vider zayn	Warsaw mine, you will once more be
A yidishe shtot vi geven.	A Jewish city as before.
Varshe mayn, du vest vider zayn	Warsaw mine, you will once more be
Ful mit yidishn kheyn.	Filled with Jewish grace.

By now it is clear that the singer is signifying truly extraordinary power, the ability
to restore a vanquished Jewish city, a Jerusalem—the messianic task itself.

In the two Willie Dixon examples cited here, and in many other blues, litany
occurs at the top of the chorus, over static harmony. In 'Varshe' Wolf uses the harmonic stasis early in the song to the same effect: recitation of attributes over a
repeated chord to amass power. The actual declaration of strength takes place not in
the litany of 'Varshe', but in the lines that follow. Wolf modifies the blues strategy
to fit Witler's composition. 'Varshe' becomes blue only through Wolf's recomposition. Wolf discovers this affinity as only one steeped in that great American vernacular idiom can.

A new litany begins each chorus of the Waters and the Allison, in strophic blues
form. While the harmonic structure of 'Varshe' permits this gesture only once on
a large scale, the chorus includes shorter lists over single chords. Short litanies
supported by long-held chords are italicized:

Unter grininke beymelekh	Under little green trees
Veln moyshelekh un shleymelekh	Moysheles and Shloymeles
Lebn un shtrebn azoy vi frier.	Will live and dream as before.
Fabrikelekh, melikhelekh,	Factories, workshops,
Khadorimlekh un shilekhlekh	Schools, and synagogues
Vider oyfboyen veln mir.	We will build up once again.

Even factories and workshops—seemingly everyone and everything—are diminutive in 'Varshe'. The suffix drags each word out: buildings levelled, loved ones
pulled kicking and screaming to their deaths.

Witler provides each diminutive a held chord and a repeated melodic riff, while
Wolf makes us care about these images as one who feels every word. He wails on

beymelekh (trees); the longing is palpable. Words may speak of rebuilding, but the music behind them is pure pain and deep blue.

A 'Dylan' moment begins the second chorus:

| Khokhme un kultur | Wisdom and culture |
| Tsu hobn aza yur. | May we have such a year. |

The words are not cryptic like Dylan's—neither surreal nor lacking in linear sense—but they are self-consciously heady and a paradigm of Yiddish multi-valence. Witler references intellectual life but in folklike, sing-song rhythms. *Tsu hobn aza yur*—literally, 'to have such a year'—is more typically ill-wishing than well-wishing ('You should have such a year'), the kind of inversion that abounds in Yiddish. To experience these multiple, potentially contradictory, layers is to be overwhelmed. (Howlin') Wolf belts them out with attitude, a cognitive dissonance one can almost taste. That Jews love both irony and vinegar is hardly coincidence.

The multi-instrumentalist Jim Armenti plays both violin and guitar on 'Varshe'. The opening violin embodies Ashkenazi place. A wonderful fiddle lick closes the litany, descending in torrential rhythmic free-for-all. The scale is Jewish, the energy jukejoint. It evokes the recitative of the *klezmer doina*, but also Doina Washington. With drums and percussion, it is the kind of anti-cadence, more like a ten-car pile-up than a final resolution, that ends countless jazz, blues, and gospel performances.

Armenti's move from violin to guitar later in 'Varshe' epitomizes the meta-narrative of *Transmigrations*: *yidishkayt* infused with American energy. When the text describes old Warsaw, violin is the 'ethnic' colour of choice. Later, a refugee, armed with his new home's national instrument, electric guitar, calmly threatens to reclaim the city and restore its former Jewish glory. The guitar break recalls the vocal riffing of the verse, though filigreed, dreamlike. Armenti's solo climaxes with bent and blue notes, used for the first time, PDs creating an emotional peak that transcends words, finally releasing the rage smouldering in Witler's text.

Wolf turns 'Varshe', a lament for a murdered Jewish city, into a vision of what should have been: a Yiddish music that trades east European etiquette for American attitude. Wolf has absorbed not only the surface of the blues, but its most profound poetry, melding two great but marginalized cultures' insistence on survival in the face of evil, as if 'Go Down, Moses' were held to a musical mirror, its timeless cry for liberation from every Egypt now in Yiddish, grooving from right to left.

WITH A LITTLE HELP FROM MY *FREMDE* (OUTSIDERS)

The myriad complexities of 'Varshe' illuminate *Transmigrations*' other songs. While poetic (professionally crafted lyrics versus folk songs) or historic (Holocaust versus other periods) are possible taxonomies, a musical classification is most natural and useful.

'Varshe' exemplifies the songs I characterize as 'blues': mournful, slow, driven by improvisatory instrumentals with a profusion of bent notes and syncopations. Most of these pieces, like most blues (but unlike 'Varshe'), eschew the women's voices.

The folk song 'Regendl' ('Little Rain') is notable for call-and-response: Armenti's multi-tracked mandolin, tenor sax, and guitar trade licks with Wolf and each other. Witler's 'Alts geyt avek mitn roykh' ('Everything Goes up in Smoke') contrasts with 'Varshe' in its formal simplicity: strophic, entirely in tempo, harmonically straightforward as a twelve-bar, three-chord blues. Wolf plays masterfully with intonation and beat; Billie Holiday comes to mind. Armenti's 'acid'-toned guitar evokes Eric Clapton at his 1960s best.

'Yeder ruft mikh zhamele' is Bernardo Feuer's setting of an anonymous poem that bluntly indicts the Nazis ('Somewhere near a fence lies my brother Shloymele murdered by a German'). A blues by virtue of its profound sadness, remarkable even by Jewish standards, it is closer to Askhenazi musical models than anything on the album. With folk-formulaic text ('I once had a dear mother . . . I once had a little sister . . . I once had a little home') and simple strophic structure, it is a slow waltz. Wolf and Armenti, on the 'European-sounding' mandolin with its unbendable strings, stay close to the melody. The relative absence of blues nuance sounds as an inability to resist either tuning system or beat. As close to despair as *Transmigrations* gets, it must be heard in a context of songs of resistance and unrestrained Jewish joy.

The album's last 'blues', Max Perlman's philosophical and imagistic 'Ven du lakhst' ('When you Laugh'), uses chorus. Its familiar message, 'laugh and the world laughs with you, cry and you cry alone', is represented quite literally: women's voices, here, then gone, simple but effective. The complexity of Perlman's lyric ('The old actor . . . leafs through all his old newspaper clippings') evokes the jazz side of the blues and Armenti rises to the occasion with tenor sax responses and a concluding solo. Ending with an instrumental solo is a motif Wolf uses often.

If 'Varshe' epitomizes Yiddish blues, its multivalence and density recall 'A Day in the Life' from the Beatles' *Sgt. Pepper*, an album *Transmigrations* resembles in stylistic breadth and conceptual depth. Wolf's other Beatles song is 'Blayb gezunt mir, kroke', Manfred Lemm's setting of Mordechai Gebirtig's posthumously discovered Holocaust lament. While bluesy, most striking is Wolf's inclusion of a 4/4 bar in a waltz, a metre change which evokes 'All You Need is Love', 'Martha, My Dear', and 'We Can Work it Out'. The latter's accordion is what lends French *chansons* sophistication—think Piaf and Brel; it is rendered in 'Kroke' by Armenti's mandolin.

The one other metre change, a 2/4 bar in the introduction to the 4/4 'Her nor, du sheyn meydele' ('Listen, Pretty Girl'), sparked by Daniel Lombardo's percussion, heats up a Latin, Santana type of groove. This folk-song duet with Fraidy

Katz has a 'love conquers all' theme remarkably similar to the Klezmatics' 'Di sapozhkelekh' ('The Boots').[36]

Shmerke Katsherginski and Abraham Brudno's 'Friling', a tango, needs no additional Latinizing. A dance genre well known to Jews at the time of the Holocaust, its erotic possibilities now bubble with despair ('I wander the ghetto from alley to alley and cannot find any rest. My beloved is gone. How can I bear it?'). Reggae accents and blues guitar heat the irony to boiling.

Transmigrations would suffer without four truly exuberant songs. Samson Kemelmakher's 'Yidishe maykholim' ('Jewish Foods') is pure fun, a discourse on holiday cuisine cast as 1950s rocker, complete with Junior Walker-like sax solo. Three high-spirited rock anthems, driven by the sexual tension between Wolf and his soul sisters, distributed in first, fifth, and final positions on the CD—beginning, middle, and end—are pillars of power that function as strategically timed messages of hope to sustain us through the jeremiads. The anthems are similar in form and feel, but remarkably different in tone. 'Tsen brider' ('Ten Brothers') and 'Shabes, shabes' are simple and touching folk songs. The former, a pitifully bitter lyric, counts backwards as each brother dies until one remains. It rocks hard; the music spites that text. 'Shabes, shabes' is naive and idyllic. 'Zol shoyn kumen di geule' is a sophisticated yet joyous discourse on redemption by Shmerke Katsherginski and Rabbi Avraham Kook, containing the album's most complex harmonies.[37] Power is expressed here quite differently from the blues-based litany of 'Varshe'. The choir, as noted, provides sexual tension; the band rocks hard and fast. Armenti ends each anthem with searing, limitlessly inventive, multiple chorus guitar solos. Hendrix here meets hasidism: signification, through guitar heroics, meets the *nign*, melody sans lyrics, ascending spiritually beyond the point where words fail, to religious ecstasy. These long jams are not the free-form essays of Cream or the Grateful Dead. Maintaining the song's harmonic structure is how Wolf keeps it Jewish; he holds text, tune, and *tam* (taste) always in mind, no matter how fervently phantasmagoric the devotions become.

LEAVING ON A JET PLANE

Having previously covered Jewish musicians in the American 'mainstream', I dedicated my last lecture at Marie Curie-Skłodowska University to explicitly Jewish music, and especially to *Transmigrations*. I knew it would both surprise and captivate my students. I first thought to choose songs that would inspire the least incredulity and challenge. I had often dealt with questions beyond either my knowledge of or patience with the theological chasm that lay between my students'

---

[36] Recorded by the Klezmatics on *rhythm + jews* (Rounder, 1992).

[37] Adrienne Cooper's version, a languorous art song with piano, on *Dreaming in Yiddish* (self-produced, 1997) is also quite effective and should be heard.

miracles and Maimonides. I was tired, ready to go home. Still, something told me that playing it safe was no way for a Jewish teacher to say goodbye to students, colleagues, or the martyred dead all over Poland for whom I'd spent every available minute saying Kaddish. Besides, a pedagogy worthy of the rock of ages must shake, rattle, and roll. I chose my tunes accordingly.

'Shabes, shabes' was an easy pick. It rocks hard, its sabbath theme easily explained in a country where the word for Saturday is *sobota*. 'Zol shoyn kumen di geule' was intended to inspire questions about differing notions of salvation. Finally, 'Varshe', so my Polish friends would hear a two-fisted Holocaust blues that literally hit home. Although I intended the message for all in attendance, I recall thinking that this tonal tower of Jewish toughness was my way of telling the rude boys who always sat in the last rows that I'd be back. And next time I wasn't coming alone.

'The Time of Vishniac': Photographs of Pre-War East European Jewry in Post-War Contexts

JEFFREY SHANDLER

IN the vast, charged array of post-Holocaust representations of pre-war Jewish life in eastern Europe, photographs seem to hold out a distinct promise of stability. Works of mechanical reproduction, they appear to offer an actuality that could rectify what personal recollections, communal lore, published memoirs, literary works, artistic renderings, songs, dramas, and even historical writings may have 'manipulated' or even 'distorted'. But, as scholars of photography have discussed at great length, the verisimilitude of photography proves to be a false friend, as deceptive as it is engaging. Like any other art form, photography has its conventions, and the meaning of photographs is as contingent as that of any other works of art—perhaps even more so, in that photographs demand some kind of commentary or narration, title or inventory label, in order to be 'read'.

No more telling illustration of this larger issue exists than the post-Holocaust presentation—in publications, films, or exhibitions—of photographs depicting east European Jews in the decades before their annihilation at the hands of Nazi Germany and its collaborators. Indeed, the post-war relationship with these photographs is rife with contradictory impulses: though highly selective and fragmentary by their very nature, they are prized as reanimating an entire 'lost world'; routine, quotidian images now often loom large as archetypal. Frequently offering glimpses of east European Jewish life as seen from without, these photographs are approached as points of entry into these Jews' inner life. Documents of actuality, they can—and now, almost inevitably, do—acquire mythic meanings. However, these contradictions do not compromise the value of these pre-war photographs and their post-war re-presentations. Rather, the contradictions provide a guide to understanding the larger cultural agendas at work in the many projects of remembrance that make use of these images.

*

Thanks to Krysia Fisher, Sherry Hyman, Andrew Ingall, Stuart Schear, Nancy Sinkoff, Marek Web, Aviva Weintraub, and Carol Zemel for their kind assistance in preparing this chapter.

In the century before the Second World War photography came to play an increasingly prominent role in representing east European Jews, both to themselves and to others.[1] While the preponderance of photographs of this community were ones they either commissioned from local studio photographers or took themselves, there were also a wide variety taken by photographers from outside their communities.[2] Especially important are the work of various professional photographers, both Jews and non-Jews, who took pictures as photo-journalists; as documentarians working for philanthropies, political parties, and other organizations; as government employees (taking photographs for identity cards, school records, etc.); or to provide images published on postcards.[3]

Today the photographs of this community are best known in quite different formats: reproduced in photograph albums, appearing in documentary films and other media, and featured in museum displays. The private, 'internal' photography of east European Jewry has become a prominent part of their public remembrance in recent years. What currently may well be the most widely seen representation of pre-war east European Jewry, the 'Tower of Faces' display in the United States Holocaust Memorial Museum in Washington, consists of reproductions of hundreds of portraits of Jews who lived in the Lithuanian town of Eyshishok (Eišiškės) before the Holocaust.[4] Another similar project is the album and travelling exhibition 'And I Still See their Faces', which presents reproductions of photographs of pre-war Polish Jewry collected in the early 1990s by Fundacja Szalom, an organization of Jews dedicated to commemorating pre-war Polish Jewish culture; many of these pictures are reported to have come from Poles who had kept them in their homes during the half-century since the war's end.[5]

But pictures taken by photographers from outside the community have been more widely familiar throughout the post-war period, none more so than the work

[1] On the history of photography of Jews in pre-war Poland, see L. Dobroszycki and B. Kirshenblatt-Gimblett, *Image before my Eyes: A Photographic History of Jewish Life in Poland, 1864–1939* (New York, 1977).

[2] Although these photographs were taken and reproduced for viewing by others, they sometimes found their way back to Polish Jews indirectly—most famously in the pages of the *Jewish Daily Forward*'s rotogravure section, which was popular with east European Yiddish readers. Several photographs depict Polish Jews reading or displaying the *Forward*'s rotogravure section; see e.g. Dobroszycki and Kirshenblatt-Gimblett, *Image before my Eyes*, 25.

[3] The number and variety of pre-war postcards depicting east European Jewry is extensive; see e.g. E. Duda and M. Sosenko, *Dawna pocztówka żydowska ze zbiorów Marka Sosenki: Old Jewish Postcards from Marek Sosenko's Collection* (Kraków, 1997); G. Silvain and H. Minczeles, *Yiddishland* (Corte Madera, Calif., 1999). See too S. Sabar's chapter in this volume.

[4] For a detailed analysis of the Tower of Faces, see J. Shandler, 'Vanishing Act: The Representation of East European Jewry in the U.S. Holocaust Memorial Museum's Tower of Faces', *Jewish Folklore and Ethnology Review* (forthcoming).

[5] *And I Still See their Faces: Images of Polish Jews. I ciągle widzę ich twarze: Fotografie Żydów polskich* (Warsaw, 1996). I discuss the role of the professional studio photographer in *shtetl* culture in 'Szczuczyn: A Shtetl through a Photographer's Eye', in L. D. Levine (ed.), *Lives Remembered: A Shtetl through a Photographer's Eye* (New York, 2002).

of one photographer, Roman Vishniac. Taken during a series of trips he made to Poland, Czechoslovakia, and Romania from the mid-1930s until the start of the Second World War,[6] some of these photographs have been republished frequently, including in five books devoted solely to the photographer's work. Vishniac's images figured prominently in the first exhibitions and books of photographs of pre-war east European Jewish life to appear in the United States after the Second World War, and not a decade has passed since without some of these photographs being published or exhibited there, as well as abroad.

Although these pictures are the product of a limited phase in Vishniac's career—he worked much more extensively as a scientific photographer—they are his best-known accomplishment. For many post-war Americans, in particular, some of his images have served as key visual points of entry into the culture of pre-war east European Jewry, appearing, for example, on the cover of the first paperback edition of Irving Howe and Eliezer Greenberg's landmark anthology *A Treasury of Yiddish Stories*.[7]

At the beginning of the new millennium Vishniac is considered 'the grand "old master"' of this genre of photography, and his images have become 'the yardstick against which all other such work is measured, even while it seems almost sacri-legious to make comparisons'.[8] The distinctive formal characteristics of his images have also influenced film-makers seeking to re-create Jewish life in pre-war eastern Europe—most notably Janusz Kamiński, the cinematographer of *Schindler's List*, who credited Vishniac's photographs as 'the guiding force' for the 1993 feature film's 'visual interpretation'.[9] The avant-garde film-maker Eleanor Antin even restaged one of Vishniac's photographs in *The Man Without a World*, a faux-1920s silent Yiddish film made in 1992. Indeed, both the photographs and their photographer have become emblematic of a cultural era that, Elie Wiesel has argued, will someday be known as 'the time of Vishniac'.[10]

[6] Different sources report a variety of dates for the initiation of Vishniac's photographing east European Jews; for example, the dust jacket of his *Polish Jews: A Pictorial Record* (New York, 1947) describes the photographs that appear therein as 'selected from the two thousand which Vishniac took in 1938'. According to Dobroszycki and Kirshenblatt-Gimblett, Vishniac took these photographs 'between 1933 and 1939' (*Image before my Eyes*, 32). The majority of photographs of east European Jews in Roman Vishniac, *A Vanished World* (New York, 1983), which contains the largest published collection of Vishniac's photographs that are dated, were taken between 1936 and 1939; a few are dated as early as 1935. The earliest photographs in the book, dated 1933 and 1934, were taken in or near Berlin.

[7] First pub. New York, 1954. Vishniac's photograph of an alley in Kazimierz appears on the cover of the paperback edition of the book, first published by Schocken Books (New York, 1973).

[8] A. Weintraub, *An Alchemy of Darkness and Light: Photographing Jewish Life in Eastern Europe* (Atlanta, 1996), 1.

[9] Interview with Janusz Kamiński in 'The Film Makers', *ABC News: Nightline* (broadcast 3346, transmitted 21 Mar. 1994), transcript, 2. For a discussion of the aesthetics of *Schindler's List*, see J. Shandler, '*Schindler's* Discourse: America Discusses the Holocaust and its Mediation, from NBC's Miniseries to Spielberg's Film', in Y. Loshitzky (ed.), *Spielberg's Holocaust: Critical Perspectives on 'Schindler's List'* (Bloomington, Ind., 1997).

[10] M. Wiesel (ed.), *To Give Them Light: The Legacy of Roman Vishniac* (New York, 1993), 14.

So familiar are the many presentations of this genre of photography now that it is important to remember they have no pre-war precedent: no book of photographs of the 'world' of east European Jewry, whether by Vishniac or any other photographer, had ever been published before the Second World War, nor had there been any public exhibition or documentary film devoted to this topic. In this respect, the post-war presentations of these photographs are part of the extensive efforts, primarily undertaken by American Jews, to represent pre-war east European Jewish life in what the folklorist Barbara Kirshenblatt-Gimblett terms the 'popular arts of ethnography'. These efforts—which also include memoirs, literary works, anthropological studies, and theatrical productions—have provided the American public, Jews as well as non-Jews, in the post-Second World War era with portraits of pre-war east European Jewish life as 'a total world'. Moreover, these works promise that, though destroyed during the Holocaust, this 'world' can be virtually reanimated.[11]

The conceptualization of photography as providing a point of entry to this pre-Holocaust 'world' is sometimes articulated in the titles of the books in which they have been published, including *The Vanished World* (1947), *The Vanished Worlds of Jewry* (1980), and *A Vanished World* (1983), all of which feature Vishniac's photographs.[12] Although the trope of east European Jewish culture as vanishing pre-dates the Holocaust by a century or more,[13] it has taken on a different dimension of meaning following the destruction of millions of lives and of Jewish communal life across the European continent. Presentations such as those offered by these and similar photograph albums foster the viewing of pre-war photographs through the lens of the Holocaust, so that east European Jewish life before 1939 is conceptualized, in the sociologist Celia Heller's words, as existing 'on the edge of destruction'.[14] As the art historian Carol Zemel observes:

the effect is to enshroud and limit the pictures' signification. Michael André Bernstein has called this sort of suggestive framing 'backshadowing . . . a kind of retroactive foreshadowing in which the shared knowledge of the outcome is used to judge the participants . . . *as though*

---

[11] B. Kirshenblatt-Gimblett, 'Imagining Europe: The Popular Arts of American Jewish Ethnography', in D. D. Moore and I. Troen (eds.), *Divergent Centers: Shaping Jewish Cultures in Israel and America* (New Haven, 2001).

[12] R. Abramovitch (ed.), *Di farshvundene velt: The Vanished World* (New York, 1947); R. Patai, *The Vanished Worlds of Jewry* (New York, 1980).

[13] B. Kirshenblatt-Gimblett, 'Problems in the Historiography of Jewish Folkloristics', paper presented at the conference 'Folklore and Social Transformation: A Dialogue of American and German Folklorists', Bloomington, Ind., 1–3 Nov. 1988, 44–6, as cited in Weintraub, 'An Alchemy of Darkness and Light', 2.

[14] C. S. Heller, *On the Edge of Destruction: Jews of Poland between the Two World Wars* (New York, 1977). So pervasive is this trope that it has also been extended to photographic portraits of post-war east European Jewish life, which is portrayed as a phantom culture—as 'remnants' (e.g. M. Niezabitowska and T. Tomaszewski, *Remnants: The Last Jews of Poland* (New York, 1986)) or 'last Jews' (B. Blue and Y. Strom, *The Last Jews of Eastern Europe* (New York, 1986); A. Gürsan-Salzmann and L. Salzmann, *The Last Jews of Rădăuţi* (New York, 1983)). On this subject, see J. Kugelmass, 'A Look at the Last Jews of Poland', *Polin*, 4 (1989), 474–81.

they too should have known what was to come.' In the backshadowed presentation, the pictures are made predictive after the fact. The Jews in these pictures, unknowing, seem marked by their terrible future; their victimization is heightened by their not sensing the tragedy ahead, and the 'character'—as depicted—seems to forecast their destiny.[15]

At the same time the trope of vanishing evoked in these book titles calls attention, if obliquely, to the limitations of photographs as instruments of recovery, by alluding to the role of photography in not merely documenting, but contributing to, the act of vanishing—what Susan Sontag characterized as the way that, 'by slicing out this moment and freezing it, all photographs testify to time's relentless melt'.[16]

*

Vishniac's photographs of east European Jews in the years before the onset of the Second World War offer an especially powerful demonstration of this issue, by virtue of both the subject of the images and the context of their creation, as reported after the war. There are multiple accounts of the circumstances that prompted Vishniac's photographic expeditions to eastern Europe offered in his own words, as well as in interviews, reportage, and the recollections of his daughter Mara Vishniac Kohn. Yet none of these published sources offers a definitive explanation of when or why he began taking these pictures. By his own account, Vishniac started to photograph east European Jews in 1936, but he dates some of these photographs a year earlier.[17] It is known that by 1937 the American Jewish Joint Distribution Committee (AJJDC) employed Vishniac to supply them with photographs for use in public relations efforts on behalf of the beleaguered Jews of eastern Europe, and that Vishniac continued to do so until the beginning of the Second World War.[18]

[15] C. Zemel, '*Z'chor!* Roman Vishniac's Photo-Eulogy of Eastern European Jews', in J. Epstein and L. H. Lefkovitz (eds.), *Shaping Losses: Cultural Memory and the Holocaust* (Urbana, Ill., 2001), 77. The embedded citation is from M. A. Bernstein, *Foregone Conclusions: Against Apocalyptic History* (Berkeley, 1994), 16; emphasis in original. My thanks to Dr Zemel for allowing me to read and cite the MS of her essay.

[16] S. Sontag, *On Photography* (first pub. 1977; New York, 1990), 15. Of Vishniac's photographs she writes, 'One's reactions to the photographs Roman Vishniac took in 1938 of daily life in the ghettos of Poland is overwhelmingly affected by the knowledge of how soon all these people were to perish' (p. 70).

[17] See E. Kinkead, 'The Tiny Landscape, II', *New Yorker* (9 July 1955), 39. This is the second of a two-part profile of Vishniac, focusing on his work as a photographer of biological subjects; the first part appeared in the *New Yorker* (2 July 1955), 28–49.

[18] Records of the AJJDC committee on publicity first discuss Vishniac's work in minutes of a report on the organization's public information programme dated 15 Nov. 1937: 'Mr. Wishniak [*sic*] originally volunteered to make photographs for the J.D.C. and his photographs are outstanding in their photographic quality and in the narrator's skill which they display.' Minutes of a meeting on 3 Aug. 1936 include a 'discussion as to the advisability of preparing a portfolio of European photographs of a striking nature for the use of field men'; this suggests that as of that date the AJJDC had no formal relationship with Vishniac (AJJDC Archive, AJJDC Administration, Committee on Publicity 1936–1940, binder 108). A letter of reference from Morris C. Troper dated 16 July 1940 explains that 'Mr. Roman Wischniak [*sic*] was engaged by the Joint Distribution Committee from time to time during the past

The AJJDC's caption on the back of one such photograph, which was distributed to the press during this period, exemplifies the organization's agenda of using these images to promote public awareness of the suffering of east European Jewry and to raise funds to provide this community with relief:

This is the most-revered rabbi among the orthodox Jews of Poland. Radjomyn Rabbi Gutterman would never consent to be photographed and the snapshot was taken without his knowledge as he was leaving a relief station. His work among the Polish Jews includes the distribution of special food required for the Feast of Passover. The American Jewish Relief Committee which is appealing for $14,000,000 for the continuance of its relief work in Eastern Europe has found in Rabbi Gutterman a worthy aide and counsellor. The man at his right is a bodyguard. Conditions are such that the Rabbi never walks alone.[19]

In addition to still photographs, Vishniac shot film footage of Jews living in villages in the Carpathian Mountains for the AJJDC, which it considered using as the basis for a promotional film; this project was never realized.[20] Some of Vishniac's still photographs were incorporated into pre-war filmstrips produced by the AJJDC, such as *Through Europe with JDC*, dated 1938.[21] Vishniac also took photographs documenting the efforts of various Jewish philanthropies working to improve the life of east European Jews during the 1930s, including an album of ninety photographs for a report on the activities of the Jewish public health organization TOZ[22] in Warsaw, entitled 'A Pictorial Visit to the Jewish Children in Poland'.[23]

In the two albums of Vishniac's photographs of pre-war east European Jews that have been published since his death, his daughter acknowledges the role of the

three years as Special Photographer in connection with the work conducted by this organization in the various countries of Europe.' This letter was one of several written by the AJJDC on Vishniac's behalf to assist him in emigrating to the United States (AJJDC Archive, Roman Vishniac Collection, no. 2886).

[19] AJJDC Archive, New York, Roman Vishniac Collection.

[20] See e.g. Public Information Program, 15 Nov. 1937, AJJDC Archive, AJJDC Administration, Committee on Publicity 1936–1940, binder 108. Footage that Vishniac recorded in the Carpathians appears in the 1990 documentary film *Chasing Shadows* (director Naomi Gryn). Vishniac also made pre-war films on European Jews emigrating to Palestine in the 1930s and on the activities of ORT in Poland, Germany, and France; see C. Capa (ed.), *Roman Vishniac*, ICP Library of Photographers, vol. 6 (New York, 1974), 95. In an interview Vishniac states that his original film was lost; only out-takes remain. This comment, as well as some of this remaining footage, are found in the television programme *Directions: The Concerns of Roman Vishniac*, ABC, 20 May 1973 (National Jewish Archive of Broadcasting, Jewish Museum, New York, item T817).

[21] *Through Europe with JDC*, General Business Films, New York, 1938.

[22] TOZ (Towarzystwo Ochrony Zdrowia Ludności Żydowskiej, the Society for Safeguarding the Health of the Jewish Population), along with CENTOS (Centralne Towarzystwo Opieki nad Sierotami, the Central Society for the Care of Orphans) and ORT (Obshestvo rasprostraneniya truda sredi evreev, the Society for Promotion of Manual Labour among Jews), were the major social welfare organizations active among Polish Jews during the inter-war period.

[23] AJJDC Archive, Roman Vishniac Collection. The undated album is labelled 'AJDC [*sic*] European Executive Office, Paris'. The handwritten captions accompanying the photographs are in English.

AJJDC in initiating this documentary project.[24] In his own published accounts, however, Vishniac characterized this as a mission that he initiated himself. More-over, he explained the agenda of his photographic expeditions in eastern Europe not as part of a public relations and fund-raising project but as an eleventh-hour effort to document communities he presaged as doomed to extermination. In an interview in 1955 he explained:

My friends assured me that Hitler's talk was sheer bombast . . . But I replied that he would not hesitate to exterminate those people when he got around to it. And who was there to defend them? I knew I could be of little help, but I decided that, as a Jew, it was my duty to my ancestors, who grew up among the very people who were being threatened, to pre-serve—in pictures, at least—a world that might soon cease to exist.[25]

Over a quarter-century later he would similarly write:

I was living in Germany in the thirties, and I knew that Hitler had made it his mission to exterminate all Jews, especially the children and the women who could bear children in the future. I was unable to save my people, only their memory.[26]

As the earlier citation above indicates, Vishniac's subjects were Jewish commu-nities quite removed, both geographically and culturally, from his own life experi-ence. Born in 1897 near St Petersburg, Vishniac grew up in Moscow in a very Russified Jewish family of well-to-do merchants. During the First World War he attended university in Moscow, studying medicine and earning a doctorate in zoology. (Combining youthful interests in the camera and the microscope, Vishniac would eventually become an important innovator in the field of biological photog-raphy, especially photomicroscopy.) After the Bolshevik revolution Vishniac and his family moved to Berlin, where he continued to conduct scientific research and to pursue his interests in photography.

As the folklorist Aviva Weintraub has observed, the story of Vishniac's creating these photographs, retold by him and others on numerous occasions after the Second World War, 'is as extraordinary as the images themselves'.[27] Various accounts characterize Vishniac's photographic expeditions in eastern Europe as being ardu-ous and fraught with perils. The very act of taking these photographs is repeatedly characterized as a risky undertaking. The photographer felt the need to keep the presence of his camera a secret, both from 'ultra-orthodox members of the [Jewish] community, [as] he had to be mindful of the suspicion with which photographers and other "image-makers" were greeted',[28] and from non-Jewish authorities: 'Once, in the Czechoslovakian village of Dunajská Streda, a policeman spotted his cam-

[24] Wiesel, *To Give them Light*, 160; R. Vishniac, *Children of a Vanished World*, ed. M. Vishniac Kohn and M. Hartman Flacks (Berkeley, 1999), p. ix.   [25] Kinkead, 'The Tiny Landscape, II', 39–40.

[26] Vishniac, *A Vanished World*, preface, unpaginated.

[27] Weintraub, 'An Alchemy of Darkness and Light', 1.

[28] Vishniac, *Children of a Vanished World*, p. x.

eras, and he was locked up in the Bratislava Prison for a month while the authorities took their time about examining his films to make sure that he had not been photographing military installations.'[29] In interviews the photographer mentioned that he was arrested eleven times during his photographic journeys.[30] Vishniac also described the great lengths he went to in order to become acquainted with his subjects. Discussing photographs of Jewish porters in Warsaw, he commented: 'For a month, I joined a group of ten porters and pulled my loads. In this way I came to understand the unquenchable spirit and endurance of my people.'[31] Eventually, Vishniac reported, most of the 16,000 photographs taken on his travels to eastern Europe were confiscated. Thus, the extant images, usually described as 2,000 photographs, are not merely documents of Jewish lives destroyed during the war, but are themselves to be valued as 'saving remnants' of the Holocaust.[32]

*

In 1947 two books of photographs of east European Jewry were published in the United States, both featuring selections of Vishniac's photographs. The earliest such publications, the books testify to the powerful meaning invested in these photographs in the immediate aftermath of the Holocaust. While both volumes are offered to readers as memorials to the same community, their scope, organization, contents, and agenda reveal differences that reflect diverging responses to the recent destruction.

Di farshvundene velt: The Vanished World, published by the Forward Association in 1947, is the more extensive of the two books, offering 530 photographs of prewar east European Jewish life as both an act of mourning for millions of recently murdered Jews and a commemoration of eastern Europe as having been 'the religious and spiritual hegemony of World Jewry' for five centuries.[33] The volume uses a diverse range of photographs, depicting 'a cross-section of the multi-colored Jewish life as it was in Eastern Europe' to represent a former entity—what 'is now a "vanished world"'. The images are drawn from a variety of sources, beginning with the archives of the *Jewish Daily Forward* (*Forverts*), including 'the remarkable documents by Alter Kacyzna [*sic*], M. Kipnis, and others who have perished, so far as we know, in the general holocaust'. In addition, 'A valuable contribution to our collection were the photos by R. Vishniak [*sic*], who now resides in New York.' Other images 'came from the Archives of the American Joint Distribution Committee, the Yiddish Scientific Institute (YIWO) [*sic*], the Yiddish Encyclopedia, and

---

[29] Kinkead, 'The Tiny Landscape, II', 40.

[30] See *Directions: The Concerns of Roman Vishniac*; *Conversations over a Glass Tea: Bruce Goldman with Roman Vishniac*, THETA (cable), *c*.1981 (National Jewish Archive of Broadcasting, Jewish Museum, New York, item T1150).

[31] Vishniac, *A Vanished World*, 'Commentary on the Photographs', photos 27 and 28.

[32] In one interview Vishniac reports that 3,000 of the 16,000 photographs were saved. See *Directions: The Concerns of Roman Vishniac*.   [33] Abramovitch, *The Vanished World*, 8–9.

others. We received also many interesting photographs from many readers of the "Forward." '[34]

The volume's introduction characterizes the assembly of these images itself as an effort of symbolic recovery:

This was not an easy task. Even if we had had at our disposal an almost unlimited collection of photographs of all cities, of all Jewish streets, of all phases of Jewish spiritual and communal life in Eastern Europe, the assignment would be a difficult one. But no such collection is at hand, and who knows if it exists? We had to make use of that which was within our own reach.[35]

The Vanished World presents its selection of photographs with minimal captions in English and Yiddish, implying an informed reader familiar with the subject matter. Photographs are grouped according to various criteria, the first and most extensive being geographic, in a section labelled 'Jewish Cities'. This opens with a selection of photographs from Poland, the largest such group, followed by the western Soviet Union, Romania, Hungary, and Czechoslovakia. Subsequent sections are organized by subject matter: types, children, work, health care, religion. These categories recall those employed to present photographs of east European Jewry in the *Forward*'s rotogravure section during the inter-war years, which frequently grouped together images from diverse locations and sources, united by topic: holiday celebrations, professional or character 'types', portraits of beautiful women, political action, etc.

Over 150 of the photographs in *The Vanished World*—almost one-third of the volume's contents—are by Vishniac; other than pictures taken by Alter Kacyzne, who had worked regularly for the *Forward* during the inter-war years, no other photographer's work is featured as extensively. Two types of images predominate among the Vishniac photographs used herein: cityscapes, which appear in the book's first section, and portraits of individuals, featured in sections entitled 'Types and Scenes', 'Jews at Work', 'Children and Youths', 'Education', and 'Religious Life'. In addition to photographs taken in Polish cities and towns, the volume features ample selections of Vishniac's photography of Jewish life in Mukachevo (Munkatsh) and Carpathian Ruthenia. A few images appear to be drawn from his assignments to document the work of TOZ, CENTOS, and ORT. Captions on these, as well as all the album's other photographs, are minimal. Through their organization and captioning the photographs in *The Vanished World* are offered primarily as ethnographic documentation. (Some of Vishniac's most affectively evocative portraits and city scenes, which would become among his best-known images in later decades, are not included.)

At the same time, the Forward Association, though an ardently secular institution, offered *The Vanished World* to the public as nothing less than an object of reverence. 'This holy record should be kept alongside the sacred books on your

---

[34] Ibid. 11–13, *passim*.   [35] Ibid. 12.

shelf,' the *Forward* exhorted its readers in an advertisement for the book.[36] *The Vanished World* thus straddles efforts to be both an encyclopaedic work of documentary value and a memorial to the dead that, evocations of sacred books notwithstanding, reflects a secular sensibility. (The volume's editor, Raphael Abramovitch, a native of Dvinsk and an activist in the Jewish Labour Bund between the wars, worked as an editor of the *Algemeyne entsiklopedye* both before the start of the Second World War and after his arrival in the United States in 1940, when he became a columist for the *Forward* and a member of its editorial board.) In this spirit, the introduction to *The Vanished World* discusses the nature of its photographs as artefacts, both materially and symbolically, taking pains to vouch for the authenticity of the images: 'The photographs have not been "improved" by retouching. We considered it our duty to reprint them as they were taken without embellishment, and restricted ourselves solely to removing stains, high-lighting faded copies, repairing torn prints, etc.' Moreover, the introduction reminds readers of the photographs' original pre-war provenance, while mindful of the shift in their significance in the post-war era, noting that these pictures were 'taken by people who could not foresee that they were photographing . . . a people on the eve of their destruction'.[37]

The creators of *The Vanished World* also recognized that the collecting, selecting, and republishing of these photographs constituted a symbolic effort, responsive to the beginning of a 'new epoch in Jewish history', in which the post-war Jewish community was charged with the

responsibility of immortalizing for future generations our common Eastern European heritage. . . . Thus we shall erect a dignified monument to it and at the same time render a service to the future. . . . It is our sincere hope that [this book] will be one of the constituent stones in that great monument which will be erected by World Jewry in memory of the world that has disappeared under the murderous blows of Hitlerism.[38]

*

In 1947 Vishniac's photographs also appeared in another volume, entitled *Polish Jews: A Pictorial Record*. Offering just thirty-one pictures taken by him over a brief period, *Polish Jews* is much narrower in scope than the Forward Association's album. Nevertheless, *Polish Jews* also strives to represent the 'world' of pre-war east European Jewry—not with an extensive inventory of its wide range, but through a concentrated presentation of its essence, defined as 'abjectly poor in its material condition, and in its spiritual condition, exaltedly religious'.[39] Thus, religion, which was but one category of images in the Forward Association's volume, becomes the nearly exclusive subject of *Polish Jews*. (In the 1955 interview mentioned earlier,

---

[36] *Jewish Daily Forward* (26 May 1947), 9; my translation. The book was published on the occasion of the *Forward*'s fiftieth anniversary. [37] Abramovitch, *The Vanished World*, 13, 11.
[38] Ibid. 10–11, 13. [39] Vishniac, *Polish Jews*, 5.

Vishniac admitted that he was not entirely satisfied with the book's highly selective approach. *Polish Jews* was 'Subsidized by a man who was primarily interested in religion . . . and, as Vishniac points out with some regret, it did not include any of the pictures he took to emphasize the economic struggle in which the Jews were engaged'.[40]

Polish Jews articulates the centrality of spirituality in pre-war east European Jewish life by prefacing Vishniac's images with a ten-page introductory essay by the philosopher Abraham Joshua Heschel entitled 'The Inner World of the Polish Jew'. This is an abridged version of a text Heschel first delivered in Yiddish at a conference of the YIVO Institute for Jewish Research in New York in January 1945. (An early exhibition of some of Vishniac's photographs took place at the YIVO Institute at the time of this conference.[41]) Eventually Heschel expanded this essay into the 1950 book *The Earth is the Lord's: The Inner World of the Jew in Eastern Europe*, which, still in print, remains one of the most widely read works on the subject.[42]

Although Heschel's text as it appears in *Polish Jews* makes token mention of a few east European locales—indeed, the use of the word 'Polish' in the book's title, a prefatory note explains, is 'for reasons of cultural (not physical) geography'[43]—it offers no discussion of the distinctive character or internal diversity of Jewish life in the particular cities or regions depicted in the photographer's images, nor is there any discussion of the specific time when they were taken. Rather, the essay provides an overview of the essence of traditional east European Ashkenazi culture, focusing, as the title suggests, on its spiritual life, as a timeless, organic entity of etherealized beauty:

Korets, Karlin, Bratzlav, Lubavich, Ger, Lublin—hundreds of little towns were like holy books. Each place was a pattern, an aspect, a way in Jewishness. When a Jew mentioned the name of a town like Medzhibozh or Berdytshev, it was as though he mentioned a divine mystery. Holiness had become so real and so concrete that it was perceptible like beauty. . . . The little Jewish communities in Eastern Europe were like sacred texts opened before the eyes of God. So close were our houses of worship to Mount Sinai. In the humble wooden synagogues, looking as if they were deliberately closing themselves off from the world, the Jews purified the souls that God had given them and perfected their likeness to God. There arose in them an infinite world of inwardness, a 'Torah within the Heart,' beside the written and oral Torah. Even plain men were like artists who knew how to fill weekday hours with mystic beauty.[44]

[40] Kinkead, 'The Tiny Landscape, II', 40.

[41] See *Yedies fun YIVO: News of the YIVO*, 7 (Feb. 1945), 7*. YIVO also exhibited some of Vishniac's photographs in March–April 1944: see 'Pictures of Jewish Life in Pre-War Poland', *Jewish Daily Forward* (19 Mar. 1944), sect. 3, 2.

[42] A. J. Heschel, *The Earth is the Lord's: The Inner World of the Jew in Eastern Europe* (New York, 1950). On the different versions of this work, see J. Shandler, 'Heschel and Yiddish: A Struggle with Significance', *Journal of Jewish Thought and Philosophy*, 2 (1993), 245–99.

[43] Vishniac, *Polish Jews*, 5.

[44] A. J. Heschel, 'The Inner World of the Polish Jew', in Vishniac, *Polish Jews*, 15–16.

Notes that appear on the back of the dust jacket of *Polish Jews* not only articulate the subject and agenda of the photographs and of Heschel's essay but imply how they echo one another. Both images and text portray a culture that is isolated from others: 'resisting influence of the outer world, these inbred Jewish communities adhered to traditional Jewish customs and values'. They focus on the spiritual aspect of Jewish life, which transcended the material: 'laboring under the burden of harsh poverty, the Jews yet succeeded in achieving a high degree of spiritual unity'. And, just as the photographs mostly depict pious old men and young boys ('That [these] two age groups ... predominate is not accidental. They were the two groups most involved in religious study'), Heschel's essay similarly assumes a pious male to be the archetypal east European Jew.[45]

The photographs in *Polish Jews* are offered with short titles indicating place and general subject (e.g. 'Old Woman', 'Yeshiva Examination'). The only statement these notes provide about the taking of these photographs is a comment by Vishniac on the dust jacket: 'These pictures ... were made without letting the subjects know of the presence of a camera.'[46] Considering this an essential feature of these images, Vishniac elaborated elsewhere his account of taking these photographs with concealed cameras, using only available light, so that his subjects would be unaware that they were being photographed. According to his notes, he 'enlarged a buttonhole in his winter coat so that the lens would fit through while the camera itself [a Rolleflex] remained hidden'.[47] He also explained in one interview that, when using a Leica, he hid the small camera in a handkerchief; pretending to mop his brow, he quickly placed the camera in front of his eyes to focus and shoot.[48] Vishniac disguised not only his camera but himself as well. In another interview he reported that he 'pos[ed] as a salesman of fabrics to explain his presence in out-of-the-way places and the suitcases in which he concealed his equipment'.[49]

Despite his assertion that the resulting images 'represent real life completely unposed', thereby validating their status as 'documents',[50] many of the photographs, especially the individual portraits, suggest that Vishniac's subjects were clearly conscious of and responsive to the photographer's gaze, if not the camera itself. Elsewhere Vishniac also acknowledged taking some of these photographs of east European Jews openly. Of a visit to the Carpathian Mountains, he reported: 'I stayed for a long time, openly taking photographs and movies. The villagers had never heard of such things. I felt myself transported several centuries back in time.'[51]

As this and other recollections indicate, Vishniac characterized photographing east European Jews as the documentation of vestigial specimens. Indeed, the notion that his subjects could only be photographed unconscious of the photographer's

[45] Vishniac, *Polish Jews*, dust jacket.   [46] Ibid.

[47] Vishniac, *Children of a Vanished World*, p. x.   [48] *Directions: The Concerns of Roman Vishniac*.

[49] Kinkead, 'The Tiny Landscape, II', 40.   [50] Vishniac, *Polish Jews*, dust jacket.

[51] Vishniac, *A Vanished World*, 'Commentary on the Photographs', photos 132 and 133.

act—even when the camera is evident—suggests a methodology similar to his approach to photographing flora and fauna. (A profile of Vishniac's work as a scientific photographer discusses the great lengths he went to in order to photograph 'a sea bass in the act of seizing a live squid. This was a very difficult project, because sea bass will not ordinarily eat in the presence of human beings, and none had ever been known to take so much as a nibble while a photographer was within working distance.'[52])

Vishniac also employed the same hidden-camera approach to documenting human subjects after the war, taking pictures for the Federation of Jewish Philanthropies in New York for use in fund-raising campaigns:

these . . . reflect the technique he developed so effectively during his rovings among the East European Jews. . . . [The pictures] are mainly of patients in hospitals and are masterpieces in the art of portraying human suffering; some that have demonstrably had the greatest appeal have been candid shots of patients describing their anguish to him as he sat at their bedside with his camera concealed under his jacket.[53]

Commercial photographers familiar with Vishniac's work in New York in the early post-war years observed of his occasional portraits of human subjects: 'he was so much under the influence of his own style that his photographs gave all his clients a lost, tortured look. He had an uncanny knack of injecting the spirit of the ghetto into every picture he took, no matter who the subject was.' This suggests that Vishniac's photographic vision of east European Jewry on the eve of the Second World War was a result as much of his personal artistic and cultural sensibility as it was, in the words of Edward Steichen, of 'a rare depth of understanding and a native son's warmth and love of his people', which made these 'among photography's finest documents of a time and place'.[54]

*

As these words of one of the pioneers of modern photography testify, Vishniac's images of pre-war east European Jews are vaunted as having iconic stature. But, as the first publication of these photographs in the two 1947 books described above evinces, their significance could be configured differently according to distinct agendas even in the early post-war years. In ensuing decades the various public presentations of these photographs has offered them to viewers in a series of shifting contexts, reflecting changes in the valuation of the images themselves, their subject, the photographer, and public remembrance of the Holocaust.

In 1969 seventeen of Vishniac's photographs (including several that appear in *Polish Jews*) accompanied another prominent writer's reflections on Jewish life in pre-war eastern Europe: Isaac Bashevis Singer's *A Day of Pleasure: Stories of a Boy*

[52] Kinkead, 'The Tiny Landscape, II', 46.   [53] Ibid. 44.   [54] Ibid. 43, 40.

Growing Up in Warsaw, a collection of stories from Singer's childhood, some of which were adapted from his memoir *In My Father's Court*.[55] Here Vishniac's images serve as illustrations to the author's personal history. Yet both text and images are offered as emblematic of pre-war Polish Jewry generally. A prefatory note explains: 'The world portrayed in these photographs is essentially the same as the one in these stories, even though the stories take place a generation earlier.'[56]

In 1971 the Jewish Museum in New York presented 'The Concerns of Roman Vishniac: Man, Nature and Science', a major exhibition of the photographer's work, curated by Cornell Capa. This proved to be a watershed in the post-war history of these images, as it called attention to the photographer's life and career. By placing Vishniac, rather than the subject of his photographs, at the centre of attention, this exhibition marked the first public effort to characterize the two major subjects of Vishniac's work as part of some larger, integrated sensibility.[57] In an ecumenical television profile recorded during the run of the exhibition, Vishniac was described as 'one of the few true Renaissance men of our time' whose photography—both of Jews and of biological specimens—'makes the invisible visible'.[58] In a volume on Vishniac published in 1974 in the ICP Library of Photographers series Capa characterized him as 'a passionate and compassionate observer of life. . . . As a man, a humanist, and a photographer, Roman Vishniac wondrously fulfills the Lewis Hine definition of what we mean to be a concerned photographer—"Things to be appreciated . . . things to be corrected." Roman Vishniac respects life and men.'[59]

The 1971 exhibition also provided the first opportunity to present to the public Vishniac's own story of his efforts to take pictures of east European Jews in the 1930s, as well as his own articulation of the photographs' significance. This was offered in an audio-visual programme that was presented as part of the exhibition, which Scholastic Magazines later published as a set of slides with an accompanying audio cassette for use in classrooms. Entitled *The Life that Disappeared*, the sixteen-minute programme features more than fifty of Vishniac's photographs. The accompanying audiotape offers Vishniac's own explanation of these pictures as his effort

[55] I. B. Singer, *A Day of Pleasure: Stories of a Boy Growing Up in Warsaw* (New York, 1969); id., *In My Father's Court* (New York, 1966).

[56] Singer, *A Day of Pleasure*, list of photographs. More recently, a selection of Vishniac's photographs were used in a similar fashion as illustrations for a German-language collection of hasidic lore (M. Keil (ed.), *So soll man Geschichten erzählen. Weisheit der Chassiden* (Vienna, 1985)).

[57] Eugene Kinkead's 1955 *New Yorker* profile of Vishniac, while dealing with both aspects of Vishniac's career, focuses primarily on his scientific photography and resists efforts to characterize the two as representing a shared sensibility. Indeed, Kinkead reports an incident, which took place in inter-war Berlin, in which Vishniac's photographic interests in biology and in Jews clashed: 'The editor of a Nazi magazine, *Volk und Rasse*, approached [Vishniac], not realizing that he was a Jew, and offered to pay him to make some microscopic photographs showing how the blood of a pure Aryan differed from that of a Jew. When Vishniac replied that there was no difference whatever, the editor contemptuously turned his back on him' ('The Tiny Landscape, II', 39).

[58] *Directions: The Concerns of Roman Vishniac*.   [59] Capa (ed.), *Roman Vishniac*, 3.

'to save the faces' of Jews whom he understood were imperilled: 'I heard from people close to the Nazi administration that the Jewish problem must be solved by killing the Jews. . . . No Jews will survive.' Vishniac goes on to discuss the life of the people in the images, providing anecdotes of their economic struggles and stigmatization ('everywhere were regulations, limitations. . . . It was not permitted to do what the others, non-Jews, could do'). In the course of his narration Vishniac makes a statement that suggests a link between his approach to documenting these Jews and his work as a natural scientist: 'I had a biological thought: Like the bees or the ants—many of them are killed and destroyed, but something—something will survive.' Vishniac's narration is punctuated by two songs: 'Afn pripetshik' ('At the Hearth'), epitomizing Jewish piety and suffering in the east European diaspora, and, at the conclusion of the programme, 'Shir hahaganah', ('Song of the Haganah'), echoing a redemptive note in Vishniac's narration that 'Only two years after all the killing stopped, a new nation was born—Israel.'[60]

During the 1970s Vishniac's work was also incorporated in other major public presentations that positioned his achievement within different photographic contexts. In 1972 Capa included Vishniac's photographs—both of Jews and of biological specimens—in a publication dedicated to 'the Concerned Photographer', which situated Vishniac's work alongside that of Bruce Davidson, Ernst Haas, Hiroshi Hamaya, Donald McCullin, Gordon Parks, Marc Riboud, and W. Eugene Smith.[61] A number of Vishniac's images also appeared in the 1976 exhibition 'Image before my Eyes', an extensive survey of the photography of Polish Jewry from the mid-nineteenth century until the eve of the Second World War, organized by the YIVO Institute for Jewish Research and exhibited at the Jewish Museum in New York; his photographs were also featured in the eponymous photograph album, published in 1977, and the 1980 documentary film.[62]

The next publication devoted exclusively to Vishniac's photographs of pre-war Jews appeared in the following decade. Though its title, *A Vanished World*, echoes the Forward Association's 1947 album, this 1983 book extends and elaborates Vishniac's particular vision of east European Jewish life on the eve of the Holocaust. And whereas the first solo presentation of these photographs in *Polish Jews* offers an elegiac, spiritualized memorial to this community—that volume's final image is of a tombstone in a Lublin cemetery—*A Vanished World* presents photographs drawn from the same stock of images according to an agenda closer to the photographer's own understanding of their significance. Both the format and inventory of *A Vanished World* is larger than *Polish Jews*: an oversized 'coffee table' volume, featuring some 180 photographs. Elie Wiesel, author of the 1983 volume's foreword, situates the viewing of these photographs as an act of Holocaust remembrance:

[60] R. Vishniac, *The Life that Disappeared: A Scholastic Humanities Unit* (teaching guide) (Englewood Cliffs, NJ, 1973), 9, 8, 13, 16.

[61] C. Capa (ed.), *The Concerned Photographer* (London, 1972).

[62] Director Joshua Waletzky, distributed by Ergo Media, Teaneck, NJ.

'Our eyes . . . see two things at once: living beings yesterday, a void today.' This perspective 'through the lens of the Holocaust' is signalled with the first image one sees upon opening the album: a small, square photograph of a kerosene lamp hanging on a plaster wall; this image is subsequently identified as 'today a torch burning in memory of the six million martyrs'.[63] In this sense, *A Vanished World* can be viewed as an extension of the process of mourning Jews murdered during the Holocaust that was initiated by *Polish Jews*: while the earlier volume ends with a symbol of burial, the latter volume begins with a metaphorical *yortsayt-likht* (memorial candle).

However, unlike previous volumes featuring these photographs, *A Vanished World* offers Vishniac's own voice prominently in the volume's dedication; in a preface that offers a brief personal history, a retrospective mission statement, and acknowledgements; as well as in an introductory section entitled 'Commentary on the Photographs', in which Vishniac offers background information on the images that follow, in an effort to explain his mission. (The photographs in *A Vanished World* are not arranged according to any taxonomy: place, date, subject, or genre. The sequence of images—linked to Vishniac's commentary—suggests that it reflects his own ordering of them.) The photographer's personal story and voice, essentially absent from *Polish Jews*, dominates *A Vanished World*, as does his reading of the images as a kaleidoscopic view not so much of the world that vanished, but of the moment of vanishing itself. This is epitomized by the volume's cover image, a portrait of an elderly Jewish man whom Vishniac photographed in a village in Carpathian Ruthenia in 1938. Half his face is lit from the side (in his commentary the photographer recalls that the scene was illuminated by firelight); the other half disappears into a shadow cast by a hand the man raised to the side of his head—a gesture that suggests an effort to shield his face from view.

In addition to an expanded selection of photographs of Jews—more portraits, street scenes, domestic interiors—in cities, towns, and villages of pre-war eastern Europe, *A Vanished World* includes several photographs taken in 1933–4 in and around Berlin, then Vishniac's home. These document the advent of Nazism (e.g. an image of his daughter standing before a shop window displaying calipers for measuring the proportions of human heads, an instrument of state-sanctioned race science) and the efforts of Jews to leave Europe (pictures of members of a Zionist youth movement preparing to emigrate to Palestine). The album's other, east European, images are linked to the Berlin photographs through captions and, especially, through Vishniac's commentary, which explain all the pictures in the volume as documents of political and economic oppression and rising antisemitism. In some instances a seemingly benign picture is rendered into an image of persecution

---

[63] Vishniac, *A Vanished World*, 'Commentary on the Photographs', unpaginated. This photograph appeared in the report Vishniac prepared on TOZ in the late 1930s (see n. 23); there it was part of a series of photographs depicting the impoverished conditions of a Jewish worker's basement home, captioned 'This only source of light'.

through Vishniac's account of what happened before or after the picture was taken, or what was taking place beyond the image's frame. For example:

Here on a street in Warsaw that is off limits to Jewish peddlers a family is selling fresh bagels. On Jewish streets nobody had money to buy anything but ordinary bread. Almost immediately after I took this picture, policemen who had been hiding behind a house gate rushed out, grabbed some of the bagels, and kicked over the basket. The peddlers shouted. I ran, with my concealed camera. The bagels lay in the gutter.[64]

What looms beyond the frame is also crucial to the final captioned images of *A Vanished World*: a pair of related photographs on facing pages. On the left the face of a bearded man peers out from a small window in a battered, heavily fortified door; on the right a small boy in a cap looks around a wall, facing in the direction of the photograph opposite, pointing towards something behind him, out of the frame. The caption to the images reads: 'The father is hiding from the Endecy (members of the National Democratic Party). His son signals him that they are approaching. Warsaw, 1938'. Vishniac comments on the photographs: 'The pogromshchiki are coming. But the iron door was no protection.'[65] Placed together, this final pair of images becomes a diptych, reminiscent in form of medieval ecclesiastical paintings of the Annunciation. This diptych is, however, an Annunciation in reverse, heralding not an advent but a disappearance, presaging not salvation but the Holocaust.

*

Since Vishniac's death in 1990 his photographs of east European Jews have continued to be prominently displayed and republished, sometimes as part of agendas of remembrance distinct from those that the photographer had articulated during his lifetime. In 1993 the International Center of Photography in New York held a Vishniac retrospective. Entitled 'The Photographs of Roman Vishniac: Man, Nature and Science 1930–1985', the installation 'recreate[d] and expand[ed] upon the landmark 1971 exhibition' of his work, incorporating 'many rediscovered images from Eastern Europe which [had] never before been shown or published'.[66] In 1993 eight of Vishniac's photographs were also installed in a special gallery within the main exhibition of the United States Holocaust Memorial Museum, which opened that year in Washington. Entitled 'On the Eve of Destruction', the gallery 'portrays traditional orthodox Jewry in prewar Eastern Europe as observed by the well-known photographer'.[67] The installation of these photographs is unique within the museum's extensive core exhibition. Individual prints are matted and framed, unlike most other photographs shown throughout the museum. The dimly lit

[64] Vishniac, *A Vanished World*, 'Commentary on the Photographs', photo 66.

[65] Ibid., photos 178 and 179.

[66] International Center of Photography press release, *The Photographs of Roman Vishniac* (New York, Dec. 1992), 1.

[67] J. Weinberg and R. Elieli, *The Holocaust Museum in Washington* (New York, 1995), 71.

gallery in which the Vishniac photographs hang contains four benches; it is one of the few places inside the museum's main exhibition where visitors are encouraged to sit. In the centre of the space is an illuminated vitrine containing a Torah scroll and pointer; they are from the hoard of Judaica confiscated by the Nazis from Jewish communities in Czechoslovakia. Displayed in a setting that evokes both an art gallery and a synagogue, Vishniac's photographs are offered as works of art and as votive objects.

That year another volume of Vishniac photographs of pre-war east European Jews was published, with the title *To Give them Light: The Legacy of Roman Vishniac*. Prefaced again by Elie Wiesel, the volume is described as 'more structured, more deliberate' than the 'magnificent, kaleidoscopic view' offered by *A Vanished World*. With its photographs organized geographically, *To Give them Light* 'takes us on a journey', though what it offers ultimately is not travel through space as much as it is through time, bringing readers across the existential frontier of the Holocaust. In this volume's preface readers are told that they will 'meet Jews in those last minutes before they were torn from history by a tempest of fire and ashes; when their lives still coursed with energy and creativity'. But in contrast to *A Vanished World*, this volume's selection of images follows the mandate of its title, offering Vishniac's photographs as redemptive works, rather than images of doom. Wiesel makes this explicit in his prefatory remarks as well, juxtaposing the achievement of Vishniac's photography against Hitler's genocide: 'Thanks to you, Roman, the executioner has not entirely prevailed. . . . The enemy gave them death; you gave them light.'[68]

The redemptive implications of *To Give them Light* are iterated—and, moreover, extended—in the most recent republication of Vishniac's photographs of pre-war east European Jews: *Children of a Vanished World*, issued in 1999 in conjunction with an exhibition of these photographs presented by the Museum of Jewish Heritage in New York in 2000. As with the aforementioned edition of Bashevis Singer's *A Day of Pleasure*, the pictures in *Children of a Vanished World* accompany texts concerning east European Jewish childhood—here a collection of Yiddish songs about children, such as Mark Warshawsky's 'Afn pripetshik', Mordechai Gebirtig's 'Yankele', and Abraham Goldfaden's 'Rozhinkes mit mandlen' ('Almonds and Raisins'), as well as examples of east European Jewish children's folklore, including a counting rhyme and an *alef-beys* (alphabetical) mnemonic.[69] *Children of a Vanished World* also recalls *Polish Jews*, in that it offers a highly selective sampling of Vishniac's œuvre, made by someone else, in which the images serve to illustrate redemptive sentiments about pre-war east European Jewry.

---

[68] Vishniac, *To Give them Light*, 13–14.

[69] This is the second public presentation of Vishniac photographs in conjunction with Warshawsky's 'Afn pripetshik'; the popular Yiddish song was also employed in the 1971 audiovisual presentation *The Life that Disappeared*, in which it signified the sorrows of traditional Jewish life in diaspora. Here the song, along with the others in the volume, is celebrated as heritage.

By showing only portraits and genre scenes involving children, this volume eschews many of Vishniac's best-known images—those of elderly Jews and crooked alleys, often photographed in dark shadows, the embodiment of impoverishment, persecution, and despair. *Children of a Vanished World* also omits the photographer's most abject images of children (notably, his portrait of a little girl in bed, in front of a wall decorated with a floral pattern, taken in Warsaw in 1939, described in *A Vanished World* as follows: 'Since the basement had no heat, Sara had to stay in bed all winter. Her father painted the flowers for her, the only flowers of her childhood'[70]). While the youngsters who appear in *Children of a Vanished World* evidently led modest, often very poor, lives, they generally appear engaged in a variety of activities—studying, working, playing—and busy with life in the immediate present. Perhaps with a child reader in mind, the editors' selection and presentation of these images avoids the 'backshadowing' effect of presenting them as 'a last-minute look' at east European Jews 'before the fury of Nazi brutality exterminated them'.[71]

Instead, the title *Children of a Vanished World* suggests generational continuity beyond the older Jews depicted prominently in Vishniac's 1983 album. In this sense, the volume resembles the spirit of Edward Serotta's *Out of the Shadows*—a 1991 photo essay of Jewish life in post-war eastern Europe that emphasizes the revitalization of these communities at the end of the cold war, most strikingly in the book's cover image of young Jews dancing at a Hanukah party in Budapest. ('What Roman Vishniac did in illuminating the vanished world of East European Jewry before the Holocaust,' comments Cornell Capa, 'Serotta's book will in its turn do for the living, breathing contemporary history of the Jews.'[72]) The photographs in *Children of a Vanished World* illustrate texts 'meant to be read or sung aloud'. The original Yiddish is both Romanized and translated with some 'attempt to provide rhyme and meter for reciting or singing',[73] and musical notation for the songs is also provided. The book becomes, in effect, a heritage production, a guide to performing the reanimation of the youngest victims of the Holocaust: 'Thanks to Vishniac's visual artistry and the editors' choice of traditional Yiddish verses,' the dust jacket asserts, 'a part of this wonderful culture can be preserved for future generations.'[74]

*

Roman Vishniac's photographs of east European Jews in the 1930s are both the product of and the progenitors of journeys. Responding to the concerns of Jewish

---

[70] Vishniac, *A Vanished World*, 'Commentary on the Photographs', photo 42.

[71] Edward Steichen, as cited in Capa, *Roman Vishniac*, 3.

[72] E. Serotta, *Out of the Shadows: A Photographic Portrait of Jewish Life in Central Europe since the Holocaust* (New York, 1991), dust jacket.   [73] Vishniac, *Children of a Vanished World*, 138.

[74] Another version of the photograph of young boys in a *kheyder* on the cover of *Polish Jews* appears in *Children of a Vanished World* as an illustration to 'Afn pripetshik'; this is one of several images to appear in both of these volumes.

philanthropies and to his own sense of crisis over rising antisemitism in Europe, Vishniac ventured eastward from his home in Berlin. For his clients, these journeys were meant to facilitate a larger rescue mission. The photographs were to communicate the urgency of east European Jewry's plight; they were a call to action on the part of viewers remote from the site where the pictures were taken. Representing a struggle to live, the images were meant to be, in their own way, life-affirming, implying hopes for a better future for their subjects.

For Vishniac, though, this was a journey to sites he understood as maintaining the vestiges of an antique way of life—once practised by his own ancestors, subsequently abandoned by his family—that had become endangered from without. The photographs would therefore not be a means to serve the end of fund-raising or political action; rather, the act of viewing the images would become the end in itself, constituting a memorial act. The images would invite viewers to look not forward, but back; the moment they document would be not one of struggling to go on with life, but one of life about to vanish. Images of urgency would become images of doom, constituting a journey to the vanishing point of east European Jewish life. Since Vishniac's death the photographs have facilitated yet another kind of journey: one that relies on their iconic value in order to move beyond this vanishing point to contact pre-war east European Jewish life reified as heritage. Indeed, in the years since Vishniac's death his photographs have found a second life, realizing the promise of heritage as a 'transvaluation of . . . the dead'.[75] From images of urgency to images of doom, these photographs have become images of legacy.

Why are Vishniac's images so distinguished among the array of photographs of east European Jews? Ultimately, the answer lies not in the images themselves but in their epiphenomena, especially the stories provided by their photographer and retold by others of the effort to create these pictures and to bring them out of war-torn Europe. Unlike Kacyzne, Menachem Kipnis, or other noted professional photographers of eastern Europe's Jews, Vishniac survived the war. His has become a tale of survival, and his photographs have taken on the privileged status of virtual survivors. Their rise in public prominence and significance parallels the ascending stature of Holocaust survivors in the 1970s and 1980s. Yet unlike the various forms of documenting survivor testimony that have flourished in the final decades of the twentieth century and beyond, the subjects of Vishniac's photographs apparently played no acknowledged, conscious role in the making of these images—none was expected by the photographer's clients, and the notion of his subjects' collaboration in the photographic process was discounted by the photographer.

The 'time of Vishniac' of which Wiesel writes is therefore more than the eve of the Holocaust. It is a time that extends beyond the moment when these pictures were taken and beyond the Holocaust itself into the dynamics of post-war remem-

---

[75] B. Kirshenblatt-Gimblett, *Destination Culture: Tourism, Museums, and Heritage* (Berkeley, 1998), 149.

brance. Like other works of Holocaust remembrance, the presentation and re-presentation of Vishniac's photographs is essential to understanding their value as objects of memory, for their significance is ultimately responsive to the concerns of those who remember more than to the lives and the deaths of those remembered.

Repopulating Jewish Poland— in Wood

ERICA LEHRER

Among the many historical sites which Poland must unearth as it comes to terms with itself and learns to situate itself with respect to its neighboring 'others,' one in particular seems to me to be extremely promising and central—the interaction of Jewish and Polish memory.

DIANA PINTO

What was done to the Jews before Polish eyes is an injury not only for the victims, but also for the witnesses.

HENRYK GRYNBERG

One doesn't struggle with ghosts; one placates them and lures them back.

RUTH GAY

JÓZEF REGUŁA broods over a vision he had in the early 1960s. He grows animated.

A path led to a wooden fence, and a man sat there, in a black cloak and hat. It was just before dusk, the distance between us was about 20 metres. This man just looked at me. I felt paralysed, as if something unnatural were happening. I turned away, and then back. There was nobody. I had never seen anybody dressed like that. I was 10 years old.

Decades later Reguła understood he had seen a Jew.

Research for this chapter was carried out with the generous support of the International Research and Exchanges Board (IREX), the Fulbright Foundation, and the Frankel Center for Judaic Studies at the University of Michigan, Ann Arbor. I am grateful to Ruth Behar, Megan Callaghan, Ania Cichopek, Jeffrey Feldman, Halina Filipowicz, Zvi Gitelman, Janet Hart, Andrew Ingall, Ellen Moodie, Doug Rogers, Niki and Steven Schindler-Rousso, and Michael Steinlauf for their thoughtful comments during earlier stages of this chapter. I am particularly indebted to Olga Goldberg-Mulkiewicz both for her insightful analysis of Jewish sculptures in Polish culture, and for her generosity in helping me further my own research and thinking on the subject. Finally, the research could not have been done without the unique hospitality shown me by the staff of the Muzeum Etnograficzne im. Seweryna Udzieli w Krakowie (Seweryn Udziela Museum of Ethnography in Kraków) (in particular Grażyna Pyla), Józef Reguła and his family, Karen Wald Cohen, and most especially Zdzisław and Lucyna Leś of the Jarden Jewish Bookshop.

The epigraphs are taken from D. Pinto, 'Fifty Years after the Holocaust: Building a New Jewish and Polish Memory', *East European Jewish Affairs*, 26 (1996), no. 2, 80; H. Grynberg, quoted in A. Bryk, 'Poland and the Memory of the Holocaust', *Partisan Review*, 57 (1990), 228; R. Gay, 'Inventing the Shtetl', *American Scholar*, 53 (1984), 349.

Fragments of the pre-war Jewish world, physical and metaphysical, linger in the Polish landscape. Tombstone shards, crumbling synagogues, troubling or puzzling memories—in the absence of a Jewish community they are up for grabs. Few Poles shoulder the weight and ambivalence such remnants merit. But tourism and economic necessity have made some the accidental custodians of orphaned Jewishness in this post-Holocaust terrain. Keepers of cemetery keys; traders of scavenged ritual items; singers of Yiddish songs; taxi drivers who subsist by ferrying visitors around the death camp loop. Józef Reguła makes wooden Jews.

An elfin man in jeans and a button-down shirt, Reguła has invited me—a Jewish student from America—to his home. He is a sculptor and soft ice cream vendor in a small Polish town. Why, I want to know, is 'Jewish culture' circulating—celebrated, even—in almost Jewless, post-communist Poland? And, in particular, what does it mean that Poles carve tiny Jewish figurines—have carved them for over a century[1]—and that these days Jewish tourists buy them? I set off in search of answers.

*

Lilliputian Jews stare out by the thousands from shop shelves in Kraków's central square. Tiny mountain-folk, Jesuses, Marys, and Devils accompany them, in segregated regiments. The Jews arc all men, traditionally coiffed and black-cloaked. In the early post-communist 1990s meaner caricatures circulated, echoing Nazi wartime propaganda: sneering lips framing a single tooth, money-clutching fists, a nose threatening to topple the piece forward. But the image has grown tamer with time and tourists. Most now are deemed by Jewish tourists as 'melancholy': with 'sad eyes', 'drooping', 'gaunt', 'haunted' faces—'prayerful' or 'resigned'—even as some play tiny violins or accordions. Through the lens of the Holocaust, these Jews seem to know their fates.

The idiom has shifted with the era, the carving tradition swelled and receded, along with the lurches of politics and the demands of memory and the market. Kraków's ethnographic museum, only a five-minute walk from the centre of the Jewish quarter, and generally empty except for shuffling older attendants who light the exhibits on demand, is not on Poland's Jewish tourist itinerary. Given the tendency of Western Jews to read all things Polish as precursors to Jewish tragedy, perhaps that's a good thing. Here grotesque masks of Jews and little puppets of Jews on sticks in elaborately decorated *szopki* (miniature Christmas puppet theatres) and a black-and-white photograph of a straw Jewish effigy hanging from a tree are interspersed with tall, ribboned Easter palms and delicate hand-painted eggs. In these dim rooms the Jew is revealed in his pre-war guise, as an ambivalent, often baneful character internal to the rituals of Christian Polish culture.

---

[1] The oldest information pertaining to Jewish figurines dates from 1874. See B. Pilichowska, 'Krakowskie zabawki odpustowe przedstawiajace Żydów', *Polska Sztuka Ludowa*, 43 (1989), nos. 1–2, 142.

Fig. 1. Figurines in a market stall, Sukiennice, main square, Kraków

Fig. 2. Figurine in a jewellery shop

Fig. 3. Figurines, Prokopek collection, Podwarszawskie Otrebusy

Grażyna Pyla, a kindly curator, presents the collection of Jewish figurines for my video camera. Behind a long pane of glass, fading and worn Jews with unkempt locks made of real fur are hard to see as anything but a proto-form of today's Jewish figurines. Made as children's toys for sale during Easter church fairs, these Jews, also in traditional garb, see-saw, swing, frolic with the Devil, or sway in 'whatever way squeezes the most buffoonery out of their moving parts'.[2]

Insisting on speaking from a prepared script for the recording, Pyla recites the museum's position on the figurines and their function in Polish culture. 'The Jew', she states pertly, is a figure of supernatural mediation in the Polish peasants' worldview; hence his prominence in their traditional cycles of ritual. Jews were one group among others who appeared in the peasant realm on the borderland between the local and the outer world. They were travelling merchants, read books, and did not work the land, inexplicably flickering in and out of the peasants' field of vision. This imbued them with a mystery and a power that the peasants tried to harness at

[2] According to Bogdana Pilichowska (ibid.), wooden figures of Jews were sold at three Kraków church fairs: at Emmaus on Easter Monday, at Rękawka on the first Tuesday after Easter, and at Skałka on 8 May (the feast of St Stanisław).

harvest time, to 'breathe new life into the whole of nature'. The see-saws, Pyla says, are symbolic of the growth of plants.

Typical of old-style ethnographic museums, 'culture' is treated as something that governs 'primitive' society, unconnected to the contemporary political and social realities of those who look at culture under museum glass. Pyla rejects my suggestion that antisemitism is a theme worth considering in relation to the figurines. And I ask her about the multitudes of figurines sold today, just a few blocks away in the tourist shops—perhaps they represent a new Polish–Jewish borderland? She looks at me a bit quizzically. 'Those are just souvenirs.'

*

How to understand today's Jewish figurines? Are they the black-faced lawn ornaments, the tobacco-store Indians of Poland? To what need, what longings—and whose—do they speak? These days it's hard to pin them down. They gape blankly across table-tops in Kraków's Polish-run 'Jewish' theme cafés at dining Jewish tourists (who then buy them). They idle between the salt and pepper shakers in the occasional Polish kitchen, and pose on the curio shelf in a Warsaw journalist's apartment. They begin intercontinental trips from shiny cases in hotel lobbies and airport duty-free shops. They even wander as far as Ann Arbor, Michigan, and balance precariously there along a moulding in a popular Polish restaurant.

Other scholars have produced detailed and fruitful formal, iconographic, and sociological analyses of Polish-made Jewish figurines. Olga Goldberg-Mulkiewicz makes the point that there can be no discussion of *the* stereotype of the Jew in Polish culture,[3] but that various stereotypes circulate both simultaneously and in different periods and sectors of society, in dialogue with various individual and institutional interlocutors. Building on her work, I use an ethnographic approach and narrative presentation to shift attention to networks of meaning and social relations associated with the creation and circulation of the figurines.[4] This approach illustrates—

---

[3] O. Goldberg-Mulkiewicz, 'Postać Żyda w polskiej rzeźbie ludowej', *Polska Sztuka Ludowa*, 34 (1980), nos. 3–4, 219. Similarly, Iwona Irwin-Zarecka notes 'the diverse literary portraits of the Jew', and states, 'If one were to judge on the basis of Polish literature in general and poetry in particular, the image of the Jew was by no means purely, or even predominantly, negative then; though there would be much disdain for the usurer, and much ridicule of the strange habits, there was also a good deal of respect for the special wisdom the Jew was seen to have' (*Neutralizing Memory: The Jew in Contemporary Poland* (New Brunswick, NJ, 1989), 37). See also A. Cała, *The Image of the Jew in Polish Folk Culture* (Jerusalem, 1995).

[4] Ethnography asks us to pay attention to the ways that abstract cultural themes are embedded in, or 'play out', their full complexity and emotion in individual lives. It pushes us beyond stereotypes or abstract predictions, revealing a broader range of cultural possibility. This is particularly important when considering Polish–Jewish relations, which too often succumb to caricature as purely antagonistic. The sheer complexity and widely scattered impact of Polish–Jewish relations today, which include my position both as an anthropologist and a Jew, is difficult to capture in concise analytical form; sometimes only a story will do.

in action—the dialogues that shape figurine production and meaning. Closely following the travels of souvenir Jewish figurines as they pass through a dynamic system of commerce illuminates how the market both constrains and influences the creation of cultural meaning in the process of commodification of cultural forms.[5]

Understanding the significance and circulation mechanisms of commercial and touristic cultural forms is particularly important when considering Jewish culture in present-day Poland, because so much of the tiny amount of Jewish culture that exists in Poland does so under the direct or indirect influence of the Jewish heritage tourist industry. Whether this 'culture' and its products should be considered Jewish, 'post-Jewish', or otherwise, is in the eye of the beholder.[6] Authenticity is an area of immense dispute, even in domains less amorphous than culture or ethnic identity.

Nevertheless, a broad, grounded focus reveals a nexus of shared cultural relevance—however varied or conflicting its associated meanings—that connects Poles and Jews in far-flung sites. The connections may be ambivalent, but they are present, suggesting a complexity of sentiment and a shifting quality to identity erased by media narratives and studies that, a priori, take Polishness and Jewishness as wholly antagonistic, or even wholly discrete, entities. I suggest that the secular tradition of Jewish figurines expresses, in part, an identification many Poles feel with Jewishness, and a need to grapple with the loss of a part of the Polish world that the Jewish Holocaust represented for Poles. This notion is also suggested by Goldberg-Mulkiewicz, who points out that the war ended both the living presence of a Jewish community in Poland, and the organic, ritualistic, and magical uses of

[5] The relationship of Jewish consumers and Polish producers of Jewish figurines is a rich topic of inquiry with respect to the specific concerns of studies on ethnic 'folk art'—a topic of long-standing interest to anthropologists. A vocabulary and set of concerns outlined more than twenty years ago by Nelson Graburn ('Introduction: The Arts of the Fourth World', in N. H. H. Graburn (ed.), *Ethnic and Tourist Arts: Cultural Expressions from the Fourth World* (Berkeley, 1976)) still sets the standard for work on the subject, of which even notable analyses continue to fall short. There is a renewed call for an understanding of ethnic arts as 'embedded in culturally plural contexts' (id., 'Ethnic and Tourist Arts Revisited', in R. B. Phillips and C. B. Steiner (eds.), *Unpacking Culture: Art and Commodity in Colonial and Postcolonial Worlds* (Berkeley, 1999), 343). Recent efforts have been made to revise studies of ethnic arts in light of newer theoretical understandings of the complex mechanisms of culture—i.e. as affected by larger political and economic systems such as colonialism, with variously positioned subjects, and likewise by various interpretations of 'authenticity'. But the 'dialogic nature' of creative activities has yet to be adequately recognized. My present work is an attempt to forge a path in this area. I am particularly interested in pursuing themes related to Graburn's anxious comment that 'The obvious danger [in the tourist art market] is that what is offered up today as a spurious artifact or souvenir might someday reemerge—in the culture of origin—as an authentic representation of one's forgotten ancestors' (Graburn, *Ethnic and Tourist Arts*, 32).

[6] This is a significant consideration when the viewer is an institution that controls resources to encourage Jewish renewal, renovation, or restitution, or a scholar of Jewish or Polish history or culture who selects areas worthy of attention and inclusion in the historical record.

Jewish images.[7] Thus, she argues, Poland's secular Jewish figurine tradition is, owing to the circumstances of its birth, memorial in character.[8]

A dialogical look at the Jewish figurine market also raises useful questions about the larger processes involved in the transformation of Holocaust memory into Jewish cultural property. We see that 'the Holocaust' is not the cultural property only of Jews, and that the Holocaust as a 'culture industry'[9] is embedded in a web of complex micro-social processes with many interpenetrating narratives and levels of meaning. The figurine trade is also a useful reminder that stereotyping Jews and their history afflicts not only non-Jews. Most Jews who buy Jewish figurines have no more direct connection to the world the figurines depict than do their Polish makers, and at least as much nostalgia. In such a robust trade any accusations of sentimentalization or historical distortion implicate the buyers as well as the producers.[10] By the same token, the Jewish figurine trade offers the opposite challenge to the traditional focus on tourists or consumers as the sole 'culprits' of cultural distortion, nostalgia, and sentimentalization in the tourist-art market.

Shelly Shenhav-Keller, using observations in an Israeli tourist shop, suggests that 'purchase of [a] souvenir becomes the legitimate framework in which to ponder, debate, expose and declare one's position in regard to the question of identity'.[11] This conception is also useful in the Polish case. But having attended equally to the meaning of Polish-made Jewish figurines to their creators, I suggest that the production, as well as the purchase, of Polish-made Jewish figurines can provide a context for such 'identity-work'. My observations suggest a circular process in which the creation and commercial circulation of symbols of Jewishness can help to animate the social and cultural processes of which they are artefacts.[12]

---

[7] The anecdotally common practice of Poles purchasing Jewish figurines as charms for luck in business may indicate the continuing influence of the older relationship of Poles to the Jewish image in some circles.

[8] She goes even further, suggesting that at times figurines represent a Polish critique of German wartime treatment of Jews. She seems to view tendencies to antisemitic caricature as anomalies, and attributes them to the external influence of German fascist propaganda. In contrast, Cała puts the blame for anti-Jewish imagery squarely on Polish culture.

[9] See T. Cole, *Selling the Holocaust: From Auschwitz to Schindler. How History is Bought, Packaged, and Sold* (New York, 1999).

[10] Goldberg-Mulkiewicz notes the overall, *market-induced* 'engagement with non-controversial, a-historical themes' as expressed by the figurines ('Postać Żyda', 225).

[11] S. Shenhav-Keller, 'The Jewish Pilgrim and the Purchase of a Souvenir in Israel', in M.-F. Lanfant, J. B. Allcock, and E. M. Bruner (eds.), *International Tourism: Identity and Change* (London, 1995), 151.

[12] My research corrects one prediction Goldberg-Mulkiewicz made. She suggested that the Jewish figurine form would 'disappear in the not-too-distant future, when there are no longer people who had direct contact with the Jewish population' ('Postać Żyda', 225), a course clearly belied by the recent explosion in figurine production. Her writings to date have dealt with figurines made, and purchased by, individuals with living memory of Jewish Poland, under the economic and ideological influences of the communist state. My research illustrates the results of both the shift to a more democratic and capitalist field of influence on figurine production, and the changes in form and meaning that occur

Indeed, taken as a whole, the trade in Jewish figurines (from maker through seller to buyer) not only reflects identity struggles, but produces them, in part in the form of contact and dialogue among, and cultural exchange between, Poles and Jews as they together try to reimagine a Polish Jewish place in the past, as well as a place for the Polish Jewish past in the present.

*

Reguła's tall kitchen shelves teem with wooden figurines, some chess-piece-sized, some a foot tall. Mostly Jews. They've stepped out of *Fiddler on the Roof*: pedlars, musicians, and worshippers, with (to my eye) zombie-like, grey-green faces ('The colour symbolizes the epoch that is gone', Reguła says). I scan the room to see bas-relief plaques on the walls, including a kneeling prisoner in striped uniform, a series of camp numbers hanging in the air around him. The words 'Auschwitz-Birkenau' arc across the top. Elsewhere a constellation of icons connoting Jewish suffering; in Poland such images almost always reference Catholic Polish martyrs.[13] Scenes from the Christian Passion define the living room and the ice cream shop. Book-shelves display miniature washerwomen, ploughmen, and pack animals carrying harvest fruits. The stairwell swims with fantastic, neon-bright fish.

when a revival of figurine production and consumption is based on inherited, second-hand memory. (In a personal communication (Sept. 1999) Goldberg-Mulkiewicz acknowledged that subsequent observations have caused her thinking on this point to shift, and her future writing will reflect the new situation.)

[13] Although each carver I spoke to cited unique inspiration and denied any knowledge of a larger tradition or of other carvers (and Schauss further substantiates their notion in his book, p. 9), it is useful to consider Jewish figurines in the context of the larger tradition of Polish folk carving. The theme of suffering Polish culture (i.e. Poland's view of itself as the 'Christ of nations') finds expression in the copious Pietàs and *Chrystus frasobliwy* (Christ in distress) figures that appear in the genre. We can see how the 'Jewish' past and 'Jewish' tragedy is Polonized, or made relevant to the Polish Catholic world-view, through the sculptural form. Indeed, it is a central stumbling block of Polish–Jewish relations that Jews generally do not understand that Auschwitz, a symbol with one exclusive meaning to most Jews (the Holocaust), has a separate, and entirely Polish (and not Jewish) meaning to most Poles, as their own symbol of Polish national martyrdom. The 'problem' can be seen vividly in Edward Kołacz's description of his recently completed figurine sculpture illustrating a concentration camp crematorium scene: 'It depicts children, pitiably thin, who bid farewell to the world and life with a primitive cross of wire' (H.-J. Schauss, *Contemporary Polish Folk Artists* (New York, 1987), 27–8). Whether a scene depicting Polish suffering, or a scene depicting Jewish suffering, or both, the cross indicates that the scene is subsumed into the framework of a Christian religious response to that suffering. Thus, regard-less of the identity of those who populate the scene, it would very likely not be accepted by many Jews as a 'Jewish' scene or memorial, because the presence of the cross violates mainstream Jewish cultural sensibilities. Beyond the Holocaust, too, Jews are important to Polish culture in ways that have either little connection, or very circuitous connections, to Jewishness as understood by Jews. 'The Abrahams, Jacobs, and Moseses presented in folk art are figures from Christian iconography, not Jewish. This is not surprising, since Jewish religious iconography simply doesn't exist, and the Polish countryside would have had no contact with secular versions. There remains, however, the fact that Moses descending with the tablets of the commandments directly in front of a church, or a dreaming Jacob, by whose side lies the holy Bible with a cross on the cover, makes a strange enough impression' (K. Gebert, 'Pamięć naiwna', *Midrasz* (Sept. 1999), 29).

Reguła unearths a photograph album from a jumble of papers on the couch. He flips it to a picture of his sister-in-law. 'She was a Jew. A *wonderful* person', he says. Her family was killed in the Holocaust. She died of cancer a few years ago. Next, Reguła's wife lays a pre-war picture of an elementary class on the table in front of me, continuing the abrupt establishment of sympathy. 'My mother's girlfriends, all Jews', she says, pointing. 'And here's my mother. She was black, too . . . yes, she was a dark one . . .'.

Reguła talks, his brow furrowed. He fills pauses with apologetic, tight-lipped smiles. He has brown hair and close-set eyes. The lids droop slightly, as do his shoulders, wearily, as he sits. He's 47. He's carved in wood since an army friend showed him how twenty-odd years before. But Reguła began with Jews about ten years ago. His brother-in-law, director of a regional museum, asked him to make some Jewish figurines; both the carvings and the request were a growing trend. Reguła discovered later that his early attempts were full of 'mistakes', such as uncovered heads. He'd worked from 'a feeling inside' about how Jews should look. Then communism waned. Films ran on television. Books became available. He indicated an album of old photographs and an *Encyclopaedia of Jewish Religion and Tradition*. His 'accuracy' improved. He includes a *minyan* (a group of ten men needed for formal prayer), *tsitses* (a ritual vest with knotted fringes), sabbath candles. He says he wants to avoid offending potential customers. By the mid-1980s Poles could finally read I. B. Singer's novels depicting *shtetl* life. Singer spent his early years in Biłgoraj, not far from Reguła's home—familiar country. Reguła is fascinated by the stories. 'So Jewish and so Polish alike', he gushes. Older local folks told Reguła that in 1942 the Germans rounded up his town's Jews, shot most, and trucked the rest away. 'Something exists and then vanishes without any trace', he says, adding softly, 'Sometimes I feel devastated when I think about it.'

Reguła, though quiet, has a taste for drama. Poverty captivates him, as does struggle. 'Happiness is boring', he says. 'Sadness is deep; a person can find much in it.' After eight years of carving Jews Reguła began reading about the Holocaust. Melded with Catholicism, the destruction shows up in fiery red-oranges that leap from the rough-hewn tops of recent pieces. He shows me a Pietà, a strong Jew holding another, collapsed in his arms. 'People around here know so little about Judaism', Reguła says. 'Christianity *came from* Judaism.'

Jewish figurines are Reguła's main business. 'I won't pretend they're not', he offers amiably. But he says he feels a mysterious connection to the Jewish world, a 'supernatural level of life'. Singer helped him comprehend that, too. Reguła half-jokes that he chose his town because of 'something in the air . . . maybe because of its Jewish inhabitants', and that he carves 'for the needs of my heart' as well as for money.

Reguła's heart was carved by a childhood confined mostly to bed, by bouts of throat infection and unpredictable bleeding. He read a lot—including Karl May, creator of the American West for generations of Europeans—about American

Indians and faraway places. 'I lived in my own world, and this developed my imagination. Sometimes illness is useful. Sometimes I think God arranged this.' Early on he sculpted the head of an American Indian, 'with a little Egyptian influence', he mused. A later statuette shows a thick-lipped African woman, and then a 'Yoruba village' with grass huts. Still, he laughed, 'The farthest I've ever been is Warsaw!'

*

Linden branches lean along the interior walls of Reguła's bunker-like workshop, soon to be cut into figurine-sized pieces. Pale light washes in through a long window. He has left his rough workbench strewn with carving tools, wood shavings, a tin with paintbrushes. On the floor lies a clutter of wood, cans of thinner and paint, unfinished plaques, and sculptures. Reguła sets a pair of glasses low on his nose. He chooses an 8-by-3 inch rectangle of wood and pencils a rough outline, following the bough's natural curve. He chisels out the basic form. When he carves, Reguła says he thinks of the River Vistula, fishing, mushroom-picking. Gripping the block between his knees—a scalpel held between his lips and another in one hand, a thick rubber thimble covering his thumb—he peels the wood, like an apple. An arm quickly emerges, holding a book. A long nose becomes visible. A beard. Finally, pupil-less, vacant eyes.

*

With post-war modernization, Polish folk traditions waned. But a new form of secular sculpture arose, encouraged (and remunerated) by a newly communist state energetically reviving and reforming national culture on a working-people's aesthetic. The Jews, so recently and suddenly wrenched from the Polish landscape—itself ravaged and in need of restoration—reappeared in wooden form, remembered by witnesses to this lost world.

An exhibition of Jewish figurines outside Warsaw in September 1999 revealed a broader conception of Jewishness than one sees in the tourist shops.[14] Jews in modern clothes: industrialists, doctors, teachers and pupils (Fig. 5), farmers—even a Jewish hunter, shotgun and dog complementing beard and cloak. A wedding. And the Nazi occupation. The best of this category are truly moving, testifying to the pain with which some neighbours watched neighbours taken to their deaths—or at least to the pain experienced upon recollection. Uniformed SS men march a baggage-laden Jew along with a pistol to his head, entitled *Polish Jew 1939* (Fig. 4). *Last Embrace before Parting* shows the carver Wacław Czerwiński's Jewish couple 'saying goodbye because in the ghetto they are going to be separated and certainly will never

[14] The exhibition was organized by the Warsaw University professor Marian Prokopek at his private ethnographic museum in Podwarszawskie Otrebusy.

Fig. 4. Nazi and Jew, Prokopek collection, Podwarszawskie Otrebusy

Fig. 5. *Kheyder*, Prokopek collection, Podwarszawskie Otrebusy

see each other again'.[15] That the Polish 'universe of obligation'[16] may be expanding to include Jews—however belatedly—is evident in the work of Adam Żegadło, a carver who did 'fieldwork' visiting synagogues to understand better the Jews he depicts. He states simply, 'I make these woodcarvings in honour of their memory . . . It is my aim not to let the traces of this ancient culture sink into oblivion.'[17]

*

Zdzisław Leś and his assistant Ania, a graduate student in Polish Jewish history, stand on either side of the sales counter in the Jarden Jewish Bookshop in Kraków. Together they wrap a shoebox full of Reguła's Jewish figurines in brown paper, securing it with packing tape. Leś completes the job by imprinting the package with his company stamp, and carefully writing the mailing address with a fat, black marker. Destination: Cornwall, Vermont. The box is going to an American couple who saw a musician figurine on a recent visit and asked for a whole orchestra to be made. They paid in advance. The shop door is a patchwork of stickers advertising acceptable credit cards.

Leś, who, like Reguła, is not Jewish, owns the bookshop in the centre of Kraków's commercially reanimated Jewish quarter, Kazimierz, a major centre of Jewish tourism in Poland because of its proximity to the primary attraction, Auschwitz, about forty minutes away by bus. He takes a chair at one of the black metal café tables on the patio in front of his shop to talk about the figurine trade. A red-and-white umbrella advertising EB beer flutters overhead, shading Leś, a tall and slim man in his fifties with a neatly trimmed brown beard. A sign behind him advertises his shop with the words 'Sefarim/Books/Książki', and 'See Places from *Schindler's List*'. Just a few metres away, beyond a row of parked cars, a ring of wrought-iron menorahs encircles a grassy patch of park, weeping willows hunching around it to form the only sunless spot in the square. A Jewish cemetery in the 1400s, today the plot is a toilet for local dogs.

Though Leś opened the bookshop in 1993, he 'discovered' Reguła and his sculptures in the late 1970s. Leś directed the local 'House of Culture', the omnipresent communist-era community arts and propaganda centre, performance and exhibit space, and shelter for local artists, all dedicated to the aesthetic uplift of the proletariat. Leś had heard of Reguła's work, visited him, and decided to organize an exhibition. Years later, when Leś opened his Jewish bookshop, he decided to sell Reguła's sculptures as well. Since then Reguła, in collaboration with Leś as his critic and muse, has specialized in the Jewish figurines. Leś has daily contact with tourists, and makes efforts to educate them aesthetically, as well as monitoring their

---

[15] Goldberg-Mulkiewicz, 'Postać Żyda', 221.

[16] This phrase was first used in this context by Helen Fein (*Accounting for Genocide: National Responses and Jewish Victimization during the Holocaust* (Chicago, 1979), 33).

[17] Schauss, *Contemporary Polish Folk Artists*, 198.

taste. He carries a few figurines by 'lesser' carvers as a 'negative background' against which he believes Reguła's artistry will shine. He shows me the roughly cut foils, turning one over in his hands. 'They're standard, without character', he says. 'They all have the same face, the same expressions, the same hands, they're static. They're sort of lightly caricatured. They have no *life* in them. With Reguła every one is different. Look at the placement of the hands', he offers, pointing at a figurine. 'It looks almost as if he's thinking. Sometimes you even see a sense of humour. You see *character* in them.'

Leś calls the figurines an example of 'post-Jewish' culture, because they depict both a world that no longer exists in Poland, and one that Reguła knows only second-hand. Reguła gets reading materials from Leś's shop (in addition to the historical albums I saw a copy of *Midrasz*, the lively new Warsaw-based magazine on contemporary Jewish life and culture, on a table in Reguła's home), and Leś acts as a reference librarian for Reguła's questions on Jewish culture ('He asked me about a Jewish wedding . . . he asked me what a *khupe* [wedding canopy] looks like . . . so I gave him a picture', Leś told me.) Leś visits Reguła often, to pick up orders, to discuss, sometimes to criticize. 'He doesn't like it,' Leś says of the latter, 'but it's good for him.'

Leś arranges a new shipment of Reguła's figurines for display. He picks them from a cardboard box he holds against his hip, piled high with the black-cloaked sculptures: a group of ten men, one *tales* encircling them all; a man clutching a goose; more *klezmorim*; a man holding a lit menorah. Leś places some next to a pile of loosely crocheted *yarmulkes*. 'Very nice, right? Aesthetic. Even the hands.' He sets a row of them across a top shelf, in front of a painting of the old synagogue that stands at the other end of the square outside: a fiddler; a merchant with a sack; a rare couple, embracing a row of children. They come alive against the backdrop.

*

During the summer Leś can barely keep Reguła's figurines on the shelves. According to Leś, they are snapped up by 'very educated' people, university professors, businessmen, and, of course, tourists—fifty Regułas for every one of the others. 'That's the most optimistic part of it. That the tourists themselves, almost intuitively, know, feel, and choose the more interesting ones. They have an aesthetic taste. Either innate, or learned. But they have it.'

Reguła speculates about why Jewish and German tourists buy his figurines (nostalgia and guilt, respectively). Poles, he says, buy them as amulets, to ensure financial success. Some complain to him that business isn't going any better. Reguła suggests harder work. He works ten hours a day, carving. One figurine takes two to four hours. He makes about 300 a year, enough to finance a large addition on his small house. He'd make more if Leś had his way, but in the warm months Reguła dons his white smock and soda jerk's twin-peaked cap and dispenses soft ice cream to local passers-by.

Fig. 6. Reguła's standard figurines

Fig. 7. Reguła's colour figurines

Leś is open about the fact that Reguła traffics in stereotypes. 'But tourists think in similar stereotypes to Reguła', Leś says. 'Reguła's stereotypes fulfil the expectations of the tourists.' And Leś has developed a keen sense of tourist expectations, of the desire on the part of visiting Jews for a particular legend; he thinks they would feel most happy if Reguła were an old man—perhaps even an old Jew—chiselling out his memories.[18]

Thus, for Reguła, imagination is tempered by marketability. At home, he has wooden Jewish women in lilac and sky blue, with red skirts and white shawls, green and yellow details, and children. But the legions of figurines he *sells* are old men in black. His Jewish world has colour, passion, possibility. The buyers' world, it often seems, has only sorrow. (See Figs. 6 and 7.)

*

Despite the popularity of wooden Jews for tourists, against the background of recent Polish Jewish history, during which the Nazis devastated the country's 3.5 million Jews and Poland's post-war pogroms and purges caused most of those who remained to flee, the stylized wooden Jews can rankle their animate counterparts.

Some Jews reject the figurines out of hand, claiming they can 'see the anti-semitism' too clearly. Zvi Engel, a 17-year-old student at Hebrew Academy in Montreal, described the figurines he saw in Kraków during a high-school trip to Poland with distaste, as 'beggars in long black coats, with big noses, big ears'.[19] Photographs I take and show to a Polish-born Jewish man in Boston elicit rage: 'Something must be done to *stop* this', he demands. He later tells me he wrote a letter to the Pope to complain and request intervention. Steven Schindler, a secular American Jew who grew up in an Orthodox household, is 'vehemently opposed' to the figurines because he feels Jews buy them out of guilt and nostalgia about their own dwindled connections to Jewishness. He also baulks at the underlying implication that traditional Jewishness—as depicted by the figurines—is dead and gone, existing only as a tourist trinket. Even Jews who do buy figurines are sometimes extremely ambivalent, both fascinated and repelled, in part purchasing 'evidence of Polish antisemitism'.

But Reguła keeps a scrapbook of comments from admiring customers. An American Jewish woman who had ordered a set of *klezmer* musicians wrote about showing the figurines to her father, who found them happily reminiscent of 'the

[18] It seems that Zdzisław has indeed identified a salient element of purchase satisfaction among some Jewish tourists. Jen Clapp, a 35-year-old Californian convert to Judaism and the daughter-in-law of a Holocaust survivor, interjected in an interview I conducted with her husband, 'Did you see the figurines? The little, mournful-looking fiddlers with long, sad faces and beards? It's just sick! These people are dead, were killed! And you want to buy a little statuette? It makes my stomach turn! I mean, unless there's some *Jewish* person making these in some artistic way . . .'.

[19] A. Riga, ' "I'm angry at what the world can do": Student Sobered by Visit to Concentration Camp in Poland', *The Gazette* (Montreal) (4 June 1992), G6.

world of his ancestors which he was denied any knowledge of'. The woman praised
Reguła for having, in the faces of the figurines, 'exactly evoked the expressions of
their souls', and thanked him 'for so tastefully bringing back a small part of our past'.

It makes sense that it matters to someone who dedicates himself to a craft how
consumers respond to the final products. Goldberg-Mulkiewicz recounts the story
of a carver whose Jewish figurine ended up in a New York shop window and was
seen by a former inhabitant of the carver's town. The man was so affected by the
image of his lost childhood world that he wrote to thank the carver, who was himself
moved 'immensely and [thus] convinced . . . of the legitimacy of his chosen path'.[20]

I have my own range of emotion to grapple with throughout my research. Even
when my visits to carvers are most graciously indulged, sometimes the weight of
history, the poverty of wooden miniatures where flesh and blood used to be, can be
blinding. The first figurine carver I interview—before I meet Reguła—is as suspicious of me as I am of him. What I learn doesn't ease my mind. A tiny Jewish head,
wearing a fur-trimmed hat, rolls across the lace tablecloth in his Kraków apartment.
It is stopped by a pack of Marlboros. The gaze points towards a disjoined arm. Its
miniature hand clutches a curling scrap of parchment lined with painstakingly
flourished Hebrew letters. Assembled, it stands about 5 inches tall, on sprung legs.
I touch it. It *shokls*, rocking in the characteristic gesture of Jewish prayer. In the
1960s the carver discovered a Torah scroll hidden in the rafters of his father's
house. He is vague on details, wary of my questions. Not an uncommon find in
Poland, the scroll was likely stashed there during the war by a doomed Jewish
neighbour—an eleventh-hour act of hope or resistance. Over the years the carver
clipped small squares from the parchment and put them in the hands of his sculptures. He's not the only one to use this method, though many carvers have turned to
photocopying. He says he stopped recently after Jewish tourists told him he was
doing something sacrilegious. His personal figurines still hold the Hebrew readings, often upside down. He chuckles. 'I can never remember which way they go.'[21]

*

Tracking Polish Jewish figurines takes me to White Plains, New York, to the home
of Karen Wald Cohen, an American Jew. Her white house is bounded by a white
picket fence and a small yard scattered with plastic tricycles and cow-shaped
planters. Jutting out above the front porch, three flags—American, Canadian, and

---

[20] Goldberg-Mulkiewicz, 'Postać Żyda', 221.

[21] The general ignorance of Catholic Poles regarding Jewish sacralia and the resulting Jewish sentiment is made clear in the following anecdote by a Holocaust survivor who returned to his Polish town in
1944, immediately after the liberation: 'I entered the store to buy some butter. It was handed to me
wrapped in sheets of the Vilna edition of the Talmud. I stood as if petrified, remembering how hard it
had been for a Jew to purchase a Vilna Talmud for his scholarly son-in-law. . . . On my way out I threw
the butter away and hid the holy scraps of text' (M. Rapaport, 'Khurbn Bilgoray', in J. Kugelmass and
J. Boyarin (eds.), *From a Ruined Garden: The Memorial Books of Polish Jewry* (New York, 1983), 221).

Israeli—flap in the winter wind. Karen and her husband, Bruce, a rabbi, run Interns for Peace, an Israeli–American organization that promotes the professional development of peace workers.

Wald Cohen, a petite, smiley woman in her early fifties, with curly red hair, a black tracksuit, and white-socked feet, invites me into the sunny, cluttered house, introducing me to its various residents over the course of the afternoon. Cohen's children—one Chinese, one white, both adopted and now Jewish—sit on the living-room floor, mesmerized by *Star Trek* playing on a wide-screen television.

The dining-room table is being set for brunch with bagels and lox, cream cheese, onions, and tomatoes. The director of Rabbi Cohen's Palestinian franchise in Gaza is visiting, and as the conversation turns to Hebrew, I wander through the house. Almost every surface bears a sign of Jewishness. In the living room, a Disney 'Happy Hanukah' wall hanging shows Pluto, Mickey, Goofy, and gang playing *dreydl*. An enormous cloth 'Shalom' drapes the hall. A scroll of the Ten Commandments hangs around the corner. On a dining-room sideboard sits a ceramic *shtetl* scene, a capped fiddler perched on the eves of a thatched house, a dancing Tevya, arms aloft, in the front yard next to a woman hawking geese from a cart. Nearby stands a matching set of Jewish man and woman salt and pepper shakers.

In the living room I find a wall of ethnic dolls, stacked in their unbreached, price-tagged plastic packaging. Mostly Barbies: Native American Barbie, Asian Barbie with her fan, African Queen Barbie with striped gown and elaborate beaded neck rings. Also a New York Yankees Barbie and a couple of Barbies in bikinis, as well as a miniature Liz Taylor in Egyptian Barbie garb. Non-Barbies include an Aunt Jemima figure with a polka-dot headscarf and curlers, and a small porcelain Japanese doll wearing a kimono.

Wald Cohen didn't 'believe in' Barbies ('too "whitebread"') until her Bosnian foster daughter began collecting them. The spectrum of the dolls' colours and ethnicities echoes the jumble of international visitors who've set up camp throughout the Cohen home ('We have an open-door policy', she says). Finally I spot what I came for. On top of a white cabinet filled with dishes, among menorahs, kosher wine, a *dreydl*, and other ritual Judaica, stand two Jewish figurines, clearly of the Polish variety. With striped and fringed *taleysim* hanging over their shoulders, they are the rarer and older 'rocking' type, their sprung necks letting their heads nod into the torn scraps of Hebrew prayer book in their hands.

After brunch a talk with Wald Cohen reveals five years of east European travel, guiding Jewish heritage travel tours, sometimes for Holocaust survivors, often visiting the camps. We finally touch on the topic of the figurines. 'I'd *love* to find out anything about the people who made these', she begins.

The real significance for me, and why I was so drawn to them—aside from the fact that you're so starved for anything Jewish in Poland, so when you see something, you *freak out*— was that I felt that they were a symbol, just sitting there, that Judaism would never die no matter what happened. That here in the midst of all this destruction that you saw, with few

Jews left, that sitting in a market were these dolls . . . That's really what it is for me. That no matter how many times you try to put the Jews down, they pop up somewhere.

*

In Poland 'a guest in the home is God in the home', and in a small town there today an American Jew sits high in the hierarchy of guests. Back at Reguła's, his wife supplies endless, steaming food: eggs and ham, *pierogi* glistening with fat, sweet tea and cake. In the afternoon local dignitaries and relatives drop by to meet me. Each adds his two cents about Jews and Poland—always emphatically rosy about the past, vaguely defensive about the present. Some brew of economics, conscience, litera-ture, and history makes me an honour, an opportunity, maybe vaguely intimidating. None of these discredit Reguła's overwhelming generosity and goodwill. (I came back months later with a three-person film crew. Rather than send us to a hotel, the Reguła family gave up their own beds—fold-down couches in the kitchen and living room—and camped out together in an attic room.) Still, a final guest trumps me.

Reguła's wife, who had been running errands, returns in a commotion with their teenage son and daughter (who'd earlier shown me small watercolour Jewish scenes she'd done). They speedily tidy themselves up, and then the house. The local priest blusters in moments later to give an annual blessing. Suddenly forgotten, I watch from the kitchen, accompanied by my wooden co-religionists. The priest pulls a surplice over street clothes, and sprinkles holy water on the Regułas, who stand in the living room with lowered heads. Everyone chants, surrounded by rustic Reguła-carved crucifixes, madonnas, popes. The priest holds out a cross. Each kisses it. Amid pleasantries, the priest accepts money and hurries out again.

Near the end of my visit Reguła disappears. He returns holding a small wooden sculpture. Jesus *frasobliwy*—in distress at the state of the world, crowned with thorns, lost in melancholy under a tree. Reguła wants to give it to me. He hopes it won't offend me. He looks at the floor as he stresses that I shouldn't think of the gift as a religious gesture. He wants me to have it because, he says, unlike the Jewish figures, 'it's something of *ours*'.

*

Secular American Jews, like me, who travel to Poland, purchase Jewish figurines, and display them in our homes, show how symbolic, how iconographic (and thus— according to some—how 'un-Jewish') a lot of Jewishness is today. But such Jewishness is not the only kind that Jews bring to Poland.

For Max Rogers, a hasidic Jew from London who travels to Poland frequently on business, Jewishness is an encompassing matter of daily practice.[22] A small and sprightly man, he dresses as his community demands: white shirt, long black jacket

---

[22] Rogers works for a foreign foundation to restore and preserve Jewish cemeteries in Poland.

and trousers, black *yarmulke* under a black fedora, long beard and *peyes* and *tsitses* (all three of which he tucks demurely away while travelling among non-Jews). He looks like one of Reguła's figurines.

Though Rogers rejects any attachment to Poland (his parents came from a small Polish town), I often catch him musing about the lilt of the Polish language, how he wishes he could speak it, how it reminds him of his mother. He listens intently to the Poles around him, straining to recognize a word or two. Rogers is one of the few Jewish visitors to Kraków who takes almost as much interest in the Jewish figurines as I do. But he simply admires Reguła's work; he can't stop talking about it. An orthodox interpretation of the Third Commandment, barring graven images, prevents him from keeping a figurine in his home. So he negotiates with Reguła to commission an acceptable piece—a landscape, a *shtetl* scene, a bas-relief without people or animals.

Rogers has some business in the area the day I travel to meet Reguła, so we ride together from Kraków, and I am dropped off at Reguła's home for my interview with the sculptor. On the drive home, after plaintively urging me not to eat the chicken Reguła's wife packed for me (not kosher), Rogers tilts his head towards the sculpture I am carrying, and complains, 'Look, when she leaves, she gets a present; when I leave, nothing!' I retort that I don't think he'd want the piece Reguła gave me. I show him the statue of the pensive Jesus—an image replicated in crossroad chapels throughout the Polish countryside. In yet another example of Jewish and Polish mutual non-comprehension, Rogers surprises me by saying, 'Why wouldn't I want this?' I answer, 'Because it's Jesus Christ.' Rogers baulks, '*Where* is Jesus Christ? For me this is a Jewish man, sitting, thinking—*beautiful*.' I laugh, but insist again that it is Jesus. Rogers demands, 'From where you think it's Jesus Christ?' I am intrigued that his world could be so insular that he wouldn't recognize a figure of Jesus. I say, for one thing, the man who made it told me it was Jesus Christ. Rogers rolls his eyes and says, 'Ah! He sees what he *wants*. I see what *I* want. He can tell you this is *Hitler*, but it doesn't *make* it Hitler . . .'. I chuckle again, at what strikes me as surprising role reversal: the subject telling the anthropologist that meaning is culturally relative.

Rogers clarifies with one of his frequent midrashes: 'If a bad man writes a Torah, it must be burned. Why? You might think, well, the words are the same, the Torah is holy, right? But where does writing come from?' He gestures as if he were writing, and points to a flow from his head through his arm to his hand and onto the imaginary page before him. 'Even the name of God written by a bad man isn't holy.' But Rogers goes on to explain that this understanding of intention and creation only applies to the Torah. For other things we make—art, for example—the intention doesn't matter. Rogers can see a beautiful Jewish man in Reguła's Jesus sculpture, and that's sufficient.

As an afterthought, though, Rogers adds that if there were a cross on the sculpture, then it would be a different story. It would be a problem because a cross is a symbol of Christianity, which Jews must avoid. 'Now, if *everyone* knows this is Jesus [pointing to the sculpture], then it would be different...' I tell him again—with our driver and our mutual Polish friend supporting me—that everyone does know it's Jesus. I point to the crown of thorns, the characteristic pensive pose, the fact that identical statues dot country roads in much of Europe. 'Oh . . .', he says reflectively, handing the figure back to me. 'Then it's not for me.'

POSTSCRIPT

I am tempted to end this chapter here, letting the reader linger on the 'limits of interethnic dialogue'.[23] The boundaries—indeed the antagonisms—between Polish and Jewish cultural memory as they most publicly find expression today often seem unbreachable, appearing as 'political and religious incommensurabilities'.[24] But as the historian Diana Pinto suggests of Jews and Poland, 'One must build a "new" memory based on a spirit of openness and mutual enrichment, two sentiments which are becoming possible thanks to the passage of time.'[25]

I would like to suggest that Jewish tourism to Poland, including the trade in Jewish figurines, be taken seriously as a site of potentially positive memory-building. Given the fact that Polish–Jewish relations exist largely at a distance, more often via media representations than through personal contact, and despite the narrow, negative ritual character that has structured much Jewish travel to Poland,[26] Jewish tourist areas in Poland are perhaps the only places in the world where Poles and Jews are in ongoing face-to-face contact in the present day. Thus such areas, and the exchanges that occur there, both social and commodity, are ideal sites for observing when and how images and meanings of Polishness and Jewishness are shared by, as well as diverge among, Poles and Jews. We should attend not only to when boundaries are invoked, but when and how they are resisted as well.

Making and purchasing Polish-made Jewish figurines clearly functions as a way of engaging with the Polish Jewish past and present, and with one's own sentiment about and identity in relation to them, for both Poles and Jews. But it is also a way that some Poles and Jews, however tentatively and ambivalently, can engage with each other. Jews and Poles are drawn into a rare dialogue, or collaboration in the production of Jewish figurines, and I would therefore suggest that both their production and their purchase can signal the desire to expand one's identity, to enlarge as well as to delimit the self.

---

[23] See J. Kugelmass, 'Bloody Memories: Encountering the Past in Contemporary Poland', *Cultural Anthropology*, 10 (1995), 279–301.

[24] This phrase was used by Jack Kugelmass in his paper 'Making Auschwitz Relevant to Jews: Can the Auschwitz Museum Serve a Multicultural Public?', presented at the Conference of the Association for Jewish Studies, Washington, 17 Dec. 2001.

[25] D. Pinto, 'Fifty Years after the Holocaust: Building a New Jewish and Polish Memory', *East European Jewish Affairs*, 26 (1996), no. 2, 81.   [26] See Kugelmass, 'Bloody Memories'.

Perhaps it behoves us to look at even such an awkward and sensitive example of 'tourist kitsch' with a less jaundiced eye, considering not only its negative, but also its potentially positive, aspects. The current trend of Jewish-figurine carving has the potential to (re)connect a new generation of Poles—Polish figurine carvers, and perhaps even Polish figurine buyers—with Jews or Jewish concerns.[27] It may be that the appearance of Jewish tourists as a customer base for Jewish figurines will both act as a check against the proliferation of more caricatured imagery, as well as attuning Polish carvers and sellers to Jewish cultural conceptions of the significance of Poland's Jewish past. Very human issues and processes occur on both sides of the tourist divide. It bears consideration that Jewish tourists (some a generation or less removed from the world the figurines are meant to depict) today have the disposable income to make a leisure trip to Poland and buy souvenirs from carvers whose financial situations are much more precarious. And beyond legitimate questions about cultural loss or degradation, assimilation or alienation, materialism or sentimentality, or stereotype or prejudice, Jewish figurines can represent longings for knowledge, social interconnectedness, tradition, and reconcilation with history on the part of consumer and producer alike.

Rather than resting on comfortably pessimistic conclusions about Poland and its Jews (real or symbolic), we might instead attend to the exceptions and sparks of possibility that exist in the cultural processes and interactions surrounding 'Jewishness', in whatever form, in Poland today. There are connections to be teased out of the conflicts between Poles and Jews, and in these connections there exists the potential for cultural change, despite enormous odds.

---

[27] Here it is worth considering Kugelmass's discussion of 'the image of the Hasid in the vernacular culture of American Jewry' in his essay 'Jewish Icons: Envisioning the Self in Images of the Other', in J. Boyarin and D. Boyarin (eds.), *Jews and Other Differences: The New Jewish Cultural Studies* (Minneapolis, 1997), 32. The hasidic image, collected and displayed by assimilated American Jews in coffee-table photograph albums, bears striking resemblance to the image of the Jew appearing in wooden figurine form in Poland. Thus we might think of Polish Jewish figurines as functioning similarly to Kugelmass's hasidic photograph albums: as 'folk ethnography', a form he suggests simultaneously strengthens group identity, distorts the cultural material in question, and creates a potential entrance leading some individuals towards deeper engagement.

The Kraków Jewish Culture Festival

RUTH ELLEN GRUBER

TWO weeks to the day before the cathartic ceremony on 10 July 2001 that marked the 1941 massacre of Jews in the north-eastern Polish town of Jedwabne, Jan T. Gross found himself in another north-eastern Polish town, dancing in the streets to the strains of *klezmer* music. Gross is the author of *Neighbors*, the book published in 2000 whose revelations that it was local Poles, not German Nazis, who slaughtered Jedwabne's 1,600 Jews, touched off an unprecedented national debate on Poland's role in the Holocaust.

Gross attended the Jedwabne commemoration, where the Polish president, Aleksander Kwaśniewski, begged forgiveness for the massacre 'in my own name, and in the name of those Poles whose conscience is shattered by that crime'.[1] But on 26 June he danced in Sejny, near the Lithuanian border, along with hundreds of other people, following the final concert of a ten-day festival and workshop that celebrated *klezmer* music and Yiddish culture in a town where no Jews have lived since the Holocaust.

Called the Musicians' Raft between New York and Sejny, the events featured public lectures and exhibits, as well as master classes by leading *klezmer* musicians from the United States, that drew participants from half a dozen countries in east-central Europe. 'It was incredible', said Krzysztof Czyżewski, the founder of the Sejny-based Borderland Foundation (Fundacja Pogranicze), which sponsored the encounter—and which was also the original publisher of Gross's book. 'The final concert was held in the White Synagogue here. There were about 500 people, and it was so crowded that people had to sit on the floor. The concert lasted about three hours and then everyone, including all the musicians, went out into the streets, singing and dancing.'[2]

The contrast between the joyousness of the concert and the intense solemnity of the Jedwabne ceremony was striking. But the two events, and others like them, form part of a related phenomenon: the exploration and even embrace of Jewish

Parts of this chapter are drawn from my article 'Brave Old World', *Ha'aretz* (Tel Aviv) (17 Aug. 2001) and my book *Virtually Jewish: Reinventing Jewish Culture in Europe* (Berkeley, 2002).

[1] Speech by President Aleksander Kwaśniewski at a memorial ceremony at Jedwabne, 10 July 2001; official English-language translation (repr. in full in *Polin*, 14 (2001), pp. xvii–xx).

[2] Telephone interview with Krzysztof Czyżewski, Aug. 2001.

culture and history as an integral part of national history and, ideally, as a necessary and urgent resurrection of national memory. 'We witness the closing of a circle that seemed broken forever, thanks to the tragic history of our times', said a prospectus for the Musicians' Raft festival. 'A new meeting, stronger than the worst prejudice and oblivion, is born from broken links, tragic conflicts, and ruined memory.'[3]

The phenomenon is particularly striking in Poland, where, the British anthropologist Jonathan Webber notes, 'the remarkable characteristic of anything to do with Jews . . . is its intensity'.[4] But it extends across Europe. Since the early 1980s, and particularly in the years since the fall of communism, there has been an explosion of interest in Jewish culture and Jewish cultural products like *klezmer* music in all corners of the continent. As part of this trend, aspects of Jewish culture (or what is perceived or defined as Jewish culture) have become visible components of the popular public domain in European countries where Jews themselves now are practically invisible.

This is manifested in a wide variety of ways, from the scholarly to the superficial. Numerous conferences are held each year on all aspects of Jewish history, culture, and tradition, and numerous academic study programmes, courses, or lecture series on Jewish topics have been established. Jewish exhibitions, festivals, and workshops of all types abound. Readings, seminars, talk shows, and films spotlight Jewish issues, and articles and programmes on Jewish subjects find frequent and prominent space in the media. Hundreds of new books on Jewish topics are published annually in local languages, and new Jewish bookshops attract a wide clientele. In addition, Jewish-themed tourism has become a solid niche market; Jewish heritage sites are being cleaned, restored, and exhibited; Jewish museums are being opened; and former Jewish quarters are being gentrified with 'Jewish-style' cafés, hotels, restaurants, and the like. In many cases the label 'Jewish' has become a category of commercial merchandise.

The Paris-based historian Diana Pinto uses the term 'Jewish space' to describe the place occupied by the Jewish phenomenon within mainstream European society, regardless of the current size, visibility, or activity of the local Jewish population.[5] 'There is a Jewish space in Europe that will exist even in the absence of Jews', Pinto told the Conference on Planning for the Future of European Jewry held in Prague in 1995. 'The "Jewish thing"', she said, 'is becoming universal.' Similarly, in the early 1990s the sociologist Y. Michal Bodemann described the emergence in Germany of a 'Judaizing terrain' made up of 'converts to Judaism, of members of joint Jewish–German or Israeli–German associations, and of many

---

[3] Introductory material provided privately by David Krakauer, the musical director of the Musicians' Raft, before the workshop. A revised version of this text is found in *Tratwa Muzykantów pomiędzy Nowym Jorkiem a Sejnami: The Musicians' Raft between New York and Sejny* (Sejny, 2001), 20.

[4] Interview with Jonathan Webber, Košice, Slovakia, Aug. 2001.

[5] See D. Pinto, *A New Jewish Identity for Post-1989 Europe*, JPR Policy Paper no. 1 (London, June 1996).

"professional almost-Jews" outside or even inside the apparatuses of the Jewish organizations and [Jewish communities]'. Jewish culture, he wrote,

is being manufactured, Jewish history reconstructed, by these Judaizing milieux—by German experts of Jewish culture and religion [who] enact Jewish culture from within German biographies and from within German history; this has an important bearing on the type of Jewish culture that is actually being produced: a culture that is not lived, that draws heavily from the museum, and that is still no less genuine for that.[6]

I think of this 'universalization' of the Jewish phenomenon and its integration into mainstream European consciousness, this emergence of a 'Judaizing terrain' and 'Judaizing milieux' in all their widely varied manifestations, as a 'filling' of the Jewish space.[7] This is a process which in turn encompasses the creation of a 'virtual Jewishness', a 'virtual Jewish world', peopled by 'virtual Jews' who perform—or, as Bodemann put it, enact—Jewish culture from an outsider perspective, alongside or often in the absence of local Jewish populations.[8]

A project undertaken by the London-based Institute for Jewish Policy Research (JPR) provided a vivid statistical illustration of this. Between May 2000 and April 2001 it attempted to 'map' Jewish cultural activities in four European countries with small Jewish communities. The countries chosen—Poland, Sweden, Italy, and Belgium—have a total Jewish population of well under 100,000 and had very different Jewish histories both before the Second World War and during and after the Holocaust. 'The results are simply astonishing, and as yet we have no idea what to make of them', Jonathan Webber, who was consultant on the project, reported in July 2001 at a conference in Budapest on Jewish identities in the post-communist era. Hundreds of Jewish cultural events, he said, took place during the surveyed period in those countries, including a 'remarkable' twenty-seven Jewish cultural festivals. This, he estimated, amounted 'to an average of one event for every 125 Jews . . . There is clearly no correlation between the considerable size of this cultural production and the percentage of Jews in a given total population of a particular country.' Across Europe, thus, a very large percentage of consumers—and, often, producers—of Jewish cultural offerings are not Jewish. It is almost as if 'once one starts to have public Jewish culture, it simply continues to generate further events'. Indeed, out of the four countries surveyed, Poland, with its tiny Jewish population (depending on how one defines 'Jew', estimates vary between 3,000 and 20,000 or more in a total population of about 40 million), was by far the Jewish cultural champion, with 196 individual events and fully seven Jewish cultural festivals,

---

[6] Y. M. Bodemann, 'A Reemergence of German Jewry?', in S. L. Gilman and K. Remmler (eds.), *Reemerging Jewish Culture in Germany: Life and Literature since 1989* (New York, 1994), 57–8. See also Y. M. Bodemann (ed.), *Jews, Germans, Memory: Reconstructions of Jewish Life in Germany* (Ann Arbor, 1996).

[7] See R. E. Gruber, *Filling the Jewish Space in Europe* (New York, 1994).

[8] This is elaborated in Gruber, *Virtually Jewish*.

including the annual Festival of Jewish Culture in Kraków—the 'largest and most important event' recorded in the JPR survey.[9]

The motives underlying this phenomenon are many, and the end results are not yet known. For some, the process has served as a means to understand, or atone for, the deeds of their parents or grandparents (for example, as part of the continuing post-war German process of *Vergangenheitsverarbeitung*), or as a key to build (or rebuild) a democratic and tolerant state or a personal or national identity. For others, it is a fashionable way of expressing multiculturalism—or, increasingly, of simply having fun. In Poland and other east European countries, where communist-era taboos prevented an objective public reflection on the Holocaust, Jewish issues, and history itself for decades, it has been a conspicuous part of the process of 'filling in the blanks' left by monolithic communist ideology. It is important to note, too, that aspects of the phenomenon can be found in countries where there are also visible and sometimes violent manifestations of grass-roots, skinhead, or political anti-semitism. (At the time of writing, the impact on the phenomenon of fallout from the renewed Israeli–Palestinian conflict that erupted in late 2000 was not clear.)

Specific history and memory have made the process in Poland particularly complex and compelling. I need not detail here that Jews have lived in Poland for 1,000 years and that the vast majority of Jews in North America trace their ancestry back to Polish lands. Nor that within its pre-Second World War borders Poland was home to the largest Jewish population in Europe, but that antisemitism was widespread and at times virulent. Nor need I detail how some 3 million of pre-war Poland's 3.5 million Jews were killed in the Holocaust, and how those who remained suffered under communist persecution. Nor how, throughout the communist period, the physical absence of Jews and their own memories and understanding of history left 'all remaining memory of this past . . . in Polish hands and thus reflected a characteristically Polish grasp of events, Polish ambivalence, and eventually even a Polish need for a Jewish past'.[10]

From Paris, the Polish Jewish intellectual Aleksander Smolar wrote in 1987, ' "The Jewish question" in Poland today exists principally as a Polish problem: that of facing history, the burden of moral responsibility, and the difficult questioning of the Polish heroic and tragic self-image, formed in the perpetual fight for freedom, independence and national survival.'[11] Similarly, as Jonathan Webber put it to me, 'There is no question that the peculiar passion by which issues relating to Polish Jewish matters, be they the debates over Jedwabne or the cultural issue, are played out is striking to the outsider. Poles are examining themselves when they examine Jewish issues. They take it very seriously.'[12]

[9] J. Webber, 'Notes towards the Definition of "Jewish Culture" in Contemporary Europe', presented at the Conference on Jewish Identities in the Post-Communist Era, Budapest, 8–10 July 2001. Results of the JPR survey have been published in R. Schischa and D. Berenstein, *Mapping Jewish Culture in Europe Today: A Pilot Project*, JPR Report no. 3 (London, 2002).

[10] J. E. Young, *The Texture of Memory: Holocaust Memorials and Meaning* (New Haven, 1993), 116.

[11] A. Smolar, 'Jews as a Polish Problem', *Daedalus*, 117 (Spring 1987), 31–2.

[12] Interview with Jonathan Webber, Aug. 2001.

The Borderland Foundation in Sejny, for example, was established in 1990 to promote awareness of minority cultures, including Jewish culture. With its head-quarters next to Sejny's large synagogue, now restored as a cultural venue, the foundation's activities have covered an impressive agenda, including publications, meetings, exhibitions, concerts, and other exchanges. It even has its own *klezmer* band, which has performed not only locally but also at venues including the annual Festival of Jewish Culture in Kraków and even, in November 2000, at a bar mitzvah reception in Warsaw. 'What's important is that the meeting takes place in a living cultural space, not limited to the past, in a space where we face modernity, where we ask the most important questions for today and tomorrow', said the Musicians' Raft prospectus.[13] The American musician Stuart Brotman, who was an instructor at the Musicians' Raft workshop, told me, 'I felt I was part of a teaching unit in which music was integrated with information in a magical proportion that could be a model for promoting cultural tolerance.'[14]

Similar ideals and motivations underlay the founding of the Kraków Festival of Jewish Culture in 1988 by Janusz Makuch and Krzysztof Gierat, two young, non-Jewish intellectuals who had independently become interested in Jewish culture and history in the early 1980s. 'Above all else, this festival is an attempt to show what we have lost as a result of the Holocaust', Makuch told the Polish Jewish students' magazine *Jidele* in 1997.

The enormity of this tragedy is such that it can only be portrayed through the presentation of a Jewish culture now extinct. People tend to flee from that which is shocking; they're able to submit to shock only for a short time. They cry, they feel better, and by the next day they've already forgotten. Considerably more difficult is the process of changing, step by step, people's awareness by introducing them to the richness of that culture. Yet such an endeavour is critical, both because of the vastness of the culture itself which was created in Poland during the course of a thousand years, and because this heritage is an integral part of Polish culture—of the culture which is ours as Poles—as well. And it is just this which we've lost, both through the Holocaust and through our own neglect.[15]

The public embrace of Jewish culture in Poland had its roots in the anti-communist dissident movements of the 1960s and 1970s and developed steadily after the success of Solidarność in 1980 opened up new cultural and intellectual freedoms that were only partially stifled by the imposition of martial law in 1981. The pervasiveness of underground networks—combined with the regime's own concerted quest for political legitimacy—forced some relaxation of official strictures, too. Many taboos remained in place, but from the early 1980s on, with official sanction that at times verged on co-option, books on Jewish topics were published, research on Jewish subjects was carried out, and exhibitions, concerts, and performances on Jewish themes were held with increasing frequency. A Jewish research institute, for

[13] Introductory material for Musicians' Raft.   [14] Personal communication, Aug. 2001.
[15] Interview with Janusz Makuch, 'VII Jewish Culture Festival in Cracow: To Knock on the Doors of Heaven', *Jidele* (Warsaw) (Nov. 1997); online version <www.jewish.org.pl/jidele/english/Door.html>.

example, was founded at Kraków's venerable Jagiellonian University in 1986. Two years later an officially sanctioned publication noted, as part of an overview of these developments, that between 1980 and 1986 more than 170 'books on the Jewish question' had been legally published in Poland.[16] The Kraków festival—founded one year before the removal of the communist regime from power—was a milestone in this process and throughout the 1990s served as an important, continuing catalyst, changing and developing as overall conditions in post-communist Poland evolved.

By now the festival is a prominent fixture in the summer calendar of a city that before the Second World War had 70,000 Jews and today has only about 200. The festival has become a week-long celebration so varied and exuberant that it has been called a 'Jewish Woodstock'.[17] Its programme includes exhibitions, lectures, theatre performances, guided tours, films, *klezmer*, jazz and cantorial concerts, workshops, and other events that feature top international Jewish artists and draw thousands of spectators and participants—most of them Polish Catholics. At the eleventh festival, in 2001, Jonathan Webber counted 'approximately 500–600 people at the main concerts, and between 50 and 100 at each of the lectures'.[18] The festival's final, marathon open-air concert as usual drew several thousand enthusiastic fans, who pressed up to the stage, clapping, swaying, and dancing, as if at a rock concert. An estimate of 10,000 fans attended the final concert of the twelfth festival, in 2002. Polish television broadcast part of the concert live nationwide. The camera focused repeatedly on the Israeli ambassador Shevach Weiss, who plunged into the crowd and danced hand in hand with other fans.

Makuch still directs the festival, which has become his consuming passion. He sees no contradiction in his role as a non-Jew running a Jewish cultural festival for other non-Jews in a former Jewish neighbourhood which today is a Jewish ghost town. He feels that he has a mission to bring contemporary Jewish artists to perform in Kraków, as a means of both honouring the dead and demonstrating Jewish survival—survival in New York or Israel, if not in Kraków itself.

On various occasions I'm asked [he says]: must I really have the Jewish Culture Festival here in Poland, in the largest Jewish cemetery in the world? And I answer: yes, it must be right here, in the largest Jewish cemetery. It must be here because Hitler desired not only to exterminate the nation, but also to exterminate all memory of that nation. The festival preserves that memory, renders it lasting. If we, here in this place, were not to have a festival of Jewish culture, we would be facilitating Hitler's endeavour, carrying out his spiritual legacy. And it is not our fault that we were born in the largest Jewish cemetery on earth. This painful awareness we carry with us every day.[19]

---

[16] D. Passent, 'Looking Each Other in the Face', in R. Piszczek (ed.), *Preserving Traces of Jewish Culture in Poland: For the Living and the Dead* (Warsaw, 1988).

[17] A. Kempner, 'Jewish Woodstock in Cracow', *Washington Jewish Week* (16 July 1992).

[18] Webber, 'Notes towards the Definition of "Jewish Culture"'.

[19] Interview with Janusz Makuch, posted in 1999 on the online 'Jews–Poles–Christians' forum on the website of Znak publishers, <www.znak.org.pl>. (The post was removed from the Znak web site in 2001 as part of regular updating.)

Makuch describes himself as a *shames*, who, like the synagogue beadle of old, knocks on the shuttered windows of public awareness. But he also knocks on the doors of Jewish performers to ask them to take part in the festival. He also sees himself as carrying out the role of a *shabes-goy* in performing activities that Jews are not able do—not because of religious restrictions, but because there are no (or not many) local Jews left.[20] He likes, too, to compare the festival to the recitation of the Kaddish, the prayer recited by Jewish mourners, in which 'there is not a word about the dead, not a word about death. Rather, Kaddish is a prayer expressing the glorification of God, the expectation of the coming of the Messiah, and the hope for common peace.'[21]

Kraków was not by any means the first Jewish cultural festival in Europe; there had been a festival in Milan in 1987, for example, and in Germany there were a number of festivals of various sorts throughout the 1980s. As indicated by the JPR survey, it is by now one of dozens of a variety of Jewish festivals that take place annually in numerous countries. Several features, however, have combined to make the Kraków festival unique amid this sometimes bewildering proliferation of festivals and other public Jewish cultural events. One is the setting. Most festival events take place in Kraków's richly evocative former Jewish quarter, Kazimierz, central Europe's most important complex of Jewish historical monuments. Kraków Jews moved virtually en masse to Kazimierz, then a separate town, when they were expelled from Kraków proper at the end of the fifteenth century. Bolstered by immigrants from Germany, Bohemia, Spain, and Portugal, the district flourished as a semi-autonomous Jewish town, protected by the king. Kazimierz today still encompasses seven synagogues that date back centuries, nearly a score of former prayer houses, two Jewish cemeteries, marketplaces, dwellings, and other buildings, many of which, until recently, still displayed the scars where *mezuzahs* were once attached to doorposts. 'Kazimierz [is] a special place and a special space, a Jewish space, where the Jewish nation created its own culture for six centuries and made a big contribution to Polish culture as well', Makuch told me.[22] Sophie Solomon, a British violinist who played at the festival in 2002, told me, 'At one point, as I was walking around, I had a rush of emotion, as if I sensed the spirits of the ages go by. I could feel the spirits on the people around me, like a culmination of all the energy and emotion at the festival.'[23]

The crowded home to 65,000 Jews before the Holocaust, the district became a run-down slum after the Second World War and was the seedy haunt of drunks and

[20] In Jewish communities in Poland in pre-modern times, the *shames* (sexton) of the synagogue would go from one Jewish house to another early in the morning, rapping on shutters to wake Jews for prayer. The *shabes-goy* was a non-Jew who performed work on the sabbath that Jews were prohibited to do.

[21] Makuch, 'VII Jewish Culture Festival'. Makuch has made similar statements elsewhere, including in conversations with me. [22] Interview with Janusz Makuch, Kraków, 1995.

[23] Interview with Sophie Solomon, Kraków, 1 July 2002.

other marginal people—as well as the ghosts of the Jewish past—when the festival was launched in 1988. Bringing new cultural life to the quarter was thus a bold as well as a symbolic move even on this physical level. Monika Krajewska, one of the pioneers of the documentation of Jewish monuments in Poland, recalls visiting the Kupa synagogue in Kazimierz in the 1970s, when it was used as a warehouse:

We stared at the walls, with their paintings: the lions, the deer, all the things that relate to the Jewish biblical tradition of synagogue decoration. And there were workers who were just installing additional shelves; they were making holes in the lion's nose, in the Levites' instruments painted on the ceiling. It seemed so inevitable that Kazimierz would crumble, brick by brick, that in a few years it simply would disappear.[24]

Over the past dozen years, however, Kazimierz has seen a remarkable revival as local entrepreneurs cashed in on history, nostalgia, and the existing infrastructure to create a tourist district whose attraction is based on its Jewish and 'Jewish-style' character.[25] Synagogues, including, most recently, the Kupa in 2001, have been restored. The main square, on Szeroka Street, is now lined with hotels and cafés with names such as Alef, Ariel, Ester, Anatewka, and Klezmer Hois, some of whose signs are written in Hebrew-style letters and most of which affect a cosy, old-fashioned, wood-panelled style of decor based on a literary image of pre-war Jewish life. Prince Charles had a drink with several local Kraków Jews in the Alef café during a visit in June 2002. A growing number of similar pubs and cafés dot nearby streets. The district consciously forms a sort of 'Jewish zone' where different rules from the rest of the city—or country—may apply: 'I feel safer with a *kipah* on my head in Kazimierz than in Warsaw', the sociologist Paweł Śpiewak once told me. 'And I would never wear a *kipah* on my head in the [main market square] of Kraków—it's a different world.'[26] The festival helped to promote this development and also drew strength from it. One guest at the 2001 festival said she felt that one of the results of the festival was, at least in Kraków, to make the word 'Jew' sound 'normal'.

Another element contributing to the festival's appeal and importance has been the breadth and the quality of its acts. They range from world-class international cantors singing liturgical music to cutting-edge or experimental groups such as the prominent American *klezmer* clarinettist David Krakauer's Klezmer Madness!. 'The festival is not just nostalgia', I was told by the New York musician Michael Alpert, a member of the group Brave Old World who has performed frequently at the festival and served as one of its musical consultants. 'It is part of the continuing

[24] Interview with Monika Krajewska, Warsaw, 1997.

[25] For a discussion of the recent Jewish awakening in Kazimierz, see 'What's to be Done?', in R. E. Gruber, *Upon the Doorposts of thy House: Jewish Life in East-Central Europe, Yesterday and Today* (New York, 1994). See also the discussion in Gruber, *Virtually Jewish*, and J. Kugelmass and A. Orla-Bukowska, '"If you Build it they will Come": Recreating an Historic Jewish District in Post-Communist Kraków', *City and Society Annual Review* (1998), 315–53.

[26] Personal communication, Warsaw, 1997.

or returning life of Jewish Kraków. It is partly a life of Jewish memory, but the festival is one of the few venues in the world that brings together young culture-makers of the new Yiddish culture.'[27]

The festival has thus become an important Jewish cultural crossroads, a Jewish cultural clearing house where performers and artists from various parts of the world can connect. It was at the festival, for example, that the Borderland Foundation in Sejny made contact with David Krakauer and began the collaboration that led to the Musicians' Raft programme, of which Krakauer is the musical director. The foundation's home-grown *klezmer* band performed at the festival's final concert in 1997 and met afterwards over 'vodka, tea, and supper' with other performers. Makuch asked the group

to take our instruments in hand and to play for a moment . . . After several pieces, we are joined by . . . David Krakauer. The musical 'moment' that Janusz Makuch requested turned into a night of *klezmer* madness. Saying goodbye after playing and dancing together, we asked David: 'And perhaps someday you'll come to Sejny?' and he came. And that is how we began to adventure together.[28]

Makuch says his aim indeed is to present Jewish culture—and Jews—as alive, not trapped behind a museum glass of nostalgia or archaeology. But he has admitted that arriving at this attitude took some evolution. At first, he said, the festival programme was devised 'under the influence of a chaotic, irrational fascination: assemble as much as possible and show it. It seemed to me that the lost culture should be found and shown, and that was all.' Early on, though, non-Jewish German performers and experts[29] were so involved as advisers and performers that the festival drew criticism from some Jews as an uncomfortable exercise in Germans teaching Poles about Jewish culture.

But meeting Alpert [in 1990] made me aware that the culture was alive, and important for many people [Makuch went on]; that despite the Holocaust, there was a flow, a continuity of that culture . . . So I tried more and more to feel at home in that Jewish culture, and at the same time to withdraw into the shadows, to avoid imposing my own feelings and dreams. Instead, I looked for ideas among the Jews themselves, and invited them. To try to make them the true creators of this festival. Some non-Jews didn't like this, while some Jews didn't like the fact that I set such high standards, that I turned so many people away, turned them down. But the importance of the festival is related to the level of the artists, and I can't squander what has been achieved.[30]

In addition, from the mid-1990s the festival gave expanded space to workshops, lectures, and hands-on participatory encounters on topics ranging from Jewish

---

[27] Personal communication, 1995.   [28] *Tratwa Muzykantów*, 28.

[29] Including Manfred Lemm of Wuppertal, who became involved with Yiddish music in the early 1980s and in particular devoted himself to resurrecting the songs of the Yiddish bard Mordechai Gebirtig, who was killed in the Kraków ghetto in 1942; on Gebirtig, see pp. 107–17 in this volume.

[30] Interview with Makuch, Znak forum.

cookery to hasidic dance and song. 'This has been an extremely important develop-ment', said Monika Krajewska. 'It brought a greater sense of Jewish life and served as a counterbalance to performance.'[31] There was an increase, too, in participation by Orthodox or otherwise overtly observant Jews, as performers or as workshop or discussion group leaders, or as members of the audience. Sabbath and Havdalah (close of sabbath) services were even listed on the festival programme. All of this brought a broader Jewish religious element into the equation: actual living—and lived—Judaism in addition to enacted Jewish culture. 'The festival is getting deep-er and deeper into cultural identity, into Jewish spirituality', Makuch said. 'It's now much more than just entertainment and more and more of a spiritual, religious experience.'[32]

The 2001 festival was a case in point. It featured meetings with rabbis, discus-sion groups on hasidism and on women in Jewish Orthodoxy, a workshop on Jewish cooking, and a well-attended workshop entitled 'Our Roots and Roads to Each Other', which explored how people felt about being Jewish—and about being at the festival. Not only that, for the first time two Habad hasidic *shelihim* (emissaries) went to Kraków during the festival. They spent the full festival week there, handing out candle-holders and prayer books from a *tefilin* booth they set up on Szeroka Street outside the Remuh synagogue. At the 2002 festival Cantor Ben Zion Miller, who is also a ritual slaughterer, attracted a standing-room audience for a workshop on *kashrut*. (Festival organizers originally announced that he would slaughter a chicken as part of his talk, but this demonstration was cancelled after protests from animal rights groups and the Polish Jewish leadership.) In 2002 Alex Jakobowitz, an Orthodox Jewish street musician who performs in a *kipah*, beard, and *peyes*, with *tsitses* hanging free from under his shirt, timed his first visit to Kraków to take place during the festival even though he was not on the festival programme. A classically trained artist, Jakobowitz, an American-born Israeli, performs the works of Bach, Vivaldi, Mozart, and other classical composers on a huge marimba, which he set up in Kraków's main market square. Local audiences compared him to one of the most famous characters in Polish literature—Jankiel, the Jewish innkeeper and cim-balom player in Adam Mickiewicz's nineteenth-century national epic *Pan Tadeusz*.

A schedule of the 2001 festival was published in a thick, illustrated souvenir pro-gramme, with a foreword by the Polish president Aleksander Kwaśniewski:

The existence, history, renown, and success of this Festival tell us something. Here is the culture of the Jewish nation, so recently sentenced to destruction, still vital and still moving minds and hearts. While upholding the remembrance of history, it continues to develop. It also offers inspiration to growing numbers of new artists, not all of whom are Jewish. This is an outstanding sign of our times.

For Poles, Jewish culture in its historical form is once again proving itself to be alive and fascinating. This vanished world is a part of what we built together. It speaks to us in the

---

[31] Telephone interview, Sept. 2001.   [32] Interview with Makuch, Znak forum.

comprehensible language of human experience born in this same land. Maintaining the memory of that world is a great merit of the Jewish Culture Festival in Cracow.

At the same time, there is also room to discover and learn about the further development of that culture as it is being shaped today in many countries around the world. This is the best proof of the degree to which the contemporary world is an open organism that combines many cultures and traditions within itself. Events like the Jewish Culture Festival in Cracow show us the living, profound bonds between different peoples, and make it easier for us to learn about and understand the diversity and all the riches of today's world.

In fulfilling this task, the Festival in Cracow has inscribed a place for itself in the process of opening up to the universal values that are one of the foundations of the new moral order, in a contemporary world that desires integration.[33]

The fact that these words came from the president of Poland was an illustration of how established—and how recognized as a symbol—the festival has become. More than that, though: the 2001 festival occurred at a sensitive moment in Polish–Jewish relations. It took place in July, immediately before the highly charged memorial ceremony at Jedwabne, an event that served as the contested culmination of months of searing national debate, which included not a little antisemitic rhetoric. Some of this antisemitism was soon to spill over into the campaigns for the Polish parliamentary elections that were held less than three months later.

Against this background Kwaśniewski used his foreword to send a political message. He echoed Makuch's almost evangelical passion as he summed up the positive reasons underlying the interest in Jewish culture in Poland, and forcefully, if optimistically, affirmed the value of this embrace—for Poland as a whole and for its future course as a democratic state. His words, however, pronounced from the pinnacle of Polish officialdom, in fact expressed a plea.

[33] Kwaśniewski, foreword to the official programme, Eleventh Festival of Jewish Culture, Kraków, 30 June–8 July 2001.

PART II

Documents

A. Litvin: Chronicler of Jewish Souls

MICHAEL C. STEINLAUF

SHMUEL HURVITS, whose pseudonym was A. Litvin, was born to a poor family in Minsk in 1862.[1] He educated himself in both Jewish and general subjects, and began to work as a teacher. But an ideological attraction to manual labour led him to give up teaching and work at paving streets, and then to take up such occupations as carpentry, woodcarving, and printing, as well as bookkeeping and peddling. He began to publish articles and poems in the 1890s, first in Russian and Hebrew, then in Yiddish. He moved to the United States in 1901, where he worked in a shoe factory, distributed newspapers, and wrote for the radical Yiddish press such as the *Forverts*, but in 1905, at the time of the first Russian revolution, he returned to eastern Europe, where he lived in Warsaw and then in Vilna. From 1909 to 1912 in Vilna he edited the left-wing nationalist monthly *Lebn un visnshaft* ('Life and Knowledge'), in which he published well-known Jewish writers such as Linetski, Mapu, Shomer, and Bialik, as well as translations from Dickens, Tolstoy, Byron, Shelley, and Lagerlöf; studies in Jewish history and folklore; and works by young Yiddish writers such as Dovid Eynhorn, S. Niger, and Leyb Naydus.

In 1911–12 Litvin began to publish articles based on his travels throughout eastern Europe beginning in 1905. After returning to the United States in 1914, he published these articles in a six-volume anthology entitled *Yidishe neshomes* ('Jewish Souls').[2] In scores of sketches of *badkhonim*, *purim-shpilers*, wandering preachers, and musicians; healers and holy men; beggars, pickpockets, and thieves in towns and cities throughout Poland, Lithuania, and Galicia, Litvin constructs an extraordinary panorama of the life of the Jewish masses at the moment when centuries-old traditions engaged modernity and either changed or vanished. He documents this world in the interests of a new generation of Jews who, he believed, needed such knowledge to build a secular yet authentically Jewish modern culture.

Litvin was also a dedicated political and social activist, one of the pioneers of the Po'alei Tsion movement, first in eastern Europe and then in the United States. He was a founder of the Jewish co-operative farming community Harmonya in Plainfield, New Jersey. He continued to contribute extensively to the Yiddish press, focusing on issues such as Jewish education and consumer and credit co-operatives.

---

[1] Biographical information about Litvin is taken from *Leksikon fun der nayer yidisher literatur*, vol. v (New York, 1963), cols. 94–7. [2] New York, 1916–17; 2nd and 3rd edns. 1922.

He also continued to gather folk tales, anecdotes, and folk songs; substantial collections of such unpublished material went to the YIVO Institute and the Jewish Theological Seminary in New York after his death in 1943.

Litvin lived an austere life in the United States, wandering from one farming community to another, and rarely referring to his personal life. He spent his last years living in a small furnished room in Coney Island.

The following two sketches are taken from volume ii, *Lite* ('Lithuania') of *Yidishe neshomes*.

EXCERPTS FROM
YIDISHE NESHOMES

⚊⚊⚊

A. LITVIN

THE JEW WITH THE 'LOOK-BOX'

THERE is a large, a very large portion of the Jewish masses for whom the entire world of aesthetics, beauty, and art is unknown. On one hand, this world is too high for their level of development. Theatre, literature, and art are not part of the experience of these thousands and tens of thousands. The cinematography theatre (moving pictures [*muving piktshurs*]) therefore has a virtue: it speaks 'mute language' [*shtum-loshn*], and in mute language the masses are already expert. But there's a drawback: it also costs money. However cheap, one still has to pay 15–20 copecks. And at best such art lovers can spare from their basic expenses a copeck, perhaps two at the most.

The Jewish folk artist comes to their help. Still today, as in the past, the aesthetic needs of the very poorest are met by the Jew with the 'look-box' [*kuk-kestele*]. The look-box is simultaneously a theatre and a museum. While remaining in one place, the viewer of the look-box travels over sea and continent, over mountains and valleys, finds himself in emperors' palaces, gazes into the bright crucible of fire-spewing mountains, and remains unharmed; cruises the ocean on the *Titanic*, observes its destruction, yet emerges cool, healthy, and—dry. The look-box also teaches history, teaches geography, and other important things. Give the needle a spin and the viewer leaps several thousand years into the past, from Gitke-Toybe's alley straight to Jerusalem, into King Solomon's palace, no more than a step from King Solomon's golden throne with the lions standing on the threshold. In another minute he is in Spain and watches the terrible Inquisition. A leap and he's at a parade of Napoleon's army in Paris. Another leap and he's in Port Arthur amid the Russo-Japanese war. The look-box serves as a newspaper. It provides you with pictures of the latest events of the day. The look-box Jew, it turns out, is a specialist in his business. He always stands in the middle of life, he lives with his time, knows 'who' and 'when'. He also knows whom to show what merchandise. Children like parades, soldiers, wars, and, in general, pictures of emperors, generals, riders with horse and chariot. An old Jewish woman will gladly catch a glimpse of Jerusalem and see the Inquisition. A peasant likes to see big cities with their magnificent palaces, bustling streets with big shop windows and dressed-up ladies [*panyenkes*].

Furthermore, the look-box is no mute panorama. In this respect it's even more interesting than the 'moving pictures' with their 'mute puppets'. Every picture and scene in the look-box is accompanied by its translator, the panorama's owner. He interprets and explains, and not like a simple translator, but with artistic flair. His speech depends on the nature of the images and their viewers. Sometimes it's in the non-Jewish language [*goyish*], sometimes in Yiddish, and always in rhyme.

Now he gives the needle on the outside a touch, and inside the box, before the viewer's eyes, appears a city with palaces, boats, and water on every side. This is the most beautiful image in the look-box and therefore the explanation is long.

> 'The city of Venice!' the box-Jew cries with rapture:
> The city all around!
> And in the middle a river!
> They're catching fish for tomorrow
> For Jews for sabbath.
> On the right, lovely trees,
> With knots on the branches
> And groups of policemen on the streets of the city.
> Whoever's interested—come on over!
> Five copecks—come here![1]

In reality the price of the show is much lower. But Venice, and the very breadth of the panorama, simply made him overvalue his own importance. What he meant is that for the privilege of seeing such a picture, even 5 copecks was not too much.

And truly, now the Kremlin in Moscow appears. Here the look-box Jew is not inspired. His explanation therefore is short and he lowers the price as well.

> 'Real cities!' shouts the translator:
> Their names are written underneath.
> Whoever has money, three copecks—
> Come here!
> And whoever doesn't—move along!
> See various cities
> And watch your pockets!

This last warning is hardly superfluous, for amid the group that gathers around the look-box lurk the boys [*khevre-layt*] with darting eyes and sticky fingers . . .

> A touch of the needle and—further:
> Gosudarsky Proezd in Moscow!
> The emperor rides a horse!
> The empress in a coach with six horses!

[1] In the original, this and the subsequent three speeches are in a Russian–Ukrainian jargon transliterated into the Hebrew alphabet and translated into Yiddish in footnotes.

> Around them hussars, ulans, and Cossacks!
> They've all come for the parade . . .
> 'The French palace in Paris!'—suddenly another lively shout:
> Gentlemen out for a walk,
> They don't take me with them.
> A baron walking with a baroness
> And leading a little girl by the hand.

'The holy city of Jerusalem!'—announced with even greater enthusiasm but still in Russian:

> The Jewish capital!
> In the middle stands the temple [*shkola*, i.e. *shul*],
> And there Jews pray to God;
> Pray for me and not for you,
> That I should make a lot of money.

The viewers of the box are generally a non-Jewish audience. Therefore the explanations are first of all in the non-Jewish language. But the Jew of the 'panorama' is, as you see further, also a master in Yiddish.

A touch of the needle. It lands on 'Stockholm'. And the artist of the look-box exclaims:

> Stockholm in Sweden!
> In mitn gas shteyen tsvey meydn [In the middle of the street stand two girls],
> Mayn bobe mit ayer zeydn [My grandma and your grandpa],
> Vel ikh zey khasene makhn beydn [So I'll marry them off to each other] . . .

The look-box is, in fact, a kind of room with a little roof, about 3 feet long and 2 feet wide. It's painted green with little painted windows and three lenses in front. The lenses are not straight and render the pictures accurately and highly magnified. The owner of this little room wanders with it from one end of Russia to another. He is seldom in the larger cities. There the audience has already been spoiled by the moving picture theatres and the other urban pleasures. So the Jew with the look-box is well received in the small *shtetl*. But he is the dearest of guests in the peasant village. There they pay, of course, not with cash but with produce: a few potatoes, a couple of eggs, a pile of pig bristles. In the *shtetl* the Jew turns this into money.

What interested me was how the Jew had acquired the look-box, and how long he had been travelling around with it.

The latter question he answered immediately: thirty years. But the first question, it turned out, was not so easy for him to answer. When he was young he had been a tinsmith. But the charcoal fumes from smelting had weakened his heart, and he had to find another occupation. At work, he says, he had always liked to think, to think things up. This was hard while tinsmithing. But the look-box frees the imagination. The business is not as simple as you might think. You need a head and an eye. You always have to stand in the middle of life, know what's going on in the big world. You have to change the pictures often according to the events of the day and the taste of your various viewers. You have to know where and from whom to get the pictures.

Then the box itself—do you think it's just a box? It's a piece of artful architecture. And he had in fact built it himself. Then the most difficult task—the lighting. For the main performances occur at night—in the viewers' homes. A simple lamp can smoke, or easily overturn and cause a fire. 'See this lamp', he points at a little tin lamp in the look-box. 'Twist it, turn it whichever way you want, it will never go out or drip out. It's something I thought up myself.'

The lamp was truly constructed in a strange and interesting way. I am certain that ever since there have been lamps in the world, there has never been such a peculiar creature. And though the look-box business has been going on, as he told me, for thirty years, its true history only begins with the little lamp, that is, since the lamp was invented.

The look-box Jew has, somewhere in Slutsk (Słuck), or in Pinsk, a wife and children. He also has several children in America who send him nothing. He comes home twice a year: for Peysekh [Passover] and Sukkes [Sukkot], after which he slings the box across his shoulders again and goes back on the road.

That's how it's been going for thirty years. The look-box Jew is close to 60 years old, but he still seems a tough little Jew. But even stronger than he is the look-box. And it seems to me it will outlive him and remain an eternal orphan. Because just as Motl the *purim-shpiler* [in a previous chapter] is the last of his trade, the look-box Jew is undoubtedly the last of this type of wandering folk artist–tramp.

AMONG BLIND MUSICIANS

The blind Jewish musicians are not born to the 'lower depths' [*dek-mentshn*], but are steered there by fate. They belong to a more solid, highly valued craft. The wandering blind Jewish musicians are nearly all former artisans. Sickness has robbed them of the ability to sit with a needle or a hammer. The physically weak among them cannot endure the darkness, cannot live without the sun, and expire after a short struggle. The stronger, more capable among them take up the fiddle and go off to wander the world. The economic situation of these unfortunates is much better than before their illness. They earn a penny more easily than when they sat healthy in their shops. Their working day is not long. 'We go out at ten in the morning,' a blind musician tells me, 'and as soon as it gets dark we go home.' That is in the winter, but in summertime they remain in the street longer. Then the work is easier and more pleasant. In the course of seven to eight hours they do not make less, in any case, then they did toiling as artisans before. The Jewish street audience likes a song and a fiddle, gathers in circles around the blind musician, gladly listens to the street concert, and doesn't begrudge the blind man a penny or a copeck. A life spent outdoors, moreover, always in the fresh air, is better for his health than his previous life sitting indoors.

From a moral perspective, the blind musician also has it better than the plain beggar. He doesn't handle the coins himself. His guide collects them and turns them over to him. Of course, it often happens that this guide and cashier quietly drops a few coins into his own pocket. But this is unavoidable. Without a guide one can't survive. And a guide who resists the temptation to steal a few copecks from the blind man is hard to find. Besides, the blind man has his own means of checking on his attendant. First of all, the latter has to turn the coins over immediately after the 'concert' right at the gate [of the courtyard]. The blind man knows that the guide would be afraid to pocket any change in front of the audience. Secondly, he knows approximately how much money has been collected from the time it takes to collect it; the longer it takes, the more copecks there should be. Thirdly, and this is the essence, the blind man, having spent some time with his guide, becomes something of an expert in his psychology. He knows what the boy is capable of, or not capable of. The guide is entirely supported by the blind man. In addition, he receives from 30 to 60 or 70 copecks a week. Including what he steals, the boy makes a rouble or a rouble and a half a week. The attendant is very rarely the blind man's child. Even when he has his own children, he usually refuses to drag them along. When they are young he sends them to *kheyder* or Talmud Torah. Older children he apprentices. The children themselves also never want to accompany their father. They consider it beneath their dignity. So one employs a stranger.

The attendant is generally half-pickpocket, half-idiot. But occasionally an unemployed worker hires himself out to a blind man, or sometimes a boy of the very dullest sort. For the most unfortunate boy who has even a drop of ambition will not drag around with a blind man. Very rarely one sees a 'partnership' between a blind man and a cripple as his guide. Not because such pairs are rare, but because the 'business' isn't worth it. The cripple or hunchback or wretch whom God has favoured with a deformity will not share with a blind man, when he can make 'business' for himself.

The blind man sings of various themes, though the tune is nearly always the same. Regardless of what he sings, or plays, about, his song is always pessimistic.

> Man doesn't know the number of his years;
> He lives and dreams in the world of lies:
> He acts with foolishness from his birth,
> Until in his dismal tent he lies—

one song philosophizes, and concludes that

> To have compassion on the vile
> Is something a man must get used to;
> Over a hundred years, when the time to die arrives,
> This will reward you with all.

A second song tells of the Odessa pogrom [in 1906]:

> Whoever read the paper
> From the famous town of Odessa,
> [Knows] what misfortune happened there,
> In two–three days and nights.

The blind man's song, in general, is not like a folk song. It has little poetry in it. These are primarily lines of prose that are rhymed, more or less successfully. The terrible scenes they depict do not make the kind of impression upon the listener that one might expect.

> The murderers sprang upon a Jew,
> Who they knew not at all;
> They hammered nails into his eyes
> And cut off both his hands.

The song goes on and makes no impression on you, for it smacks of the newspaper. Though whatever the blind man sings, he often returns to his own song—the song of the blind man:

> O bitter, bitter to be blind
> What is there that is worse?
> When one can't see one's wife and children
> Nor the light of the shining sun.

The words are ordinary, but these simple verses make a powerful impression on you. You scarcely close your eyes for a second and you are in the situation of the blind man. This song is not 'composed' [*ferfast*] like others, but suffered through.

'Who makes up the songs for you?' I asked one blind man from whom I transcribed the song of the pogrom.

'The song I tell you,' answers the blind man, 'I made up myself. I make up all my own songs, I've got stacks of them.'

'How do you make up the songs?'

'If a pogrom happens, or some other horrible occurrence, I buy all the Yiddish papers on that day. I have them read to me, and then make a song out of them. Rhymes I can make easily because I've got stacks of printed songs by all the composers.'

This blind man is still young. He had been a shoemaker. Swam in a river and—lost his sight. Another told me that a wind caused it. A third—a case of typhus. The first song was dictated to me by a blind woman, who doesn't play but only sings in courtyards. She used to be a seamstress. She became blind after a pregnancy. When she lost her sight, her husband left her. She was left with a little daughter and a sick old mother. And she supports them both. Doctors have told her that she can regain her sight with an operation. As I understand it, she is not hurrying to have the operation because as a blind woman she can make a living much more easily.

One blind man I visited at home. He lives no worse than a poor worker. This blind man is also a former shoemaker. Now he no longer goes out on the street. He sits at home, and his two daughters, who previously accompanied him on his wanderings, go out alone. Without him, they perform for passengers on the train and in this manner feed the family. This is the only case I know of Jewish girls travelling alone on the train and performing in the cars. But more recently the real breadwinner is just one of them, the younger, a girl who's 11 years old. The elder, who is 14, began to get embarrassed and left to work—knitting stockings. The younger, Yehudiske, travels alone and doesn't do badly. She doesn't look at all like a Jewish child: flaxen hair and lashes—a real Gentile girl [*shiksl*]. Except for the conductors, no one knows she's Jewish. Christians gladly give her a coin, thinking they're giving it to a Christian girl. Yehudiske charms everyone on the train. She plays well, has a delicate sympathetic face, holds herself proudly, like an artist. When she has finished, she never begs, never stretches out her hand. When she takes a coin, she never thanks anyone, doesn't even move her head. She takes it as though she's doing you a favour, and moves on without giving you another glance. But at home Yehudiske is very different. She is quite spoiled and behaves like an only child.

'She has a dear little head,' her mother complains, 'but what's there to do? She doesn't want to study at all, nor even to play! She doesn't take the violin into her hand.'

Yehudiske is embarrassed to have her mother praise her in this way. She throws her hands over her mother's mouth and cries:

'Be quiet, be quiet [*Svayg*, Lithuanian Yiddish, instead of *shvayg*]! I tell you! Who cares if I play or don't play . . . She has to tell everything.'

At first Yehudiske refused to talk to me at all. She turned her head bashfully to one side and remained silent, slyly biting her lips. But somewhat later she felt more comfortable and with her elder sister played the fiddle for me. After that she showed me cards from her four brothers who were in America as well as a card from one of their brides.

'Do the children send you any money?' I asked the blind man and his wife.

'On holidays they send a bit. They're not set up themselves yet. Two of them have just left. But they are good children. If we need more, they will send it. Still *this* winter Yehudiske will work on the train, but after that no more. She will also knit stockings. How will we manage then? They, the children in America, will have to help.'

This same blind man told me that the actual writer of the songs that the blind musicians sing is a blind violinist in Odessa. 'Oho!' he exclaimed. 'That one doesn't go around as we do, and lives a bit better than we. He goes around in a top hat and gold watch, and doesn't collect pennies or copecks.'

When the Odessa poet has sung his songs, he puts them into a treasury for all the blind, not for free, but for a coin.

There are blind men who go all the way to Odessa and spend a lot of money to obtain the Odessa blind poet's songs. They make this money back with interest when they return home. Each song of the Odessa poet becomes sweetened. There are songs that are worth no less than 3 roubles each.

Translated from Yiddish by Michael C. Steinlauf

Urke Nachalnik: A Voice from the Underworld

GWIDO ZLATKES

URKE NACHALNIK belongs to the underworld, perhaps even more so today than in his own time in Poland between the wars. Equally out of place in the sentimental-ized *shtetl* and among the heroes and heralds of progress, he belongs to the unwrit-ten part of the Jewish past that has nearly faded from collective memory.

We are venturing into uncharted territory. There is very little written about the Jewish underworld or Jewish criminals in Poland. The *Encyclopedia Judaica* entry for crime gives only a summary of crime statistics in the Diaspora. Practically the only scholarly work on the subject is a statistical study by Liebman Hersch of the University of Geneva, written as a series of articles in 1936–8 and published in book form in Polish translation in 1938.[1] Hersch analysed official Polish statistical data for 1924–5 and found a lower level of criminal activity among the Jewish population compared to the general population. This applied to both the frequency and the gravity of criminal acts committed by Jews in two of the three examined categories: crimes against the person and crimes against private property. Only in the third cat-egory, crimes against the legal order (namely, avoiding conscription, profiteering, and begging), was the level of crime higher among Jews than non-Jews. According to Szyja Bronsztejn, the same trend continued in the 1930s.[2]

We lack some of the most basic biographical facts about Urke Nachalnik, not to mention an authoritative biography. Two reference works, a new dictionary of Polish Jewish history and culture and an essential monograph on Jewish literature between the wars, do not mention him at all.[3] There are two accounts of Nachal-nik's life, an apologetic one by Abram Karpinowicz and a critical one by Stanisław

I would like to thank Katarzyna Raczkowska of the Biblioteka Narodowa (National Library) in Warsaw for her invaluable help in gathering material for this introduction.

[1] L. Hersch, *O przestępczości wśród Żydów w Polsce*, trans. G. Jaszuński (Warsaw, 1938).

[2] S. Bronsztejn, 'O przestępczości wśród Żydów w Polsce w latach dwudziestych XX wieku (W pięćdziesięciolecie ukazania się książki Liebmana Herscha)', *Biuletyn Żydowskiego Instytutu Historycznego w Polsce*, nos. 3–4 (1988), 135–47.

[3] A. Cała, H. Węgrzynek, and G. Zalewska, *Historia i kultura Żydów polskich: Słownik* (Warsaw, 2000); E. Prokop-Janiec, *Międzywojenna literatura polsko-żydowska* (Kraków, 1992).

Milewski. Both, however, are literary in character.[4] They lack sources, they differ in significant details, and they are inconsistent with other sources including Nachalnik's own autobiography. Even Nachalnik's real name differs in the accounts of his life; it is variously given as Icchok Farberowicz, Icek Boruch Farbarowicz, and Icek Senderowicz from Białystok.[5]

Urke Nachalnik was the underworld nickname that he retained as a pen name. The linguist Maria Brzezina tells us that the first name derives from the thieves' argot, *urka* meaning a seasoned thief, in a form adjusted to the morphology of Yiddish (and the Yiddish-influenced Polish of Jews), and the second name comes from the adjective *nachalny*, meaning brazen or impudent.[6] But Milewski's assessment both of Nachalnik's professional accomplishments and of his credibility as a criminal and a writer undermines this interpretation. Nachalnik, according to him,

was convinced that in thieves' slang the word *urke* meant 'an internationally prominent thief', as he himself explained in a footnote in his principal book. This already calls into question his reliability as a self-proclaimed expert in the clandestine affairs of thieves. This was a myth he created for himself in his writings and conversations. Yet respected professional pickpockets and other 'professionals' reserved the term *urka* for 'inferior thieves, botchers, thieves who would not shy away from banditry'.... It is noteworthy that the word *urka* found its way into some dictionaries of criminal slang with the definition given by Nachalnik, apparently owing to the influence of his books, whereas among thieves and prisoners even today the word *urka* is used with the [other] meaning.[7]

The following facts can be established with a relative degree of certainty. Nachalnik was born in 1897 in Nowogród, near Łomża; his father was a reasonably well-to-do miller. His mother wanted him to become a rabbi, apparently against his inclinations. Immediately after her death he dropped out of the yeshiva in which he had been studying and entered the criminal underworld, where he passed through all the stages of initiation, from *konik* (little horse, i.e. apprentice) to seasoned criminal. Nachalnik's self-portrait from the period of his imprisonment in Mokotów Prison in Warsaw in 1923 reads as follows:

> Prisoner's Description:
> Age: 27
> Height 172 cm. [5 feet 8 inches]
> Body: strong
> Hair: dark blond
> Beard: shaven

---

[4] A. Karpinowicz, 'Urke Nachalnik', trans. N. Krynicka, *Midrasz: Pismo żydowskie*, 12/32 (Dec. 1999), 53–6 (an excerpt from Karpinowicz, *Geven, geven amol Vilne* (Tel Aviv, 1997)); S. Milewski, *Złodziej i literat: Życie i sprawki Urke Nachalnika* (Warsaw, 1988).

[5] Karpinowicz, 'Urke Nachalnik', 53; Milewski, *Złodziej i literat*, 7; R. Dzieszyński, *Ciemna, węsząca, żerująca: Pitaval* (Rzeszów, 1986), 224.

[6] M. Brzezina, 'Słownictwo złodziejskie w *Życiorysie własnym przestępcy* oraz w *Żywych grobowcach* Urke Nachalnika', *Zeszyty Naukowe Uniwersytetu Jagiellońskiego, Prace Językoznawcze*, no. 97 (1988), 76.   [7] Milewski, *Złodziej i literat*, 7.

Face: pale
Brow: high
Eyes: blue, normal, set deep
Eyebrows: thick, black
Nose: small
Ears: medium
Mouth: medium, protruding lower lip
Teeth: 8 missing
Hands: medium, medium fingers
Palm: wide
Legs: medium
Stature and walk: straight
Pronunciation: normal
Languages: proficient in Polish, Russian, German, Hebrew, and Yiddish
Tattooing: none
Special features: spectacles
Education: secondary school[8]

In 1927 Nachalnik began an eight-year sentence in Rawicz Prison for a bank robbery in Warsaw. Stanisław Kowalski, a young graduate of the pedagogical institute at the University of Poznań, held a series of lectures for inmates of the prison at this time and asked them to bring their writings. Nachalnik responded with two novels and the beginning fragment of an autobiography written in Polish. He had already submitted the novels to the Rój publishing house, where he had received a positive response as well as the recommendation that he write an autobiography. Kowalski encouraged Nachalnik to continue writing and then edited the manuscript, minimally correcting spelling and grammar.[9] *Życiorys własny przestępcy* ('The Autobiography of a Criminal') was published in 1933 in Poznań by the Towarzystwo Opieki nad Więźniem 'Patronat' Oddział Rawicz ('Patronat' Association for the Care of Prisoners, Rawicz branch).

Nachalnik was released in the same year, two years before completing his sentence. He moved first to Vilna and then to Otwock, a suburb of Warsaw. He became a full-time writer, got married, and fathered a son. According to Karpinowicz, he was in the Otwock ghetto during the war. He talked two young men into derailing German trains with him, and during one of these actions they were caught by the Germans. After interrogation and torture, while being led to his death, Nachalnik hit the escorting officer in the face and was shot on the spot. His wife and son were last seen in the Warsaw ghetto.[10] Milewski, more critical of Nachalnik, states only

---

[8] U. Nachalnik, *Żywe grobowce* (Warsaw, 1934), 154–5. As Milewski notes, Nachalnik doubtless counted his yeshiva studies as a secondary-school education since he attended no other schools and learned written Polish only when in prison (see *Złodziej i literat*, 56).

[9] S. Kowalski, 'Wstęp: Jak zdobyłem rękopis', in U. Nachalnik, *Życiorys własny przestępcy* (Poznań, 1933).   [10] Karpinowicz, 'Urke Nachalnik', 55–6.

that during the war Nachalnik 'perished without a trace like millions of Holocaust victims'.[11]

Despite the popularity of Nachalnik's writings in inter-war Poland, his bibliography is rather difficult to reconstruct. According to a reviewer of his collection of short stories *Miłość przestępcy* ('A Criminal's Love'),[12] Nachalnik's autobiography was printed twice in 1933 and serialized in a daily newspaper.[13] It was later translated into several languages including Yiddish and Russian, and was reprinted in 1989 by Wydawnictwo Łódzkie. The book covers the period from Nachalnik's childhood to November 1918 and the restoration of an independent Poland, a moment that finds him in the Czerwoniak (Red) prison in Łomża. The autobiography is continued as *Żywe grobowce* ('Living Tombs'), most of which describes Nachalnik's incarceration in Mokotów Prison in Warsaw, where he was transferred from Łomża. The book was first published in 1934 by Rój in Warsaw and was reissued in 1990 by Wydawnictwo Łódzkie. Karpinowicz mentions another title, *Zmartwychwstanie* ('Resurrection'), possibly the third instalment of his autobiography, describing his break with the underworld. Milewski writes about two mystery novels published in 1938 by the W. Fruchtman publishing house in Warsaw, *Rozpruwacze* ('The Safecrackers') and *W matni* ('Trapped'), as well as an unnamed play staged at the Scala Theatre in Warsaw.[14] 'Wyjście z sytuacji' ('A Solution') is the title of a short story published in the satirical journal *Szpilki* ('Pins'). According to Milewski, its hero, Boruch, seeks a *rebbe*'s help because his wife cannot have children. 'No problem,' responds the *rebbe*, 'you will have two boys but beware—one of them will become a pimp and the other a thief.' Boruch departs saddened, but then returns to the *rebbe* and says, 'I found a solution. I'll build a fancy hotel near the main railway station for the pimp, and a publishing house for the thief. It will be almost the same . . .'.[15] Milewski often mentions Nachalnik's contacts with American publishers and the money he received for publishing in American magazines. I was unable to confirm this, nor was I able to trace any of the works mentioned above, with the exception of *Życiorys*, *Żywe grobowce*, and 'Wyjście z sytuacji'.

Nachalnik was certainly not a great writer and he probably never had the ambition to become one. His style bears all the characteristics of popular novels of the period. It is heavily sentimental and filled with clichés, especially with respect to descriptions of nature and the author's emotions. His characters are one-dimensional, and he does not even try to penetrate their motives. When he sometimes ventures into 'philosophizing', as he calls it, he addresses the reader directly with a self-serving sermon of dubious profundity.[16] Still, both of his autobiographies provide very lively and entertaining reading. He is at his best when he simply relates events: who

---

[11] Milewski, *Złodziej i literat*, 84.   [12] Warsaw, 1933.

[13] Lektor, 'Przestępca w roli pisarza', *Nasz Przegląd* (31 Dec. 1933).

[14] Milewski, *Złodziej i literat*, 33, 83, 6.   [15] Ibid. 7.

[16] Milewski notes that Nachalnik's self-analyses seem to illustrate popular contemporary theories of criminology (see ibid. 42 ff.).

stole what and how. He also writes effective dialogue, in which he often uses criminal slang, sometimes providing explanations in footnotes. According to Maria Brzezina, he offers the lexicographer of underworld argot a treasury of some 300 words.[17]

Nachalnik's importance extends well beyond literature. There are four particularly important aspects to his writings. First, he provides an insight into the underworld, its structure and customs. He provides rich information about relations among the various elements of this world—thieves, fences, pimps, prostitutes, etc., and the codes that governed their lives. The sociological value of his testimony is great even if he sometimes distorted particular facts. His colleagues, in fact, accused him of boasting. In 1933 a Warsaw daily wrote that

prominent representatives of the criminal world have alleged that Senderowicz [*sic*] was not an *urke* but a *łachudra*, a petty thief held in contempt by others. He claimed others' actions to boost his literary career. 'Surely, a *dintojre* [thieves' court] awaits him', they have quipped. Senderowicz is said to have been so frightened by this that he has gone into hiding in the outskirts of Vilna.[18]

But Nachalnik's editor Kowalski writes about verifying the content of the memoirs in his introduction: 'During our frequent conversations I did not notice any inconsistencies with the text of the autobiography. Nachalnik himself admitted that he omitted many things and assured me that all he wrote was true.'[19] It seems that Nachalnik more often inflated the importance of his criminal accomplishments than invented them outright. He often puts himself at the centre of the action, yet a closer look shows that he generally served as an auxiliary, a lookout or an accomplice.

Secondly, Nachalnik's descriptions of prison life are even more detailed and reliable than his descriptions of life on the streets. Milewski points out that he 'was . . . in the criminal underworld for a year at the most, whereas he learned Russian, Prussian, and finally Polish prisons really well'.[20] By the age of 36 he had spent more than half his life behind bars. His expertise about this world cannot be questioned. He offers, for example, one of the first accounts of the homosexuality that was widespread in prisons, and pioneers in detailing the mechanisms of incarcerated communities.

Thirdly, Nachalnik offers an entirely unsentimental, probably accurate even if one-sided, account of the Polish Jewish world. The description of his *kheyder* in an airless, damp, and filthy basement where the *rebbe* dispenses humiliating punishments is a world far removed from the accounts of Sholem Aleichem or the images

[17] Brzezina, 'Słownictwo złodziejskie', 100. She also notes: 'Urke Nachalnik, who operated in the ethnically integrated criminal community, could not fully recognize the distinction between Polish criminal slang (which contained a significant number of yiddishisms [*żydowizmy*]) and Jewish criminal slang; or perhaps this difference was already fluid in his times' (p. 102 n. 10).

[18] *Ilustrowany Kurier Codzienny* (16 June 1933), cited in Dzieszyński, *Ciemna, węsząca, żerująca*, 224.   [19] Nachalnik, *Życiorys*, p. xiv.   [20] Milewski, *Złodziej i literat*, 42.

of Roman Vishniac. His warm words about his yeshiva do not conceal its desperate backwardness.

Finally, Nachalnik provides evidence of the underworld as an advanced outpost of cultural exchange, a kind of democratic avant-garde. He sleeps indiscriminately with Jewish and non-Jewish women, prostitutes and non-prostitutes, and nobody seems to mind. His partners and accomplices are people with names like Staszek or Wojtek; his fences are Jews. He steals equally from Jews and non-Jews.

Nachalnik is the best-known Polish Jewish criminal, but by no means the only one. Notorious Jewish criminals are recorded as early as the beginning of the nineteenth century. Milewski writes that

Kurier Warszawski in its first year of publication [1821] announced that a very dangerous thief had been caught, 44-year-old Judy Icek Goldstein, married, father of two, who came to a fair in Warsaw 'in the hope of big gains'. According to the *Kurier*, he had snatched purses and watches from crowds even as a 6-year-old child carried around by his father. Later he was caught together with his gang. He was to be executed in Kraków but managed to escape from the strongest fortress in Silesia. He was famous because of his thefts, and the greatest thieves considered him their master. 'He was amazingly clever and bold', we further read in the *Kurier*. He eluded prison many times. Another trace of him is found in the *Kurier* in 1827. The paper reports that the appeals court sentenced him to twenty years of confinement, branding, and exposure on the pillory. He probably escaped beforehand; another report states that owing to his cleverness he managed to escape twenty times from various prisons.[21]

Ryszard Dzieszyński presents a gallery of Jewish characters from the inter-war underground, among them Abram Sycowski, reputedly Al Capone's sidekick, who returned to Poland and masqueraded in Warsaw as Prince Aleksei Romanov; another Chicago mobster named Symche Majer Eichenbaum, or 'Bloody Sam', who had once studied at the Sorbonne; Tewel Gromb and his gang, who 'protected' businesses in Warsaw's Muranów district; Izrael Mossak, a pimp who supplied white slaves to provincial brothels; and Chil Tennenbaum, an international drug dealer.[22]

In the memoirs of his childhood in Bałuty, the proletarian quarter of Łódź during the second decade of the twentieth century, the communist activist Wacław Kuchar provided a fascinating description of the Jewish underworld. His account deserves to be quoted at length:

Besides the groups of impoverished children playing in the gutters and looking for a momentarily unattended stand, Bałuty was different from the rest of Łódź because of the prostitutes walking their 'beats' from early morning until late at night. For a long time my 11–12-year-old mind didn't realize what kind of job some of my neighbours' daughters had. They just dressed a little flashier, which I rather liked. I had a classmate living in the other part of our house who was an excellent student, and whose two sisters were prostitutes.

[21] S. Milewski, *W świecie występku i zbrodni: Z dziejów przestępczości i jej zwalczania* (Warsaw, 1996), 85–6.   [22] Dzieszyński, *Ciemna, węsząca, żerująca*, 86–90, 121, 191, 201.

They worked in a brothel on an adjoining street, and there they paraded around and found their patrons. They helped their parents with a portion of their earnings. I liked a particular girl with auburn hair a lot; I often visited and talked with her and her sisters, who regretted that they could never go to school and didn't have real jobs.

On some Bałuty streets prostitutes walked about who were not much older than I was. They had their pimp protectors, who defended them against overly aggressive clients, obtrusive drunkards, and various degenerates. Generally, every girl working in this oldest of the world's professions needed a protector, who took the lion's share of her earnings and often mistreated her, but at the same time served as a shield protecting her from the blows of the hostile environment. In a brothel an older, worn-out prostitute would govern and enforce unwritten but firm rules. Pimps were the organizers and owners of the brothels, and their wealth and importance grew depending on the number of girls they employed. They were judges who instantly resolved all conflicts, and executioners immediately implementing merciless punishments. Woe to a girl who tried to escape her Argus-eyed protector! In that capacity they ruled the streets of Bałuty, co-operated among themselves, made alliances, assigned turfs, proclaimed and fought bloody wars. Every once in a while decaying corpses were found in ponds outside the city, butchered beyond recognition, the result of a relentless war among various factions of what today we would call gangsters.

Besides prostitutes working in brothels, there were sometimes girls who tried to work on their own. Usually they were new, attempting to enter the ranks of the profession, and did not yet know the rules and regulations strictly observed in it. But they soon learned. Through their colleagues, pimps from the immediate neighbourhood would efficiently force the girl to give up her independence. And if she tried to resist, either the pimp himself or a decoy pretending to be a client would beat her up, making her unable to work for many weeks. After such a bloody lesson the starved and submissive girl would either come on her own to the protector or go to a brothel—which she did didn't matter.

Less visible than prostitutes on the streets of Bałuty were gangs of thieves. Actually, Bałuty was only their residence, not their workplace. Loosely associated, they formed groups of highly specialized professionals who did not depart from their narrow speciality. They were all linked in many ways to prostitution, the world of love-for-pay. However, these groups of specialist thieves did not have much to do with each other except in the narrowly defined sense of the expropriation of someone else's possession. A shoplifter [*szopenfeldziarz*] wouldn't work with a housebreaker. A burglar had contempt for a pickpocket [*doliniarz*], and the entire society of thieves highly respected the aristocracy of the profession, the safe-crackers. A true thief wouldn't disgrace himself with a dirty job such as armed robbery or banditry. That was an entirely different profession.

In Bałuty there were schools for thieves with different specialities. Veterans of the profession taught the next generation, and it appeared to me that volunteers were never lacking. The Łódź thieves, as professionals, were well known in all the cities of Europe, where they could always find booty. They used their own language understood only in their community. Neither in Bałuty nor later in prisons have I encountered a single occurrence of national animosity among thieves, something, regretfully, I cannot say about other social groups. The world of thieves followed its own moral code with strictly enforced rules, according to which the worst crime was informing on others. Any other transgression against their code could have extenuating circumstances, but there was no pity for an informer. He placed himself outside the law governing the community, and if found out, the *dintojre* judgement over him was often quick. In serious cases, if the informing occurred among the elite, *dintojre* was performed with full ceremony, by the light of black candles. The sentence could be merciless and instantly carried out with a knife.

Old thieves were highly respected in the Bałuty community. You could borrow money from them and they gave to charity more than others. It could happen that one of them, or several from one family, would be the sole support of a house of prayer, a *shul*. If a daughter began to age in a poor family and couldn't find a husband because she had no dowry, or if someone needed funds for doctors for a sick child, these older thieves would help. This way they 'bought good deeds from God', hoping thereby for a good inscription in the book of life on Yom Kippur.

Fences recruited receivers of stolen goods most often from that old guard. They sent out merchandise stolen from shops or goods from emptied apartments to other towns through channels known only to them; they skilfully covered their tracks and sold everything. Without a well-organized network of fences the thieves' profession could not have operated effectively. It often happened that a victim found his way to the fence without notifying the police, and either himself or through middlemen bought his property back.

At the time of my adolescence there were two famous centres of underworld power in Bałuty. One was of a thief–fence nature, and was controlled by the authoritative patriarch of a large family, Shaye (nicknamed the Magnate), who owned several houses in Bałuty and a kosher butcher's. The other was governed by the co-owner and patron of several brothels, Moyshe (nicknamed Poytc). Their spheres of influence were strictly divided. They chaired at *dintojres*. Their authority was limitless, and when they walked on a street everyone respectfully gave way before them. Even some members of the police recognized their prestige, and it happened more than once that fines or penalties meted out to a poor worker or shopkeeper were averted as a result of the intercession of one of the two.[23]

There is a great store of source material available on the Jewish criminal world before the Second World War. There are crime chronicles in the daily press, an inexhaustible source of information about the spectacular cases that preoccupied all of Polish and Jewish society as well as the everyday petty crimes and misdemeanours; there are court and prison records, at least partially preserved; there are some memoirs and literary testimonies. It is imperative that this part of the past be regained and analysed to show the scope and function of Jewish crime, the processes occurring within it that affected both Jewish and Polish societies. This chapter, with the following excerpts from Urke Nachalnik's autobiography, are small steps in that direction.

[23] W. Kuchar, MS trans. as 'Memoirs of Łódź' by F. L. Vigoda.

EXCERPTS FROM
ŻYCIORYS WŁASNY PRZESTĘPCY

~~~~~

URKE NACHALNIK

Confessing evil requires more courage than committing it.

BEFORE I begin the sad story of my life I feel bound to give at least a summary of the circumstances that led me away from the straight and narrow. I ask the reader's forgiveness for first starting with a picture of my entrance into the world.

I see this as through a fog—a little town on the banks of the River Narew. A two-storey brick house lies in the centre of the town, almost on the market square. From the outside it is distinguishable only for having a porch with two benches at the entrance to a store. Above the entrance is the Russian sign 'Flour Shop', along with the woman proprietor's name, N.N.

The owner of the house is a tall man of 30, healthy-looking with soft, disarming eyes. These features are usually found in extraordinarily strong people. His wife is a woman of 25 with an intelligent look—a typical blonde. This rather well-matched couple belongs to the Jewish intelligentsia of this small town.

In my mind's eye I see this house on a beautiful day in June 1897. The store is closed because of the birth of the first-born son. Friends and relatives are congratulating my parents; I see great joy all around.

I see my mother lying in the bedroom, all in white with a triumphant maternal smile playing on her somewhat pale face. I lie on her right side, bundled in my blankets. My father stands in the centre of the room receiving congratulations. He's serious and thoughtful; his eyes shine with happiness.

I see people come and go from the house. On every face I see joy, both sincere and insincere.

More people gather in front of the house. They comment on the miracle of my birth. I hear snippets of conversation: 'God showed His mercy and listened to them, giving them a son.' Now I hear whispers: 'The rich always have luck!' The woman listening nods her head, and lifts her hands reverently, saying, 'A real wonder, five years after the wedding, *nu, nu*. God can do anything—for Him nothing is impossible!' Another pale Jewish woman with black hair, looking like an old slave, peers around shyly and asks in a timid whisper, 'Is it true that she went to the *tsadik* in Libawa [Liepāja] and returned a month ago?'

I see a plump Jewess taking her aside and saying mysteriously, 'Nobody can produce miracles like that *tsadik* in Libawa. My cousin hadn't had a baby in fifteen years, and then on her rabbi's advice she went to him and had a son shortly after.'

'Maybe I should go to him too.' The pale woman blushes. 'As you know, I also somehow can't . . .'. And lowering her voice she adds, 'seven years after my wedding . . . !'

'You, my dear,' answers the other disdainfully, 'you are too poor to receive his blessing.' These and other conversations revolved around my arrival into the world.

On my eighth day of life I see a stir in the house along with preparations for a celebration. On that day the ritual of introduction into the ranks of believers in the commandment of Israel is to be held. The rooms shine with cleanliness; candles in brass and silver candlesticks burn on the tables. Women's laughter comes from a room full of friends and relatives where my mother lies. Men sit in another room at tables arranged in a semicircle. My father and our relatives serve as hosts and try to sit every newcomer in an appropriate place, depending on his position in the town hierarchy.

The rabbi with a long grey beard and beautifully curled sidelocks sits in the place of honour and recites something aloud. Everyone listens intently.

Then the door opens and a Jew with the imposing look of Abraham carries me in. I lie on a pillow and scream with all my might, as if aware of what awaits me. The pillow, along with me, is passed from hand to hand. A Jew with red hair bends over me with the ritual knife. With dirty hands, he starts the procedure . . . My cries die on my lips and complete silence seizes the room. The old rabbi prays, moving his lips soundlessly. Then, as if woken from a dream, he breaks the silence with a cry, 'Mazl tov, mazl tov!' Everybody present hugs and congratulates my father.

'God, give him health!'

'God, let me see his wedding!'

'God, let him become a *tsadik*!'

'God, let us see the times of the Messiah!'

My father receives this all with a glowing face and my mother wants me returned to her, a demand met immediately. Now I'm back by her side.

After the celebration is over, various dishes and beverages appear on the table. The feast begins. They toast me and tell racy jokes, thoroughly exploiting the occasion by talking about local events and interests, prolonging the feast long into the night.

*

Five years had passed since the day I joined the believers in the Mosaic faith. These were not just the best years of my childhood, but of my life. During that time my fate regarding my elementary education was decided.

I remember it as if it were yesterday. At my fifth birthday dinner I noticed my mother and father were keeping something from me, arguing about it. From a few overheard words I realized the conversation concerned me, but I didn't know the issue. Later I learned that the controversy concerned my future. My father wanted my intellect to be developed, rather than fed with fairy tales about miracles, devils, and wondrous acts; he wanted me to attend our town's public school. Whereas my mother, a hasid's daughter, firmly believed that the Lord God gave her a son through the *tsadik*'s intercession, and not a son to be raised as a *goy* but as a servant of the Lord. She was adamant about this. She even claimed that I would become a *tsadik* or at least a rabbi. Towards this end she insisted that I begin my education in a traditional *kheyder*. Unable to reach agreement, they resolved to ask me which I preferred: a school or a *kheyder*.

To convince me of their respective desires, both father and mother outdid themselves giving me presents and treats. Therefore, on the day I had to decide my future, my mother gave me a pretty toy horse, a lead soldier, and a chocolate bar to boot, so I fell under her influence and agreed to go to the *kheyder*.

I clearly remember the day my mother took me to the *kheyder* for the first time. I see myself through the mists of time—a little boy squeezed behind a large table among several tykes in colourful outfits whose appearance reflected the means of those who sired them.

We bend over a book and recite in a variety of voices. In the middle on a dirty clay floor several girls sit in various positions. They are playing, each in her own way. In the corner of the *kheyder* the silhouette of the *rebbe*'s wife flickers in the smoke; she mutters something under her breath about her husband. The room is rather small, located in the basement, and is never aired. The students constantly breathe in smoke and fumes. The smoke irritates eyes, not to mention that it is unbearably hot and stuffy.

Standing upright in the middle of the *kheyder*, almost threateningly, the *rebbe*[1] reigns over this pack of children. In his right hand he holds his nine-tailed sceptre, the almighty whip. From time to time he tries his unchecked power, lashing the backs of the boys closest to him, more for practice than necessity. We huddle into a tight group so that not a needle can be squeezed between us. The *rebbe* swings his whip over our heads and waves it menacingly in the air.

That's what this temple of learning that my father had opposed looked like. Yet, because gifts had bought my consent, I had to stay there every day from eight in the morning to nine at night. Every day was the same as the next, with no variety. The *rebbe* never allowed us to open the windows, claiming that he would lose his voice

---

[1] In this context, the term *rebbe* is used to mean *kheyder* teacher (*melamed*).

with which he graced Saturday services in the synagogue. Nor did the sun ever peek into our *kheyder*, as there was a pen in front of the window where the *rebbe* kept his livestock, consisting of two goats and four kids. The *rebbe*'s goats truly plagued the entire town. These pests would never stop bothering the local peasants who came to town for church or shopping. The goats were everywhere. Sometimes they even stole the breakfasts we brought from home from the windowsill. Because the *rebbe* asked us to put them there, we didn't know if he was doing this on purpose or not. But it made things easier for the goats and they helped us eat our breakfasts. The *rebbe* claimed there was no nicer creature in the whole world than a goat; you never need to feed it and it gives good milk.

The bleating of goats and the screaming of children annoyed me so much that I would have gladly run away from that paradise to the ends of the earth, but my fear of the *rebbe* was greater. This is what kept me there. Still, some days we breathed fresh air. This was when we played in the yard and the sun shone on us with its soothing rays. Unfortunately there were very few such days—this depended on the number of traditional weddings when the *rebbe* took on an extra role singing to the newlyweds as a *badkhn*.

On such days he freed us from his company and allowed us to play in the yard. The yard was a dump, but for us it was nice because it had everything that we need-ed for play. No wonder that we regularly looked for notices of new engagements.

Already then, despite our youth, the question would come up—why do people marry? Each of us had an explanation. Finally, the cobbler's son, who was the old-est—already 10 when he came to the *kheyder*—started saying that he knew why, basing this on his observation of his parents. He told us what his father and mother did at night. As for me, I firmly rejected this and called him a liar. Srulek (this was his name) did not give up, and immediately showed us how to do it. Obviously he was 'Tate' [daddy] and chose a girl to serve as the 'Mame' [mummy]. An obstacle arose—in order to marry one needed a bed. At least this is what Srulek claimed. Seeing his hesitation, we all decided that the broken trunk standing by the window could be the bed. The girl, however, having no idea what was going on, baulked and refused to get into the trunk. Srulek grabbed her by the waist and forced her into the trunk while she valiantly defended herself. When she saw that she was over-powered, she started crying with terrified screams, as though calling for help from all of us. Without thinking, I stood up for her, which caused a fist fight with Srulek. In the end I won, so the performance did not occur.

When the *rebbe* returned and learned about this incident, he gave me ten lashes on that part of the body which, as he said, won't hurt the head and actually makes it smarter.

*

[At the age of 13, after completing *kheyder*, the boy is sent to the yeshiva in Łomża.]

*

The yeshiva building was located more or less in the centre of the town on a large cobbled square near the rector's residence. The yeshiva itself consisted of a large room, so large that the architect added a row of columns in the middle to support the ceiling. By the wall, across from the foot of the stairs, was the *orn-koydesh* [ark] and the altar [*sic*]. There were rows of benches on both sides of the hall where even at night you saw students of different ages, some even with long beards, engrossed in the Talmud.

The yeshiva was divided into four grades. Each grade had its days of classes, that is, the first grade had classes every day, the second had classes every other day. The third grade met twice a week and the fourth consisted of the students who studied on their own most of the time. There were even some among them who by now could have been rabbis. I always looked with envy at their ascetic figures because nobody from the first grade could easily reach the fourth grade; learning in each grade took several years at least. The first grade was taught by an old man with a white beard and a holy face. He lectured slowly and clearly, but when we reached a chapter in the Talmud that talked about men's relations with women he would tell us to skip a page or two so that we did not touch upon this topic. However, we would take every opportunity to peek secretly at what was hidden there. Scared and fearful we would read the prohibited passage, but were not always able to understand the content and interpreted it in different ways. Woe to him who got caught by the teacher studying and deliberating on these matters. This was why everybody kept on guard and looked behind his shoulder as if committing a crime.

It was not unusual that the old man did not lecture on these topics. It stemmed from the custom in the yeshiva not to talk about what was considered too complicated for young people. They thought that, if a teacher touched upon sensitive issues, this would show an easy way to sin instead of protecting you from it. They saw the greatest of evil in anything concerning that impure creature called woman . . .

All in all I liked the order and mood of the yeshiva. I was proud to be the youngest of 200 students. Also I was aware that I was well liked by my classmates, which made me feel good. On the other hand I missed what I had left behind, the sun and woods of the River Narew. Constant compulsory study of the Talmud was tiresome, and I was only too happy when classes were over and I could leave the gloomy walls of the yeshiva. [. . .]

*

In the yard of the yeshiva was a ramshackle shed. One half of it sheltered those without a 'day place'[2] and a place to sleep at night. These students could stay in the shed

---

[2] It was a custom that poor students were treated to dinner each day in a different Jewish home (*esn teg*: eating days); thus the term 'day place'.

overnight sleeping on dirty bunks. The other half of the shed had been occupied for years by a cobbler who would repair the shoes of the future redeemers of Israel for five copecks. He was a 40-year-old Jew with a pockmarked face. His wife looked just like him. They were extremely poor but luckily they were childless. For once God was just, because no child could grow up in such a stench. The cobbler was a pious hasid, a follower of the Libawa *tsadik* who had bestowed on him this post of court cobbler, despite his poverty. He was always cheerful. His wife did the poorer students' laundry and sold half-rotten fruit.

He had no furniture save a broken workbench, a stool, a table, a trunk, and a bundle of bedding in the corner, but he was good at telling stories about the miracles of his *tsadik*. Of course, as future *tsadiks* we loved to listen to him.

I remember him once being asked why he wouldn't ask God or his *tsadik* to make him rich if he believed in miracles so much. He gave us a sad smile and answered full of faith, 'I'm not worthy of his grace.' I jokingly asked, 'Reb Leyzer' (this was his name), 'if the Libawa *tsadik* told you to become a thief, would you listen to him?' He looked at me and put aside a muddy boot he held in his hand. After a pensive moment he responded steadfastly, 'I would not hesitate to do whatever the *tsadik* asks of me.' I interrupted, 'Even eating *khazer* [pig]?' Everybody started laughing. 'Yes, he said, I would do even the worst thing if he ordered me, even jump into fire! Do you know why? He knows what comes out ahead of time; therefore whatever he commands is surely for the good, even if it looks bad at the time. If I had time I would tell you about one such case . . .'.

There were maybe ten of us there, as this was on Friday, when everybody is free, and we all started to press him to tell us the story until he finally gave in. He told us to believe that everything he was about to tell was true. We gave our word that we would believe every word he said, and so he started.

'In a large town in Poland there was a very rich hasid. He owned several factories and a bank. Every year during the high holidays he visited his *tsadik*, to whom he gave large sums of money for charity. It was like this for many years. One year he came to the *tsadik* for the holidays and he was very upset. When the holidays were over and he was leaving for home, the *tsadik* gave him his blessing. But the man started crying and told the *tsadik* that he had had very bad luck the last year. He had lost a great portion of his riches and asked the *tsadik* for advice how to improve things.

The *tsadik* looked at the sky and then he said these words to the hasid: "Listen, Khayim, I have some advice for you that can make you rich again, but I know you won't do it."

Khayim answered, "*Rebbe*, if I can't do it, I don't want to know about it . . .".

Next year he came again and threw himself at the *rebbe*'s feet.

"*Rebbe*, help! I have already lost more than half my property, what can I do?"

The *tsadik* told him to rise and said: "I told you, I have a solution but I believe you would never do it, so it's better that you don't know . . .".

And again Khayim returned home sad and depressed.

He came back again in yet another year. He looked destitute. He fell at the *tsadik*'s feet. "*Rebbe*, I lost all I had. My wife and children are crying for bread. I am a beggar. Save me!"

The *tsadik* responded, "I already told you and I can repeat it again."

"*Rebbe*," cried Khayim, "command me. I'll do anything not to die of starvation."

"Fine," answered the *tsadik*, "listen to me. Go home and become a thief!"

"I, a thief?" cried Khayim, "Never, never ever. I'd rather die of hunger with my wife and children than become a thief . . ."

"I told you," said the *rebbe*, "you would not want to do this. So be it, I don't have any other advice for you."

Khayim left sad and frustrated but firmly convinced that he would rather perish than take someone else's property.

Two weeks had passed since he returned home. His wife and children kept asking for bread. What could he do? He would never do this for himself, but what about his wife and children—was this their fault? "I have to do it for them", he thought. "I can't stand their tears." But here the poor guy had a problem. "How can I go about it? Money doesn't lie on the street ready to be stolen, so even if I decide to do it, I don't know how . . . But there's no choice and one must try." He prayed, and then he dressed up in his last good *kapote* and tied up his *tsitses*. He went to the attic, found a nail, and waited until midnight. "Come what may, I'll try."

At midnight, when he started out on his mission, the whole town was fast asleep. He sneaked past the houses. Finally, barely knowing what he was doing, he started fiddling with the lock to a shop. Suddenly the lock opened and he got in. He pulled out a drawer in the counter which contained many gold, silver, and small coins. He found a copper 5 copeck piece and said, "God, I'm borrowing these 5 copecks for bread; I'll return them as soon as I can." And so he left the shop. In the morning the owner found the door open and raised alarm. The police arrived, but it turned out that only 5 copecks were missing. They couldn't understand what this meant.

The same thing happened the next night, and so it went on. An uproar started in town that there was a break-in at a different shop every night, and each time only 5 copecks were missing, even from steel boxes. The news reached the governor-general. He ordered a soldier to be placed on guard at each shop, but even this did not help. Five copecks disappeared as before, and all the bolts and locks were opened. The governor-general ordered the soldiers who guarded the shops that had been robbed to come before him so he could interrogate them in person. Each soldier swore that he had been awake all night and had noticed nothing. The general decided to check this himself. In the evening he disguised himself as a night burglar and went to investigate. He patrolled the wealthy streets where the 5 copeck thefts usually occurred, but he couldn't find anything. He was about to return home when he noticed a Jew boldly approaching a jeweller's. The iron door soon opened and the Jew walked in.

The general followed and saw the Jew open a safe, find a 5 copeck coin, and say, as usual, that he was just borrowing it for bread and would return it with interest as soon as he could. The general stood quietly behind him, put his hand on his shoulder, and said, "Don't be scared, I am a thief too. We're in the same trade—no need to be afraid of me." Noticing that the Jew was frightened, the general continued, "I see you can open locks. Let's work together. Why steal only 5 copecks at a time? What do you say?" The Jew did not want to agree. He explained that he was just borrowing and wanted to leave. The general told him, "If you don't want me as a partner I will hand you over to the police. It's up to you", and he grabbed him by the collar. The Jew did not want to be caught, so he accepted the offer, but under the condition that they wouldn't take anything else from that shop.

The general laughed, "I have a better job for you. If it works we will be the richest people in the town. Listen, I have been looking for someone like you for a long time, someone who can be invisible and overcome any obstacle. With you I can put my old plan to work. As you know, the governor-general lives in our town and he is very rich. He has a million roubles in cash and many precious stones. We have to go together. I know every nook in the palace and where the treasury is. You will get in unnoticed past the soldier who is on guard there. We will share the loot and become rich once and for all. What do you say?"

At first the Jew did not want to agree, but he gave in under threats and pressure. They went to the palace and upon entering the general showed the Jew the way to the treasury. He stayed behind waiting in the shadows of the palace walls. After half an hour the Jew returned with empty hands. The angry general asked him what this meant. The Jew responded, "I was just by the treasury when I heard a man who looked like a servant talking to the soldier on guard. 'When the general comes,' said the servant, 'we will give him poisoned tea or coffee, then we will take the money and escape abroad.' The soldier agreed."

"So how could I take anything? No, I couldn't. It's better that we write to the general so he will not drink the tea. He is a good man. I feel sorry for him . . ."

The general tried to insist that the Jew go back, but to no avail. Finally he said to him, "I don't want to deal with such a stupid thief", and on this they parted.

The dawn was grey when the general returned to the palace. He entered his study and rang up his servant ordering him to bring him something to drink. The servant asked if the general wanted tea or coffee. "Tea", said the general. The servant brought the tea in a flash, and the general asked him if it was sweet enough. "Yes", answered the servant. The general, pretending to skim casually through his papers said, "Please, try it!" The servant baulked, but the general looked at him menacingly and ordered him to try it. The servant tried to back towards the door. The general called the guard, and several soldiers ran into the room. He ordered them to put the servant and the soldier who guarded the treasury in chains. Then, in order to convince the eyewitnesses, the general gave some tea to the dog. The dog did not even manage to swallow it before he dropped dead on the floor. After this the general ordered the soldiers to bring the Jew to him. The general already knew where he lived. When the soldiers led the Jew in chains across town, nobody who knew him could guess what the charge was against such a noble person. It did not occur to them that he was the 5 copeck thief sought by the police for so long. He was brought to the general, who ordered him unchained and asked if he recognized him. The Jew responded that he didn't. The general turned to him with these words:

"Do you remember? I was the thief that night who told you about the job at the general's palace. I am the general. I wanted to try you, and you saved my life. If not for you, these worthless fellows would have poisoned me. I owe you my salvation. For this you get half that money, half a million roubles, just as if we stole it together." He gave the money to the Jew, who from that day on became even richer than before. He returned all of his 5 copeck loans with generous interest.

This was the aim of the *tsadik* who had told him to become a thief. The *tsadik* knew beforehand what would come of it. So whatever he commands, even if it seems not to be very good at first, must be done at once.'

We were thrilled with this story. It remained in my memory and I could repeat it word for word.

*

[Nachalnik receives news about the death of his mother but is urged not to return home. He struggles to support himself and finds board at the house of a prostitute with whom he has a relationship. As a result he neglects his studies. He returns home for the following Passover.]

*

The first Passover after my mother's death was sad, even if my stepmother tried hard to be good to us to help us in our grief. Alas, although my brother and sister seemed to miss our mother less than I, I was not able to trust my stepmother completely.

When the holiday was over, I learned from my father what had caused our relationship to cool. In a letter my cousin had complained that I was taking life easy while neglecting my studies. He suggested that my father keep me impoverished so that I would become a man sooner. He also told my father about my adventures. When I learned about this, I was so angry with my cousin that I told my father everything I knew about him.

My father laughed at my revenge and asked me what my plans were for the future. I didn't answer. From my silence he concluded that I planned to stay at home. He indicated to me what direction he thought I should take: 'You can't stay at home. I'm going to apprentice you because it seems to me you've had enough of this yeshiva learning.' These last words were said in a rather nasty tone.

I am not sure if I disliked all manual work already by then, but I did not want to become an artisan. I wondered why my father did not want me to stay home, and I put the blame squarely on my stepmother. I suspected this was her idea. To prove that her scheme wouldn't work, I firmly told my father that I had decided to return to the yeshiva to fulfil the promise made to my mother.

My father was not pleased with my answer. He became angry with me and said I could go wherever I liked but he wouldn't give me a penny more because he was convinced that I would never be a rabbi. On this note my quarrel with my father ended.

The next day he sent me to one of his debtors to collect 82 roubles for flour. When I got the money, a foolish thought popped into my mind: 'You have money so you can go wherever you like . . . '. Initially I was scared by this thought, but the memory of my father's words, 'you can go wherever you like', stirred such bitterness in me that all my thoughts turned towards the idea of going away into the world. At the same time this thought was challenged by the words of the commandment 'you shall not steal'. But I even found a way of getting around this warning, namely, by telling myself that the money was my father's, and that by taking it I wasn't harming anyone. Thus, struggling with myself I walked out of town instead of returning home.

It was a beautiful day. Without even realizing what I was doing or where I was going I found myself on the road to the town of R. I had never before had such a sum of money on me; this reassured me that I would somehow cope in life. Thinking like this and constantly checking to make sure the money was still there, I found myself near the ferry, which was located two versts beyond the town. The ferryman looked at me suspiciously and asked where I was going. He recognized me because sometimes he came to our house. To avoid telling him the truth, I lied as well as I could. I told him that my father had sent me on business to the estate G., to the squire. I mentioned this estate because I knew it was 2 kilometres away.

I was surprised at my own ability to lie so smoothly. Nobody taught me this and it was against my nature. I thought about the maxim from the Talmud, 'Aveyro greges aveyro' ['A sin leads to a sin'].[3]

I thought, 'Maybe I should go back, there is still time', because I realized the consequences of what I had done, for instance what an uproar it would cause at home and what gossip would fill the town. But I crossed the Narew and went on, as if pushed by some unknown evil force. In the next town I learned that the railway station was nearby and that the train came once a day, stopping at the station just for a brief moment. I joined a few other passengers going to the train, and, having paid 10 copecks, climbed on a horse-drawn carriage going to the station. We arrived too early and had to wait until midnight for the train.

It was a strange thing, you could say the earth was burning beneath my feet. Every time someone asked where I was going, or even just looked at me, I was certain he knew who I was and where I was coming from, could read the word 'thief' written on my face, and was ready to give me over into the hands of a mean 'Matvei'

---

[3] The actual citation, in Ashkenazi Hebrew, is 'Aveyro goyreres aveyro' (Mishnah, *Pirkei avot* 4: 2).

[policeman]. I was scared of my own shadow. I regretted my thoughtless step. But it was impossible to turn back. Probably everybody in my town was already talking about my escape. So 'bridges were burned', and what will be will be. For a while I thought about where I should go. One thing was resolved, I wouldn't go back to the gloomy embrace of the yeshiva. I would go into the world. No matter where it led! I felt money in my pocket, which to me meant that somehow I would manage.

Within two days I was in the large, strange city of Vilna. Most of the day I walked the streets without purpose. When I felt hungry I went to one tea-shop or another. In one of them I made the acquaintance of a Jew who claimed to be from my area. I believed him because he talked about people I knew. After half an hour of conversation I was so taken by him that I confessed my travel intentions to him, and also that I had money and how I got it. On hearing this the Jew took so much of a liking to me that he decided to accompany me on my travels.

From that moment he wouldn't leave me. In the evening he led me to a house on a distant street where a relative of his supposedly lived and where I could be safe from my father's pursuit.

I was met by a young woman. After introducing us my friend told me to make myself at home. Then he excused himself and left to take care of some urgent business.

As soon as we were alone, the young woman gave me a mysterious smile and asked me to sit next to her on the couch. This invitation surprised me, but after a little hesitation I did as she asked. I noticed that she was very pretty, or at least she seemed pretty to me. I readily answered her questions and did not resist much when she took my hand and pulled me closer to her. Her hints that I be bolder made my head spin and I was ready to proceed.

An abrupt shake brought me back to my senses. I turned round. An older man stood before me with a threatening gesture. The frightened woman jumped back, while I sat there helpless, surprised, and scared, not knowing what was going on. The man raised his fist above my head and yelled, 'You snot-nose . . . You came here to mess around with my wife! . . . I'm going to teach you . . .'. Seeing that I was in danger, the woman jumped between us to protect me.

The story ended quickly with me being thrown out on the street without a penny in my pocket because my whole fortune was taken from me. Only then did I realize that I had fallen prey to what they call a 'scam'. I had heard about such things before. The whole farce was cleverly devised and well acted, and it was initiated by the fellow I met in the café.

Later, when I became a part of that world and familiar with its secrets and the tricks of the trade, I met that 'good' company several times. They laughed at me and my naivety. I laughed with them and shared their principle that one should 'suck the soul from a fool like the last breath from your horse', which more or less meant that if somebody lets you dupe him, you should go all the way. [. . .]

*

It was the beginning of May. I arrived in the village of G. on the River Niemen, flanked on both sides by beautiful forests and hills. This was a resort especially liked by Jews. The house, or rather villa, that was pointed out to me had a glass veranda and stood out among the others. Upon entering I was met by an imposing man of 46 and his large family. I was expected and received very well.

After initial greetings, they invited me to their table and served me tea and preserves. During the conversation the owner subtly inspected me, asking where I came from and about my family, and then he asked about my education. My answers were excellent and I saw they pleased him. Then he started to discuss the conditions. As for me, I knew from the beginning that the outcome would be good because I was much better educated than the examiner; this was confirmed by loud applause after every satisfactory answer. Also, his appraisal of my appearance was favourable, a conclusion I came to after observing the discreet looks that the villa owner's daughter Sonia gave me now and then.

The deal was that at New Year I was to receive the salary of 50 roubles. Until then I was to get bread and board, first at Mr B's and then at the villa [thereby apparently tutoring in two households]. For this I was to teach four pupils for a few hours each day about the Pentateuch and the Prophets, as well as how to write in Hebrew and Yiddish. [. . .]

*

One day late in the afternoon, the word went out in the village that a vacationer had disappeared. He was an elderly man, the owner of a bank in Kaunas (Kowno) who had gone to the woods early in the morning and had not returned. They thought he had lost his way. The entire village went out to search for him. Of course I was among the first to join the expedition. As you can guess, Sonia was by my side.

The search party was all over the woods. Now and then someone would call, 'Yoo-hoo, yoo-hoo!' Echoes multiplied the voices and they were heard all over. The noise was such as to raise the dead. Perhaps the lost man heard it as well, but he didn't respond . . . But I am not going to write much about him here; I'll just tell you what happened. He was found dead in the woods. The doctors said he died of a stroke. He had a large sum of money on him that his soul forgot to take while joining the angels and it was left for his heirs.

To return to my story—initially Sonia and I participated in the search and even yelled together with the others with all our might. But we gradually left the rest of the company and walked along the edge of the woods on the banks of the Niemen. We stopped calling and became preoccupied with each other . . .

It was already dark. The September evening delightfully enveloped the woods and the river. The calls of the searchers had long stopped reaching our ears. Arms around each other, we walked on and on, listening to the eternal murmur of our natural surroundings and breathing the refreshing scent of herbs and resin.

We climbed a little hill that was like an island amid the sea of green. There Sonia stopped. She felt tired and suggested that we rest, so we sat down. She held me even closer. A damp, chilly breeze was coming off the river. She just had a light scarf on, and was shivering with cold. I took off my coat and covered my companion.

I was completely happy with my beloved at my side and listening to the beating of her heart. I wanted time to stop for ever.

I was awakened from this dream by her asking me to tell her something about myself. I started telling her about my family—my mother and my home. I did not tell her about my father because this particular memory always brought that bad thing concerning the money to my mind. I was surprised that Sonia listened, but she seemed to ask questions more to pass the time than out of genuine interest.

I felt uneasy. I lost my composure and fell silent. Suddenly, what a shock—I couldn't believe my ears when I heard her ask, 'Tell me, *rebbe*. Have you ever been with a woman?' I was stunned. I thought the forest had fallen on my head. I couldn't believe that my beloved Sonia could actually ask about something like this. I did not understand at all what she wanted from me. As for me, it never crossed my mind that I could harm my love . . . A great love for her burned in me and I acted like a slave before a princess . . .

'Tell me . . . tell me . . .', she insisted, clutching my hand passionately. 'Come on, come on . . . 'N-o, n-e-v-e-r', I choked out the answer, my voice trembling with emotion. 'Would you like to try it now?' she asked innocently, wrapping her body around me.

Instead of answering I started to tear off her clothes . . . And so it happened . . . Calling as witnesses the stars shining above us so beautifully, the woods and the River Niemen, which also saw the mystery of our love, I pledged that I would love her until death and that nothing would ever separate us. Hearing the confessions of my love, she just smiled and said, 'That's not necessary . . . Just keep your mouth shut . . . I will be with you again when the opportunity arises.' I shivered at these words. I did not understand their meaning. Until then I thought that a young woman, especially somebody like Sonia, would treat the act of love as a sacred thing or at least expect from a man honest feelings that would secure her future.

The flippancy with which Sonia treated the whole thing put me completely out of kilter. I could not gather my thoughts. To tease me even more, she laughed at my naivety on our way back as if nothing had happened. Then, to top it off, she noted cynically that I had ripped her panties.

We arrived home past midnight. Everybody was asleep. I quietly crept to my room and lay down in bed. But there was no way I could fall asleep. The emotions of the adventure that had just ended were too strong. For the hundredth time I relived the evening in my thoughts, and each time I reached the same words which I could hardly understand, 'That's not necessary. Just keep your mouth shut.'

Yet I was completely at peace with myself about one thing; I was aware that for the first time I had tasted the real pleasure that a woman gives . . . I totally agreed with the Talmud, which describes this as being equal to the delights of paradise. I had not known 'paradise', but now I could imagine it more precisely. I had to say that being eternally in paradise would be a rather pleasant thing. I began to envy those who are taken directly there after death.

These and other thoughts ran through my head until I collapsed with exhaustion and fell asleep. I was dreaming I was in paradise. I was sitting among beautiful, completely naked girls shaped like the ancient goddesses I once saw in a book in the library, and I delighted in their beauty. The women tried to seduce me with their bodies . . . I embraced one of them, pulled her closer to me, and she returned my embrace. I felt pleasure and delight spreading through my body . . . and I woke up. The dark room made me realize how far I had drifted from reality. I felt angry with myself, but tried to calm down.

But there was no way I could. My imagination, once unleashed, was conjuring up fantastic images and wouldn't let my mind rest. Such thoughts and plans emerged that I would never have dared to imagine before.

A wild thought came to me and became more and more pressing—to go to Sonia's room. I could not struggle any more with the mysterious force that pushed me. I got up from my bed and, creeping like a shadow through the corridor and dining room, I proceeded towards her bedroom. With my heart pounding after passing all the obstacles, I stood at the door to my goal. I froze, because it seemed to me that I heard whispering. I moved closer to the door and was all ears.

No, I was not mistaken. This was not my imagination. I clearly heard the quiet whispering and subdued laughter of two people. In my divine Sonia's room was the student who taught her French, an ordinary man of 25.

Only then did I realize the nature of his frequent visits to Sonia's room. I was so naive that I had never thought these visits were also repeated at night. This was not difficult because his room was next to Sonia's.

The pain of disappointment seized my heart. I leaned against the door in order not to fall. I felt tears of sorrow for lost happiness rising in my throat and choking me. I staggered towards the student's room. It was empty. His clothes were scattered all over the chairs and on the floor. He had left his room in just his underwear.

I was boiling; my blood beat hotly, hammering away in my swollen temple and veins. Now I knew what her words, 'That's not necessary . . . Just keep your mouth shut' meant. She did not love me. She was just a harlot!

The contradictory feelings of disappointed love and jealousy which had tormented me before began to turn into a desire born in hell—the desire for revenge! This idea would not leave me alone and I started to look around for the opportunity to implement it.

I did not know what my revenge would be, but I decided to do something. Suddenly my eyes spotted a gold watch hanging from the wall, teasing me with its shiny surface as if sneering at my helplessness. 'Take it', a tempting voice whispered to me. 'There is also a wallet with money under his pillow . . . take it! After the spasms of love, such a loss will hurt him even more. You can't stay here anyway. He sneered at you, constantly mocked you and you were the butt of his nasty jokes . . . You could not stand him before . . . and now, after what you witnessed . . . take it and run away!'

Overcome by these thoughts I approached the bed and reached for the watch. I quietly took it from the wall, and with equal skill dug the wallet out as if I were already a professional thief. Seized by some inexplicable fear I sneaked out of the door, and then returned to my room the same as before. Here I immediately put on my clothes, quickly gathered my belongings, and slipped out onto the street like a snake.

It was past midnight. I walked, no—ran, driven by an unknown fear. I was by turns sweating buckets and shivering with cold; I trembled. A strange pressure bore down on my head, and my legs were leaden. At times I stopped and was almost unable to move on. I was making superhuman efforts not to fall. My mouth was completely dry and my heart was pounding so hard and fast that I could barely breathe.

I was furious with myself for my cowardice. What is the use of nerve if it produces such suffering? For once, make it stop . . .

The way I took led to a railway station 10 kilometres away. I had just one thought, to be there as soon as possible. The feeling of satisfied revenge together with the watch and stuffed wallet in my pocket propelled me and pushed me on and on. Yet at the same time the fear of a chase paralysed me. At moments my legs refused to carry me and I had to stop. I tried to forget about what had happened, but, despite all my excuses, my conscience refused to be silent. The call of 'thief! . . . thief! . . . stop . . . you still can . . .' rang in my ears.

I forced my legs like a madman, and again ran breathlessly towards the saviour railway station. Finally the tracks appeared and the lights of the small station buildings shone before me. I breathed a sigh of relief and slowly walked towards my destination.

The oil lamp in the station shed dim light. The tobacco smoke in the air made the room even darker. Only after a while could I see the people waiting for the train. A few dozen peasants and several women sat on the floor by their bundles. None wore town clothes. I cautiously looked around and tried to spot a far corner where I would not draw any attention to myself. But first I wanted to find out about the train. So I approached a *babushka* who was swaying, half asleep. After some mumbling she told me that the train would arrive in two hours. I realized that staying in the station for so long could be dangerous for me and I changed my mind. I decided to pass the time outside the building. I moved towards the door.

Suddenly a guard appeared in front of me. 'Vy kuda?' ['Where are you going?'] he asked. I was speechless with fear and couldn't even open my mouth. Noticing my fear the guard became even more suspicious and, to the surprise of a few night passengers, he took me by the collar and dragged me to the sentry room. The gendarme who was dozing at the table lazily raised his head when he saw us and was visibly angry that his sweet dream had been interrupted. He stared at me with his evil, bloodshot eyes. The guard reported that he had brought in a suspicious person (myself) who had probably done something wrong since he wanted to run and did not have his passport on him.

The gendarme yawned several times while listening to this rather long report. He stretched his body, which was stiff from sleep. He apparently did not completely trust the guard's investigative intuition. Yet when he heard, 'net pasporta' ['no passport'], he livened up and ordered, 'Search him!'

I fell to pieces! I had just experienced so many emotions, and so many new things had happened to me recently, and now I was in the hands of an evil guard and an equally dangerous gendarme. All at once, this was just too much for my nerves. I couldn't answer the questions they asked me—just cried aloud with streams of tears running down my cheeks.

First the watch was put on the table, followed by the wallet, in which I found out there were 30 roubles and some papers. The guard and the gendarme looked at all of this with keen interest, especially at the watch, which they unanimously decided was 'gold'. Now they were convinced they had a *vor* [thief] on their hands. They could not work out where these things came from and whose they were, because, as I mentioned above, I was crying the whole time. The gendarme ordered me to be locked up for further investigation. The door locked behind me with a slam and I fell on the floor crying. I tore my hair and wailed.

*

[Nachalnik spends several weeks in prison and is finally bailed out by his father. He returns to his town, where his father keeps humiliating him by telling everybody about his thievery; he wants to escape and tries to steal his father's wallet. His father then sends him to work for his uncle as an apprentice in his bakery. Overworked, he falls sick with 'brain fever'. After recuperating, he is supposed to return home but instead remains and becomes a horse-drawn-cab driver (*dorożkarz*).]

*

At first I liked my job. But after a month I had had enough of it. I was not happy with the meagre income I was making in this business. My circle of friends had grown, and so had my expenses. I was jealous of my peers, who had nice clothes, hung around with pretty girls, and had a good time. They would not even avoid large bills.

I figured out how some of them made money. I wanted to have an easy life too, and for the time being suppressed this desire, but I felt that sooner or later I would give in to temptation. In fact it happened before I even noticed it. Owing to a coincidence that had nothing to do with me, I was gradually driven into participating in forays which, had they failed, could easily have landed me in prison.

One day my boss told me to take three 'respectable gentlemen' (as he called them) to a place some 18 kilometres away. They were quite well-dressed young men, pleasant, and in good humour. We arrived at the 'place' at midnight. I say 'place' even if this is not exactly right, because I was told to stop on the road by a tree and wait for their return. I was instructed how to act in case of a *poruta* [bungling]. I noticed that, before they left the cab, they distributed among themselves some strange things whose names I did not know.

When they left, I was alone in my cab. I was thinking scary and worrisome things. I was afraid to move. Time dragged on endlessly. Hours passed and they hadn't come back. I listened for the faintest of sounds and finally heard running steps. The silhouettes of my passengers appeared in the fading night. They carried a rather large suitcase.

They jumped into the cab and ordered me to drive like a bat out of hell. They did not need to repeat this twice—I wanted to leave the spot where I had experienced so much fear and uncertainty right away. I did not spare the whip on my boss's pair of well-rested horses, who leaped forward. In no time at all we were far from the 'job'. The horses slowed down. Now I could listen to the conversation behind me. I had no doubts about the kind of 'work' they had just done. They openly made 'professional' comments. Still, the most convincing evidence was the present I got in the form of a silver watch on a gold chain. To relax my nerves I was also given vodka and a piece of sausage.

I went on several such expeditions at the request of my boss, and they all ended well. Each time I was paid in money and given small items of value. But I have to admit that I did not retain much from this easy gain. Most of the time I lost everything on cards in the underworld bars where I went more and more often with my new pals. I did not care about my losses because I knew that in a few days I would 'make money' again. I was pleased that I was trusted and admitted into the thieves' hideaways.

This first close contact with a world whose representatives I had briefly encountered before inside prison walls made a great impression on me. The world attracted me with its mystery. I liked the carefree life of people who did not think about tomorrow.

I'm not sure how it happened, but one day I told my boss I wasn't going to work for him any more. He wasn't surprised at all because he had figured out my intentions. But since I had exceeded his expectations and brought him a good profit, he tried to bargain with me. He promised to give me a rise. Then he started explaining that, if I wanted to be a thief, I should at least have a job 'for appearances' sake', so that the police would not bother me. Because as soon as the *hinty* [police] find out that someone *kinderuje* [steals] professionally, they won't leave him alone and will follow his every step. They will constantly demand *mone* [money], and the thief will end up working all the time just to pay them off.

'I went through this myself', he said pensively. 'I was in *kicz* [prison] twice when

I was young. But after that God let me "earn" a nice sum of money. I got married and became a cab driver. At first the *hinty* tried to harass me, but when they saw I was a working man, which gave me a pretence of the legitimate life, they left me alone. Now, as you know, I'm making more than before. Listen to me and you will be well off. Stay with me "for appearances", and you can make money on the side without attracting attention. I know that Cwajnos [Twonose] has talked you into becoming his *konik* [lit. 'horsey', thief's apprentice]. His sister has been after you for some time as well. So it's because of them that you want to leave. But I'm telling you as a Jew, you won't be at large for long. If you join his gang you will perish soon because the *hinty* know him all too well.'

All his urging did not change my mind. As my boss rightly guessed, a conversation with Cwajnos aided my decision. This is what I learned from him. 'You take unnecessary risks', he said. 'Your boss takes the same share without even leaving his house. He is also a fence and gets rich on thieves' blood, but you get pennies. You say nothing and that's why they consider you a good guy. For that reason your boss won't let you go that easy. He knows he can rely on you when he sends you on all these trips. But don't be a fool, you're worth more than that. You can be a good *jeke*;[4] you have everything it takes. All you need is to get into the right hands. You know, in our trade one needs physical strength, cold blood, and tight lips. I have noticed that you have all these qualities, and that's why I like you. I've decided to take you in.' He also let me know that his sister took an interest in me as well.

In the light of such arguments, how could I remain a cab driver? I must admit that it was less the desire to become Cwajnos's companion that attracted me, than his sister's charming dark eyes. They were the main reason I left my old job.

The friendship with Cwajnos and his pals was formalized the same day at his place. According to the rules, several bottles of schnapps were emptied along with some snacks to seal the *Bruderschaft*. I also moved under the tender protection of Cwajnos's sister, and I must say I thought I was in paradise.

I need to say a few words here about the noble company in which I found myself. Cwajnos, so-called by his companions and also his nickname in the police records, was a professional burglar of about 30 years of age. He lived with his mother and two sisters, one of whom was a quite successful *kontrolna* [registered prostitute]. In other words she was an *oficerska* [officer's girl] and would not go with anyone from the street. The army was stationed in the town, so her business ran smoothly.

My participation in the initiation party was rather passive, and limited to a few glasses of vodka. I was preoccupied with my Hanka. My honeymoon with her was rather sweet. Hanka was still an apprentice and not as licentious as her sister. She confessed to me that she had once had a fiancé who had seduced her and she had made a pledge to stay away from men. But, as she said, she liked me so much that

---

[4] *Jeke*, a term for an international thief but not one of the highest rank; something like *złodziejaszek* (petty thief) [Nachalnik's note].

she decided to try once more. If she felt that I deserved her heart, she would really love me and I would be the only man whom she would trust. [. . .]

*

The booty was unexpectedly large. The next day we sold all the jewellery and the more valuable things to a jeweller, who also readily fenced them. We took the rest of the silver, a substantial amount, to another less wealthy fence. He was an elderly Jew. He examined everything piece by piece, looking at us askance again and again. He mumbled something under his breath and shook his beard with sadness as if to say, 'I expected something more valuable from you; you can just take it back!'

After he had looked through everything, he turned to Cwajnos, whom he knew well, and from whom he had bought similar stuff many times before. With a baffled expression on his face he asked, 'How much do you want for this junk?' He pointed his finger contemptuously at the things on the floor.

'What junk?' answered Cwajnos, as if surprised. 'Everything is brand new, never used, and straight from the factory. It's not junk!' He twisted his face into something like a smile.

'What? Are you crazy?' protested the fence. 'I have to melt this. I can't keep it like this and I don't want to go to gaol. For me this is junk and nothing more.'

'Okay, buddy! Don't be so nervous', said Cwajnos soothingly. 'Tell us what you can really pay.'

'Five roubles a pound', answered the fence firmly. 'For me this is not worth any more.' And he looked at me suspiciously because he had never seen me before.

Cwajnos pondered for a moment and said, 'Give me 10 roubles a pound and we have a deal.' And he added softly, 'You know I don't like bargaining.'

'What? Ten roubles a pound? Are you sick or what? You can take it away.' The fence was jumping up and down crazily on his seat waving his hands. After a moment he said, 'As I am a Jew', and he pounded his chest, 'I can't pay you more than 6 roubles. Or you can go to Jankiel with this, he has more money.'

Cwajnos thought for a moment and said to me, 'Pack it up. We're going to Jankiel. He will give us more.'

I witnessed bargaining for the first time in my life. Until then I was never present when the loot was sold to a fence. I realized that a thief steals for a fence. I wanted to act on Cwajnos's command, but the fence leaped towards me and pushed me so hard that I landed against the wall.

'What a half-wit you brought with you!' he yelled at Cwajnos. 'He doesn't even know that a fence may bargain, but he never lets the *szoria* [loot] leave his house even if he has to put all his money into it. I will give you 7 roubles a pound. You know that this is junk I have to melt. Okay?' And he extended his hand to my partner, who smiled slyly.

I wanted to get even with the fence for pushing me and calling me a half-wit. I saw that my partner was ready to take the offer, so I went to the kitchen and took a cleaver from the wall. Without saying a word to Cwajnos and the fence, who watched me with surprise, I approached the pile of silver. I picked up a chalice and raised the cleaver. I was about to strike and crush the chalice. The fence turned pale. He jumped at me and grabbed my hand.

'*Nu*! What are you doing, crazy?'

'I'm making it junk! If you pay 7 roubles for a pound of junk, I will give you junk!' And I pushed him away, ready to destroy the silver.

Now the fence looked me straight in the eye. He turned to my partner, who was laughing aloud. 'Why the hell did you bring him here? He's nuts, stop him!' My partner was amused and started teasing him.

'Well, you bumped into quite a lad! I'm out of it now—he's selling.'

The fence calmly turned to me. 'Drop it. I will pay 9 roubles, but you must always bring things to me. I like you. I will take it all, as is, the whole thing.'

'Twelve roubles a pound. If not, I'm crushing it.'

The fence moaned and fell back on a chair. 'What a thief!' he cried, looking at Cwajnos accusingly. 'If you bring him here ever again I will throw you out along with him. I won't buy anything from you any more.'

'So', I asked, indifferent to threats, 'should I crush it?'

'No, no! Go to hell! I will give you twelve, but don't come to me any more, you two', he cried to Cwajnos.

The deal was done. There was 30 pounds of silver. My partner looked at me with awe.

From that day on, fences hated me. They said, 'This *litvak* is too smart, he won't leave a fence alive!'[5] Cwajnos entrusted me to do all our dealings with them. The fences tried to bribe me and wanted to give me a share behind my partners' backs, but this didn't work. From that day on Cwajnos respected me. I got an equal *dola* [share]. He did not cheat on me as before. He often praised me in front of the others while drinking vodka. He would point to me saying, 'Look at my apprentice. Not so long ago he was a cab driver, and now he is a fully fledged *jeke*. He'll grow to be a great *urke*.'[6]

His words 'During a war it's easier to steal' proved true. [After the First World War began] we had 'jobs' almost every day, all making a good profit. It seemed as if the Russian police only arrested those thieves who did not know how to steal or had no skill and just botched jobs. Once I was there during a burglary of a shoe shop. We were busy emptying shelves and boxes when suddenly someone opened the door and said, 'Ladno, ladno, rebyata! Mozhete dal'she rabotat' tol'ko na zavtra nuzhno mne piat'desyat'rublei, nu i paru sapog' ['All right, you lads! You can carry on, but tomorrow I need 50 roubles and a pair of shoes']. And the door closed quietly. I was scared and asked my partner what it meant. He calmed me down. 'Keep working',

---

[5] Litvaks (Lithuanian Jews) were noted, among other things, for their intellectual (i.e. talmudic) acuity.

[6] *Urke*, a prominent international thief [Nachalnik's note].

he said. 'That was the patrolman from this quarter. He's on our payroll and *błatny* [takes bribes]. He just let us know that he knows who is here and who is doing the job. He'll get his share tomorrow.'

Thus we stole boldly left and right. The police got their *dola*; this gave us courage. Cwajnos always knew how to approach an officer. If someone was too shy to take cash openly, he was sent gifts to his home. Of course, Cwajnos did not buy these gifts. To others we sent a pretty woman. If somebody was still stubborn, Cwajnos tried playing cards to lose some money to them. A certain Al—ov was such a lucky player.

Once it happened that a member of our gang was caught red-handed. He was taken to gaol and the prospect of at least four years loomed. It seemed that this time everything was lost and nothing could be done. A new investigating officer took over the district. He did not take *błat* and vigorously pushed the case to catch the accomplices as well. But something was found on him too—he had a weak point. This seemingly stern and incorruptible man was a sexual deviant. We managed to get our hands on him in such a way that he was afraid of scandal and accepted the conditions dictated to him. He had to dance our way, and our partner was released. [...]

*

One day I went to the town of G. on the German border along with Stasiek. We were taken there by a Jew. We arrived at his house early in the evening, around ten o'clock. As a prosperous cattle merchant he lived quite well. He had spent a year in prison because of some *szmuk* [jewellery] and I had met him in gaol. Now when he ran into me he mentioned a job concerning a loan shark. He wanted us to help him get even, as he put it. This was the same fellow who had testified against him and thus sent him to gaol.

We spent the night at his place and didn't show our faces to a soul for the whole of the next day, except in the evening, when we went to see the town. The merchant pointed out the loan shark's house. We were to steal a pair of horses, taking off immediately after. With just a bit of extra effort the job came off well. We hit the road with a wagon harnessed to a pair of pretty chestnuts.

Next morning at eleven we showed up at a fence 9 miles away from the site of the job. The fence looked over the horses and harness, and shook his head. 'I can take the goods from you, but you won't get the money until Sunday. I will be in Łomża and I'll pay you there.'

'Why Sunday?' I asked him.

'Because, sweetheart, judging from the harness, I think these are Jewish horses.'

'So what if they're Jewish?' I tried to ask.

The fence looked outraged and responded in Yiddish, '*Nu*, this wouldn't surprise me from a *goy*, but from you? I'm amazed!'

'I don't understand', I said.

The fence looked at me in disbelief and asked, 'How long have you been a horse thief?'

'Never, this is a one-time deal.'

'That's different, then. So I'm telling you, no honest fence would take horses stolen from Jews—even for free. Now peasant horses are a different story. Bring me as many as you find and I'll always buy them.'

With this explanation and despite our solemn assurances that the horses came from *goyim*, the fence wouldn't give us the money. We drank a bottle of Passover vodka together and, after agreeing on the final amount, his farmhand took us in his carriage to Łomża.

On Sunday I went to the inn where we were to meet; he paid the agreed sum with brand-new 100 rouble notes, without a word, and told me to bring him more horses like these—that he would always buy them. Privately I thought that I finally had the fence, because the horses were indeed Jewish. I was surprised that in the four days he hadn't discovered it.

Perhaps two weeks passed. One day a fence nicknamed Gold Tooth met me on the street. 'That you, Nachalnik? I've been all over town looking for you. Come with me.'

'Where to?' I tried to ask, sensing his excitement.

'Oh, just hurry up, we're going to Jechon, you'll find out there.'

We went to Jechon, where the fences always gathered. At once I spotted the fence who had bought the Jewish horses from us. Upon my entrance, he jumped on me immediately. 'You damned *sheygets* [gentile scamp], those horses were Jewish. What are you going do about it now?'

'What will I do?' I asked ironically. 'The Jew bought himself two more.'

'Don't try to kid with me', he threatened. 'Sit down. We have to talk.'

I noticed that one of the men in the room, whom I didn't know, locked the door. It's a *dintojra* [thieves' court], I thought.

'If you keep going on like this, no good will come of it. A fence must be told honestly where loot comes from so he knows where he can sell it. Did you know those horses were Jewish?'

'It was the first time I had ever been in that town, I took the job blind; how could I tell if the horses were Jewish or not? They didn't speak Yiddish or Polish when I let them out of the stable', I joked.

The fences looked at each other, and one with a goatee shouted, 'Don't be such a *fetniak* [smart-arse]. If you don't watch it, we will stop your know-all antics.'

Completely unafraid, I looked at him provocatively. Who knows what would have happened next if the fence who had bought the Jewish horses had not suddenly taken my side? 'Listen, Schmerke, don't threaten him. He's a good *urke* and well known among our people. We can deal with this in a peaceful way. He knows the thieves' law better than you.' And he turned to me.

'You sold me horses, and what about the *szmuk* you stole? Who did you sell it to?'

He jokingly threatened me with his finger.

'I didn't know you take Jewish jewellery', I answered.

'Why not?' he cried, 'Me not buy *szmuk*? Such a deal! So what are we going to do now?'

'Where are your sidekicks? Maybe we should call them in too?' asked one of the judges.

'That's not necessary', I said. 'They accept whatever I do.'

'Listen then, I'm telling you what happened', said the fence. 'I kept the horses until Sunday, and I heard nothing. I came across a buyer by chance and sold them to Germany for 2,400 roubles. Just three days ago, in the early evening, I went to the synagogue and what do I see? A Jew I don't know standing in a circle telling all the Jews about a rich moneylender living in his house who's been robbed. At the time he was robbed, his horses were his sole possession. These Jews told him to turn to me, and my conscience moved me. I took him to the *rebbe* and returned the value of the horses to him. I told him to swear not to reveal who paid him—otherwise the moneylender would come to me for his jewellery, which I knew nothing about. My 2,000 roubles all went to hell', he finished, his voice full of sadness.

'Who told you to confess, if nobody else knew anything about it?'

'Do you think my conscience would let me take Jewish horses just for money? Up until now, praise God, during my twenty-five years as a fence, I've never had anything like that on my conscience and I never want to!'

Everyone present smiled at this reasoning. He was a well-known fence and a rich horse-trader. He owned some 200 houses in town. Also, in Russian times he had served in a penal unit in the army for five years. It is worth mentioning why he was there—I've heard it from him personally.

He had a feud with the chief of the Russian secret police because he gave too little in bribes, so they decided to investigate him. The chief himself ran the investigation. But it was impossible to catch the horse-trader red-handed. Whole gangs of Gypsies brought him their spoils and he sold everything to Germany, getting richer and richer. Once a pair of highly valued racehorses was stolen from a local nobleman. The word was that the chief of police found them in the horse-trader's stable. He always kept a hundred or more horses there. The chief of police asked for the horses' certificate. The horse-dealer answered that he could not produce it until the next morning because his son, who had the certificate, was away. The chief detained the horses until morning. In the morning the horse-trader reported with the certificate. They went to the stable to check the description against the horses, but the horses were gone, though all the locks and bars were in place. The police had to pay him for the horses! But they swore revenge upon him. For half a year the chief roamed the local horse markets in disguise. One day, dressed as a Gypsy, he caught the horse-trader receiving horses from Gypsies and arrested him on the spot. So he had many different things on his conscience that didn't disturb him at all; yet he considered stealing Jewish horses a sin.

After long deliberations, during which some three geese were consumed along with a few bottles of vodka, naturally the bill was on me. It was decided that Stasiek and I were to provide a pair of good horses within a week, for which we were to receive no payment. I agreed, knowing that provoking a fight wasn't clever. Later when I told Stasiek everything, he agreed with me at once, saying that from the beginning he knew this would happen because fences never bought Jewish horses.

Translated from Polish by Frank L. Vigoda

PART III

New Views

Making a Space for Antisemitism: The Catholic Hierarchy and the Jews in the Early Twentieth Century

BRIAN PORTER

THE study of Catholic antisemitism in Poland is complicated by two competing but equally problematic assumptions. The first is that some fundamental characteristic of the Church in Poland (or perhaps Christianity more generally) has inevitably and necessarily generated hostility towards the Jews. Jacob Katz reports, for example, that

> it has been cogently argued by critics of the trend to eradicate antisemitic inferences [from Christian teaching] that such a revision would subvert the whole doctrinal edifice of Christianity. It has also been pointed out that the presentation of Christian doctrine even by the most sophisticated modern theologians retains the idea of Christian superiority, implying a concomitant negative evaluation of Jews and Judaism.[1]

In reference to Poland specifically, Ezra Mendelsohn claims that 'both Polish nationalism and Polish Catholicism were *by their very nature* exclusive, anti-pluralistic, and antisemitic'.[2] The second, alternative approach to Catholic antisemitism is an inversion of the first: the claim that the Church as such has been entirely innocent of prejudice, and that only a small handful of non-representative clerics have propagated hatred or intolerance. The best example of this defensive stance came from Cardinal Józef Glemp, the Polish primate, in a much-publicized sermon delivered in May 2000. Pope John Paul II had earlier instructed all Catholic institutions and local churches to confess publicly their historical sins, so as to approach the new millennium in a spirit of humility, contrition, and reconciliation.[3]

---

[1] J. Katz, *From Prejudice to Destruction: Antisemitism, 1700–1933* (Cambridge, 1980), 326. Haim Hillel Ben-Sasson also argued, in his survey of Jewish history, that intolerance is a basic and irredeemable feature of Christianity (see H. H. Ben-Sasson, *A History of the Jewish People* (Cambridge, 1976), 403).

[2] E. Mendelsohn, *The Jews of East Central Europe between the World Wars* (Bloomington, Ind., 1984), 82; my italics.

[3] The Pope's initial call for contrition came in the bull *Incarnationis mysterium*, issued on 29 Nov. 1998, <www.vatican.va/jubilee_2000/docs/documents/hf_jp-ii_doc_30111998_bolla-jubilee_en. html>. The Vatican then published, in Dec. 1999, a seminal text entitled *Memory and Reconciliation: The Church and the Faults of the Past*, <www.vatican.va/roman_curia/congregations/cfaith/ documents rc_con_cfaith_doc_20000307_memory-reconc-itc_en.html>.

Cardinal Glemp's sermon of apology was presented during an open-air mass in the centre of Warsaw. After some words of praise for the Polish clergy, the primate offered his 'confession':

Yet not every priest is saintly. That is why the flaws rooted in humanity are also reflected in the clergy. . . . I am moved to regret by those clergy who have lost their love for humanity and have cultivated their own private lives, focusing on holidays or comfortable apartments instead of devoting all their time to the poor, and particularly to the young. The loss of love for humanity is sometimes manifest in disrespect for people of other faiths, or in tolerating manifestations of antisemitism. I apologize for those who have not carried out faithfully their duties, particularly their pastoral or pedagogical duties, and who have neglected the teaching of religion.[4]

Prejudice appears here as an individual character flaw that can be redeemed by a more rigorous adherence to the Church's doctrines. Moreover, Cardinal Glemp admitted only that the clergy had 'tolerated' antisemitism, not that it had generated it. In the end, the primate's 'apology' served only to shift the blame for antisemitism away from the Church and onto individual sinners—by definition exceptions to the virtuous rule.

   Both of these approaches to Catholic antisemitism suffer, on the most basic level, from the same conceptual weakness. Both presume that we are dealing with a pair of static and coherent entities called 'the Polish Church', and 'Antisemitism'. Both imply that the Church is historically unchanging and internally homogeneous (fundamentally, despite isolated exceptions), and that antisemitism is an easily identifiable attribute which is either present or absent. It is much more productive, I would argue, to approach both antisemitism and Catholicism as *historical* phenomena, recognizing that both are historically contingent and always embedded in a rich context. Antisemitism is not something that essentially and eternally 'belongs' to any institution, any religion, or any community; it is not something that can be defined in a historically static or unchanging manner. Antisemitism is *historical* rather than *structural*. That is, it cannot be said to reside in or emanate from any particular institutional form, ideological or theological perspective, or social formation. Institutions, ideologies, theologies, and social structures can be configured in such a way as to make antisemitism more or less likely, but even then the actual emergence of hatred as a significant public phenomenon is dependent upon a vast array of historical contingencies. Groups like Catholics or Poles cannot be said to 'be' antisemitic, because the verb 'to be' here implies a degree of historical constancy and collective homogeneity that does not *ever* exist.

   It does not follow from this, however, that every incident of antisemitism has to be described in isolation, for generalizable conclusions are possible even when

---

[4] The text of Cardinal Glemp's sermon can be found in 'Prymas Polski wyznaje winy Kościoła', *Katolicka Agencja Informacyjna* (20 May 2000), <www.kai.pl/nowyserwis/newsroom.xml?id=64896>.

we abandon the simplicity of overgeneralization. Granting all due importance to contingency and variability, we can still recognize that certain discursive frameworks are more or less resistant to antisemitism, and others are more or less amenable to it. That overused and often misunderstood concept the 'discursive framework' is here meant to signify a set of ideas, terms, and rhetorical practices that structure and limit what we can say and (as follows) what we can think and imagine. As long as one remains within a given discursive framework, one's thoughts and actions are constrained in ways that are difficult to transcend; difficult, but not impossible, for such frameworks are always subject to change, expansion, contraction, and reconfiguration. These changes occur on the margins (virtually by definition, a discursive framework cannot undergo a sudden, fundamental transformation), but if you play at the margins long enough, you can profoundly alter the whole framework.[5] If we approach both Catholicism and antisemitism as examples of discursive frameworks—as bounded yet malleable conceptual spaces, not as static objects—then we can assess with more subtlety the relationship between Christianity and antisemitism in Poland.

And this leads to the main argument of this chapter: as recently as the 1880s Catholicism, *as it existed in Poland at the time*, was still somewhat resistant to expressions of antisemitism, *as it existed in Poland at the time*. Catholicism, in other words, was configured in such a way in the late nineteenth century as to make it hard for antisemites to express their views without moving to the very edges of the Catholic framework.[6] Catholicism and antisemitism did overlap at the time, but the common ground was much more confined than it would later become. If we move forward fifty years, to the 1930s, we see a different picture: the discursive boundaries of Catholicism in Poland had shifted to such a degree that antisemitism became not only possible, but also difficult to avoid. The upshot of this argument is that Catholicism in Poland isn't antisemitic in any sort of essential way, and that religion did not directly *generate* the forms of hatred that would become so deadly and virulent in the early twentieth century. None the less, Catholicism did *become* amenable to antisemitism in Poland, so much so that the Church in Poland between the wars was one of the country's leading sources of prejudice and animosity.

[5] For the theoretical background to this approach, one must cite the obvious seminal texts: P. Bourdieu, *In Other Words: Essays towards a Reflexive Sociology*, trans. M. Adamson (Cambridge, 1990); id., *Language and Symbolic Power*, ed. J. B. Thompson, trans. G. Raymond and M. Adamson (Cambridge, 1991); M. Foucault, *The Archeology of Knowledge*, trans. A. M. Sheridan Smith (New York, 1976); id., *Politics, Philosophy, Culture: Interviews and Other Writings, 1977–1984* (New York, 1988); id., *Power/Knowledge: Selected Interviews and Other Writings, 1972–1977* (Brighton, 1980).

[6] Léon Poliakov makes a similar claim in describing Catholicism during the papacy of Pius IX, but argues that the situation began to change under Leo XIII. In Poland, as I will argue, the change came just a bit later. (L. Poliakov, *The History of Antisemitism*, vol. iv: *Suicidal Europe, 1870–1933*, trans. G. Klim (New York, 1985), 33.) Peter Pulzer makes a similar set of arguments about late 19th-century Germany, although he suggests that Catholicism became more amenable to antisemitism over time in the Habsburg empire (see P. Pulzer, *The Rise of Political Antisemitism in Germany and Austria*, 2nd edn. (London, 1988), 156, 266).

To find out when and why this happened, let us turn to 1883, one of the most important years in the history of antisemitism in Poland. Prior to the 1880s modern antisemitism was perceived in Poland as a foreign problem, unlikely to disturb Poland's Jews seriously. Writing later, the magazine *Izraelita* looked back fondly to those years:

Until a short time ago, the main context for the attitude of the Christian population towards the Jews was a dislike rooted only in the distinctiveness of the Jewish population. . . . We do not think we would be mistaken in stating that this mutual dislike lacked any deep psychological foundation, that stronger feelings or emotions did not come into play, and that, had things gone well, this dislike could have easily been softened and even uprooted. . . . Antisemitism in its modern form is not the creation of local social conditions, but a symptom of a sickness incubated in foreign societies and carried to our land as part of an epidemic.[7]

Starting in the 1880s, this 'epidemic' would spread to the Polish lands. When a pogrom broke out in Warsaw in 1881, the city's intelligentsia was shocked. Riots shook the city for three days in December of that year, and the Russian authorities arrested 2,600 people before the violence ended. The pogrom left two people dead, twenty-four injured, and almost a thousand families financially devastated. In the months that followed, about 1,000 Jews from Warsaw alone emigrated to the United States.[8] The liberal journalist Aleksander Świętochowski was forced to admit, in an article revealingly entitled 'Without Illusions', that 'among the European nations we do not constitute an ideal exception'.[9] The novelist Eliza Orzeszkowa responded to the pogrom with a small book called *On the Jews and the Jewish Question*. As she put it, her reaction to the 'Warsaw tempest' could be summarized in three words: disgrace, pity, and regret: 'disgrace over the antisocial and anti-civilized acts; extreme pity for the suffering; burning regret that the fruits of so many years of effort by noble and enlightened minds had once again fallen into the flames of hatred'.[10] In 1881 there was still a sense of disjuncture between the liberal tolerance of the mainstream intelligentsia and the 'anti-civilized' behaviour of the violent mob, but a little more than a year later the 'flames of hatred' would be ignited in the polite world of the Warsaw press. In January of 1883 a little-known journalist named Jan Jeleński was catapulted into notoriety when he bought a weekly magazine called *Rola* and immediately transformed it into Poland's first programmatically antisemitic periodical. This was a vile publication, preaching

[7] *Izraelita*, 4 (1887), repr. in A. Żbikowski (ed.), *Dzieje Żydów w Polsce: Ideologia antysemicka, 1848–1914. Wybór tekstów źródłowych* (Warsaw, 1994). For more on the attitudes and ideas expressed in the Jewish press of the time, see M. Fuks, *Prasa żydowska w Warszawie, 1823–1939* (Warsaw, 1979), 41–123.

[8] On the pogrom, see A. Cała, *Asymilacja Żydów w Królestwie Polskim, 1864–1897: Postawy, konflikty, stereotypy* (Warsaw, 1989), 268–78.

[9] A. Świętochowski, 'Bez złudzeń', *Prawda*, 1 (19–31 Dec. 1881), 625–7.

[10] E. Orzeszkowa, *O Żydach i kwestyi żydowskiej* (Vilna, 1882), 5.

an amoral struggle for survival with the Jews (and the Germans), and spreading hate-filled antisemitic imagery. A columnist for *Rola* recited the major themes of 'modern' antisemitism:

The source of antisemitism is much deeper than its opponents think. It burst forth from the soul of humanity. That humanity, tyrannized, oppressed, defiled, and demoralized by the golden calf, has opened its eyes. We have had enough materialism, greed, enrichment; enough positivism, atheism, and bestial exploitation; we have had enough wallowing in the mud. . . . That humanity has risen up in anger against the demoralization of materialism and gold, and has turned against those who love Mammon the most. That's antisemitism![11]

Here was the dehumanization of the Jews (they were 'tyrannizing' humanity, but they were clearly not part of it); here was the equation of Jews with capitalist liberalism; here, on the pages of *Rola*, was the whole ideological structure built in the 1870s by Wilhelm Marr, Adolf Stöcker, Eugen Dühring, and the like.

Significantly, the leading Catholic magazine of the Warsaw archdiocese, *Przegląd Katolicki*, was unambiguous in its condemnation of Jeleński and *Rola*. Denouncing the whole concept of a 'struggle for survival' as anti-Christian, an anonymous editorialist urged *Rola* to take a different path:

Rola is fulfilling its civic duty when it complains about our lack of attention to industry and trade, when it calls for competition in these areas with the Jews, when it criticizes Jewish usury, etc. But it can do all of this without descending from the position of Christian love, without soaking its pen in hatred. . . . The German, and the Jew, and every human is a brother to the Pole, if the Pole recognizes God as his Father . . .[12]

In another article *Przegląd Katolicki* reiterated that it was acceptable to criticize the specific actions of any individual or group, but that one must 'never forget that the Jews are our neighbours'.[13] This is not to say that the late nineteenth-century Catholic press was a bastion of enlightened tolerance. Catholic papers did occasionally repeat very old Judaeophobic prejudices, some of them quite loathsome. For example, later that same year (1883), *Przegląd Katolicki* discussed 'the question of the ritual use of Christian blood', accepting the possibility that some 'fanatics' among the Jews might indeed participate in such rites, even though most Jews did not know about this.[14] But this type of article was rare; for the most part the Catholic press of the day simply was not interested in the Jews. There were numerous articles attacking liberalism, urban growth, capitalism, and modernity in general, but in almost all cases the connection between these evils and Judaism was left in the silent margins—perhaps implied to those reading between the lines, but

[11] Pancerny [T. Jeske-Choiński], 'Na posterunku', *Rola*, 6 (29 Jan.–10 Feb. 1883), 7.

[12] 'Walka o byt', *Przegląd Katolicki*, 7 (3–15 Feb. 1883), 105.

[13] 'Objaśnienie "Roli" ', *Przegląd Katolicki*, 10 (24 Feb.–8 Mar. 1883), 155.

[14] 'W kwestji rytualnego używania krwi chrześcijanskiej', *Przegląd Katolicki*, 13 (17–29 Mar. 1883), 204.

rarely articulated. Even extended critiques of that old Catholic *bête noire* free-masonry passed without reference to the Jews.[15]

Now let us move forward several decades. In 1920, during the Polish–Soviet war, a group of Polish bishops composed a letter outlining their understanding of the ongoing military campaign:

The race which has the leadership of Bolshevism in its hands has already in the past sub-jugated the whole world by means of gold and the banks, and now, driven by the everlasting imperialistic greed that flows in its veins, is already aiming at the final subjugation of the nations under the yoke of its rule. . . . The hatred of Bolshevism is directed against Christ and his Church, especially because those who are the leaders of Bolshevism bear in their blood the traditional hatred for Christianity. Bolshevism is in truth the embodiment and incarnation of the spirit of Antichrist on earth.[16]

This passage exemplified Catholic discussions of the Jews in the inter-war years. Even the most virulent antisemites in the Church condemned physical brutality, but such protestations were usually hedged with expressions of understanding for those who engaged in violence. This 1936 announcement by the Katolicka Agencja Prasowa (Catholic Press Agency of Poland) was typical:

All excesses and brutal means of war are unworthy of the name Christian, and ultimately do not attain their goal. The Catholic clergy certainly does not approve of any violence and does not neglect to remind the faithful that the highest commandment of Christian ethics is the commandment to love God and love one's neighbour without regard to race, nationality, or religion. . . . But Jews who complain about excesses ought to remember that they are not without fault in this regard.[17]

The official stance of the Polish hierarchy towards the Jews was articulated in Cardinal August Hlond's pastoral letter of 29 February 1936, *On Catholic Moral Principles*. Here he wrote:

It is a fact that Jews are waging war against the Catholic Church, that they are steeped in free-thinking and constitute the vanguard of atheism, the Bolshevik movement, and revo-lutionary activity. It is a fact that Jews have a corrupting influence on morals, and that their publishing houses are spreading pornography. It is true that Jews are perpetrating fraud, practising usury, and dealing in prostitution. It is true that, from a religious and ethical point of view, Jewish youth are having a negative influence on the Catholic youth in our schools. But let us be fair. Not all Jews are this way.

Having said this, he did emphasize that

one may love one's own nation more, but one may not hate anyone. Not even Jews. . . . One should stay away from the harmful moral influence of Jews, keep away from their anti-

---

[15] See e.g. the long series of articles from 1897 entitled 'Masonry and Socialism': Cam. Segr., 'Masonerya i socyalizm', *Przegląd Katolicki*, 1–8 (7 Jan.–24 Feb. 1897); or, from the same year, K. W. M. Dębicki, 'Owoce pozytywizmu', 1–4 (7–25 Jan. 1897).

[16] This document is translated in R. Modras, *The Catholic Church and Antisemitism: Poland, 1933–1939* (Chur, 1994), 118.   [17] As cited ibid. 316.

Christian culture, and especially boycott the Jewish press and demoralizing Jewish publications. But it is forbidden to assault, beat up, maim, or slander Jews.[18]

This text is disturbing enough, but it appears as a voice of calm and restraint when compared to the popular Catholic press of the inter-war years. Catholic newspapers like *Mały Dziennik* and demagogues like Father Stanisław Trzeciak were among Poland's most influential sources of antisemitic vitriol throughout the inter-war years, and they were rarely restrained by Cardinal Hlond's efforts to be 'fair'.

All of this compels us to look again at the initial reluctance of Catholics in the 1880s to embrace modern antisemitism when it first appeared in Poland. It turns out that the configuration of Catholicism—the boundaries of Catholic thought, the limits of Catholic rhetoric—*changed*, and continues to change, and always will change. Discursive frameworks (and Catholicism is one such framework) are indeed constitutive of thought and imagination, but they are also mutable; indeed, mutability lies in their very nature. The change in this case did not constitute a reversal of Catholic teaching—prejudice was abundant enough in the 1880s, and even in the 1930s Catholic antisemitism differed in significant ways from secular antisemitism—but there was none the less an important evolution in the shape and the limits of Catholic discourse.

If we return to the late nineteenth century, we see that the public declarations of the official institutions of the Catholic Church were characterized by a vehement opposition to 'modernity' (a term that particularly merits quotation marks in this case, since Catholic authors cultivated their own idiosyncratic, and somewhat phantasmal, definition of modernity). Leo XIII made some gestures towards the modern world with seminal texts like *Rerum novarum*, but even he was a deeply conservative man.[19] Pius X was even more resolute and unyielding in his resistance to the dawning twentieth century. His encyclical *Pascendi dominici gregis* (1907) was one of the most sweeping condemnations of modernism to emerge from the Church.[20] The problem with antisemitism around the turn of the century, from a Catholic perspective, was that it was quintessentially modern. As historians have noted for a long time now, the antisemitism that emerged in the late nineteenth century was quite new, even though it drew upon some older traditions of Judaeophobic rhetoric. It was different because of its biological, pseudo-scientific racism; it was different because of its links to a Spencerian vision of a struggle for survival; it

[18] August Kardynał Hlond, 'O katolickie zasady moralne', in *Na straży sumienia narodu: Wybór pism i przemówień* (Warsaw, 1999), 164. An English version of Hlond's letter is reprinted in Modras, *The Catholic Church and Antisemitism*, 346.

[19] Leo XIII, *Rerum novarum*, in C. Carlen (ed.), *The Papal Encyclicals 1878–1903* (Raleigh, NC, 1981).

[20] Pius X, *Pascendi dominici gregis*, in C. Carlen (ed.), *The Papal Encyclicals 1903–1939* (Raleigh, NC, 1981). On Pius X's campaign against modernism, see M. R. O'Connell, *Critics on Trial: An Introduction to the Catholic Modernist Crisis* (Washington, 1994). See also the somewhat sensationalist account in T. Bokenkotter, *Church and Revolution: Catholics in the Struggle for Democracy and Social Justice* (New York, 1998).

was different, in sum, because it was *modern*.[21] Of course antisemitism was *also* profoundly reactionary: people like Jeleński in Poland, the anti-Dreyfusards in France,
Wilhelm Marr in Germany, and so many others, were resolutely anti-liberal; but
this was not necessarily the same as being anti-modern.[22] To be more precise (and
to avoid getting hung up on defining 'modernism'), late nineteenth-century antisemitism presumed an essentially secular, scientific, worldly approach to human
communities, and for Catholics this constituted the founding sin of modernism.
Before the First World War there was simply no space within Catholicism for *any*
flirtation with modernism or modernity—not even an anti-liberal modernity. As
the Polish priest Jan Rostworowski put it in 1906,

That which the proponents of coming to terms [with modernity] will never be able to understand fully enough is that the very *spirit*, the very direction of mind and heart that modern
education produces, is anti-Christian. . . . The Church . . . if it allowed that spirit in any
form, in even the most holy and lustrous garment, to penetrate its ranks, would have to deny
[the Church's] very essence as the Kingdom of God on Earth.[23]

   Jan Jeleński and his ilk were not content with religious conversion; they were not
even terribly interested in religion. Of course, many antisemites used the expression 'Christian' a lot, but they employed it only as a code word for 'not-Jewish'.
Jeleński tried in vain to placate his clerical critics with a short article entitled 'A
Misunderstanding', in which he insisted that 'from our first issue we stood on a
foundation of "Christian love", and we will continue to do so'.[24] Without trying
to assess Jeleński's capacity for 'love', it is clear that he was committing three basic
sins from a Catholic perspective: first, he based his world-view on science and
reason (albeit a twisted science, and some highly irrational reasoning); secondly, he
divided the world into Poland and its enemies, rather than into believers and non-
believers; thirdly, and above all, he treated Christians and Jews as rival human
communities, without recognizing the Church's status as a spiritual body that was
only *partially* of this world. In his 1876 book *The Jews, the Germans, and Us* Jeleński
introduced a new way of talking about international relations: 'It is not enough to
know if the Jews and Germans, as strata made up of individuals, are this way or that,
are bad or good, are guilty or innocent', he wrote. 'It is, rather, necessary above all *to
consider what sort of position we have to take right now in regard to those two elements*.'[25]
Jeleński dismissed the long tradition of itemizing the negative characteristics of

---

[21] For a relatively recent affirmation of this position, see H. A. Strauss (ed.), *Hostages of Modernization: Studies on Modern Antisemitism, 1870–1933/39* (Berlin, 1993).

[22] I am thus somewhat more restrictive in my use of the term 'anti-modernism' than is Shulamit
Volkov in her work *The Rise of Popular Antimodernism in Germany: The Urban Master Artisans,
1873–1896* (Princeton, 1978).

[23] J. Rostworowski, *Liberalny katolicyzm* (Kraków, 1906), 48.

[24] 'Nieporozumienie', *Rola*, 8 (12–24 Feb. 1883), 11.

[25] J. Jeleński, *Żydzi, Niemcy i my* (Warsaw, 1876), 5–6.

Judaism, and he was particularly opposed to that old Enlightenment project to 'improve' the Jews. Instead, he argued that the 'nature' of the Jews should be set aside as irrelevant; it was not a question of how the Jews could be made more like the Poles, but how 'we' should deal with 'them'. Turning to the Germans, Jeleński asked rhetorically:

When have we ever been in a state of agreement and friendship with the Germans? History will answer us: *never*. For centuries Germanism has set upon the peaceful inhabitants along the Elbe, Oder, and Vistula, who have nothing rapacious in their nature, and for centuries struggle has been unavoidable. . . . From those prehistoric epochs to the present moment the intention of the Germans has not changed at all, and therefore today the struggle seems to be as necessary and unavoidable as it is necessary for one who is attacked to preserve his own individuality, his own existence.[26]

Jeleński described a 'struggle between tribes', in which it was pointless to try to reform the other side. Instead, it was necessary to resolve 'our' weaknesses so as to better compete with 'them'. A close colleague of Jeleński, Konstanty Wzdulski, wrote several years later that the Poles themselves were responsible for the 'Jewish question' as long as they refused to recognize the Jews as foreigners. 'We let the wolf into the sheep pen, and the wolf did what wolves do,' he wrote, 'but the shepherd did not fulfil his obligation—he did not defend the flock entrusted to him—and the responsibility falls on him, not on anyone else.' Just as wolves had an unchanging nature, so would the Jews always be dangerous aliens. To imagine that one could reform or assimilate the Jewish community was as absurd as trying to domesticate wild beasts.[27] Thus we see two fundamental innovations: the Jews were reconceptualized as an eternal other and (even more importantly) as an irreconcilable foe. This acceptance of the Spencerian 'struggle for survival' distinguished Jeleński from the traditional right, and *Rola*'s contributors regularly used the phrase 'modern conservatism'.[28]

At the same time, paradoxically, *Rola* tried to exemplify an older conservatism based on tradition, stability, authority, and faith, and Jeleński regularly praised the Church, the nobility, and even the tsar.[29] It was not easy to reconcile the conservative ideals of the aristocracy and the clerical hierarchy with the construction of a 'modern' conservatism based on 'science' and an amoral vision of eternal struggle. When Wzdulski proposed the immediate expulsion of all Jews, he apologetically admitted that 'such seemingly inhuman ostracism' would return Polish law to the

---

[26] Ibid. 26.

[27] K. Wzdulski, *Żydzi polscy w świetle prawdy* (Warsaw, 1887), 40.

[28] The expression 'modern conservatism' can be found in Pancerny [T. Jeske-Choiński], 'Na posterunku', *Rola*, 1 (17–28 Apr. 1883), 8–9; Pancerny, 'Na posterunku', *Rola*, 1 (15–26 May 1883), 7–8; Pancerny, 'Na posterunku', *Rola*, 1 (18–30 June 1883), 7–8.

[29] C. Reklewski, 'Z teki wieśniaka', *Rola*, 1 (22 Jan.–3 Feb. 1883), 3–5; 'Czego chcemy? II', *Rola*, 1 (1–13 Jan. 1883), 1.

Middle Ages. He was angered by the 'need' to adopt a brutalized Spencerism in his war with the Jews.

[The Jews] are the most dangerous and most threatening representatives of the struggle for survival, against which gentleness, sweetness, patience, and above all justice and Christian morality are only infantile illusions. The Jews are a nation of positivists—and they will never betray the principle of 'whoever is stronger is better'. For several thousand years before the appearance of today's positivist–materialist science, they were total positivists in practice—and aside from matter, that is, earthly wealth, they saw nothing loftier.

This reasoning drove Wzdulski to a point of frustration often demonstrated on the pages of *Rola*: he wanted to embrace an unqualified vision of struggle, but he could not do so. He believed that 'the idea of brotherhood is a false idea. . . . It has brought those societies which believe in it not gains, but losses.' None the less, Wzdulski described this as a 'Christian' idea, for which countries like Poland had to pay a heavy price. The same 'moral' principles that he offered as the mark of Christian superiority were also, in his view, the cause of Poland's downfall.[30] Similarly, the antisemitic publicist Teodor Jeske-Choiński recognized the conflict between an ideology of struggle and any ethical system, be it Christian or 'modern':

The struggle for survival is not a song of forgiveness and mutual love, because [it involves] a defence of the exploited against the exploiters. And wherever people defend themselves, the meaning of 'humanitarian considerations', even the most just, vanishes. . . . Unqualified tolerance, particularly regarding religion, is a valuable achievement of our century. It is only unfortunate that the struggle for survival has formed us differently, that it forces us necessarily to exclusivity. There are too many Jews among us and we have too little time to attempt to incorporate them into our organism. Anyway, would such an experiment be successful? . . . Let us learn solidarity and exclusivity from the Jews.[31]

This tone of regret was common. It was as if Jeske-Choiński were accepting a doctrine of unending struggle and exclusivity against his will, with the understanding that it contradicted his Catholic upbringing. This embrace of Spencerian rhetoric continued as the radical-right national movement developed and grew, but the undertone of regret faded away. Roman Dmowski, the leader of the radical right in the early twentieth century, even attacked Jeleński for being *too* eager to appease the Church. In the 1903 party platform of the Stronnictwo Demokratyczno-Narodowe (Democratic National Party, the forerunner of the Endecja), we find the promise to 'establish the principle of control by public opinion over the policies of the Church hierarchy and the behaviour of the civic clergy'. This was identical to the position of liberals all over Europe: the Church was being cast as a civic institution, not a sacred body. But, more disturbingly, Dmowski was unapologetic in his embrace of the 'struggle for survival'. In 1902 he described his world-view as 'a

[30] Wzdulski, *Żydzi polscy w świetle prawdy*, 16, 32, 37–8.
[31] Pancerny [T. Jeske-Choiński], 'Na posterunku', *Rola*, 1 (22 Jan.–3 Feb. 1883), 8–9.

philosophy of national struggle and oppression. Perhaps. But what if that struggle and that oppression are realities and universal peace and universal freedom are fictions? One must have the courage to look the truth in the eye.'[32]

The official representatives of the Church could not tolerate this position. A Poznań priest by the name of Ignacy Geppert wrote in 1903 (in a small book bearing the Church's *imprimatur*) that the nationalists had to be 'stifled and destroyed' because their main loyalty was to the nation, not to their faith. This was demonstrated by their effort to place the 'struggle for survival' above Christian morality. 'Just as in the world of nature one may not act against the laws governing the universe,' Geppert wrote, 'so in the world of the spirit one must always and everywhere take into account the eternal commandments of morality.' The nationalists were drawn to such moral relativism, Geppert believed, because they had fallen victim to the allure of modernism. 'The whole membership of the Stronnictwo Demokratyczno-Narodowe, in so far as they agree with the spiritual theories of their leaders, are outside the limits of the Catholic Church,' he wrote, 'and a considerable portion of them might even be outside the limits of Christianity. The vast devastation in the Endek mind was caused, albeit unconsciously, by that which is today so energetically attacked and defended: modernism.' Geppert went on to cite Pius X's *Pascendi* for support in his argument that nationalism was just another form of the modernist plague which the Church dedicated itself to resisting.[33]

Catholic authors, publicists, and clerics were thus in a unique situation in the late nineteenth and early twentieth centuries. On the one hand, Catholics *did* have a tradition of Judaeophobia, and there are plenty of examples of hostility that one could cite. On the other hand, there was a gap between the antisemitism of the day and the Catholicism of the day, because of the former's focus on that quintessentially modern doctrine, the amoral struggle for survival. Back in 1896 a priest named Maryan Morawski had tried to balance his own antipathy towards the Jews with the Church's principled opposition to modern antisemitism, and it was not easy. Writing in the Kraków paper *Przegląd Powszechny*, Morawski affirmed that Jews were guided by a moral code 'lower than that of Christianity', and that they had for centuries been 'preparing for the rule of free-thinking and atheism'. He feared the effective organizational skills of the Jews, and believed in the conspiratorial myths familiar to all antisemites. Significantly, however, Morawski's 1896 article was entitled 'Asemitism', and he struggled to find a way to fit his prejudices within the limitations of Catholic teaching by creating a form of Judaeophobia distinct from the antisemitism of his day.[34] This was difficult, for as Morawski himself

---

[32] R. Dmowski, *Myśli nowoczesnego Polaka* (Lwów, 1902), 87. For more on this topic, see B. Porter, *When Nationalism Began to Hate: Imagining Modern Politics in Nineteenth-Century Poland* (New York, 2000).

[33] F. Kujawiński [Ignacy Geppert], *Stronnictwo Demokratyczno-Narodowe w świetle nauki katolickiej* (Poznań, 1913), 7, 40, 47. The identity of F. Kujawiński was revealed later that same year in Hozakowski, *O katolickie podstawy Narodowej Demokracyi* (Poznań, 1913), 141.

[34] M. Morawski SJ, 'Asemityzm', *Przegląd Powszechny*, 49 (Feb. 1896), 161–89.

stated, 'the Christian conscience, to which both philosemites and antisemites appeal, sometimes vacillates, not knowing where duty lies'. One should favour fellow Christians in one's economic dealings, one should fight liberalism (which Morawski considered quintessentially Jewish), and one should avoid excessively close social relations with Jews. But any repeal of legal equality was out of the question, in Morawski's opinion, and violence was most certainly to be avoided:

A crime is always a crime, a greater evil for society than any material harm. Abuse of the Jews can be psychologically explained, but never morally excused. Every Christian and every Christian society ought to condemn such acts thoroughly and without reservations. And if, God forbid, [a pogrom] would happen here, [the Christian] could do nothing better than go out into the streets and, at the risk of his own life, defend the Jews from harm—and protect our people from committing a crime. If it is wrong to allow violence against the Jews, it is therefore also wrong to incite [*hecować*] the populace against them—that is, to provoke the hatred of the people with the spoken or written word, to rouse [the people] to anger, bitterness, or revenge against the Jew. . . . Even if there were no other way [to resist Jewish influence], goals never justify evil means.

Morawski's argument casts some light on the seemingly paradoxical behaviour of Christian antisemites like Zofia Kossak, who demonstrated phenomenal courage during the Holocaust by defending Jews against Nazi violence.[35] But more interesting here than Morawski's call for non-violence is his refusal to accept racialist thinking. 'Much is said today about race,' he wrote, 'but perhaps not enough attention is paid to history.' Racial thinking led, in Morawski's view, to a tendency towards unjust overgeneralization: 'An ethical type, however correct on average, cannot and must not be taken as a measure for judging in advance an individual Jew; that would be a gross injustice [*krzycząca niesprawiedliwość*].' And although Morawski rejected the possibility of secular assimilation, he repeated the long-standing Christian argument that converts from Judaism be welcomed into the Christian community.[36] Morawski's article proved influential; his terminology was taken up (with attribution) by Warsaw's *Przegląd Katolicki* specifically in the context of refuting *Rola*'s antisemitism. Jeleński might claim to be Christian, this anonymous author (identified only as a priest) wrote, but there was ample evidence that *Rola* was outside the bounds of Catholicism.

A Christian periodical ought to be characterized by two things: truth and love. Let us defend truth without violating love; let us defend love with respect for the truth. Yet what about that mockery of the Jews and that abusiveness for the entertainment of the readership? Is that an act of Christian love, a constructive act? Would *Rola* not be better off to work in a positive manner, developing serious principles along the lines, for example, of Father Morawski's article, 'Asemitism?'[37]

---

[35] Kossak's story is discussed in Modras, *The Catholic Church and Antisemitism*, 397.

[36] Morawski, 'Asemityzm'.

[37] K. A. Z. 'W odpowiedzi "Roli" ', *Tygodnik Katolicki*, 44 (29 Oct. 1896), 703.

Morawski himself offered an example of this sort of 'positive work' two years later (1898) in a special supplement to *Przegląd Powszechny* published in response to the declaration of martial law in Galicia after violent pogroms racked the province. In an appalling foreshadowing of the tendency between the wars to blame the victims of antisemitic violence, Morawski lamented that 'the Jews were formally adopting a provocative stance, which will only worsen the situation'; but this wasn't his primary message. Rather, his main concern (in good conservative fashion) was to avoid further violence and re-establish order. To do this, he argued, Catholics needed to work harder to improve the lot of the peasants, to 'consider their economic and moral interests, and together with them to work for the improvement of the country'.[38]

At the end of this article Morawski offered a hint about how one gets from this more guarded rhetoric to the naked antisemitism and the inter-war Polish Church. He did so by calling for 'modern Catholic social action' (using the Polish word *nowożytny*, which established at least a little distance from the dangerous term *modernizm*). In Poland, as elsewhere, once Catholic publicists and clerics began to realize that the modern world was here to stay, they had to figure out how to live with it. They needed to find a way to become modern themselves, without sacrificing any of their basic ideals; they needed to work out what elements of their hitherto reactionary views could be sacrificed in the name of reconciling themselves with modernity. They did this by accepting one key principle of the modernist repertoire –the idea that human communities were locked in a struggle for survival—while continuing to reject the rest. This, in turn, allowed Catholics to slide more easily towards the rhetoric of modern antisemitism.

As recently as the 1880s the very expression 'struggle for survival' could never have appeared in any Catholic text (at least not any approved Catholic text). This is precisely what angered the authors in *Przegląd Katolicki* about Jan Jeleński's *Rola* in 1883, and inspired the latter to insist that 'by the slogan "the struggle for survival", which the commentators of *Przegląd Katolicki* consider a reason to make unfair accusations about us, we understand not a ruthless, materialist struggle, but quite the contrary, a struggle of spiritual forces against the forces of the golden calf'.[39] As we have seen, this was not entirely correct, but even if it had been, the very phrase was still considered too dangerous among Catholics in the early 1880s. The whole idea was simply too tied up with liberal visions about progress through struggle. The whole Social Darwinist school of thought was rooted in the presumption that competition led to the collapse of the weak and the advance of the strong, in turn generating 'progress'—a word that was anathema to Catholics at the time. But in the 1890s there appeared a new version of the struggle for survival, one which was entirely severed from its liberal moorings. The new concept of struggle—

---

[38] M. Morawski, 'Co teraz robić?', *Przegląd Powszechny*, 58 (Aug. 1898), 1–8.
[39] 'Nieporozumienie', *Rola*, 8 (12–24 Feb. 1883), 11.

represented in Poland by the early National Democrats, and all over Europe by the antisemitic movement—posited an image of struggle that implied no progress. Societies were locked in eternal conflict—conflict that was going nowhere and accomplishing nothing. If we read Catholic publications from the 1890s and early 1900s, we see a striking development. From a position of unyielding resistance to antisemitism because of its links to Social Darwinism, we see the appropriation of this *new* ideology of struggle.

The earliest example that I have found comes from 1900, from the pages of *Przegląd Katolicki* itself. In May and June 1900 there appeared in this magazine a multi-part essay called 'On Antisemitism' by an author who signed his name only as 'J.b.P.'. Like Morawski before him, this author initially insisted that Catholicism had nothing in common with antisemitism, which was 'a specifically Protestant product'.[40] With each successive instalment in this series, however, J.b.P. slid closer and closer to an identifiably modern antisemitism, evolving as it were from week to week. In the second article he argued that the papacy had long been sympathetic to the Jews on the grounds that 'the justice which is owed to everyone is also owed to the Jews', but he went on to itemize the many reasons why the Jews might merit persecution from institutions less virtuous than the Holy Church. Among these Jewish vices, the author maintained, were unethical trading practices, profanation of the Sacred Host, and ritual murder (a charge he considered 'proven').[41] As odious as all this was, it was nothing new; indeed, what is striking here is the anachronistic nature of J.b.P.'s charges. But soon he took the step that distinguished traditional Catholic Judaeophobia from modern antisemitism: the conviction that human communities were immutable, that conflict was inevitable and eternal, and that sin resided in races rather than individuals:

The Jews are entirely distinct; they are a society which, in their opinion, is the only one which deserves to exist, because they believe that they possess the absolute truth. They demand power for themselves in the name of that truth, and since they do not have their own fatherland beneath their feet, they regard the whole earth as their fatherland and want to be supreme on [the earth] and command others. Money, for them, is never a goal, only a means for attaining power. . . . There is really only one path to the conquest of the earth for the Jews . . . the steady destruction of Christianity in its religious and social aspect. There is, simply put, not a single method for undermining Christianity which the Jews have missed. Be it anti-Christian periodicals or newspapers, or pornography, or providing the means for decadence or drunkenness, or the trade in live human products, or providing the means for minors to cheat their parents, or the bribing of public and private servants and bureaucrats—in all these areas the leaders, if not the only practitioners, are Jews.[42]

After this litany of evil, J.b.P. returned to the topic of 'Protestant' antisemitism, which he claimed was distinguished by its use of 'improper means' to combat the Jewish menace. Moreover, antisemites refused to recognize that the Jews had their

[40] J.b.P., 'Coś o antysemityźmie', *Przegląd Katolicki*, 22 (31 May 1900), 339.
[41] Ibid. 23 (7 June 1900), 360.   [42] Ibid. 361.

good side, too: their piety, their strong families (with 'the absolute dominance of the husband, the deep submissiveness of the wife, and the discipline and obedience of the children'), their strong social bonds, and their devotion to their community.[43] J.b.P. did indeed want to retain his self-image as a man free of antisemitic sentiments, and he insisted that Christians must never employ violence or hatred in their struggle with the Jews. He even cautioned that economic struggle was both futile and morally problematic, because immoral means would be needed to beat the Jews at their own game. However, in the last instalment of the series J.b.P. fell into the dangerous language Catholics had previously tried to avoid: 'this is a struggle, a struggle which will be a matter of life or death'.[44] To my knowledge, this is the first appearance in the Catholic press of this previously anathematized Spencerian concept. J.b.P. worked hard to dissociate the 'struggle for survival' from its links to 'modern' social thought, but he had helped to introduce this virus into the world of Catholic rhetoric in Poland.

It would only take another decade or so for this sort of language to spread throughout Catholic circles in Poland. By the 1920s one could find struggle-for-survival terminology in the pastoral letters of the bishops, in the Catholic press, in sermons, etc. Catholics would typically try to contain the implications of this rhetoric, usually by saying that the struggle for survival with the Jews had to be limited to non-violent means, but such protestations faded alongside the unrestrained hatred and fear that emanated from the Church—from the primate down to the parish priests. The Church continued to condemn most manifestations of modernity—indeed, they identified the Jews as the primary agents of modernity (much as antisemites had been doing all along)—but they had found their point of contact with the twentieth century, and for several decades they clung to it as one of the central tropes of their public activities. They had enmeshed themselves in this world by accepting a vision of social interaction according to which communities battled incessantly with other communities. What Father Rostworowski had characterized as the battle between the 'spirit of modernity' and Christianity became a battle between the Masonic–Jewish–Bolshevik conspiracy and the Catholic Church. What had been a battle of ideas and ideals (modernity versus Catholicism) came to be portrayed as a very earthly struggle for supremacy between two human communities.

[43] Ibid. 24 (14 June 1900), 375–7.   [44] Ibid. 25 (21 June 1900), 395.

Polish 'Neighbours' and German Invaders: Anti-Jewish Violence in the Białystok District during the Opening Weeks of Operation Barbarossa

ALEXANDER B. ROSSINO

SINCE the early 1990s, research about the genocide of the Jews in eastern Europe has focused increasingly on developments in the so-called 'regional periphery' of Nazi-dominated Europe, rather than on the decision-making process at the 'centre' in Berlin. As a result of this shift, a number of scholarly studies have begin to take into account the role east Europeans played in the destruction of Jewish communities during the German occupation.[1] One book in particular, *Neighbors: The Destruction of the Jewish Community in Jedwabne, Poland*, by Jan T. Gross,[2] sparked a storm of debate in Poland about the complicity of non-Jewish Poles in the murder of Polish Jews. By writing that Poles in Jedwabne and other small towns west of Białystok had taken part in the murder of local Jews, Gross challenged the long-cherished notion in Poland that all Poles—Christians and Jews—had suffered equally under the Nazis. Gross's description of the spontaneous massacre of Jedwabne's Jews by their Polish neighbours also deeply offended Poles, who considered his version of events one-sided and inaccurate. Indeed, *Neighbors* contributed to an ongoing re-examination of the history of the Holocaust in Poland, but Gross's failure to examine German documentary sources fundamentally flawed his depiction of the events. The result was a skewed history that did not investigate either SS operations in the region or German interaction with the Polish population. This chapter therefore attempts to redress this oversight by describing the

---

[1] C. Gerlach, *Kalkulierte Morde. Die deutsche Wirtschafts- und Vernichtungspolitik in Weissrussland 1941 bis 1944* (Hamburg, 1999); S. Spector, *The Holocaust of Volhynian Jews 1941–1944* (Jerusalem, 1990); M. Dean, *Collaboration in the Holocaust: Crimes of the Local Police in Belorussia and Ukraine, 1941–44* (New York, 2000); B. Musial, *'Konterrevolutionäre Elemente sind zu erschiessen'. Die Brutalisierung des deutsch-sowjetischen Krieges im Sommer 1941* (Berlin, 2000); S. Cholawsky, *The Jews of Bielorussia during World War II* (Amsterdam, 1998); and D. Pohl, *Nationalsozialistische Judenverfolgung in Ostgalizien 1941–1944. Organisation und Durchführung eines staatlichen Massenverbrechens* (Munich, 1997). [2] Princeton: Princeton University Press, 2001.

historical context within which the pogroms in Jedwabne and elsewhere in the
Białystok district occurred. For in fact a detailed exploration of SS activities in the
region reveals that the outbreak of 'popular' violence against Jews was directly
related to policies that the SS implemented during the brief 'transitional phase'
from the targeted killing of Jewish men in June–July 1941 to the comprehensive
annihilation of Soviet Jewry in August 1941.[3]

The Nazi regime defined the war against the USSR as a conflict of mutually
antagonistic ideologies, the ultimate aim of which was to destroy what Adolf Hitler
commonly referred to as the 'Judaeo-Bolshevik' system. Because National Socialism conflated notions of ideological identity and racial–biological origin, however,
the attack on the Soviet Union (code-named Operation Barbarossa) was not a
normal military offensive in which the sole objective was the destruction of the Red
Army. Rather, officers in the Wehrmacht, SS, and police were also determined to
carry out a war against elements of the civilian population, and to eliminate the
alleged biological carriers of communism, meaning Jews in the Soviet military,
political, and police apparatus. The documentary evidence for this is abundant and
irrefutable. On 3 March 1941, for example, Hitler approved orders drawn up by the
Oberkommando der Wehrmacht (Armed Forces High Command, OKW) stipulating
that one of the offensive's primary objectives was the elimination of the 'Jewish-
Bolshevik intelligentsia'.[4] SS and police units received similar instructions that
described in still greater detail the segments of Soviet society that were to be liquidated, including members of the Comintern; functionaries in the upper, middle, and
lower levels of the Communist Party; political commissars attached to the Red Army;
Jews in party and state positions; saboteurs; propagandists; partisans; agitators; and
the like.[5] Additionally, SS and police units carried into Soviet territory specially
prepared ledgers (*Fahndungslisten*) containing the names of specific individuals
whose arrest was considered particularly important.[6] The decapitation of Soviet
society through the liquidation of officials in the state and Communist Party apparatus, especially those of Jewish background, was therefore a firmly established
Nazi goal before the German attack.

---

[3] C. R. Browning, *Nazi Policy, Jewish Workers, German Killers* (New York, 2000), 29 ff., discusses
in detail the notion of a 'transitional phase' in the process of murdering Soviet Jewry, which transpired
in June–July 1941.

[4] Richtlinien auf Sondergebieten zur Weisung Nr. 21, 3 Mar. 1941, quoted in J. Förster, 'Das
Unternehmen "Barbarossa" als Eroberungs- und Vernichtungskrieg', in Militärgeschichtliches
Forschungsamt, *Das Deutsche Reich und der Zweite Weltkrieg*, vol. iv: *Der Angriff auf die Sowjetunion*
(Stuttgart, 1983), 414.

[5] A. Angrick, 'Die Einsatzgruppe D. Struktur und Tätigkeit einer mobilen Einheit der Sicherheitspolizei und des SD in der deutsch besetzten Sowjetunion', Technische Universität, Berlin,
D.Phil. thesis, 1999, 68.

[6] See Fahndungslisten für die UdSSR, United States Holocaust Memorial Museum Archive,
Washington (USHMMA), RG 14.016M (Bundesarchiv, Records of the RSHA, R58/574), fiche 2,
p. 189, which contains 4,508 names.

Once the invasion commenced, however, what might be termed ideologically conditioned pragmatic concerns caused a further radicalization of German policy from the selective killing of Jews to full-scale genocide. As Jürgen Förster has noted, to Hitler and others in the Third Reich the 'Jewish-Bolshevik intelligentsia' was not only the biological pillar upon which communism rested, it also formed the nucleus (*Keimzelle*) of potential opposition to German administration of the eastern territories.[7] This view of Jews as insurgents who would instinctively resort to partisan warfare was integral to the National Socialist 'concept of the enemy', or *Feindbild*, and it directly influenced the way in which the SS, police, and Wehrmacht treated the Jewish civilian population.[8] As a result, the SS and army responded to even the slightest civilian resistance by shooting Jews. The killing began with Jewish men during the initial weeks of Operation Barbarossa and then came to include women and children by late July and August 1941. In addition to the use of violence against Jews in reaction to civilian attacks, SS and Wehrmacht units also employed violence 'preventively' against Jews. Klaus-Michael Mallmann concludes that because many Germans on the eastern front automatically assumed Jews were hostile, the SS and army resorted to mass shootings as a prophylactic measure to deter expected Jewish resistance.[9] German security concerns in the early stages of the invasion thus brought together the twin objectives of destroying the Soviet bureaucratic and police apparatus and pacifying the occupied territories, with violence employed against Jews on an increasingly radical scale to achieve these goals.

What then was the context within which this process of radicalization took place? Beginning in spring 1941, negotiations between Reinhard Heydrich, chief of the Sicherheitspolizei (SS Security Police), and the army quartermaster-general, Lieutenant-General Eduard Wagner, led to the conclusion of several agreements delineating the security responsibilities of the SS and Wehrmacht in areas behind the battlefront. The antisemitic and anti-communist ideological affinity of the SS and Wehrmacht informed their institutional co-operation above all, but, as Geoffrey Megargee has also recently demonstrated, the Oberkommando des Heeres (Army High Command, OKH) expected the Red Army to collapse within the first few weeks of the invasion.[10] The end of Soviet resistance would clear the path for a rapid German advance to the Ural Mountains, resulting in the occupation of vast stretches of territory inhabited by a large number of Jews. In the event that this scenario actually came to pass, and many German officers were absolutely convinced it would, insufficient forces would remain behind to secure the newly occupied territory. The military therefore agreed to share responsibility with the SS for

[7] Förster, 'Das Unternehmen "Barbarossa"', 414.

[8] K.-M. Mallmann, 'Die Türöffner der "Endlösung". Zur Genesis des Genozids', in G. Paul and K.-M. Mallmann (eds.), *Die Gestapo im Zweiten Weltkrieg. 'Heimatfront' und besetztes Europa* (Darmstadt, 2000), 445.   [9] Ibid. 508.

[10] G. P. Megargee, *Inside Hitler's High Command* (Lawrence, Kan., 2000), 124.

security measures behind the front until these areas were transferred entirely to civilian control.

According to the agreement reached by Heydrich and Wagner on 26 March 1941, units composed of Sicherheitspolizei and men from the Sicherheitsdienst (Security Service, SD) of the Nazi Party would be responsible for so-called 'special tasks' in German army rear areas, including the use of 'executive measures' (i.e. shootings) to combat 'activities hostile to the state and Reich'.[11] Heydrich's Sicherheitspolizei and the SD were combined into *Einsatzgruppen* (Operational Groups) and instructed to co-ordinate their activity with army security forces. Four of these *Einsatzgruppen* were deployed on the Eastern Front altogether, with one *Einsatzgruppe* assigned to each *Heeresgruppe* (Army Group) area (North, Centre, and South) and one to the Romanian sphere of operations. Each *Einsatzgruppe* was in turn composed of several smaller *Einsatzkommandos* and *Sonderkommandos*, which could operate in the field autonomously. Lastly, Waffen-SS units, battalions of the Ordnungspolizei (Order Police, Orpo) and formations of Schutzpolizei from the General Government were called up to support rear area security operations. Security in the Białystok district and Belarus was the responsibility of Einsatz-gruppe B, which was commanded by SS-Gruppenführer Arthur Nebe. Nebe's *Einsatzgruppe* was constituted in Poznań (Posen) during the third week of June 1941 and included 655 officers and men from the Sicherheitspolizei, Gestapo, Kriminalpolizei (Criminal Police), SD, Waffen-SS, and the 2nd Company of Reserve Police Battalion 9. These SS and police personnel were organized into Nebe's Einsatzgruppe Staff; Sonderkommandos 7a and 7b, under the command of Walter Blume and Günther Rausch respectively; Einsatzkommando 8, led by Otto Bradfisch; and Einsatzkommando 9, under Alfred Filbert.[12]

The destruction of Soviet forces in the Białystok district involved a simultane-ous eastward advance by the German Ninth Army in the north and the Fourth Army in the south. Two German divisions, the 87th Infantry Division and 221st Security Division, entered the area between these two armies and advanced on Białystok from the north-west and south-west respectively. In the north-west two regiments of the 87th Infantry Division, the 173rd and 187th Infantry Regiments, began the attack from East Prussia between Szczuczyn and Kolno on 22 June 1941. After passing through Stawiski on 23 June, Radziłów and Jedwabne on 24 June, and Osowiec on 25 June, these units moved to the north and east of Białystok.[13] To the south, meanwhile, the 221st Security Division occupied Łomża on 24 June and was

---

[11] Förster, 'Das Unternehmen "Barbarossa"', 422.

[12] Tätigkeitsbericht des Chefs der Einsatzgruppe B für die Zeit vom 23.6.1941 bis zum 13.7.1941, 14 July 1941, repr. in P. Klein (ed.), *Die Einsatzgruppen in der besetzten Sowjetunion 1941/42. Die Tätigkeits- und Lageberichte des Chefs der Sicherheitspolizei und des SD* (Berlin, 1997), 377–8.

[13] Zwischenmeldung an Heeresgruppe B, AOK 9, Abt. Ia, 23 June 1941, National Archive and Records Administration, College Park, Md. (NARA), RG 242, T-312, r. 274, fr. 7833353. See also Morgenmeldung an Heeresgruppe B, AOK 9, Abt. Ia, 24 June 1941, NARA, RG 242, T-312, r. 274, fr. 7833346.

in Białystok by 27 June. Red Army resistance east of Białystok then finally collapsed at the beginning of July, bringing an end to fighting in the region.

Nebe's group moved into the Białystok district shortly after the opening of Operation Barbarossa. Blume's Sonderkommando 7a and Filbert's Einsatzkommando 9 moved east behind the Ninth Army, arriving independently in Vilna on 27 June and 1 July. Sonderkommando 7a remained in Vilna until 3 July, when it relocated to Krewo, which lay 75 miles to the north-west of Minsk.[14] Filbert's command continued to operate in Vilna, Grodno, and Lida throughout July, and in the middle of the month also deployed an advance command in Wilejka, 15 miles southeast of Minsk. For its part, Rausch's Sonderkommando 7b advanced to Brześć Litewski (Brest-Litovsk) on 26 June, moved into the vicinity of Prużana two days later, where it carried out 'Sicherheitspolizei tasks' until 2 July, and then advanced to Słonim and Baranovicze on 3 July 1941.[15] Finally, on 1 July Bradfisch's Einsatzkommando 8 arrived in Białystok, where it stayed only briefly until 5 July, before moving to Słonim, Baranovicze, and other points further east.[16]

In comparison to the large-scale killings that would later occur, Nebe's men shot relatively few Jews during this early stage of the campaign.[17] For example, the Sicherheitspolizei shot nearly 200 Jews in Wilejka, while in Minsk between fifty and seventy Jews were murdered, ostensibly as punishment for an incident of arson.[18] In contrast, the Orpo in Brześć Litewski and in Białystok carried out significantly larger shooting actions throughout July.[19] Białystok was occupied on 27 June, but even after the Red Army retreated, shooting could still be heard in the streets as units with the 221st Security Division destroyed isolated pockets of resistance that remained behind. It was during this fighting in Białystok on the first day of the German occupation that the synagogue was burned to the ground, supposedly after German troops had come under fire from the building.[20] One day later Orpo Battalion 309 entered Białystok and searched the Jewish quarter for weapons. Thousands of Jewish men were arrested during this action and interned in a hastily erected camp until 8 July, when perhaps as many as 3,000 of them were shot on direct orders from Heinrich Himmler, who visited the city on that day.[21] Several elements of the terrorization and murder of Jews in Białystok illustrate the close connections between the campaign against the Jews and the war against communism. On 30 June 1941 General Johann Pflugbeil, the commander of the 221st Security Division, ordered the formation of a Jewish labour battalion to demolish

---

[14] Tätigkeitsbericht des Chefs der Einsatzgruppe B für die Zeit vom 23.6.1941 bis zum 13.7.1941, in Klein (ed.), *Die Einsatzgruppen in der besetzten Sowjetunion 1941/42*, 377.

[15] Ibid.   [16] Ibid.

[17] Such is the conclusion expressed in C. Gerlach, 'Die Einsatzgruppe B 1941/42', in Klein (ed.), *Die Einsatzgruppen in der besetzten Sowjetunion 1941/42*, 54.

[18] R. Ogorreck, *Die Einsatzgruppen und die 'Genesis der Endlösung'* (Berlin, 1996), 114.

[19] Details on the shootings in Brześć Litewski can be found in Browning, *Nazi Policy*, 119 ff.

[20] Entry for 27 June in Kriegstagebuch 2 der Sicherheitsdivision 221, 6.5.1941–13.12.1941, NARA, RG 242, T-315, r. 1666, fr. 135.   [21] Ogorreck, *Die Einsatzgruppen*, 123.

all of the Lenin and Stalin monuments in Białystok.[22] Einsatzkommando 8 then reported two weeks later that '215 Jewish and Bolshevik functionaries' had been liquidated, along with '15 agents of the NKVD'.[23] These 'enemies' were identified with the help of the local Polish populace, who pointed out 'Jewish, Russian, and even Polish Bolsheviks'.

The killings in Białystok and several other larger towns in the region were relatively isolated events in this early phase of the German invasion. Even by mid-July 1941 Nebe's men had not entered a majority of the villages that dotted the surrounding countryside. This was generally due to the rapidity of the German advance and the small number of men in each *Sonder-* and *Einsatzkommando*. In fact, the records show that Einsatzgruppe B moved so quickly through the southern, central, and eastern regions of the Białystok district that on 1 July Heydrich reprimanded Nebe for not stationing a detachment of the Sicherheitspolizei in Grodno, which he and Heinrich Himmler had visited on 30 June.[24] Given the shortage of personnel available for security it became increasingly apparent that additional forces were needed in the regions adjacent to Germany's eastern border and the General Government. Precisely this concern had prompted the deployment of Police Battalion 309 in the Białystok district and the establishment of military command posts in Łomża, Śniadowo, Wygoda, and Sokoły.[25] In addition, for part of the first week of the campaign, several Waffen-SS combat regiments patrolled the area west of the River Biebrza, from Augustów southwards to Wizna, before Himmler ordered them back into East Prussia on 27 June.[26]

Concerns among SS commanders about partisan warfare developing along the eastern frontier of the Reich heightened significantly on 25 June after Dr Eberhard Schöngarth, the commander of the Sicherheitspolizei and SD in the General Government, filed a report noting that Red Army troops dispersed by the Wehrmacht's sudden attack had turned to guerrilla warfare and were inflicting

---

[22] Entry for 30 June in Kriegstagebuch 2 der Sicherheitsdivision 221, NARA, RG 242, T-315, r. 1666, fr. 143.

[23] Ereignismeldung UdSSR Nr. 21, 13 July 1941, USHMMA, RG 14.016M (Bundesarchiv, Records of the RSHA, R58/574), fiche 1, p. 150.

[24] Gerlach, 'Die Einsatzgruppe B 1941/42', 53.

[25] Entry for 3 July in Kriegstagebuch 2 der Sicherheitsdivision 221, NARA, RG 242, T-315, r. 1666, fr. 145. Although the 221st Security Division established these *Orts-* and *Feldkommandanturen* (local and field commands), the 580th rear army area commander, General Max von Schenckendorff, exercised overall military authority in the area.

[26] These units included the 10th SS Infantry Regiment, 8th SS Infantry Regiment, 8th Motorized SS Infantry Regiment, 1st SS Infantry Brigade, 2nd SS Infantry Brigade, and 1st SS Cavalry Regiment. See F. Baade *et al.* (eds.), *Unsere Ehre heisst Treue. Kriegstagebuch des Kommandostabes RFSS. Tätigkeitsberichte der 1. und 2. SS-Inf.-Brigade, der 1. SS-Kav.-Brigade und Sonderkommandos der SS* (Vienna, 1965). See also Tagesmeldung, AOK 9, Abt. Ia, 22 June 1941, NARA, RG 242, T-312, r. 274, fr. 7833357, and Operationsbefehl Nr. 3 zur Einleitung der Vernichtung des Feindes im Raum Bialystok-Wolkowysk, AOK 9, Abt. Ia, Nr. 3340/41 geh., 26 June 1941, NARA, RG 242, T-312, r. 274, fr. 7834705.

casualties.[27] Christopher Browning has also noted that on 5 July Major Stahr, the commander of Police Battalion 307, and Major General Stubenrauch, the local military commander in Brześć Litewski, 'sent alarming reports concerning the very insecure situation in and around Brest. There were many Soviet soldiers still roaming the area . . . [and] extra manpower was desperately needed.'[28] Jews were of course immediately suspected of helping cut-off Soviet soldiers to sustain their resistance behind German lines. As the intelligence officer of the 299th Infantry Division recorded in his daily report on 24 June, 'guerrilla activity is especially intense in areas that are thickly settled by Jews'.[29]

Consequently, within days of the war's outbreak the combination of legitimate threats to rear area security, the danger that Jews allegedly presented to German personnel, the fundamentally anti-Jewish animus of SS activities, and the paucity of German security forces proved decisive in radicalizing SS anti-Jewish policy. The result of this radicalization was the introduction of measures against the Jews living in areas adjacent to the eastern frontier of East Prussia and the General Government. The earliest of these measures to be implemented was the mobilization of Gestapo and Sicherheitspolizei frontier posts for 'cleansing' border areas of Jews. This process began in Lithuania, where on 24 June Dr Walther Stahlecker, the chief of Einsatzgruppe A, agreed with the suggestion of Hans-Joachim Böhme, the head of the Sicherheitspolizei office in Tilsit, that all Jews and communists along the East Prussian frontier should be killed.[30] Within days of the decision being made, Böhme's men had shot hundreds of Jews in the towns of Gargždai, Kretinga, and Palanga. Incidentally, Christoph Dieckmann has shown that the impetus for these murders arose from rumours that Jewish civilians had participated in the Red Army's defence of Gargždai.[31] The other measures introduced included the formation of additional *Sonder-* and *Einsatzkommandos* for service in the occupied territories, and a systematic effort by the SS to enlist the help of Lithuanians, Latvians, Ukrainians, Belarusians, and Poles against the Jews.

Turning first to the mobilization of native Poles against the Jews, no small number of Wehrmacht and SS documents note that upon entering former Soviet-occupied eastern Poland the non-Jewish population greeted German troops as liberators. According to a report filed by the Ninth Army on 22 June 1941, 'the Polish and Lithuanian population expressed great joy at being liberated [by the

---

[27] Ereignismeldung UdSSR Nr. 4, 25 June 1941, USHMMA, RG 14.016M (Bundesarchiv, Records of the RSHA, R58/574), fiche 1, p. 21.   [28] Browning, *Nazi Policy*, 119.

[29] Mallmann, 'Die Türöffner der "Endlösung"' 445.

[30] W. Scheffler, 'Die Einsatzgruppe A 1941/42', in Klein (ed.), *Die Einsatzgruppen in der besetzten Sowjetunion 1941/42* (Frankfurt am Main, 1996), 57.

[31] C. Dieckmann, 'The War and the Killing of the Lithuanian Jews', in U. Herbert (ed.), *National Socialist Extermination Policies: Contemporary German Perspectives and Controversies* (New York, 2000), 242–3.

German Army]'.[32] An entry in the war diary of the 221st Security Division similarly noted that upon entering the village of Kleczkowo, south-west of Łomża, 'the
civilian population hailed our troops with flowers, salt, and bread as liberators from
the Soviet yoke'.[33] And the XXXXII Corps reported that civilians in Łomża,
Stawki, and Kolno were all 'friendly to Germans' (*Deutschfreundlich*).[34] The pro-
German reaction of the Poles did not escape the attention of the Sicherheitspolizei,
who reported to Berlin, 'The Polish population in the occupied Soviet-Russian area
has in places joyfully greeted German troops.'[35]

Several scholarly analyses of the Soviet occupation of eastern Poland from late
September 1939 until the middle of June 1941 offer an insight into the reasons why
Poles welcomed the Wehrmacht with such warmth. By some indications, the
Soviet occupation of eastern Poland was nearly as brutal as the German occupation
of western Poland. According to Bernhard Chiari's history of Belarus at this time,
including the Białystok district, which was formally incorporated into the Belarusian Soviet Socialist Republic (BSSR) in 1940, the Red Army's arrival in the area
was chaotic and violent. Some locations, such as the city of Grodno, were reduced
to rubble after Polish army units attempted to defend themselves against the Soviet
invaders.[36] Chiari also notes that from the very beginning agents with the Soviet
Secret Police, the NKVD, embarked upon a campaign of terror against the civilian
population in search of reputed 'anti-Soviet' enemies.[37] The targets of NKVD
operations were political and so-called 'class' enemies, such as large landholders,
business owners, Polish soldiers and military officers, the members of Polish political parties, any Pole reputed to have nationalist tendencies, Catholic clergymen,
and officials in the Polish administrative elite.[38] On this subject, Bogdan Musial has
provided telling figures on the extent of the arrests carried out in the Białystok
region over the nearly two-year period of Soviet rule. Looking at just the NKVD
prisons in Białystok, Grodno, and Łomża, Musial found that a total of 8,389 people

[32] Anlage zu AOK 9, Abt. Ia, Nr. 3320/41 geh. Op-Befehl Nr. 1, 22 June 1941, Feindnach-
richtenblatt, NARA, RG 242, T-312, r. 275, fr. 7834728. See also Ic-Morgenmeldung VIII A.K.,
27 June 1941, Beilage zum Kriegstagebuch, AOK 9, Anlage III zum Tätigkeitsbericht der Abt. Ic/AO,
21.6.41–31.7.41, NARA, RG 242, T-312, r. 277, fr. 7837401: 'Vor 8 I.D. die bis zu Wolpujanka-
abschnitt vordrang und Wolpa 20.10 Uhr besetzte, nur vereinzelte feindliche Spähtrupps. Truppe
wurde beim Einrücken in dem stark zerschossenen Wolpa von der Bevölkerung freudig empfangen.'
[33] Entry for 23 June in Kriegstagebuch 2 der Sicherheitsdivision 221, NARA, RG 242, T-315,
r. 1666, fr. 112.
[34] Ic-Morgenmeldung XXXXII A.K., 25 June 1941, Beilage zum Kriegstagebuch, AOK 9, Anlage
III zum Tätigkeitsbericht der Abt. Ic/AO, 21.6.41–31.7.41, NARA, RG 242, T-312, r. 277, fr.
7837475.
[35] Ereignismeldung UdSSR Nr. 4, 25 June 1941, USHMMA, RG 14.016M (Bundesarchiv,
Records of the RSHA, R58/574), fiche 1, pp. 23–4.
[36] B. Chiari, *Alltag hinter der Front. Besatzung, Kollaboration und Widerstand in Weissrussland
1941–1944* (Düsseldorf, 1998), 36.   [37] Ibid. 37.
[38] Cholawsky, *The Jews of Bielorussia*, 10–11.

had been incarcerated by 20 March 1941.[39] These arrests were followed by a final wave of detentions in the vicinity of Łomża and Białystok on 19–20 June 1941, which led to the incarceration of another 2,059 people.[40] Furthermore, of the twenty-one prisons in Belarus Musial examines, only the prison in Brześć Litewski held a higher number of internees (3,239) than the three gaols listed above.

Yet arrest by the NKVD was not the only means of repression employed by Soviet occupation forces; deportation was another. Limited deportations of civilians were initially carried out in areas adjacent to the German–Soviet demarcation line. A document cited by Martin Dean in his study of eastern Poland, Belarus, and Ukraine shows that the inhabitants of all villages located within 800 metres of the demarcation line were forcibly resettled eastwards during the establishment of the Soviet security zone.[41] Bogdan Musial concludes, based upon the most recent research of this subject, that in the BSSR this number totalled 35,300 people.[42] Of still greater social consequence, however, was the permanent deportation of large parts of the civilian population to Siberia. According to the latest scholarly estimate, by the time of the German invasion the Soviets had deported as many as 381,000 people (permanent inhabitants and refugees) from occupied eastern Poland to Siberia.[43] Poles made up about 60 per cent of these deportees, which was by far the largest segment of any ethnic group. In what seems to have been a disastrous coincidence, the Soviets carried out extensive deportations in the Białystok district during the week prior to the German invasion on 22 June 1941. Soviet documents cited by the Polish scholar Michal Gnatowski reveal that as a result of these deportations on 19–20 June a total of 22,353 Poles, including entire families, were deported to Siberia from the regions of Łomża and Białystok.[44] Among these deportees were also families from Jedwabne and Wizna.[45] Bernhard Chiari's conclusion that deportation was a 'daily threat' hanging over the heads of all civilians in the BSSR is thus a valid appraisal of the situation.[46] And although we cannot be certain, the fear elicited by this final wave of deportations was surely fresh enough in the minds of many local Poles to suggest the murder of Jews in retaliation.

Lastly, the economic impact of the Soviet occupation was ruinous to the already poor and backward agricultural regions of eastern Poland. Red Army troops requi-

---

[39] Musial, '*Konterrevolutionäre Elemente sind zu erschiessen*', 95. J. T. Gross, 'The Sovietisation of Western Ukraine and Western Byelorussia', in N. Davies and A. Polonsky (eds.), *Jews in Eastern Poland and the USSR, 1939–46* (New York, 1991), 72, offers the even more staggering estimate of *c*.500,000 people arrested in western Ukraine and western Belarus during the twenty-one months of Soviet rule.

[40] M. Gnatowski, *W radzieckich okowach: Studium o agresji 17 września 1939 r. i radzieckiej polityce w regionie łomżynskim w latach 1939–1941* (Łomża, 1997), 115. I am grateful to Bogdan Musial for this citation, as well as the information in nn. 46, 56, 57, 61.

[41] Dean, *Collaboration in the Holocaust*, 4.

[42] Musial, '*Konterrevolutionäre Elemente sind zu erschiessen*', 33.   [43] Ibid.

[44] Gnatowski, *W radzieckich okowach*, 115.

[45] Katolika Agencja Informacyjna, ISSN 1426–1413, 23 Feb. 2001; and interview with Jadwiga Szymanowska, 23 Feb. 2001, Wizna.   [46] Chiari, *Alltag hinter der Front*, 48.

sitioned everything in sight, from foodstuffs to other goods, often leaving behind useless receipts for the seized items.[47] The collectivization of small farms into large agricultural enterprises was also universally resented by the rural population and led to severe shortages of grain as production dropped. In the words of Jan Gross, this 'radical redistribution of property . . . undercut nearly everyone's material basis of existence'.[48] Bernhard Chiari substantiates this statement, noting that the black-market price of grain after the Soviet occupation rose to fifteen times the state-mandated price.[49] Collectivization initially exacerbated class tensions as well given that 'the heaviest burden of Soviet economic policy fell on the well-to-do strata of Polish society [which] . . . had the things that could be taken away'.[50] Peasants suffered too, Jan Gross points out, as those who had been encouraged to take land and goods from the middle and upper classes were soon heavily taxed by the authorities, resulting in the continued build-up of anti-Soviet resentment across all segments of Polish society.

Given the considerable economic and social impact of the Soviet occupation, the delight expressed by Poles at the arrival of German forces is quite comprehensible. But the communist occupation left deep psychological scars as well. These mani-fested themselves in the resentment that many Poles quickly turned against their Jewish neighbours, whom they blamed for Soviet depredations. This reaction was fostered in part by the fact that many Jews had welcomed the Red Army as it rolled into eastern Poland. Stories abound in the scholarly and memoir literature of Jews dancing in the streets at the arrival of Soviet tanks in their towns. For example, Shalom Cholawsky recounts the comments of a Jew from the town of Dereczyn who stated, 'It is hard to describe our joy. It seemed to us that this was the happiest day in our lives. All of the Jewish population, and also many non-Jews, came out to welcome the Soviet saviors.'[51] The Polish scholar Andrzej Żbikowski cites similar evidence from the underground archive of the Warsaw ghetto that reinforces the conclusion that Jews initially welcomed Soviet forces. Jews in Vilna, for instance, were seen showing great enthusiasm for the arriving Red Army.[52] And in the town of Lutsk 'The majority of [Jewish] youth expressed great enthusiasm. They kissed the soldiers, climbed the tanks, [and] they gave an ovation.'[53] Finally, Jan Gross cites the story of one Polish witness from Jedwabne who recalled that a local Jewish family and several Polish communists set out bread and salt for Soviet troops as well as a banner that read 'We Welcome You'.[54]

Scholars generally agree that the sight of Jews greeting the Red Army was abhor-rent to Poles, but until recently there was little evidence to suggest that Jews had

---

[47] Chiari, *Alltag hinter der Front*, 41.

[48] Gross, 'The Sovietisation of Western Ukraine and Western Byelorussia', 67.

[49] Chiari, *Alltag hinter der Front*, 40.

[50] Gross, 'The Sovietisation of Western Ukraine and Western Byelorussia', 67.

[51] Cholawsky, *The Jews of Bielorussia*, 4.

[52] A. Żbikowski, 'Jewish Reaction to the Soviet Arrival in the Kresy in September 1939', *Polin*, 13 (2000), 66.   [53] Ibid. 67.   [54] Gross, *Neighbors*, 45.

participated directly in the crimes of the Soviet occupiers. Detailed research carried out by Bogdan Musial over the past few years has resulted in a more nuanced understanding of Jewish involvement with Soviet occupation forces. Musial has been criticized for suggesting that Jews in eastern Poland were over-represented in the Soviet administrative and police apparatus, but after examining numerous eye-witness reports taken from the inhabitants of eastern Poland, including Jews who survived the German occupation, Musial found that in many cases Jewish militia members directly participated in mass arrests and deportation actions. Take, for example, the statement of Aleksander Kotowski, a Polish inhabitant of Jedwabne. Kotowski recalled after the war that in October 1939 the NKVD released 'Jews and [Polish] Communists' who had been held in Polish prisons and then utilized these people as informants to denounce 'Polish patriots'.[55] Another witness from Jedwabne testified that during the deportation of local Poles to Siberia in the third week of June 1941 'an armed Jew sat on every wagon'[56] onto which the deportees were loaded. Correspondingly, Michel Mielnicki from the village of Wasilków, which lay near Białystok, remembered that his father, Chaim Mielnicki, hosted a gathering of NKVD commissars from Moscow in the family's home. According to Michel, his father 'served as advisor to the NKVD about who among the local Poles was to be sent to Siberia, or otherwise dealt with'.[57] As Michel explained, his father had at the time claimed that Polish 'fascists' were 'not good for the Jewish people' and deserved to be sent to Siberia.[58]

Other leading scholars corroborate Musial's conclusions. Yitzhak Arad, for one, writes of extensive arrests by the NKVD in his home town of Święciany: 'although there were also thousands of Jews among the exiles [who were arrested], Jews played a relatively large role in the Communist Party apparatus that was behind the action'.[59] Dov Levin has similarly concluded 'the labeling of the Soviet administration as a "Jewish regime" became widespread when Jewish militiamen helped NKVD agents send local Poles into exile'.[60] Furthermore, Jan Gross himself wrote in 1983 that 'Jewish collaboration' with the Soviet authorities was behind the sudden upsurge of antisemitism among the non-Jewish population in eastern Poland.[61] It is worth noting here as well the findings of Evgeny Rozenblat, who concluded in a recent essay that the percentage of Jews in the Soviet administrative apparatus rose during the two years from 1939 to 1941 in the Pinsk oblast, which is located to the

[55] Report of Polish Deportees, no. 2675, Archive of the Hoover Institution on War, Revolution, and Peace, Stanford University, Calif.

[56] Cited by D. and A. Wroniszewski, *Kontakty: Łomżyński Tygodnik Społeczny*, no. 10 (July 1988).

[57] M. Mielnicki, *Bialystok to Birkenau: The Holocaust Journey of Michel Mielnicki as Told to John Munro* (Vancouver, 2000), 82 ff.   [58] Ibid.

[59] Y. Arad, *The Partisan: From the Valley of Death to Mount Zion* (New York, 1979), 26–7.

[60] D. Levin, *The Lesser of Two Evils: Eastern European Jewry under Soviet Rule, 1939–1941*, trans. N. Greenwood (Philadelphia, 1995), 63.

[61] J. T. Gross and I. Grudzinska-Gross (eds.), *'W czterdziestym nas Matko na Sybir zesłal—': Polska a Rosja 1939–42* (London, 1983), 28 ff.

south-east of the Białystok district. In his examination of various sectors of local society, Rozenblat found that, despite the fact that Jews comprised only 10 per cent of the regional population, they held 49.5 per cent of the leading administrative positions in the Pinsk oblast, including 41.2 per cent of those in the judicial and police administration.[62]

Polish Jews had good reason to greet the Soviets, as life under communist rule was preferable to that under Nazism. Moreover, Poles had by and large never accepted Jews as equal citizens in inter-war Poland, and the threat of pogroms lurked constantly beneath the seemingly placid surface of Polish–Jewish relations. As Jan Gross notes, the destruction of Poland allowed some Jews to show openly their resentment of Polish antisemitism by stating ironically, 'You wanted Poland without Jews, so now you have Jews without Poland.'[63]

The uniform characterization by Poles of Jews benefiting from the Soviet occupation was nevertheless patently unfair because Jews too suffered under Soviet rule. By the time of the German invasion between 60,000 and 70,000 Jews had been deported from eastern Poland to Siberia, although it should be noted that the vast majority of these Jews were refugees who had fled the German invasion in September–October 1939.[64] In his analysis of the 'Sovietization' of Jewish communities, Ben-Cion Pinchuk remarks that because Jews generally 'occupied themselves with commerce, crafts, and services for the surrounding peasant population', the elimination of private commerce by the communists may in reality have hit Polish Jews much harder than Polish non-Jews.[65] Pinchuk similarly notes that the religious practice of both Polish Catholic and Jewish communities was frowned upon by the Soviets, who viewed displays of faith as 'act[s] of defiance'.

It seems then that outbursts of Polish antisemitism in reaction to the arrival of German forces had their origin in the conflation of traditional anti-Jewish feeling and recent experience with Soviet oppression. The membership of some Jews in the Soviet police apparatus and the participation of Jews in Soviet crimes fed into the overall stereotype of the 'Jewish communist', which in turn reinforced the notion of 'Jewish treason' against the Polish nation and its citizens. In effect, all Jews were tarred with the same brush and blamed for the crimes committed by some of their brethren. The image of Jews greeting the Red Army, and of Jews in militia uniform assisting the NKVD, appeared to bear out the deepest suspicions of a nefarious Jewish–Bolshevik alliance. And despite the reality that many Jews also endured the horrors of Soviet occupation, 'the sight of a few Jews in the police and administration' raised the ire of Poles whose communities had been terrorized and

[62] E. Rozenblat, 'Evrei v sisteme mezhnatsional'nykh otnoshenii v zapadnykh oblastyakh Belarusi 1939–1941 g.', *Białoruskie Zeszyty Historyczne*, no. 12 (2000), 96–7.

[63] Gross, 'The Sovietisation of Western Ukraine and Western Byelorussia', 66.

[64] Musial, *'Konterrevolutionäre Elemente sind zu erschiessen'*, 32, 62.

[65] B.-C. Pinchuk, 'Sovietization of the Shtetl of Eastern Poland, 1939–1941', in J. W. Strong (ed.), *Essays on Revolutionary Culture and Stalinism* (Columbus, Ohio, 1990), 72–3.

whose nation had been destroyed within the space of one generation.[66] Indeed, concerning events in Jedwabne and the surrounding area, this Jewish policeman may have been the head of the Soviet Secret Police office in nearby Łomża, who was a Jewish man named Urwiez.[67] The evidence clearly demonstrates that, just like Poles and other native east European peoples with communist sympathies, a certain number of Jews collaborated with Soviet occupation forces. But when speaking of an unholy union between all Jews and communists, one can only conclude that scholars are dealing with a fantasy imagined by resentful Poles, a perceived reality that proved to be more influential than reality itself.

In practical terms, the open expression of anti-Soviet sentiment by Poles and other east European peoples presented Heinrich Himmler and Reinhard Heydrich with the opportunity to enlist collaborators against Jews in the Soviet Union. For his part, Heydrich seems to have anticipated this development, informing *Einsatzgruppen* commanders in Berlin on 17 June that in an effort to achieve German objectives (i.e. the destruction of Judaeo-Bolshevism) they should exploit long-standing ethnic tensions between eastern peoples.[68] Understandably Einsatzgruppe B's rapid movement through the Białystok district had not allowed Nebe's men to take full advantage of these tensions. This subject arose during a meeting between Himmler, Erich von dem Bach–Zalewski, and several other SS and police leaders, which took place on 28 June in East Prussia.[69] At this meeting Himmler asked Bach–Zalewski, the commander of Polizeiregiment Mitte (Police Regiment Centre) and the SS officer responsible for anti-partisan operations behind Heeresgruppe Mitte (Army Group Centre), why pogroms against the Jews had not yet broken out in the Białystok district as they had in the Baltic States just to the north. The next day Heydrich added to his earlier instructions about exploiting ethnic tensions by issuing orders for the Sicherheitspolizei to 'intensify' and 'move in the correct direction' all 'efforts at self-cleansing by anti-communist and anti-Jewish activists'.[70] Heydrich cautioned, however, that there should be 'no trace' of SS involvement in the pogroms that erupted. He also made it clear that any operations of this kind had to take into account the opinion of local military authorities. Finally, Heydrich's order stated that the outbreak of so-called 'popular pogroms' (*Volkspogrome*) was preferable at this stage of the campaign to the formation of Polish auxiliary police units like those that had been created in Lithuania.[71]

Returning now to the connection between these orders and the formation of supplemental *Sonder-* and *Einsatzkommandos*, it is surely no coincidence that on

[66] Dean, *Collaboration in the Holocaust*, 13.

[67] Fahndungslisten für die UdSSR, USHMMA, RG 14.016M (Bundesarchiv, Records of the RSHA, R58/574), fiche 2, p. 189.   [68] Angrick, 'Die Einsatzgruppe D', 68.

[69] This meeting with Himmler was recounted by Bach–Zalewski in his testimony at the trial of Nazi war criminals in Nuremberg. See the copy of this testimony in Zentrale Stelle der Landesjustizverwaltungen, Ludwigsburg (ZStL), 5 AR-Z 56/1960, Verfahren gegen Wolfgang Birkner u.a., p. 4.

[70] Fernschreiben Heydrichs an die Einsatzgruppenchefs vom 29.6.1941, repr. in Klein (ed.), *Die Einsatzgruppen in der besetzten Sowjetunion 1941/42*, 319.   [71] Ibid.

30 June Eberhard Schöngarth in Kraków initiated the creation of four small operational groups for deployment in the Białystok district within two days of Himmler and Heydrich expressing a desire to stimulate pogroms.[72] Schöngarth probably received orders from the Reichssicherheitshauptamt (Reich Security Main Office, RSHA) to form these groups and he immediately transmitted the instructions to Sicherheitspolizei and SD commanders in Warsaw, Radom, and Lublin.[73] Within three days, four auxiliary Sicherheitspolizei and SD groups had been created and placed under the command of Adolf Bonifer, Erich Engels, Johannes Böhm, and Wolfgang Birkner. Events were now quickly moving in the direction Himmler and Heydrich desired. On 1 July Nebe reported to Berlin that he had visited the headquarters of the Heeresgruppe Mitte and as a result the 'self-cleansing efforts of anti-communist and anti-Jewish circles were to be intensified' in his area of command.[74] With the military's co-operation now secure, Heydrich explicitly authorized the Sicherheitspolizei to organize pogroms. These pogroms were to be initiated using small groups of local agitators, particularly members of the Polish intelligentsia reputed to be fervently anti-Jewish.[75] Similar consultations held between the army and *Einsatzgruppe* chiefs elsewhere on the Eastern Front revealed that other Wehrmacht commanders also agreed with the organization of indigenous antisemitic elements against the Jews.[76]

A day later (on 2 July) Arthur Nebe travelled to Warsaw from Białystok to meet the commanders of the new *Sonder-* and *Einsatzkommandos* and to familiarize them with their impending duty. It was probably at this point that Nebe informed them about their responsibility for instigating pogroms.[77] Nebe then departed for Białystok early the next day along with Bonifer's and Böhm's groups.[78] Arriving in Białystok in the afternoon of 3 July, Nebe immediately dispatched Böhm's *Einsatzkommando* to Grodno and Adolf Bonifer's *Einsatzkommando* to Bielsk.[79] A 'pogrom' then broke out in Grodno two days later.[80] The *Sonderkommandos* of Engels

[72] Pohl, *Nationalsozialistische Judenverfolgung*, 53, notes that Schöngarth claimed to have raised these auxiliary police units on his own initiative, but Pohl argues this was unlikely.

[73] Blitz-Fernschreiben, BdS Krakau Nr. 6285, 30 June 1941, USHMMA, RG 11.001M.15 (Records of the Osoby archiv, Moscow, 1932–1945), reel 80, *fond* 1323, *opis'* 1, folder 59, fr. 237.

[74] Ereignismeldung UdSSR Nr. 9, 1 July 1941, USHMMA, RG 14.016M (Bundesarchiv, Records of the RSHA, R58/574), fiche 1, p. 48.   [75] Ibid. 53.

[76] Ereignismeldung UdSSR Nr. 10, 2 July 1941, USHMMA, RG 14.016M (Bundesarchiv, Records of the RSHA, R58/574), fiche 1, p. 52.

[77] According to Ereignismeldung UdSSR Nr. 11, 3 July 1941, USHMMA, RG 14.016M (Bundesarchiv, Records of the RSHA, R58/574), fiche 1, p. 63, the RSHA required that contact be established between *Einsatzgruppen* chiefs and the new supplemental units in order to ensure that these new commanders were properly aware of their new tasks.

[78] Bericht der Einsatzkommando z.b.V., Warschau, 2 July 1941, USHMMA, RG 11.001M.15 (Records of the Osoby archiv, Moscow, 1932–1945), reel 80, *fond* 1323, *opis'* 1, folder 59, fr. 243.

[79] Tätigkeitsbericht des Chefs der Einsatzgruppe B für die Zeit vom 23.6.1941 bis zum 13.7.1941, 14 July 1941, repr. in Klein (ed.), *Die Einsatzgruppen in der besetzten Sowjetunion 1941/42*, 378–9.

[80] Ereignismeldung UdSSR Nr. 13, 5 July 1941, USHMMA, RG 14.016M (Bundesarchiv, Records of the RSHA, R58/574), fiche 1, p. 74.

and Birkner also arrived in Białystok late in the day on 3 July. Engels's group was sent on to Nowogrodek a day later (4 July), while Birkner's command remained in the city. Little information exists about Wolfgang Birkner and the men of his *Sonderkommando*, but the unit was made up of twenty-nine Sicherheitspolizei and Gestapo officers altogether. Birkner and his men co-ordinated their work with a small group of Sicherheitspolizei from Einsatzgruppe B that Nebe had left behind in Białystok. By the way of background, it is interesting to note that Birkner and seven of the other members of his *Sonderkommando* were veterans of Einsatzgruppe IV, which had occupied Białystok briefly at the end of the Polish campaign in 1939, before the city was turned over to the Soviets. According to reports filed by Nebe with the RSHA in Berlin, Birkner's men participated in several shooting actions in and around Białystok, which by 28 August had claimed the lives of 1,800 Jews.[81]

As for evidence concerning the participation of Birkner's *Sonderkommando* in inciting pogroms, this is very slim. West German prosecutors investigating Birkner in 1960 initially suspected that his men were involved in the murder of Jews in Jedwabne, Radziłow, and Wąsosz.[82] These suspicions were based on the research of the Polish historian Szymon Datner, but the investigators turned up little hard evidence directly implicating either Birkner or his men in these events.[83] It is perhaps interesting to note in this context the statement of Polizeimeister N., who was a witness in the West German investigation. Polizeimeister N. recalled that the head of the small gendarmerie post in Jedwabne was a police officer named Henning and not the gendarme named Adamy, whose name appears in Jan Gross's book *Neighbors*.[84] In his retelling of events leading up to the Jedwabne pogrom, Gross quotes the post-war testimony of Władysław Miciura, who stated that on the day of the killings one of the German gendarmes ordered him 'to go to the square and to watch the Jews'.[85] Miciura's testimony suggests that the gendarmes were at least involved in guarding the Jews assembled on the marketplace, if not with actually collecting the Jews. But Gross dismisses this evidence, concluding that the Germans in Jedwabne on the day of the pogrom limited their activity to 'taking pictures'.[86] One of the members of Birkner's *Sonderkommando* was SS-Oberscharführer

[81] Auswertung der Ereignismeldungen zu den Judenerschiessungen in Bialystok im Juli 1941 in ZStL, 5 AR-Z 67/1960, pp. 4 ff.

[82] I am grateful to President Leon Kieres, the director of the Institute of National Remembrance (INR) in Warsaw, and Dr Paweł Machcewicz, the director of the INR's Public Education Office, for providing me with archival documentation relevant to events in Jedwabne and other locations in the Białystok district.

[83] Vorläufiges Ermittlungsergebnis, 13 Apr. 1960, ZStL, 5 AR-Z 56/1960, p. 2.

[84] Vernehmung von Paul N., 6 September 1960 in ZStL, 5 AR-Z 56/1960, p. 129. N. also stated that three Germans and two Poles staffed the gendarmerie post in Jedwabne, not the eleven men claimed in Gross, *Neighbors*, 76, 112. The discrepancy between N.'s and Gross's accounts of the Jedwabne gendarmerie post may be the result of timing, as N. did not take up his post until Sept. 1942.

[85] Gross, *Neighbors*, 77. [86] Ibid. 78.

Gerhard Henning, but there is no direct proof as yet that this man was the Henning referred to during the West German investigation.[87]

More evidence exists to indicate that Sicherheitspolizei and Gestapo detachments other than Birkner's were responsible for instigating pogroms and shooting Jews in the western half of the Białystok district. In addition to ordering the formation of supplemental *Einsatzkommandos* at the very beginning of July, the Reichssicherheitshauptamt also authorized the Gestapo offices in Tilsit and Olsztyn (Allenstein) to pull personnel from subordinate posts along the East Prussian border and deploy these detachments in the 'newly occupied territories' that lay just to the east of the frontier.[88] These detachments of Gestapo and Sicherheitspolizei were instructed to establish contact with the *Einsatzgruppen* in the areas where they were deployed and to commence 'cleansing' operations (i.e. destroying Jewish communities).[89] The murders carried out along the Lithuanian–German border by Gestapo personnel from Tilsit have already been mentioned, but in their post-war investigation of Birkner's *Sonderkommando* West German authorities discovered that the Gestapo office in Ciechanów (Zichenau) had also deployed personnel in the area. Specifically, a German witness, who had been the *Kreiskommissar* in Łomża, recalled that when he arrived in the city at the beginning of August he found a detachment of Gestapo personnel from the office in Płock (Schröttersburg) stationed there.[90] This unit from the Płock substation of the Ciechanów Gestapo headquarters was under the command of SS-Obersturmführer Hermann Schaper.

Upon investigating further, the West Germans located a Jewish witness from the village of Tykocin who positively identified Schaper as the man who had directed a shooting action in his town in August 1941.[91] Even more important was the discovery in Israel of a female Jewish witness from Radziłów, who recognized photographs of Schaper as the man who had overseen the murder of Jews in her village in early July 1941. In *Neighbors* Jan Gross quotes at length the testimony of Menachem Finkelsztajn, who recounted to Polish investigators on 14 April 1946 what had taken place in Radziłów on 7 July 1941, three days before the pogrom in Jedwabne.[92] According to Finkelsztajn, for several days before the massacre in Radziłów, German soldiers stationed in the village joined local Poles in torturing, beating, and otherwise tormenting the village's Jews. Events in Radziłów then concluded with a pogrom, during which several hundred Jews were killed.[93] The part of Finkelsztajn's testimony that described the pogrom itself was missing, leaving Gross unable to provide details about the killings. It is important to note,

---

[87] Stärkemeldung des Einsatztrupps Bialystok, 28 July 1941, USHMMA, RG 11.001M.15 (Records of the Osoby archiv, Moscow, 1932–1945), reel 80, *fond* 1323, *opis'* 1, folder 59, fr. 252.

[88] Ereignismeldung UdSSR Nr. 11, 3 July 1941, USHMMA, RG 14.016M (Bundesarchiv, Records of the RSHA, R58/574), fiche 1, p. 63.   [89] Ibid.

[90] Vernehmung von Oberregierungsrat Graf von dem G., 2 Sept. 1960, ZStL, 5 AR-Z 13/62, p. 11.

[91] Zwischenbericht No. 5 der Untersuchungsstelle für N.S. Gewaltverbrechen beim Landestab der Polizei Israel, 23 Jan. 1963, ZStL, 5 AR-Z 13/62, p. 70.   [92] Gross, *Neighbors*, 54 ff.

[93] In Gross, ibid. 57, the number of Jews killed in Radziłów is estimated at between 800 and 1,500.

however, that Finkelsztajn never actually saw these events with his own eyes.[94] Yet, this fact did not keep him from stating categorically: 'the Poles were in charge, since not even a single German was present'.[95]

Gross presents Menachem Finkelsztajn's account of the Radziłów massacre in its entirety and accepts it at face value, including its portrayal of local and regional Poles as the perpetrators of the crime. By contrast, West German and Israeli investigators looking into this incident discovered another version of the story that is at odds with Finkelsztajn's portrayal. According to Menachem Finkelsztajn's mother, Chaja Wasersztajn Finkelsztajn, the female Jewish survivor from Radziłów who witnessed the violence from the window of her home:

On 7 July 1941, three automobiles bearing Gestapo functionaries entered Radziłów and in cooperation with the [local] Polish police, rousted all of the Jews from their homes and collected them on the marketplace. After all the Jews were assembled, they were forced to march to a barn that lay around two kilometres from the town. The barn was set alight and the nearly 2,000 Jews were burned alive.[96]

The West Germans suspected that one element of this testimony was incorrect. Specifically, they did not believe that there was a barn large enough in the area to have held 2,000 people. On the other hand, they thought the witnesses' recollection of Hermann Schaper was very credible, given that she had met him face to face. As Chaja Wasersztajn Finkelsztajn recounted.

This Gestapo officer entered my home along with Grzynk, who was the chairman of the local council in Radziłów and the commander of the Polish police . . . I saw from my window that Gestapo functionaries were standing in front of my house shortly before the beginning of the action. I saw also the Gestapo functionary (i.e. Schaper), who I recognized in the photograph. I saw how he gave orders to the Gestapo men and the Poles working with them. I also saw how he gave orders on the marketplace . . . he gave the impression of leading the action.[97]

Additional testimony uncovered by the Polish researcher Anna Bikont also supports the theory that the Gestapo co-ordinated the massacre of Radziłów's Jews with local Polish antisemites. According to an eyewitness, Maciej F.,

Three Germans arrived in an open car. I stood nearby. They said: 'it stinks of Jews here too much. When we return some days later it shouldn't stink so!' They [the Germans] put Feliks Mordasiewicz in charge. He asked 'How should I do it?' So they gave him five rifles.[98]

Another witness, named Hanna Z., corroborated the statements of both Maciej F. and Chaja Wasersztajn Finkelsztajn:

[94] A. Bikont, 'They Had Vodka, Weapons and Hate—before Jedwabne: The Murder of Jews in Radziłow', trans. David W. Dastych, available online at <www.radzilow.com/gazeta1.htm>; first pub. as 'Mieli wódkę, broń i nienawiść, in *Gazeta Wyborcza* (15 June 2001).

[95] Gross, *Neighbors*, 65.   [96] Vermerk, 2 Sept. 1965, ZStL, 5 AR-Z 13/62, pp. 2–3.

[97] Zwischenbericht Nr. 5 der Untersuchungsstelle für N.S. Gewaltverbrechen beim Landestab der Polizei Israel, 23 Jan. 1963, ZStL, 5 AR-Z 13/62, p. 70.

[98] Bikont, 'They Had Vodka', no page number.

Four Germans arrived at the marketplace in two cars . . . they had caps on with the death's head [insignia], and they brought rifles to distribute. Mostly young lads went to listen to them. The Germans said: 'Here you have Jews who are responsible for the fact that your families will freeze in Russia. Bring them all to the marketplace for weeding the pavement.'[99]

Lastly, Bikont notes that in the post-war memoir of Chaja Wasersztajn Finkelsztajn (held in the archive of Yad Vashem in Israel), a 'Gestapo man' and a local Pole named Stanisław Grzymkowski

went together to look for a proper place to burn the Jews. At first they planned to do it in the Jewish prayer house, but it was too close to other houses and the fire could harm them . . . I was a witness to how the Germans organized Poles from the town and the Poles were the executors of the whole action.[100]

This version of events in Radziłów clearly contradicts that of Finkelsztajn as repeated by Gross. According to the testimony above, the murder of Jews in Radziłów was most likely a massacre orchestrated by Hermann Schaper's Gestapo unit and carried out with the co-operation of a group of local Poles. The massacre was not a spontaneous uprising of the Polish population against local Jews as portrayed by Gross in *Neighbors*.[101] For reasons that remain unclear, Chaja Wasersztajn Finkelsztajn was not killed during the action, but then again in the version of events cited by Jan Gross the Germans saved eighteen of Radziłów's Jews from death that day.[102] The evidence collected by the West Germans, including the positive identification of Schaper by witnesses from Łomża, Tykocin, and Radziłów, thus suggested that it was indeed Schaper's men who organized the killings in those locations.[103] Investigators also suspected, based on the similarity of the methods used to destroy the Jewish communities of Radziłów, Tykocin, Rutki, Zambrów, Jedwabne, Piatnica, and Wizna between July and September 1941, that Schaper's men were to blame. But, lacking absolutely watertight evidence placing Schaper's men in Jedwabne on the date of the murders, the West Germans could only tentatively conclude, 'it is highly probable that the *Einsatzkommando* from

---

[99] Bikont, 'They Had Vodka', no page number.   [100] Ibid.   [101] Ibid.

[102] Gross, *Neighbors*, 69.

[103] More than sixty years after the massacre in Radziłów, German and Polish investigators managed to locate Hermann Schaper, who was still alive and living in Germany. On 11 Apr. 2002 Radosław Ignatiew, prosecutor from the Brand Commission for the Prosecution of Crimes against the Polish Nation in Białystok, interrogated the 90-year-old former SS officer about the murder of Jews in Radziłów, Jedwabne, and other locations in July 1941. During the interrogation Schaper admitted that he and his unit of ten to fifteen Gestapo men had been deployed in the region 'to search for Russian agents and to secure documents'. However, Schaper denied any involvement in the murder of Jews, claiming instead that, while he was stationed in the area, 'there were wild actions [against the Jews] by the local people and some [unidentified German] units'. The interrogation was then called off owing to alleged health problems the elderly Schaper claimed to be suffering. For a summary, see 'Information on the Interrogation of Hermann Schaper', 11 Apr. 2002, available on the website of the Institute of National Remembrance at <www.ipn.gov.pl/index_eng.html>.

Schröttersburg' was responsible for the killing of Jedwabne's Jews on 10 July 1941.[104]

Despite Gross's depiction of Jedwabne's Poles as the sole perpetrators of the massacre in their town, some of the evidence he cites actually supports the West German investigation's conclusion that Schaper's men were deeply involved in the slaughter. For one thing, Gross writes, 'we can also infer from various sources that a group of Gestapo men arrived in town by taxi on either that day or the previous one'. To the inhabitants of a rural village like Jedwabne, the automobiles driven by the Gestapo may have appeared to be taxis, and the exact dates of incidental events like the arrival of a car often slip the minds of eyewitnesses. What is certain, though, is that witnesses in Radziłów, Tykocin, and other locations not far removed from Jedwabne all remembered Gestapo men driving into their villages in two or three automobiles.[105] Secondly, Gross cites the testimony of Czesław Lipiński, Władysław Miciura, and Feliks Tarnacki, all of whom mentioned that German police brought them to the town square to guard the Jews.[106] Thirdly, the witness Danowski stated to Polish investigators in 1953 that 'several dozen men assembled in front of the city hall in Jedwabne and were equipped by the German gendarmerie and Karolak (the mayor) and Sobuta (Karolak's accomplice) with whips and clubs'.[107] Fourthly, just as the Germans had forced the Jews of Białystok to demolish the monuments of Lenin and Stalin, the Jews of Jedwabne were compelled to rip up the village's monument of Lenin and parade it around before being led to their deaths.[108] Finally, the method used to kill most of the Jews of Jedwabne was exactly the same that had been employed by the Gestapo to kill the Jews of Radziłów only three days earlier. The Jews of Jedwabne were collected on the town square, forced to pull up weeds, driven by physical violence to the place of their murder, and then burned to death.

In short, while Gross marshals considerable evidence to prove the involvement of Jedwabne's Poles in the murder of their Jewish neighbours, he plays down evidence that suggests the Gestapo too might have played a significant role in the killings. As Gross concludes concerning the direct involvement of the Germans in the mass murder of the Jews, 'one must admit that it was limited, pretty much, to taking pictures'.[109] The findings of the Branch Commission for the Prosecution of Crimes against the Polish Nation in Białystok investigating the massacre suggest that the story is more complicated than Gross describes. According to the chief prosecutor of the commission, Radosław Ignatiew, the Germans, 'who were

---

[104] Abschlussbericht, 17 Mar. 1964, ZStL, 5 AR–Z 13/62, p. 164.   [105] Ibid. 158, 160, 161.

[106] Gross, *Neighbors*, 77.

[107] Ibid. 91. See also p. 112, where Gross quotes Irena Janowska, the wife of one of the men accused of having murdered Jedwabne's Jews: 'on the critical day German gendarmerie walked around together with the mayor and the secretary [of the town council] Wasilewski, and chased out males to go and guard Jews who were assembled in the square'.   [108] Ibid. 88.

[109] Gross, *Neighbors*, 78.

probably in a small group, assisted in driving the victims to the marketplace'.[110] Ignatiew goes on to state that, owing to discrepancies in the testimony, it is unclear if the Germans participated any further in the killings. He believes it is clear, however, that a considerable number of local Poles (about forty men) were responsible for carrying out the murders, after arrangements with the Gestapo had been completed. In Ignatiew's view, therefore, 'It may be assumed that the murders at Jedwabne were perpetrated upon German inspiration. At this stage it . . . is justified to ascribe, in legal and criminal terms, the complicity *sensu largo* of the mass murder to the Germans.'[111]

What conclusions should be drawn from this examination of the killings in Jedwabne and elsewhere in the region? To begin with, whether events in Jedwabne and Radziłów can honestly be classified as 'pogroms' is doubtful. Spontaneous anti-Jewish violence did erupt, but this bloodshed did not escalate into wholesale slaughter until the Gestapo became directly involved. Given the clear links between the larger SS policy of inciting local populations (Polish, Lithuanian, Ukrainian, Russian, and others) against the Jews, it makes far more sense to classify the massacre of Jedwabne and Radziłów's Jews as SS killing actions in which local Poles were mobilized to do the dirty work. Gross acknowledges that the SS may have been involved in the crimes, but he divorces events in Radziłów and Jedwabne from the broader framework of Nazi anti-Jewish policy. He also minimizes German involvement while maximizing the responsibility of Jedwabne's Polish inhabitants for the murders. The graphic descriptions offered by Gross of the violence against the defenceless Jews of Jedwabne and Radziłów are proof enough that many Poles were involved in these heinous crimes. Nevertheless, the historical context within which the killings occurred strongly suggests that the murder of the Jews in this region by Poles did not occur without the knowledge, consent, and even direct participation of the SS. Moreover, that SS units may have been more deeply involved than Gross acknowledges does not exonerate those Poles who acted as the Germans' accomplices.

It is important to remember that the SS deliberately collected information to determine where 'pogroms' could be incited and where they could not. Reinhard Heydrich noted specifically in his 1 July order that 'in the newly occupied areas, particularly those that formerly belonged to Poland, Poles have shown themselves to be anti-communist and anti-Jewish as a result of their recent experiences [during the Soviet occupation]'.[112] Where individuals could not be found to foment anti-Jewish violence, Orpo and Wehrmacht propaganda units attempted to inflame

---

[110] R. Ignatiew, quoted in 'Press Release on the Final Findings of Investigation S 1/00/Zn into the Killing of Polish Citizens of Jewish Origin in the Town of Jedwabne on 10 July 1941', 9 July 2002, available on the website of the Institute of National Remembrance at <www.ipn.gov.pl/index_eng.html>.   [111] Ibid.

[112] Heydrichs Einsatzbefehl Nr. 2 vom 1.7.1941, repr. in Klein (ed.), *Die Einsatzgruppen in der besetzten Sowjetunion 1941/42*, 320.

antisemitism using loudspeaker announcements, photographs, public lectures, and films like *The Eternal Jew* to raise the ire of local non-Jews.[113] In effect, SS authorities were well aware of the historically strong anti-Jewish feeling in the territories that formerly comprised the Pale of Settlement, and they found local populations generally willing to assist in the liquidation of the Jewish communities in their midst. The Germans were further aided in their destructive mission by nearly two years of brutal Soviet occupation of the region that dramatically inflamed native antisemitic sentiment.

German documents offer several telling clues about the extent to which the anti-Jewish policies of the SS met with success in the western region of the Białystok district. Among these documents is a report of 9 July from the intelligence officer of the V Corps, which ominously refers to the 'threatening attitude' that the Polish population in his sector had recently adopted towards the Jews.[114] Three days later officers with the Sicherheitsdivision 221 noted in the unit war diary that pogroms had broken out in Kolno and Szczuczyn, both located to the north of Łomża.[115] The pogrom in Kolno resulted in the deaths of thirty Jews, while in Szczuczyn as many as 400 were killed. Similarly, the commander of the rear army area for Heeresgruppe Mitte reported on 20 July that pogroms had broken out 'in several localities near the border with the General Government'.[116] Further evidence provided by Dieter Pohl, Shmuel Spector, Martin Dean, Bogdan Musial, and Shalom Cholawsky also clearly demonstrates the ease with which Heydrich's Sicherheitspolizei were able to mobilize massacres among the Lithuanian, Polish, and Ukrainian civilian populations in the regions adjacent to East Prussia and the General Government.[117]

These killings were stimulated in many places by small groups of individuals whom the Sicherheitspolizei had identified as dependable collaborators. By employing agitators to whip up anti-Jewish sentiment to the point of explosion, German propagandists were then able to depict the massacres as spontaneous outbursts of popular violence. This portrayal supported the Nazi propaganda message that Jews were criminals and oppressors. Citing outbursts of 'spontaneous' violence as evidence that Jews were exploiting and terrorizing the non-Jewish population, the SS was then able to justify its own murderous attacks on Jewish communities. This

---

[113] Gerlach, *Kalkulierte Morde*, 536–7, notes that films and lectures on 'Die Juden, das Unglück Russlands' were shown in Belarus from July 1941 to 1943. These efforts did not meet with success in the eastern sections of Belarus, where Nebe complained that it had been impossible to initiate anti-Jewish violence among Belarusians.

[114] Ic-Morgenmeldung V A.K., 9 July 1941, Beilage zum Kriegstagebuch AOK 9, Anlage III zum Tätigkeitsbericht der Abt. Ic/AO, 21.6.41–31.7.41, NARA, RG 242, T-312, r. 277, fr. 7837267.

[115] Anlage 50, Sicherungsdivision 221, 12 July 1941, Anlagen zum Kriegstagebuch, 1.5.41–16.12.41, Bundesarchiv-Militärchiv, Freiburg, RH 26-221/84.

[116] Der Befehlshaber des rückwärtigen Heeres-Gebiets Mitte, Abt. Ia, Br.B.Nr. 393/41 geh. An OKH, Gen.Qu., 20 July 1941, Anlagen Sonderband zum Kriegstagebuch 1 der Befehlshaber d. rückwärtigen H.Geb. Mitte, Abt. Ia, NARA, RG 242, T-501, r. 1, fr. 503.

[117] See n. 1 for a listing of these scholars' publications.

dynamic of German agitation, Polish 'pogrom', and SS killing action was integral to the anti-Jewish policy implemented by the SS in the Białystok district and elsewhere in eastern Poland during the first eight weeks of Operation Barbarossa. The elimination of Jews in regions of Lithuania and eastern Poland along the frontier of East Prussia and the General Government was also central to the progressive radicalization of SS anti-Jewish policy in the summer of 1941 that ultimately resulted in genocide. Given German fears about the development of partisan warfare and the widely held belief (the *Feindbild*) that Jews presented a dire threat to security in the newly occupied territories, the use of the local non-Jewish population to counter this threat was a logical step to the SS. It is safe to say, however, that the dynamic of agitation, 'pogrom', and reprisal would not have developed were not a considerable number of Lithuanians, Latvians, Poles, Ukrainians, Belarusians, and Romanians prepared to join in the destruction of Jewish communities. By mid-summer 1941 the powder keg of anti-Jewish feeling in eastern Europe was set to explode in the wake of the Soviet occupation, but in the final analysis it was the SS and not the indigenous non-Jewish population that struck the match and lit the fuse.

Jews in the Polish Security Apparatus: An Attempt to Test the Stereotype

ANDRZEJ PACZKOWSKI

IN the course of my research into the security apparatus in the Polish People's Republic, I have often thought about writing on the ethnic make-up of the organization, but somehow I could not summon the courage to do so.[1] After all, the subject is problematic in terms of the degree of its mystification, its moral and political delicacy, and poverty of access to relevant sources. But given the centrality of the issue in recent discussions of the extent and intensity of antisemitism in Poland, I feel I cannot avoid it.

I shall not become entangled here in the problem of Jews and communism, which continues to engage academics of all types and in many languages. Neither do I have any ambition to enter the area of Polish–Jewish relations, which has been hotly researched. However, the issue of Jews in the Urzędy Bezpieczeństwa (Polish security apparatus, UB) includes that of the relationship of Jews to communism as well as of Poles to Jews, and also perhaps of Jews to Poles.

The disproportionate number of Jews in the communist movement and in radical leftist movements in general is unquestioned, though the time frame is difficult to define: from a certain moment, and certainly from the 1950s, there was an outflow of Jews from these movements rather than the reverse. Furthermore, only a (usually insignificant) minority of Jews laid claim to the possibility of entry (for example, in the Jewish state itself). In spite of this, and regardless of their many and varied motivations, this disproportionate number influenced the attitude of Poles and other nationalities towards Jews in general, and was at times the subject of controversy among Jews themselves.

Since the 1980s the issue has often been addressed in Polish literature and commentary.[2] Although I know of no bibliography on the subject, my impression is that

---

[1] I have given a lecture on the subject at the Żydowski Instytut Historyczny (Jewish Historical Institute) and mentioned it in a couple of texts; e.g. 'Terror und Überwachung. Die Funktion des Sicherheitsdienstes in Polen von 1944 bis 1956', *BF Informiert*, 23 (Berlin, 1999), 8.

[2] One of the first was the essay by Stanisław Krajewski (using the pseudonym Abel Kainer), 'Żydzi i komunizm', *Krytyka*, 15 (1982), 178–206. Also noteworthy is the group of texts apearing in *Aneks*, 41–2 (1986), including articles by Jakub Karpiński, Jan T. Gross, and Aleksander Smolar, as well as Roman Zimand's pamphlet *Piorun i popiół: Czy Polacy i Żydzi wzajem się nienawidzą?* (Warsaw, 1987), trans. as 'Wormwood and Ashes (Do Poles and Jews Hate Each Other?)', *Polin*, 4 (1989), 313–53. See also

there are significantly more antisemitic texts devoted to it than texts that try to analyse or justify the choices made by Jews. The narrower goal of this short chapter is merely to follow up a statement by 'Abel Kainer' that 'some of the[se] speculations . . . should be confronted with the most detailed factual data possible'. Thus, I would like to confront with evidence from archival sources one 'speculation' by Stanisław Krajewski[3] relating to Jewish participation in the Polish security apparatus in the years 1944–56.

First, however, to provide context I will present data from the Soviet Union, whose security apparatus was the model for similar services in other communist countries. I believe that these data are known to only a very few Polish historians. In an article entitled 'Evrei v apparate VChK–OGPU v 20-e gody' ('Jews in the Cheka–OGPU Apparatus in the 1920s'), L. Krichevsky analyses the ethnic structure of the Soviet security apparatus, not only in relation to its Jewish officials.[4] The data he selects indicate that people from minority backgrounds played a key role during the period when the Cheka was set up. In September 1918, of all the functionaries of this organization, 35.6 per cent were Latvians, 6.3 per cent Poles, and 3.7 per cent Jews; thus these three nationalities made up 45.6 per cent of all *chekisty*. But among the 'responsible workers' they made up 69.9 per cent.[5] With time the *apparat* became gradually Russified, so that, for example, in 1924 in the central apparatus of the OGPU (consisting of 2,402 people) Russians made up 69.5 per cent, Latvians 8.7 per cent, Jews 8.5 per cent, and Poles 3.7 per cent.[6] At the beginning of 1940 in the central apparatus of the NKVD (approximately 3,600 people) Russians made up 84 per cent, Ukrainians 6 per cent, Jews 5 per cent, and Belarusians 1.2 per cent.[7] A slightly different picture is presented in *Kto rukovodil NKVD 1934–1941* (Who Ran with NKVD 1934–1941) by Nikita V. Petrov and Konstantin V. Skorkin.[8] This book contains, among other things, biographical information on more than 500 officials fulfilling directorial functions both in the central office (from department heads to the *narkom* (people's commissar)) and in the field (from directors of *oblast* offices upwards). During the years covered by this work the number of *rukovodyashchie kadry* (cadre leaders) gradually grew from ninety-six in 1934 to 182 in 1941. According to the authors' calculations, in 1934 (as at 10 July[9]) Jews made up 38.5 per cent, Russians 31.2 per cent, and Latvians 7.3

K. Kersten, *Polacy, Żydzi, komunizm: Anatomia półprawd 1939–1968* (Warsaw, 1992). An important monograph which for unknown reasons has yet to be published in Polish is Jaff Schatz's broad sociological work *The Generation: The Rise and Fall of the Jewish Communists of Poland* (Berkeley and Los Angeles, 1991). ³ See n. 2.

⁴ In O. V. Budnitsky (ed.), *Evrei i russkaya revolyutsiya* (Moscow, 1999) (OGPU: Obshcherosiiskoie Glavnoe politicheskoe upravlenie, All-Russian Main Political Office). I am grateful to Prof. Szymon Rudnicki for providing me with a copy. ⁵ Ibid. 328. ⁶ Ibid. 334. ⁷ Ibid. 344.

⁸ (Moscow, 1999), 502.

⁹ This is the date of the liquidation of the OGPU and its incorporation (as the Glavnoe upravlenie gosudarstvennoi bezopasnosti: Main Administration of State Security, GUGB) into a unified NKVD.

per cent.[10] In 1941 (as at 26 February[11]) Jews were 5.5 per cent and Russians 64.8 per cent; Ukrainians (15.4 per cent) and Georgians (6.6 per cent) overtook the Jews. A fundamental change took place in the ethnic make-up in late 1938 and early 1939: on 1 September 1938 Jews still constituted 21.3 per cent of the management cadre, but as at 1 July 1939 they were only 3.9 per cent. (From 1938 Poles, who made up 4.2 per cent of the management cadre in 1934, disappeared from this category of *chekist*.)

Comparing Krichevsky's data with those of Petrov and Skorkin, it seems certain that the higher the position, the greater the participation of *inorodtsy* (foreigners). Krichevsky emphasizes that in the 1920s the role of Latvians declined and their place was taken by Jews; at the same time he asserts that the changes in ethnic make-up 'were not the result of a central personnel policy, but were the effect of objective changes in Soviet society'.[12] The data collected by Petrov and Skorkin seem to indicate, however, that, at least with regard to the category on which they focused, the key agent of change was the Great Purge. They did not calculate by ethnic group, but it is possible to infer that the sudden outflow of Jews in 1938 was connected with the fact that this was the year of the greatest repression[13] of the heads of the apparatus of repression themselves: of the 241 officials on record as having been convicted in the period 1933–40, 107 were caught up in the Stalinist machine in 1938 and fifty-seven the following year.[14] This change was connected with Beria's campaign to 'purge' the apparatus of 'Ezhov's people' and 'old cadres'.

The party leadership was constantly drawing attention to the ethnic make-up of various state organs, but communications on this subject are sporadic. Among others, Leon Trotsky was concerned that the presence of too many *inorodtsy* among the officials would prompt 'chauvinist anti-Soviet agitation'. At a meeting of the Politburo of the Central Committee of the Bolshevik party in April 1919 there was a debate over the disproportionate number of Latvians and Jews in the institutions of the 'rear' compared with those fighting at the front.[15] However, Krichevsky asserts, following his examination of primary sources, that successive attempts to regulate the ethnic make-up of the state and party apparatuses did not significantly alter the

---

[10] Petrov and Skorkin, *Kto rukovodil NKVD*, p. 495, table 4.

[11] This is the date of the separation of the security section from the NKVD and the creation of the NKGB. [12] Krichevsky, 'Evrei v apparate VChK–OGPU', 345.

[13] 'Repression' virtually always meant a death sentence.

[14] Petrov and Skorkin, *Kto rukovodil NKVD*, p. 500, table 9. Beria took the office of first deputy *narkom* on 22 Aug. 1938, became the chief of the GUGB on 29 Sept., and the *narkom* on 25 Nov. of that year. In 1933–9 a total of 22,600 *chekisty* were arrested. On the scale of the entire apparatus, 1935 was the record year, during which more than 6,200 officials were arrested; 5,600 were arrested in 1938 (ibid. 501).

[15] Krichevsky, 'Evrei v apparate VChK–OGPU', 339. Of course there were more in rear positions—otherwise there would have been nothing to discuss.

situation. Thus, before there was the issue of Jews in the UB there was the issue of Jews in the Cheka as well as that of Latvians in the Cheka.[16]

Unfortunately, in Polish archives I was unable to obtain the kind of materials that Krichevsky used. The only Polish historian so far who has been able to find original precise statistics on the officials of the UB, and then only for a single time period and in one *województwo* (voivodeship), is Leszek Piłat.[17] In the few works dealing with the local UBs at either the *województwo* or *powiat* (district) levels there is a dearth of information on the subject.[18] Neither Tadeusz Walichnowski, the editor of the official collected history of the department,[19] nor Henryk Dominiczak, the author of the most extensive monograph on the security apparatus,[20] mentions this issue. In some analyses and reports (including the insistent statements by Józef Światło) there are isolated references and general evaluations, but no primary statistical data.

One of the few reliable sources is a report sent by Nikolay Selivanovsky, the chief Soviet adviser at the Ministerstwo Bezpieczeństwa Publicznego (Ministry of Public Security, MBP), to Beria on 20 October 1945. According to this report, Jews made up 18.7 per cent of the ministry's workforce and held half of the managerial positions. In certain sections their presence was even greater: in Department I (counter-intelligence) they made up 27 per cent of the staff and occupied all of the managerial positions, and in the Press Control Department they were 'up to 50 per cent'. It is unclear why, in addition to the MBP, the report mentions 'the Radom office', in which 82.3 per cent of the officials were apparently Jews.[21] It is difficult to doubt the competence and access to information of a person who was de facto head of the ministry; thus we must accept these data, at least initially, as reliable. They are, however, random and there are no definitive figures among them. For the same period (25 November 1945) there is a note, drawn up by Bolesław Bierut on the basis of information provided by Stanisław Radkiewicz, minister of the MBP, according to which Jews made up 1.7 per cent of the total workforce of the MBP (438 out of 25,600) and held about 13 per cent of the managerial positions (67 out of 500).[22]

---

[16] Even today some Russians justify their animosity towards Latvians (and independent Latvia) by pointing to the role that their forebears played in the creation of the Cheka and the 'Red Terror' of the civil war period.

[17] L. Piłat, 'Struktura organizacyjna i działalności Wojewódzkiego Urzędu Bezpieczeństwa Publicznego w Lublinie 1944–1945', *Studia Rzeszowskie*, 6 (1999), 77–92.

[18] There are no systematic data even in the wide-ranging monograph—the only one of its kind to date—on a regional apparatus (Z. Nawrocki, *Zamiast wolności: UB na Rzeszowszczyźnie 1944–1949* (Rzeszów, 1998)).

[19] T. Walichnowski (ed.), *Ochrona bezpieczeństwa państwa i porządku publicznego w Polsce 1944–1988* (Warsaw, 1989).

[20] H. Dominiczak, *Organy bezpieczeństwa PRL 1944–1990: Rozwój i działalność w świetle dokumentów MSW* (Warsaw, 1997).

[21] T. Cariewskaja et al. (eds.), *Teczka specjalna, J. W. Stalina: Raporty NKWD z Polski 1944–1946* (Warsaw, 1998), 421.

[22] Krystyna Kersten used these data in her chapter 'Żydzi—władza komunistów', in her *Polacy Żydzi, komunizm*, 83–4.

There is thus a discrepancy between these two articles: Selivanovsky's report speaks of '50 per cent of the managerial positions' while Bierut's asserts that the figure is 13 per cent. The difference is probably due to the fact that in the former the figure referred to the ministry itself, while the latter referred to the entire apparatus (including regional offices).

Some time ago, on the basis of a 1978 analysis by Bureau C of the Ministerstwo Spraw Wewnętrznych (Ministry of Internal Affairs, MSW) entitled *Służba Bezpieczeństwa Polskiej Rzeczpospolitej Ludowej 1944–1978: Centrala* ('The Security Service of the Polish People's Republic 1944–1978: Head Office'),[23] statistical research was conducted on people who in 1944–56 occupied the position of section (*wydział*) head or higher in the head office (originally the Department, then the Ministry of Public Security, and then the Committee for Public Security).[24] This is obviously a source of limited usefulness as it concerns only a part of the managerial apparatus. It does not cover, for example, officials who occupied managerial positions—even the highest, such as heads of the Wojewódzki Urząd Bezpieczeństwa Publicznego (Voivodeship Office of Public Security, WUBP)—in regional offices but who never reached higher positions in the head office. This category includes 447 people. For 131 of these—or 29.3 per cent—their 'nationality' was listed as Jewish. In 1944 and 1945 people of this nationality made up 24.7 per cent of the total. This is thus half the number given by Selivanovsky in his report. This discrepancy may be due to Beria's envoy using different criteria for 'managerial position', but since we do not know what criteria he used, it is difficult to verify his information. The data contained in Bierut's note cannot be compared here, since they included the entire managerial apparatus, including the regional offices.

In the head office the involvement of Jewish officials remained more or less constant and, with the exception of the years 1944 and 1945, wavered around 30 per cent. This reflects a general stabilization at all levels of the apparatus. Poles made up 63.5 per cent while other nationalities were present in insignificant numbers (Russians 2.7 per cent, Ukrainians 2.2 per cent, Belarusians 2 per cent). The discussion here is exclusively about ministry officials and so leaves out *sovetniki* (advisers), among whom the ethnic make-up was probably entirely different. I was not able to establish whether there were (Soviet) Jews among these advisers.

[23] A reprint with introduction by Mirosław Piotrowski was published as *Ludzie Bezpieki w walce z Narodem i Kościołem: Służba Bzpieczeństwa w Polskiej Rzeczyspospolitej Ludowej w latach 1944–1978. Centrala* (Lublin, 1999). The calculations under discussion were conducted in SPSS/PC+ by Jarosław Pawlak in the framework of a research project under my direction entitled 'Institutions of a Totalitarian State: Poland 1944–1956'. In the course of this research, unfortunately, I made an error which I have been unable to correct: the number of Jews in 1957 (and later years) was not counted, and so I am lacking data for a quantitative description of one of the most essential facts: the purge of Jews from the security apparatus after 1956.

[24] The calculations were carried out this way because the analysis contained biographical information only for people in these positions, and not for all of the department's personnel. One category in the biographies was 'nationality'.

In his article Leszek Piłat states that, as at 1 February 1946 in the Lublin *województwo*, of 1,122 UB officials at all levels there were nineteen of Jewish nationality, that is, 1.7 per cent (this corresponds, coincidentally, to the proportion for the whole department noted by Bierut several months earlier). A clear majority (fourteen) occupied higher positions and worked in the WUBP.[25] Biographical information in Zbigniew Nawrocki's monograph serves as an indicator of the proportions of various nationalities in the security apparatus in the Rzeszów *województwo*.[26] According to this information, of the 102 people who in 1944 to 1949 were in managerial posts—managers, directors, and deputy directors of sections in the WUBP—four (i.e. 4 per cent) were of Jewish 'nationality'. Doubtless there were significant regional or local differences. We cannot exclude the possibility that in Silesia in 1945 there really were 150–225 Jewish officials, as estimated by John Sack.[27] It seems much less likely that Jews constituted half of the Łódź UB, as reported by an inspector from the Central Committee of the Polska Partia Robotnicza (Polish Workers' Party, PPR) in August 1945,[28] or that Jews constituted 82.3 per cent of the Radom UB, as Selivanovsky reported.

This completes all I was able to find in the sources and reliable analyses that was amenable to statistical treatment. The question is whether it is possible to make any generalizations on this basis. We may guardedly assert what is not contested—that Jews were over-represented, occupied higher rather than lower positions, and that the higher the level, the greater their proportion. Many other issues connected with this are worthy of consideration, but I will limit myself to just a few.

One is the matter of ethnic identification. In the course of research on the subject of Jews in the UB I have several times come across questionable biographical and statistical data created and gathered in the department. For example, the data contained in the article by Bureau C have raised doubts because it would be reasonable to suspect that the 'nationality' category was filled in later by the authors of the publication in 1978—thus, during a period in which a strong antisemitic tendency had existed in the security apparatus (and also in the party apparatus) for more than twenty years. It would therefore be logical for them to have exaggerated the number of Jewish officials working in the department during the period when the UB committed its most serious crimes (1945–56). However, after checking several

---

[25] Piłat, 'Struktura organizacyjna', 88. It is not impossible that all of the other *województwa* had a similar composition. This would be very interesting if it were true.

[26] Nawrocki, *Zamiasat wolności*, *passim*.

[27] J. Sack, *Oko za oko: Przemilczana historia Żydów, którzy w 1945 r. mścili się na Niemcach* (Gliwice, 1995), 279. Zygmunt Woźniczka, in his article 'Wojewódzki Urząd Bezpieczeństwa Publicznego w Katowicach (1945–1956)', *Kronika Katowic*, 8 (1999), 140–76, does not provide figures for the officials of the UB in the Silesia–Dąbrowski *województwo*. If we assume, taking into account the significance of the region and the size of its population, that the Silesian *bezpieka* (UB) numbered perhaps 1,500 people, then the figure given by Sack would represent 10–15%, which is possible.

[28] K. Lesiakowski, *Mieczysław Moczar, 'Mietek': Biografia polityczna* (Warsaw, 1998), 101.

sources,[29] I have come to the conclusion that this information was simply taken from personnel forms. In these forms, as in similar forms around the country and covering the whole population, including elementary school students, for many years (probably until 1980) there was a box for nationality which had to be filled in in some way. So we should accept that the authors of the guide to the department used authentic records along with other types of statistical data. In one instance—that of the Lublin *województwo* in 1946—figures on religion were introduced into the statistics and there was such a category in personnel forms (I was unable to determine how long this item remained in such forms, but I remember filling it in myself several times).

A separate problem, and one that is unusually complex, is that of ethnic self-identification. I will not go into this question in depth, but for the sake of completeness I should mention that the conviction that the communist Jew was primarily a communist, and even ceased by definition to be a Jew, has been repeated many times. (Others have made use of this manipulation as well, asserting, for example, that one is either a communist or a Pole.) A certain number of Jews in the UB and other branches of the apparatus of the communist state—perhaps even the majority—did not consider themselves Jews. They not only broke off all cultural ties with Jewishness, but were also positively anti-Jewish in that they fought against not only the religion, but also other elements of Jewish culture (especially Jewish languages, and particularly Yiddish). They were culturally Polonized and ideologically communized.[30]

In my opinion there is no possibility of reaching statistically valid conclusions on this subject as the only objective research conducted *in situ* at the end of the 1940s covered all Polish Jews, without distinguishing categories such as communist Jews, far less Jews in the UB. It is worth recalling, however, that, according to the forms examined by Irena Hurwic-Nowakowska, 22 per cent of those asked responded that they were Poles (2.1 per cent said that they were both Jewish and Polish, 1.7 per cent asserted that they did not belong to any national community, and 73.9 per cent considered themselves Jews).[31] In the statistics from the Lublin WUBP, sixteen out of nineteen Jews answered 'Mosaic' in the religion category.[32] It is not clear whether this means that they were practising, but they can be said to have thus

---

[29] I checked among other places in *Słownik biograficzny działaczy polskiego ruchu robotniczego*, vols. i–iii (Warsaw, 1978–92); in the *Polski słownik biograficzny*, vols i–xl (Kraków, 1939–); and in personal papers from the Central Committee of the PZPR filed in the Archiwum Akt Nowych, Warsaw, in 1990.

[30] This is one of the key elements of the analysis in the aforementioned monograph by Jaff Schatz. Schatz analyses the issue of 'the Generation's' participation in the security apparatus in *The Generation*, 222–8. He identifies four motives for entry into the UB: identification with the new system; party discipline ('the party has placed me in this position'); a desire for revenge (against anti-communists, antisemites, collaborationists); and a 'pure lust for power'.

[31] I. Hurwic-Nowakowska, *Żydzi polscy (1947–1950): Analiza więzi społecznej ludności żydowskiej* (Warsaw, 1996), p. 179, table 6. [32] Piłat, 'Struktura organizacyjna', 89.

confirmed their national identity. Unfortunately I have no data that indicate how
widespread this position was among Jews in the UB. It is not possible, after all, to
get into the skin of Józef Różański, for example, who in 1981, twenty-seven years
after his removal from the UB and seventeen years after he was released from his
(deserved) prison sentence, requested that he be buried in the Jewish cemetery,
asserting that he had considered himself a Jew in 1945 and 1953. Nor can we tell
how his communism related to his Jewishness.[33] Perhaps one way out would be to
replace the designation 'Jew' with the designation 'person of Jewish descent'.
However, there are no data for applying such distinctions in quantitative research,
and that is precisely what interests us here.

The security apparatus was a distinct element in the state apparatus, and the
selection of candidates for employment in it, at least in the first years of its existence, was particularly vital. Those who were drawn into or rather delegated to it
enjoyed a high degree of trust and had had their loyalty tested. Of course this was
especially true of those at the highest level, while things were done differently lower
down. One of the guarantees was a long-lasting organizational connection with the
communist movement. As a result, of the 447 more senior officials in the head
office, 21 per cent had been members of the pre-war Komunistyczna Partia Polski
(Polish Communist Party, KPP). Among those who entered 'Jewish' as their
nationality, there was a significantly higher proportion of KPP members: 35.1 per
cent. Among Poles there were decisively fewer: only 16.2 per cent. No research has
been conducted on this question, but it seems very likely that former KPP members
felt something like an *esprit de corps*, and doubtless also had higher aspirations concerning their place in 'serving the cause'. It is also possible that maintenance of
close social contacts, which was (and is) treated as 'national (Jewish) kinship', was at
least partially an expression of the group loyalty of 'old communists' instead.

Following on Trotsky's concerns, it is worth pausing for a moment over the
issue of 'improper proportions' in the security apparatus, for in Poland this
question really refers only to Jews. The simple fact that data on nationality were
gathered cannot be treated as an act directed against anyone. After all, the statistics
analysed on the basis of the aforementioned forms covered a broad range of
categories: age, gender, education, party affiliation, and the infamous 'social background'. In the data and articles known to me there is little to indicate that
Trotsky's dilemma played a more significant role before 1948. Some data can be
found in the report by Selivanovsky, who wrote that 'the situation arouses serious
dissatisfaction among Poles, who speak of [the Jews] lording it over them',[34] and in
the report mentioned earlier by the inspector from the Central Committee of the
PPR sent from Łódź. But in both of these cases the authors are concerned with
society's attitude towards the UB Jewish communists and not with the mood

[33] No clear answer is offered in the interesting monograph by Barbara Fijalkowska, *Borejsza i
Różański: Przyczynek do dziejów stalinizmu w Polsce* (Olsztyn, 1995).
[34] Cariewskaja *et al.* (eds.), *Teczka specjalna*, 422.

within the party and apparatus. However, they corroborate the documents from the period of the 'struggle with the right-wing nationalist deviation'. In August 1948 Mieczysław Moczar was accused of antisemitism in connection with statements about the number of 'Jewish comrades' in the security apparatus being too high.[35] The problem must have been the subject of disagreement significantly earlier, and the fact that Gomułka cited the question of 'attitude towards Jewish comrades' as one of four reasons why he rejected Stalin's proposal that he become a member of the Politburo that was being formed in the Polska Zjednoczona Partia Robotnicza (Polish United Workers' Party, PZPR) testifies to the weight of these differences.[36] That the disagreements also (and perhaps mainly) concerned the situation in the security apparatus is apparent from a speech by Gomułka (which admittedly was given much later and in a specific context). In the course of the March 1968 campaign he asserted that twenty years earlier the struggle against him had begun when he tried to change the leadership of the MBP.[37] We may therefore suppose that one of the reasons for unfavourable personnel decisions in this period was a dislike of Jews or outright antisemitism.[38]

One of the innumerable paradoxes of communism, at least in its Soviet version, was the drastic changes in the party line. One such change concerned the position on Jews. Without entering into irrelevancies, I mention here a report by the Soviet ambassador in Warsaw, Viktor Lebedev, sent to Moscow on 10 July 1949. Among the addressees were Stalin, Molotov, and Beria. Ambassador Lebedev, whose knowledge of Poland was good, warned the recipients of his letter of the presence of 'agents of the pre-war intelligence and counter-intelligence services' at the highest levels, and hinted that Minister Radkiewicz was 'a nationalist' and that his wife was 'a passionately anti-Soviet person'. He emphasized also that Minc, Berman, and Zambrowski still supported Jewish nationalism; that is, those who a year earlier, with the assistance of the Kremlin, had unseated Gomułka for Polish nationalism. He also drew attention to the fact that in the MBP, 'beginning with the vice-ministers through the department directors, there is not a single Pole. They are all Jews.'[39] It

[35] Lesiakowski, *Mieczysław Moczar*, 100.

[36] T. V. Volokhtina *et al.* (eds.), *Vostochnaya Evropa v dokumentakh rossiiskikh arkhivov 1944–1953*, vol. i: *1944–1948* (Moscow, 1997), 940–1.

[37] Quotes from this speech can be found in D. Stola, *Kampania antysyjonistyczna w Polsce 1967–1968* (Warsaw, 2000), 127. In the summer of 1948 Mieczysław Moczar, the long-time chief of the Łódź WUBP and member of the Central Committee of the KPP during the period of conspiracy, was transferred to the MBP to the position of de facto vice-minister. Gomułka was certainly exaggerating when he said that he became the subject of an attack originating in Moscow; the first analyses of the right-wing nationalist deviation were prepared in the Central Committee of the Bolshevik party by the spring of 1948.

[38] Zbigniew Girzyński discusses this and other reasons for being fired from the MSW in his article 'Czystki polityczne w Ministerstwie Spraw Zagranicznych w latach 1947–1956', *Czasy Nowożytne*, 6 (1999), 31.

[39] A. Kochański *et al.* (eds.), *Polska w dokumentach z archiwów rosyjskich 1949–1953* (Warsaw, 2000), 46.

was thus not a matter of a better image for the party (and the security apparatus) in the eyes of society; it was pure—albeit intra-party—antisemitism. Lebedev believed that 'the time has not yet come for a fundamental resolution to the question of the battle with Jewish nationalism in the Polish party. We can only think about a gradual preparation for such a resolution.' Of particular interest to the subject here, Lebedev added that he felt the situation was worsening, and that this 'concerns in particular the apparatus of the Ministry of Public Security'. He concluded by saying that 'restoring the leadership of the MBP to health would be an important step on the road to restoring the situation in the leadership of the Polish party to health'.[40]

Certain steps were taken by the leadership of the PZPR: a new vice-minister, Wacław Lewikowski, appeared within the elite staff of the MBP. Lewikowski was not only Aryan but also a long-time functionary of the Comintern. Also, Różański was removed from the investigation of the Lechowicz–Jaroszewicz case (which, as we know, was the origin of the Gomułka and Spychalski proceedings); Romkowski personally took over.

However, this was too little. Far more important was the decision of February–March 1950 on the establishment of a Secretariat of the Organizational Bureau of the Central Committee, which was to become the highest and most important decision-making organ for several years. Neither Berman nor Minc, whom Lebedev had mentioned among those who 'had not freed themselves of strong nationalist prejudices',[41] was included in this body. Of the threesome thus evaluated, only Zambrowski was included in the Secretariat of the Organizational Bureau. Although it has not been proved, it seems to me that from that time at least until Stalin's death the role of Minc and Berman was in fact reduced. Their place under Bierut was taken by Edward Ochab, Zenon Nowak, and Franciszek Mazur, all of whom were Aryans. After the first reading at a session of the Politburo of the draft on the establishment of this office Lebedev wrote directly to Stalin—which was quite astonishing—presenting the following justifications: Bierut 'should free himself from the "confusion" in which he finds himself, draw two or three Polish comrades close, and rely on them more boldly'.[42] Bierut thus found comrades of a more suitable background. Unfortunately, I do not know whether he consulted with Moscow in this matter. On 12 April 1950 the secret section of TASS communicated to Stalin (with copies to Molotov and Malenkov) its commentary on the composition of the personnel of the new office. Drawing on the opinions of Stefan Matuszewski and Wacław Wolski, who as we know from other documents were perhaps the most frequent guests of the Soviet embassy in Warsaw, the author of the commentary asserts that 'many Jewish workers in the Central Committee consider [the decision on the ethnic make-up of the new office] an attack against

---

[40] Ibid. 47. The phrase 'fundamental resolution' (*korennoe reshenie*) is disturbingly reminiscent of the Nazi 'final solution', but there is no evidence that the antisemitism of the Soviet leadership (and of course not only the leaders) might have led to a new Holocaust.   [41] Ibid. 45.   [42] Ibid. 74.

Jewish party workers', but, according to Matuszewski, 'it was enthusiastically supported by the entire party'. Wolski was more sceptical, believing that there was still a 'Jewish clique' in the party, which 'not only hindered the advancement of Poles, but also baited leading party activists like Franciszek Jóźwiak-Witold'.[43] Thus, as the wave of antisemitism was rising in the Communist Party and the Soviet apparatus after 1948, there appeared in Poland the first of those who wanted to ride it to higher positions. None of them succeeded, however, and Wolski experienced an ignominious defeat: shortly after his next denunciation, he was removed not only from the Central Committee, but also from the party itself.

From the second half of 1949 references appear in Bierut's (preserved) notes, some of which had a point, regarding the presence of Jews in the security apparatus.[44] Though there was no lack of encouraging examples from fraternal countries (Czechoslovakia, Hungary) and in the Soviet Union itself,[45] the antisemitic purge in the UB focused almost exclusively on functionaries of the intelligence service headed by its long-time chief, Wacław Komar; these were mainly people from the Second Department of the General Staff and not from the Seventh Department of the MBP.[46] Although Lebedev had communicated to Stalin his opinion on the necessity of 'replacing' the leadership of the MBP in 1950,[47] the nucleus of the security apparatus remained untouched and all of the department directors remained in their positions or in other positions at the same level.

Until 1956 none of the major changes in the MBP were connected with the antisemitic campaign.[48] The first purges in 1948–9 were directed against 'carriers' of the right-wing nationalist deviation, including Moczar and Grzegorz Korzyński. The next wave came with the thaw after the death of Stalin. The first to lose his job,

---

[43] Ibid. 76. Wolski added dramatically that 'because of the campaign conducted against him, Jóźwiak was rumoured to have mentioned suicide'.

[44] For example, there is his note on the uselessness of Jews as intelligence officers in a situation in which one of the tasks of intelligence was to penetrate Polish political emigration.

[45] One of the victims of the antisemitic purge of the party organs in 1950 was Aron Palkin, chief of the special group that participated in the falsification of the results of the referendum of 1946 and the elections of 1947. See R. Pikhoya, *Sovetskii Soyuz: Istoriya vlasti 1945–1991* (Moscow, 1998), 87.

[46] In the course of this purge the well-known German literary critic of later years Marceli Raich-Ranicki was accused among other things of being a Trotskyist. In a similar context in 1949 people connected with Noel or Hermann Field—either in reality or on the supposition of the UB—were arrested. The conduct of antisemitic purges may have been complicated in Poland by the fact that they started with the struggle against the Polish 'nationalist deviation'.

[47] Kochański *et al.* (eds.), *Polska w dokumentach*, 74.

[48] The reservations of the party leadership about the ethnic make-up of the Ministerstwo Spraw Zagranicznych (Ministry of Foreign Affairs, MSZ) also seem not to have been acted on. That there were such reservations can be seen from 'Notatka o stanie kadr MSZ i wnioski w sprawie zmian personalnych' ('Note on the State of MSZ Cadres and Conclusions in the Matter of Changes in Personnel'), in which it was asserted that 'in terms of nationality the make-up of the managerial staff is unsatisfactory': of eight department directors five were Jews; of four vice-directors three were Jews; and of twenty-eight department heads eighteen were Jewish (W. Borodziej, *Wydział Zagraniczny KC PZPR (1949–1970)* (Warsaw, 1999), 45).

at the beginning of 1954, was Anatol Fejgin (for allowing the 'loss' of Światło), and immediately after him came Różański (for 'violating the people's law and order'). The most serious purge took place in the autumn of 1954 but was not directed at Jews; rather, as a result of the reorganization of the ministry, the vice-ministers Romkowski and Mietkowski were removed (but so was the Aryan minister Radkiewicz). The 'barons' of the security service—the department directors and heads of the regional offices—remained in their posts regardless of their nationality. This does not mean that the security apparatus consisted exclusively of Jews and philosemites, but antisemitic attitudes were not apparent. This was probably because the party leadership, which tightly controlled the security apparatus, did not agree to it. These tendencies did not reveal themselves in their true colours until 1956, when the real campaign against 'Jewish comrades' began in earnest. Whether this occurred as a result of a weakening of this control, or because someone higher up gave the green light, is not clear. It is a fact that all the leading officials of Jewish descent who had survived the period of the antisemitic purges in Prague, Budapest, or Moscow unscathed—although perhaps with trepidation in their hearts—said farewell to the department in late 1956. Indiscriminate and fairly overt antisemitic attacks by recent subordinates and colleagues accompanied these departures. It was in this period that antisemitism rooted itself in the security service for good and lasted throughout the rest of its existence.

The problem of Jews in the UB thus disappeared, to be replaced by the problem of antisemites in the reformed security apparatus. But that is an entirely different story.

Translated from Polish by Claire Rosenson

PART IV

Reviews

REVIEW ESSAYS

Some Remarks on Leszek Hońdo's Study of the Old Jewish Cemetery in Kraków

ANDRZEJ TRZCIŃSKI and MARCIN WODZIŃSKI

FOR CENTURIES the old Jewish cemetery in Kraków has attracted the special attention of researchers on Jewish antiquity and pious pilgrims to holy grave sites, as well as ordinary travellers and the simply curious. Recently, the need for a detailed inventory of the grave sites has become ever more urgent, particularly with the pace of erosion of the headstones. Following the publication by earlier historians of several incomplete descriptions of the cemetery in Kraków, Leszek Hońdo took a full inventory between 1994 and 1997. On the basis of this work he has published a volume entitled *Stary żydowski cmentarz w Krakówie: Historia cmentarza, analiza hebrajskich inskrypcji* ('The Old Jewish Cemetery in Kraków: History of the Cemetery with Analysis of the Hebrew Inscriptions').[1]

Hońdo's work was intended as a general introduction to the full inventory of Kraków's old Jewish cemetery. It consists of three chapters (with an introduction and summary) dealing respectively with the history of the cemetery, the current state of research on the cemetery, and general characteristics of the inscriptions. The last chapter is by far the longest and discusses the language of the inscriptions, the formulaic structure of epitaphs, abbreviations, and the connection between the text and images on the gravestones. The section entitled 'The Formulaic Structure' constitutes a third of the whole book. It deals with many issues beyond the subject of structure, addressing elements of style, the deceased's titles, identifiers (names, nicknames, works, patronymics), forms of presenting data, and formulaic elements on the epitaphs. The book is interspersed with samples of inscriptions, with a photograph, transcription and translation of the epitaph, sometimes a short description of the tombstone, and a discussion of other places where it is described. At the end of the book are a list of references, sketch map of the cemetery, and index.

We have many reservations about this volume, beginning with its conceptualization and composition and ending with the orthography and editorial analysis. In writing this review, however, our purpose is not so much to list the mistakes

[1] Kraków, 1999.

evident in this particular work, but rather to discuss the wider methodological issues arising in the analysis and description of Jewish cemeteries.

The primary weakness of Hońdo's volume is its lack of documentation (a gap partially filled a year later with the publication of the first of five planned volumes of documentation, with photographs of 174 gravestones together with the text of their inscriptions in Hebrew and in Polish translation[2]). The book contains a discussion of materials that are not made available to the reader, and this lack of source materials (texts of inscriptions or photographs of gravestones) leaves the volume inaccessible, at least for the time being, particularly for researchers who are interested in Hebrew epigraphy. Many of the theses Hońdo puts forward are unverifiable. The introduction includes no information on the scope, character, or timetable of any forthcoming supplements to the work. It is not until page 22 (n. 11) that we learn that 'materials in the form of a database are currently ready for publication', and later, on page 82 (n. 209), we read: 'Work is now under way on the preparation of the documentation of the cemetery (including photographic documentation) as a computerized database.'

There are also serious omissions in the descriptions of sample gravestones and their inscriptions that Hońdo uses as a model for further documentation of other gravestones in future publications. Most importantly, in the heading of each tombstone's description there is no information about the date of death. Because of the significant number of grave sites with two *matsevot* (tombstones) or with *matsevot* that have been restored, data on the completion or renovation of a particular gravestone and references to secondary gravestones dedicated to the same person should also be given here. Details of the previous publication of the drawings or photographs of the described tombstone would also be helpful. The 'concise description' of gravestone 147, which is presented as the model, contains no specific features to distinguish it from several hundred other gravestones in the collection under discussion,[3] and the list of references relating to gravestone 147 is also incomplete.[4] It is also not clear whether the given dimensions of a gravestone refer to that part of the original that has been preserved or whether it also includes a recent addition. The proposed order of entries, by inventory number rather than chronological, would make use of the catalogue difficult and necessitate an additional chronological list.

The information provided for the sample gravestone inscriptions is also insufficient, and the descriptions are inconsistent. For example, we do not know whose version of the sample finally appears on page 22: is it Friedberg's, Wet-

---

[2] L. Hońdo, *Inskrypcje starego żydowskiego cmentarza w Krakowie* (Kraków, 2000).

[3] The author did not make use of the (not too carefully considered) classification he criticizes (pp. 76–8) contained in I. Rejduch-Samkowa and J. Samek (eds.), *Katalog zabytków sztuki w Polsce*, iv/6 (Warsaw, 1995). This work does contain, though, sensible models of synthetic descriptions for specific objects.

[4] The following article is missing: E. Duda, 'Stary cmentarz żydowski w Krakowie: Materiały inwentaryzacyjne', *Krzysztofory*, 15 (1988), 104.

stein's, or Hońdo's? It is also not clear which version of Michael Kalahora's inscription is reproduced on page 110. Furthermore, when gravestones are discussed in the text, references to their catalogue numbers are often omitted (as on pp. 35, 44, 50, 52, 143, and 144).

The sample inscriptions and photographs provide little help since there is no list of illustrations, and there are no cross-references to them in the text. Their captions are also inconsistent and fragmentary; for example, the gravestones described in the text are identified by their inventory numbers, but these are not supplied in the captions, except for gravestones in the wall. This means that even if a photograph of a gravestone discussed by Hońdo is reproduced in the book, the reader has no way of matching the text to a photograph without flipping through the entire book. This type of work would also benefit from a list of gravestones, and indexes, at least of persons and geographical names. We hope that these will be added to future publications, together with cataloguing materials.

But the work is incomplete and fragmentary not only on account of the absence of reliable samples of texts. Hońdo's aims, stated in the subtitle of the book (*History of the Cemetery with Analysis of Hebrew Inscriptions*), were to deal with the history of the cemetery, to describe in detail the current state of research, and to analyse the Hebrew inscriptions. The first two points are covered, but treatment of the last is only partial and superficial. The book addresses only a few aspects of the epitaphs, limiting itself to cataloguing typical formulations and a description of the structure of the monuments. On questions such as 'the iconography, typology of gravestones, and poetics of the texts' Hońdo tells us only that 'they require further analysis' (p. 214); however, he does not say when and by whom this analysis will be conducted. He does not even refer to the technical features of the lettering, the ornamentation (including painting), versification, orthography, or many other elements of the cemetery monuments. Without a section devoted to the technical features, or an analysis of the iconography and the poetics of the inscriptions, the work cannot be considered complete or its theses reliable. It is difficult to accept the conclusions in the section characterizing the inscriptions (which occupies more than half the volume) as the author barely mentions their literary contents (e.g. versification, stylistic features, and stylistic traditions). It is even more difficult to accept that 'there is a similarity between the majority of the stylistic methods in the Kraków inscriptions and those found in Silesian inscriptions' since the Kraków style is not characterized, and all the comments on it are contained in one small paragraph (pp. 94–5). Rather, it appears that the author, having failed to offer a stylistic analysis of the Kraków epitaphs, refers to their 'similarity' to the Silesian texts because this is the only group of modern Hebrew inscriptions known to him that have been described in detail.[5] And what of the epigraphy of Małopolska and Ruthenia? Are the Kraków

---

[5] Marcin Wodziński, *Hebrajskie inskrypcje na Śląsku XIII–XVIII wieku* (Wrocław, 1996).

texts not similar to those of the gravestones of Lesko, Przemyśl, or Olkusz? Or perhaps to the old Polish *matsevot* of Lublin or Szczebrzeszyn? Not only here, but also in the chapters devoted to the analysis of epitaph formulations, one senses that Hońdo is insufficiently knowledgeable about epitaphs found in other Jewish cemeteries, particularly those in the Polish–Lithuanian Commonwealth. It seems that, other than the published Kraków *matsevot*, he is unaware of either the preserved monumental materials from the old Polish period,[6] or the inscriptions published earlier, for example from L'viv, Dubno, or Kolomyja (even though these publications are listed in his bibliography). Moreover, although he makes use of materials published by the end of 1998, he does not take into account several recently published substantial collections of inscriptions and valuable studies that would have been primary material for comparison, particularly for the oldest, sixteenth- and seventeenth-century, inscriptions.[7]

In discussing the sources used, it should be mentioned that Hońdo refers to unpublished catalogues and studies without citing them in the text; the references in the notes are incomplete and do not allow for identification of sources (for example, p. 67 n. 157 reads: 'On the basis of catalogue cards'). The bibliography lists only published material, and there is no list of manuscript sources, although there are imprecise references in the footnotes. There is also no list of references to iconographic archival collections. The list of archival photographs reproduced from the cemetery in Remu is also incomplete.[8] What is more, in several places Hońdo paraphrases or even reproduces fragments of works by other authors without acknowledging them, thus taking credit for their authorship.[9] This is especially unsatisfactory as these private manuscripts were provided to Hońdo as a courtesy.

As we mentioned earlier, Hońdo focuses his attention on the structure of the epitaph and on the inventory lists of its elements. Unfortunately, he does not

---

[6] An impressive collection of documentation (particularly photographic) can be found in the Żydowski Instytut Historyczny (Jewish Historical Institute) in Warsaw.

[7] For example, several articles from J. Woronczak (ed.), *Studia z dziejów kultury żydowskiej w Polsce*, ii (Wrocław, 1995); A. Trzciński and J. P. Woronczak, 'Nagrobki z XVI wieku na cmentarzu żydowskim w Szczebrzeszynie', in Krzysztof Pilarczyk (ed.), *Żydzi i judaizm we współczesnych badaniach polskich: Materiały z konferencji, Kraków, 21–23 XI 1995* (Kraków, 1997); A. Trzciński and J. P. Woronczak, 'Nagrobki z XVI wieku na starym cmentarzu żydowskim w Lublinie przy ulicy Siennej', in T. Radzik (ed.), *Żydzi w Lublinie: Materiały do dziejów społeczności żydowskiej Lublina* (Lublin, 1998); A. Trzciński and M. Wodziński, 'Nagrobki z XVII wieku na starym cmentarzu żydowskim w Lublinie przy ulicy Siennej', in Radzik (ed.), *Żydzi w Lublinie*.

[8] See e.g. archival photographs published in L. Dobroszycki and B. Kirshenblatt-Gimblett, *Image before my Eyes: A Photographic History of Jewish Life in Poland* (New York, 1977), 57, not mentioned by Hońdo.

[9] For example, on p. 34 (third para.) and p. 54 (first para.) Hońdo uses a text that is being prepared for publication: A. Trzciński, 'Formalne cechy nagrobków', in J. P. Woronczak (ed.), *Cmentarze żydowskie w Polsce: Vademecum opracowania i opisu* (forthcoming). On p. 164 we find fragments borrowed from Woronczak's article 'Kalendarz żydowski', in the same volume. On p. 172 the author imperceptibly paraphrases Wodziński's *Hebrajskie inskrypcje*, 153.

elaborate or apply the relevant tools to the analysis and characterization of source materials; neither does he refer to methodologies developed by other authors researching Jewish epigraphy in Poland, including our own most recent works and those of Jan Paweł Woronczak. As a result, the work under discussion contributes surprisingly little to the development of the study of cemeteries. Although the author discusses–or rather criticizes–current publications on the subject of the Kraków necropolis in great detail, at times discussing unpublished material for many pages (e.g. pp. 66–80), he takes no note of the methodologies used in these or other works, concentrating his criticism exclusively on the correctness of the transcription or even on spelling errors. What does he propose instead? His suggested analysis leads mainly to a succession of examples and lists of the formulaic structures of inscriptions. This presentation does not give a clear picture of the materials discussed, and is of exceptionally little use for further comparative studies. Researchers in the field are interested above all in the frequency with which particular elements occur in different regions and the characteristics of those elements in the context of other elements of the demographics and social status of the deceased. At the same time Hońdo remains, for the most part, silent on the diachronic aspect of the phenomena he describes, and, in the few fragments in which the time factor is taken into consideration, the smallest unit of measure is the century. It is obvious, however, that the periods of the development of epigraphy do not coincide with these units of time, and that a penetrating analysis would adopt a different and more precise demarcation of the phases in the development of Kraków epitaphs. On the basis of materials known to us we can affirm, for example, that there is a significant difference in formulaic structure between the oldest *matsevot* from the middle of the sixteenth century and the gravestones from the end of that century. Conversely, the late sixteenth-century inscriptions do not differ in any significant way from epigraphs from the first twenty or thirty years of the following century. Perhaps it would therefore make sense to compare the development of the oldest Kraków epitaphs to other collections of sixteenth- and seventeenth-century *matsevot* from Małopolska, in which we find similar phases of development. Such a study would be particularly useful since it seems that sepulchral forms and epigraphy evolved more rapidly in the Kraków metropolitan cemetery than in the provincial cemeteries, and thus served as models for them. Such research would enable us to define the directions of development of Jewish sepulchral art in Poland.

In the section on language the use of Hebrew in epitaphs (in Europe?) is dealt with in a generalized single sentence (p. 97). Hońdo directs the reader only to a superficial and outdated work published in 1931. The discussion of other languages in the rest of the paragraph is more satisfactory, although Hońdo's information is limited to a few sentences cited from very general works on the subject. The single-sentence treatment of Yiddish based on examples from two cemeteries (n. 5) does not adequately capture the real state of affairs.

The discussion of the use of acrostics is very superficial and contains some contradictions. On pages 94–7 Hońdo says that 'acrostics appear on only a few of the preserved gravestones',[10] but on page 107 he contradicts this statement, saying that 'very often the expansive terms of praise form an acrostic'. The only comparative reference here is a mention of Frankfurt am Main, but the use of acrostics in epitaphs in the old Polish period, although infrequent, was equally significant (an aspect of the epigraphy that has to date not been adequately researched).

The failure to deal with the diachronic element leads the author to make several serious errors in his description of epitaph formulations. For example, in describing introductory formulas[11] he states that the custom of putting funereal wording in the form of the abbreviation פ"נ began with sixteenth-century gravestones and became common on men's gravestones in the seventeenth century (p. 112). Although it is possible that a few gravestones with precisely this abbreviation appeared as early as the sixteenth century,[12] such a claim demands solid evidence, and not reliance on one illegible sixteenth-century gravestone (which is mentioned without any indication of the source of the information and is therefore impossible to verify[13]). Hońdo gives only one example of a seventeenth-century gravestone beginning with this formula (no. 336; this is an epitaph dated 1695). However, from analysis of many Hebrew inscriptions in Poland it is evident that the abbreviation appeared only towards the end of the seventeenth century (earlier in Wielkopolska and in Silesia than in central and eastern Poland), and became widespread only in the eighteenth century.[14] This is therefore an

---

[10] Nine epitaphs are listed here, including five from the 19th century, two from the 17th, and one—supposedly the oldest—'from the end of the sixteenth century'. However, on the legible stones from before the 19th century we found more examples, including an unlisted one from 1583 with a double acrostic (no. 180) and one from 1588 (number unknown).

[11] According to the terminology of the author, unfortunately taken from the German (see M. Brocke, *Der alte jüdische Friedhof zu Frankfurt am Main* (Frankfurt am Main, 1996)) rather than the more explanatory Polish, these are funereal formulations.

[12] In Prague the abbreviation reportedly appears in 1540, in Frankfurt in 1596. See Wodziński, *Hebrajskie inskrypcje*, 133.

[13] Hońdo writes only: 'number 227 (wording illegible)'. We managed to establish that the gravestone belonged to David, son of Ephraim Saba; its transcription was published in 1900 by B. Friedberg ('Neue auf dem jüdischen Friedhof in Krakau aufgefundene Grabschriften', *Monatsschrift für Geschichte und Wissenschaft des Judentums* (1900), 359), who actually gave the abbreviation פ"נ. But as we know, in the past, for collectors of antique Judaica, the difference between the full and the abbreviated form was not essential, as they were interested in epitaphs only for the biographical information they contained. Thus in 19th- and early 20th-century works, this type of abbreviation appears often, along with other errors of transcription. It is surprising that Hońdo, who is very critical of earlier authors, including Friedberg, has so uncritically accepted the version given by him.

[14] For instance, from the second half of the 17th century we have examples from Krotoszyn (1670), Cieszyn (1692), and Biała, near Prudnik (1700); for the 1720s from Leszno, Osobłoga, Mikołow, Brzeg Dolny, Tarnów, Lesko, Przemyśl, and Lubaczów; for the 1730s from Głogów, Baligród, and Sieniawa; for the 1740s from Nowy Żmigrod, Lublin, and Szczebrzeszyn. I (A.T.) take this opportunity to admit, after broad comparative studies, that the illegible fragments of

important element in the dating of damaged and unclear epitaphs. From this perspective, as well, the history of the abbreviations seemed important to us, and we decided to test Hońdo's thesis at the cemetery in Kraków. The results confirmed our expectations. Among the 153 seventeenth-century inscriptions we researched (all in areas 4–7) only three (nos. 710, 612, and 569) contained this abbreviation, and all of these dated to the end of the century. As it turns out, not only was the abbreviation not widely used in the seventeenth century (as the author claims), but it appears in the cemetery in Kraków about the same time as it appears in other necropolises in this part of Europe.

In the next part of the section on 'funereal formulations' Hońdo focuses on 'the separation of names or dates and their transference to the head of the inscription', something which already appears on the oldest gravestones in the cemetery in Remu, and lists many variants of this type of opening to epitaphs. The long list of variants is of little value, however, because once again only examples from outside the Polish–Lithuanian Commonwealth are drawn on for comparison. Meanwhile, a comparison of the Kraków inscriptions with other sixteenth- and seventeenth-century gravestones in Poland can yield interesting data: in the oldest preserved monuments the practice of beginning an epitaph with the date of death (sometimes with compositional separation) is in evidence in Przemyśl in 1591–2, in Lesko in 1595, and in Lublin in 1605, though in Szczebrzeszyn it does not appear in either the sixteenth or the seventeenth centuries. The practice of beginning an epitaph with personal information on the deceased appears in Lublin around the middle of the sixteenth century and later, in 1593–4 (but subsequently not until the 1630s). In the other cemeteries mentioned this variant is not found in either the sixteenth or the seventeenth century.

This same bookkeeping method of description (which is, in fact, just cataloguing) means that the substantial list of honorary titles on pages 129–44 says almost nothing about the functioning of these titles in the Kraków epitaphs, and thus in Jewish society in Kraków. The fundamental question that has occupied researchers of Jewish epigraphy for more than 150 years is the function of the title *morenu* (literally 'our teacher', a traditional title of higher religious education) and its gradual devaluation. Hońdo refers only marginally to this problem, telling the reader that 'according to B. Wachstein, the title *morenu* retained its meaning until the nineteenth century' (p. 131); however, Wachstein was describing Viennese, not Kraków, inscriptions. And what of the devaluation of this title in the Polish lands and in Silesia, which was already recognized in the eighteenth century? Surely the rich Kraków material (verified by information from sources other than epitaphs) allows us to determine the function of this title in Kraków? We would have expected to find in this volume, particularly where reference is made to honorary titles, an indication of the frequency with which the title *morenu* appears over a period of time in the context of other titles, epithets, and *kahal* functions that capture the social status of the deceased. This would allow researchers to investigate the true functioning and significance of honorary titles over a particular period and provide evidence of its eventual decline. But Hońdo only mentions (following Leopold Zunz) that in the sixteenth century the title מהר״ר predominated, and that this holds also for the cemetery in Remu (which is true), 'with three exceptions'—numbers 174, 180, and 646 (which is incorrect).[15] The author then presents theoretical variants of titular abbreviations containing the element *morenu* in connection with epithets (p. 132). But there is no reference here to epitaphs in the cemetery in Remu, although the title כמר in particular (with various abbreviation indicators) appears with great frequency in sixteenth-century epitaphs. The problem awaits resolution, and no doubt someone will have to take it up following the publication of the collection of Kraków inscriptions.

The titles of officers of the Va'ad Arba Aratsot are equally poorly treated: from the cemetery in Remu we are given only one example of such a title (p. 137), which seems strange for such a large community. The list should be supplemented by at least the most important titles.[16]

Similarly, the section on abbreviations (pp. 180–204) is not much more than a substantial catalogue of variants found in the cemetery in Kraków. Its short introduction contains a high number of errors, and the remarks on abbreviation symbols with which the section begins are superficial. In note 1066 it is unclear what Hońdo is talking about—surely not about the methods of noting abbreviations in the cemetery in Remu (which we would have expected) or about contemporary methods of standardizing notation. Elsewhere the author makes the imprecise and illogical assertion that letters are differentiated 'by full stops or marks'.[17] Also untrue is the assertion that in eighteenth- and even nineteenth-century inscriptions the difference between the abbreviation for one word and the abbreviation for several words was 'consistently applied' on the gravestones in the cemetery in Remu (p. 181).[18] On the same page Hońdo reports that לפ״ק in the form of a ligature is present from the sixteenth century, and offers three examples (n. 1067):

---

[15] On gravestone 180 we find the exceptional abbreviation מוהר״ר (there is an unreadable three-letter abbreviation and another: כמר), neither is this abbreviation found on gravestone 646 (there is the typical מהרר), and we did not check gravestone 174. We observed other exceptions, however: on *matsevah* 150 (p. 98, transcription, and p. 100, photograph) the abbreviation מוהרר appears, and מהר׳ appears on the gravestone of Moses Menachem, son of Asriel (d. 1557).

[16] פרנס הוועד דד״א—marshal of the Sejm of the Four Lands—appears in at least four epitaphs in Lublin: 1760, 1762, 1766, and about the middle of the 18th century, and ראש לועד הנבחרים — marshal of the Sejm tribunal—appears in Lublin in 1616.

[17] The full stop is one of a broad inventory of various marks. In Hońdo's photographs we notice four types of abbreviation mark: the v-shape, the tilde, the *geresh* (single dash), and the *gershayim* (two dashes) in various graphic variants. These marks serve at the same time to indicate chronograms, chronostics (a poetic chronogram), and acrostics.

[18] Verification is possible only by examining the inscription on the stone or by looking at legible photographs, because in Hońdo's transcriptions the shape and position of the marks are standardized.

number 335 (on the map of the cemetery marked as sixteenth-century), number 394 (marked as seventeenth-century), and number 510 (marked as eighteenth-century). But gravestone 335 is much later (probably 1675 or 1775),[19] gravestone 394 (1646) has no ligature but instead the abbreviation לק, and gravestone 510 dates to the end of the eighteenth century (1794). In the subsequent discussion of the abbreviations for the name of God, which are quite characteristic for epitaphs, he mentions only the conventional symbol consisting of two *yods*, and gives only four examples. He does not even mention two other abbreviations: the ה' and the conventional sign ד'. These first appear in the list of abbreviations (p. 182 nn.), and in addition Hońdo transcribes the symbol ד' as השם (as if this were a first-letter abbreviation of this expression, when in fact it is a conventional symbol for the Tetragrammaton). It would have been very useful to have these abbreviations presented in chronological order and by frequency, since the periods of their usage are essential.

The list of abbreviations itself is decidedly better than the introduction, and the abbreviations have been expanded correctly.[20] However, the list is clearly longer than necessary as Hońdo has also included as abbreviations letters that are merely the remaining parts of words that have otherwise been obliterated, for example a possessive suffix, a fragment of an inflected ending, or the last letter of the root. This part of the list is completely unnecessary as abbreviations of this type do not appear regularly (almost all are unique) and their inclusion contributes no information but rather makes it more difficult to use the rest of the index.

The only fundamental question of Hebrew epigraphy that Hońdo discusses in detail is that of the significance, and thus the proper translation, of the concluding formula תנצב"ה. The discussion turns out to be fruitless, however, as he presents no new arguments. The assertion that the word בצרור should be translated as 'to the wreath' because this was its meaning 'at the time when the inscriptions were written' (p. 174) is unfounded. In support of this translation Hońdo offers only one twentieth-century dictionary as well as an article by Iwona Brzewska dated 1995 and two of his own texts with some translations of Hebrew inscriptions. Moreover, he himself is inconsistent in his translation of the phrase, translating it, curiously, as 'And the wreath of life will be bound his soul' (p. 46), and soon after as 'May his soul be bound into the wreath of life!' (p. 50). This time he makes use of broad comparative materials (including two cemeteries within the Polish–Lithuanian Commonwealth), pointing out early incidences of this formu-

---

[19] In the case of the first date this would be the earliest of the epitaphs recognized so far that uses this ligature. In other cemeteries in the Polish–Lithuanian Commonwealth its earliest application that we know of is in 1787–8 in Lublin; in many cemeteries it does not appear before the beginning of the 19th century.

[20] It should be attributed to Frowald Gil Hüttenmeister and his dictionary of abbreviations (*Abkürzungsverzeichnis hebräischer Grabinschriften* (Frankfurt am Main, 1996)). But even in this section there are errors. היתומים means 'orphans' rather than 'scholars'.

lation in the form of an abbreviation; we are not told, however, what year this formulation dates to in Kraków.[21]

In the introduction to the section on the structure of word formations (p. 97) Hońdo takes issue with the thesis that the oldest Kraków inscriptions were relatively short and simple, but we are not told who, if anyone, actually holds this thesis. The assertion that the content of the epitaph depended on the social status of the deceased is correct, but we are not given the inventory numbers of epitaphs of important persons or of ordinary citizens included in the collection discussed (cf. p. 107) so that this thesis could be checked in the relevant material. The 'evaluation of the length of the inscriptions' (p. 99) leads only to a listing of a few individual examples (two from the sixteenth century, four from the seventeenth, and two from the eighteenth). Among the seventeenth-century examples the 'oldest [inscription] on a sarcophagus', from the tomb of Natan Note Spiro, is given as an example of short inscriptions (cf. pp. 63 and 64). But this is only a fragment of stone, containing part of an informational epitaph, the complete text of which could have been spread over different parts of the gravestone. There is also some doubt about whether this is an original inscription.[22] Hońdo presents the typical structure of an epitaph on the basis of the example of the gravestone of Gitel, the daughter of Moses Auerbach, who died in 1552 (p. 104). In reality, though, the inscription comes from a secondary *matsevah*, erected probably in the nineteenth, not the sixteenth, century, and therefore cannot serve as an example of a typical epitaph.[23] But it does not end here. Citing this 'typical' epitaph, Hońdo has made many mistakes, changing the order of the elements in it to suit his proposed arrangement of the formulation. Here are the differences:

Hońdo has:	On the gravestone:
פה טמונה	פה
כל עין תזל	טמונה אשה
הגונה	הגונה כל מעשיה
כל מעשיה היה באמונ(ה)	היה באמונה מרת גיטל
נדיבה היתה לעניים	בת ר':משה אוערבך ז"ל
כל ימי חיית'	כל עין תזל : נדיבה היתה
לבית הכנסת השכימה	לעניים כל ימי חיית'

---

[21] As a supplement we offer the earliest examples on the evidence of materials preserved from the territory of the Polish–Lithuanian Commonwealth: Szczebrzeszyn, 1545; Lesko, 1565; Lublin, 1570; Przemyśl, 1574.

[22] These doubts are raised by the notation of the introductory formulation in the form of an abbreviation, as well as by the characteristics of the script.

[23] The dissimilarity of the formulation of a secondary *matsevah* is well known to researchers and has been written about extensively. See esp. J. Woronczak, 'Inskrypcje nagrobne z cmentarza żydowskiego w Białej Prudnickiej', *Annales Silesiae*, 19 (1989), 71–3; see also M. Wodziński, 'Inskrypcje', in Woronczak (ed.), *Cmentarze żydowskie w Polsce* (this text is known to Hońdo).

והעריבה	לבית הכנסת השכימה
מרת גיטל בת ר' משה	והעריבה בשיבה טובה
אוערבך ז"ל	הלכה לעולמה
בשיבה טובה הלכה	ביום ראשון כ"ז
לעולמה ביום ראשון	סיון שי"ב לפר"ק
כ"ז סיון שי"ב לפר"ק	עם ש' צ' ע' בגן עדן
עם ש' צ' ע' בגן עדן	

Since the arrangement of the elements even in the example cited as a model differs so significantly from Hońdo's model, and since he failed to find an epitaph that corresponded to his proposed schema, we have to wonder whether this schema is at all reliable. We doubt that it is, also because the nineteenth-century example—even though it is a secondary gravestone—cannot have much in common with inscriptions from the sixteenth, seventeenth, or eighteenth centuries that make up the vast majority of the Kraków *matsevot*.

Our remaining reservations about the accuracy of the transcriptions are less serious. Above all, Hońdo leaves out or adds segmentation marks and symbols of abbreviation, for example on page 45 lines 1, 4, 5, 7, 15 (cf. p. 47, photograph); on page 69 lines 7, 9, 12, 13, 14, 16, 18–20, and 22 (cf. p. 70, photographs); on page 72 line 4 (cf. p. 73, photograph); on page 75 lines 4 and 11 (cf. p. 74, photograph); on page 85 line 3 (cf. p. 88, photograph); and on page 98 lines 9, 16–18 (cf. p. 100, photograph). Sometimes, too, he separates the abbreviations (e.g. on p. 45 no. 7: מהור"י becomes מהר"ר י; cf. p. 47, photograph; p. 63: במהור"ר becomes ב' מהור"ר; cf. p. 64, photograph; and p. 87 no. F41), assuming that such complex abbreviations do not exist; sometimes he corrects the errors of the stonemason (e.g. p. 101 line 5: לומבלא becomes לובמלא). He is not hindered in this even by the inscriptions on the gravestones. Sometimes lines of text are omitted (e.g. p. 87 no. F41 line 1: . . . פה הנעלה הר).[24] These are all less important errors, but in light of the fact that Hońdo provides only a dozen or so inscriptions, the number of errors is surprisingly great.

Worse than the transcriptions themselves are the translations. On numerous occasions Hońdo is unable to manage the translation of Hebrew images into Polish; on page 67 we read, for example: 'with them our eyelids come to be sprinkled with water because of death'. Twice, on pages 63 and 103, the abbreviation שליט"א is treated as a surname, even though Hońdo knows its meaning and gives it beside the translation. He translates the phrase ויצתה as 'and [the holy

---

[24] For example, in the inscription on p. 45 we have הוגות instead of הגות (line 3); בפתחו instead of ובפתחו (line 9); ובידו instead of בידו (line 12); ברחובתינו instead of ברחובותינו (line 17). In the inscription on pp. 68–9 we have ורגלים instead of ורגלם (line 4), מרוצה instead of מרצה (line 10), שניהם instead of שנים (line 15), כ"ו instead of כ"ג (line 21), למרחקי instead of למרחק (line 22). In the inscription on p. 101 we have כלה instead of כולה (line 5), חיים instead of דים (line 6), עדיף instead of עודף (line 6).

and pure soul] was consumed by fire' (p. 24),[25] not realizing that in the Hebrew of Polish Jews there was a vacillation between final ה and א, which in this formulation would yield ויצתה, rather than ויצאה ('and emerged' in the typical periphrase for death).[26] According to Hońdo, Michael Kalahora died a martyr's death 'because of the holiness of God' (p. 110), and not 'for sanctification of the name of God'. There are many such instances. However, the greatest number of errors of translation arise because Hońdo ignores the loftier style of inscriptions, often translating them too narrowly; for example, 'was acquainted with learning' (p. 69) or 'a skilled worker' (p. 117). We address the issue of stylistic and grammatical errors later.

The rules for transcribing Hebrew proper names in the work are unclear and inconsistent. It is true that there is a lack of agreement on this among the many researchers, and accepted methods vary from complete Polonization, through intermediate solutions, to transcription bristling with diacritical marks following Polish norms. Since there is no agreement, it is not necessary to adopt any particular one of these variants; the only requirement is consistency. In Hońdo's work, however, we find transcription that is standard for Sephardi pronunciation ('Marguliot', p. 83) right beside transcription for the Ashkenazi pronunciation of the same name ('Margulies', p. 82); we find the Polonized ('Mojżesz') and the transcribed ('Mosze') versions of the very same name on a single line (p. 79), as, throughout the work, Szmuel and Samuel; both declined and undeclined elements of a patronymic (p. 120: 'Synaj syn Menachem Mendla' (Synaj, son of Menachem Mendel)); a free mixture of Polonized and transcribed first names (p. 34: 'Debora', 'Riwka', and 'Jakub'); and even completely incomprehensible forms ('Leibusz', p. 41; 'Codek' instead of 'Cadok', p. 181). The words 'ben' and 'bar' are also inconsistently translated or not translated (e.g. 'Szymon, son of Szmuel Zanwil . . . Szmuel bar Meszulam', p. 130). This creates a completely chaotic picture and prevents one from even guessing at the author's assumptions.

Hońdo's next constantly repeated error is his rendering of the Hebrew days of the week in literal translation; thus, 'the first day' rather than Sunday, 'the second day' rather than Monday, and so on. The error arises from a naive incomprehension of the idioms of the language and a tendency towards word-for-word renderings of phrases with entirely different linguistic constructions.[27] According to this logic, we would have to render the English 'Saturday' in Polish as 'the day of Saturn', and the Russian word for Sunday as 'resurrection'. Even stranger is Hońdo's argument that 'the Jewish day begins and ends at sundown. Thus the first day does not correspond to Sunday, since it begins on Saturday evening and ends on Sunday evening' (p. 18, and again on p. 162). Following Hońdo's argument, we

---

[25] This yields the absurd image of a soul in flames, and thus a soul condemned!

[26] Compare Wodziński, *Hebrajskie inskrypcje*, 145–6.

[27] Similarly, on p. 171 Hońdo wants to translate the phrase בן ע״ה שנה as 'son of 75 years', again missing the fact that this is a typical Hebrew construction meaning '75 years old'.

would have to translate every Hebrew date as 'between . . . and . . .'; for example, 11 Elul 5603 would become 'between sundown on November 5 and sundown on 6 November 1843'. Even the author himself could not bring himself to such an absurdity. Since we keep in mind the adjustments arising out of differences in calendars in translating dates, there is no reason to come up with new linguistic devices to replace the current names for the days of the week. Beyond all this, Hońdo's notation is difficult to read; for example, 'was buried 4 day 3 Adar of the same [year]' (p. 87).

The next major structural shortcoming in this work that must be mentioned is the method of dating gravestones. To be sure, Hońdo asserts on pages 83–5 that, for stones without dates, secondary *matsevot*, and other doubtful cases, he used formal analogies to determine the age. However, the dating here is limited to the century, and the only place where we can acquaint ourselves with a list of *matsevot* (though it gives only the number of each gravestone) is the map of the sections of the cemetery on pages 225–8. According to the map, there are as many as fifty-five *matsevot* (though, according to the table on page 85, the number is fifty-seven) with no indication of date (and in regard to twenty-two gravestones the following term is used: 'gravestone consisting of various elements dating to various periods'). Thus Hońdo implies that formal analysis does not allow for even approximate dating. But this is not so. For example, an analysis of the script of inscription 133 dates this stone unequivocally to the seventeenth century. Many formal characteristics of gravestones 81 and 83 indicate that they date from the nineteenth century, and characteristics of gravestone 300 date it to the seventeenth century. On gravestone 374, which is not dated by Hońdo, 13 Nisan 5430 (i.e. 3 April 1670) can be seen.

In comparing Hońdo's work with the gravestones in the cemetery we noticed several other errors in dating. For example, gravestone 84 is labelled nineteenth-century, but the two dates visible on it are 1758 and 1800. Gravestone 183, in memory of Menachem Nachum, who died in 5650 (1889–90), is designated as eighteenth-century. Gravestone 335, which is designated as sixteenth-century, has a date of either 1675 or 1775. Gravestone 388 is dated 5551 (1790–1) but is designated seventeenth-century. The formal characteristics of gravestone 601, designated as eighteenth-century, indicate rather the first half of the seventeenth. Gravestone 649, designated as sixteenth-century, has a not completely legible date indicating the second half of the seventeenth century. These were the corrections that we were able to make in the course of a visit of several hours to the cemetery. Unfortunately, further systematic correction was impossible in the absence of a sourcebook on the basis of which we could have determined and analysed the rest of Hońdo's work.

On more than one occasion the dating is contradictory. One example is the gravestone that is allegedly the oldest, that of Kala, the daughter of Mordecai, who died in 1549 (pp. 22–4, transcription and translation) or 1592 (p. 23, the caption to the photo). Of the gravestone for Moses Eberles, who died in 1557, Hońdo writes on page 62 that it certainly was not erected in the sixteenth century; on the map, however (no. 221), he designates it as sixteenth-century, though, according to his stated principles, this gravestone should be labelled as consisting of various elements dating to various periods (sixteenth and eighteenth to nineteenth centuries). Similar contradictions and unclear statements are made in regard to other gravestones, and particularly to those that have undergone renovation; for example, in the descriptions of the gravestones of Shalom Shakhna and Natan Note Spiro (p. 63). As a result the author permanently avoids dating stones with no preserved date and secondary *matsevot* (these appear mainly in the captions to the illustrations and on the map of the cemetery), which makes reading of the work extremely difficult.

Hońdo's declaration mentioned above, that 'the scope of the work does not in principle extend to considerations of art history, except for the cases when these considerations were necessary to explain inscriptions' (p. 11), may be understood as referring to questions connected with the formal characteristics of the gravestone (shape and ornamentation, characteristics of the print) and the contents of artistic features. As it turns out, however, discussion of the contents of an epitaph without reference to the formal characteristics of the gravestone is impossible, and, despite the established incompleteness of the work, the author has not managed to avoid an encroachment into this territory. Each time the results are lamentable. For example, in his three-sentence digression on the subject of segmentation marks in the text (p. 54), Hońdo lists only three marks, without indicating the date of their appearance. In fact, the epitaphs in the cemetery in Remu contain perhaps the richest collection of such marks in Poland. Changes in these forms over time can serve as an excellent aid to dating inscriptions with illegible dates, and in the photographs reproduced in the volume under discussion we find at least six types, not counting variations.

Equally disastrous are the comments on the connection between text and symbolic content (pp. 204–8). The introduction to this section contains superficial information concerning artistic elements, with reference to only one popular study. We cannot agree with the assertion here that 'in Jewish cemeteries in Europe, large letters in relief were at first the only decorative element on *matsevot*' (p. 204), because by the first half of the sixteenth century concave inscriptions had become widespread, and framing had become an essential element of decoration. Nor can we agree with the groundless assertion that 'symbolic motifs became universal only in the second half of the nineteenth century' (p. 204), because in central and eastern Europe in particular they had become much more widespread in the course of the seventeenth century. There is evidence of this in many of the works listed in Hońdo's bibliography. Perhaps it is only through linguistic clumsiness that the author maintains that the Levite or priestly symbol 'was not obligatory on the gravestones of daughters whose fathers were Levites and priests' (p. 205); in reality, not only are such symbols not obligatory on women's gravestones, they are extremely rare.[28] The broad iconological question concerning the symbolism of the bird (p. 207) is contained here in one sentence, with reference to only one quite interesting but very general work.

There are other incomprehensible errors in Hońdo's work. For example, on page 12 the author notes that the work of Muneles and Vilimková on the old cemetery in Prague covers inscriptions for the years 1539–1787, whereas the epitaphs published in it are for the years 1439–1588.[29] On page 31 he claims that social position had no influence on the location of the grave, though the phenomenon of the so-called 'rabbi's hill' is well known. On page 87 he refers to the non-existent verse 15 of Psalm 16 (this should read 'Prov. 16: 15'). On page 107 he asserts that 'there are no texts which can be said to have grammatical or stylistic errors', while in the footnote to this remark he notes that 'of course errors occur'. On page 149 he introduces the name of Horowits from the unknown Czech town of Gurowice (instead of Hořovice).

Finally, a few words on the linguistic make-up of the work. The long list of shortcomings begins with lexical errors; for example *lunearny* instead of *lunarny* on page 161; the use of the word *werset* ('verse') to mean a line of an epigraph on pages 44 and following (the author appears not to know that *werset* is a biblical term); on page 10 surely *reprezentatywny* rather than *reprezentacyjny*, because it is difficult to imagine that the author really wanted to say that the necropolis in Kraków, the state capital, was representative of little, provincial towns in the Commonwealth. No doubt the following errors are stylistic: that the Kraków gravestone inscriptions are 'the result of the author's cataloguing' ('wynikiem prac inwentarysacyjnych autora', p. 17); that the object of description is 'the analysis located on the sarcophagi' ('analiza inskrypcji znajdująca się na tumbie', p. 80); that the personal tone of the Viennese lamentations 'present[s] the most objective aspect of the monument, precisely where the entirety speaks, lamenting owing to loss' ('przedstawia najbardziej obiektywną stronę pomnika, mianowicie tam, gdzie całość opowiada, lamentując z powodu straty', p. 116); that the likenesses of priestly palms and Levite pitchers 'appeared universally in Kraków at the beginning of the seventeenth century' (p. 205);[30] and that on the majority of the gravestones in the cemetery in Kraków information can be found about when and by whom they were made (p. 35).[31] Numerous stylistic and grammatical

[28] The few examples known to us are the *matsevah* of a woman (d. 5406) in the cemetery in Remu (see Rejuch-Samkowa and Samek (eds.), *Katalog zabytków*, fig. 215), and the 19th-century *matsevah* of a woman, with hands raised above candles, in Sandomierz (surely a symbol connected with the sabbath blessing, but the fingers are arranged as in the priestly blessing; unfortunately the lower half of the inscription is missing, so we do not know whether her father was a *cohen* (priest)).

[29] O. Muneles and M. Vilimková, *Starýžidovský hřbitov v Praze* (Prague, 1955).

[30] Of course these images did not appear universally, but only on the gravestones of priests and Levites.

[31] Such information is extremely rare and appears only now and then on secondary *matsevot*, which is perhaps what Hońdo had in mind.

errors are to be found also in the translation of Hebrew inscriptions; for example, on page 113: 'may his grave rest here beside me' ('tutaj niech spocznie obok mnie jego grób'), and on page 99: 'they lie in the dust with joy' ('leżą w prochu z radością').

What can we say in summation? The long-awaited work of Leszek Hońdo is incomplete owing to its faulty construction and its fragmentary approach to its subject. A representative collection of epigraphs, an analysis of the formal characteristics of the gravestones, and many basic elements in the description of inscriptions are all absent from this work. It does not address many of the most essential problems in the field of research on Jewish cemeteries in Poland, and where such questions are raised, it is done ineffectively because the author consistently disregards the diachronic character of the inscriptions. Methodologically, Hońdo's book is closest to the works of nineteenth-century collectors of antique Judaica, and although he repeatedly criticizes the publications of authors like Friedberg and Wetstein, he does not propose a new methodology of description. Moreover, he completely ignores recent methodological achievements and the many current research questions. When it comes to his major subject, the construction of inscriptions, it seems that other than a listing of the formulations found in Kraków, the treatise says nothing either about the construction and development of the formulations themselves (the inscription used as a model is clearly inappropriate) or about the history (that is, functioning) of specific formulations. Hońdo seems to have failed to define properly his subject of study or to develop an appropriate methodology for it, and, even worse, he did not know what is entailed in describing a Jewish cemetery.

Translated from Polish by Gwido Zlatkes

The Last Controversy over Ritual Murder? The Debate over the Paintings in Sandomierz Cathedral

ANNA LANDAU–CZAJKA

A SERIES of religious paintings hangs in the old cathedral in Sandomierz. One of them, depicting a ritual murder, is currently the subject of controversy. In 1710 the Revd Stefan Żuchowski commissioned a huge painting (10 square metres) on the topic from Karol de Prevot; Żuchowski emphasized that he wanted the picture to serve as 'clear evidence of Jewish cruelty'.[1] The painter did an excellent job. A Jew with a bloodthirsty grimace drives his knife into the body of a child lying on a table; a child is cut up and the pieces are thrown to a dog; and a child is trapped in a barrel spiked with nails.

The painting has hung there for a long time. In 2000 a debate began over what should be done with a painting whose message was so clearly and unambiguously antisemitic. Should a depiction of ritual murder be on display in a church even though Church doctrine has long recognized that Jews never killed children for matzah? On the other hand, should works of art be censored? If they are illegal or immoral, should they be removed?

The subject of the painting in Sandomierz Cathedral soon ceased to be merely a local issue when discussion of it filled the Polish press for several weeks. The main problem seemed to be that the myth of ritual murder, though it should by now have been relegated to the past along with that of the existence of witches, was a subject whose interest, in Poland at least, was by no means confined to historians and folklorists. This should come as no surprise, since the issue of ritual murder was still taken seriously by the press in the period between the two world wars. Despite official Church prohibitions, accusations against the Jews were still being made during that period. Indeed the Kielce pogrom, which is still alive in people's memory, was sparked by a rumour that a Christian boy had been killed for matzah.

Even today it is not unknown for articles to appear in the press in which the author—sometimes a priest—expresses his or her uncertainty about secret practices

---

[1] Quoted by the Revd S. Musiał SJ ('Droga Krzyżowa Żydów sandomierskich', *Gazeta Wyborcza* (5–6 Aug. 2000), 21).

within the Jewish community or tries to unravel the mysteries of alleged ritual murders. For example, in 1997 the newspaper *Głos Rzeszowa* provoked outrage when it published an interview between a spokesman for the president of Rzeszów and a priest about the search for the grave of a 9-year-old girl who died in 1945.[2] The rumour was that she had been murdered by Jews. While the priest noted that he personally did not believe that children were murdered for matzah, he said that 'had blood been necessary for the matzah, the Jews would not have had to murder anybody. . . . Polish villages were so poor the Jews could have bought as much blood as they wanted.'[3]

Unfortunately, many people still believe that ritual murder took place. During a meeting of Polish, Jewish, and Swedish youth in Kazimierz Dolny on the Vistula, one participant, an older man, said, to the horror of listeners: 'I know Jews don't drink blood, but a drop of Christian blood in the matzah is necessary.'[4] Similar attitudes were recorded by Józef Myjak, a journalist from Sandomierz, during his research on folklore. Myjak discovered that, until recently, mothers in villages would frighten children who wanted to stay outside in the evening with the threat that a Jew would come and draw their blood for matzah.[5]

The events related to the painting in Sandomierz Cathedral began in 1997. According to a report by the historian Jerzy Tomaszewski, a guide showing a group of tourists round the cathedral explained: 'This picture shows that the Jews kill Catholic children and drink their blood.'[6] Outraged, the tourists reported the comment to the nuncio, the primate, and the Catholic weekly *Tygodnik Powszechny*. Instead of the expected apology, they received a letter from a bishop (whose name Tomaszewski did not disclose) expressing doubts about whether ritual murder was in fact a myth. In the bishop's view,

among the scholars of Judaism there is a hypothesis about a sect in Judaism whose believers, relying on the study of the Talmud, actually committed the crime of ritual murder of which they were accused. . . . Will this problem ever be clarified? We can ask endless questions to which we cannot give clear answers given today's knowledge.

A few months later the case became widely known, and the new head of the Polska Rada Chrześcijan i Żydów (Polish Council for Christians and Jews), the Revd Michał Czajkowski, commented on the bishop's statement with apparent embarrassment: 'I know the whole letter and I know the response of the bishop, who showed a great deal of concern but apparently did not have a good historical background.

---

[2] The Związek Żydów Rzeszowskich w Izraelu (Union of Rzeszów Jews in Israel) protested, among others. See 'Głos rzecznika', *Gazeta Wyborcza*, suppl., *Gazeta w Rzeszowie* (2 Aug. 1997), 1.

[3] 'Jestem antysyjonistą', *Głos Rzeszowa* (Mar. 1997), 3.

[4] B. Michalski, 'Dialog nadziei', *Rzeczpospolita* (3 Dec. 1998).

[5] J. Myjak, 'Lekcja antysemityzmu', *Gazeta Wyborcza* (25 Aug. 2000).

[6] The event is related by Jerzy Tomaszewski, 'Mord rytualny dawniej i dzisiaj', *Midrasz*, 1 (2000), 46–7.

I believe that the diocese of Sandomierz will take steps to end this matter, which compromises our whole Church, not just the Sandomierz branch.'[7]

There were three ritual murder trials in Sandomierz—a record number. The Revd Stanisław Musiał also found there to be the largest number of depictions of ritual murder on display to the public in Poland. One such picture is in the old collegiate church, now the cathedral, and seven can be found in the stalls of the presbytery of St Paul's Church. In August 2000 the Revd Musiał wrote a strongly worded protest in *Gazeta Wyborcza* against having these pictures on display, asserting that it was absolutely unacceptable and that to see a picture with such content in a holy place would offend anyone's sensibilities: such a picture should immediately be removed. To deflect arguments from art conservators and historians about the need to preserve antiquities, the Revd Musiał emphasized he was not advocating the destruction of the picture—just its removal. He pointed to a precedent: a church built in Germany in the seventeenth century was named after Andrew of Rinn, a boy aged two and a half who was supposedly the victim of ritual murder. The church was of artistic value and the paintings on its ceiling unique. Nevertheless, after the Second World War Bishop Reinhold Stecher ordered all paintings and sculptures of little Andrew to be removed from the church. The relics were gathered together and exhibited with labels explaining about Jewish–Christian dialogue. The ceiling was painted over with the approval of the office of the preservation of antiquities, and it was no small matter since this was the only surviving painting by the brothers Franz and Josef Giner.

In his article the Revd Musiał argued that the same should be done in Sandomierz Cathedral. Good use could be made of the empty wall by giving it over to a memorial to the Jews of Sandomierz who were murdered as a result of accusations of ritual murder. He ends his article with a dramatic plea: 'Pictures of alleged ritual murders perpetrated by Jews do not belong in cathedrals, or in parish churches, or even in roadside chapels. As a Catholic, as a member of an order, as a priest, I would like to live within a Church that does not tolerate slander in its temples.'[8]

This article initiated a heated discussion among priests and laymen, both Catholics and Jews. Bishop Stanisław Gądecki, the chairman of the Rada Episkopatu Polski do spraw Dialogu Religijnego (Conference of Polish Bishops' Council for Religious Dialogue), soon issued a statement, which was published in *Gazeta Wyborcza*. Characteristically, its title ('Jews did not Murder') and most of its contents were devoted to explaining why ritual murders never happened and could not have happened in light of Jewish religious doctrine.

It is interesting but at the same time saddening that senior Church officials still feel the need to explain to believers that 'the accusation of "ritual murder" is a great misunderstanding resulting from a fundamental ignorance of Jewish religious law, which not only does not approve of shedding innocent blood, but also very firmly

[7] The Revd M. Czajkowski, 'Zmieniajmy nasz wizerunek w świecie', *Rzeczpospolita* (18–19 Nov. 2000).   [8] Musiał, 'Droga Krzyżowa Żydów sandomierskich'.

condemns any murder as well as any ritual desecration through contact with blood'.[9] We must recognize that the continually repeated explanations that ritual murders never happened are the gloomiest element of the discussion. In a way, the apparent need for these benevolent explanations demonstrates that this belief has not altogether disappeared, and indirectly reinforces the arguments of those who believe that the painting in Sandomierz Cathedral should no longer be on show.

In his statement Bishop Gądecki ponders what should be done with the painting and proposes several potential solutions without adopting any single 'proper one'. It might be possible to treat the picture as evidence of a kind of religious fanaticism that is uncharacteristic of Catholicism, and the bishop emphasizes that Catholicism has many saints, some of whom rescued Jews during the war (he also does not omit to mention that the Jewish religion has had its own fanatics). The picture might also be regarded as a work of art inseparably connected with its location, in which case its removal would be 'impossible'. A better solution might be to place a label near it clarifying its history, or else to do nothing since 'it could be said that one does not visit someone's house demanding that he remove furniture that is unpleasant or has negative connotations for the guests'.[10] Finally, Bishop Gądecki suggests, one might adopt the solution suggested by the Pope to all Christians: repentance and return to God.

The Sandomierz paintings were to be a matter of priority, together with Jedwabne and the anti-Jewish headings in the Millennial Bible, for the Polska Rada Chrześcijan i Żydów. In an interview for the newspaper *Rzeczpospolita*, the council's chairman supported the Revd Musiał's proposal to create a museum of antisemitism and to place the pictures there. As a compromise, he would allow the placing of an explanatory plaque near the picture, a proposal which had appeared in the press two years before the present discussion started.[11] This was to be 'a minimum programme', and the council was prepared to sponsor the plaque. It suggested the following text:

The events depicted on this picture are not historical truth. Jews never committed ritual murders. The popes forbade the propagation of such accusations. This picture presents an alleged Jewish ritual murder which was supposedly perpetrated for the purpose of adding the blood of Christian children to the matzah used during Passover. Because of such accusations, Jews were often persecuted and murdered. The accusation is nonsense because the laws of Judaism forbid the consumption of blood, and matzah can be made only from flour and water. Since the thirteenth century the popes have defended the Jews against this accusation. The pagans in antiquity issued a similar accusation against the Christians: that they supposedly practised cannibalism by eating a newborn baby during the Eucharist.[12]

Those who are against exhibiting the painting in the cathedral point to the shock it provokes among visiting tourists. They express concern that, for many Jews, the

[9] Bishop Stanisław Gądecki, 'Żydzi nie mordowali', *Gazeta Wyborcza* (18 Aug. 2000), 5.
[10] Ibid. [11] Czajkowski, 'Zmieniajmy nasz wizerunek w świecie'.
[12] S. Krajewski, 'Kaplica sandomierska—minimum to tablica', *Gazeta Wyborcza* (8 Nov. 2000).

decision to leave it in place may be proof of Polish antisemitism, and that the painting itself could be used as 'evidence' in educating Israeli youth. This issue was raised by Józef Myjak, the journalist from Sandomierz mentioned above. He pointed out that Israeli groups visiting Sandomierz are always taken to the cathedral, where they pause for some time in front of the picture. He asks whether this is not 'a conscious lesson on Polish antisemitism, perfectly illustrative from the pedagogic point of view'.[13] The art conservator Marek Juszczyk expressed a similar opinion, stating that groups from Israel are specially 'programmed' to see this particular picture and to use it as an occasion to discuss Polish antisemitism.[15]

Of course *Gazeta Wyborcza* and the opponents of the painting were not the only participants in the discussion. It also had numerous defenders. For example, Professor Ryszard Bender wrote polemics in *Nasz Dziennik* and *Głos: Tygodnik Katolicko-Narodowy* strongly criticizing the Revd Musiał's views.[14] Bender asserted that his demand for the painting to be removed threatened national and world culture, and the Revd Musiał himself was an iconoclast who brought shame on the Church, his order, and Poland. In *Nasza Polska* he argued

This is a dangerous idea. It leads to a degradation of culture. We must realize that if the historical paintings in both churches in Sandomierz were actually to be removed, it would represent irreparable loss and damage to the churches. It would compromise the Church in Poland. In the future the very people from the free-thinking and liberal circles whom the Revd Musiał wants to please with his proposal will complain to the Church that this decision—should it be made—was detrimental to Polish and world culture.[15]

In response, the art critic and publicist Andrzej Osęka observed that the discussion did not simply revolve around the picture itself but had a broader context concerning the belief in ritual murder, which, contrary to what Bender claimed, was not merely an example of thirteenth-century attitudes. In fact, 'this mentality still has a hold in Poland at the end of the twentieth century. It can be seen, among other things, from the passion with which its relics are defended. . . . Now Bender compares [the Revd Musiał] to Hitler. Many people demand the right to repeat freely the tales of Jewish ritual murders that are rooted in our national tradition . . .'.[16]

However, in another issue of *Nasza Polska* Stanisław Michałkiewicz echoed Ryszard Bender in accusing the Revd Musiał of wanting to 'please' the Jews and of obsessively looking for instances of antisemitism in Poland. Michałkiewicz went even further, suspecting a plot in which the Revd Musiał took part by consciously 'discovering' pictures and publicizing the cases. The author argued:

This time the thing is about the restitution of 'Jewish' private property. . . . At precisely this moment the Revd Musiał appears with his discovery from Sandomierz. What a deal! If

[13] Myjak, 'Lekcja antysemityzmu'.

[14] R. Bender, *Głos: Tygodnik Katolicko-Narodowy* (4 Nov. 2000).

[15] R. Bender, 'Ks. Stanisław Musiał gani Kościół polski', *Nasza Polska* (23 Aug. 2000).

[16] A. Osęka, 'Troska o mord rytualny', *Gazeta Wyborcza* (10–12 Nov. 2000).

the experiment in Sandomierz works (if he refuses to remove the pictures, the Sandomierz bishop ordinary will immediately be accused of 'condoning antisemitism'), it will be possible to demand the creation of a mixed Catholic–Jewish commission (with the Catholic side represented by Father Musiał, of course) to review pictures in all churches. Such a demand will stir protests, so there will be another opportunity to launch accusations of antisemitism in the hope that the authorities, for the sake of peace ('take this, take that, take it all!'), will accept that second claim; then the 'Jewish side' will graciously give up on appointing the commission and will—temporarily—leave the pictures alone.[17]

The defenders of the painting never say that ritual murders might have happened; on the contrary, they vehemently deny it. Instead they offer different arguments: the picture is a work of art, a document of its time, the depiction of an event that is part of Sandomierz tradition.

Jarosław P. Kazubowski writes in *Nasz Dziennik*: 'Today nobody claims that the murder depicted in the picture in the cathedral ever happened. None the less, the story of this event, like it or not, belongs to local tradition. The attempt to eradicate or eliminate it instead of rationally explaining it is reminiscent of the Soviet censorship that eliminated the name of Katyń from maps and geography.'[18] This reasoning is astonishing. Although in the first sentence the author denies the reality of such murders, he compares their 'eradication' from society's memory to the murders in Katyń. This leads to the conclusion that either ritual murders actually took place, or Katyń is a myth. The author opposes the claim that displaying the picture affects the image of Poland. He states simply: 'If Jewish tourist groups are so offended by the picture, perhaps it would be better if they bypassed Sandomierz Cathedral.'

Not all of those who favour leaving the painting where it is use antisemitic arguments. Much more convincing are the arguments of art historians and conservationists. They are concerned that removing antiquities simply because they show things that are untrue, controversial, or incompatible with today's knowledge or with 'political correctness' may have tragic consequences. It is difficult to deny some justification to this argument. In a letter to *Gazeta Wyborcza* Dr Jakub Sitko of the Instytut Sztuki Polskiej Akademii Nauk (Institute of the Arts at the Polish Academy of Sciences) argued that the controversial picture is part of a larger artistic entity, and that its removal would destroy the whole body of work. Dr Sitko pointed out that paintings with content that is antisemitic from today's perspective can be found in baroque ecclesiastical buildings throughout Europe. If they were all to be removed, the authentic interiors of many ancient churches would be destroyed. The author ends his letter:

Allow these ancient objects of art, including those with content that is unacceptable today, to remain in those places for which they were made. There have been far too many undesirable

---

[17] S. Michałkiewicz, 'Musiał Musiał?', *Nasza Polska* (30 Aug. 2000).

[18] J. P. Kazubowski, 'O księdza Musiała braku wiedzy historycznej słów kilka, czyli . . . nadgorliwiec walczy z "ciemnogrodem" ', *Nasz Dziennik* (30 Aug. 2000).

or fateful relocations in Poland. I think that in the case of both Sandomierz objects a plaque placed nearby with clarification of the Church's stand on antisemitism and a proper explanation of the events in the picture would be sufficient.[19]

A discussion published in *Gazeta Wyborcza* summed up the debate. The newspaper's editors invited people involved in Polish–Jewish relations and the problem of the painting in Sandomierz Cathedral—both supporters and opponents of its removal—to participate. Taking part in the discussion were the Revd Stanisław Musiał, the sociologists Professor Hanna Świda-Zimba and Professor Krzysztof Kiciński, the Catholic publicist Halina Bortnowska, Dr Jakub Sitko, Marek Juszczyk, Joanna Barańska of the Polish–Israeli Friendship Association, the journalist Dariusz Bugalski, and Anna Wereszczyńska, a high-school student from Sandomierz. Understandably absent were the most ardent supporters of leaving the picture where it is, i.e. the journalists of *Nasza Polska*.

The discussion was very heated; it began with a provocative proposal by Professor Świda-Zimba simply to burn the picture. Although this proposal was immediately rejected, a row ensued about whether a picture portraying a ritual murder could be seen as a work of art or only as the work of a hack, as the Revd Musiał bluntly put it (he was rebuked by the art critics). The Revd Musiał added that leaving the picture in place was out of the question because it was an incitement to crime. This opinion provoked an argument over the extent to which a picture could influence people to commit antisemitic actions or hold antisemitic attitudes. Halina Bortnowska leaned towards the Revd Musiał's view. 'The mechanism is simple,' she said; 'people who look at the picture are convinced that it portrays the truth. And they continue to believe that the Jews needed blood for matzah.'[20] Several people initially applauded the idea of moving the picture to a proposed museum of antisemitism. However, Marek Juszczyk pointed to the example of the museum of atheism located in the former Dominican church in Lviv, and this analogy discouraged even those who had initially favoured the idea.

Both art historians were against removing the painting, especially Marek Juszczyk, who argued on the grounds that the picture was part of the cultural heritage and an antique. Similarly, in the later part of the discussion Dr Sitko supported the claim that its removal would destroy the church's interior (to which the Revd Musiał retorted: 'Don't you think the murdered people justify this removal, this aesthetic gap?'[21]) This in turn sparked another exchange, in which it was disclosed that the cathedral guides described the painting as depicting a scene of ritual murder. Often they could not answer tourists' questions about whether such murders took place in reality; they sometimes appeared to confirm it by saying that, although there was a sect that practised ritual murder, one should not accuse all Jews of this crime. Seen in this light, the picture was dangerous, and the more so as

[19] J. Sitko, 'Czy usuwać obrazy z kościołów?', *Gazeta Wyborcza* (4 Sept. 2000), 16.
[20] 'Sąd nad obrazem', *Gazeta Wyborcza* (27 Oct. 2000), 18–20.   [21] Ibid.

the Church had not responded to the proposal for an explanatory plaque. Besides, a plaque alone would not suffice because it would require that all foreign tourists know Polish, and it would be difficult to put the inscription in a number of European languages and Hebrew. On the other hand, there were few antiquities left in Poland, and to destroy the ones that were left would be a crime. In addition, the empty space left by the picture's removal would stir emotions as powerful as those provoked by the picture itself. The historians raised images of tour guides telling people that a picture of ritual murder had hung here but that the Jews had ordered it to be removed, or of protesting antisemites occupying the cathedral or chaining themselves to the painting. They expressed concern that the removal could start a domino effect: once you started censoring works of art you might end up censoring *Pan Tadeusz*, in which Adam Mickiewicz wrote about Jews piercing children with needles.

The participants came to no conclusions. Still, we can sum up with the statement made by Halina Bortnowska at the end of the discussion:

A church is a living place serving to educate believers and those practising their religion, and not a museum space. . . . If something desecrates this sacred place—and this picture desecrates it because it commemorates the unrepented crime against the Jews—then that place cannot serve the populace. It needs to be closed as a place of worship and given a sign saying 'Museum'; then anyone can display in it whatever he wishes.[22]

Whatever the varying views of journalists, and even of the Church authorities, canon law rules that the person with the authority to make the final decision about the painting is the bishop ordinary of the diocese of Sandomierz, Wacław Świerzawski. Since he answered the letter of an outraged tourist from Australia by saying that 'certainly the whole Jewish nation cannot be blamed for such crimes. The matter needs to be investigated further and a joint explanation and a solution need to be found',[23] it is no wonder that the painting is still hanging. It will probably hang 'until the matter is investigated'.

Translated from Polish by Gwido Zlatkes

---

[22] 'Sąd nad obrazem'.
[23] Quoted in R. Jarocki, 'Biskup bada . . .', *Rzeczpospolita Plus–Minus* (4–5 Nov. 2000).

The Anti-Zionist Campaign in Poland of 1967–1968: Documents

WŁODZIMIERZ ROZENBAUM

THE anti-Zionist campaign in Poland which culminated in March 1968 has been given much attention in the last few years by historians. However, for the most part, published works have focused on anecdotal evidence rather than analysis, mainly because of restricted access to the archives, lack of familiarity with primary sources, and insufficient knowledge of the period. Furthermore, the Jewish aspect of the events of March 1968 has been relegated to the status of an almost secondary, 'embarrassing' factor, and the authentic heroes of the events who chose to remain in Poland 'Polonized' the character of these events in their own recollections and analyses. A monograph by Dariusz Stola, a historian at the Instytut Studiów Politycznych Polskiej Akademii Nauk (Institute of Political Studies, Polish Academy of Sciences) in Warsaw, is a remarkable departure from the standard literature on the subject published to date.[1]

Stola sets the record straight in his introduction, referring to the perverse character of the anti-Zionist campaign:

The name '*anti-Zionist* campaign' is misleading on two counts, because . . . [First, it] began as anti-Israeli, but soon it became anti-Jewish, and this clearly anti-Jewish designator remained until the end. In 1968 the words *Zionism* and *Zionist*, repeated in hundreds of propaganda publications and in thousands of meetings, were not meant to characterize properly a certain variety of nationalism, but served as substitutes for the words 'Jew' and 'Jewish'. Secondly, a *Zionist* meant a 'Jew' even when the person branded as such was not Jewish. . . . The events discussed had two acts: the summer of 1967 and the spring of 1968. (p. 7)

How was such a campaign possible in Poland? Stola offers the following major reasons:

1. The Soviet origins of the instruments of power in communist Poland.

2. The struggle with the right-wing nationalist deviation in 1948–9, when local communist leaders were replaced by leaders from Moscow—Stola takes a traditional, one-sided view of this. There is no doubt that Gomułka's abrasive and uncompromising character contributed to the strong animosity felt towards him by

---

[1] D. Stola, *Kampania antysyjonistyczna w Polsce 1967–1968* (Warsaw, 2000).

the party leadership, and his complaints to Stalin about Jewish comrades caused additional strain in his relationship with party leaders.

3. The events of October 1956, when Gomułka played both the Puławska (liberal) and the Natolin (Stalinist) factions. Stola points out that Gomułka ultimately opted for the latter, which brought back to power former well-known exponents of anti-semitic views. But he fails to mention that Gomułka's decision to sideline comrades of Jewish descent, such as Roman Zambrowski, Stefan Staszewski, Antoni Alster, and Wacław Komar—to mention just a few of the more prominent ones—helped to create an antisemitic climate in the party apparatus. Embracing the Natolin faction had its dramatic repercussions later when Gomułka began to push for the 'disper-sal' (*rozrzedzenie*) of Jews by removing them from their positions or blocking pro-motions in the foreign service, foreign trade, security services, the military, and other key government sectors. Gomułka referred to these attempts later at the Politburo meeting on 8 April 1968.

4. Moczar and the 'partisans'. Stola does not discuss this phenomenon in great detail, but throughout the book he provides many examples demonstrating that Major-General Mieczysław Moczar, minister of the interior, was Gomułka's loyal 'national policeman' (this phrase was first used by Colonel Władysław Tykociński, former chief of the Polish military mission in West Berlin, who defected to the United States in the early 1960s). Stola fails to mention that Gomułka's personnel decisions during October 1956 created favourable conditions for the partisans in the security services, the military, and other key agencies. Furthermore, Moczar's use of the Związek Bojowników o Wolność i Demokrcji (Union of Fighters for Freedom and Democracy, ZBOWiD) veteran organization to further nationalist ideology was an open secret, and, as members of the ZBOWiD's supreme council, Gomułka and other party leaders were well aware of it.

5. The status and activities of the Pax Christian Association. Stola correctly draws attention to its support in 1956 for the Natolin faction, which blamed Jews for the excesses of the Stalinist period. This benefited Pax later, when Gomułka appointed a number of prominent Natolin faction members to important party and government positions. Stola aptly observes that 'For the anti-Semitic tendencies in Poland, Pax was an institutional connection between the old times and the present' (p. 22).

Stola maintains—and the documentation he has assembled bears him out—that Polish political leaders had no qualms about applying racist criteria when launching the anti-Zionist campaign. After all, the conditions for it had already been created in 1956, when anti-Jewish sentiment forced the emigration of 50 per cent of the Jewish population in Poland. Later, even though the situation of the Jewish com-munity appeared to be relatively stable, the Towarzystwo Społeczno-Kulturalne Żydów w Polsce (Civic and Cultural Association of Jews in Poland, TSKŻ) 'remained under the watchful eye of the Ministry of the Interior and the party leadership' and 'the Jewish topic . . . was an ever present undercurrent in the imagination, gossip, and intrigues of the party establishment' (p. 24).

The outbreak in 1967 of the Six Day War was no doubt a shock to Gomułka, but it was an even greater shock than Stola implies. In fact, notification of the war by the Israeli government was followed by a delay of two days before the Polish government responded. During this hiatus Gomułka must have consulted the Kremlin, but, as Stola points out, he wasted no time and avidly read confidential Ministry of the Interior reports on attitudes to the war among Polish Jews. Although he knew these reports to have been fabricated, a few days later, while in Moscow, he nevertheless shared this information with Brezhnev and other communist leaders assembled for the summit. However, it was of no interest to the participants. Brezhnev himself expressed concern that the war might lead to antisemitic excesses and require government action against the perpetrators of such acts.[2]

Gomułka did not share Brezhnev's concerns and came up with a plan on his own, which he began to implement as soon as he returned to Warsaw. As Stola tells it, Gomułka immediately reported to the Politburo on the Moscow summit. He then met with the provincial party chiefs and Central Committee department heads, to whom he issued a stern warning: 'many of our organizational units show dangerous signs of liberalization. This was also demonstrated during the events in the Middle East. Such anti-party attitudes, which are in direct contradiction of our policies, cannot be tolerated' (p. 38). The anti-Zionist campaign clearly acquired an internal aspect, and Gomułka's instructions were not lost on the party administration. The Warsaw Party Committee convened a meeting of local party activists and quickly published a pamphlet, for distribution in Warsaw party organizations, condemning the Israeli aggression, as well as the adventurist and imperialist policies of the Jewish state.

On 19 June, just two weeks after the Six Day War, Gomułka's rhetoric moved from being anti-Israeli to anti-Zionist, or rather anti-Jewish. That day, at the Sixth Trades Union Congress, he issued the following warning: 'we cannot remain indifferent towards people who, in the face of a threat to world peace and thus to the security of Poland and the peaceful work of our nation, speak out for an aggressor and a wrecker of peace, and for imperialism. . . . We will not tolerate a Zionist fifth column in Poland' (p. 40).[3] According to Stola, the issue of 'internal Zionists' was not discussed at subsequent meetings with the Soviet leaders. To my knowledge, the 'Polish variant' was discussed by the Soviet Politburo, but ultimately rejected. And yet, as Stola points out, Gomułka continued to emphasize the internal character of the anti-Zionist campaign despite objections from some Polish Politburo members. He was 'clear in these matters', and said so at a meeting on 27 June 1967.

---

[2] See also M. Zaremba, 'Breżniew, Żydzi, Polska: Gorąca linia', *Polityka* (10 Mar. 2001), 72–3.

[3] The text quoted by Stola differs from the copy I managed to obtain from a *Trybuna Ludu* reporter. My version was also published in *L'Unità* (the Italian communist party organ) by their Warsaw correspondent, Franco Fabiani. The Polish government retaliated by withdrawing his accreditation.

To understand better the significance of Gomułka's policy it is necessary to look at the turmoil Warsaw party activists were experiencing at the time, something that neither Stola nor other historians have paid sufficient attention to. This turmoil manifested itself in the June 1967 party membership verification drive instituted in connection with the forthcoming congress of the Polska Zjednoczona Partia Robotnicza (Polish United Workers' Party). The verification process presented an opportunity to remove all those who were critical of Gomułka's trade union speech or who were not supporting it forcefully enough. In the heat of the campaign party organizations were quick to use defamatory information from the Ministry of the Interior and even from non-party members (who voluntarily supplied it) without bothering to verify it. A few months later, in accordance with party statutory regulations, city and provincial party committees reported the results.

On 25 July Józef Kępa, propaganda secretary of the Warsaw Party Committee, reported at a plenary meeting that party members had divergent views on party policy with regard to the Middle East conflict. Some were very disturbed by its antisemitic aspects, vigorously demonstrated at many rallies and meetings. Kępa defended the campaign and maintained that the party could not remain indifferent to those who did not support the new line. His speech was greeted with a round of applause. The next speaker, Stanisław Kociołek, first secretary of the Warsaw Party Committee, expressed concern about the campaign, saying:

People's Poland has always recognized Israel's right to exist. Therefore, we have never agreed with reactionary Arab nationalism bent on the destruction of Israel. . . . While respecting family, cultural, and ethnic ties, we have the right to demand a citizen's concern for the affairs of the People's Poland, peace, and progress. At the same time we reject and deplore all activities that may engender real antisemitism.[4]

Kociołek's speech did not go down well with Gomułka, who posted his formerly favourite party secretary to a similar position in the province of Gdańsk, selecting Kępa to replace him. Always a quick student, Kociołek realized his mistake; he performed well in Gdańsk, and at the Fifth Party Congress in November 1968 Gomułka rewarded him with membership of the Politburo.

Stola maintains that the party chief in Poland had absolute power. The years 1967–8 illustrated this poignantly, particularly with regard to the security activities of the Ministry of the Interior, which played the major role in the anti-Zionist campaign. At the ministry the campaign was strictly supervised by the top-level Kolegium (executive board). Documents put forward by Stola clearly indicate that the Kolegium understood Gomułka perfectly and was ready to satisfy his demands: Moczar made it clear to his subordinates that this should be the case. This did not guarantee that in the course of identifying the 'new, influential, and cunning adversary' the Ministry of the Interior would be objective (p. 53). As subsequent

---

[4] *Trybuna Ludu* (26 July 1967).

events showed, the ministry spared no effort to manufacture evidence of a Zionist conspiracy. Thus, as Stola emphasizes, the anti-Israeli campaign, which was transformed by Gomułka into an anti-Zionist one, became antisemitic. Stola further maintains that the conditions must already have existed for this to have come about in just three weeks.

Stola presents ample information on the methods employed to watch the Jewish community. At the same time he does not believe that, from the interest in Jewish organizations, we can conclude that a special 'Jewish' branch, division, or department was formed, as has commonly been thought. He raises the possibility that a Jewish section may have existed at the National Minorities Division in the Third Department, responsible for monitoring anti-state subversive activities. However, the issue is not as simple as that. A Jewish branch was established in the late 1940s at the Ministry of Public Security, the predecessor of the Ministry of the Interior. Its first chief was Anatol Liberman, who was Jewish. Initially the branch focused on surveillance of correspondence and on monitoring telephone conversations. The unit was most likely phased out during the reorganization of the ministry in 1954. Many of its employees were absorbed by Bureau W (surveillance of correspondence). Others were reassigned to Bureau T (technological). After the upheaval of October 1956 Jewish matters were dealt with by a variety of sections within the Ministry of the Interior. Jews continued to be watched by, among others, Bureaus W and T; the Department of Social and Administrative Affairs; the Second Department (counter-intelligence); special sections within provincial militia commands; Centralne Biuro Ewidencji Ludności Komendy Głównej Milicji Obywatelskiej (Central Census Office of the Headquarters of the Citizens' Militia); and the First Department (intelligence). A crucial moment—missed by Stola—came with Yury Andropov's elevation to the chairmanship of the KGB in 1967. One of his first decisions was to establish the Fifth Directorate to Combat Ideological Subversion with a focus on Zionism. Later that year, hardly by coincidence, Lieutenant-Colonel Tadeusz Walichnowski was transferred from the First to the Third Department as deputy director in charge of combating Zionism. He had just acquired a reputation as an expert on Zionism after defending his Ph.D. thesis entitled 'Izrael a Niemiecka Republika Federalna' ('Israel and the Federal Republic of Germany'). It is important to remember, however, that Jewish matters were also handled by other sections and organizations before and after 1967. These were the internal affairs departments of people's councils (departments managed by officials in the Ministry of the Interior); military counter-intelligence (officially in order to investigate and prevent defections to the West by Jewish officers); and personnel and administrative departments at the party Central Committee.[5]

---

[5] Based on a series of interviews with middle-ranking Ministerstwo Spraw Wewnętrznych (Ministry of the Interior) officials who were involved in activities concerning the Jewish community in Poland and were very familiar with Jewish organizations in Poland. The interviews were conducted in 1967–76.

And yet, as Stola rightly points out, despite an atmosphere that was favourable to them, and despite continued efforts, the activities of all these organizations were haphazard and unco-ordinated. The major reason was undoutedly the lack of proof that Jews were engaged in either open or clandestine activity against the state. This made it difficult to secure additional funding and establish a viable system. The situation was further complicated by competition among various sections to obtain evidence and to win the support of the party leadership for funding their activities. Documents presented by Stola indicate that the Ministry of the Interior was very cautious and even referred to senior party officials for advice. This cautious approach supports Stola's contention that the ministry supposedly did not have information on Zionists in top government positions. But the problem was not so much with information as with jurisdiction. Top positions came within the domain of the party leadership, so that the party already had the information and did not need it from the secret police. In order to obtain such information the Ministry of the Interior needed special 'operational tasking' from the Politburo or the Secretariat, which was not forthcoming. Gomułka made it clear several times during the campaign that he decided personnel matters, and that is why, when in the autumn of 1968 the Ministry of the Interior began to disseminate disparaging material about several top party and government officials without the approval of Gomułka, Walichnowski and several other officers from the Third Department had to go. After all, at the meeting on 28 June 1967 Moczar reminded the Kolegium that they served the party. Stola documents that, while the Ministry of the Interior played a crucial role in shaping decisions of the party leadership, its reports and findings were not automatically believed unless they confirmed the leadership's expectations.

It may be worth mentioning here (though Stola does not do so) that the issue of national minorities had been of serious concern to the party leadership and the Ministry of the Interior before the Six Day War. A meeting of the Kolegium on 11 April 1967 was devoted to policy on national minorities. It was attended by the deputy director of the party Central Committee administrative department, which supervised the ministry. A draft of the new policy was presented by the head of social and administrative affairs at the ministry. The minorities were to be subject to more stringent control by provincial and local administrations as well as the Milicja Obywatelska (Citizens' Militia, the police). The head of the Third Department stated that the goal was to achieve complete assimilation of national minorities, while the director of the Second Department questioned the need for national minorities' organizations and institutions.[6]

With the demands of the anti-Zionist campaign, co-operation between the party leadership and the Ministry of the Interior substantially improved. In July ministry reports contributed to the punishment of fifteen Warsaw journalists, who were

[6] E. Mironowicz, *Polityka narodowościowa PRL* (Białystok, 2000).

either dismissed or given party sanctions. Several months later Leon Kasman, the editor-in-chief of the party organ, *Trybuna Ludu*, was dismissed. Stola's information about the reasons is incorrect. Kasman, a Central Committee member, lost his job at Gomułka's direction for refusing to publish a review of Walichnowski's book *Izrael a NRF* ('Israel and the FRG') and for his criticisms of inadequate measures taken by the party to fight antisemitism in Poland. Kasman also happened to be Jewish. His deputy and several other staff members who happened to be of Jewish descent had already been dismissed. An enthusiastic review of Walichnowski's book appeared after Kasman's departure. It was written by a distinguished reporter who, although of Jewish descent, had retained his job on the paper. Ironically, a year later the Ministry of the Interior was trying to implicate him in intelligence activities for West Germany.

It is a pity that Stola was unable to elicit information on the activities of the Third Department from Walichnowski, who subsequently returned to the Ministry of the Interior as deputy minister and was rewarded with the rank of general and membership of the party Central Committee. His department caused a lot of grief to the Jewish community. One of its most contemptible actions was the 'unmasking' of Jews who had concealed their Jewish roots. Many of them had survived the Nazi occupation under assumed Polish names, sometimes converting to Catholicism.

Particularly valuable are chapters in which Stola analyses the events of March 1968. He shows that these events were characterized by aggressive antisemitic propaganda, rallying the masses against Zionists, and mass, high-profile purges of Jews from the party and jobs. Stola emphasizes that the campaign acquired these characteristics within a few days, but it is clear that the authorities focused on the student revolt and attempts to crush it. Stola further maintains that the March revolt and the repressions that followed need not have become an inherent part of the anti-Jewish campaign started in 1967. There is no evidence, according to Stola, that the student revolt was instigated by a Zionist conspiracy aimed at overthrowing the government. Documents suggest that the Ministry of the Interior came up with this theory in January 1968 at the latest and embarked on collecting evidence to support it. Stola wonders if this had anything to do with the transfer of Walichnowski to the Third Department. Considering the changes in the KGB at that time, there should be little doubt about it. These changes may have made Moczar's requests for support from the Politburo more persuasive, but then again, by that time the party leadership had already decided to use the anti-Jewish angle to deal with student dissent. In fact, in early 1967, at the plenary meeting of the Związek Młodzieży Socjalistycznej (Union of Socialist Youth), its leader proclaimed that the party would no longer tolerate the 'Szlajfers, Blumsztajns and other sztajns',[7] and to make sure that the party line was followed a hardliner was put

[7] Based on an interview in Feb. 1967 with a party journalist who attended a special briefing on the plenary meeting at his newspaper.

in charge of the organization. But the party did not want to miss any opportunity to push its policy. Stola discusses the contacts between the party and the Pax Christian Association at the beginning of the March campaign which led to the publication in *Słowo Powszechne* of a list of 'Jewish' ringleaders of the student unrest.

As Stola points out, Gomułka had a clear concept of the campaign, and he knew how to manipulate the party rules and regulations to achieve his goals without consulting the Politburo. This approach explains the character of the campaign and its zigzags. It allowed him to step in at any time he felt that amendments needed to be made, such as when his friends or favourites were treated unjustly. Thus, he facilitated the selection of Artur Starewicz, the secretary of the party Central Committee, who happened to be Jewish but was also a strong Gomułka supporter, as a delegate to the Fifth Party Congress; and he restored jobs and party membership to several family friends who had been fired for allegedly celebrating Israeli victories.

According to Stola, Gomułka, Moczar, and Gierek—who are considered to be the main actors of the March events—saw the need for an anti-Jewish campaign. The idea, at least initially, was to stop the student revolt and dissent among intellectuals on the one hand, and effect personnel changes on the other. Thus, anti-Zionism was linked with an attack on 'bankrupt politicians' who no longer played any role in politics. Stola does not understand this approach. But it seems obvious that an attempt was being made to provide evidence for a Jewish conspiracy. That is why the media drew attention to positions held by parents of Jewish students from 'banana' (well-to-do) families: they were exposing to the general public the 'Zionist' change of guard. Zambrowski was a perfect target because of his son's dissident activities and because Gomułka and other 'deviationists' from 1948, as well as the Natolinists of 1956, held a grudge against him. To make the conspiracy theory more persuasive, Staszewski's name was added. The public already knew him from the campaign against the 'encyclopaedists', who were accused of falsifying Polish history. This was leading straight to the officers in Soviet uniforms. Ochab, a former general with a Jewish wife, and Szyr, a Jew, were still in the Politburo and had attacked Gomułka for his 'Zionist fifth column' speech in June 1967. They were also prominent members of the liberal 'Puławska' faction in 1956. This conflict in the Politburo was to be one of the main engines of the anti-Zionist campaign, in Stola's view. It also helped Moczar in his intrigues.

Stola maintains that it is still impossible to establish clearly the source and role of the anti-Zionist aspect of the events of March 1968. Undoubtedly, stifling dissent among intellectuals, making personnel changes, consolidating the party leadership, and even crushing the student revolt would have been possible without using anti-Zionist slogans and introducing an atmosphere of hysteria. Antisemitism helped, but it was not a necessity, and Stola exposes the obsessions of Gomułka, Kliszko, Moczar, and other major personalities. But the campaign was not accidental in any way. Attacks against alleged Zionists and other selected individuals leave no doubt that Jews were the target from the beginning. The authorities wanted to remove them from positions of importance, to marginalize them in public life, and, if possible, to force them out of Poland. Stola comments that the campaign was motivated by rationally defined interests coupled with a paranoid vision of the world. This sounds like a very damning reason, but after all, if it looks like a duck, walks like a duck, and talks like a duck, it is a duck.

Stola focuses extensively on a description of the campaign. It was a fusion of two historically opposite trends in their worst manifestations: a communist purge and antisemitism of the nationalist right, says Stola. Paradoxically, the 1968 campaign, waged by communists, utilized the anti-communist concept of Judaeo-communism in accusing Jews of being communists. Stola notes that it was as if the Stalinist period of physical terror was replaced by psychological terror of greater ferocity than the pre-war antisemitism of the chauvinist right. He calls it a symbolic or verbal pogrom, a bloodless one.

Stola was unable to unearth any guidelines or instructions for the campaign, but materials he was able to examine indicate that the party propaganda apparatus was the guiding spirit and the main engine. Documents from the press bureau of the Central Committee show that the campaign, directed from above, produced huge quantities of publications and radio and TV broadcasts, as well as many thousands of rallies and meetings in public places, places of employment, and in party organizations. In Warsaw alone, during the first two weeks of the campaign, party meetings were held in 1,900 organizations and institutions, mostly open to the public, some 400 rallies, 700 meetings of party functionaries, and 600 meetings of party groups. At these functions invited speakers and participants frequently made antisemitic attacks without any intervention from the authorities. Stola found one example of a lecturer who was punished for his presentation: the authorities objected not to his antisemitic remarks, but to his comment that all Politburo members were Jewish (there was only one at the time).

The Ministry of the Interior provided various institutions and organizations with lists of Jews to help with campaigns against individuals employed there. Only rarely did such lists go unused, asserts Stola. 'Unmasked' Jews often declared support for party policy, but usually their declarations were rejected and they were disciplined by the party, often as well as being dismissed from their jobs. According to statistics gathered by Stola, by 28 May in Warsaw 360 persons had been expelled from the party and at least 483 from managerial positions (not counting the military and the Ministry of the Interior, where several dozen people lost their jobs). Among those dismissed were critics of the antisemitic policy and opponents of the purge of Jews in their offices.

Particularly vicious were purges in the military and the Foreign Ministry, and Stola provides plenty of information about them. Both sectors had been of particular interest to the party leadership for many years. The anti-Zionist campaign of 1967–8 provided a good opportunity for the Polish *hunweibins*, as they were called, to stage their own cultural revolution. To hide the racist aspect of the purges, the

Polish party leadership informed Communist Party leaders in other countries of a foiled Zionist plot in the Polish military organized by Jewish officers with intent to undermine the socialist armed forces and to assist the Israeli army. One such letter was made public by the Czechoslovak general Jan Sejna, who in 1968 defected to Britain. Also, contrary to Stola's information, the purges in the Foreign Ministry were not a 'local' affair. According to published memoirs of the deputy minister, Józef Winiewicz, the party meeting called to eliminate Jewish officials in the ministry was supervised by telephone by an unnamed Politburo member (probably Zenon Kliszko, Gomułka's right-hand man, or Ryszard Strzelecki, who was responsible for security and a close friend of the party leader).

Stola repeats Paweł Wieczorkiewicz's plausible explanation for the purge: that it was designed to settle accounts with Edward Ochab and Marian Naszkowski, both former chiefs of the main political administration in the military after the war and thus responsible for the bloody repressions of Polish officers. Also, both went to Poland after the war with the Soviet army, where they had served as political officers in the Polish division. The problem with this theory is that one of the main animators of the antisemitic campaign was General Kazimierz Witaszewski, head of the party Central Committee administrative department, supervising the military and security services. Witaszewski, like Ochab and Naszkowski, had served as a political officer in the Polish division of the Soviet army. At the height of Stalinism in Poland, in 1952, he was elevated to chief of the army main political administration and deputy minister of defence. In 1956 he was a prominent member of the Stalinist Natolin faction in the party. He is one of many illustrious examples of party and military officials who contributed significantly to the Stalinist terror in Poland. However, their Polish backgrounds did not fit the campaign, which was directed against Jews.

A separate chapter in Stola's book is devoted to the social aspects of the anti-Zionist campaign. Stola's findings are as interesting as they are revealing. He points out that party policy and activities proved to be highly attractive to the masses. Not only were meetings on Jewish topics very popular, but party membership grew as well. In 1968, in Warsaw alone, the number of candidates for party membership increased by five times in comparison with 1967. This was a consequence of the spread of what at the time was called an 'anti-Zionist psychosis'. Stola is careful about sweeping generalizations, but he believes that there was clearly an eruption of antisemitic prejudices and emotions in Polish society. The reasons for this are quite complex, but there is no doubt that anti-Zionism became in March 1968 the glue that bound together several other problems that evoked great emotion among the people. Stola rightly points out that one of the main goals of the March campaign was to channel prevailing social frustrations into aggression against identifiable enemies. Customs within the party allowed Poles to violate more than one established taboo. Encouraged to offer sincere, open, and critical comments, and to vent their frustrations, people blamed and attacked Jews who had been elevated to membership of the establishment. In other words, attacks against Jews and other alleged enemies were interpreted and perceived by many as 'renewal', a completion of the unfinished de-Stalinization process or personnel-based alternative to institutional reform of the system. And yet the racist character of the campaign was clear. Although the authorities claimed that it was the Zionists who had caused the increase in meat prices, refusal to reverse the increase was proof that blaming Jews was just a pretext for the anti-Jewish campaign. Sometimes the enthusiasm for anti-Jewish purges was motivated by a desire for advancement in the party and government bureaucracy.

The campaign was characterized by a high degree of opportunism and conformism, hence the term 'a March antisemite'. Pressure from the authorities and from one's peers cannot be ignored, however, and Stola illustrates this by quoting a popular joke of the period: 'What is the difference between antisemitism before the war and today? It was not compulsory then.' Stola gives examples of people who were punished for their public criticism of the campaign and refusal to fire Jews. Such people not only lost their jobs, but had difficulty in finding new ones. Small wonder that sympathy for Jews and desire to help them were expressed by rather few people, usually privately and with circumspection.

One of the most disturbing aspects of the campaign was the emigration of Jews from Poland. This started with Gomułka's 'programmatic' speech of 19 June 1967. He repeated it, foaming at the mouth, on 19 March 1968, when addressing a hostile crowd of Warsaw party activists. Gomułka believed that emigration would solve the Jewish problem in Poland, and the Politburo instructed both the Ministry of the Interior and the Foreign Ministry to prepare guidelines for 'departures from Poland of Polish citizens of Jewish descent'. The prime minister, Józef Cyrankiewicz, repeated Gomułka's call at a session of the Sejm. The guidelines were supposed to streamline the emigration of Jews, but if anything they made the procedure painful and humiliating. In order to obtain permission to emigrate, Jews had to declare Jewish nationality, to select Israel as their destination, and to renounce Polish citizenship. In return the Polish authorities issued useless travel permits, which stated that their holders were no longer Polish citizens, an act in violation of international law. More importantly, potential Jewish emigrants had to deal with a highly restrictive and discriminatory application of the regulations with regard to property that could be taken out of Poland. Customs officials routinely confiscated various personal items and made capricious decisions.

Stola estimates that a little over 13,000 Jews left Poland in the years 1968–71. He gives the following reasons for the emigration: (1) the atmosphere, including a 'wave of verbal aggression', news about mistreatment of friends and relatives, personal painful experiences, and a feeling of hopelessness; (2) the internal dynamics of emigration, sometimes manifested as mass flight, and fear of remaining alone in Poland; (3) the destruction of Jewish institutions; and (4) 'de-Polonization'—depriving people who, judged by all civilized standards, were in fact Polish of a Polish self.

Documents examined by Stola indicate that there were already attempts to slow down the campaign in April 1968, but they cannot be taken at face value. Judged by the public manifestations of the campaign in the media, such attempts—if they were made at all—meant very little. The campaign had its own dynamics, which the party could not fully control. Gomułka and Kliszko supervised the 'dispersal' process aimed at removal of Jews from management positions, which in a government agency could mean a department director, but in a small organization, a filing clerk. Gomułka, while reportedly irritated by the scope of the purges, actually intervened only rarely. His interventions, involving—with very few exceptions—non-Jews, discouraged no one from sacking Jews. Stola tells us that in response to complaints from dismissed Jews and disoriented Polish managers, the Central Committee Secretariat established a special commission for employment of people dismissed from senior positions. He fails to mention, however, that this commission did not review the decisions leading to dismissal and had no authority to restore (or interest in restoring) anybody to his or her original position. Its purpose was to make sure that the dismissed managers did not get a similar position and to help with their retirement. There were a few cases of dismissed Jews being offered positions managing small, faltering companies, but in general, many dismissed professionals were denied work in their fields even if their skills were badly needed in Poland at the time (e.g. solid-state physicists).

Stola has gathered much interesting information on sometimes successful attempts to remove such prominent personalities as Jerzy Morawski, Marian Naszkowski, Marian Spychalski, and Czesław Mankiewicz—all Poles, but hardly typical cases. Gomułka was very unhappy about attacks on these people. Meanwhile, Walichnowski, the Zionist expert at the Ministry of the Interior, who was in the midst of these activities, quietly waited until December to leave, even though he had been advised to do so by Gomułka's secretary in May. In a meeting in the second half of May 1968 Gomułka admonished the leaders of the Warsaw Party Committee about campaign abuses, but at the end of the meeting praised the Warsaw party organization for passing the test in March with flying colours. He advised the leaders to 'take steps to correct the mistakes, particularly in dealing with the Jewish question and in other personnel matters'. But there was no follow-up and the Warsaw committee continued the campaign as if nothing had changed. Gomułka never returned to this problem and in the plenary session of the party Central Committee he praised the campaign. At the Fifth Party Congress in November three of the most active provincial party chiefs (Stanisław Kociołek, Władysław Kruczek, and Jan Szydlak) were rewarded with seats in the Politburo, and the person in charge of the media campaign, Stefan Olszowski, was promoted to secretary of the Central Committee. Stola's comment that Moczar's removal from the Ministry of the Interior was a slap on the wrist for his conduct of the campaign is not very convincing either. He moved to the Politburo, where he was given responsibility not only for security but for the military as well. Clearly,

Gomułka felt that Moczar could do more in the Politburo, and he did. This was reflected in a ministry directive issued on 15 February 1969 in which the Kolegium instructed the security services to 'establish operational control over persons identified as revisionists or Zionists'. By then the term 'revisionist' was already synonymous with the term 'Zionist'. The 'operational control' went beyond individuals and survived until the end of the communist regime in Poland, but its consequences are felt to this day.

Stola's outstanding monograph should be of major interest to historians, sociologists, psychologists, and anyone interested in crucial episodes in the history of communist Poland. It is a multidimensional work delving boldly into controversial and less well-known moments. Stola is the first scholar of the events of March 1968 to have consulted foreign publications and interviewed Jewish emigrants. An impressive selection of primary archival documents and excellent historical analysis make this book a must for any serious student of communist Poland. It is a treasure trove of topics and ideas to be studied and analysed further.

An excellent literary companion to Stola's historical analysis is *Memorbuch*, a new book by Henryk Grynberg, the leading Polish Jewish American writer.[8] This is docufiction at its best.

The title *Memorbuch* refers to the tapes and memoirs written by Adam Bromberg, a Polish Jew. Born to a very wealthy family, he tried his skills in business before the war, only to be seduced by the communist ideology, which took him to prison in prewar Poland, into Soviet *stroibaty* (militarized construction units for unreliable elements), into the Polish communist army (as a political officer and participant in the bloodiest battles), into a publishing empire in communist Poland as its chief, to prison during the antisemitic campaign, and finally to emigration to Sweden.

Grynberg, with his unmistakable style, draws vivid pictures of Bromberg's travails, painting the great and not so happy times. By the time Grynberg embarked on his writing project, Bromberg had been dead for five years, making it impossible for the writer to discuss certain events, or to ask questions generated by the recordings. Grynberg has compensated for this with research and his own imagination. Thus, he provides historical sketches of Jewish life in Poland before the Second World War with dramatic excerpts from parliamentary debates on the Jewish question. We learn about Jewish history in various cities and get glimpses of Jewish experiences in the Communist Party and the communist system. Grynberg admits to using poetic licence in much of the dialogue throughout the book, and to drawing his own interpretations and conclusions: this is docufiction, after all. And yet the reader is not short-changed in any way. On the contrary, the book makes the events more human and dynamic. It helps that Grynberg was born in Poland and lived there for many years until 1967. His personal experiences and outstanding writing ability make the story of Bromberg so much richer, more vivid, and more credible.

[8] H. Grynberg, *Memorbuch* (Warsaw, 2000).

The book was not intended as a hagiography of a very accomplished person. Grynberg is not glossing over negative aspects of Bromberg's life and career. But he succeeds admirably in presenting an honest picture of a Jewish communist, who, while seduced by ideology, had his doubts, was not proud of everything he did, and ultimately chose a career that allowed him to compromise with an oppressive system without sacrificing his dignity and harming his fellow men. In Bromberg one can recognize many Jewish communists in Poland who joined the movement for unselfish reasons: to make life better for the poor, the disadvantaged, the discriminated against. Like Bromberg they had faith in the party and suffered for their convictions before the war, then lived through the Holocaust, with no family to speak of and barely surviving themselves, and trying to rebuild their lives in communist Poland.

Bromberg seems to have had the makings of a successful party functionary. In the military he reached the position of chief of the political administration in the navy. But he was not a yes-man and had no interest in political infighting. He went on to the publishing business, which he loved and had honed his skills in before the war. The job was not easy, and yet the obstacles thrown at him by party bureaucrats, Polish and Jewish alike, did not deter him. He managed to build a powerful and highly reputable publishing house that won universal recognition abroad. And yet his career did not bring him any measure of security. With the rising tide of antisemitism in the party apparatus he became one of the many victims of the anti-Zionist campaign of 1968. He was imprisoned for his alleged activities against the Polish state, but none of the charges were proved.

This panoramic view of Bromberg's life allows us to get glimpses of his friends and relatives, Jews and Poles, whose lives, ideologies, and careers were often very different from his. We also get personal views of some very dramatic moments in communist Poland's history, such as prison life and communist politicking before the war, the Jewish question in the Polish army in the USSR, war experiences, and the purges of Jewish officers after Marshal Rokossovsky became the Polish minister of defence. One of the most powerful sections in the book is the last chapter, entitled 'The Expulsion'. There Grynberg details the experiences of a dozen Polish Jews who were forced to leave their homeland as a result of the antisemitic campaign of 1967–8. It is frightening to see how far the Polish authorities were willing to go to solve the Jewish problem, and it certainly gives pause in the context of current Polish–Jewish debates. The events of 1967–8 may, in fact, be the last chapter of Jewish life in Poland.

Stola and Grynberg offer a unique look at the Jewish experience and Polish–Jewish relations in Poland. They enrich our knowledge and offer new perspectives, and their books are indispensable for anybody wishing to get a better understanding of the anti-Zionist campaign in Poland of 1967–8. They belong on the shelf of anybody who is seriously concerned about the future of Polish–Jewish relations.

BOOK REVIEWS

HILLEL J. KIEVAL

Languages of Community: The Jewish Experience in the Czech Lands

(Berkeley and Los Angeles: University of California Press, 2000); pp. xii + 312

One thinks of the Czech Jews of the inter-war period, perhaps like the Italian Jews of the Renaissance, as uniquely charmed: at a time when elsewhere in central and eastern Europe Jews were subjected to ever-increasing antisemitism, the Jews of the new Czechoslovak Republic enjoyed extraordinary cultural integration and social acceptance. Moreover, they carved out identities as Czech Jews not only by assimilation, but also in other forms. In an epilogue to this richly textured, extensively researched, and theoretically sophisticated work Hillel J. Kieval relates an anecdote, told to him years after the fact, from Max Brod's visit to Prague in 1963. While Brod was meeting a number of old friends in the home of the playwright František Langer, someone noted that each of those present represented a different form of Czech Jewish identity: Brod had opted for Zionism; Langer for Czech acculturation; Eduard Goldstücker, a professor of Germanics, for identification with German culture; and Arnost Kolman, a philosopher and mathematician, for communism. Kieval points out that these identities were chosen rather than inherited, and also that they overlapped: Brod, for example, was as much a representative of Jewish–German synthesis as of Zionism.

Kieval's *Languages of Community* both confirms this image of the Czech Jews and undermines it by demonstrating that the development of this community in the period before the First World War was fraught with intense struggles against emerging Czech nationalism. In these interlinked essays Kieval's primary emphasis is on the way in which the conflicts over language shaped the identities of the Czech Jews—a persuasive emphasis given the centrality of language in the definition of nationalisms in the Habsburg empire. The fact that German was the primary spoken and written language of urban Jews was a particular irritant to Czech nationalists, who in the nineteenth century were seeking to turn Czech into the language of a new national culture. Like other Jews in the multi-ethnic empire, Czech Jews were caught between the German culture of the regime and the culture of their indigenous environment. However, unlike the Hungarian Jews, who underwent Magyarization in the mid-nineteenth century, Czech Jews in the major cities and towns remained wedded to German culture (even as those in the countryside were much more linguistically Czech). Until emancipation in 1867 and beyond, the Jews were perceived as—and indeed often acted as—allies of ethnic Germans and of the Habsburg regime. Towards the end of the nineteenth century a Czech Jewish movement emerged which favoured the adoption of the Czech language and culture. But Kieval argues that this movement had only modest success, which was limited primarily to the abolition of German Jewish schools in the villages. The gradual adoption of Czech by Jews was not so much the product of this kind of ideological movement as it was the result of the influx of Czech-speaking Jews from the countryside into the cities.

In addition to the essays on social and political developments such as these, Kieval's most interesting essays concern the role of myth both in the creation of Czech Jewish identity and in the conflict between Czechs and Jews. In particular, he is fascinated by the role of forgeries in the creation of myths of national identity. Between 1816 and 1830 Czech nationalist intellectuals 'discovered' a series of manuscripts (later proved to be forgeries) which purported to demonstrate the antiquity of the Czech nation. Romantic historiography based on these manuscripts left the Jews out of Czech history. In response, in the 1860s, a Jewish writer named Markus Teller published an anonymous pamphlet claiming that the Jews pre-dated the Czechs in Bohemia, but that the Jews had always been loyal allies of the Czechs. This pamphlet generated a response in the form of another anonymous pamphlet entitled *Die Juden und die Nationalen*, which purportedly was also written by a Jew, but which, Kieval argues, corresponded neatly to the historiography of the forged manuscripts. The pamphlet contains the claim that Jews and Czechs had lived in harmony until the arrival of the Germans created a division between them. But *Die Juden und die Nationalen* turns viciously anti-Jewish in its criticism of contemporary Jews who refused to abandon German culture. Kieval concludes that the claim that it was written by a Jew was also false; the pamphlet was rather the disingenuous product of an anti-Jewish Czech nationalist.

Another myth that involved forgery was that of the Golem of Prague. In the 1830s and 1840s Jewish and Czech ethnographers independently recorded the legends of Rabbi Judah Loew ben Bezalel (the Maharal of Prague) and of the creation of the Golem—legends which have no grounds in what is known of the historical Maharal. Kieval argues that these legends were attempts by both Jews and Czechs to construct a usable past in the form of a figure who ostensibly symbolized the integration of the Jews in Bohemia. On the Czech side this folklore bespeaks a philosemitic bent to Czech romantic nationalism that would support the image of a Czech–Jewish symbiosis. However, Kieval does not adequately square this image with the anti-Jewish hostility he chronicles elsewhere in nineteenth-century Czech nationalism. But the most spectacular forgery of a Golem story appeared in the first decade of the twentieth century, when Yudl Rosenberg, a Polish rabbi, published various manuscripts allegedly written by the Maharal, including one on the Golem who saved the Jews of Prague when they were accused of ritual murder. These manuscripts were demonstrably forged by Rosenberg, but this Golem story became the source for subsequent stories and films. Ironically, the most recent version was accepted by many as the oldest.

That Rosenberg's Golem fights a blood libel is the giveaway for Kieval, since such accusations were not made against Bohemian Jews in the sixteenth century, but were made against Czech Jews in the late nineteenth century. Kieval devotes a chapter to the way in which the resurgence of the blood libel and of Czech nationalism reinforced each other as two forms of 'social discourse' or 'social knowledge'. The blood libel, as a medieval legacy, in a negative way fed the nationalist desire to recover ancient roots. Kieval might have said a good deal more about why this latest type of 'forgery' emerged when it did and where it did. Why did some antisemitic nationalisms, such as the French, not produce blood libels while others did?

As a result of the Hilsner blood libel case in 1898, Thomas Masaryk came to be seen as the great Czech champion of the Jews. Indeed, the myth of Czech–Jewish symbiosis owes much to Masaryk's liberal nationalism. But Kieval demonstrates that Masaryk's own position on the Jews was extremely complicated and ambivalent. He favoured Zionism because he saw the Jews as a legitimate national group, but he was highly critical of the assimilationist Czech Jewish movement. It is in the story of Masaryk that Kieval convincingly shows both the truth and the limitations of the symbiosis myth—a creative tension that animates his outstanding account of the history of this singular Jewish community.

DAVID BIALE
Emanuel Ringelblum Professor of Jewish History,
University of California, Davis

JACOB GOLDBERG

Haḥevrah hayehudit bemamlekhet polin–lita

('Jewish Society in the Polish–Lithuanian Commonwealth')

(Jerusalem: Zalman Shazar Center for Jewish History and the Center for Research on the History and Culture of Polish Jews, Hebrew University, 1999); pp. 312

The latest book by Professor Jacob Goldberg, an outstanding scholar who focuses on the history of Jews in the Polish–Lithuanian Commonwealth in the early modern period, consists of fourteen articles. The articles were published in various periodicals and collective works, mostly in Polish, with some in English and German (a list of the original titles and places of publication is included). The texts are translated into Hebrew. The book contains an index of persons and an index of places; place names are given in both Hebrew and Polish.

The great value of this book is that it collects in one volume texts that are widely dispersed and (for linguistic reasons) inaccessible and makes them available to Israeli scholars and students interested in the history of Jews in old Poland. The texts illustrate many important aspects of Jewish life in the Polish–Lithuanian Commonwealth.

The book contains the following articles:

'The Attitude of Polish Society towards Jews'. The author examines the image of the Jew in Polish society, anti-Jewish literature, the policy of the Catholic Church towards Jews, and ritual accusations against them (above all, the blood libel). The various subgroups within Polish society—noblemen, peasants, and townspeople—differed in their attitude towards Jews, and the transformation of Polish society in the eighteenth century brought about a change in attitude towards them. The demographic factor—that is, the fact that the Jews constituted 10 per cent of the population—determined Polish attitudes towards the Jews to a much greater extent than it had before and influenced ideas for Jewish reform at the time of the Four-Year Sejm.

'De non tolerandis Iudaeis'. Anti-Jewish regulations in Polish towns and the struggle against them—the case of Wieluń in the sixteenth to nineteenth centuries. The author discusses rights of *de non tolerandis Iudaeis* granted to Polish towns (Wieluń was granted the right in 1566). When a town obtained this right, it did not mean that all Jews were expelled; often they continued to live on the private properties of noblemen in the town (*jurydyki*) and in other properties excluded from municipal authority. In towns which had been granted this right, it was also possible for Jewish merchants to conduct limited trade.

'The Legal Status of Polish Jews and Privileges Granted to the Jewish Communities in the Polish–Lithuanian Commonwealth in the Sixteenth to Eighteenth Centuries'. The privileges granted to the Jews outlined their rights concerning residence and trade, communal institutions, the construction of synagogues, and the establishment of cemeteries; they also defined the relationships between the Jews and the ruling authorities and between Jews and the rest of the population. Jewish privileges may be divided into general privileges (valid for the whole country), regional privileges, and community privileges. The latter, issued by a king for royal properties and by the owners—mostly noblemen—for private properties, are the basic source for study of the position of the Jews in the Polish–Lithuanian Commonwealth. The rights granted to Jewish communities were frequently opposed by the local townspeople.

'The Va'ad Arba Aratsot (Council of Four Lands) in the State and Social System of the Polish–Lithuanian Commonwealth'. The author presents the history of the institution from its beginning in the second half of the sixteenth century to its dissolution in 1764. The Jewish parliament was an integral part of the fiscal apparatus of the state and occupied an accepted place among other autonomous institutions in the Polish–Lithuanian Commonwealth at that time. The institution was of great importance for the Polish Jews and enjoyed the respect of Jewish communities throughout Europe.

'The Jewish Community in the Social and State System of the Polish–Lithuanian Commonwealth'. The situation of the Jewish people in royal towns was different from the situation of those in towns owned by noblemen. (A decision of the Sejm in 1539 made the Jews who lived on private properties subject to the landowners.) The *kehalim* in private towns were much more dependent on the landowners than their equivalents were on the royal officials in the royal towns. In the seventeenth and eighteenth centuries the owners interfered in the internal life of the communities much more than they had earlier. The landowners also used the *kehalim* to enforce their regulations. The Jewish marriage markets (created by the owners' prohibitions against marrying Jews from other properties) and the territorial range of the *kehalim* generally corresponded to the area of the magnate's or nobleman's property. Noblemen strove to incorporate 'their' arendars into *kehalim* in their towns and supported efforts of 'their' *kehalim* to subordinate arendars from other properties.

'The Rights of Jewish Arendars and their Rule over Peasants'. In the social structure of the Polish–Lithuanian Commonwealth there were three groups of Jews engaged in agriculture: arendars of liquor production, who generally leased auxiliary farms together with taverns and breweries; Jews who ran farms (following a Sejm decision of 1775); and Jews who held various kinds of land on lease. The prohibition against renting land to Jews was not observed in practice. The conditions of renting a property varied according to whether the arendar was a nobleman, a townsman, or a Jew. Generally, Jews were obliged to pay rent in advance for the whole period of the lease. The text of the contract made the peasants subject to the arendar, so that in the case of the Jewish arendars it conflicted with the law forbidding Jews to rule over Christians. Thus, jurisdiction over peasants was frequently taken away from the Jews and handed over to the landowners. This fact did not eliminate the negative attitude of the peasants towards the Jewish arendars, which gave rise to numerous conflicts and riots.

'Marriage among Polish Jews in the Eighteenth Century'. Marriage played an important role in the economic life of Polish Jews. The author reports the opinions of contemporary writers, both Christian and Jewish, concerning Jewish marriage. Generally the writers evaluated the institution of Jewish marriage very highly, while 'enlightened' observers were critical of the fact that many Jews married very young. On the basis of the 1791 census, the author discusses the average age of marriage and the marriage market. Several tables are included, showing among other things the age distribution of Jewish men and women, the married Jewish population, and early marriages among Jews. The author deals also with the

'father's table' (Yiddish: *kest*), a widespread custom among the Polish Jews, according to which the wife's or husband's parents fed and housed the newly married
couple and their children for a certain period of time.

'From *Shtadlanim* to Politicians: Representatives of Communities at the Time of
the Four-Year Sejm (1788–1792)'. Representatives appointed by the *kehalim* and
regional assemblies differed from the *shtadlanim*, who acted individually or in small
groups, and whose activity was limited to emergency situations and interventions.
The representatives, of whom there were about 120, continued the tradition of
central representation of the Polish Jews in a new form. Their activity was extensive
and forward-looking and concerned among other things the 'reform of the Jews'.
The representatives presented to the authorities a list of postulates concerning the
Jews which would influence other documents prepared in that period.

'Jews and Rural Taverns'. The author examines the production and sale of liquors
(Polish: *propinacja*) and the outstanding importance of Jewish arendars in this
market. He presents the factors that inclined the majority of owners and arendars of
land properties to develop production of liquors and beer and, as a consequence, to
increase the profits of their taverns. Jews were engaged in this branch of activity,
both as general arendars leasing all taverns and breweries in the whole complex of a
magnate's properties, and as arendars of one or several taverns in a village, with the
liquors supplied by the manor. The Jews played an integral part in the manor's
economy, and their services were used not only on the magnates' or noblemen's
properties, but also on the properties of the Church. For this reason the Jewish
tavern-keeper was the most widespread image of the Polish Jew in the seventeenth
and eighteenth centuries.

'Jews and Urban Taverns in Podlasie'. A characteristic feature of Podlasie was the
particularly high percentage of Jews engaged in the production and sale of liquors.
Podlasie had a developed network of urban taverns, and almost all of them were
leased by Jews. The author stresses the differences between leasing a rural tavern
and leasing an urban one. In towns a Jewish lease embraced not only the production
and sale of the liquors, but also other branches of economy, and arendars often
entered into partnerships. Moreover, arendars of urban taverns did not have exclusive rights to produce and sell liquors. The conditions of a tavern's lease varied
from town to town, and to enlarge income from urban taverns many more limitations were placed on the town's inhabitants, both Christian and Jewish.

'Jewish Enterprises in Polish Industry in the Eighteenth Century: A Priest and a
Jew Establishing a Factory in Wielkopolska'. Jews who were active in developing
industry in the second half of the eighteenth century had to overcome social and
economic obstacles. There was a lack of necessary capital; thus, for a Jew who
wanted to establish a factory, a partnership with a landowner or royal official was
the best solution. The author tells the story of the establishment and management
of an ironworks in Chocz by Shlama Ephraimowicz, who co-operated with the

owner (who was the parish priest) and with the local nobleman. This was the only enterprise of its kind to be found in Wielkopolska at that time.

'Taxes Paid by the Jews in Towns of the Polish–Lithuanian Commonwealth in the Sixteenth to Eighteenth Centuries'. The author surveys the taxes paid by the Jews in towns: in royal towns to the *starostas* and in private towns to the owners. Taxes were paid for the rights to reside in the towns, to observe religious practices, and to engage in trade, artisanship, and other professions. In addition, Jews had to pay a separate fee for selecting community elders, appointing a rabbi for betrothals, marriages, and burials, ritual slaughter, trading in partnership with Jews from other towns, and so on. Apart from the taxes paid to the royal official or landowner, Jews were forced to make payments to the Catholic Church and clergy, and in some private towns they had to work in the landowners' manors. A common practice was to collect taxes from Jews as a lump sum.

'The Attitude of the Jews towards Enemies of the Polish–Lithuanian Commonwealth'. The subject embraces the following problems: forms of Jewish support for the Polish army; the traditional Jewish aversion to military service (above all, because it made observance of Jewish religious laws impossible); motives inclining Jews to fight state enemies; and legal and social limitations which made it difficult or even impossible for Jews to perform military service. Despite the stereotype of the military ineffectiveness of the Jews, in the eastern parts of the Polish–Lithuanian Commonwealth, which was imperilled by Tatar and Cossack invasions, Jews had much experience in battle. It was also common for the inhabitants of Jewish towns to be required to perform various services of a military character, such as the defence of the town's walls or the repair of fortifications. Nevertheless, the Jewish presence in the Polish army did not reach a high level.

'The Memoirs of Moses Wasercug, a *Shoḥet* [ritual slaughterer] in Wielkopolska'. Wasercug's memoir is one of three memoirs of Polish Jews dating to the eighteenth century. The author describes Wasercug's life and his travels to neighbouring countries, and notes that the Jews were at that time the most mobile group in the Polish–Lithuanian Commonwealth.

ANNA MICHAŁOWSKA
Warsaw University

KRISTI GROBERG and AVRAHAM GREENBAUM (EDS.)

A Missionary for History: Essays in Honor of Simon Dubnow

Minnesota Mediterranean and East European Monographs, no. 7

(Minneapolis: University of Minnesota, 1998); pp. xvi + 158

In the English-speaking world the historian Simon Dubnow has never been as widely read as his German predecessor Heinrich Graetz. This is due, above all, to the ready availability of the Jewish Publication Society translation of Graetz's multi-volume *History of the Jews*, which has remained in print for over a century, and, to a lesser degree, to Graetz's spirited prose and vigorous judgements. The editors of this volume of essays would like to redress the balance and stimulate interest in Dubnow, whose work as historian, ideologue, and advocate has not received extensive attention in Anglophone academic circles. This is a laudable object, but whether the slim volume under review here, however well-meaning the intentions of its editors, will boost Dubnow's stock is doubtful.

Most of the contributions to this volume first saw life a decade ago, at a conference in 1991 at the University of Illinois at Champaign-Urbana marking the fiftieth anniversary of Dubnow's death, and most still bear the marks of their birth as conference papers. They are unusually short, ranging in length from four to eight pages, and, while prolixity in itself is no virtue, there is a point at which brevity becomes a liability. In several cases contributors summarize research and conclusions that they have published elsewhere. Michael Hamm's 'Kiev: Dubnow's Inferno of Russian Israel' reproduces material from his *Kiev: A Portrait, 1800–1917* (1993). Joseph Goldstein's 'Fathers and Daughters: Dubnow and Ahad Ha-Am', which compares the reactions of the two men to the marriages of their daughters to non-Jews, is based on Goldstein's *Aḥad ha-am: biografiyah* (1992) and Isaac Remba's *Banim akhlu boser* ('The Children have Eaten Unripe Grapes', 1973). Shlomo Lambroza's 'Simon Dubnow and the Pogroms in Late Imperial Russia' restates views that he has elaborated elsewhere. Other essays, such as Mikhail Beizer's 'Dubnow's St Petersburg', essentially a list of buildings associated with Dubnow's career in the imperial capital, and Viktor Kelner's paper on the historian and Jewish nationalist Aleksandr Braudo, whose importance for Dubnow's work is never made clear, are charitably described as modest contributions to the topic.

The most useful cluster of essays is the trio on Dubnow and the pogroms. Hamm, Lambroza, and John Klier (who, in 1992, co-edited with Lambroza a collection of studies on pogroms in modern Russian history) show that there is little evidence to support Dubnow's view that the pogroms of the late imperial period were carefully prepared and centrally directed, in part to discredit and intimidate

liberals and revolutionaries, and in part to divert peasant discontent. Most importantly, they explain how Dubnow's understanding of the pogroms, which still
enjoys enormous influence and informs many synthetic accounts of modern Jewish
history, derived from his lack of access to important sources as well as to his lack of
distance from the events and his own involvement in Russian Jewry's political
struggles. Stimulating as well is Israel Bartal's essay on how Dubnow's diaspora
nationalism influenced his view of medieval Jewish autonomy, leading him to
reverse the Haskalah's negative attitude towards communal autonomy and, at the
same time, to describe this autonomy in thoroughly anachronistic terms. Still,
despite these useful essays, this volume as a whole does not shed much new light on
the topic. Readers seeking an up-to-date, historically contextualized analysis of
Dubnow's work would be well advised to look at the relevant pages in Benjamin
Nathan's recently published essay 'On Russian-Jewish Historiography' in the
collection edited by Thomas Sanders, *The Historiography of Imperial Russia: The
Profession and Writing of History in a Multinational State* (1999).

TODD M. ENDELMAN
University of Michigan, Ann Arbor

ISRAEL KLEINER

*From Nationalism to Universalism: Vladimir Ze'ev
Jabotinsky and the Ukrainian Question*

(Edmonton, Alta.: Canadian Institute of Ukrainian Studies Press,
University of Alberta, 2000); pp. xvi + 200

Born in Odessa, V. Z. Jabotinsky (1880–1940) was one of the most colourful and
controversial Zionist activists of the inter-war period. Fluent in half a dozen
languages, he was first of all a man of letters. From a career in journalism he moved
on to become a celebrated translator as well as a poet and novelist. In 1903
Jabotinsky brought his very considerable literary and rhetorical skills into the camp
of Russian Zionism, and in the tumultuous period of 1903–6 he took an active leading role in that movement. He then moved onto the larger stage of Zionist politics in
both Europe and the Middle East, delineating and energetically championing an
activist and confrontational Zionist ideology. In 1935, after a decade of criticizing
the established leadership and its policy orientations, Jabotinsky broke with the
World Zionist Organization to found the New Zionist Organization in order to
appeal directly to the Jewish masses and to pursue an independent Zionist agenda
in international affairs.

In this monograph Israel Kleiner focuses our attention on Jabotinsky's views of Ukrainian nationalism both in the period before the First World War and in the aftermath of the Bolshevik revolution and the ensuing civil war. Kleiner examines Jabotinsky's writings and actions at three critical moments: in 1911–14, when Ukrainians were celebrating the life and work of the Ukrainian national poet Taras Shevchenko; in September 1921, when Jabotinsky reached an agreement with Maksym Slavinsky, a representative of Symon Petlyura's Ukrainian People's Republic, to create a Jewish police force in Ukraine to protect the community against possible assaults should there be renewed hostilities between Ukrainian and Bolshevik forces; and in 1926, when Shalom Schwartzbard was placed on trial for the assassination of Petlyura, who was widely blamed by Jews for the wave of pogroms suffered by Jewish communities in Ukraine during the civil war.

After establishing Jabotinsky's general views on nationalism and cultural identity, Kleiner examines closely what he identifies as the courageous positions adopted by Jabotinsky in these three instances. In Kleiner's view, Jabotinsky's support for Ukrainian nationalism was fully consistent with his fierce opposition to Jewish cultural assimilation. Jabotinsky not only condemned the Polish policies of active Polonization in Austrian Galicia, but also rejected tsarism's efforts to Russify the ethnic communities of the western borderlands of the empire. Instead, he welcomed the full development of Ukrainian cultural life and championed those expressions of Ukrainian nationalism that he believed would eventually result in an independent Ukraine. In Kleiner's exposition Jabotinsky envisioned a future in which democratic nationalist movements would achieve their goals, thereby producing a non-threatening international order in which individuals could realize their own full potential as human beings without loss of national culture or ethnic identity.

Jabotinsky's interaction with Slavinsky was based upon his understanding of antisemitism as a product of circumstance, or what he called 'the antisemitism of things', rather than as a function of personality or long-standing cultural heritage. Therefore, he concluded that the assaults on Ukrainian Jewry after the First World War were rooted in the economic structure of Jewish life in Ukraine and not in putative anti-Jewish attitudes that were presumably deeply entrenched in the religious and cultural world-views of the Ukrainian people. This approach distanced Jabotinsky from most contemporary Jewish leaders in the West and allowed him to negotiate directly with those identified by the masses as hereditary antisemites.

Kleiner's admiration for Jabotinsky is clear throughout the essay. He presents him in heroic terms as a visionary possessing an ideology that was consistent and uncompromising. In doing so, Kleiner's effort is harnessed to a broader contemporary agenda: Jewish–Ukrainian understanding and co-operation. Kleiner is especially committed to refuting the kind of scholarship that views Ukrainian–Jewish relations as thoroughly and irretrievably conflict-ridden owing to attitudes and postures that are based upon stereotypical assumptions; namely, that all

Ukrainian nationalists are instinctively antisemites and that all Jewish political behaviour is inherently hostile to the existence of an independent Ukraine. His positive depiction of a committed Jewish nationalist known to be fully sympathetic to Ukrainian cultural and political development demonstrates Kleiner's belief that a harmonious and mutually beneficial Ukrainian–Jewish relationship was quite possible.

Certainly Kleiner's goal is laudatory. However, as in most instances where scholarship is linked to an agenda, something is generally lost along the way. Extrapolating specific positions espoused by Jabotinsky at a particular moment without carefully contextualizing them does not allow for a full discussion of his views. For instance, the manner in which Jabotinsky balanced, or some would say compromised, his commitment to Jewish emigration to Palestine with Diaspora Jewish politics needs to be analysed much more closely and critically. At the same time, the assessment of the Jabotinsky–Slavinsky agreement and Jabotinsky's public statements at the time of the Schwartzbard trial need to be related to Jabotinsky's simultaneous involvement in contemporary Yishuv developments, and especially the question of Jewish self-defence against Palestinian Arab assaults.

Jabotinsky was a complex man. As an orator he was unsurpassed in his ability to move and energize his audience by reducing complicated issues to clear and simple options. As a writer he passed effortlessly from language to language without loss of meaning or cultural nuance. Even though he is often associated with strength (Samson) and with militancy (steel), and even though he expressed admiration for some of the practices associated with Italian fascism, he articulated a vision of the future in which individual freedoms were to be vouchsafed and human potential could be realized. His views and thoughts are deserving of a full and critical discussion.

ALEXANDER ORBACH
University of Pittsburgh

KONRAD ZIELIŃSKI

Żydzi Lubelszczyzny 1914–1918

('Jews of the Lublin Region 1914–1918')

(Lublin: Wydawnictwo Lubelskiego Towarzystwa Naukowego, 1999); pp. 392

Among Polish historians interested in Jewish issues there is a move away from topics solely concerned with the twenty years between the two world wars. Until recently research into Jewish history in Poland has concentrated mainly on the inter-war period and has merely scratched the surface of earlier times, especially the nineteenth and early twentieth centuries. Konrad Zieliński's book breaks this silence. The author focuses on the period of the First World War and its influence on the Jews living in the region of Lublin at the time, more specifically in the area under Austro-Hungarian occupation. A pertinent question would be how to extend this research to cover the area within the province of Lublin–Chełm that was under German occupation, particularly Podlasie. It would then be possible to compare the processes of development of national and political awareness among the Jews living under the two different occupying forces in the region of Lublin. It is worth noting that the Austro-Hungarian administration was decidedly more liberal than the German.

Zieliński bases his study on numerous sources from several dozen historical records found in archives in Warsaw, Lublin, Kraków, and Zamość. His research draws on an impressive number of memoirs and diaries (including some published in Yiddish and Hebrew in the memorial books of particular towns in the Lublin region), as well as on periodicals from the Lublin region, Galicia, and as far away as the Prussian sector of partitioned Poland. He has managed to reconstruct a detailed picture of Jewish life at the time, not only in large towns such as Lublin, Chełm, and Zamość, but also in the tiny *shtetls* about which very little has been written in either Polish or foreign historical studies. The diverse sources Zieliński uses complement one another to present a comprehensive picture of how the Jewish minority functioned in the region of Lublin during the First World War—a period of great change for this particular community.

The layout of the book is coherent, and includes graphs containing statistical, economic, sociopolitical, and cultural information on the Jewish inhabitants of the region. However, the reader does not feel overwhelmed by the volume of factual information the book contains, and wherever there are gaps in the source material, Zieliński does not hesitate to make his own comparisons and present his own hypotheses.

Zieliński does not restrict himself to the period of the Great War, as it was called then. In writing about various developments, such as the shaping of Jewish political and cultural life, he draws on earlier materials dating to the end of the nineteenth century, when, in large towns such as Lublin, Chełm, and Zamość, the seeds of the Jewish political parties were sown. The revolution of 1905 proved to be of great importance for the region of Lublin because, to the surprise of both Poles and Jews, it demonstrated that the latter were capable of engaging in mass sociopolitical movements and often displayed great national awareness. But the decisive period for the shaping of Jewish identity in the provincial towns of the region of Lublin was the First World War, when news of Zionism, socialism, and communism reached such places as Markuszów, Biłgoraj, Hrubieszów, and Tomaszów Lubelski. It was also a time when the younger generation became politically active and initiated a cultural and religious revolution by rebelling openly against their Orthodox or hasidic parents.

All of these developments are examined in Zieliński's work. He unfolds before the reader a vivid panorama of Jewish life in the region in all its historical, ethnographic, and social aspects, relating events such as the emergence of local political party committees and the establishment of cultural and educational associations, centres, and periodicals, and introducing some of the individuals working within these organizations. In addition, there are detailed descriptions of the everyday life of the Jewish inhabitants of large and small provincial towns. Zieliński outlines the particular character of the Jews living in the region of Lublin as compared with those living in other regions of Poland. This group was strongly influenced by hasidism, and was thus more conservative than analogous communities in Warsaw, Łódź, and the western provinces of the Kingdom of Poland. Few among the group had received a secular education or belonged to the intellectual elite in the larger towns of the region, and the process of assimilation was slower here as a result not only of Jewish conservatism and the poor economic standing of the Jews, but also of the conservatism of provincial Christian (mainly Polish) society.

In this study Zieliński introduces an important aspect of Polish–Jewish relations and of Christian–Jewish relations in general. Jews in the region of Lublin came into contact not only with Poles but also with Ukrainians and German functionaries of the Austro-Hungarian administration during the period of the war. The relationship was not a happy one, but was full of tension and prejudice. The Jews were confronted with Polish nationalism, whose most popular aspect was antisemitism, while Polish reactions to the Jews' increasing consciousness of their national identity were many and varied. These developments, which are approached objectively in this study, are extremely complex and probably require additional research. Not only did they find their expression in economic antisemitism, as Zieliński emphasizes, but they also became increasingly more ideological. The First World War itself, however, was not the cause of the increasing antisemitism among Poles and Ukrainians, or of the nationalism of the Jews; it served only to escalate and radicalize these tendencies. Unfortunately, in describing these processes Zieliński does not take into account the rise of Polish nationalism from the 1905 revolution onwards, or the increasingly difficult atmosphere in Polish–Jewish relations, especially in 1911 and 1912, when, for the first time on Polish soil, the Stronnictwo Narodowo-demokratyczne (National Democratic Party) declared a general boycott against the Jews. The call for a boycott met with a significant response in the conservative and provincial area of Lublin. Polish–Jewish relations during the First World War had their roots in these earlier events, and rich information on the topic may be found in the provincial press of the period.

Zieliński's book also contains examples of Polish–Jewish collaboration, as well as accounts of Jews consciously involving themselves in Polish political and cultural life. Despite their rarity, and the fact that they were regarded with disapproval within right-wing political circles, such activities extended beyond the city and the region. It is important to note that, official antisemitic policy notwithstanding, everyday life demanded that Polish–Jewish relations remain at least tolerable, if not friendly, especially in the small towns, where the Jews comprised the majority. The two groups were interdependent administratively, economically, and simply as neighbours.

Zieliński provides an extensive appendix of tables and photographs found in private collections and archives. However, the table of information on the present state of Jewish monuments in the region of Lublin should not have been included. Although it is based on relevant sources, it contains a number of errors arising from the fact that the original compilers of the inventories never visited the sites mentioned, and thus had no first-hand information on their condition. In Zieliński's defence, it would be difficult to demand that he personally inspect all of the monuments, but he could have made use of archival material from the inter-war period, which includes statistical information on properties belonging to the Jewish community during and directly after the First World War.

Despite these shortcomings, the work as a whole is extremely valuable and contributes a great deal of new information on the Jewish community, both in the region of Lublin and in Poland in general. It clarifies the situation of Polish Jews in the early twentieth century not merely from the perspective of great urban centres such as Warsaw, Kraków, Łódź, and Lviv, but also at the provincial and regional level.

ROBERT KUWAŁEK
Majdanek State Museum, Lublin

JERZY MALINOWSKI

Malarstwo i rzeźba Żydów polskich w XIX i XX wieku

('The Painting and Sculpture of Polish Jews in the Nineteenth and Twentieth Centuries')

(Warsaw: Wydawnictwo Naukowe PWN, 2000); pp. 434 + vi, 554 illus.

One can only admire the energy and learning of Jerzy Malinowski, an authority on Polish art and Polish Jewish culture, whose beautifully produced work on the painting and sculpture of Polish Jews is over 400 two-column pages long and includes 554 illustrations, many of them in colour (although they are small). Among the men (and a few women) he discusses are many unknown or virtually unknown artists, while relatively few are well-known figures such as Mark Antokolsky, Maurycy Gottlieb, Samuel Hirszenberg, and Ephraim Moses Lilien.

Malinowski begins his story in the mid-nineteenth century with the appearance of the first Polish artists of Jewish origin, of whom Aleksander Lesser (born in 1814) was the most prominent. This was an easy decision, but other decisions made by the author are more difficult and more problematic. What exactly does he mean by *Polish* Jewish artists? Obviously, those artists born and active in the Kingdom of Poland and in Galicia qualify, but it is difficult to justify the inclusion of Mark Antokolsky (here spelled Marek Antokolski), the important sculptor born in Vilna (Wilno, Vilnius) and universally regarded as a Russian Jew. Malinowski admits that Antokolsky's cultural orientation was Russian, as is clearly expressed in his choice of subject matter. So why is he, along with other artists from the Russian Pale of Settlement, such as Yehudah Pen and Mordecai Zvi Mane, included in this volume? This tendency towards 'Polish imperialism' may also be noted in the author's decision to reproduce and discuss the work of Lesser Ury, surely a German Jewish artist, since he was born in the Poznań region, then part of Prussia. On the other hand, another outstanding artist of Jewish origin from a region once Polish, Isaac Levitan, is not discussed at all, and neither is Chagall, Pen's pupil in Vitebsk.

More significant is the question of what Malinowski means by 'Jewish artists' and 'Jewish art'. In his very brief introduction he tells us that he has included artists who identified themselves as belonging to the Jewish national camp, and artists who, even if they did not identify themselves in this way, took an active part in Jewish life (p. 3). Those who qualify on neither of these grounds are branded as 'assimilationists' and omitted. Perhaps this is why Levitan does not appear, although this 'assimilated' artist, known above all for his depictions of the Russian countryside, did paint at least one picture of Jewish interest: a remarkable scene of a Jewish graveyard. This principle of selection seems reasonable enough, although it is never entirely clear what such terms as 'national' and 'assimilation' really mean. Malinowski also seems to imply throughout the book that 'Jewish artists' were those who at least occasionally, and sometimes predominantly, selected Jewish themes as the subject of their work. One problem here has to do with the definition of 'Jewish themes'. For example, are portrayals of the life and death of Christ, remarkably common in 'Jewish art', Jewish subjects? Another difficulty is that numerous Polish (non-Jewish) artists have also portrayed Jewish subjects, sometimes in a most moving and profound manner (this is the subject of a fine book edited by Marek Rostworowski: *Żydzi w Polsce: Obraz i słowo* (Warsaw, 1993), vol. i). One needs only to think of the beautiful paintings of Aleksander Gierymski. Was he, then, a Jewish artist, a creator of Jewish art? Obviously, Malinowski does not think so, but he does not say why. At any rate, I suppose that we cannot blame him for failing to define satisfactorily what 'Jewish art' is all about. No one, so far as I know, has resolved this conundrum.

It is a pity that Malinowski has chosen not to go very deeply into the various historical and artistic contexts so important for an understanding of the emergence of Jewish artists in Poland. We are told precious little about modern Jewish history in the Polish lands, and what we are told is rather simplistic. He mentions nationalists and assimilationists, but ignores the important camp of Jewish integrationists, who combined a commitment to modernization and acculturation with a pride in their

Jewishness. I would argue that it was in this camp that Maurycy Gottlieb, one of the fathers of Polish Jewish art, belonged, and I therefore cannot agree with Malinowski's assertion that he was a 'national' Jewish artist. Gottlieb died, after all, in 1879, before the emergence of a modern Jewish national movement. (Malinowski argues that Gottlieb became a nationalist under the influence of Rubin Bierer, whom he met in Lwów. But the meeting took place in 1878, before the emergence of Zionism in Galicia, and Bierer's suggestion that Gottlieb devote himself to Jewish historical subjects is hardly an indication of a 'national' position. See p. 36.)

The great changes that took place after the First World War, with the emergence of an independent Polish state and the upheavals in Jewish life during that time, are glossed over, although they clearly had an important impact on the cultural activities of Polish Jews. Nor, surprisingly, are we given an adequate guide to modern Polish art, a subject on which Malinowski is an authority. Examples of Polish (non-Jewish) art are lacking here, which is a great pity since, as the author himself notes, most of the artists referred to themselves as Polish as well as Jewish artists (see p. 4). Moreover, Malinowski does not concern himself with the role of Jews as publishers of cultural journals, as gallery owners, or as patrons and purchasers of art. For example, the name of Salomon Lewental, publisher of *Kłosy*, a leading nineteenth-century Polish cultural journal, does not appear in his index. Nor does the author delve deeply into the history of the reception of his artists in the Jewish and the non-Jewish worlds, a fascinating subject that would undoubtedly shed much light on the Jewish cultural world and on relations between Poles and Jews.

These failings are offset by many obvious strengths. The author provides interesting and informative readings of the works of numerous artists, whose artistic language ranges from nineteenth-century academism to expressionism, cubism, and abstraction, and whose subject matter is equally diverse. He tells us a great deal about the influences that helped to shape their style, and his quotations from contemporary critics give us at least some sense of how they were understood and evaluated. Their 'Jewish' paintings are explicated in the light of wider Jewish concerns and prevailing Jewish ideologies—as in the case of the many portrayals of scenes from the life of Jesus and the surprisingly numerous representations of the enigmatic figure of the seventeenth-century philosopher Uriel Da Costa, who became in the nineteenth century a potent symbol of Jewish intellectual heterodoxy and of free thinking. Malinowski is a particularly valuable guide to the diverse ideologies and modes of expression of the artists associated with the Yung Yidish (Young Yiddish) group of the early years after the First World War, a subject on which he has published an important monograph. Although he fails to tell us much about Polish art, he does highlight the bonds that linked the Jewish artists to their non-Jewish Polish colleagues.

Particularly important, in my estimation, is the emphasis Malinowski places on the growing tendency among Jewish artists in the period between the wars to form their own explicitly Jewish organizations and to exhibit together. This was surely the result of the rise of secular Jewish nationalism of both the Zionist and autono-mist, sometimes Yiddishist, varieties, whose influence on at least some artists, such as Lilien and Hirszenberg, is already clearly discernible in the years before the First World War. It may also have to do with the triumph of exclusivist Polish national-ism, which held out little hope for the kind of coexistence and integration cham-pioned by such early practitioners of 'Polish Jewish art' as Lesser and Gottlieb. Malinowski is an excellent guide to the many Jewish exhibitions held in Warsaw and elsewhere, and he is also good in pointing to the emergence of different Jewish 'schools' in the major artistic centres of Łódź, Kraków, and Lwów. He is no doubt right to emphasize the central importance, in this period, of the search for a style that was both Jewish, even Jewish nationalist, and 'modern', a search that led many Jewish artists to embrace the language of expressionism and to create a unique artistic movement here labelled 'Jewish expressionism'.

The author follows the careers and achievements of his selected Jewish artists up to 1939. It is heartbreaking to be reminded of the activities of so many creative people whose lives were cut short by the Holocaust. A second volume is planned, to be devoted to the life and work of Polish Jews who lived abroad, and particularly those who belonged to the famous École de Paris.

Malinowski's book belongs to a well-known genre, which includes books on African American writers and distinguished Americans of Polish origin. In all these cases one is confronted by the nagging question whether such projects, based on the principle of segregation, are really justified, and whether all the figures brought to our attention are really worthy, on their artistic merits alone, of being remembered. There is undoubtedly something slightly ludicrous about these compilations, which must be counted as a species of apologetics, and Malinowski's book often reads like an endless encyclopaedia of artists and the exhibitions in which they took part. There are inevitably a few inconsequential errors, and a claim, which I have never encountered before, that Oskar Kokoschka was of Jewish origin (p. 149).

On the other hand, it is undeniably interesting, even amazing, that so many Polish Jews were active in the world of the fine arts. Malinowski's unearthing of this vast array of personalities may be compared to an archaeological excavation shed-ding considerable light on the historical process of Jewish modernization, accultur-ation, and the search for a usable new Jewish identity in the Polish lands. He presents for our inspection a large number of men and women who wished both to be European artists and also to proclaim, in various ways, an attachment to their Jewishness; and gives us ample evidence of a Jewish stratum within Polish art, just as there is, no doubt, a 'southern school' in American literature and an African American tradition within American music. For all this he deserves our gratitude. His book should not be ignored by anyone interested in the history of modern Polish Jewry.

EZRA MENDELSOHN
The Hebrew University

KADYA MOLODOWSKY

Paper Bridges: Selected Poems of Kadya Molodowsky

TRANSLATED, EDITED, AND INTRODUCED BY

KATHRYN HELLERSTEIN

(Detroit: Wayne State University Press, 1999); pp. 544

In *Paper Bridges* the poet, translator, and Yiddish scholar Kathryn Hellerstein has selected poems from the six books of Yiddish poetry Kadya Molodowsky (1894–1975) published between 1924 and 1974. In her introduction Hellerstein mentions that, according to Jewish legend, when the messiah comes, the Jews will cross into paradise over a paper bridge (p. 32). Molodowsky's use of this folk motif as a theme in her poetry exemplifies its double character, which embraces both social realism and messianic utopianism. The poems are presented in their original Yiddish version and in precise, often evocative, translations. Endnotes elucidate ambiguous meanings of Yiddish words. This allows the reader to partake in some of the choices Hellerstein faced as translator.

In her note on the translation Hellerstein describes some of the difficulties in translating Yiddish literature into English. The primary obstacle, she writes, is a basic incompatibility between Yiddish, which is rooted deeply in Jewish tradition, and English, with its strong Romance influence, embedded in Christian tradition. The impossibility of conveying the multifaceted Jewish associations in the vocabulary that stems from the Hebrew–Aramaic component of Yiddish is perhaps the strongest argument for the necessity of bilingual editions of Yiddish poetry. Words such as *agune* ('abandoned wife') or *tume* ('ritually unclean') in 'Froyen-lider' ('Women Poems') from Molodowsky's first collection, *Kheshvndike nekht* ('Nights of Heshvan', 1927), cannot merely be left in their English translation. The translation instead becomes a gateway to the original with the translator as guide, interpreter, and, to a large extent, custodian of a Yiddish poetic language which is mostly obscure and hidden in today's American literary landscape.

In his introduction to a 1991 selection of poems by Abraham Sutzkever, Benjamin Harshav, another excellent translator of Yiddish poetry, remarks: 'We felt that in this almost lost, hardly accessible language of literary Yiddish (unlike the lower-class jargon that many Americans still remember), we should convey the original meaning as closely as possible.'

The question remains, of course, as to what the original meaning actually was. Bilingual editions give the reader the opportunity to compare the translations with the original. Even if the reader has no knowledge of Yiddish, he or she must still confront the otherness of the Hebrew alphabet. It is hoped that this will spur the reader to look for the corresponding words in the original, which will—again, it is hoped—lead to a quest into the lost world of Yiddish. Scholarly works on individual Yiddish writers require elaborate notes and literary historical context rarely needed to the same degree for better-known writers from other cultures, such as German or Italian. Similarly, Hellerstein is faced with the Herculean task of resurrecting a whole literary historical universe in order to place Molodowsky and her work in a meaningful context.

Considering the still nascent scholarly treatment of Yiddish women's poetry, Hellerstein succeeds in outlining the main biographical and literary influences on Molodowsky's work in her introduction. She should be credited for highlighting the feminist themes and styles of Molodowsky's earlier poetry, such as 'Froyenlider'. After emigrating to the United States, and especially following the Holocaust, Molodowsky shifted her focus from the particularity of women's issues, styles, and voices to that of 'unified Jewish peoplehood. This led to a strong emphasis on manifestations of *plain yidishkayt,* and an identification with the universal, the mainstream which had a male-identified voice' (p. 49). A good example of this tendency in Molodowsky's poetic response to the Holocaust is the poem *El khonen* ('Merciful God') from the collection *Der dovid melekh aleyn iz geblibn* ('King David Alone Remained', 1946). Here it would have been helpful to compare her response to the Holocaust with that of other Yiddish poets, such as Yankev Glatshteyn, Chaim Grade, Rokhl Korn, and Malka Heifets-Tussman.

The balance between situating the poems in their original framework and making them speak eloquently to today's reader is the major challenge of translating Yiddish poetry. Hellerstein has given us a comprehensive sample of one of the most important Yiddish women poets that is, as I can attest, an excellent introduction to Yiddish poetry for college students. *Paper Bridges* is a major contribution to the still relatively small library of Yiddish poetry in English translation and a reliable introduction to the poetics of Yiddish.

JAN SCHWARZ
Department of Germanic Languages and Literatures,
University of Illinois, Urbana-Champaign

JULIAN TUWIM

Utwory nieznane. Ze zbiorów Tomasza Niewodniczańskiego w Bitburgu: Wiersze, Kabaret, Artykuły, Listy

('Unknown Works. From the Bitburg Collection of
Tomasz Niewodniczański: Poems, Cabaret, Essays, Letters')

EDITED BY

TADEUSZ JANUSZEWSKI

(Łódź: Wydawnictwo Wojciech Grochowalski, 1999); pp. 320

The title of this volume of miscellany by Julian Tuwim, *Utwory nieznane* ('Unknown Works'), is somewhat misleading. The book is largely made up of cabaret pieces that were performed and known to the public; they simply were never published in written form. Still, the book's publication in 1999 was an important event, not only for poetry lovers and historians of literature, but also from a Jewish perspective. Jewish topics appear prominently and in many forms in this collection of poems, facsimiles, juvenilia, cabaret skits and songs, and private letters from various periods of the poet's life. This is in clear contradiction to the stereotype, predominant in Jewish historiography, of the pre-war Polish Jewish intelligentsia as thoroughly assimilated and uprooted. Tuwim's example demonstrates that the opposite was the case. Like many other writers he was in constant dialogue with his Jewishness, defending it when attacked, but also critical of Jewish obscurantism. 'Far from antisemitism', he wrote in his *Wspomnienia o Łodzi* ('Memoirs from Łódź', 1934), 'I was always, and will always be, an enemy of men uniformed in beards with their Hebrew-German hotchpotch and traditional butchering of the Polish tongue. It is high time, gentlemen, to trim your long kaftans and curly sidelocks, and learn respect for the tongue of the nation in whose midst you live.' (From today's perspective Tuwim's evaluation of Yiddish and traditional garb is questionable, but his appeal to overcome Jewish exclusivity is not.) This is one side of Tuwim's dialogue with Jewishness. The other is represented by one of the finest epigrams published in this book:

Usłyszałem od tej gnidy,	I heard this bastard say
Żem żydowski jest krwiopijec.	I'm a Jewish leech.
A ja—szlachcic między Żydy,	Well, I'm a Jewish prince
Gdy on gudłaj, choć aryjec.	While he's an Aryan kike.

Many of the poems presented in *Utwory nieznane* are satirical comments on the political situation of the time. In his response to growing radical nationalism in pre-war Poland, Tuwim resorted to all literary means—including parody, pastiche, and buffoonery—to mock and ridicule the adversary. His irony was sometimes misunderstood, which occasionally left him open to misinterpretation and to the accusation that he was taking an antisemitic stand.

Among the large selection of Tuwim's productions for cabaret presented in the book, the most revelatory are his monologues for the Quid Pro Quo theatre. In all of them—even those that do not feature a Jewish speaker (for example, *Exposé pana prezydenta* ('Mr President's Speech')—the idiom of Jewish *szmonces* (the traditional self-mocking cabaret monologue) is clearly discernible. For example, Tuwim constantly plays with mispronounced words, as if repeating the inventiveness of the Jewish 'butchering of the language'. Cabaret, enormously popular in pre-war Poland and an influential factor in shaping cultural patterns, has been very little researched. If I am not mistaken, only one journalistic account exists in English (Ron Nowicki's *Warsaw: The Cabaret Years* (San Francisco, 1992)). Cabaret's saturation with the Jewish idiom was probably much greater than we imagine; indeed, it was quite possibly one of the main venues of Polish–Jewish cultural osmosis.

The longest text in the book, 'Smorgoński Savonarola: Humorystyczniak o K. Ild. Gałczyńskim' ('Savonarola from Smorgonie: A Satire on K. Ild. Gałczyński'), on fellow poet Konstanty Ildefons Gałczyński, was written after Gałczyński had published an antisemitic diatribe in the nationalist *Prosto z mostu*. Tuwim builds his argument on the fact that Gałczyński worshipped him as a poet in private, while publicly besmirching him as a Jew in *Prosto z mostu*. While paying respect to Gałczyński's poetic talent, Tuwim denounces his duplicity and questions his self-appointed authority to set, or discuss, moral standards. Tuwim's article was prepared for publication in *Wiadomości Literackie*, and we do not know why it did not appear. Perhaps Tuwim himself withdrew it at the last moment, or his editor did so, or some outside factor prevented its publication. Had it been published, it would certainly have become a classic among polemics against antisemitism. In *Utwory nieznane* it appears in print for the first time, reprinted from surviving galley proofs.

The texts published in the book come from a single source: the collection of Dr Tomasz Niewodniczański of Bitburg. Unfortunately, the book provides no information about him or about his collection and its origins. The editor's introduction is limited to a general description of the works and a brief discussion of the authorship of the texts, which in some cases is presumed and in some cases appears to be collaborative. The footnotes are uneven and the documentation of the provenance of the texts is fragmentary. In some cases the footnotes provide trivial and unnecessarily encyclopaedic data, while in others they fail to provide information indispensable to understanding the text (as, for example, in the footnote to the letter to Władysław Besterman about Tuwim's conflict with a friend of twenty-five years; we are given no clue to who this friend might have been). This lack of editorial supervision is surprising, considering that the volume's editor, Tadeusz Januszewski, is the curator of the Museum of Literature in Warsaw. A possible reason for it may be that the publisher, Wydawnictwo Wojciech Grochowalski, which is new in the market, is not equipped to handle such a complex task as a critical edition of a major classic requiring extensive human and financial resources. As a result, *Utwory nieznane* can hardly be considered a definitive edition of this very important part of Tuwim's work. Still, the book can be greatly enjoyed and appreciated by the lay reader. Few things age as badly as humour, yet, surprisingly, many of Tuwim's satirical texts have preserved their flavour and freshness for some seventy years. Nor should this volume be bypassed by the specialist.

GWIDO ZLATKES
Brandeis University

STANISŁAW WIELANEK
Szlagiery starej Warszawy: Śpiewnik andrusowski
('Hits of Old Warsaw: A Songbook of the Streetwise')
(Warsaw: Wydawnictwo Boston, 1994); pp. 504

A Warsaw street music band might not appear to be an obvious place for a Jewish historian to look for materials or inspiration. But this would be a mistake, and it took me some six years to realize it. *Szlagiery starej Warszawy: Śpiewnik andrusowski* by Stanisław Wielanek was published in 1994 and should have been acknowledged in the subsequent volume of *Polin*. Fortunately, the present volume on Jewish popular culture in Poland presents an ideal opportunity to make up for that omission.

Stanisław (Stasiek) Wielanek, born about 1950, is the leader of Kapela Warszawska, a street band that usually performs for tips in an underpass near the Hotel Forum in the centre of Warsaw. They play mainly pre-war Warsaw urban folk music: songs like 'U cioci na imieninach' ('Auntie's Name-Day Party') and 'Bal na Gnojnej' ('Party on Gnojna Street'). This is the repertoire for which Stanisław Grzesiuk is known as the last original master; Jarema Stępowski later presented a watered-down version to the public through the mass media. In other words, this music is regarded today as lowbrow culture of questionable authenticity. Wielanek recorded more than two dozen records with Kapela Czerniakowska and Kapela Warszawska, yet none of them seems to have had lasting artistic value. Few people would suspect that he is also a serious, passionate, and versatile collector of urban folklore. His 500-page volume contains a richness of material that is not only musical—including both scores and lyrics—but also literary and iconographic: from cabaret monologues and vignettes, jokes, bon mots, and (not always accurate) biographical and contextual information, to drawings, posters, photographs, and postcards. Alongside old Warsaw songs and criminal or lumpenproletarian ballads, the book includes a separate section on Jewish folklore in Polish which is nearly 100 pages long, and another fifty-page section on Lwów.

In the Jewish section, among some thirty songs, we find classics like 'Mein Yiddishe Mame' with Polish lyrics by Julian Tuwim, 'Bełz' with lyrics by L. Frey and J. Roman, and 'Yidl mitn Fidl' ('Yidl with a Fiddle') with lyrics by Józef Aleksandrowicz. Some lesser-known songs include 'Komorne' ('Rent') by Mieczysław Miksne, 'Balia' ('Laundry Tub') by Moryc Gebaj, and 'Rebeka' with lyrics by Andrzej Włast (Gustaw Barmitter). Not long ago 'Rebeka' was a popular hit in a magnificent rendition by Ewa Demarczyk. One of my favourites in this section is the song 'Madagaskar', also by Miksne, a satirical response to the idea of resettling the Jewish population on that island. I already knew this song, but thought of it as a pure nonsense piece—its Jewish context was lost on me, and only Wielanek's book brought it out. There are more surprising discoveries. For instance, I always thought that the song 'Bal na Gnojnej' was an anonymous folk tune; in fact it is by a Jewish composer, Fanny Gordon.

The contribution, or even over-representation, of Jews in pre-war Polish popular culture is clearly visible well beyond the Jewish section in Wielanek's book. In the section on Lwów we of course find Marian Hemar, but also Emanuel Szlechter, Anna Kitschmann, and Henryk Vogelfänger (who was Tońko of the famous comedic duo Szczepko and Tońko). The section 'Szemrane kawałki' ('Shady Ditties') includes many songs about the lower echelons of Warsaw society written by Władysław Szlengel, who later wrote poems in the Warsaw ghetto and songs for the Jewish cabaret there, and died in 1943. The names Dawid Glik, Bolesław Mucman (Micmacher), Konrad Tom, and Andrzej Włast, to list just a few personalities almost forgotten today, appear many times throughout the book. The name index at the end of the book is an alarming reminder that the field is virtually neglected; monographs on pre-war popular culture in Poland and the Jewish participation in it are badly needed.

Szlagiery starej Warszawy is published in a quarto format, which is very convenient when using the musical scores. It has an attractive hard cover with a collage of pre-war postcards and photographs. The most serious flaw is that the book is printed on inferior paper, yellow and coarse. This badly affects the illustrations, which are not only grey but also blurred, disqualifying it as a coffee-table book, which was apparently one of the publisher's aims. Also, occasional factual and typographical errors and editorial imperfections signal the need for caution if the book is to be used as a scholarly source. Still, the wealth of rare material more than compensates for these flaws. *Szlagiery starej Warszawy* by Stanisław Wielanek is an invaluable presentation of pre-war popular culture, and makes very enjoyable reading.

GWIDO ZLATKES
Brandeis University

STANISŁAW WIELANEK
Party na Nalewkach
('A Party in Nalewki Street')

(ZicZac Music; 2001; distributed by BMG Poland)

Tracks: 1. 'Rebe', 2. 'Bajgełe', 3. 'Kochaj mnie', 4. 'Madagaskar', 5. 'Paczka',
6. 'Balia', 7. 'Dlaczego ja', 8. '12 rodzin', 9. 'Sardinenfisz', 10. 'Szabasówka',
11. 'Mein Jidisze Mame', 12. 'Ameryka', 13. 'Oj bidy da', 14. 'Rebeka',
15. 'Kupcie jaja', 16. 'Srulek', 17. 'Jojne karabin', 18. 'Pipek', 19. 'Stary Josel',
20. 'Dalej Jojne żydowskiego', 21. 'Bełz'

No one interested in Stanisław Wielanek's songbook of inter-war hits should miss his recording of Yiddish-tinged 'oldies' *Party na Nalewkach*. Released on vinyl in 1980 and later available on cassette, until recently the album was hard to find in either format. Reportedly, the publisher let it go out of print after receiving complaints from Jewish tourists (apparently a target audience) that songs such as 'Jojne karabin' evoked unattractive stereotypes or even summoned up the spectre of the deferential singing and dancing little Jew associated with the term *majufes*. Whatever the reason for its disappearance, Wielanek's album has now reappeared on CD with a new cover and title (it was first known as *Szmonces i Lyrika*), and with five new selections added to the earlier version's sixteen. Aficionados of Jewish popular song will find a veritable lost continent of fascinating repertoire attractively arranged and performed by Wielanek and his band, Kapela Warszawska. Something of an archaeologist and troubadour, Wielanek first discovered the genre of *szmonces* as an ardent collector of musical folklore from Warsaw. The encounter was inevitable, since, as Wielanek says, Jewish songwriters dominated the field of popular music in Poland between the wars.[1] Scholars and performing artists alike should be grateful to him for reviving this repertoire and bringing to light the names of its sadly forgotten creators, both with this CD and with its most useful accompanying book.

BRET WERB

---

[1] Interview with Ewa Cichowicz, *Południe*, 16 (16 Apr. 2001); <www.poludnie.com.pl/16_1.htm>.

JAN TOMASZ GROSS

Sąsiedzi: Historia zagłady żydowskiego miasteczka

(Warsaw: Fundacja Pogranicze, 2000), pp. 158 + 36 illus., 1 map

ENGLISH EDITION

Neighbors: The Destruction of the Jewish Community in Jedwabne

(Princeton: Princeton University Press, 2001); pp. 262 + 27 illus., 3 maps

Think of a short, accusatory book on a Jewish topic that has galvanized and divided a whole nation. If your first thought was Zola's *J'accuse*, your second should be *Neighbors*, by Jan T. Gross.[1] The story that Gross tells is well known by now. On 10 July 1941, two weeks after the Germans arrived, a pogrom took place in the small town of Jedwabne, near Białystok. With the acquiescence of the German police, perhaps at their instigation, but without their major participation, townspeople and peasants from the surrounding countryside attacked the town's Jews. After several hours of beatings, torture, and individual murders, the remaining Jews were first assembled in the town square, and then herded into Bolesław Śleszyński's barn, three streets away, which was doused in petrol and set alight. But for a few who managed to run away and hide, all the town's Jews perished that day, at the hands of their Polish neighbours.

Although townspeople had always known who the perpetrators were, and spoke about it openly among themselves, the facts of the case were not widely disseminated. The trials of twenty-three Poles in 1949 and 1953 took place without publicity, and the official line throughout the communist era, reflected in a commemorative plaque displayed in the town until recently, was that the Germans had done it. Historians during that era did not question the official view: even the Jewish historian Szymon Datner, in a 1966 survey of the Holocaust in the Białystok region, felt free to say only that some 'social outcasts' had been involved.[2] Not until nearly a decade after the end of communism did Agnieszka Arnold's 1998 documentary *Gdzie mój starszy brat Kain?* ('Where is my Elder Brother Cain?') finally break the

---

[1] This analogy was first suggested by Andrzej Leder, 'Jedwabne: Polska sprawa Dreyfusa?', *Nowa Res Publica*, 7 (July 2001). Leder writes that 'the basic conflict—in the Dreyfus case as in the dispute over Jedwabne—is over social consciousness, over which set of imaginings will decide people's attitudes in each of these societies. Hence the passions. The battle over one's own imagination awakens violent emotions.'

[2] S. Datner, 'Eksterminacja ludności żydowskiej w okręgu bialostockim', *Biuletyn ŻIH*, 60 (1966), 1–29.

silence. An interview in the film with Śleszyński's daughter, who spoke of the events candidly, spurred Gross to write the first full historical treatment, nearly sixty years after the event. Ironically, Gross's opponents accuse him of 'hasty judgements'.

Gross allowed a year to elapse between the publication of the Polish and English editions, to give Poles a chance to debate the matter before the international spotlight fell on it. He was not disappointed: the appearance of *Sąsiedzi* in May 2000 set off an unprecedented 'affair', which was still simmering more than two years later. There have been other heated debates on Polish–Jewish issues in recent years, for example over Michał Cichy's article 'Czarne karty powstania warszawskiego' ('Black Pages of the Warsaw Uprising'[3]), about the massacre of Jews by an AK unit during the 1944 Warsaw Uprising, or in 1986, occasioned by Jan Błoński's 'Biedny Polak patrzy na getto' ('A Poor Pole Looks at the Ghetto'), in the liberal Catholic weekly *Tygodnik Powszechny*; but these discussions were limited to a small circle of intellectuals, and each lasted only a few weeks. The reaction to *Sąsiedzi* was of an entirely different order. Over the next two years nearly a thousand articles appeared in the Polish press, many of them heatedly polemical; debate raged in public meetings and on the Internet, and there was extensive coverage in the electronic media. An official investigation was launched, and the highest authorities of Church and State became involved. The Jedwabne affair has represented really the first mass public airing of Polish–Jewish issues since the Holocaust.

As in the Dreyfus affair, the debate pitted truth against national honour and pride. One of the right-wing splinter parties launched an abortive lawsuit against Gross for 'insulting the Polish nation' (Zola was also sued for libel: he lost, and had to flee to England). The right-wing press was full of headlines like 'J. T. Gross's 100 Lies about Jedwabne', 'Gross's Anti-Polonism', 'To Humiliate Poland', and 'Anti-Polish Propaganda Action': in general, the extreme right represented the book as part of a conspiracy designed to squeeze money out of Poland. These were marginal voices, to be sure, but there was also a more respectable opposition, whose position will be analysed in more detail below. The Jedwabne affair differed from its French predecessor in one important respect: the official reaction was on the whole appropriate and free of defensiveness. The Instytut Pamięci Narodowej (Institute of National Memory, IPN) launched an investigation, releasing interim reports from time to time and its 'final findings' in July 2002;[4] the full two-volume 'White Book' appeared in October 2002.[5] With the IPN's interim reports leaving less and less doubt that the story was true, President Aleksander Kwaśniewski

---

[3] *Gazeta Wyborcza*, 29–30 Jan. 1994.

[4] IPN, 'Końcowe ustalenia śledztwa w sprawie zabójstwa obywateli polskich narodowości żydowskiej w Jedwabnem w dniu 10 lipca 1941 r.', published on the IPN's web site (www.ipn.gov.pl) but since removed. All quotations in this review that pertain to these findings are drawn from this document, portions of which were reproduced in the 10 July 2002 editions of *Gazeta Wyborcza*, *Rzeczpospolita*, and other newspapers.

[5] P. Machcewicz and K. Persak (eds.), *Wokół Jedwabnego*, i: *Studies*; ii: *Documents* (Warsaw, 2002).

Table 1. Comparison of responses to the Jedwabne affair polls, April and August 2001

Presumed responsible	(%)	
	April 2001	**August 2001**
Only Germans	34	28
Germans with the help of Poles	11	12
Poles under German pressure	2	4
Maybe Poles	2	2
Poles	5	8
Others (e.g. Soviets, Russians)	2	5
Haven't heard about it	17	10
Hard to say	26	30

proposed to offer a symbolic apology as a way of acknowledging some form of collective responsibility for the crime, and this soon became the touchstone of the discussion (an opinion poll in March 2001 found 40 per cent in favour of such an apology, 35 per cent against, and 25 per cent undecided). The mainstream press, too, generally accepted Gross's conclusions: *Tygodnik Powszechny*, its monthly counterpart *Więź*, the news magazine *Wprost*, and the intellectual monthly *Polityka* all took editorial lines in support of Gross. The two leading dailies, the left-wing *Gazeta Wyborcza* and the conservative *Rzeczpospolita*, both dispatched reporters to Jedwabne (Andrzej Kaczyński and Anna Bikont, respectively), whose stories left no doubt that at least some of the townspeople remembered the events just as Gross had recounted them. A further documentary by Arnold, also entitled *Sąsiedzi* (Gross had borrowed the title with Arnold's permission), was screened on Polish television, allowing a national audience to see and hear these eyewitnesses for themselves.

There is no doubt that all this activity had its effect: a poll conducted in August 2001 by the Centrum Badania Opinii Społecznej (Centre for Social Opinion Research, CBOS) found that 90 per cent of respondents had heard of the massacre and 70 per cent knew that the victims were exclusively Jews. Beyond these basics, however, the Polish public displayed considerable confusion. Asked who the perpetrators were, respondents answered as in Table 1.

Thus only 10 per cent believed that the perpetrators were, or might have been, exclusively Poles, and only a further 16 per cent accepted that Poles had played some part; 40 per cent thought that the Germans had played the leading role, of whom 28 per cent held the Germans alone responsible; 9 per cent thought that some of the victims were Poles.[6] In short, after more than a year of discussion, only

---

[6] In this they were not entirely wrong: a Polish communist named Eliasz Krawiecki was killed on 25 June 1941, during the first disturbances that followed the arrival of the Germans ('Jedwabne—Ciszej nad tą zbrodnią', *Gazeta Wyborcza*, 22 Aug. 2002).

one Pole in ten was convinced by Gross's version of events, only one in four would concede that Poles had played any role at all, and nearly half did not know what to think. A comparison with the April poll results suggests, however, that public opinion was slowly coming around.

The public's ambivalence was mirrored by the Catholic Church, deeply divided between liberals, who backed Kwaśniewski's call for atonement, and conservatives, who resisted the book's message, occasionally in tones that were distinctly anti-semitic.[7] Cardinal Glemp, the primate of Poland, seemed torn between the two positions. Glemp vacillated over whether he should take part in the sixtieth anniversary commemoration in Jedwabne, at first declining on the grounds that the massacre was a 'local tragedy', then changing his mind, then changing it again. In the end Kwaśniewski attended the ceremony, but there was no official Catholic presence, and the parish priest. Father Edward Orłowski, led the townspeople in a conspicuous boycott of it. The climax of the ceremony was the unveiling of a new plaque, whose controversial wording papered over the same divisions. The new inscription, in Hebrew, Yiddish, and Polish, reads: 'In memory of the Jews of Jedwabne and surrounding areas, men, women, and children, fellow dwellers [współgodarze] of this land, murdered and burned alive at this site on 10 July 1941. Jedwabne 10 July 2001.' This curt epitaph left the identity of the perpetrators up in the air.

Glemp offered, as an excuse for his absence, that his participation would have turned the ceremony into a 'spectacle', and that he had already offered an apology at a solemn commemorative mass in Warsaw on 27 March. Glemp's apology was hedged about with qualifications, however. It was directed, not to the Jewish people, but to God, and asked forgiveness, not specifically for the massacre, but in vague terms, for all 'evils' that Jews had suffered at the hands of Christians, in Jedwabne or elsewhere. Glemp ascribed the massacre to people who had gone against the teachings of the Church, but said nothing about the anti-Jewish phobias that the Church had actively promoted at the time (much less their persistence even today). He also expressed his hope that the Jews would come round to apologizing to the Poles for their role in bringing communism to Poland.

The public's confusion was in large part understandable, given the mixed messages emanating from the country's spiritual leaders, and given that most people had not read the book and had no real basis on which to form a judgement.

---

[7] The parish priest of Jedwabne, Father Edward Orłowski, made a particular exhibition of himself, claiming that he had secret documents that proved German responsibility, which he could not reveal because of the seal of the confessional, and telling reporter Anna Bikont the following: 'As we learned in the Bible, the priest told us: "The Jew has a cap on a stick and says: watch out, there are two of us." That's the Jewish soul for you. In New York I was with a Jewish multimillionaire, and he was bragging that he had a huge factory and during the war sold it to the Germans. "They gave us a lot of gold, and took us by car to Hamburg, and from there we went by boat to America", he told me. Here their people were dying and they were like that; it was just a swindle. These are facts' ('My z Jedwabnego', *Gazeta Wyborcza*, 23 Mar. 2001).

Many Poles felt that one ought to wait until the IPN's results were in—perhaps not unreasonably, but the issue was forced in the spring and summer of 2001 by the approaching sixtieth anniversary, which clearly demanded some form of public response. Many thus felt themselves under unfair pressure to take a stand in a matter that they had only just heard about, and about which the experts seemed to disagree.

The experts, on the other hand, had no such excuse. The eminent historian Tomasz Strzembosz, in particular, had spend several decades studying the Białystok region during the Soviet occupation, yet this largest pogrom in Polish history, which happened days after the end of that occupation, had somehow escaped his attention. In acknowledgement of Strzembosz's expertise, Gross had submitted a preliminary article on the massacre for the Festschrift marking Strzembosz's retirement in 1998; Strzembosz had thus had two years to consider his position. Yet in his first article on the subject, in January 2001, he declared that 'the documentation in my hands does not permit me to take a position on this key question' (that is, on whether the perpetrators had been Germans or Poles). This self-confessed ignorance did not prevent him from claiming, in the same article, that 'Gross's assertions seem in the light of certain sources to be not entirely true', or from emerging shortly as an expert on the subject and Gross's chief adversary.[8] Other respected historians of the wartime period in Poland, including Tomasz Szarota and Bogdan Musiał, joined in on Strzembosz's side. (On the other hand, Gross had numerous supporters, among them Andrzej Żbikowski, who had earlier alluded to the massacre in an article of his own.)

Though they remain politically potent, most of the objections to Gross's book have been rendered irrelevant by the IPN's 'final findings', which on the whole support Gross's version of the story. Szarota offered the following concession in the light of this report:

There is no disagreement between us as to the fundamental question: in the crime committed against the Jews in Jedwabne (and not only in that locality) their Catholic neighbours took part. We both agree that, knowing the truth about these events, the fault of the Poles can no longer be reduced to that of the role of the passive witness, looking upon the Jewish tragedy with indifference, since unfortunately the German perpetrators found helpers among us in the work of extermination.

'There, he added, 'the consensus probably ends.'[9] Strzembosz, for his part, wrote that 'Polish perpetration of the crime in Jedwabne is indisputable,' adding, perhaps to save face: 'but it was the participation of the Germans that made it at all possible . . . It wouldn't have happened without the Germans.'[10] But Strzembosz might just as easily have quoted Gross, who had written: 'it is . . . clear that had Jedwabne not been occupied by the Germans, the Jews of Jedwabne would not have been

[8] T. Strzembosz, 'Przemilczana kolaboracja', *Rzeczpospolita*, 27–8 Jan. 2001.
[9] *Tygodnik Powszechny*, 19 (2002).   [10] *Polska Agencja Prasowa*, 9 July 2002.

murdered by their neighbors'.[11] Gross's critics persistently misrepresented Gross as having said that the Germans had played no role at all in the massacre, and thus claimed every indication of German involvement as a victory, whereas his position was actually only that the Germans had not actively participated in the killing itself. The critics regularly set up such straw men, attributing to Gross theses that he never put forward. Szarota, for example, puts in Gross's mouth the opinion that 'the Holocaust was prepared for the millions by the Germans and Poles in partnership'.[12] Musiał, who lived and works in Germany, compared *Sąsiedzi* to Daniel Goldhagen's *Hitler's Willing Executioners*, a justly criticized book that drew far-reaching conclusions about German society on the basis of another group of 'ordinary men'. Gross makes no such claims about Polish society in general, however. There is a grain of truth behind Musiał's criticism: the Polish edition ends with the statement that the 'community' (*społeczeństwo*) was responsible for the massacre, meaning the Polish community of Jedwabne as it existed in 1941. The word *społeczeństwo*, ambiguous when taken out of context, was misrepresented as meaning Polish society in general by some early commentators. In the English translation Gross replaces it with 'neighbors'.

If the 'consensus' ends, as Szarota writes, with conceding the substance of Gross's case, what is there left to discuss? Only two substantive issues remained unresolved after the IPN report: the exact number of victims, and the number and representativeness of the perpetrators. Gross had accepted the established figure of 1,600 victims (another misrepresentation is that this figure was his own estimate), which was the number that appeared on the original commemorative plaque, for example; but exhumations at the site seemed to point to a much smaller number, perhaps 300. Gross is reluctant to accept this conclusion: although he admits that it will probably never be possible to establish exactly how many Jews were in Jedwabne on the day, he points to numerous estimates that fall between 1,400 and 1,600. If these are accurate, then a large number of Jews are unaccounted for, and the most likely explanation of the discrepancy is that the exhumation did not uncover all the remains. Gross points out that the exhumation was carried out hastily, in only five days, and incompletely, because the rabbinic authorities would not give permission for a complete exhumation. (The right-wing press immediately seized on this fact as evidence of a cover-up, even though further exhumations could only have made their case look worse.) The IPN unfortunately does not give details of how its estimate was arrived at, referring only to a panel of unnamed 'anthropological and archaeological' experts, using 'established methods'.[13] It may be that the 'White Book' will have the answers; in the meantime I have carried out some rough calculations of my own, on the basis of figures published by the IPN, which seem to cast some doubts on this finding. Thus, the IPN's expert panel

[11] *Neighbors*, 77.   [12] *Tygodnik Powszechny*, 19 (2002).
[13] 'Jednak sąsiedzi', *Rzeczpospolita*, 10 July 2002.

estimated that grave 2, the larger of the two burial pits, contained the ashes of 100–150 victims. A call to a local crematorium established that the complete cremation of an adult typically yields three litres of ashes, so that this number of victims would correspond to 450 litres of ashes at most—probably considerably less, since some of the victims were children, the cremation was not complete, there would have been some settling and compaction, and some of the ashes must have been lost in the course of being transferred to grave 2, which was located outside the perimeter of the barn. But grave 2 measured 8×2 metres and was filled with ashes, in places to a depth of 1.6–1.7 metres, for a total volume of something like 10,900–20,000 litres. No doubt the human remains were mixed with wood ashes from the barn; nevertheless, we can see that the IPN's determination can only have been an estimate, subject to numerous kinds of error. It was based, for instance, on a sample taken from the upper layers of the pit, which was thus probably unrepresentative. It is therefore difficult to see how the IPN can put forward its figures with such confidence. These technical questions are mere quibbles, however. Despite the disagreement over numbers, the IPN did concede the essential point: that nearly all the Jews who were present in Jedwabne on that day were killed, with only 'tens' of survivors.

As to the perpetrators, the IPN concurred with Gross's main contention, that the 'decisive role' in the massacre was played by Poles, but it left unresolved the questions of how many Poles were directly involved and of how widely the circles of responsibility spread. Gross had estimated that there were ninety-two direct perpetrators, while according to the IPN report there were 'at least' forty. Szarota and other critics have seized on this latter number as vindication for their own contentions and a rebuff for Gross; but of course 'at least' forty does not rule out ninety-two. In fact, Gross's estimate may well prove to be conservative. The IPN's legal consultant, Andrzej Rzepliński, on whose investigation of the post-war trial records the IPN had based its conclusions, pointed out in a subsequent interview that witnesses had named more than ninety people as perpetrators in the course of their interrogation. He added that the interrogators, not having been interested in that kind of information, had often cut short the witnesses' recitations of names. Rzepliński sharply criticized the slovenly procedures of both the prosecutors and the judge, which seemed to be aimed at disposing of the matter as quickly and quietly as possible; he added that, in his opinion, 'sto kilkadziesiąt' (a hundred and a few tens) of people should have been charged.[14] This number would have represented about one-quarter of the adult male Polish population of the town, certainly much too large a proportion to be written off as a marginal or criminal element, as Strzembosz tries to do. In any case, none of the critics have come to terms with the evidence that Gross puts forward as to the identity of the perpetrators, drawn from the trial records:

[14] 'Jedwabne—ciszej nad tą zbrodnią', *Gazeta Wyborcza*, 22 Aug. 2002.

mostly small farmers and seasonal workers . . . [including] two shoemakers, a mason, a carpenter, two locksmiths, a letter carrier, and a former town-hall receptionist. Some were family men (one a father of six children, another of four), some unattached. The youngest was twenty-seven years old, the oldest sixty-four. They were, to put it simply, a bunch of ordinary men.[15]

In addition to the direct perpetrators, of course, one has to take into account others, whose actions were insufficient to warrant prosecution:

Everyone who, that day, pulled a hiding Jew from behind a bush, pointed out someone hiding behind a coal-pile, grabbed someone fleeing across a field, kicked someone who was being hurried along in the crowd, threw a stone at those being led to their deaths, swore at them, spat on them—took part in the crime of genocide. That was the reality of the events in Jedwabne, and I gave written expression to that reality in the statement that on that day the Polish half of the inhabitants of the town murdered the Jewish half.[16] Rzepliński, too, thought that indirect participants should be considered accessories: According to pre-war legal practice, all those who were at the marketplace were perpetrators of the crime. It was enough if they stood in the second row as spectators: their very presence ensured, for example, that the Jews had no possibility of escaping, that they felt more terrorized.[17]

The IPN, however, evidently considered such minor perpetrators to be outside its remit.

That there was broad sympathy for an anti-Jewish action is not only conceded but stressed by Gross's critics. Szarota writes:

Was this a mob? No. Among the participants in the pogrom were also victims of Soviet persecution. Some had only just got out of the NKVD prison in Łomża, others had come out of the forests [where they had been hiding with the Polish underground], still others remembered the Soviet deportations, whose final phase had after all just taken place in June 1941. These people hated the Communists, and believed in the slogan 'Żydokomuna' [Judaeo-communism].[18]

This is meant to put the massacre in its 'historical context', which, according to the critics, Gross fails to do. (Gross in fact devotes five chapters to 'historical context', before, during, and after the war.) Szarota's explanation is apposite (and could again have been quoted from Gross), but it is not sufficient: belief in the 'Żydokomuna' myth and in Jewish collaboration with the Soviets was widespread in Poland, and if that were enough 'historical context', then we should expect such incidents to have broken out in thousands of towns, not just a few. Gross, on the other hand, describes—as Szarota omits to do—the one purely local incident that probably explains why a number of such pogroms broke out in the Jedwabne area and not elsewhere. In June 1940, a Polish underground group hiding in the forests

---

[15] *Neighbors*, 14–15.

[16] *Tygodnik Powszechny*, 18 (2002).

[17] 'Jedwabne—ciszej nad tą zbrodnią'.

[18] 'Jedwabne bez stereotypów', *Tygodnik Powszechny*, 17 (2002). It might be noted parenthetically that the June 1941 deportees were mostly Jews.

near Jedwabne, Radziłów, and Wizna was betrayed to the NKVD. Many people were killed in the resulting shoot-out, and 250 more were later rounded up and imprisoned. In view of the 'Żydokomuna' myth, this betrayal was naturally—and, as it turns out, unjustly—ascribed to the Jews.[19] It is probably no coincidence, therefore, that German efforts to encourage a pogrom elicited a ready response in these three towns and not elsewhere.

It is therefore the critics who do not look deeply enough into the 'historical context'; Strzembosz, in particular, repeats allegations of Jewish collaboration with the communists in a completely uncritical manner, as if the views and generalizations of his witnesses were not coloured by pre-war preconceptions. Here, for example, is one witness from Jedwabne:

Immediately after the entry of the Soviet Army a town committee arose spontaneously, made up of Polish communists (the leader was the Pole Czesław Krystowczyk, but the members were Jews). The militia was made up of Jewish communists. At first there were no repressions, since they didn't know the population, only after denunciations by local communists did the arrests start.[20]

A historian taking a properly critical view of his sources might have noticed an inconsistency: here we have, apparently, a spontaneously arising committee made up of local Jews and communists, yet in the next breath we are told that 'they' do not know the local population. His suspicions might have been deepened by the fact that the only person mentioned by name is a Polish communist: the others are generically 'Jews' and 'communists'. One might expect that people in a small town might have known the names of at least one or two of their oppressors, but in the five testimonies that Strzembosz cites, not a single Jewish name is mentioned. When pressed, present-day townspeople are similarly unable to come up with concrete names or details. A witness in Arnold's documentary says: 'You know, I, I don't know any proofs of this. I only repeat what was, so to speak, a well-known secret. This is what people said. Well, someone had to do it. But I cannot guarantee this with my . . . No, I didn't see anyone do it. I didn't personally know.'[21]

Here is another testimony: 'I was not present when the Red Army entered, Jews were admitted to [positions of] power, and also Polish communists, who had been in jail for being communists, they led the NKVD to people's houses and denounced

---

[19] *Neighbors*, 47–53. Subsequent research in the KGB archives turned up a list of eighteen informers from the Jedwabne area, none of them Jews. With regard to this accusation, Leder ('Jedwabne') draws another analogy with the Dreyfus affair, in ironic tones: 'Captain Dreyfus is a traitor. For a huge part of French society he is that even before the court has issued its verdict, before any evidence whatsoever has been put forward, in a certain sense even before he was arrested, in other words, before the 'affair' even began. A Jew in the French army must be a traitor. Similarly, the Jews in Jedwabne are traitors. Taking advantage of the Soviet occupation, they spit on the churches, inform on the Poles and volunteer to help with the deportations. Fundamentally this is only a manifestation of what they constantly do in secret, sponging off the Poles in trade, sucking out their blood—literally and metaphorically—and, finally, simply regarding their neighbours . . . in an evil, unfriendly way.'

[20] 'Przemilczana kolaboracja', *Rzeczpospolita*, 27–8 Jan. 2001. [21] Quoted in *Neighbors*, 46.

patriotic Polish citizens.'[22] Again the vagueness of this testimony is notable, but we might also be struck by the conjunction, which occurs in most of these accounts, not of 'Polish and Jewish communists', but of 'Polish communists and Jews'. Polish communists, it seems, are communists, but Jewish communists are Jews. This perception is really the essence of the 'Żydokomuna' myth, which Strzembosz appears to share. Strzembosz seems to want to characterize the pogrom as an anti-communist rather than an antisemitic act; but Polish communists were not burned alive: on the contrary, ex-communists presently form the government.

Whether they believe in the myth themselves or not, the critics do in any case agree that there was a widespread animus against the Jews, which simmered during the Soviet period and exploded once the Germans arrived. It is inconsistent to put this scenario forward and to maintain at the same time that the perpetrators of the massacre were isolated individuals with no support among the crowd.

Besides the perpetrators, their accomplices, and those who looked upon the events with malicious satisfaction, there must have been many others who were simply passive onlookers. The excuse is offered that they were impotent in the face of German pressure and the frightening behaviour of the perpetrators. But there were, after all, a few people who did extend help to a few of the victims, and this would seem to refute the claim that there was nothing that the others could do. It is perhaps for this reason that people who helped Jews during the war often became pariahs afterwards: their presence served as a constant goad to their neighbours' uneasy consciences. The IPN, however, as a prosecutorial rather than a historical agency, did not seem to be interested in dealing with such questions. Prosecutor Radosław Ignatiew concluded only that 'it is not possible to determine the causes of the passive behaviour of the majority of the inhabitants of the town in the face of the crime. In particular it cannot be prejudged whether this passivity was a result of the acceptance of the crime, or whether it resulted from fright at the brutality of the perpetrators' actions.'[23]

Finally, the IPN waffled on the role of the Germans. Ignatiew wrote that a small group of Germans had 'probably . . . assisted in the action of leading the victims to the marketplace, and their active role was limited to that. It is not clear . . . whether they took part in escorting the Jews to the place of the crime or whether they were present at the barn. The testimonies of witnesses vary fundamentally on this point.' By this, Ignatiew means that while some eyewitnesses (those who appear in Arnold's documentaries, for example) say that there was no direct German partici-pation in the day's events, others claim that the town was 'swarming with Germans'. Whom to believe?

At the time of the post-war trials, the only person who claimed to have seen a larger number of Germans in Jedwabne was the cook for the German police detach-ment, Julia Sokołowska; but her testimony was contradicted by her own previous

<hr>

[22] Quoted in *Neighbors*, 46.   [23] *Gazeta Wyborcza*, 10 July 2002.

statement, and was flatly denied by one of the convicted perpetrators (Karol Bardoń), who at the time was appealing his sentence and, if anything, should have embraced Sokołowska's account as tending to exculpate him. Apart from Sokołowska's story, the 'swarming with Germans' version did not begin to appear until after the IPN investigation had started. It seemed at first to be confirmed by a claim put forward by the IPN's prosecutor in Białystok, Waldemar Monkiewicz, who asserted that a 232-man Ordnungspolizei (Order Police) detachment, commanded by a certain Wolfgang Birkner, had arrived in red vans on the day of the massacre. Although Birkner was real enough, the rest of Monkiewicz's story turned out to be a fabrication. Later, the exhumations turned up bullets and casings which seemed to indicate that Germans had fired shots at the barn: these discoveries were greeted triumphantly by the critics, but their joy was short-lived: some of the bullets turned out not to be bullets, and others were of a type not introduced until 1942 or later.

The one piece of evidence discovered by the IPN that did point to a German presence was documentation in the German archives that showed that a small *Einsatzkommando* headed by Hermann Schaper had been operating in the Jedwabne area around that time. In addition, a witness from Radziłów, where events took a very similar course, had picked Schaper out from a photo dossier as having been present at the massacre there. Schaper proved to be still alive; when interviewed, he said that his unit had consisted of about a dozen men and had travelled in passenger cars. This is consistent with eyewitness testimony, which Gross cites, that a small group of Germans had arrived in two passenger cars, either on the day of the massacre or on the day before. There is still, however, nothing that places these men at the site of the burning, and, indeed, good reason to believe that they stayed at arm's length. The role of Schaper's commando was to organize 'self-cleansing' actions, in other words, to induce local populations to carry out pogroms, not to carry them out themselves. It would have been entirely consistent with this role to have taken propaganda photographs, or even filmed the events, as some witnesses say they did; some witnesses also speak of their having met with the town council to discuss the planning of the event. But there is nothing to suggest that they played an active role either at the marketplace or at the barn. Gross was therefore quite correct to discount Sokołowska's testimony, and to ignore all the latter-day witnesses who agree with her. Briefly, those who put forward the 'swarming with Germans' story are simply not credible. Besides the lack of any support for the story, it is also perfectly obvious why some witnesses would want to remember Germans who were not there, but there is no obvious reason why Polish eyewitnesses would want to incriminate their neighbours by insisting that the Germans were not involved if they were.

The IPN's unwillingness to take a stand on these conflicting testimonies—to say, flatly, that some of the witnesses were lying—as well as its reluctance to draw conclusions about the townspeople's behaviour, were probably a political decision.

Even thus toned down, the 'final findings' drew angry responses from the right: the Liga Polskich Rodzin (League of Polish Families, LPR) even threatened to sue the IPN for 'slandering the Polish nation'. The LPR could at least see clearly enough that the IPN's report had gone against them, but the academic critics were quick to claim the opposite: that, despite the 'consensus', it was their point of view that had prevailed.

But what exactly was their point of view? There was more than a difference of opinion between Gross and his critics; there was a fundamental difference in approach. Though his book is short and in some ways sketchy, Gross went about his business in the proper scholarly manner: that is, he gathered evidence and let it guide his conclusions. There is nothing to suggest that Gross was motivated by a prior agenda, let alone an anti-Polish one. Gross also states clear theses: that though the Germans played a role in initiating it, the massacre itself was carried out by Poles acting of their own free will; and that the perpetrators were ordinary people, not social deviants, who acted at least with the passive acquiescence of the community as a whole. Right or wrong, these are testable propositions, which have so far not been contradicted by any of the credible evidence. Gross's opponents, on the other hand, not having looked into the matter themselves, were united only by the prior conviction that Gross must be wrong. They were never, however, able to produce a coherent theory that both differed significantly from Gross's and accounted for all the facts. The propositions that they put forward in the course of the debate were impressive in their variety, but all equally inadequate. The Germans had done it; or perhaps they had not actually done it, but only instigated it: if so, then the actual perpetrators were not really Poles but Volksdeutsche; or if they were Poles, then they were social deviants. Or if not social deviants, then they had been coerced; or their actions could be explained, perhaps even justified, by the fact—or perhaps it was only a belief—that the Jews had collaborated with the communists. And if these excuses did not suffice, then the crime could be minimized: there were fewer victims than Gross claimed, only a few hundred, and also fewer perpetrators.

It is in the IPN's findings on these last two points that the critics now claim victory; on all other points they either agree with Gross or stand defeated. But even if these conclusions stand up, they first of all change nothing fundamental about our understanding of the event, and, secondly, they were at best lucky guesses on the part of the critics, who had certainly not based them on any careful investigation of their own. In fact their entire position, being based on an a priori belief, was not science but metaphysics, and it is not surprising that science has carried the day.

Metaphysics, on the other hand, has a strong following among the Polish public and within the Catholic Church. Bishop Stanisław Stefanek, whose diocese includes Jedwabne, was ready with his explanation of the massacre, and of the IPN's conclusions:

The enemies of God made Jedwabne a place of martyrdom. First they murdered Poles, deporting them to the East, and then they burned the Jews. Today they arouse hatred there, precisely in Jedwabne, they want to create a laboratory of human hatred . . . Unfortunately this laboratory includes even such authorities as the Institute of National Memory.[24]

There we have it, then: the Soviets (or was it the Jews?) who deported Poles to the east, and the pogromists, and Gross, and now the IPN, are all allies in the business of creating hatred, and all equally enemies of God. As to Gross's book, here is Stefanek's assessment: 'it is at best belletristic, dangerous because it is easy to read. It has the ability to deceive, despite its often demonstrated errors.'[25]

It has indeed been a constant refrain among the critics that Gross had committed egregious 'workshop' (i.e. methodological) errors; but what are these errors supposed to have been? First, he is accused of relying uncritically on Szmul Wasersztajn's description of the massacre, which he does indeed quote in full early on in the book. The critics point out that Wasersztajn could not have been an eyewitness, since he was in hiding, so that his whole testimony must be a fabrication; this is supposedly proven by the existence of two different versions of it, differing on points of detail. But Wasersztajn does not claim to be offering an eyewitness account, except in a few places where he says: 'I saw with my own eyes . . .'. Elsewhere he is trying to set down the history of what happened, as he heard it 'from people'—that is, from Poles in the town. And it would have been very surprising—indeed, suspicious—if in telling his story twice he had told it exactly the same way.

In any case, Wasersztajn's testimony is only a starting point: Gross sets it out as an accusation, and then proceeds to test it. And he does not, in the end, agree with Wasersztajn on all points. Despite a much derided statement in the introduction of his book which seems to imply that memoirs should be accepted without corroboration, Gross does offer considerable supporting evidence. He uses three main kinds of sources—the testimony of Jewish survivors (Wasersztajn among others), the records of the post-war trials, and the testimony of present-day residents of Jedwabne—and tries to reconcile them, just as historians normally do. In the process, he decides who is telling the truth, who is mistaken, and who he thinks is lying, going to rather more trouble than historians usually do to explain his reasons. The critics call this 'selective use of sources', but it is really the judicious use of sources: it is the critics who use sources selectively, or rather, tendentiously, picking what fits their theory of the moment and ignoring the rest—just as people with prior agendas usually do. Gross is next accused of not having consulted all the relevant sources: specifically, of not having delved into the German archives to find out which German units were operating in the vicinity. But since the eyewitness evidence did not point to a large German presence, Gross had no reason to go looking for one, and when the IPN did carry out this inquiry, it is not surprising that it found nothing of much interest. It certainly did not find support for Monkiewicz's story about Birkner and his 232 men in red vans, which successfully deceived

---

[24] *Niedziela*, 18 Aug. 2002.　　[25] Ibid.

Szarota, or any of the equally fanciful stories now circulating in right-wing circles. At best, we now know the identity of the dozen men in passenger cars, but the German records will not tell us either exactly when they were in Jedwabne or what they did while they were there. The only people who can tell us that are the towns-people who saw the events and participated in them, and anything that might turn up in the archives has to be reconciled with their testimony—in other words, with Gross's book. That is to say: even if some document were to turn up which shows, let us say, that some large unit was dispatched to Jedwabne, the eyewitness evidence would suggest that they never got there. Szarota has criticized Gross for relying on oral history rather than German archival records, with the sarcastic remark that 'history is not written by going around bars'.[26] But this is an odd observation from someone who made his reputation as a historian of everyday life, and has necessarily had to lean heavily on oral history himself. In fact that sort of evidence is critical, as Szarota should know better than anyone.

In the end, the 'workshop' criticisms are as wrong as they are often repeated. The critics have attacked Gross's methods, his sources, his credentials, and his person, but they have not been able to challenge his conclusions: the IPN's investigation has shown that in all essentials he got the story right. *Sąsiedzi* may be an easy read, as Bishop Stefanek says, but neither 'belletristic' flights of fancy nor metaphysical speculations could have stood up to rigorous reality-testing. Gross's book has done so.

In the end, it can be said that while science has won the intellectual battle, in the popular mind it makes headway only slowly against metaphysics. 'Given a choice,' Jedwabne's mayor, Krzysztof Godlewski, has said, 'people will opt for the easier truth.' But why should well-tested findings about this event be so hard for so many Poles to accept? After all it is not they, personally, who stand accused, and the facts are clear enough. The sticking point, I think, is not the facts themselves, but the conclusions that are to be drawn from the facts; in particular the question of who, in the larger sense, was to blame. Those who resist the weight of the evidence most doggedly are those who believe that all Poles, or Poles in general, or the Polish nation, or the present residents of Jedwabne, are being held responsible for this crime. But neither Gross, nor anyone else of any repute, has made such an accusation. The massacre that took place in Jedwabne on 10 July 1941 was committed by Poles, but not only Poles did such things: the Iaşi pogrom in Romania took place at almost the same time (26–9 June 1941), and there were scattered outbreaks of anti-semitic violence in other communities that had newly come under German occupation, in Latvia and Ukraine as well as in Poland. That spring Jews had also been massacred by Hungarian troops in Novi Sad and Transylvania. Naturally, as Gross is at pains to point out, the Nazis were the engine of the destructive machine of which the Jedwabne massacre was part, and they destroyed Jewish lives in vastly

[26] 'Jedwabne bez stereotypów'.

greater numbers than any local group of bigots. What all these events have in common is not the ethnic identity of the perpetrators, which was diverse, but anti-semitism. In each of them the alleged link between the Jews and communism, a staple of antisemitic propaganda since the 1880s, played an important part. The fear of communism, or the actual experience of life under communism, produced easily mobilized passions that were expended against, not the communists themselves, but the Jews.

The ultimate responsibility for these crimes thus rests with antisemites, including those antisemites who merely fanned the flames while, in theory, opposing violence. Indirectly, it also rests with those who, without sharing this ideology, tolerated it or regarded it as a respectable shade of political opinion, even if not one that they personally shared. In a word, the ultimate responsibility for the Jedwabne massacre rests with almost the whole of Polish society in the 1930s and 1940s, and rests today with those who have not cleanly broken from those traditions but continue to defend them. Much of the opposition to acknowledging the facts set out by Gross originates with those who know perfectly well on whose foot this shoe fits.

Far from being an insult to Poland, *Sąsiedzi* has represented an opportunity for Poles to deal with the facts with courage, honour, and dignity. All nations, after all, have various unsavoury episodes in their past: the Jedwabne pogrom was not different in kind from an American lynching or the Amritsar massacre: these are crimes that belong to a bigoted past that the civilized world is trying to acknowledge and put behind it. There is no shame in having such a past, since it is the common heritage of mankind. There is shame, however, in trying to whitewash or deny it. A headline in the *New York Times* expressed the encouragement that many observers felt on watching the Polish debate in its early stages: 'Poland Faces its Past, and Does not Blink'. It was the self-appointed defenders of Polish honour who did blink; whose panic and rhetorical antics undid much of the good that this long-overdue book had done for their country's reputation.

GUNNAR S. PAULSSON
Imperial War Museum

Burning Questions

A FILM BY
MISHAEL POREMBSKI

(Smyrna, Ga.: Matchlight Productions Inc., 1999)

Nearly six decades have passed since VE Day in May 1945, but personal and family stories continue to tumble out of the Holocaust and the Second World War. Every one is unique and demands our attention. The children of the survivors perhaps best understand the need to tell these stories. Parents and relatives have often resisted revisiting this past, but their children sense that those most dear to them are troubled. They too are troubled that gaps in the family history are not open to discussion, and remain as shadows separating the generations. A daughter's desire to bridge such a gap is the genesis of the film *Burning Questions*.

Jan Porembski was born in pre-war Poland and lost his father during the Second World War. After the Warsaw uprising he was deported, along with tens of thousands of others, to the Bergen-Belsen concentration camp. He did not return to Poland after the war, but eventually made a career as a network cameraman in America. It was his daughter Mishael who sensed that something was troubling her father and who persuaded him to return with her to Poland. This is the story of a daughter's efforts to understand her father, whom she loves. In the process, a family story is transformed into a meditation on Poland, on Polish–Jewish relations, and on humanity.

Mishael knows the basic outline of her father's story, but asks whether he, as a Polish Catholic, is as much a survivor of the Holocaust as a Polish Jew. Reflecting the popular perception of the Holocaust in America, Mishael asks why her Catholic family had experiences that seem similar to those of the Jews. The return to Warsaw, where Jan's aunt Stefania still lives, provides the occasion for Jan to share with Mishael scenes from his childhood and wartime experiences. For Mishael, the purpose of the trip to Poland is to find her father. However, the journey becomes something larger: an exploration of the 'Holocaust' of Polish Catholics, and particularly of the Nazis' efforts to eliminate the Polish elites and reduce the rest of the population to slave labourers. Jan recounts the story of how the Germans took his father away. It was the last time his father kissed him and said goodbye. 'I never saw him again', he says. This moving, tragic personal story, repeated many times, epitomizes what Richard Lukas has called the 'forgotten' Holocaust in his book of that name (1986).

This personal documentary does not stop with the Polish Catholic 'Holocaust'. Mishael remains in Poland after her father departs. She visits Auschwitz and Bergen-Belsen, and reflects on Polish–Jewish relations. She sees Auschwitz as a place of both Jewish and Polish martyrdom. She returns to the camp with Jan and visits Stefania's cousin Marysia, who spent two years in Auschwitz and who is filmed with her tattooed number in clear view. Mishael is told that Poles did not kill Jews in the camps, while her aunt asserts that those who denounced Jews can be counted 'on your fingers'. Mishael also discusses the difficult issue of the two victim groups with Rabbi Michael Schudrich, the Ronald S. Lauder Foundation's representative in Poland. Rabbi Schudrich tells her that there were Poles who became accomplices of the occupiers and that some did participate in genocide, while others assisted Jews. This is difficult to put in rational perspective because the pain is so great. Szymon Szurmiej, vice-president of the World Federation of Polish Jews and director of the Jewish Theatre in Poland, also appears in the film. Szurmiej invokes the great number of Polish names listed as 'Righteous among Nations' at Yad Vashem, and warns that one should not generalize or make accusations about nations.

A dual healing takes place in this documentary. Jan comes to terms with his past. Mishael does not return with a magic fix for Polish–Jewish relations, but she is less judgemental and looks rather to the future. Jan tells Michael about the rebuilding of Warsaw and about how the capital's citizens rebuilt it with love, brick by brick. We also have that option. Beginning with broken buildings and broken lives, we too, if we choose, can pick up the old, broken bricks to rebuild and 'say to ourselves there is always hope'.

The ending may sound melodramatic, but *Burning Questions* is a thoughtful and at times deeply moving personal meditation set within the vexing American context of Polish–Jewish tensions over what occurred between these two communities in Nazi-occupied Poland. As Rabbi Schudrich remarks, 'if people don't know about your suffering, your obligation is to talk about it. It is nobody else's obligation.' The documentary does tell some of the Polish Catholic story of the Holocaust, and in this sense it is an apologia. Mishael, through her father, brings the often overlooked or misrepresented Polish perspective to the screen. On the other hand, she moves into the larger problem of Polish–Jewish wartime relations and tries to find hope. For that she deserves to be highly commended. However, it must be noted that while enquiring into the Polish Catholic 'Holocaust', the producer skirts some difficult issues. The distinction between Jewish and Polish victimization could have been drawn much more sharply. Local Polish collaboration in the round-up of Jews is glossed over by the emphatic (and correct) assertion that there was no collaborationist government in occupied Poland. The question of individual collaborators, or of villagers collaborating in the round-up of Jews for deportation, is not raised. Polish Jews' view of the *szmalcownicy* (blackmailers) cannot be overlooked if one wishes to understand the passions surrounding Polish–Jewish relations. Furthermore, there is no doubt that there were instances in which Poles killed Jews during the war—for example, in Jedwabne in July 1941. Finally, the producers do not address what some scholars assert was the seeming indifference of most Poles to the wartime fate of their Jewish neighbours.

Apart from these omissions and the unequal weight assigned to different topics, there are errors of fact. The Polish government did not flee to England in September 1939, but rather sought safe passage through Romania, where it was interned. Authority was passed to Polish exiles in France; they formed the government-in-exile, which moved to England when France fell.

These errors do not diminish the value of this documentary as a teaching resource in Holocaust education, however. While not exhaustive, *Burning Questions* reminds its viewers of the Polish Catholic 'Holocaust' sympathetically and in a very personal way. It would be challenging and worth while for students to compare *Burning Questions* with Marian Marzyński's controversial *Shtetl* (1996). Both documentaries are rough-hewn and direct, and they address the issue of Polish–Jewish relations during the Second World War from different perspectives. One challenges us to rebuild with hope, while the other reaches a pessimistic conclusion. One producer is ready to be a partner in dialogue, while the other appears uninterested. It sometimes seems that contradictory conclusions predominate in discussions of Polish–Jewish relations. Historians know that this is not the case. However, the divergent directions of *Burning Questions* and *Shtetl* tell us that Jewish and non-Jewish Poles, and particularly their diasporas in America, still have a distance to travel. The personal journey of Jan Porembski and his daughter Mishael is reason to continue the pilgrimage.

STANISLAUS A. BLEJWAS
Central Connecticut State University

MARTIN DEAN

Collaboration during the Holocaust: Crimes of the Local Police in Belorussia and Ukraine, 1941–44

(New York: St Martin's Press and the United States Holocaust Memorial Museum, 2000); pp. xx + 242

Martin Dean's book is about local police participation in the murder of the Jews in certain regions of Belarus and Ukraine which were part of Russia until 1918, then part of Poland or the Soviet Union until 1939, and then part of the Soviet Union until 1941.

The book does not cite a single source, not even an article, in any Slavonic language. The author claims at one point to have 'used extensively' the archival collections in Moscow, Minsk, Brest, and Zhytomyr (p. xi), but one wonders how he could have oriented himself among the many documents that would have been written in the local languages. At another point he scales down his claim: he 'examined only a tiny sample' of the 'vast' archival collections (p. 204 n. 97). The footnotes show relatively little use of the former Soviet archives. Certainly they are not exploited to the extent that they were in Dieter Pohl's study of the Holocaust in nearby eastern Galicia, *Nationalsozialistische Judenverfolgung in Ostgalizien 1941–1944* (Munich, 1997), a work that is cited several times in the book under review.

It is difficult to pronounce definitively on Martin Dean's use of archival sources, because he never gives a clear account of what he used, as most academic historians would. We never learn, for example, what kind of records he had from the police themselves. For Galicia such records are very well preserved, but it is not at all clear from Dean's text what exists for the parts of Belarus and Ukraine he is interested in, and whether he used what exists. His archival references are generally devoid of any date or description of content (for example, WCU D9317), and favoured sources seem to be memoirs and relatively recent court cases. In other words, he does not follow the basic methods of academic historians, and this makes his book difficult to assess.

Dean was formerly a policeman in Scotland Yard's War Crimes Unit. He describes his methodology as 'forensic history'. Its key feature, he says, is the comparison of conflicting accounts, 'testing each against the totality of evidence available' (p. xi). Judging by its application in this book, forensic history is less insistent upon criticism and differentiation of sources than is academic history.

What results does Dean arrive at? He points to the importance of a 'second wave' of killings, at least in the parts of the former Soviet Union he addresses. Generally, he notes, the historiography of the Holocaust has focused on the 'first wave', which took place in the summer and autumn of 1942. This period has attracted the attention of historians because of the detailed (and easily accessible) documentation compiled by the perpetrators themselves, the infamous *Einsatzgruppen*. But the great majority of the murders took place later, in 1942 and 1943, as ghettos were systematically cleared. In this deadly 'second wave', local Ukrainian and Belarusian police forces played an essential role, primarily in rounding up and hunting down Jews for execution, but also from time to time as gun men. The Germans relied heavily on these policemen to find the Jews since they had the advantage of knowing the intended victims personally—after all, they were neighbours.

The policemen were recruited largely from the most dangerous form of the human species: young males. About half were under 25 and only 6 per cent were over 35. Many volunteered for the police in the early stages of the units' formation, but later there was considerable conscription. The social composition of the police force was largely peasant (75 per cent), and the vast majority (95 per cent) had at most a basic education. They were, then, 'ordinary men', though at the lower end of the social scale. Some volunteered for the force because they hated communism, others because they wanted a steady pay cheque. Some enjoyed killing.

Dean wonders to what extent these particular perpetrators were motivated by antisemitism, and attempts to answer the question by exploring whom they killed other than Jews and how they did it. He writes a chilling chapter on the murder of the families of partisans and of suspected sympathizers. The police entered their homes and killed every member of these families, without regard to sex or age; they often ended their killing spree by looting the property of their victims. In other words, they did not behave this way towards Jews alone. Dean also wonders about the role of nationalism, and concludes that it does not seem to have influenced the behaviour of the police: the Ukrainians were generally imbued with a nationalist consciousness, while the Belarusians were not, yet the behaviour of both police forces was quite similar.

The book is interesting and clearly written. One hopes that it will inspire scholars to return to these important issues, but next time using the proper tools.

JOHN–PAUL HIMKA
University of Alberta

JERZY TOMASZEWSKI (ED.)

Studia z dziejów i kultury Żydów w Polsce po 1945 roku

('Studies on the History and Culture of Jews in Poland after 1945')

(Warsaw: Wydawnictwo TRIO, 1997); pp. 202

This volume consists of three short monographs by Polish graduate students in the
early stages of their professional development. Two were originally written as MA
theses: one by Maciej Pisarski on Jewish emigration from Poland from 1945 to
1951, and the other by Albert Stankowski on Jewish emigration from western
Pomerania from 1945 to 1960. The third, by August Grabski, on the organization of
Jewish religious life in Poland during the communist and (primarily) post-communist eras, originated as a seminar paper.

On the whole, postgraduate writing of this type, if it is published at all, appears
in limited-circulation journals for an audience of academics. The fact that these
studies were published in book form, especially in paperback with the aid of a sub-
sidy from the Polish Ministry of Culture, offers further testimony of the keen interest in the history of Jews in Poland evident among the Polish public in recent years.
The conviction appears to be growing, as Jerzy Tomaszewski puts it in his introduction to the volume, that 'it is difficult to understand Polish culture without
knowledge of Jewish culture' (p. 10). Those in Poland seeking to acquire such
knowledge, however, have been limited by a dearth of reliable literature on the subject in the Polish language. According to Tomaszewski, 'until recently studies on
the history and culture of the Jews in Poland after 1944 have been especially
neglected' (p. 8). That neglect provides the ostensible justification for publishing
this collection of papers in their present form.

Such a rationale prompts the question: precisely what sort of knowledge of the
history and culture of Jews in Poland after 1944 is needed to raise the level of understanding of Polish culture? A brief book review is not the place to undertake a
general discussion of this issue, but the point has to be made, unfortunately, that
whatever sort of knowledge may be required, the studies in the present volume
seem unlikely to provide it.

It is not that they fail to bring to light much hitherto unknown data. Indeed, all
three researchers have examined formerly inaccessible or unexploited archives and

report extensively on their contents. This preliminary spadework will certainly be welcomed by future scholars wrestling with historical issues raised by these documents. The problem is that, for the most part, the authors themselves have made no effort to engage with these issues or even to define them. Instead they have provided three fairly random collections of details, statistics, and comments by contemporary observers, without placing them in a context that could lend them significance. Thus readers may learn, among other things, the procedure by which Polish Jews obtained emigration documents, the parties and organizations represented in the Koordinacja Syjonistyczna (Zionist Co-ordinating Committee) in Szczecin in 1946–7, and the names of the officers and board of the Związek Religijny Wyznanin Mojżeszowego (Religious Association of the Mosaic Faith, ZRWM) elected in December 1948. But it is not clear why we are being provided with this information or what might be learned from it beyond the facts themselves.

Some obvious, elementary historical questions are prompted immediately by the materials. For example, why did Jewish emigration from Poland assume the particular forms and dimensions that it did? How are we to account for the variations in its pace over time and its intensity in different regions of Poland? Is there any way of determining what sorts of Jews were more or less likely to emigrate at a particular time, along a particular route, or within a certain framework? What social functions did the Jewish religious community serve under the communist regime in Poland in its successive manifestations? Did those functions change over time? How can the changes be explained? What continuities and discontinuities between the communist and post-communist eras are manifested in the history of the religious community? Seasoned historians would put these questions almost instinctively in response to the material disclosed in this volume. But where the authors consider them at all, they offer only the most cursory answers, which for the most part have already been suggested, mainly by participants in the events described. They do not address, to any appreciable extent, the problem of whether the new information uncovered in the course of their research compels a rethinking of those answers.

To be sure, the three authors are still in the midst of their training, and it is to be hoped that they will be encouraged to use the findings of their archival research for interpretative, as well as strictly informational, purposes. While the desire to publish the volume and bring the material presented in it to light is understandable, it would have been more profitable, both for the authors and for the academic community as a whole, to publish a well-annotated, broad-ranging documentary compilation. As for the wider Polish public seeking to illuminate its own experience through the study of Polish Jewish life, it would benefit far more from the considered interpretation of mature scholars than from the fruits of research plucked before their time.

DAVID ENGEL
New York University

DAGMAR C. G. LORENZ (ED.)

Contemporary Jewish Writing in Austria: An Anthology

Jewish Writing in the Contemporary World

(Lincoln: University of Nebraska Press, 1999), pp. 362 + xxxiv

Jewish literature is a fascinating phenomenon. It has developed as three branches of one tree: in Hebrew, in the Jewish languages of the Diaspora (mainly Yiddish), and in the national languages of the countries where Jews lived. No wonder that it is often difficult to grasp cross-references and connections between various works. To understand Jewish literature in all its complexity one should be able to read Hebrew, Yiddish, and at least a dozen European languages. Of course, one should not only have a thorough knowledge of the Jewish culture and tradition but also of the traditions and the ways of life of other nations. Not surprisingly, the culture of the people among whom the Jews of the Diaspora have lived has influenced Jewish authors, often very profoundly.

Among winners of the Nobel Prize for literature two wrote in Jewish languages: Samuel Joseph Agnon, who wrote in Hebrew and was awarded the Nobel Prize in 1966, and Isaac Bashevis Singer, who wrote in Yiddish and received the award in 1978. But many other Jewish winners of the prize wrote in national languages; for example, Henri Louis Bergson (French, 1927), Nelly Sachs (German, 1966), Saul Bellow (English, 1976), Elias Canetti (German, 1981), Yosif Brodski (Russian, 1987), and Nadine Gordimer (English, 1991).

To understand them better, to grasp the roots and connections between various works and writers, one needs a broad overview of the full phenomenon. This is the idea behind the series Jewish Writing in the Contemporary World, which aims at presenting authors and their works, as well as the influences and historical events that shaped them in a particular homeland.

Austrian Jews and Austrian Jewish writing has always been an intriguing subject. The once powerful country in the heart of Europe has attracted attention with its tolerance and multiculturalism dating back to the period of the empire and with the charm of Vienna, the unquestionable cultural capital of the region throughout the centuries; but also with its many difficult political problems. The Jewish community in Austria can be traced back to the ninth century. Its history is tragically similar to that of many others in Europe, with a series of immigrations and expulsions, such as those in 1421 and 1670. In 1782 Emperor Joseph II issued his Edict of Tolerance, which revoked many anti-Jewish laws, but on the other hand promoted complete assimilation. In 1867 Austrian Jews obtained equal political rights. On the eve of the Second World War the Jewish population in Austria numbered more than 185,000. After the Holocaust only 7,000 remained, and, while many had fled, it is estimated that about two-thirds of Austrian Jews perished in Nazi concentration camps. Today there are only about 8,500 Jews living in Austria.

Austrian Jewish literature reflects both the history of Austria and the history of the Jews in Europe. Some of the major events in Jewish cultural and political life took place in Austria, including the 1908 Czernowitz Conference, which was decisive in the development of Yiddish literature, and the founding of political Zionism in Vienna by Theodor Herzl. The Jews of Austria can even boast a Nobel Prize-winner: in 1911 the Austrian Jewish publicist, politician, and founder of European peace organizations Alfred Hermann Fried received the Nobel Prize for peace.

Austrian Jews have written in various languages, but mainly in Hebrew, Yiddish, and German. There are numerous examples of Jewish poets and writers living in or originating from the Austrian Empire. Yiddish literature, which developed and flourished in those times, yielded such talents as Shmuel-Yankev Imber and David Königsberg. Itzik Manger, the greatest Yiddish troubadour, was born in Chernovits (Czernowitz, now Chernivtsi in Ukraine). The two most prominent Israeli authors, Samuel Joseph Agnon and Uri Zwi Greenberg, one of the greatest Hebrew poets of our time, were both born in the late nineteenth century in Galicia. Avigor Hameiri, a well-known Hebrew poet and novelist, even served as an officer in the Austrian army during the First World War.

However, much better known to the outside world were German-language Jewish authors such as Franz Kafka, Arthur Schnitzler, Stefan Zweig, Franz Werfel, Elias Canetti, Friedrich Torberg, Paul Celan, and Ilse Aichinger. It is tragic that out of this plenitude only the literature written in German continued in Austria after the Holocaust. For the Jews writing in German, Nazism also signified another tragedy: the fall of German culture and the corruption of the language that fascinated them. Then came the inevitable question: how could one possibly continue to write, to express oneself, in the language of the murderers? A number of authors emigrated and settled outside Austria, among them Erich Fried, Jakov Lind, Georg Kreisler, and Elias Canetti. Some, like Stefan Zweig, Paul Celan, and Jean Améry, committed suicide either during the war or in the post-war years. Others began to write in other languages (Hebrew, English, and others, depending on the country to which they emigrated) or even ceased to write (or at least to publish), as in the case of Veza Canetti.

Many events in the extremely rich history of Austria in the twentieth century, such as the fall of the empire, the Anschluss, the Second World War, the Waldheim case, and even more recently the Haider debate, have had an enormous impact on Austrian Jews. To be able to see these historic events through the eyes of Jewish Austrian writers is a thrilling prospect.

Contemporary Jewish Writing in Austria is an anthology of the writings of Jewish authors from five generations whose works have been published in recent decades. Dagmar C. G. Lorenz provides a very interesting introduction to her book, sharing with the reader her profound understanding of the complexities of Austrian Jewish literary history. She introduces the problems that faced Austrian Jews after the Holocaust: that they were not invited to return from exile, and if they decided to return to their home country, they were expected to assimilate to the dominant culture. Fascinating and tragic is the fact that still, despite all adversities, some Jews do not mind living in Vienna and identify themselves with this city as the only beloved home they have ever had. The author of the anthology also broaches the subject of the dual emotional loyalties of Austrian Jews and European Jews in general: loyalty to their home country and emotional ties to Israel. The predominant themes of post-war Jewish literature are (as well documented in the anthology) the Holocaust and relationships with non-Jews and possible identification with the non-Jewish homeland. There is also a tendency to present and preserve the varieties of Jewish life and traditions before the Holocaust. In her overview the editor stresses the fact that contemporary Austrian Jewish writers participate in world and Austrian literature but at the same time remain, by their own choice, distinct and unassimilated.

Lorenz also discusses the influence of Austrian and European history on Austrian Jews and on Jewish writers and intellectuals in particular. She reveals the impact of historical and political events on Austrian Jewish literature as well as the connections between Jewish and non-Jewish literary works. The texts included in the anthology are used to exemplify the issues discussed, and the editor provides many references not only to other works, but also to other critical literature on the subject.

While the introduction provides the background necessary to understand the anthologized works, it might be wondered whether Lorenz does not simplify some views and topics. For instance, it is unfortunate that she cannot sometimes abstain from stereotypes: in raising the complex subject of antisemitism, she speaks in one breath about the Romanian Iron Guard, Stalinist antisemitism, and Polish Jew-hatred (exemplifying the latter with the film *Shoah* by Claude Lanzmann, which was quite controversial for many viewers and critics).

The writers are divided into five groups: the pre-First World War generation (Albert Drach, Elias Canetti, Veza Canetti, Friedrich Torberg, Hans Weigel, Simon Wiesenthal, Hilde Spiel, and Jean Améry); the inter-war generation (Elisabeth Freundlich, Paul Celan, Ilse Aichinger, Erich Fried, Georg Kreisler, Eva Deutsch, and Jakov Lind); the generation of Austrian fascism, the Second World War, and the Holocaust (Ruth Klüger Angress, Peter Henisch, and Robert Schindel); the post-Holocaust generation (Elfriede Jelinek, Nadja Seelich, Anna Mitgutsch, and Ruth Beckermann); and the generation of the Second Austrian Republic (Robert Menasse, Doron Rabinovici, and Matti Bunzl).

One might wonder about the reasoning behind this selection of authors. Although Austria is evidently the common factor, the connections between them vary a lot. Some of the authors, though born there, have long since left the country. Others have simply chosen Austria as their place of residence, though they were not born there and their mother tongue is not German; they can hardly be called

Austrian (a good example is Polish-born Eva Deutsch, who was not able to publish her book in German by herself and had to co-operate with an Austrian writer, or Nadja Seelich, a native Czech-speaker born in Prague, whose grandmother refused to speak German after the Holocaust). However, this problem illustrates the enormous complexity of Austria. Should we call everyone who was born on Austrian soil and writes in German an Austrian writer (one could ask further whether writing in German and not in any other language of the former Austrian Empire should be a decisive factor—in her introduction the editor concentrates only on Austrian Jewish literature written in German, as though German was the only language in which Austrian Jews were writing)? According to this guideline, Elias Canetti (born in Bulgaria), Simon Wiesenthal (born in Ukraine), and Paul Celan (born in Romania) are Austrians, but Eva Deutsch, Nadja Seelich, and Doron Rabinovici (born in Israel) are not. The anthology would have to lose the texts of Canetti, Celan, and Wiesenthal if we were to refer to Austria according to its borders as they were drawn after the fall of the empire. Since the subject is contemporary (meaning post-Second World War) Austrian writing, we could use this guideline to select those authors who live in Austria today. This would, however, exclude the emigrants Elias and Veza Canetti, Jean Améry, Paul Celan, Erich Fried, Georg Kreisler, Jakov Lind, Ruth Klüger Angress, and Matti Bunzl (the latter currently living in the United States), but would explain the presence of Simon Wiesenthal, Eva Deutsch, Nadja Seelich, and Doron Rabinovici.

Of course, it is extremely difficult to identify 'citizens of the world', among whom there is a high percentage of Jews, with any particular country in today's multicultural and open world. In any case, the author of the anthology seems to be using her own guideline: if a Jewish writer has any connection to Austria, either as a birthplace, a place of temporary residence or citizenship, or by the themes of their literary works, then he or she is an Austrian author. This enables Lorenz to include in the anthology a broad spectrum of very interesting works and authors. One even wonders why she stops at this point and does not discuss other Jewish authors originating from Austria or the Austrian Empire and writing in other languages such as Hebrew, Yiddish, and English.

The short biographical notes are followed by excellent translations of the carefully chosen excerpts reflecting the respective eras that shaped the authors emotionally and intellectually. Some of this material, such as memoirs and historical essays, is on the borders of literature. It is to Lorenz's great credit that she incorporates them into her anthology, as they help the reader to understand contemporary Austrian Jews.

The material presented introduces a wide range of themes, including, among others, a typically warm and witty portrait of Aunt Jolesch by Friedrich Torberg; and Hans Weigel's *The Draped Window* and *It is Impossible to Speak about it Dispassionately*, which demonstrate his deep humanity in preaching forgiveness and understanding for the German generation born after the Second World War. The extremely interesting inside view of the Waldheim case by Simon Wiesenthal should be recommended reading for all involved in the protests and condemnation of Austria following the Haider affair. It brings to light some less well-known problems of the contemporary Austrian Jewish community, which has had to struggle not only with memories of the past but also with the consequences of the grotesque behaviour of American Jewish organizations, which, mainly for political reasons, have ruined (as Wiesenthal states) years of post-war education in Austria.

The high point of the anthology is the famous *Death Fugue* by Paul Celan; followed by impressions of Claude Lanzmann's *Shoah* by Ruth Klüger Angress; the study of the permanent problem of rapprochement between West and East by Nadja Seelich in her *Film, State, and Society in Eastern and Western Europe—and I*; an account of growing up Jewish in Vienna by Ruth Beckermann, which resembles the famous Arthur Schnitzler's *My Youth in Vienna* not only in its title; two stories by one of the most distinctive young Jewish writers, Doron Rabinovici; and, finally, *From Kreisky to Waldheim* by Matti Bunzl, in which he discusses the situation of contemporary young Austrian Jews.

The problem of the selection of authors notwithstanding, the anthology is a highly interesting record of the presence of Austrian Jews in contemporary literature and gives the reader insight into what life has been like for Austrian Jews. This selection also sheds light on another significant phenomenon that is common to Austrian Jewish literature and world Jewish literature after the Second World War. Jewish authors remain, as Lorenz rightly observes, distinct and unassimilated. It is the only way possible after the Holocaust.

MAGDALENA SITARZ
Jagiellonian University, Kraków

ROMUALD JAKUB WEKSLER-WASZKINEL

Błogosławiony Bóg Izraela

('The Blessed God of Israel')

(Lublin: Towarzystwo Naukowe Katolickiego Uniwersytetu Lubelskiego, 2000); pp. 280

This is an unusual book—perhaps as unusual as the fate of its author. A child, or as he himself put it, 'an infant' of the Holocaust, born in the ghetto, is offered to a Christian woman with the words: 'You are a believing person, a Christian . . . and he [Jesus] was a Jew. So save this Jewish infant on behalf of that Jew, in whom you believe. When this baby is grown up, you will see, he will become a priest; he will teach people . . .'. The child, surrounded by the enormous love of his Polish foster parents, grows up unaware of his origin, his conscience pricked by momentary doubts about overheard antisemitic remarks. During his teenage years he is asked what he may eventually become, and a surprising answer escapes his lips: 'A priest!' He has no idea at the time why he has said it. Upon graduation, he enters a theological seminary, and, as he observes, in some way ends up keeping his word. After six years of study he is ordained to the priesthood. While still in the seminary, he experiences a divine prodding to deepen his faith, and begins to dream about being a Jew in order to come even closer to Christ. Finally, in the thirty-fifth year of his life, he hears from the woman he believed was his mother that his real parents were Jewish. Eleven years later, in 1989, he learns of the existence of an uncle and an aunt, the brother and sister of his Jewish father. In 1992 he takes a double name to honour his parents as well as his foster parents. From then on, as prophesied, he 'teaches people', from the perspective of his own life experience, about Christ's love for the Jews and about the need for Christians also to love the Jews. A prophecy, possibly made to enhance the mother's persuasiveness, is fulfilled.

The book itself, Weksler-Waszkinel's first, is a collection of texts published from 1992, the year he achieved 'full integration' of his past with his new-found Jewish heritage. The texts differ in character according to the aims for which they were written: there are cultural essays and short treatises on post-Auschwitz theology, reports from historical-theological conferences, transcripts of radio and university interviews, and the response to a questionnaire from a religious magazine as well as personal memoirs.

The volume is divided by subject into three parts, outlined in the author's introduction. The first contains more specialized, although easily accessible, writings on Catholic theology regarding Judaism. It opens with Pope John Paul II's prayer for the Jewish people, written for the Polish Catholic Church on the occasion of the Church's celebration of its International Day of Judaism on 17 January. This introduction is indicative of the author's perspective: that of the post-conciliar opening of the Church to the Jewish liturgy, its proclamation and invocation of its Jewish roots, and the efforts of the Pope to build bridges of mutual understanding and prayer between Jews and Christians. Weksler-Waszkinel is not out to invent a new theology, wholly inclusive of Judaism and all of its practices. Rather, he brings to light certain anti-Jewish tendencies found in elements of the pre-conciliar Church, as embarrassing as they may be for Christians, in order to point out not only their obsolescence, but also their utter incompatibility with the attitude of full respect for Judaism and its confessors that is expressed by the Church today (and principally by its Pope).

In the opening essay, which presents Pope John Paul II's views on the Jews and Judaism, the author analyses the basic differences between Judaism and Christianity. The Pope had not hesitated to characterize these differences as forming 'a profound division, present in the very centre of the great monotheistic tradition'. This division consists, as Weksler-Waszkinel puts it, in the transition 'from the faith of Jesus to faith in Jesus', and, as the Pope puts it, in love, 'which gives itself, which lets itself be seen, heard, and followed as a man, which lets itself be bound, slapped in the face and crucified').[1] In spite of this division, however, there has been no 'tearing away of the roots'. 'Faith in Jesus', according to Weksler-Waszkinel, 'presupposes the whole heritage of the faith of Abraham.' Following the Pope, Weksler-Waszkinel asks whether the position of the Jewish authorities at the time of Jesus should really come as a surprise to us. After all, 'Peter himself had trouble with that. The mystery of God in the Holy Trinity, of God crucified, might have seemed unacceptable for the believers in one God, to whom Abraham was a witness.' The choice of Christianity, then, which from the author's perspective was as much a work of grace as of human initiative, ought to be respected, just as the choice and presence of Judaism ought also to be respected. While Weksler-Waszkinel is not silent concerning the responsibility of some Jews for the persecutions of the earliest Christians, he then turns at once to a treatment of what Jules Isaac, regarding a later time, has called 'the teaching of contempt', beginning as far back as the Constantinian Edict of Tolerance. He further outlines the history of anti-Jewish tendencies in Catholicism and antisemitic tendencies in European culture in general, grounding himself throughout in a discussion of historical references and sources. The body of literature that he cites is made up mainly of Francophone scholars like Jules Isaac, Emmanuel Levinas, Henri de Lubac, and Marcel Simon. It suggests that he is attempting to do for the Poles what Isaac has already done for the French; that is, to 'disenchant' Polish Catholicism from holding on stubbornly to the conviction that its members have been wholly innocent, rather than recognizing that it is part of a Church that has always considered itself 'a holy community of sinners'.[2]

In diagnosing the various causes and conditions that led to the Holocaust in Europe, Weksler-Waszkinel approaches Isaac's position in *The Genesis of Antisemitism*. Isaac concludes that anti-Jewish attitudes nurtured over the years among lower-ranking members of the clergy, and fed by the popular antisemitism of the masses, facilitated the eventual realization of the Nazi genocide. Weksler-Waszkinel often analyses history from this perspective, but because the position from which he observes this depressing phenomenon is that of a Catholic priest, he does not give up in despair at this point of his analysis. After the example of the Pope, he draws attention to the presence of an 'ecumenical consciousness among divided Christians' which sprang up in the wake of the exterminations. He presents the positive development of Christian consciousness along the path marked by the Second Vatican Council: 'the sons of Israel are our *elder brothers*'. Such a complete presentation of the post-conciliar attitude of the Church towards Judaism—an attitude to some extent recovered in its original relationship to authentic Catholic

---

[1] Pope John Paul II, *Crossing the Threshold of Hope*, ed. V. Messori (New York, 1985), 10–11.

[2] Weksler-Waszkinel (p. 186), attributes this quotation to the Revd J. S. Pasierb, without citing him specifically.

teaching—is a second important theme of the book. In fact, the most often quoted ecclesiastical statement therein is this sentence, from the conciliar declaration *Nostra aetate*: 'In her rejection of every persecution against any man, the Church, mindful of the patrimony she shares with the Jews and moved not by political reasons but by the Gospel's spiritual love, decries hatred, persecutions, displays of antisemitism, directed against Jews at any time and by anyone.' What in English is rendered as 'the Church . . . decries' is rendered in Latin as the expressive 'Ecclesia deplorat'. Weksler-Waszkinel repeats these words as a kind of incantation, and tenderly, longingly, embraces them like a child who, having repeatedly suffered the rejection of his own mother, hears from her lips for the first time words of repentance and love.

The second part of the book is written, according to the author, to demonstrate the closely rooted relationship of Christianity to the Bible and Judaism. It contains texts presenting a Christian vision of the human person and Christian universalism, as well as very interesting essays presenting three great adventurers of the religious frontier: Henri Bergson, Emmanuel Levinas, and Edith Stein. While the first two texts, unfortunately, do not explore deeper references to Judaism, the perspective from which the author looks at these three philosophers of Jewish origin is revealing—particularly as far as Bergson is concerned—and should necessarily evoke self-critical reflection on the part of all European Christians. By bringing the question of the relationship between Judaism and Christianity down to a personal level, the author has sketched a more profound portrait of it; I, for one, must confess that this was the part of the book which I read with by far the greatest interest.

The most moving part, though, is the third part, which reveals the personal lot of the author. Like the story of every child of the Holocaust, his story is at once painful and amazing; its placement towards the end of the book makes it all the more compelling.

An appendix providing Church documents on the relationship between Christianity and Judaism provides an interesting supplement to Weksler-Waszkinel's theological considerations. Contained therein are a key chapter from the conciliar declaration *Nostra Aetate*, three important texts of the Commission for Religious Relations with the Jews (of the Pontifical Council for Promoting Christian Unity), several of Pope John Paul II's allocutions, and one of the pastoral letters on the subject from the Polish bishops. These documents comprise an interesting and perhaps indispensable starting point for research into the historical development of the Church's position regarding its relationship to Judaism.

Again, considered as a whole, Weksler-Waszkinel's book is made up of an interesting combination of different styles and genres, so much so that Michał Czajkowski, in his epilogue, calls it 'a mixture of theology and autobiography'. There are advantages as well as disadvantages to such a mixture. Among the disadvantages may be counted a tendency to repetition and a certain impression of incoherency, regarding both the subject matter and the perspective from which the author looks at the relationship between Christians and Jews and between Christianity and Judaism. A few essays seem to be so far removed from the scope of the subject matter defined in the introduction that they could conceivably exist independently and exclusively as Catholic pastoral or theological texts. Among the advantages we may also count a redeeming aspect of what I have just called an impression of incoherency: Weksler-Waszkinel's multifaceted perspective enables him to place a strict representation of Catholic teaching according to the Catechism of the Catholic Church side by side with moving personal accounts and poignant memories, and to succeed in creating an impression of consonance. The presentation of Weksler-Waszkinel's thought in this way leaves us with the impression of a man coherent to the core, who feels, experiences, and thinks as one, and whose lot in life led him to a kind of personal theological reflection in which his theology became the perfect expression of his faith. The result is a first-person portrayal of a Catholic priest for whom the internalization of the truths of faith is in accord with his own lived experience of personal integration with the fate of the Jewish people. To ignore his voice, his calls for conversion and change, would be our loss.

Weksler-Waszkinel writes a very difficult book, and it is difficult for various reasons. First of all, it is difficult for Poles and for Catholics, for whom it is an inescapable call to self-examination, to a reconsideration of history, and to the recognition of the general degeneration of Catholic Europe into pockets of post-Christian nationalism. The book is not lacking in harshly worded accusations of anti-Judaism in the history of the Church and of antisemitism in that of Poland. Anti-Judaism, for example, is referred to as a catalyst of the detonation of an explosion of antisemitism which indirectly abetted those who perpetrated the Holocaust. The author even goes so far as to assert that individual Christians might thus be considered, in some way, bearers of the first and foremost responsibility for the terrible persecutions that resulted. Such words may sound like heresy to Christian ears; no true follower of Christ could ever in any way consider a Nazi persecutor to be a brother in faith. Certain Protestant churches in Germany, it is true, escaped persecution for the most part, but what of the brutal oppression of the Catholic Church in Germany, in which many priests, nuns, and ordinary faithful were tortured and murdered in the camps? There were, of course, the inevitable quislings, members and even clergy of Christian denominations who collaborated with a Nazi regime—whether out of fear of intimidation, pursuit of personal advantage, or even baser motives. And just as some who called themselves Christian engaged in such actions, so also, as surprising as it may seem, did some who called themselves Jews. Nevertheless, such individual betrayals do not support a general conclusion that the Church as a whole co-operated with the evil of Hitler's regime of terror.

The book is also difficult, however, for Jews. It presents a point of view that is simply Catholic, and although it seeks to approach Judaism and its attitudes in a most open and positive manner, it will be understandably difficult for Jewish readers to separate the authentic Catholic position that the author seeks to support from the deformation of Catholicism known as anti-Judaism—with the many negative associations and connotations that inevitably result.

From a theological standpoint, the book is a compendium of references to the teachings of Pope John Paul II. The references to the Pope throughout the work serve as a testimony to his attitude of cordial friendship towards Jews and Judaism, from the earliest days of his childhood friendships with Jews.

Finally, Weksler-Waszkinel's is a difficult book because it presents apparently impossible phenomena and seeks to unify elements that appear to be mutually exclusive. If, however, it is possible in one life 'to love Poland and the Poles' and at the same time 'to love Israel and the Jews', then it is equally possible within a religious perspective for Christian and Jewish Poles to pray together. This is the road Weksler-Waszkinel seems to be taking when he recalls the prayers of Pope John Paul II, when he recollects the Jewish sources of Christian liturgy and prayer, and finally when he himself prays together with the community of the messianic Jews in Israel. There is reason to hope that many prejudices might melt away in the reading of this book: the confrontation with the voice of true experience (that of a true Jew and a true Christian, one feels tempted to say) is simply too demanding not to respond to. There is reason to hope that Christian biases might be rendered harmless under the gaze of this ordained Jew; and Jewish defences might fall at the feet of this son of Israel, whose life is also filled with love for Jesus as the Christ. One has reason further to hope that the encounter with such a puzzling and yet unifying paradox might result in the acknowledgement of a common origin in the 'free choice' of the one Source, whom Jews call 'the God of our Fathers', and Christians, 'God, our Father'.

Weksler-Waszkinel is a fascinating person, a sign and a source of hope that finding this unity in a common Source may be possible and may provide a more tangible response than mere, and possibly sterile, theoretical considerations regarding 'the Christian–Jewish dialogue'.

MONIKA RICE
Ballina, Co. Mayo, Ireland

CORRESPONDENCE

Exchange between Józef Lewandowski and Joanna Rostropowicz Clark

The Editors
Polin: Studies in Polish Jewry

Dear Sirs,

In *Polin* volume 13 Joanna Rostropowicz Clark published an article, 'Krzysztof Kamil Baczyński: A Poet-Hero'. The theses of the article and the material used to exemplify them are well known and came from my work on Krzysztof Kamil Baczyński. I published them in *Aneks* (London), volume 22 (1979), and discussed them at more length in my *Szkło bolesne, obraz dni* (Uppsala, 1991). I dealt there with the taboo on the discussion of the Jewish origins of the most outstanding poet of the Polish underground and, in particular, his feelings of solidarity with the murdered Jews.

It is on these topics that Joanna Rostropowicz Clark has written. I should have been happy that she has taken up this theme and made use of my work, but I am not, since she failed to provide the source of her knowledge and quotations. It is difficult to imagine that without my work Ms Rostropowicz Clark would have turned her attention to the Jewish motifs in Baczyński's work. Moreover, her article does not add anything significant to what I had already set out.

The author had already written on this subject in *Teksty drugie* (Warsaw), when she also failed to mention my name. I pointed this out to her. She wrote that she had been in the wrong, that she regretted this, and that she would correct this in the reprint. As is evident from the present case, she has not done so.

My work on Baczyński was the product of many years' work, and its publication encountered strong resistance from people who were important in the Polish opposition of those days, who could not swallow the idea that the poet of the underground should have shown solidarity with the murdered Jews. It has been the subject of unrestrained attacks, which have continued until today. For this reason, the appropriation of the results of my work is clearly something that I resent.

Yours faithfully,
Józef Lewandowski

6 February 2002

The Editors
Polin: Studies in Polish Jewry

Dear Sirs,

In my article 'Krzysztof Kamil Baczyński: A Poet-Hero' (*Polin*, volume 13) I neglected to mention Józef Lewandowski's pioneering study about the Jewish origins of the poet and the Holocaust-related content of a significant number of his poems. He presented his seminal research in an article published in *Aneks*, volume 22 (1979), and in his collection of essays about Baczyński, *Szkło bolesne, obraz dni* (Uppsala, 1991). I most sincerely apologize to the author and to the readers for this omission.

I should also like to emphasize that the inspiration for my own essay did not come from Józef Lewandowski's work, but from Natan Gross's book *Poeci i Szoa*, which I do quote in the first paragraph of 'A Poet-Hero'. And since my intention was not to write a scholarly study, but an account of a personal rereading of Baczyński's poems, I deliberately chose to do it 'on my own', in order to demonstrate the transparency of their meaning: that it indeed is strikingly obvious to any open-minded reader that Baczyński wrote about the martyrdom of Poland's Jews. The full credit of being the first unbiased reader of Krzysztof Kamil Baczyński belongs to Józef Lewandowski. I am but a yet another one, though directed there by Natan Gross.

   Yours faithfully.
      Joanna Rostropowicz Clark   *23 February 2002*

Exchange between Dina Porat and Roni Stauber, and Alina Cała

The Editors
Polin: Studies in Polish Jewry

Dear Sirs,

In volume 13 of *Polin*, on the Holocaust and its aftermath, you published a series of book reviews by Alina Cała, under the title 'Analyses of World Antisemitism Published between 1991 and 1997'. In her article Dr Cała included two paragraphs about *Antisemitism Worldwide 1994*, published by Tel Aviv University (the Stephen Roth Institute for the Study of Contemporary Antisemitism and Racism). These outrageous passages raise serious doubts not only about Dr Cała's professionalism but also about her integrity as a scholar.

The author focused in her review on the chapter about Poland, from which she concluded that the whole book was 'superficial, and contains . . . errors and stereo-typical oversimplifications'. Moreover, in the first paragraph she charged that the information in *Antisemitism Worldwide* was derived from a similar report published by the Institute of Jewish Affairs (IJA). This accusation is not supported by any evidence whatsoever, and it is unclear why the editor agreed to publish such passages, which defame serious scholars.

Since the end of 1991 the Stephen Roth Institute has monitored antisemitic manifestations and the activities of extremist movements worldwide, and operated a unique computerized database based on information collected from throughout the world. The chapters in *Antisemitism Worldwide* are based on this information, and also include special reports written by experts from various countries. In 1994 the part on eastern Europe was written by Professor Raphael Vago, a distinguished scholar known for his professionalism and integrity.

Dr Cała did not inform her readers that *Antisemitism Worldwide 1994* was not a one-time publication, but the first volume of a yearly review. It has continued to appear years after the IJA ceased updating its review annually. Each yearly edition of *Antisemitism Worldwide* contains updated information on the chapters reviewed in the previous years. Had Dr Cała been a serious and unbiased scholar, she would have reviewed the 1997 volume, instead of the first one (her article reviewed publications appearing from 1994 to 1997). It is uncommon, to say the least, to publish a review on a book that appeared several years previously when new editions have appeared since. It should also be noted that, as of 1997, besides the worldwide reviews, research articles written by leading scholars in the fields of racism and anti-semitism have also been included in *Antisemitism Worldwide*

While we share her praise of the publications of the Vidal Sassoon International Center, which, incidentally, gave her a scholarship and published her research, Dr Cała does not even bother to mention that as of 1994 the Stephen Roth Institute has published a series of monographs, in addition to *Antisemitism Worldwide*, among them pioneering studies on various aspects of current antisemitism.

But neither the details nor a fair review are Cała's concern. From the second paragraph, the reader learns that the review of the book is merely a pretext for her recurring claim about the stereotypic perception of the Poles in Israeli public opin-ion that is allegedly reflected in *Antisemitism Worldwide*.

What are the 'errors and stereotypical oversimplifications' that Cała found in the chapter about Poland? She mentions two: first, that the author did not write enough about important antisemitic parties and concentrated too much on minor groups or parties that are not antisemitic per se; secondly, that he described '*all* Poles . . . [as] antisemites, since they deny (justly) the claim that during the Second World War they collaborated with the German occupation authorities'. While Cała's first claim is a matter of evaluation, her second is again pure defamation. It is clear that the author did not label all Poles antisemites and distorters of history, but certain elements within Polish society ('antisemitic voices', p. 118). Moreover, today, after the publication of Jan Gross's *Neighbors*, the charge about the collab-oration of Poles and Germans, including in the actual killing of Jews—which has aroused Cała's fury—seems even more rooted in the history of the German occupa-tion of Poland.

To sum up: it is a pity that an important publication such as *Antisemitism Worldwide*, a product of unique co-operation between scholars and Jewish and non-Jewish organizations, and which has been praised by scholars and non-govern-mental organizations all over the world, was attacked in such a biased and even unethical way in your journal.

Yours faithfully,
    Dina Porat
    Roni Stauber   *20 January 2002*

The Editors
Polin: Studies in Polish Jewry

Dear Sirs,

My survey of publications monitoring antisemitism in the contemporary world had as its goal a short presentation of examples of the documentary material they contained as well as of the analyses they provided. It was not my intention to discuss all the publications in this area—that would take up a whole volume. As result, I was able to devote only a few sentences to several serial publications, among them *Antisemitism Worldwide*, published by the Stephen Roth Institute for the Study of Contemporary Antisemitism and Racism at the University of Tel Aviv. I chose the first volume of this series because one could expect that it would be in that volume that the interests and manner of research would be made clear.

I concede that I indeed was very critical in my assessment of this volume, but I am convinced that my criticisms are justified. In the section dealing with Poland one can indeed find the outrageous claim that 'In Poland, where only several tens of thousands of Jews out of 3.3 million survived, and where six extermination camps were located, the Holocaust *per se* cannot be denied. However, antisemitic voices have been raised denying *cooperation with the Germans*, or alternatively, justifying cooperation, with all the differences implied between cooperation in German allied states, such as Slovakia, Hungary, or Romania, as opposed to Poland' (p. 118; my italics). If we compare the discussion of Poland with the reports of the Institute of Jewish Affairs in London, one can perceive similarities, both in the information provided and in the way it is assessed, that cannot be the result of accident. This can be seen in the discussion of antisemitic organizations. In 1994 there were considerably more of these than were mentioned in *Antisemitism Worldwide*. There were six organizations with the name 'National Party' and the 'senioral National Party, was by no means the largest of them. In parentheses, one might mention that the word 'senioral' was not part of the official name of the party, but was given to it by others to distinguish it from the other parties of the same name. In fact, these parties, whose programmes were almost entirely limited to antisemitism, did not achieve any electoral success. This did not mean that there were no antisemitic activists in the Sejm, including activists of the various National Parties, who were elected on other party lists. From 1989 antisemitic activists have sat in every Sejm, and some popular parties have in a more or less open manner tolerated or even favoured antisemitism. At times they have even exploited it. The failure to mention this problem gives a totally false impression.

The picture of Poland set out in *Antisemitism Worldwide* is, in fact, too positive. I would be very happy if in my country there were active only five antisemitic parties, not including the skinheads (who in 1994 certainly numbered more than a thousand individuals). I would also be very happy if the Catholic Radio Maryja (which actually started broadcasting in 1994) stopped propagating antisemitism. The reality is much gloomier: these circles have established their own university and publish newspapers with a mass circulation—these phenomena require much more careful observation than is revealed in *Antisemitism Worldwide*, which, if one is to judge from the list of contributors and institutions involved, has the ambition to establish itself as a prestigious publication summing up annually the global state and extent of antisemitism.

I have examined the two subsequent publications in the series *Antisemitism Worldwide* and, to my regret, I did not find that the analyses that they contain have significantly improved in depth. As in the first issue, there is a large discrepancy between the way conditions in western and eastern Europe are described, in spite of the fact that much has been published recently on conditions in the east of our continent. Unfortunately, I have not had access to the most recent issues—I very much hope they are better, as I am sure is also the desire of those who are preparing them.

Antisemitism in contemporary Poland is a serious problem and requires constant observation, the search for methods to counteract it, and, in view of the way it is ignored by official bodies and the courts, also international pressure. It is such a serious problem that one cannot permit serious flaws in its analysis, which only make it more difficult to counteract. This is a matter about which I feel passionately, as may have been evident in the tone of my criticism.

I should like to underline that, in spite of the insinuations of Professor Porat and Dr Stauber, there were no personal motives in my criticism of *Antisemitism Worldwide*. This also applies to my favourable assessment of the Vidal Sassoon International Center for the Study of Antisemitism, which, I hasten to add, has not published any of my research. I have not received a scholarship from this institution, although I must confess I should be honored to do so. I have participated in research sponsored by it. The argument that my opinions are dictated by material motives would have strength had I attempted to curry favour with the Stephen Roth Center, since its financial resources seem to be considerably greater than those of the Vidal Sassoon International Center.

I cannot avoid, in conclusion, adding a personal remark. Professor Porat and Dr Stauber have cast doubt on my 'professionalism' and 'integrity as a scholar'. I have to admit that I do not have as much self-confidence as them. I do not regard myself as an Einstein, but I have participated in many studies of antisemitism. Both personally and together with other scholars I have published a number of analyses of this phenomenon in Poland. It was our hope that these would be consulted by serious institutions responsible for monitoring antisemitism—indeed this was why they were often published in English. We expected in this way that they would be able to advance beyond oversimplified explanations of complex phenomena.

Yours faithfully,
Alina Cała

15 June 2002

OBITUARIES

Władysław Szpilman
1911–2000

WŁADYSŁAW SZPILMAN, pianist and composer, was born on 5 December 1911 in Sosnowiec, Poland. His parents were Samuel and Estera (*née* Rappaport) Szpilman. He married Halina Grzecznarowska on 30 June 1950 in Warsaw. Together they had two sons, Andrzej and Christopher.

Szpilman's initial training as a pianist was at the Akademia Muzyczna im Frederyka Chopina (Frederick Chopin Academy of Music) in Warsaw under two former students of Liszt, Józef Śmidowicz and Aleksander Michałowski. In 1931 he enrolled at the Akademie der Künste (Academy of Arts) in Berlin, where he studied piano under two of the most distinguished players of the day, Artur Schnabel and Leonid Kreuzer, and composition under Franz Schreker, the renowned composer of *Der ferne Klang* and other similarly successful operas. During this time he wrote a number of compositions, including the piano suite *Życie Maszyn* ('The Life of Machines'), a concertino for piano with orchestra, a symphonic suite, a violin concerto, many works for piano and violin, and several songs.

On his return to Poland in 1933, Szpilman formed a highly successful duo with the violinist Bronisław Gimpel, the basis, twenty-nine years later, of the Warsaw Piano Quintet. In addition to Szpilman (piano), and Gimpel (first violin), the Warsaw Piano Quintet was comprised of Krzysztof Jakowicz (second violin), Stefan Komasa (viola), and Aleksander Ciechański (cello). Their worldwide tours, with some 2,500 concert performances, soon earned the group a reputation as an ensemble of world standing. Szpilman, the core and founder of the group, played with the quintet for twenty-four years until 1986. He was employed by Polish Radio from 1935 until 1963, except during the years of the Second World War. From 1936 he composed approximately 500 songs, about 150 of which were in the Polish pop charts and are popular even today. He also composed the scores for *Wrzos* (1937), *Dr Murek* (1939), and *Pokój zwycięży świat* (1957), among other films.

During the Second World War Szpilman managed to continue practising his art in the Warsaw ghetto, primarily as a pianist and composer. He was playing a Chopin nocturne at Polish Radio when the Germans seized Warsaw. It was the same piece that would later save his life when a German officer, Captain Wilm Hosenfeld, heard him playing and spared him the tragic fate of many others.

When the Nazis invaded Warsaw, Szpilman was working on a concertino for piano and orchestra—a jazz-flavoured, Gershwinesque piece remarkably good-natured for the circumstances of its origin. The score went with him from hiding-place to hiding-place before he had to sacrifice it in order to survive. After the war he reconstructed the piece entirely from memory. This work recently had its American debut as part of a Holocaust memorial observance on 29 April 2001. The date represented the end of the Month of National Remembrance in Poland (dedicated to the memory of the victims of Nazi Germany). The programme of this special concert, entitled 'Remembrances: Reflections on the Holocaust', included works connected to this tragic event either thematically or through the composer's personal experience.

Most notable from the Polish point of view was the American première of a piano concertino composed by Szpilman in 1940 in the Warsaw ghetto. The piece was performed confidently and enthusiastically by the Los Angeles Jewish Symphony conducted by Noreen Green. The concertino was played masterfully by Artur Abadi, a remarkable and talented 16-year-old. The composition has been compared to 'Rhapsody in Blue' by George Gershwin, an American Jewish composer with family roots in Poland.

From 1945 Szpilman appeared in numerous concerts as a soloist and with chamber groups in Poland, throughout Europe, and in America. In 1946 he published his book *Śmierć miasta* ('Death of a City'), which was the original version of and precursor to his later autobiography, *The Pianist*; unfortunately it was in print only briefly.

In the 1950s Szpilman wrote some forty popular songs for children. He also wrote many orchestral pieces including ballets, a short overture, musicals, and music for children's theatre. His light music was particularly successful. For decades Poles sang the songs from his three musicals, his fifty or sixty children's songs, and his 600-odd popular songs as they went about their daily lives.

In 1955 the Związek Kompozytorów Polskich (Polish Composers' Union) bestowed a highly prestigious honour on Szpilman. In 1961 he initiated and organized the International Festival of Song in Sopot. He also founded the Polish Union of Composers of Popular Music. Since 1964 he had been a member of the presidium of the Związek Kompozytorow Polskich and ZAIKS (the Polish equivalent of the American ASCAP or the British Performing Rights Society). Szpilman is mentioned in the *International Who's Who*, the *Music and Musicians' Directory*, and *Who's Who in the Socialist Countries of Europe*.

A CD released in 1998 by the German label Alina (run by Szpilman's son Andrzej) testifies to both his fluency as a composer and his excellence as a pianist. It includes an archive recording of that life-saving Chopin nocturne. A five-CD set was released subsequently by Alina (in conjunction with Polish Radio) containing a recording of this concertino, performed by Szpilman himself with the Polish Radio orchestra and conducted by Stefan Rachon in 1969, one year after the antisemitic purges that prompted many Jews to leave Poland. Amazingly, Szpilman was able to stay and continue his illustrious career as a composer, musician, performer, and well-respected contributor to Polish culture. These CDs document his career by giving us an example of his superb talents as a composer of concert pieces, children's music, and popular songs, and ultimately as a performer. With luck, his last-minute fame as a writer will bring his music the wider currency he would have wished for it during his lifetime.

Many versions of *The Pianist*, his award-winning bestseller and miraculous story of survival, have been published internationally: in Britain, Canada, France, Germany, Israel, Italy, Japan, the Netherlands, Poland, Spain, and Sweden. His compelling autobiographical account of the war years brought him well-deserved accolades and much attention worldwide. The initial publication, in Germany in 2000, became a bestseller and featured the commentary of the famous German poet and writer Wolf Biermann. In Britain the book was awarded the *Jewish Quarterly–Wingate Prize* for 2000 in the non-fiction category. This prestigious annual award is bestowed on newly published books that stimulate interest in and awareness of themes of Jewish concern among a wider reading public. A feature film, *The Pianist*, directed by the Auschwitz survivor Roman Polanski, won the prestigious Palme d'Or prize at the 55th Cannes Film Festival in 2002.

Władysław Szpilman, the sole member of his family to survive the Holocaust, died in Warsaw on 6 July 2000. He is survived by his wife, Halina, his son Andrzej, his daughter-in-law Anna Grabka-Szpilman (who is principal ballerina of the Hamburg Ballet), their children, Daniel and Alina, his son Christopher, and his daughter-in-law Cittose.

In Poland Szpilman was known as 'a man in whom music lives'; music was his entire essence and his soul. His contribution to Polish culture will be a long-lasting and important one. According to Jewish beliefs, one does not die as long as one is remembered. Władysław Szpilman, thanks to his gift of music and the preservation of his miraculous story of survival, will live and be remembered for ever in the hearts of generations to come.

GARY FITELBERG

Stanislaus A. Blejwas
1941–2001

Professor Stanislaus A. Blejwas, one of the foremost scholars of Polish and Polish American history in the United States, and a member of the editorial board of this journal, died at his home on 23 September 2001 at the age of 59. His death leaves a professional and personal void in the lives of the many colleagues, friends, and family he touched in a distinguished and fruitful academic career. He is survived by his wife of thirty-five years, Lucy, and two children, Andrzej and Carol, as well as his mother and five brothers.

Stan Blejwas was born on 5 October 1941 to Polish immigrant parents in New York City and grew up in New Jersey. He received his bachelor's degree in history summa cum laude from Providence College in 1963. He then enrolled at Columbia University, where, in 1966, he earned a master's degree in history and a graduate certificate from the university's Institute on East Central Europe. He conducted research for his dissertation at the University of Warsaw in 1967–8 and 1969–70. In 1973 he received his Ph.D. in modern East European and Polish history from Columbia. He was assistant director of the Institute on East Central Europe in 1974.

In the same year Blejwas accepted a position in the history department at Central Connecticut State University (CCSU) in New Britain. He remained there until his death, holding the position of assistant professor (1974–9), associate professor (1979–84), professor (1984–9), and finally university professor (1989–2001). From 1974 until his death he was coordinator of Polish studies. In 1987 he became the holder of an endowed chair in Polish and Polish American studies at CCSU, the only such chair in the world (which he created). He also served at various times as a visiting professor at several colleges and universities, including Columbia University, Wesleyan University, Hartford College for Women, Alliance College, and the University of Connecticut.

As a scholar, Blejwas was widely respected and well known both in the United States and in Europe. He received numerous awards and honours. He was decorated by the Polish president Aleksander Kwaśniewski with Officer Swords of the Order of Merit of the Republic of Poland in July 1996. In October 2000 Władysław Bartoszewski, minister of foreign affairs of the Republic of Poland, presented him with the Foreign Minister's Diploma of Recognition for the promotion of Polish culture abroad. He was awarded the Mieczysław Haiman Medal by the Polish American Historical Association (PAHA) for his lasting contribution to the study of Polish Americans. He was three times awarded PAHA's Joseph Swastek Prize for the best published article on Polish Americans (1981, 1985, 1998). No single individual has won this award as many times.

At the time of his death Blejwas was serving his second consecutive term as a member of the United States Holocaust Memorial Council, having been first appointed by President Bill Clinton in 1994, and was also president of PAHA. He served in numerous offices within PAHA and played a key role in PAHA's development as a professional scholarly organization. He was also on the board of directors of the Polish Institute of Arts and Sciences in America, the Józef Piłsudski Institute, the Kosciuszko Foundation, and the National Polish American–Jewish American Council. He also served as president of such local Polish community groups as the Polish Cultural Club of Greater Hartford, the Connecticut District of the Polish American Congress, and the 44 Club. He was on the editorial boards of *Polin*, *Polish American Studies*, and Ohio University Press's Polish–Polish American Monographs series.

Blejwas was also deeply involved in the affairs of his university. Remarking on his career President Richard L. Judd of CCSU noted:

The sudden death of Professor Blejwas is a profound loss for the Central Connecticut State University community. The *ojciec* [father] of our Polish-American program, Professor Blejwas was respected globally as an eminent historian. It was Stan Blejwas who, over thirty years ago, developed the Copernican Fund in the University's Foundation, and who tirelessly worked with citizens state-wide to build the University's first endowment. In 1996, his dream of establishing an endowed chair in Polish-American studies was realized. Professor Blejwas was the first holder of that chair.

In an academic world given over to ever greater specialization, Blejwas had the skill to integrate divergent viewpoints and sources. He was one of the few American scholars who was well versed in both Polish and US history. He was comfortable with theory and the history of ideas but was also a consummate local historian. While understanding the social-scientific approach to the past, he retained a keen interest in the impact of literature and music on how people in the past thought and acted. This quality made him a unique asset to all the fields in which he worked. It also made him a scholar who was not estranged from the community in which he lived, and allowed him to bridge divisions of class, ethnicity, and religion. In a time when it has become fashionable for scholars to follow their political instincts rather than evidence, and to show studied contempt for ordinary people, Blejwas's writing stood out in its rigour, fairness, and sympathy for the common man and woman. Yet, his even-handedness would never be mistaken for lack of passion. He was a man who stood on principle, who cared deeply about his profession.

Blejwas's early work was on Polish positivism. As an important alternative in Polish intellectual and cultural life during the partitions, positivism attempted a 'progressive' and even 'scientific' reading of Poland's situation that allowed educated elites to work for the good of the nation without perpetual, bloody revolt on one hand, or collaboration with the partitioning powers on the other. He illustrated both the promise and the flaws of positivism through an examination of the positivist approach to the 'Jewish question': while the positivists opposed antisemitism and fought for a place for Jews in Polish society, they had little understanding of their Jewish neighbours and saw complete assimilation as the price for Jewish integration.

A second major area of Blejwas's research was on the relationship of communist Poland to Poles living abroad, as well as the development of Diaspora institutions such as the Polish American Congress (PAC) in response to threats to Poland's independence. He was one of the first American scholars to conduct significant research in newly opened government archives in Poland after the fall of communist power. (In 1995 he received grants from both the Polish Ministry of Education and the Kosciuszko Foundation to support this work.) He found that, despite a public façade of indifference, the communist regime was highly interested in developments in Polonia, particularly among politically active émigrés. He also shed new light on the details of the founding of the PAC.

Blejwas was the most important historian of the Polish immigrant experience in New England, producing a steady stream of articles and monographs on the subject. He was among those who pioneered the study of immigrants through literature and music. He had also begun to develop an interest in the relationship between Polish and Jewish immigrants in the United States, and at his death was preparing a volume for the monograph series Biblioteka Polonijna on this topic.

Through his involvement in the United States Holocaust Memorial Council and the National Polish American–Jewish American Council Blejwas worked tirelessly to improve Polish–Jewish relations in the United States. He strongly opposed both antisemitism and anti-Polonism. Thanks in part to his work, the portrayal of the victimization of Polish Christians by the Nazis was improved at the Holocaust Museum, a task which took gradual and patient work. Despite obstacles from all sides and the fact that many in his own community could not or would not understand what he was doing on their behalf, he knew far better than most that there was no real future in endless Polish–Jewish dispute and, that despite claims to the contrary, Poles and Jews had far more in common than they had in conflict.

The notion that academic scholarship and academics themselves should play an important role in public discourse was something that came naturally to Blejwas. His example, however, demonstrates that the proper role of academics is not to sermonize from the ivory tower or to make research captive to ethnic or political interest, but to serve their communities. He often wrote not about ordinary people, but for them as well, giving them back a usable past. He was not afraid to engage in the occasional polemic, some of which have become famous. Yet, he never wrote to attack or degrade others, but because he cared deeply about the truth and understood that loving truth does not always mean being popular.

On 29 September 2001 he was laid to rest following a funeral Mass at Holy Cross Catholic Church in New Britain, fittingly a parish whose history he had chronicled. The chair that he founded and to which he dedicated much of his professional life was named in his honour. It is in vain for a single short piece to try to summarize a person's life: the work he did, the lives he touched, the younger scholars he encouraged. However, it is the dedication to his profession, his community, and to the truth that will remain the lasting legacy of Stan Blejwas.

JOHN RADZILOWSKI
University of Minnesota

SELECT BIBLIOGRAPHY OF BLEJWAS'S WORKS

'The Adam Mickiewicz Chair of Polish Studies: Columbia University and the Cold War (1948–1954)', *Polish Review*, 36/3–4 (1991), 323–37, 343–50.

'Alternatives to Romanticism: KOR and the Traditions of Polish Positivism', *Canadian Slavonic Studies*, 31/2 (1989), 194–210.

'A Polish American Fellow Traveler', *Polish Review*, 36/2 (1991), 169–77.

'A Polish Community in Transition: Holy Cross Parish, New Britain, Connecticut, 1927–1977', *Polish American Studies*, 24/1 (1977), 26–69, and 25/1–2 (1978), 23–53.

Choral Nationalism: The Polish Singers Alliance of America, 1889–1999 (forthcoming).

'Cold War Ethnic Politics: The Polish National Catholic Church, the Polish American Congress, and People's Poland, 1944–1952', *Polish American Studies*, 55/2 (Autumn 1998), 5–24.

'Danuta Mostwin, *Odkrywanie Ameryki*', *Polish Review*, 39/1 (1994), 85–90.

'"Equal with Equals": The Polish National Catholic Church and the Founding of the Polish American Congress', *Polish American Studies*, 19/2 (Autumn 1987), 5–23.

'The Evolving Polish Parish in the United States: St. Stanislaus Kostka, Bristol, Connecticut', *Analecta Cracoviensia* (Kraków), 27 (1995), 383–94.

The 44 Club: 1939–1989 (New Britain, Conn.: Art Press, 1989).

'The "44" Club: Second Generation Polonia', *Polish American Studies*, 51/1 (Spring 1994), 49–64.

From Lithuanian to American: A Centennial History of St. Andrew's Parish, New Britain, Connecticut, 1895–1995 (forthcoming).

'The Historiography of Organic Work', *Surabu Kenku* (Slavic Studies, Slavic Institute, Sapporo, Japan) (1974), 191–205.

'The Inherited and the Disinherited: The New England Literary Image of the Polish Peasant Immigrant', *Connecticut Review*, 14/2 (Fall 1992), 49–60.

'The Inherited and the Disinherited: The Polish Peasant Farmer in New England Literature', *Polish Anglo-Saxon Studies*, 3–4 (1992), 81–93.

'Introduction' to Sister Mary Amadeus Ruda, *Blazing New England Trails: Love and Service: A History of the Felician Sisters of Our Lady of the Angels Province, Enfield, Connecticut, 1932–1970* (Enfield, Conn.: Felician Sisters, 1998).

'Jews in the Mental World of Polish Immigrants: Przewodnik Katolicki of New Britain, Connecticut, 1907–1920', in T. Gladsky, A. Walaszek, and M. M. Wawrykiewicz (eds.), *Ethnicity, Culture, City: Polish-Americans in the USA. Cultural Aspects of Urban Life, 1870–1950, in Comparative Perspective*, Polska Akademia Naukowa, Biblioteka Polonijna, 33 (Warsaw: Oficyna Naukowa, 1998).

'The Jews in the Theory and Practice of Polish Positivism', in J. Micgiel *et al.* (eds.), *Poles and Jews: Myth and Reality in the Historical Context*, Conference Proceedings, 6–10 Mar. 1983 (New York: Columbia University, Institute of East Central Europe, 1986).

'List w sprawie tłumaczenia tekstu w Polonii Amerykańskiej', *Przegląd Polonijny*, 16/1 (1990), 129–32.

'The Local Ethnic Lobby: The Polish American Congress in Connecticut, 1944–1974', in F. Renkiewicz (ed.), *The Polish Presence in Canada and America* (Toronto: Multi-cultural Society of Ontario, 1982).

'Milosz and the Polish Americans', *New York Times Book Review* (22 Nov. 1987).

'Nowa i Stara Polonia: Napięcia w społeczności etnicznej', in H. Kubiak, E. Kusielewicz, and T. Gromada (eds.), *Polonia amerykańska: Przeszłość i wspolczesność* (Wrocław: Ossolineum, 1988).

'Old and New Polonias: Tensions within an Ethnic Community', *Polish American Studies*, 38/2 (Autumn 1981), 55–83.

'The Origins and Practice of "Organic Work" in Poland: 1795–1863', *Polish Review*, 15/4 (1970), 23–54.

'Pastor of the Poles: The Second Generation', in S. A. Blejwas and M. B. Biskupski (eds.), *Pastor of the Poles: Polish American Essays* (New Britain, Conn.: Polish Studies Monographs, 1982).

'Patriotism Misunderstood: Warsaw Positivism, 1863–1890', *Polish Review*, 27/1–2 (1982), 47–54.

'Polemic as History: Shmuel Krakowski, *The War of the Doomed. Jewish Armed Resistance in Poland, 1942–1944*', *Polin*, 3 (1988), 391–404.

A Polish American Ethnic Parish: St. Stanislaus Kostka Parish, Bristol, Connecticut, 1919–1994 (New Britain, Conn.: Art Press, 1994).

'Polish Positivism and the Jews', *Jewish Social Studies*, 46/1 (Winter 1984), 21–36.

'The "Polish Tradition" in Connecticut Politics', *Connecticut History*, 33 (Nov. 1992), 61–98.

'Polska Ludowa i Polonia Amerykańska (1944–1956)', *Przegląd Polonijny*, 22/1 (1996), 9–41.

'Przeszczepieni', *Akcent: Literatura i sztuka*, 14/4 (54) (1993), 29–37.

'Puritans and Poles: The New England Literary Image of the Polish Peasant Immigrant', *Polish American Studies*, 42/2 (Autumn 1985), 4–88.

Realism in Polish Politics: Warsaw Positivism and National Survival in Nineteenth Century Poland (New Haven: Yale and Slavic and East European Monographs, 1984).

'Researching Ethnic History in Connecticut: The Polish Question', *Connecticut History*, 22 (Jan. 1981), 31–5.

A Rhode Island Ethnic Group: Polish Americans (Providence, RI: American Polish Exchange Commission of Rhode Island, 1995).

St. Stanislaus B. & M. Parish, Meriden, Connecticut: A Century of Connecticut Polonia, 1891–1991 (Meriden and New Britain, Conn.: Polish Studies Program Monographs and St Stanislaus Parish Council, 1991).

'Spadkobiercy i wydziedziczeni: Polski chłop w literaturze Nowej Anglii', *Res Publica*, 4/10 (36) (1990), 58–66.

' "To Sing Out the Future of the Beloved Fatherland", Choral Nationalism and the Polish Singers Alliance of America 1889–1939', *Journal of American Ethnic History*, 19/1 (Fall 1999), 3–25.

'The Wallingford Schism: The Origins of St. Casimir's Polish National Catholic Church, Wallingford, Connecticut', *PNCC Studies*, 12 (1991), 4–61.

'Why Polka and Jazz were "Banned in Hartford" ', *Hartford Courant* (5 Aug. 2001).

Notes on the Contributors

MICHAEL AYLWARD is an English translator and discographer whose most recent work includes *Beyond Recall: A Record of Jewish Musical Life in Nazi Berlin, 1933–1938*, by Horst Bergmeier, Ejal Eisler, and Rainer Lotz (Bear Family Records, 2001; the book is accompanied by eleven CDs and a DVD of extremely rare recordings made by artists associated with the Jewish 'Kulturbund'). He is also currently working on an anthology of travellers' accounts of Jewish life in Europe.

NATHAN COHEN, Professor Chone Shmeruk's last student at the Hebrew University, teaches Yiddish literature and culture at Bar Ilan University and is an associate editor of *Yad Vashem Studies*. His research focuses on Jewish cultural life in inter-war Poland. His book *Books, Writers and Newspapers: The Jewish Cultural Center in Warsaw 1918–1942* was published in Hebrew in 2003 by Magues Press.

WALTER ZEV FELDMAN researches Ottoman Turkish and Jewish music, as well as the literature of the Ottoman and central Asian Turks. His book *Music of the Ottoman Court: Makam, Composition, and the Early Ottoman Instrumental Repertoire* (1996) is currently being translated into Turkish. He has taught at Princeton University, the University of Pennsylvania, New York University, and Bar Ilan University. He is also a leading performer of *klezmer* music, particularly on the cimbalom (*tsimbl*); his CD *Khevrisa: European Klezmer Music* was issued by Smithsonian-Folkways in 2000. He is currently preparing a monograph on *klezmer* music.

NATAN GROSS is a film director, writer, poet, translator, and journalist who has lived in Israel since 1950. The more than 100 documentary films he has produced include *Mir lebngeblibene* and *Undzere kinder*, the last Yiddish films made in Poland. His books include *The Jewish Film in Poland* (Hebrew and Polish editions), the autobiographical *Who are You, Mr Grymek?* (Hebrew, Polish, and English editions), *Mayn fayfele*, a collection of Mordechai Gebirtig's previously unpublished songs, and, most recently, *Żydówski Bard*, on Gebirtig's life and work. His many awards include that of the Israeli Film Academy for lifetime contributions to Israeli film.

RUTH ELLEN GRUBER is an American author and journalist who has been based in Europe for many years. She was chief correspondent in Poland for United Press International in 1981–3. Since the later 1980s she has written extensively on contemporary Jewish issues in Europe and is the senior European correspondent for the Jewish Telegraphic Agency. Her books include *Virtually Jewish: Reinventing Jewish Culture in Europe* (2002), *Upon the Doorposts of thy House: Jewish Life in East-Central Europe, Yesterday and Today* (1994), and *Jewish Heritage Travel: A Guide to East-Central Europe* (1992, 1994, 1999).

FRANÇOIS GUESNET, associate fellow at the Simon-Dubnow-Institut für jüdische Geschichte und Kultur at Leipzig University, is the author of *Polnische Juden im 19. Jahrhundert. Lebensbedingungen, Rechtsnormen und Organisation im Wandel* (1998). He specializes in east European Jewish history.

ELLEN KELLMAN is a lecturer in Yiddish at Brandeis University. She writes on Yiddish literature and its history. Among her publications is 'Sholem Aleichem's Funeral (New York, 1916): The Making of a National Pageant', *YIVO Annual*, 20 (1991). She is currently preparing a monograph on Abraham Cahan as arbiter of American Yiddish fiction.

ARIELA KRASNEY holds a doctorate in Yiddish literature from Bar Ilan University. She has taught at the Technion and the Teachers' College in Haifa. She is the author of *Habadhan* (1998). Her research interests include Jewish popular literature and folklore.

ANNA LANDAU-CZAJKA is a docent in the Institute of History of the Polish Academy of Sciences. She received her doctorate from the Sociological Institute of the University of Warsaw and her habilitation from the Institute of History of the Polish Academy of Sciences (1999). Her research interests are the Jewish community in Poland and antisemitism in inter-war Poland. She has published a number of articles on these topics as well as *'W jednym stali domu': Koncepcje rozwiązania kwestii żydowskiej w publicystyce polskiej lat 1933–1939* (1998).

ERICA LEHRER is completing her doctoral dissertation in cultural anthropology at the University of Michigan, Ann Arbor. Her thesis concerns the intersections of Jewish cultural revival, identity, and tourism in Poland. She did her fieldwork in Kraków as a Fulbright and IREX grant recipient during 1998–2000. Her writing and photographs have been published in the *Pakn Treger, Bridges*, the *International Institute Journal*, and elsewhere. An exhibition of her photographs, with accompanying text and artefacts, entitled 'The Motives of Memory: Commercializing the Jewish Past in Poland', was shown at the University of Michigan and Grinnell College.

ALEX LUBET is Morse Alumni distinguished teaching professor of music and adjunct professor of American and Jewish studies at the University of Minnesota. His research on Jewish and American music, music and film, and disability studies have appeared in such journals as *Ethnomusicology*, the *Annual Review of Jazz Studies*, and *Medical Problems of Performing Artists*. In 1999 he was a visiting professor at Marie Curie-Skłodowska University in Lublin, where he taught Jewish contributions to American musical culture. He is also an active composer, guitarist and bassist, and theatre artist.

YAAKOV MAZOR was born and brought up in the Batei Rand neighbourhood of Jerusalem, the centre of Tsanz hasidism. He holds degrees in violin studies and music theory from the Rubin Academy of Music and in musicology from Bar Ilan

University. He has been recording, collecting, and studying hasidic and other Jewish music since 1966. His publications include over two dozen articles and books, including *The Klezmer Tradition in the Land of Israel* (Hebrew, 2000), and four recordings of Jewish music (1974, 1992, 1997, 1999). He is currently a research associate at the Jewish National and University Library in Jerusalem.

BARBARA MILEWSKI completed her Ph.D. dissertation on the mazurka and Polish musical nationalism at Princeton University in 2002. Most recently she was awarded a Center for Advanced Holocaust Studies fellowship by the US Holocaust Memorial Museum in Washington, in order to do archival research on music of the Nazi concentration camps. With her colleague Bret Werb she is currently working on a CD recording of songs composed in Sachsenhausen.

ANDRZEJ PACZKOWSKI was born in 1938 in Krasnystaw, Poland. He is a historian and specialist on the contemporary history of Poland and holds the position of professor at the Institute of Political Studies of the Polish Academy of Sciences. He is the author of many monographs, including *Prasa polska w latach 1918–1939* (1980), *Pół wieku dziejów Polski 1939–1989* (1995; Eng. trans. forthcoming), and *Droga do 'mniejszego zła': Strategia i taktyka obozu władzy, lipiec 1980-styczeń 1982* (Warsaw, 2002). He is a member of the board of the Institute of National Memory.

GUNNAR S. PAULSSON was born in Sweden to a Swedish father and a Polish Jewish mother whom the Red Cross had rescued from the camps. After a lengthy career as a computer software developer he returned to historical studies, gaining his MA from the University of Toronto in 1992 and D.Phil. from the University of Oxford in 1998. His D.Phil. thesis won the 1998 Fraenkel prize for contemporary history. He was a lecturer in Jewish studies and Holocaust studies at Leicester University from 1994 to 1998 and was subsequently the senior historian of the Holocaust Exhibition Project at the Imperial War Museum, London, and an honorary research fellow at the University of Warwick. He is the author of *Secret City: The Hidden Jews of Warsaw* (London, 2003) and numerous articles. He currently lives and works in Canada.

ANTONY POLONSKY is Albert Abramson professor of Holocaust studies at Brandeis University and at the United States Holocaust Memorial Museum. Until 1991 he was professor of international history at the London School of Economics and Political Science. He is chair of the editorial board of *Polin*, author of *Politics in Independent Poland* (1972), *The Little Dictators* (1975), and *The Great Powers and the Polish Question* (1976), and co-author of *A History of Modern Poland* (1980) and *The Beginnings of Communist Rule in Poland* (1981). He is co-editor, with Monika Garbowska, of *Contemporary Jewish Writing in Poland: An Anthology* (2001).

BRIAN PORTER is associate professor of history and director of Polish studies at the University of Michigan. He is the author of *When Nationalism Began to Hate:*

Imagining Modern Politics in Nineteenth Century Poland (2000). He is now working on a book provisionally entitled 'For God and Fatherland: Catholicism, Poland, and Modernity'.

EDWARD PORTNOY is a Ph.D. candidate in modern Jewish studies at the Jewish Theological Seminary in New York. He is writing his dissertation on cartoons of the Yiddish press in New York and Warsaw from the turn of the twentieth century to 1939. He received an MA in Yiddish Studies at Columbia University in 1997 with a thesis on the lives and work of artists and puppeteers Zuni Maud and Yosl Cutler. An article based on this research was published in *TDR (The Drama Review)* (Fall 1999).

ALEXANDER ROSSINO is a research historian at the Center for Advanced Holocaust Studies of the US Holocaust Memorial Museum. He received his doctorate from Syracuse University and has published a number of scholarly articles on the German occupation of Poland in the Second World War. He is the author of the monograph *Hitler Strikes Poland: Blitzkrieg, Ideology, and Atrocity* (2003).

WŁODZIMIERZ ROZENBAUM is the author of 'The Anti-Zionist Campaign in Poland, June–December 1967', *Canadian Slavonic Press*, 22/2 (June 1978), as well as other articles about Jews in communist Poland.

SHALOM SABAR, professor of Jewish art and material culture, is chair of the department of Jewish and Comparative Folklore at the Hebrew University in Jerusalem. He is the editor of *Rimonim* and co-editor of *Jerusalem Studies in Jewish Folklore*. He has published numerous articles and several books on subjects such as *halakhah* and art, biblical themes in Jewish, Christian, and Islamic art, Hebrew script in European art, Jewish ceremonies and rituals, the image of Jerusalem in art, and the relationship between Jews and their host societies as reflected in Jewish art.

JEFFREY SHANDLER is an assistant professor in the department of Jewish studies at Rutgers University. He is the author of *While America Watches: Televising the Holocaust* (1999); the editor of *Awakening Lives: Autobiographies of Jewish Youth in Poland before the Holocaust* (2002); and the co-editor, with Dina Abramowicz, of *Profiles of a Lost World: Memoirs of East European Jewish Life before World War II* by Hirsz Abramowicz (1999). He is currently writing a book on Yiddish culture after the Second World War.

JOSHUA SHANES received his doctorate in history at the University of Wiconsin-Madison in 2002 with a dissertation entitled 'National Regeneration in the Diaspora: Zionism, Politics and Jewish Identity in Late Habsburg Galicia, 1883–1907'. A past Fulbright fellow, and fellow at the Center for Advanced Judaic Studies of the University of Pennsylvania, his area of specialization is modern Jewish nationalism and its European context.

MICHAEL C. STEINLAUF is associate professor of history at Gratz College and senior consultant for the Museum of the History of Polish Jews in Warsaw. His book *Bondage to the Dead: Poland and the Memory of the Holocaust* (1997) has recently appeared in Polish. His articles on the Jewish theatre and press in eastern Europe and Polish–Jewish relations have been translated into Hebrew, Polish, German, and Italian. He is currently working on a social and cultural history of Jewish theatre in Poland, and editing the theatre section of the *YIVO Encyclopedia of Jewish Life in Eastern Europe*.

ANDRZEJ TRZCIŃSKI is a lecturer in the department of arts, Marie-Curie Skłodowska University of Lublin. He has written widely on Jewish art in the Polish Common-wealth, Jewish symbols, and Hebrew epigraphic script. He is the author of *Symbole i obrazy: Treści symboliczne na nagrobkach żydowskich w Polsce* (1997), and co-author of *Cmentarz żydowski w Lesku*, i: *Wiek XVI i XVII* (2002).

BRET WERB has produced a series of recordings of ghetto, camp, and partisan songs for the US Holocaust Memorial Museum in Washington, where he has worked as music specialist since 1992. A contributor to the recent edition of *The New Grove Dictionary of Music and Musicians*, he is currently curating an online exhibition (www.ushmm.org/museum/exhibit/online/music) showcasing the sic collection at the Holocaust Memorial Museum. He earned his MA in ethno-musicology at the University of California at Los Angeles with a thesis on the American Yiddish stage composer Joseph Rumshinsky, and is currently a Ph.D. candidate at the same institution.

MARCIN WODZIŃSKI is chair of the Research Centre for the Culture and Languages of Polish Jews at the University of Wrocław. He is the author of *Hebrajskie inskrypcje na Śląsku w XIII–XVIII wieku* (Wrocław, 1996); *Groby cadyków Polsce: O chasydzkiej literaturze nagrobnej i jej kontekstach* (Wrocław, 1998); *Oświecenie żydowskie w Królestwie Polskim wobec chasydyzmu: Dzieje jednej idei* (Warsaw, forthcoming); and co-author of *Cmentarz żydowski w Lesku*, i: *Wiek XVI i XVII* (2002).

SETH L. WOLITZ has for the past twenty years held the Gale Family Chair of Jewish Studies at the University of Texas at Austin, where he is also professor of French, Slavic, and comparative literature. He has published widely on Jewish literature, as well as Provençal, French, Portuguese, and German literature. In recent years he has devoted particular attention to the literary and artistic works of Yiddish modernism. His most recent volume is *The Hidden Isaac Bashevis Singer*.

GWIDO ZLATKES studied Polish literature at Warsaw University and Jewish stud-ies at Hebrew College and Brandeis University. He currently works at Harvard's Tozzer Library. His recent publications include 'Czterech weszło do Pardes', an annotated translation of the mystical chapter in Mishnah, Ḥagigah, in *Studia Judaica*, 1–2 (2001), and 'The Fourth Warsaw Mystic—Aleksander Wat's Encounter with the Devil in History', in M. Freise and A. Lawaty (eds.), *Aleksander Wat und 'sein' Jahrhundert* (2002).

Glossary

arendar A lessee of monopoly rights, usually of a landed estate or some of its enterprises (for example, mills, fishponds, breweries, taverns), which were then administered by the arendar.

badekn (Yiddish; lit. 'to cover') The groom's veiling of the bride in a traditional Jewish wedding; the ceremony is known as *badekns*.

badkhn (Yiddish; pl. *badkhonim*; Hebrew: *badhan*) Traditional Jewish performer and master-of-ceremonies at weddings and other celebrations.

badkhones (Yiddish) The repertoire of a *badkhn*.

bazetsn (Yiddish) The seating of the bride in a traditional Jewish wedding; the ceremony generally includes veiling. The entire ceremony is known as *bazetsns*.

bimah (Hebrew) The podium at the centre of a traditional Ashkenazi house of prayer from which the Torah is read.

Broder zingers (Yiddish) Semi-professional itinerant performers who toured eastern Europe from the mid-nineteenth to the early twentieth century, performing in taverns and wine cellars. They took their name from the Galician city of Brod.

Bund Abbreviation and popular designation for the Algemeyner Yidisher Arbeter Bund in Poyln un Rusland (General Jewish Workers' Alliance in Poland and Russia) Jewish socialist party founded in 1897; it joined the Russian Social Democratic Labour Party, but seceded from it when its programme of national autonomy was rejected. In independent Poland it adopted a leftist, anti-communist posture, and from the 1930s cooperated increasingly closely with the Polish Socialist Party.

Commonwealth (Polish: Rzeczpospolita) The term Rzeczpospolita is derived from the Latin *res publica*. It is sometimes translated as 'Commonwealth' and sometimes as 'Republic', often in the form 'Noblemen's republic' (*Rzeczpospolita szlachecka*). After the Union of Lublin in 1569 it was used officially in the form Rzeczpospolita Obojga Narodów (Commonwealth of Two Nations) to designate the new form of state that had arisen. In historical literature this term is often rendered as the Polish–Lithuanian Commonwealth. It ceased to exist after its partition by the Prussian, Austrian, and Russian empires at the end of the eighteenth century.

Endecja, Endek Endecja was the popular name of the Polish National Democratic Party, a right-wing party that had its origins in the 1890s. Its principal ideologue was Roman Dmowski, who advocated a Polish version of the integral nationalism that became popular in Europe at the turn of the nineteenth century. The Endecja advanced the slogan 'Poland for the Poles' and called for the exclusion of the Jews from Polish political and economic life. Its adherents were called Endeks.

gaon, geonim, geonic (Hebrew; lit. 'genius') A term originally used to designate the heads of the academies of Sura and Pumbeditha in Babylonia from the sixth to the middle of the eleventh centuries. It was later used to describe a man who had acquired a phenomenal command of the Torah.

gematriye (Yiddish; Hebrew: *gematriyah*; from the Greek word for 'geometry') A method of interpreting biblical passages by explaining a word or group of words according to the numerical value of the Hebrew letters or of substituting other letters of the alphabet for them in accordance with a set system.

golus (Yiddish; Hebrew: *galut*) Exile. In eastern Europe the term, as used in vernacular speech, acquired a metaphysical tinge as a synonym for the Jewish condition.

halakhah (Hebrew; lit. 'the walking' or 'going') Denotes Jewish law, that is, the entire prescriptive part of Jewish tradition. It defines the norms of Jewish behaviour and religious observance on a daily, weekly, and annual basis. Individual rules are called *halakhot*.

hasidism A mystically inclined movement of religious revival based in distinct groups with charismatic dynastic leadership. It arose in the borderlands of the Polish–Lithuanian Commonwealth in the second half of the eighteenth century and quickly spread throughout most of eastern Europe. The hasidim emphasized joy in the service of God, whose presence they sought everywhere. Though their opponents, the mitnagedim, pronounced a series of bans against them beginning in 1772, the movement became normative Judaism in most of eastern Europe by the mid-nineteenth century.

Haskalah (Hebrew; lit. 'learning' or 'wisdom') A movement that arose in the wake of the general European Enlightenment in the second half of the eighteenth century and continued into the second half of the nineteenth century. Its adherents were known as maskilim. The Haskalah began in Germany, where its most prominent representative was Moses Mendelssohn (1729–86), and spread to the Slavonic lands. It advocated secular education, the acquisition of European languages, the adoption of 'productive' occupations, and loyalty to the state. Maskilim venerated Hebrew and attacked the use of Yiddish.

kahal (Hebrew; pl. *kehalim*), *kehilah* (Hebrew; pl. *kehilot*; Yiddish *kehile*, pl. *kehiles*) Although both terms mean 'community' *kahal* was generally used to denote the autonomous Jewish council in a particular locality, while *kehilah* denoted the organized community of Jews who lived in that town. The *kahal* was the lowest level of the Jewish autonomous institutions in the Polish–Lithuanian Commonwealth. Above the local *kehilot* were regional bodies, and above these a central body, the Va'ad Arba Aratsot (Council of Four Lands) for the Kingdom of Poland and the Va'ad Medinat Lita (Council of Lithuania). The Va'ad Arba Aratsot was abolished by the Polish authorities in 1764, but autonomous institutions continued to operate legally until 1844 and in practice for many years after this date in those parts of the Polish–Lithuanian Commonwealth directly annexed by the tsarist empire and until the emergence of the Polish state in the Kingdom of Poland and Galicia. Here the reorganized communal body, which no longer had the power to punish religious heterodoxy, but administered synagogues, schools, cemeteries, and *mikva'ot*, was often called the *gmina* (commune). In inter-war Poland the legal status of the *kehilot* was regulated by statute in October 1927 and March 1930. The legislation gave them control over many aspects of Jewish communal life with both religious and social functions. All adherents of the 'Mosaic faith' were required to belong to a *kehilah*, and one could not withdraw except through baptism or by declaring oneself an atheist.

kapote (Yiddish) The long black coat worn by traditionally dressed Jewish men.

kehile (Yiddish) See *kahal*.

khadorim (Yiddish) See *kheyder*.

kheyder (Yiddish; pl. *khadorim*; Hebrew: *heder*, lit. 'room') Denotes the traditional Jewish elementary school, in which teaching was carried on by a *melamed*, who was paid by the families of his students. Poorer students attended the *Talmud toyre*, a school run by the Jewish community. See also *melamed*.

klezmer (Yiddish; pl. *klezmorim*) East European Jewish professional instrumental musician indispensable at weddings and other celebrations.

magid (Hebrew) Itinerant preacher of homilies on religious themes.

Małopolska (Polish; lit. 'Lesser Poland' or 'Little Poland') Southern Poland, the area around Kraków. Also referred to under the Habsburgs as (western) Galicia.

maskil (Hebrew; pl. *maskilim*) See Haskalah.

matseyve (Yiddish; pl. *matseyves*; Hebrew: *matsevah*, pl. *matsevot*) Tombstone.

melamed (Yiddish; pl. *melamdim*) A teacher in a *kheyder* or *Talmud toyre*. A distinction was made between a *dardekey-melamed*, who taught children of both sexes to read and write Hebrew and also a chapter or two weekly from the Pentateuch, and a *gemore-melamed*, who taught Bible and Talmud to boys and also, when they were older, the *Shulhan arukh* or code of Jewish law. See also *kheyder*.

midrash (Hebrew; pl. *midrashim*) A story that expands and/or reinterprets a biblical or talmudic text.

mikve (Yiddish; pl. *mikves*; Hebrew: *mikvah*, pl. *mikvaot*) A pool or bath of clear water, immersion in which renders ritually clean a person who has become ritually unclean through contact with the dead or any other defiling object or through an unclean flux from the body, especially menstruation. An indispensable social institution in east European Jewish communities, in particular use on Friday afternoons before the sabbath.

mitnaged (Hebrew; pl. *mitnagedim*; Yiddish: *misnagid*, pl. *misnagdim*; lit. 'opponent') Defenders of rabbinic Judaism against supposed hasidic heresy in the late eighteenth and early nineteenth centuries, originally led by R. Elijah, known as the Gaon of Vilna.

mitsvah (Hebrew, pl. *mitsvot*; Yiddish: *mitsve*, pl. *mitsves*) One of the 613 positive and negative commandments incumbent upon a traditional Jew. Colloquially, any celebration or act of kindness.

muser (Yiddish; Hebrew: *musar*) Refers to both a ritualized form of moralizing, as in the expression *muser-zogn* (saying *muser*), and to a genre of popular Jewish homiletical literature that developed from the sixteenth to the eighteenth centuries. In the nineteenth century the Lithuanian rabbi Israel Salanter tapped into these traditions to found a religious movement known as Musar that sought to renew Judaism from an ethical perspective. Its influence remained strong in Lithuanian yeshivas until the Second World War.

orn-koydesh (Yiddish; Hebrew: *aron hakodesh*; lit. 'Holy Ark') A covered opening in the east wall of a synagogue or a cupboard placed against the east wall where the scrolls of the Torah are kept.

oyfrufn (Yiddish) 'Calling up' the groom to the reading of the Torah on the sabbath before his wedding; the ceremony itself is known as *oyfrufns*.

peyes (Yiddish) Ritual sidelocks worn by traditional Jews.

purim-shpil (Yiddish) A play, typically parodic and bawdy, performed in connection with the carnivalesque Jewish holiday of Purim.

Reb (Yiddish) Traditional honorific form of address, abbreviated R.

rebbe (Yiddish; lit. 'my teacher') Charismatic dynastic leader of a hasidic group, also known as a *tsadik*. Also honorific form of address to (and synonym for) *melamed*.

rosh-khoydesh (Yiddish; lit. 'head of the month') Monthly celebration of the new moon, first day of the month of the traditional lunar Jewish calendar.

rov (Yiddish; Hebrew: *rav*) Rabbi. Refers to the officially appointed leader of a Jewish community.

Ruthenia Region of western Ukraine south of the Carpathian Mountains. In older literature, used as a synonym for Ukraine.

Sanacja (Polish; from Latin *sanatio*: 'healing', 'restoration') The popular name taken by the regime established by Józef Piłsudski after the coup of May 1926. It referred to Piłsudski's aim of restoring health to the political, social, and moral life of Poland.

seder (Hebrew) Traditional feast held on Passover during which the Haggadah, an account of the Exodus and its traditions, is read.

sefirah (Hebrew; pl. *sefirot*, from Hebrew *safor*, to numerate, because of its relationship to the ten primordial numbers) A fundamental term in kabbalah (Jewish mysticism) used to designate one of the ten emanations that emerged from Ein Sof (God transcendent) in his pure essence, and which continue to form the realm of God's manifestations in his various attributes.

shtadlan (Hebrew; pl. *shtadlanim*) A representative of the Jewish community with access to high dignitaries and legislative bodies of the non-Jewish world.

shtetl (Yiddish: 'small town') The characteristic small town of central and eastern Poland, Ukraine, Belarus, Lithuania, and adjacent lands, which had a substantial Jewish population which sometimes amounted to a majority of the inhabitants of the township. Many *shtetls* were originally 'private' towns under the control of the *szlachta* although the term is widely used to mean any small settlement with a Jewish population.

shund (Yiddish) Popular, 'low', that is, uncanonized literature or theatre.

starosta (Polish) A royal administrator, holder of the office of *starostwo*. From the fourteenth century there were three distinct offices covered by this term: the *starosta generalny* (general *starosta*) represented the Crown in a particular region; the *starosta grodowy* (castle *starosta*) had administrative and judicial authority over a castle or fortified settlement and its surrounding region; and the *starosta niegrodowy* (non-castle *starosta*) or *tenutariusz* (leaseholder) administered royal lands leased to him.

szlachta (Polish) Polish nobility. A very broad social stratum making up nearly 8 per cent of the population in the eighteenth century. Its members ranged from the great magnates, such as the Czartoryskis, Potockis, and Radziwiłłs, who dominated political and social life in the last century of the Polish–Lithuanian Commonwealth, to small landowners (*szlachta zagrodowa*) and even to landless retainers of a great house. What distinguished members of this group from the remainder of the population was their noble status and their right to participate in political life in the dietines, the Sejm, and the election of the king.

szmonces (Polish; Yiddish: *shmontses*) A Jewish skit, routine, or joke particularly popular in Polish cabarets of the inter-war period.

tales (Yiddish; pl. *taleysim*; Hebrew: *talit*, pl. *talitot*) Prayer shawl used in synagogue services.

Talmud toyre See *kheyder*.

Tisha Be'av (Hebrew) Jewish holiday occurring in July or August lamenting the destruction of the temples in Jerusalem.

tsadik (Yiddish; lit. 'righteous person') Term used to designate the charismatic leader of a dynastic hasidic sect, used interchangeably with *rebbe*. See also hasidism.

tsitses (Yiddish; Hebrew: *tsitsit*) Ritual fringed garment worn by traditional Jews against the body and meant to protrude into outerwear.

Va'ad Arba Aratsot (Hebrew) See *kahal*.

Wielkopolska (Polish; lit. 'Great Poland' or 'Greater Poland') Western Poland, the area around Poznań.

yarmulke (Yiddish; Hebrew: *kipah*, pl. *kipot*) Skullcap worn by Orthodox Jews.

yeshiva (Hebrew) Rabbinical college, the highest institution in the traditional Jewish system of education.

Index